Experiencing Childhood and Adolescence

Experiencing Childhood and Adolescence

Janet Belsky

macmillan education

FOR DAVID AND SHELLY

Vice President, Social Sciences and High School: Charles Linsmeier
Director of Content and Assessment, Social Sciences: Shani Fisher
Executive Program Manager: Christine M. Cardone
Developmental Editor: Elaine Epstein
Assistant Editor: Melissa Rostek
Senior Marketing Manager: Lindsay Johnson
Marketing Assistant: Morgan Ratner
Director of Media Editorial, Social Sciences: Noel Hohnstine
Lead Media Project Manager: Eve Conte
Senior Media Editor: Laura Burden
Assistant Media Editor: Nik Toner
Director, Content Management Enhancement: Tracey Kuehn
Managing Editor, Sciences and Social Sciences: Lisa Kinne
Senior Content Project Manager: Vivien Weiss
Senior Workflow Supervisor: Susan Wein
Senior Workflow Project Manager: Paul Rohloff
Photo Editor: Sheena Goldstein
Photo Researcher: Krystyna Borgen, Lumina Datamatics, Inc.
Director of Design, Content Management Enhancement: Diana Blume
Interior Design: Lumina Datamatics, Inc.
Art Manager: Matthew McAdams
Illustrations: Lumina Datamatics, Inc.
Composition: Lumina Datamatics, Inc.
Printing and Binding: LSC Communications

ISBN-13: 978-1-319-18774-3
ISBN-10: 1-319-18774-9

© 2018 by Worth Publishers
All rights reserved.

Printed in the United States of America
First printing

Worth Publishers
One New York Plaza
Suite 4500
New York, NY
10004-1562

About the Author

Born in New York City, Janet Belsky always wanted to be a writer but was also very interested in people. After receiving her undergraduate degree from the University of Pennsylvania, she deferred to her more practical and people-loving side and earned her Ph.D. in clinical psychology at the University of Chicago. Janet spent her thirties in New York City teaching at Lehman College, CUNY, and doing clinical work in hospitals and nursing homes. During this time, she wrote one trade book, *Here Tomorrow: Making the Most of Life After 50*, got married, adopted a child and, with the publication of the first undergraduate textbook in the psychology of aging, began what turned into a lifelong developmental science textbook writing career. In 1991, Janet moved to Tennessee with her family to write and teach undergraduate courses in psychology at Middle Tennessee State University. After her husband died in 2012, Janet enrolled in the Master's Program in Liberal Arts at the University of Chicago (a beginning graduate student again, after 45-plus years!). Still, she remains committed to her life passion—exciting readers in the marvelous story of development through writing this book.

ABOUT # Brief Contents

Preface xv

PART I ## The Foundation 1

Chapter 1 The People and the Field 3

Chapter 2 Prenatal Development, Pregnancy, and Birth 33

PART II ## Infancy and Toddlerhood 69

Chapter 3 Physical and Cognitive Development in Infants and Toddlers 71

Chapter 4 Emotional and Social Development in Infants and Toddlers 105

PART III ## Childhood 131

Chapter 5 Early Childhood 133

Chapter 6 Middle Childhood 163

Chapter 7 Settings for Development: Home, School, and Community 191

PART IV ## Adolescence 221

Chapter 8 Physical Development in Adolescents 223

Chapter 9 Cognitive, Emotional, and Social Development in Adolescents 251

PART V   The Next Step: Emerging into Adulthood 283

Chapter 10   Emerging into Adulthood 285

Final Thoughts 317

Glossary 319
References 329
Name Index 367
Subject Index 383

Contents

Preface xv

PART I The Foundation 1

Chapter 1 The People and the Field 3

Who We Are and What We Study 4

Setting the Context 5
- Tracking the Evolution of Childhood 5
- The Impact of Socioeconomic Status 8
- The Impact of Culture and Ethnicity 8
- The Impact of Gender 9

Theories: Lenses for Looking at Children and Adolescents 10
- Behaviorism: The Original Blockbuster "Nurture" Theory 10
- Psychoanalytic Theory: Focus on Early Childhood and Unconscious Motivations 13
- Attachment Theory: Focus on Nurture, Nature, and Love 14
- Evolutionary Psychology: Theorizing About the "Nature" of Human Similarities 14
- Behavioral Genetics: Scientifically Exploring the "Nature" of Human Differences 14

HOW DO WE KNOW . . . that our nature affects our upbringing? 16
- Nature and Nurture Combine: Where We Are Today 16

HOT IN DEVELOPMENTAL SCIENCE: Environment-Sensitive Genes and Epigenetically Programmed Pathways 17
- Emphasis on Age-Linked Theories 18
- The Ecological, Developmental Systems Approach 20

Research Methods: The Tools of the Trade 23
- Two Standard Research Strategies: Correlations and Experiments 23
- Designs for Studying Development: Cross-Sectional and Longitudinal Studies 25
- Critiquing the Research 27
- Emerging Research Trends 27
- Some Concluding Introductory Thoughts 27

Chapter 2 Prenatal Development, Pregnancy, and Birth 33

Setting the Context 34

The First Step: Fertilization 34
- The Reproductive Systems 34
- The Process of Fertilization 35
- The Genetics of Fertilization 36

Prenatal Development 37
- First Two Weeks: The Germinal Stage 37
- Week 3 to Week 8: The Embryonic Stage 37
- Principles of Prenatal Development 38
- Week 9 to Birth: The Fetal Stage 39

Pregnancy 41
Scanning the Trimesters 41
Pregnancy Is Not a Solo Act 42
What About Dads? 43

Threats to the Developing Baby 44
Threats from Outside: Teratogens 44

HOT IN DEVELOPMENTAL SCIENCE: The Long Shadow of Prenatal Stress 48
Threats from Within: Chromosomal and Genetic Disorders 49

HOW DO WE KNOW . . . about the gene for Huntington's disease? 53
Interventions 53
Infertility and New Reproductive Technologies 55

INTERVENTIONS: Exploring ART 56

Birth 58
Stage 1: Dilation and Effacement 58
Stage 2: Birth 58
Stage 3: The Expulsion of the Placenta 58
Threats at Birth 59
Birth Options, Past and Present 59

The Newborn 61
Tools of Discovery: Testing Newborns 61
Threats to Development Just After Birth 62

EXPERIENCING CHILDHOOD AND ADOLESCENCE: Marcia's Story 63
A Few Final Thoughts on Resilience 64

PART II Infancy and Toddlerhood 69

Chapter 3 Physical and Cognitive Development in Infants and Toddlers 71

Setting the Context 72
The Expanding Brain 72
Neural Pruning and Brain Plasticity 72

Basic Newborn States 75
Eating: The Basis of Living 75

EXPERIENCING CHILDHOOD: A Passion to Eradicate Malnutrition: A Career in Public Health 77
Crying: The First Communication Signal 79

INTERVENTIONS: What Quiets a Young Baby? 80
Sleeping: The Main Newborn State 80

INTERVENTIONS: What Helps a Baby Self-Soothe? 82
To Co-Sleep or Not to Co-Sleep? 83

HOT IN DEVELOPMENTAL SCIENCE: SIDS 84

Sensory and Motor Development 85
What Do Newborns See? 85
Expanding Body Size 88
Mastering Motor Milestones 89

INTERVENTIONS: Baby-Proofing, the First Person–Environment Fit 90

Cognition 90
- Piaget's Sensorimotor Stage 91
- Critiquing Piaget 94
- Tackling the Core of What Makes Us Human: Infant Social Cognition 95

Language: The Endpoint of Infancy 97
- Nature, Nurture, and the Passion to Learn Language 97
- Tracking Emerging Language 98

Chapter 4 Emotional and Social Development in Infants and Toddlers ... 105

Attachment: The Basic Life Bond 106
- Setting the Context: How Developmentalists (Slowly) Got Attached to Attachment 106
- Exploring the Attachment Response 107
- Is Infant Attachment Universal? 112
- Does Infant Attachment Predict Later Relationships and Mental Health? 113
- Exploring the Genetics of Attachment Stability and Change 113

HOT IN DEVELOPMENTAL SCIENCE: Experiencing Early Life's Worst Deprivation 114
- Wrapping Up Attachment 115

Settings for Development 115
- The Impact of Poverty in the United States 115

INTERVENTIONS: Giving Disadvantaged Children an Intellectual and Social Boost 117
- The Impact of Child Care 117

INTERVENTIONS: Choosing Child Care 120

Toddlerhood: Age of Autonomy and Shame and Doubt 121
- Socialization: The Challenge for 2-Year-Olds 122

HOW DO WE KNOW . . . that shy and exuberant children differ dramatically in self-control? 123
- Being Exuberant and Being Shy 123

INTERVENTIONS: Providing the Right Temperament–Socialization Fit 124
- Some Concluding Thoughts: Giving Is Built into Being Human, Too 126

PART III Childhood ... 131

Chapter 5 Early Childhood ... 133

Setting the Context 134
- Special "Mind Reading" Talents 134
- Age of Exploration 134

Physical Development 135
- Two Types of Motor Talents 136
- Threats to Preschool Physical Skills 137

Cognitive Development 138
- Piaget's Preoperational Stage 138

EXPERIENCING CHILDHOOD: Animism and the Power of Stephen King 141

INTERVENTIONS: Using Piaget's Ideas at Home and at Work 143
- Vygotsky's Zone of Proximal Development 144

INTERVENTIONS: Becoming an Effective Scaffolder 145
- Language 145

Emotional Development 148
Constructing Our Personal Past 148
Making Sense of Other People's Minds 149

INTERVENTIONS: Stimulating Theory of Mind 151

Social Development 152
Play: The Work of Early Childhood 152
Girls' and Boys' Play Worlds 154

HOW DO WE KNOW . . . that pink gives girls permission to act like boys? 157

HOT IN DEVELOPMENTAL SCIENCE: Autism Spectrum Disorders 158

Chapter 6 Middle Childhood 163

Setting the Context 164

Physical Development 165
Brain Development: Slow-Growing Frontal Lobes 165
Motor Skills, Obesity, and Health 165

Cognitive Development 167
An Information-Processing Perspective on Intellectual Growth 168

INTERVENTIONS: Using Information-Processing Theory at Home and at Work 169

HOT IN DEVELOPMENTAL SCIENCE: Attention-Deficit/Hyperactivity Disorder 170

INTERVENTIONS: Helping Children with ADHD 171

Emotional Development 172
Observing and Evaluating the Self 172

INTERVENTIONS: Promoting Realistic Self-Esteem 175

Doing Good: Morality and Prosocial Behavior 175

INTERVENTIONS: Socializing Moral Children 177

Doing Harm: Aggression 178

INTERVENTIONS: Taming Excessive Aggression 180

Social Development 181
Friendships: The Proving Ground for Relationships 181
Popularity: Rising in the Peer Ranks 182
Bullying: Moral Disengagement in Action 185

EXPERIENCING CHILDHOOD: Middle-Aged Reflections on My Middle-Childhood Victimization 186

INTERVENTIONS: Attacking Bullying and Helping Rejected Children 186

Chapter 7 Settings for Development: Home, School, and Community 191

Setting the Context 192

Home 193
Parenting Styles 193

INTERVENTIONS: Lessons for Thinking About Parents 195

How Much Do Parents Matter? 196

HOT IN DEVELOPMENTAL SCIENCE: Resilient Children 196

INTERVENTIONS: Lessons for Readers Who Are Parents 198

Spanking 198
Child Abuse 200

INTERVENTIONS: Taking Action Against Child Abuse 201

Divorce 202

School 205
    Unequal at the Starting Gate 205
    Intelligence and IQ Tests 205

EXPERIENCING CHILDHOOD: From Dyslexic Child to College Professor Adult 208

INTERVENTIONS: Lessons for Schools 211
    Classroom Learning 212

HOT IN DEVELOPMENTAL SCIENCE: Communities Matter in Children's Success 216

PART IV Adolescence 221

Chapter 8 Physical Development in Adolescents 223

Puberty 224
    Setting the Context: Culture, History, and Puberty 224
    The Hormonal Programmers 226
    The Physical Changes 226

HOW DO WE KNOW . . . how puberty progresses? 228
    Individual Differences in Puberty Timetables 230
    An Insider's View of Puberty 232
    Wrapping Up Puberty 235

INTERVENTIONS: Minimizing Puberty Distress 235

Body Image Issues 237
    The Differing Body Concerns of Girls and Boys 237
    Eating Disorders 238

INTERVENTIONS: Improving Teenagers' Body Image 240

Sexuality 241
    Exploring Sexual Desire 242
    Who Is Having Intercourse? 242
    Who Are Teens Having Intercourse With? 244

HOT IN DEVELOPMENTAL SCIENCE: Is There Still a Sexual Double Standard? 244
    Wrapping Up Sexuality: Contemporary Trends 245

INTERVENTIONS: Toward Teenager-Friendly Sex Education 246

Chapter 9 Cognitive, Emotional, and Social Development in Adolescents 251

Setting the Context 252

Cognitive and Emotional Development: The Mysterious Teenage Mind 253
    Three Classic Theories of Teenage Thinking 253
    Studying Three Aspects of Storm and Stress 258

HOW DO WE KNOW . . . that adolescents make riskier decisions when they are with their peers? 259

HOT IN DEVELOPMENTAL SCIENCE: A Potential Pubertal Problem—Popularity 263
    Different Teenage Pathways 264
    Wrapping Things Up: The Blossoming Teenage Brain 266

INTERVENTIONS: Making the World Fit the Teenage Mind 266

EXPERIENCING ADOLESCENCE: Innocently Imprisoned at 16 267
    Another Perspective on the Teenage Mind 270

Social Development 271
Separating from Parents 271
Connecting in Groups 274
A Note on Adolescence Worldwide 278

PART V The Next Step: Emerging into Adulthood 283

Chapter 10 Emerging into Adulthood 285

Setting the Context 286
Culture and History 286
Beginning and End Points 288

Constructing an Identity 291
Marcia's Identity Statuses 292
The Identity Statuses in Action 293
Ethnic Identity, a Minority Theme 294

Finding a Career 295
Entering with High (But Often Unrealistic) Career Goals 295
Self-Esteem and Emotional Growth During College and Beyond 296

EXPERIENCING EMERGING ADULTHOOD: A Surprising Path to Adult Success 297
Finding Flow 297
Emerging into Adulthood Without a College Degree (in the United States) 298

INTERVENTIONS: Smoothing the School Path and School-to-Work Transition 299
Being in College 301

INTERVENTIONS: Making College an Inner-Growth Flow Zone 301

Finding Love 302
Setting the Context: Seismic Shifts in Searching for Love 303

HOT IN DEVELOPMENTAL SCIENCE: Same-Sex Romance 303
Similarity and Structured Relationship Stages: A Classic Model of Love and a Critique 305

HOT IN DEVELOPMENTAL SCIENCE: Facebook Romance 307
Love Through the Lens of Attachment Theory 309

HOW DO WE KNOW . . . that a person is securely or insecurely attached? 310

INTERVENTIONS: Evaluating Your Own Relationship 311

Final Thoughts 317

Glossary 319

References 329

Name Index 367

Subject Index 383

Preface

I spent my thirties and forties writing textbooks on adult development and aging. I spent almost two decades surveying the lifespan in writing four editions of a human development text. My mission in *Experiencing Childhood and Adolescence* is simple: to excite students about children's and adolescents' lives.

This book showcases cutting-edge research—from state-of-the art studies exploring the genetics of development to path-breaking findings tracking upward mobility in every U.S. county. It also pays full attention to the world-class twentieth-century geniuses who revolutionized our field, such as Bronfenbrenner, Bowlby, Erikson, and Piaget. I've been striving to write a book that is both intellectually rigorous and tells a riveting story. I believe that by talking directly to readers, textbooks can convey sophisticated concepts in terms that any person can understand. My goal is to have students look at children and society differently, to energize, to inspire, and hopefully to change readers' lives. Here are the features that make this pinnacle textbook in my *own* career stand out.

What Makes This Book Special?

- *Experiencing Childhood and Adolescence* **unfolds like a story.** The main quality that makes this book stand out is the writing style. *Experiencing Childhood and Adolescence* reads like a conversation rather than a traditional text. I've begun each chapter with a vignette constructed to highlight the material I will be discussing. I've designed my narrative to flow from topic to topic, and I've planned every chapter to interconnect. In this book, the main themes that underlie development flow throughout the *entire* book. I want students to have the sense that they are reading an exciting, ongoing story. Most of all, I want them to feel that they are learning about a coherent, *organized* field.

- *Experiencing Childhood and Adolescence* **is uniquely organized to highlight development.** A second passion that drives my writing is to demonstrate exactly how children change. What qualities distinguish toddlerhood from infancy, and why are 8-year-olds much more mentally mature than 4-year-olds? What agendas drive elementary schoolers, preteens, and emerging adults, and how do the worldviews of children change as they travel from babyhood to adult life?

  To give readers a vivid sense of lives unfolding, I follow the characters in the chapter-opening vignettes throughout each book part. I continually stress how everything—from motor skills to social cognition to executive functions—blossoms over the years. Yes, this textbook (mainly) moves through childhood and adolescence chronologically, stage by stage. But because it's designed to capture the magical strides in *development* that define the childhood years, I believe my text captures the best features of the chronological and topical approaches.

The fact that toddlers naturally take joy in giving suggests that giving is built into being human.

The blissful rapture, the sense of being totally engrossed with each other, is the reason why developmentalists use the word *synchrony* to describe parent–infant attachment.

- *Experiencing Childhood and Adolescence* **is both short and in-depth.** This overarching emphasis on how children develop makes for a more manageable book. I don't feel compelled to cram in a litany of disparate topics. At 10 chapters and just under 330 pages, this textbook *really* can be mastered in a one-semester course! But focusing on how children change offers me the luxury to describe central topics in our field in special depth. As you will discover while reading my comprehensive discussions of attachment, parenting, puberty, theory of mind, and teenage storm and stress, omitting superficial coverage of "everything" encourages students to explore the defining questions in developmental science in a more thoughtful way.

- *Experiencing Childhood and Adolescence* **actively fosters critical thinking.** Guiding students to reflect on what they are reading is another of my writing goals. A great advantage of engaging readers in a conversation is that I can naturally embed critical thinking into the narrative. For example, as I move from discussing Piaget's ideas on cognition to exploring Vygotsky's theory, I point out the gaps in each perspective and highlight *why* each approach offers a unique contribution to understanding children's intellectual growth. By exploring selected studies in depth, I can bring home the complexities involved in interpreting developmental data, and so teach students to critically assess the "facts" in our field. This same evaluative attitude applies to society. Whether discussing day care, bullying, parenting, or getting at-risk teenagers connected to high school, my mission is to get readers to step back and ask a basic question: How is our culture and its institutions fostering children's development, and where might society be falling short?

- *Experiencing Childhood and Adolescence* **has a global and historical orientation.** Intrinsic to getting students to evaluate our culture is the need to highlight alternate perspectives on children's developing lives. Therefore, *Experiencing Childhood and Adolescence* is a firmly international book. I introduce this global orientation in the first chapter when I spell out the differences between collectivist and individualistic cultures and between the developed and developing worlds. When discussing topics from pregnancy to parenting, I pay special attention to cultural variations. (In fact, "How do other groups handle this?" is a question that crops up when I talk about practically every topic in the book!) Another feature that makes this book stand out is its historical perspective on childhood. How did parents treat children in the nineteenth century? What was adolescence like in the past, and how have our attitudes toward spanking or childrearing or divorce evolved? It's tempting to assume that the way we currently think about development is set in stone. I believe it's vital to bring home the fact that society, like human lives, is a work in progress. More than just enlarging their views about children, I hope to widen students' views about the world.

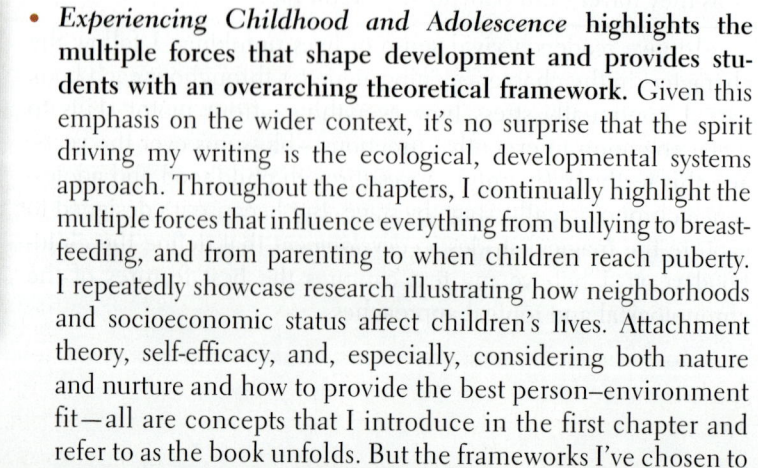

This young girl in Thailand is learning to weave just by observing her mother—a strategy that we might find unusual in our teaching-oriented culture.

- *Experiencing Childhood and Adolescence* **highlights the multiple forces that shape development and provides students with an overarching theoretical framework.** Given this emphasis on the wider context, it's no surprise that the spirit driving my writing is the ecological, developmental systems approach. Throughout the chapters, I continually highlight the multiple forces that influence everything from bullying to breastfeeding, and from parenting to when children reach puberty. I repeatedly showcase research illustrating how neighborhoods and socioeconomic status affect children's lives. Attachment theory, self-efficacy, and, especially, considering both nature and nurture and how to provide the best person–environment fit—all are concepts that I introduce in the first chapter and refer to as the book unfolds. But the frameworks I've chosen to drive home how children *change* are Piaget's and Erikson's landmark theories. Because I believe these master theorists can help students put each life stage into context, tables that showcase each relevant Piaget and Erikson stage, accompanied by compelling examples, flow through this book.

- *Experiencing Childhood and Adolescence* is applications-oriented. Having a background as a clinical psychologist, my other mission is translating research into applications through end-of-section **Interventions** that spell out practical implications of the research. With its varied Interventions—such as "What Gets Babies to Self-Soothe?" (Chapter 3) or "Using Piaget's Theory at Home and at Work" (Chapter 5)—and regular summary tables—such as "How to Produce Prosocial Children" (Chapter 6) or "Succeeding in College/Finding a Career Identity: Tips for Young People and Society" (Chapter 10)—this text emphasizes how we can use scientific findings to improve people's lives.

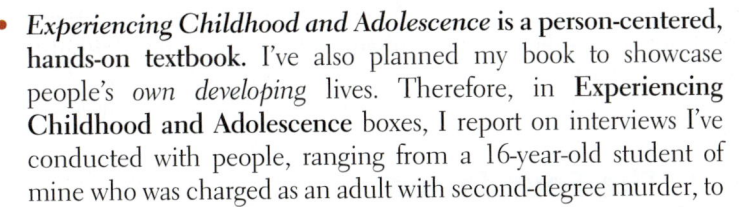

- *Experiencing Childhood and Adolescence* is a person-centered, hands-on textbook. I've also planned my book to showcase people's *own developing* lives. Therefore, in **Experiencing Childhood and Adolescence** boxes, I report on interviews I've conducted with people, ranging from a 16-year-old student of mine who was charged as an adult with second-degree murder, to another student born very premature and who is coping with cerebral palsy. I interviewed a colleague with dyslexia about her childhood, and, in the section on peer victimization, I even described my own experience being bullied at age 8! Because personal examples best flesh out the research, I liberally use anecdotes to illustrate concepts and regularly encourage readers to see life from the perspective of real-world parents, toddlers, and teens.

These teens are taking great pleasure in serving meals to the homeless as part of their community-service project. Was a high school experience like this life-changing for you?

Another strategy I use to make the research vivid and personal are **questionnaires** (often based on the chapter content) that get readers to think more deeply about their own lives. For example, I've created a "Checklist for Identifying Your Parenting Priorities" table (Chapter 7); a questionnaire on "Evaluating Your Own Relationship: A Section Summary Checklist" (Chapter 10); and a true/false quiz at the beginning of the chapter on adolescence (Chapter 9) that provides a hands-on preview of the content, enticing students into reading the chapter so that they can test the scientific accuracy of their ideas.

- *Experiencing Childhood and Adolescence* is designed to get students to learn the material while they read. The chapter-opening vignettes, the interventions sections with summary tables, the hands-on exercises, and the end-of-section questionnaires are part of an overall pedagogical plan. As I explain in my introductory letter to students on page 2, I want this to be a textbook that readers don't have to struggle to decode—one that helps people *naturally* cement the concepts in their minds. Two centerpieces of this effort are the **Learning Outcomes** and **Tying It All Together** quizzes, which bracket each major chapter section. These short, introductory statements summarizing the topics to come, along with concluding section mini-tests, serve as guideposts that highlight the core messages students need to learn.

Admiring each other's talents in their shared life passion predicts future happiness for this young couple. It also may make these actors feel as if they are becoming better performers just from being together—and it certainly helps if they inflate each other's talents, too ("My partner is sure to be the next Denzel Washington!").

I've also carefully planned the photo program in *Experiencing Childhood and Adolescence* to bring home the terms and concepts in the book. As you page through the text, you may notice that the pictures and their captions feel organically connected to the writing. They visually bring together the main text messages. When it's important for students to learn a series of terms or related concepts, I may provide a summary series of photos, such as photographs illustrating the different infant and adult attachment styles on pages 110 and 310 and the table highlighting Jean Piaget's infant circular reactions on page 92.

As you scan this book, you will see other special features: **How Do We Know . . . ?** boxes delve deeply into particular research programs; **Hot in Developmental Science** sections in each chapter showcase cutting-edge research on diverse topics from prenatal stress to preteen popularity; timelines pull everything together at the end of complex sections (such as the chart summarizing the landmarks of pregnancy and prenatal development in Chapter 2, on pages 54–55).

What will make this text a pleasure to teach from? How can I make this book a joy to read? These are questions I have been grappling with as I've been glued to my computer—often seven days a week—during this labor of love.

What Makes Each Chapter Special?

Now that I've spelled out my general writing missions, here are some highlights of each chapter.

This actress, working with refugee children, shares a core mission of developmental science: to help traumatized children around the world.

PART I: The Foundation

CHAPTER 1: The People and the Field

- Outlines the basic contexts of development: cohort, social class, culture, and ethnicity.
- Traces the evolution of childhood over the centuries and explores the classic developmental science theories that have shaped our understanding of life.
- Spells out the concepts, perspectives, and research strategies I will be exploring in each chapter of the book.

CHAPTER 2: Prenatal Development, Pregnancy, and Birth

- Discusses pregnancy rituals and superstitions around the world.
- Highlights the latest research on fetal brain development.
- Fully explores the experience of pregnancy from both the mother's and father's points of view and discusses infertility in depth.
- Looks at the experience of birth historically and discusses policy issues relating to pregnancy and birth in the United States and around the world.

PART II: Infancy and Toddlerhood

CHAPTER 3: Physical and Cognitive Development in Infants and Toddlers

- Covers the latest research on brain development.
- Focuses in depth on basic infant states such as eating, crying, and sleep.

- Explores breast-feeding and scans global undernutrition.
- Provides an in-depth, personal, and practice-oriented look at infant visual perception, motor development, Piaget's sensorimotor stage, beginning language, and social cognition.

CHAPTER 4: Emotional and Social Development in Infants and Toddlers

- Provides unusually in-depth coverage of attachment theory.
- Explores research tracking orphanage-reared babies.
- Offers an honest, comprehensive look at day care in the United States and discusses early-childhood poverty.
- Highlights exuberant and shy toddler temperaments, explores research on the genetics of temperament, and stresses the need to promote the right temperament–environment fit for each child.

PART III: Childhood

CHAPTER 5: Early Childhood

- Begins by exploring why we have childhood, illustrating what makes human beings qualitatively different from other species.
- Offers an overview of preschool motor development and discusses threats to motor skills.
- Showcases Piaget's and Vygotsky's theories—with examples that stress the practical implications of these landmark perspectives for parents and people who work with children.
- Discusses autobiographical memory and theory of mind in depth.
- Describes pretend play, tracks the development and causes of gender stereotyped play, and offers a section on autism spectrum disorders.

CHAPTER 6: Middle Childhood

- Organizes the research on this landmark first "adult-like" age, by discussing industry, concrete operations, and the expanding frontal lobes.
- Outlines issues relating to middle childhood motor development.
- Describes the growth of memory and executive functions.
- Explores the features and treatments for ADHD.
- Discusses emotion regulation, internalizing and externalizing disorders, emerging self-understanding, and self-esteem.
- Offers an in-depth look at prosocial behavior, aggression, friendships, and popularity.
- Discusses bullying and cyberbullying.

CHAPTER 7: Settings for Development: Home, School, and Community

- This final childhood chapter shifts from the process of development to the major settings for development—home, school, and community—and tackles important controversies in the field, such as the influence of parents versus peers versus genetics in shaping development, and the pros and cons of intelligence testing.

Imagine buying this device, guaranteed to propel your child into a kindergarten star. How would you like your child spending his time?

- Offers extensive discussions of ethnic variations in parenting styles and immigrant families and describes the latest research on how to stimulate intrinsic motivation.
- Explores spanking, child maltreatment, and divorce.
- Showcases schools that beat the odds and targets the core qualities involved in effective teaching.
- Stresses the impact of communities on children's development and describes path-breaking research relating to upward mobility and the long-term impact of having *one* excellent elementary school teacher.

PART IV: Adolescence

CHAPTER 8: Physical Development in Adolescents

- Offers an in-depth look at puberty, including the multiple forces that program the timing of this life transition, and looks at historical and cultural variations in puberty timetables.
- Explores the emotional experience of puberty (an "insider's" view) and the emotional impact for girls of maturing early.
- Provides up-to-date coverage of teenage body image issues, eating disorders, and emerging sexuality.

CHAPTER 9: Cognitive, Emotional, and Social Development in Adolescents

- Covers Elkind's, Piaget's, and Kohlberg's theories; the developmental science research on teenage brain development; and various facets of adolescent "storm and stress."
- Spells out the forces that enable adolescents to thrive and explains what society can do (and also may not be doing!) to promote optimal development in teens.
- Explores parent–teenage relationships and discusses adolescent peer groups.
- Discusses why at-risk teens may drop out of school and join gangs.

What are the teens who avidly scan the photos on a social network site likely to do? The surprise is that girls may decide to post more assertive, sexually oriented comments than boys.

PART V: The Next Step: Emerging into Adulthood

CHAPTER 10: Emerging into Adulthood

- Devotes a whole chapter to emerging adults.
- Offers extensive coverage of diversity issues during this life stage, such as forming an ethnic and biracial identity, changes in interracial dating, and issues related to coming out gay.
- Gives students tips for succeeding in college and spells out career issues for non-college emerging adults.

- Introduces topics—such as the concept of "flow" and identity—and provides extensive coverage of the research relating to selecting a mate and adult attachment styles.

Final Thoughts
This one page wrap-up summarizes my top insights from surveying the current research.

What Teaching and Learning Aids Support This Book?

When you decide to use this book, you're adopting far more than just this text. You have access to an incredible learning system—everything from tests to video clips that bring the material to life. The Worth team and several dozen dedicated instructors have worked to provide an array of supplements to my text to foster student learning and make this course memorable: Video clips convey the magic of prenatal development, clarify Piaget's tasks, and highlight child undernutrition. My publisher has amassed a rich archive of developmental science materials. For additional information, please contact your Worth Publishers sales consultant or visit the company website at http://www.macmillanlearning.com. Here are descriptions of the supplements.

LaunchPad with *LearningCurve* Quizzing and *Developing Lives*

A comprehensive web resource for teaching and learning child and adolescent development, **LaunchPad** combines Worth Publishers' award-winning media with an innovative platform for easy navigation. For students, it is the ultimate online study guide, with rich interactive tutorials and videos, as well as an e-Book and the *LearningCurve* adaptive quizzing system. For instructors, LaunchPad is a full course space where class documents can be posted, quizzes easily assigned and graded, and students' progress assessed and recorded. LaunchPad for *Experiencing Childhood and Adolescence* includes all the following resources:

- *LearningCurve* adaptive quizzing system is based on the latest findings from learning and memory research. It combines adaptive question selection, immediate and valuable feedback, and a gamelike interface to engage students in a learning experience that is unique to them. Each *LearningCurve* quiz is fully integrated with other resources in LaunchPad through the Personalized Study Plan, so students will be able to review using Worth's extensive library of videos and activities. And state-of-the-art question analysis reports allow instructors to track the progress of individual students, as well as their class as a whole.

- *Developing Lives* is a robust and sophisticated interactive experience in which each student "raises" a virtual child from sperm-and-egg to teenager—fully integrated into Launchpad. With *Developing Lives*, each student creates a personal profile, selects a virtual partner (or chooses to be a single parent), and marks the arrival of his or her newborn (represented by a unique avatar based on the parents' characteristics). As the child grows, the student responds to events both planned and unforeseen, making important decisions (nutrition choices, doctor visits, sleeping location) and facing uncertain moments (illness, divorce, a new baby), with each choice affecting how the child grows. Throughout, *Developing Lives* deepens each student's attachment and understanding of key concepts in the field with immediate, customized feedback based on child development research.

It integrates more than 200 videos and animations and includes quizzes and essay questions that are easy to assign and assess.

- **Immersive Learning Activities:** *Something to Consider* activities apply the research to everyday life and to possible future careers for students. Each activity concludes with a quiz to assess what students have learned.
- **Videos**—in collaboration with dozens of instructors and researchers, Worth has developed an extensive collection of video clips. The collection covers the full range of the course, from classic experiments (like the Strange Situation and Piaget's tasks) to investigations of children's play to adolescent risk-taking. Instructors can show these videos in class, assign them to students through LaunchPad, or choose one of the **video activities** that combine videos with short-answer and multiple-choice questions.
- **An interactive e-Book** allows students to highlight, bookmark, and add their own notes on the e-Book page, just as they would in a printed textbook.
- The *Scientific American* **News Feed** delivers weekly articles, podcasts, and news briefs on the very latest developments in psychology from the first name in popular science journalism.

Assessment and Other Instructor's Resources

The Instructor's Resources are fully integrated with LaunchPad. This rich collection of resources includes learning objectives, springboard topics for discussion and debate, handouts for student projects, course-planning suggestions, ideas for term projects, and a guide to audiovisual and online materials.

- **Downloadable Diploma Computerized Test Bank (for Windows and Macintosh).** This Test Bank offers an easy-to-use test-generation system that guides you through the process of creating tests. The Diploma software allows you to add an unlimited number of questions; edit questions; format a test; scramble questions; and include pictures, equations, or multimedia links. The Diploma software will also allow you to export into a variety of formats that are compatible with many Internet-based testing products.
- **Lecture Slides** are available in two slide sets for each chapter of *Experiencing the Adolescence and Childhood*—one featuring a comprehensive chapter lecture, the other featuring all chapter art and illustrations.

LMS Integration

Deep integration is available between LaunchPad products and Blackboard, Brightspace by D2L, Moodle, and Canvas. These deep integrations offer single sign-on, asset-level linking, and assignment-level automatic grade sync.

Who Made This Book Possible?

This book was a completely collaborative endeavor engineered by the finest publishing company in the world: Worth (and not many authors can make that statement)! Firstly, again heartfelt thanks go to Elaine Epstein. Elaine, whom I have been fortunate to have as my "developmental editor" for most of my books, meticulously pores over every sentence of this manuscript multiple times, helps prepare all the figures and tables and select the photos, and is guiding this book into print as we speak. Elaine, as usual, is my real, unseen, full partner on this book.

The other collaborator on my books is my masterful hands-on editor Chris Cardone, who *also* delves into this manuscript line by line. After decades spent working with editors, I can honestly say that in terms of attentiveness to authors, sensitivity to their needs, reliability, and genuine good smarts, Chris ranks as the best. Since we started working together more than 15 years ago, I count Chris and Elaine as lifelong friends!

Then there are the talented people who transform this manuscript into print. Thanks go to Vivien Weiss, my hardworking Senior Content Project Manager, for coordinating this intricate process; to Melissa Rostek, Assistant Editor; and to Paul Rohloff, my Senior Workflow Project Manager, for helping to ensure everything fit together and stayed on schedule. It's been my great fortune to rely on the advice of Worth's accomplished Director of Content Management Enhancement, Tracey Kuehn. Thanks also to eagle-eyed copy editor Beth Rosato and proofreader Paula Pyburn for meticulously picking through the manuscript for accuracy and ensuring that each sentence makes grammatical sense.

Then there are the talented people who make *Experiencing Childhood and Adolescence* look like a breathtaking work of art. As you delight in looking at these fabulous pictures, you can thank Sheena Goldstein and Krystyna Borgen for coordinating the photo program, and Matthew McAdams for coordinating the art. The Director of Design, Diana Blume, is responsible for planning this book's gorgeous design.

Thanks to Laura Burden, Senior Media Editor, and to the supplements and media authors. Without good marketing, no one would read this book. And, as usual, this arm of the Worth team gets my A+ rating. Kate Nurre, our Executive Marketing Manager, and Lindsay Johnson, Senior Marketing Manager, do an outstanding job. They go to many conferences and spend countless hours in the field advocating for my work. Although I may not meet many of you personally, I want to take this chance to thank all the sales reps for working so hard to get "Belsky" out in the world.

I am grateful to student readers of my previous lifespan book who took the time to personally email and tell me, "You did a good job," or "Dr. Belsky, I like it; but here's where you went wrong." These kinds of comments really make an author's day! My writing has benefited from the insights of an incredible number of reviewers over the years. I especially want to thank the reviewers of this new book in its early stages:

Deborah Chapin, University at Albany

Tyra Edwards-Rowell, Holmes Community College

Patrick Frato, Cleveland State University

Eugene Geist, Ohio University

Nanci Monaco, SUNY Buffalo State

Jackie Nelson, University of Texas at Dallas

Natalia Potapova, Washington State University

Christine Weinkauff, California State University-San Bernardino

I also want to thank the instructors whose feedback I relied on in preparing my lifespan books, and so have implicitly made *Experiencing Childhood and Adolescence* a far better book:

Heather Adams, Ball State University

Daisuke Akiba, Queens College

Cecilia Alvarez, San Antonio College

Andrea S. Anastasiou, Mary Baldwin College

Emilie Aubert, Marquette University

Pamela Auburn, University of Houston Downtown

Tracy Babcock, Montana State University

Harriet Bachner, Northeastern State University

Carol Bailey, Rochester Community and Technical College

Thomas Bailey, University of Baltimore

Shelly Ball, Western Kentucky University

Mary Ballard, Appalachian State University

Lacy Barnes-Mileham, Reedley College

Kay Bartosz, Eastern Kentucky University

Laura Barwegen, *Wheaton College*

Jonathan Bates, *Hunter College, CUNY*

Don Beach, *Tarleton State University*

Lori Beasley, *University of Central Oklahoma*

Martha-Ann Bell, *Virginia Tech*

Daniel Bellack, *Trident Technical College*

Jennifer Bellingtier, *University of Northern Iowa*

Karen Bendersky, *Georgia College and State University*

Keisha Bentley, *University of La Verne*

Robert Billingham, *Indiana University*

Kathi J. Bivens, *Asheville-Buncombe Technical Community College*

Jim Blonsky, *University of Tulsa*

Cheryl Bluestone, *Queensborough Community College, CUNY*

Greg Bonanno, *Teachers College, Columbia University*

Aviva Bower, *College of St. Rose*

Marlys Bratteli, *North Dakota State University*

Bonnie Breitmayer, *University of Illinois, Chicago*

Jennifer Brennom, *Kirkwood Community College*

Tom Brian, *University of Tulsa*

Sabrina Brinson, *Missouri State University*

Adam Brown, *St. Bonaventure University*

Kimberly D. Brown, *Ball State University*

Donna Browning, *Mississippi State University*

Janine Buckner, *Seton Hall University*

Ted Bulling, *Nebraska Wesleyan University*

Holly Bunje, *University of Minnesota, Twin Cities*

Melinda Burgess, *Southwestern Oklahoma State University*

Barbara Burns, *University of Louisville*

Marilyn Burns, *Modesto Junior College*

Joni Caldwell, *Spalding University*

Norma Caltagirone, *Hillsborough Community College, Ybor City*

Lanthan Camblin, *University of Cincinnati*

Debb Campbell, *College of Sequoias*

Lee H. Campbell, *Edison Community College*

Robin Campbell, *Brevard Community College*

Kathryn A. Canter, *Penn State Fayette*

Peter Carson, *South Florida Community College*

Michael Casey, *College of Wooster*

Kimberly Chapman, *Blue River Community College*

Tom Chiaromonte, *Fullerton College*

Yiling Chow, *North Island College, Port Albernia*

Toni Christopherson, *California State University, Dominguez Hills*

Wanda Clark, *South Plains College*

Judy Collmer, *Cedar Valley College*

David Conner, *Truman State University*

Deborah Conway, *University of Virginia*

Diana Cooper, *Purdue University*

Ellen Cotter, *Georgia Southwestern State University*

Deborah M. Cox, *Madisonville Community College*

Kim B. Cragin, *Snow College*

Charles P. Cummings, *Asheville-Buncombe Technical Community College*

Karen Curran, *Mt. San Antonio College*

Antonio Cutolo-Ring, *Kansas City (KS) Community College*

Ken Damstrom, *Valley Forge Christian College*

Leslie Daniels, *Florida State College at Jacksonville*

Nancy Darling, *Bard College*

Paul Dawson, *Weber State University*

Janet B. Dean, *Asbury University*

Lynda DeDee, *University of Wisconsin, Oshkosh*

David C. Devonis, *Graceland University*

Charles Dickel, *Creighton University*

Darryl Dietrich, *College of St. Scholastica*

Stephanie Ding, *Del Mar College*

Lugenia Dixon, *Bainbridge College*

Benjamin Dobrin, *Virginia Wesleyan College*

Delores Doench, *Southwestern Community College*

Melanie Domenech Rodriguez, *Utah State University*

Sundi Donovan, *Liberty University*

Lana Dryden, *Sir Sanford Fleming College*

Gwenden Dueker, *Grand Valley State University*

Bryan Duke, *University of Central Oklahoma*

Trisha M. Dunkel, *Loyola University, Chicago*

Robin Eliason, *Piedmont Virginia Community College*

Traci Elliot, *Alvin Community College*

Frank Ellis, *University of Maine, Augusta*

Kelley Eltzroth, *Mid Michigan Community College*

Marya Endriga, *California State University, Stanislaus*

Lena Ericksen, *Western Washington University*

Kathryn Fagan, *California Baptist University*

Daniel Fasko, *Bowling Green State University*

Nancy Feehan, *University of San Francisco*

Meredyth C. Fellows, *West Chester University of Pennsylvania*

Gary Felt, *City University of New York*

Martha Fewell, *Barat College*

Mark A. Fine, *University of Missouri*

Roseanne L. Flores, *Hunter College, CUNY*

John Foley, *Hagerstown Community College*

James Foster, *George Fox University*

Geri Fox, *University of Illinois, Chicago*

Thomas Francigetto, *Northampton Community College*

James Francis, *San Jacinto College*

Doug Friedrich, *University of West Florida*

Lynn Garrioch, *Colby-Sawyer College*

Bill Garris, *Cumberland College*

Caroline Gee, *Palomar College*

C. Ray Gentry, *Lenoir-Rhyne College*

Carol George, *Mills College*

Elizabeth Gersten, *Victor Valley College*

Linde Getahun, *Bethel University*

Afshin Gharib, *California State University, East Bay*

Nada Glick, *Yeshiva University*

Andrea Goldstein, *Kaplan University*

Arthur Gonchar, *University of La Verne*

Helen Gore-Laird, *University of Houston, University Park*

Tyhesha N. Goss, *University of Pennsylvania*

Dan Grangaard, *Austin Community College, Rio Grande*

Julie Graul, *St. Louis Community College, Florissant Valley*

Elizabeth Gray, *North Park University*

Stefanie Gray Greiner, *Mississippi University for Women*

Erinn L. Green, *Wilmington College*

Dale D. Grubb, *Baldwin-Wallace College*

Laura Gruntmeir, *Redlands Community College*

Lisa Hager, *Spring Hill College*

Michael Hall, *Iowa Western Community College*

Andre Halliburton, *Prairie State College*

Laura Hanish, *Arizona State University*

Robert Hansson, *University of Tulsa*

Richard Harland, *West Texas A&M University*

Gregory Harris, *Polk Community College*

Virginia Harvey, *University of Massachusetts, Boston*

Margaret Hellie Huyck, *Illinois Institute of Technology*

Janice L. Hendrix, *Missouri State University*

Gertrude Henry, *Hampton University*

Rod Hetzel, *Baylor University*

Heather Hill, *University of Texas, San Antonio*

Elaine Hogan, *University of North Carolina, Wilmington*

Judith Holland, *Hawaii Pacific University*

Debra Hollister, *Valencia Community College*

Heather Holmes-Lonergan, *Metropolitan State College of Denver*

Rosemary Hornak, *Meredith College*

Suzy Horton, *Mesa Community College*

Rebecca Hoss, *College of Saint Mary*

Cynthia Hudley, *University of California, Santa Barbara*

Alycia Hund, *Illinois State University*

David P. Hurford, *Pittsburgh State University*

Elaine Ironsmith, *East Carolina University*

Jessica Jablonski, *Richard Stockton College*

Sabra Jacobs, *Big Sandy Community and Technical College*

David Johnson, *John Brown University*

Emilie Johnson, *Lindenwood University*

Mary Johnson, *Loras College*

Mike Johnson, *Hawaii Pacific University*

Peggy Jordan, *Oklahoma City Community College*

Lisa Judd, *Western Wisconsin Technical College*

Tracy R. Juliao, *University of Michigan Flint*

Elaine Justice, *Old Dominion University*

Steve Kaatz, *Bethel University*

Jyotsna M. Kalavar, *Penn State New Kensington*

Chi-Ming Kam, *City College of New York, CUNY*

Richard Kandus, *Mt. San Jacinto College*

Skip Keith, *Delaware Technical and Community College*

Michelle L. Kelley, *Old Dominion University*

Richie Kelley, *Baptist Bible College and Seminary*

Robert Kelley, *Mira Costa College*

Jeff Kellogg, *Marian College*

Colleen Kennedy, *Roosevelt University*

Sarah Kern, *The College of New Jersey*

Marcia Killien, *University of Washington*

Kenyon Knapp, *Troy State University*

Cynthia Koenig, *Mt. St. Mary's College of Maryland*

Steve Kohn, *Valdosta State University*

Holly Krogh, *Mississippi University for Women*

Martha Kuehn, *Central Lakes College*

Alvin Kuest, *Great Lakes Christian College*

Rich Lanthier, *George Washington University*

Peggy Lauria, *Central Connecticut State University*

Melisa Layne, *Danville Community College*

John LeChapitaine, *University of Wisconsin, River Falls*

Barbara Lehmann, *Augsburg College*

Rhinehart Lintonen, *Gateway Technical College*

Nancy Lobb, *Alvin Community College*

Martha V. Low, *Winston-Salem State University*

Carol Ludders, *University of St. Francis*

Dunja Lund Trunk, *Bloomfield College*

Vickie Luttrell, *Drury University*

Nina Lyon Jenkins, *University of Maryland, Eastern Shore*

Christine Malecki, *Northern Illinois University*

Marlowe Manger, *Stanly Community College*

Pamela Manners, *Troy State University*

Kathy Manuel, *Bossier Parish Community College*

Howard Markowitz, *Hawaii Pacific University*

Jayne D. B. Marsh, *University of Southern Maine, Lewiston-Auburn College*

Esther Martin, *California State University, Dominguez Hills*

Jan Mast, *Miami Dade College, North Campus*

Pan Maxson, *Duke University*

Nancy Mazurek, *Long Beach City College*

Christine McCormick, *Eastern Illinois University*

Jim McDonald, *California State University, Fresno*

Clark McKinney, *Southwest Tennessee Community College*

George Meyer, *Suffolk County Community College*

Barbara J. Miller, *Pasadena City College*

Christy Miller, *Coker College*

Mary Beth Miller, *Fresno City College*

Al Montgomery, *Our Lady of Holy Cross College*

Robin Montvilo, *Rhode Island College*

Peggy Moody, *St. Louis Community College*

Michelle Moriarty, *Johnson County Community College*

Wendy Bianchini Morrison, *Montana State University-Bozeman*

Ken Mumm, *University of Nebraska, Kearney*

Joyce Munsch, *Texas Tech University*

Jeannette Murphey, *Meridian Community College*

Lori Myers, *Louisiana Tech University*

Lana Nenide, *University of Wisconsin, Madison*

Margaret Nettles, *Alliant University*

Gregory Newton, *Diablo Valley College*

Barbara Nicoll, *University of La Verne*

Nancy Nolan, *Nashville State Community College*

Harriett Nordstrom, *University of Michigan, Flint*

Wendy North-Ollendorf, *Northwestern Connecticut Community College*

Elizabeth O'Connor, *St. Mary's College*

Susan O'Donnell, *George Fox University*

Jane Ogden, *East Texas Baptist University*

Shirley Ogletree, *Texas State University*

Claudius Oni, *South Piedmont Community College*

Randall E. Osborne, *Texas State University, San Marcos*

John Otey, *Southern Arkansas University*

Carol Ott, *University of Wisconsin, Milwaukee*

Patti Owen-Smith, *Oxford College*

Heidi Pasek, *Montana State University*

Julie Hicks Patrick, *West Virginia University*

Margaret Patton, *University of North Carolina, Charlotte*

Evelyn Payne, *Albany State University*

Ian E. Payton, *Bethune-Cookman University*

Carole Penner-Faje, *Molloy College*

Michelle L. Pilati, *Rio Hondo College*

Meril Posy, *Touro College, Brooklyn*

Shannon M. Pruden, *Temple University*

Ellery Pullman, *Briarcrest Bible College*

Samuel Putnam, *Bowdoin College*

Jeanne Quarles, *Oregon Coast Community College*

Mark Rafter, *College of the Canyons*

Cynthia Rand-Johnson, *Albany State University*

Janet Rangel, *Palo Alto College*

Jean Raniseski, *Alvin Community College*

Frances Raphael-Howell, *Montgomery College*

Celinda Reese, *Oklahoma State University*

Ethan Remmel, *Western Washington University*

Paul Rhoads, *Williams Baptist College*

Kerri A. Riggs, *Lourdes College*

Mark Rittman, *Cuyahoga Community College*

Jeanne Rivers, *Finger Lakes Community College*

Wendy Robertson, *Western Michigan University*

Richard Robins, *University of California, Davis*

Millie Roqueta, *Miami Dade College*

June Rosenberg, *Lyndon State College*

Christopher Rosnick, *University of South Florida*

Trisha Rossi, *Adelphi University*

Rodger Rossman, *College of the Albemarle*

Lisa Routh, *Pikes Peak Community College*

Stephanie Rowley, *University of Michigan, Ann Arbor*

Randall Russac, *University of North Florida*

Dawn Ella Rust, *Stephen F. Austin State University*

Tara Saathoff-Wells, *Central Michigan University*

Traci Sachteleben, *Southwestern Illinois College*

Douglas Sauber, *Arcadia University*

Chris Saxild, *Wisconsin Indianhead Technical College*

Barbara Schaudt, *California State University, Bakersfield*

Daniela E. Schreier, *Chicago School of Professional Psychology*

Pamela Schuetze, *SUNY College at Buffalo*

Donna Seagle, *Chattanooga State Technical Community College*

Bonnie Seegmiller, *Hunter College, CUNY*

Chris Seifert, *Montana State University*

Marianne Shablousky, *Community College of Allegheny County*

Susan Shapiro, *Indiana University, East*

Elliot Sharpe, *Maryville University*

Lawrence Shelton, *University of Vermont*

Shamani Shikwambi, *University of Northern Iowa*

Denise Simonsen, *Fort Lewis College*

Penny Skemp, *Mira Costa College*

Peggy Skinner, *South Plains College*

Barbara Smith, *Westminster College*

Valerie Smith, *Collin County Community College*

Edward Sofranko, *University of Rio Grande*

Joan Spiegel, *West Los Angeles College*

Jason S. Spiegelman, *Community College of Baltimore County*

Carolyn I. Spies, *Bloomfield College*

Scott Stein, *Southern Vermont College*

Stephanie Stein, *Central Washington University*

Sheila Steiner, *Jamestown College*

Jacqueline Stewart, *Seminole State College*

Robert Stewart, Jr., *Oakland University*

Cynthia Suarez, *Wofford College*

Joshua Susskind, *University of Northern Iowa*

Josephine Swalloway, *Curry College*

Emily Sweitzer, *California University of Pennsylvania*

Chuck Talor, *Valdosta State University*

Jamie Tanner, *South Georgia College*

Norma Tedder, *Edison Community College*

George Thatcher, *Texas Tech University*

Shannon Thomas, *Wallace Community College*

Donna Thompson, *Midland College*

Vicki Tinsley, *Brescia University*

Eugene Tootle, *Barry University*

David Tracer, *University of Colorado, Denver*

Stephen Truhon, *Austin Peay Centre, Fort Campbell*

Dana Van Abbema, *St. Mary's College of Maryland*

Mary Vandendorpe, *Lewis University*

Janice Vidic, *University of Rio Grande*

Steven Voss, *Moberly Area Community College*

William Walkup, *Southwest Baptist University*

Anne Weiher, *Metropolitan State College of Denver*

Robert Weis, *University of Wisconsin, Stevens Point*

Lori Werdenschlag, *Lyndon State College*

Noel Wescombe, *Whitworth College*

Andrea White, *Ithaca College*

Meade Whorton, *Louisiana Delta Community College*

Wanda A. Willard, *Monroe Community College*

Joylynne Wills, *Howard University*

Nancy A. Wilson, *Haywood Community College*

Steffen Wilson, *Eastern Kentucky University*

Bernadette Wise, *Iowa Lakes Community College*

Steve Wisecarver, *Lord Fairfax Community College*

Alex Wiseman, *University of Tulsa*

Rebecca Witt Stoffel, *West Liberty State College*

Nanci Woods, *Austin Peay State University*

Chrysalis L. Wright, *University of Central Florida*

Stephanie Wright, *Georgetown University*

David Yarbrough, *Texas State University*

Nikki Yonts, *Lyon College*

Ling-Yi Zhou, *University of St. Francis*

On the home front, I have been indebted to my colleagues at Middle Tennessee State University and to thousands of students over the past 25 years. As any teacher will tell you, I learned as much—or more—from you each semester as you did from me. I want to thank my student reference checkers, Kin Leong Chan and Sydney Reichin, for performing the difficult task of ferreting out the source of every new citation. I'm grateful to my baby, Thomas, for giving my life meaning and for offering me terrific parental bragging rights as he moves into his robust thirties (no longer an emerging adult!). But the real credit for this book belongs to Shelly Gertzfeld, my new life love since I moved to Chicago three years ago (yes, we met online!) and my late husband David for putting this book and my happiness center stage.

Janet Belsky
September 9, 2017

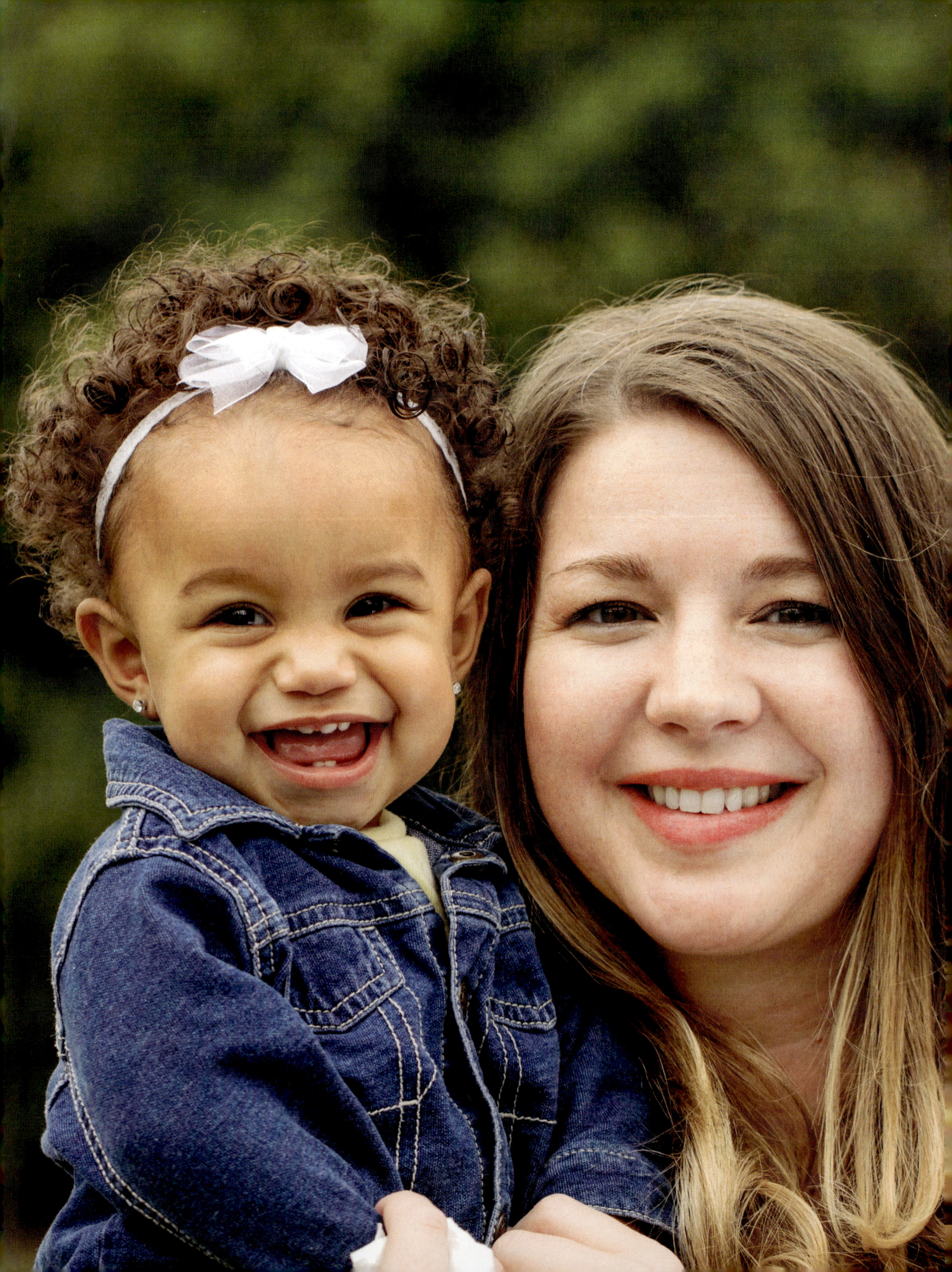

The Foundation

PART I

This two-chapter part offers the foundation for understanding children and adolescents.

Chapter 1—**The People and the Field** introduces all the major concepts in this course. Here, I'll describe our discipline's basic terminology, provide a history of childhood, and highlight basic markers that influence children's lives. Most important, this chapter describes the themes, theories, and research strategies that have shaped our field. Bottom line: Chapter 1 gives you the tools you need for understanding this book.

Chapter 2—**Prenatal Development, Pregnancy, and Birth** lays the foundation for children's developing lives. Here, you will learn about how a baby develops from a tiny clump of cells, and gain insights into the emotional experience of pregnancy from the point of view of mothers and fathers. This chapter describes pregnancy rituals in different cultures, discusses the impact of prenatal issues such as stress and infertility, and offers an in-depth look at the miracle of birth.

Application to Developing Lives Parenting Simulation: *Introduction and Prenatal Development*

In the Introduction module of *Developing Lives*, you will begin to customize the developmental journey of your child with information about your personality, cognitive abilities, and demographic characteristics. Below is a list of questions you will answer in the Prenatal simulation module. As you answer these questions, consider the impact your choice will have on the physical, cognitive, and social and emotional development of your baby.

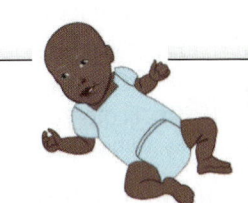

Physical	Cognitive	Social and Emotional
• Will you modify your behaviors and diet during pregnancy?	• Are you going to talk to your baby while he or she is in the womb?	• How will you and your partner's relationship change as a result of the pregnancy?
• Will you find out the gender of your baby prior to delivery?	• How much does your baby understand during prenatal development?	• Will you begin bonding with your baby prior to birth?
• What kind of delivery will you and your partner plan for (in the hospital with medication, at home with a doula, etc.)?		

Left: pixelheadphoto/Shutterstock

CHAPTER 1

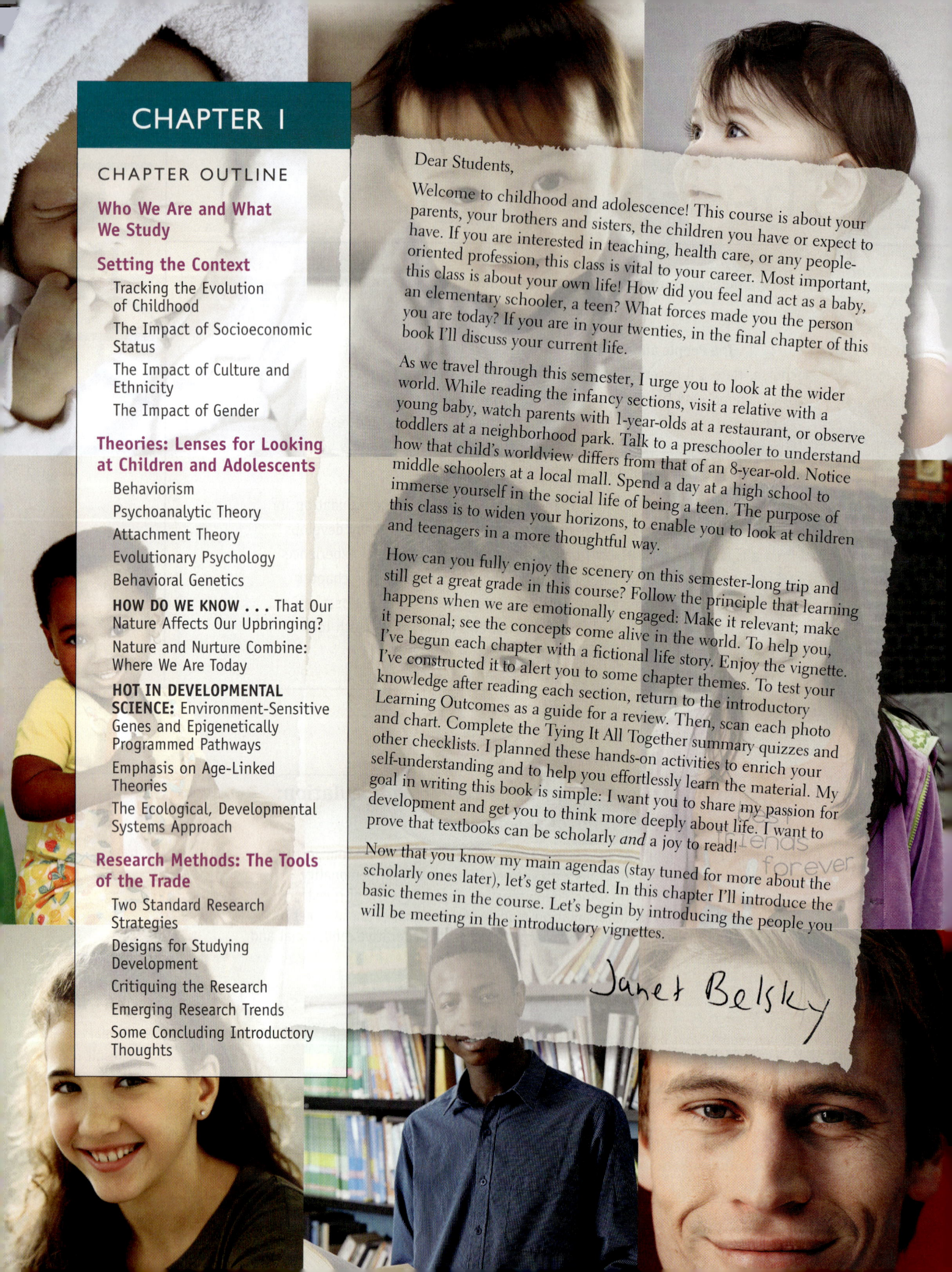

CHAPTER OUTLINE

Who We Are and What We Study

Setting the Context
Tracking the Evolution of Childhood

The Impact of Socioeconomic Status

The Impact of Culture and Ethnicity

The Impact of Gender

Theories: Lenses for Looking at Children and Adolescents
Behaviorism

Psychoanalytic Theory

Attachment Theory

Evolutionary Psychology

Behavioral Genetics

HOW DO WE KNOW . . . That Our Nature Affects Our Upbringing?

Nature and Nurture Combine: Where We Are Today

HOT IN DEVELOPMENTAL SCIENCE: Environment-Sensitive Genes and Epigenetically Programmed Pathways

Emphasis on Age-Linked Theories

The Ecological, Developmental Systems Approach

Research Methods: The Tools of the Trade
Two Standard Research Strategies

Designs for Studying Development

Critiquing the Research

Emerging Research Trends

Some Concluding Introductory Thoughts

Dear Students,

Welcome to childhood and adolescence! This course is about your parents, your brothers and sisters, the children you have or expect to have. If you are interested in teaching, health care, or any people-oriented profession, this class is vital to your career. Most important, this class is about your own life! How did you feel and act as a baby, an elementary schooler, a teen? What forces made you the person you are today? If you are in your twenties, in the final chapter of this book I'll discuss your current life.

As we travel through this semester, I urge you to look at the wider world. While reading the infancy sections, visit a relative with a young baby, watch parents with 1-year-olds at a restaurant, or observe toddlers at a neighborhood park. Talk to a preschooler to understand how that child's worldview differs from that of an 8-year-old. Notice middle schoolers at a local mall. Spend a day at a high school to immerse yourself in the social life of being a teen. The purpose of this class is to widen your horizons, to enable you to look at children and teenagers in a more thoughtful way.

How can you fully enjoy the scenery on this semester-long trip and still get a great grade in this course? Follow the principle that learning happens when we are emotionally engaged: Make it relevant; make it personal; see the concepts come alive in the world. To help you, I've begun each chapter with a fictional life story. Enjoy the vignette. I've constructed it to alert you to some chapter themes. To test your knowledge after reading each section, return to the introductory Learning Outcomes as a guide for a review. Then, scan each photo and chart. Complete the Tying It All Together summary quizzes and other checklists. I planned these hands-on activities to enrich your self-understanding and to help you effortlessly learn the material. My goal in writing this book is simple: I want you to share my passion for development and get you to think more deeply about life. I want to prove that textbooks can be scholarly *and* a joy to read!

Now that you know my main agendas (stay tuned for more about the scholarly ones later), let's get started. In this chapter I'll introduce the basic themes in the course. Let's begin by introducing the people you will be meeting in the introductory vignettes.

Janet Belsky

The People and the Field

It's a hot July afternoon, and María has invited a few neighbors to a barbecue. Moving to Shady Groves was a financial stretch, but María was determined to live in a town where her son, José, could go to a top-rated school, and—most important— grow up having the right kind of friends. A decade ago, María and her ex-husband left Honduras when the gang situation became dire. After years of struggle and a difficult divorce, María got refugee status, became fluent in English, and (finally) found a decently paying job. Now it's time to nurture the familylike relationships she misses from home.

First to ring the doorbell are Kim, her husband Jeff, and baby Elissa. For the past year, María has been thrilled to witness Elissa blossom from lying in a stroller, to toddling around. The downside is feeling jealous when Jeff expertly takes over the child care. It brings home how difficult life can be as a single mom.

Next to arrive are Samantha and Sam, the teenage twins from María's church youth group. María takes credit (but she is too humble to broadcast this fact) for helping Samantha blossom, too. Last year, Samantha was involved in drugs and running around with older boys. After María enticed her "second daughter/ assistant" to volunteer for community service during winter break, Samantha's grades and self-esteem have soared.

Now, María's real baby runs in. Yes, mothers can be biased, but everyone agrees that José is a special boy. Since preschool, José has been exceptionally caring. Now, at age 9, her child is amazingly adult in the way he thinks about life.

After José excuses himself to give Elissa backyard horsey rides—amidst gales of joy—the talk turns to deeper issues. Kim shares her worries about day care. Hasn't María noticed how clingy Elissa gets when she and Jeff leave the room? How will her precious child handle spending hours away each day, when Elissa can't let her parents out of sight?

Sam admits to having separation anxiety, too. This September he must leave for college and enter the real world. Is it normal to be almost 18 and not have a clue about what you want to do in life?

María has her own worries about this next school year. How will her sensitive child handle the bullying she knows is so common in fifth grade?

Still, as a wise "old" woman of 40, María can keep things in perspective. In Honduras, many children have no future. Despite her fears for her baby, how blessed she is to live in the United States and, best yet, to have new familylike friends!

Are María's worries about bullying realistic? Why do babies such as Elissa get so clingy around age 1, and what mental leaps make 9-year-olds like José seem so grown up? What can keep adolescents, such as Samantha, from going down the wrong path, and what college experiences will help Sam connect with his passions in life? **Developmentalists,** or **developmental scientists**—people who study development—are about to answer these questions and hundreds of others about children's unfolding lives.

developmentalists (developmental scientists) Researchers and practitioners whose professional interest lies in development.

Who We Are and What We Study

LEARNING OUTCOME
- Describe developmental scientists' interests.

Although philosophers have speculated about children for millennia, the research discipline called *developmental science* is relatively new. In 1877, Charles Darwin published an article based on notes he had made about his baby during the first years of life. In the 1890s, a pioneering psychologist named G. Stanley Hall established the first institute in the United States devoted to research on the child. Child development began to take off between World Wars I and II (Lerner, 1998). It remains the passion of thousands of scientists working in every corner of the globe. Who works in this huge field, and what passions drive people who study children's and adolescents' lives?

This actress, working with refugee children, shares a core mission of developmental science: to help traumatized children around the world.

- **Developmental science is multidisciplinary.** It draws on disciplines as different as neuroscience, nursing, psychology, biology, education, and economics to understand how children develop and grow. A biologically oriented researcher might examine toddlers' output of salivary cortisol (a stress hormone) when they arrive at day care. An anthropologist might look at what cultural values shape day-care choices. An economist might explore the impact on adult wages of offering government-funded day care in Finland and France.

A biochemist studying puberty could examine the molecular structure of the hormones unleashing the body changes. An educator might focus on innovative ways to teach middle school boys. A psychologist might study peer-group formation or bullying among young teens. A culturally oriented adolescent specialist could compare how different societies treat the pubertal years.

- **Developmental science explores the predictable milestones that punctuate human growth,** from walking to speaking, to Elissa's sudden shyness and attachment to her parents. What normally happens physically and intellectually at age 8 or 18? What makes a 9-year-old child's worldview totally different from that of a 3-year-old?

- **Developmental science focuses on the individual variations that give spice to life.** Why do some boys, such as José, seem especially caring, and what causes the differences in temperament we can see almost from birth? When do normal variations in the rate of development shade into problems? Should parents be worried if their 3-year-old isn't speaking or their 10-year-old seems particularly aggressive or unable to sit still? What parenting strategies and life conditions best mold babies into loving, accomplished adults?

- **Developmental science explores the impact of specific child-rearing practices and life conditions.** How does spanking, or sleeping in the same bed, or divorcing, or day care affect children? What is it like to grow up in a single-parent family, and is María right that moving to Shady Groves will make a difference in José's life? In what ways do boys and girls adapt to entering middle school?

Developmentalists realize that living at our unique time in history determines whether children enter day care or middle school, or if people are likely to divorce. They understand that child-rearing practices such as spanking or sleeping in bed with a child vary, depending on our social class and cultural background. They know that children's development is influenced by several basic **contexts of development,** or overall conditions of life.

contexts of development Basic markers that shape children's (and adults') lives.

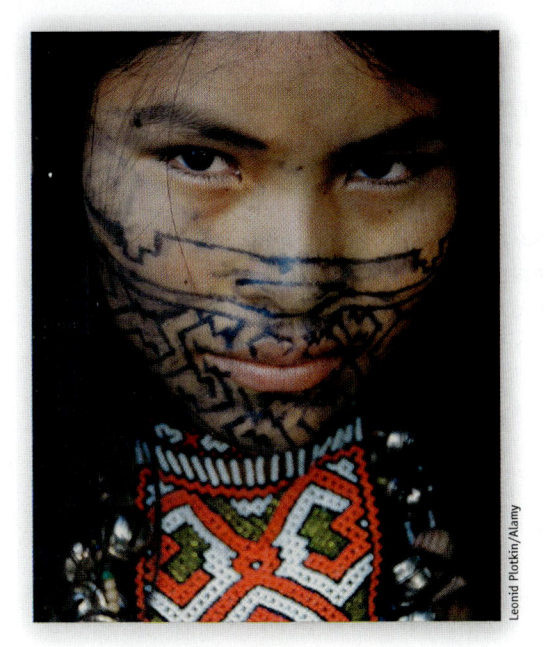

Because societies vary in how they treat puberty, culturally oriented developmentalists might study how this coming-of-age ritual affects a girl's feelings about her body during this watershed time of life.

This blissful family is making a nontraditional choice—but only in the West. In Chapter 3, you will learn how bed sharing affects families.

Setting the Context

Now it's time to introduce several basic contexts that shape children's lives. The most important is what developmentalists call our **cohort**, the age group and *time* in history when we travel through life.

Tracking the Evolution of Childhood

> At age ten he began his work life helping . . . manufacture candles and soap. He . . . wanted to go to sea, but his father refused and apprenticed him to a master printer. At age 17 he ran away from Boston to Philadelphia to search for work.
>
> His father died when he was 11, and he left school. At 17 he was appointed official surveyor for Culpepper County in Virginia. By age 20 he was in charge of managing his family's plantation.
>
> (Mintz, 2004)

Who were these boys? Their names were Benjamin Franklin and George Washington.

Imagine being born in Colonial times. In addition to reaching adulthood at a much younger age, your chance of having *any* childhood would be far from secure. In seventeenth-century Paris, roughly 1 in every 3 babies died in early infancy (Ariès, 1962; Hrdy, 1999). As late as 1900, almost 1 in 5 U.S. children died during their first years of life (Gordon, 2015).

The incredible childhood mortality rates, plus tremendously hard lives, may explain why child-rearing practices that today are considered "abusive" used to be routine. In the past, parents felt free to hit their children and abandon their babies at birth (Konner, 2010; Pinker, 2011). In the early 1800s in Paris, about 1 in 5 newborns was "exposed"—placed in the doorway of churches, or left outside to die. In cities such as St. Petersburg, Russia, almost one in two infants faced this fate (Ariès, 1962; Hrdy, 1999).

LEARNING OUTCOMES

- Describe developmental contexts that shape children's lives, including four changes during the twentieth century.
- Identify the core difference between developed and developing nations.
- Contrast individualistic and collectivist cultural worldviews.

cohort People born during the same historical time period.

In the nineteenth century, children as young as age 5 or 6 worked in factories such as this cannery. Clearly, we have come a long way in our attitudes toward childhood.

In addition, for most of history, people did not share our modern view that childhood is a special life stage (Ariès, 1962; Mintz, 2004). Children, as you saw above, began to work at a young age. During the early industrial revolution, poor boys and girls made up more than one-third of the labor force in British mills (Mintz, 2004).

In the seventeenth and eighteenth centuries, enlightenment philosophers such as John Locke and Jean Jacques Rousseau spelled out a different vision of childhood (Pinker, 2011). Locke believed that human beings are born a *tabula rasa*, a blank slate on which anything could be written, and that the way we treat children shapes their adult lives. Rousseau argued that babies enter life totally innocent. He felt that we should leave babies alone to naturally develop their gifts. However, this kinder, more permissive child-rearing style could only resonate when the early-twentieth-century explosion of technological advances—from indoor toilets to washing machines, from refrigerators to cars—allowed us to enter our modern age (Gordon, 2015).

Demographic Shifts

demographic Relating to the statistical study of populations.

What **demographic** (population) shifts made the twentieth century unique for children?

AN EXTENSION IN LIFE EXPECTANCY The main change revolutionizing childhood relates to health. In the nineteenth century, before pasteurization and refrigeration, contaminated milk and impure foods ensured that many infants did not survive (Gordon, 2015). In 1900, most people died of bacterial or viral illnesses—diseases such as dysentery or diphtheria that strike in youth and early adult life. When doctors were able to cure these illnesses (through vaccines), people could count on *all* their sons and daughters living to adulthood. Parents felt more comfortable getting attached to their babies and could seriously limit their family size (more about this soon).

In addition, as Western nations grew affluent, children no longer had to work to help the family from an early age. Education became essential to constructing a secure adult life.

In the not-so-distant past, these twenty-something women would have been labeled "old maids." Today, it is normal to put off marriage and parenthood for a decade after leaving one's teens.

AN ESCALATION IN EDUCATION Education sets the limits of childhood because as long as we are in school, we must depend on our parents to provide care. In the nineteenth century in Western Europe and much of the United States, primary school became mandatory (Ariès, 1962). Still, as late as 1915, only 1 in 10 U.S. children attended high school; most people began their work lives after seventh or eighth grade (Mintz, 2004; Gordon, 2015).

At the beginning of the twentieth century, psychologist G. Stanley Hall (1904/1969) identified a stage of "storm and stress" between childhood and adulthood, which he named **adolescence.** However, it was only during the Great Depression of the 1930s, when President Franklin Roosevelt signed a bill mandating high school attendance, that adolescence became a standard U.S. life stage (Mintz, 2004). Our famous teenage culture has existed for less than 100 years!

adolescence Stage of life lasting from puberty through high school graduation (roughly age 12 to 19).

emerging adulthood The phase of life that begins after high school, lasts through the late twenties, and is devoted to constructing an adult life.

In recent decades, with college and graduate school, we have delayed adulthood to an older age. Developmentalists (see Tanner & Arnett, 2010) have identified a new in-between stage of life in affluent countries. **Emerging adulthood,** lasting from age 18 through the twenties, is devoted to exploring our place in the world.

A DECREASE IN FAMILY SIZE Throughout history, it made sense for people to get married right after puberty and then have 6 or 10 children, because few babies would survive. Then, beginning in the late nineteenth century, along with the medical advances I just discussed and more access to contraception and abortion (Lahey, 2014), parents began to limit their childbearing. Births in affluent nations started to decline.

Today, **fertility rates** (childbirths per female) in every European nation have slid below the number needed to replace the population (2.1 children). Although, as Figure 1.1 suggests, child birth rates still vary dramatically worldwide, in East Asia fertility has dipped alarmingly close to one child (Central Intelligence Agency, 2015).

During the past half-century, a similar trend has occurred in poorer regions of the globe. Only 3 percent of the world's population is still giving birth at rates that greatly exceed the level needed to replace the population today.

Having one or two babies, and waiting until our thirties to give birth, has incredible benefits. Older, more affluent couples have the luxury to lavish total attention on each precious daughter and son. But another family change affecting children has had more mixed effects—the late-twentieth-century decline in traditional marriages.

A DECLINE IN THE TRADITIONAL WESTERN TWO-PARENT FAMILY When I was growing up in my middle-class suburb during the 1950s, women who dared to get pregnant without a wedding ring were forced to give up their babies for adoption or endure "shotgun" marriages. Once people got married, gender roles were set in stone. Wives stayed home to raise children while husbands worked.

Then, during the 1960s and 1970s, when the mammoth bulge in the population called the **baby boom** (people born from 1946–1961) became teenagers, we rebelled against these rigid gender roles. The *women's movement* encouraged wives to have careers. Everyone felt liberated to leave an unhappy marriage. People no longer felt they needed to be married to become parents at all.

Today, with more than half of U.S. married women in the workforce, a minority of parents fit the traditional roles of breadwinner husband and homemaker wife. Today, with alternate family forms, such as single motherhood (and fatherhood), adoption, and gay parenthood, out-of-the-closet children are growing up in a variety of family forms. We need to celebrate this beautiful diversity (and resilience) of twenty-first-century Western families. However, the fact that as of 2014 in the United States, more than 2 in 5 babies were born to unmarried women (Child Trends Databank, 2016) has a serious downside. Imagine the challenges of supporting a family alone, and you will understand why, for the past 40 years, young children have been the poorest segment of the U.S. population (Economic Policy Institute, 2011). Unfortunately for millions of struggling single parents, economic deprivation can be a family's fate.

The timeline at the bottom of this page summarizes these four historic twentieth-century demographic changes. In this book, I will also explore two twenty-first-century transformations in children's lives: the growth of **income inequalities,** or the widening gap between the very rich and everyone else in the United States, and how

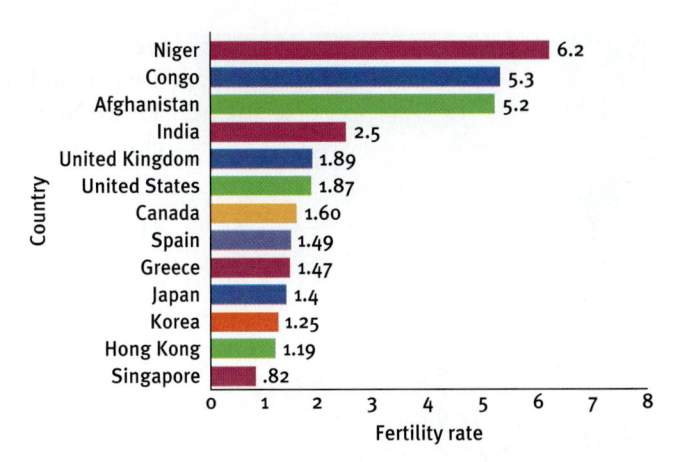

Country	Fertility rate
Niger	6.2
Congo	5.3
Afghanistan	5.2
India	2.5
United Kingdom	1.89
United States	1.87
Canada	1.60
Spain	1.49
Greece	1.47
Japan	1.4
Korea	1.25
Hong Kong	1.19
Singapore	.82

FIGURE 1.1: Snapshot of fertility rates in selected nations in 2016 Although worldwide, fertility has dramatically declined; notice that childbearing rates still vary greatly from nation to nation today.

Data from Central Intelligence Agency, The World Factbook, 2015.

fertility rate In a specific nation, the average number of children a woman gives birth to during her lifetime.

baby boomers Age group born from 1946–1961, after soldiers returned from world War II.

income inequality The gap between the very rich (or top 1 percent of the population) and everyone else.

TIMELINE: Selected Twentieth-Century Milestones and the Progress of the Huge Baby Boom

	1900	1910	1920	1930	1940	1950	1960	1970	1980	1990	2000	2010	2020	2030
MAJOR SOCIETAL CHANGE	Life expectancy takes off — Deaths shift from infectious to chronic diseases								Decline of traditional family — Women's movement/rise in divorce/unmarried motherhood/gay parents					
EDUCATION					Adolescence becomes life stage				College			Emerging adulthood		
FERTILITY	Begins to decline				Baby boom							Below replacement		

8　PART I　The Foundation

technology, in particular **social networking sites**—such as Facebook, Twitter, and Instagram—are altering the lives of teenagers and emerging adults. Now it's time to focus on another powerful enduring force shaping children's lives—socioeconomic status.

The Impact of Socioeconomic Status

Socioeconomic status (SES)—a term referring to education and income—affects development even before we leave the womb. Low-income children are often vulnerable to a cascade of problems—from being born less healthy to attending lower-quality schools, from living in more dangerous neighborhoods to being less likely to finish college than their middle-class peers. Not only do developmentalists rank children within nations by socioeconomic status, they rank nations, too.

Developed-world nations are defined by their affluence, or high median per-person incomes. Babies born in these countries have widespread access to education and state-of-the-art medical care. In these nations, childhood often lasts for decades, family sizes are tiny, and parents assume that their newborns will live to old age. Traditionally, the United States, Canada, Australia, New Zealand, and Japan, as well as every Western European nation, are classified in this "most affluent" category, although its ranks are expanding as the Asian economies explode.

Developing-world countries stand in sharp contrast to these most privileged nations. In the world's worst-off regions, such as sub-Saharan Africa (recall from Figure 1.1 on page 7), fertility remains high. Pregnancy is hazardous and children may die from contaminated foods or normally curable infectious diseases. In many ways, babies born in these most impoverished nations have lives similar to the ones children faced before we entered our twentieth-century modern age.

This consequence of the social-media revolution is familiar. In Chapter 6, you will learn what forces promote bullying and what makes these anonymous messages more distressing than peer harassment of the face-to-face kind.

The Impact of Culture and Ethnicity

Children growing up in developing nations lead more difficult lives. Still, if you visited these places, you might be struck by a sense of community we don't see in the West. Can we categorize societies according to their basic values, apart from their wealth? Developmentalists who study culture answer yes.

Collectivist cultures place a premium on social harmony. The family generations live together, even as adults. Children are taught to obey their elders, to suppress their feelings, to value being respectful, and to subordinate their needs to the good of the wider group.

Individualistic cultures emphasize independence, competition, and personal success. Children are encouraged to openly express their emotions, to assert themselves, and to stand on their own as self-sufficient and independent adults. Traditionally, Western nations score high on indices of individualism. Nations in Asia, Africa, and South America rank higher on collectivism scales (Hofstede, 1981, 2001; Triandis, 1995).

As we scan children's lives worldwide, I will distinguish between collectivist and more individualistic societies. I also will highlight the issues families face when they move from these traditional cultures to the West and will explore research relating to the beautiful multicultural mosaic that defines childhood in the twenty-first-century United States (see Figure 1.2).

As you read this information, keep in mind that the *similarities* among children far outweigh minor distinctions based on socioeconomic status, world region, culture, or race. Moreover, making diversity generalizations is particularly hazardous because of the diversity that exists *within* each country and ethnic group. In the most individualistic country (no surprise, that's the United States), people have a mix of

---

social networking sites Internet sites whose goal is to forge personal connections among users.

socioeconomic status (SES) A basic marker referring to status on educational and, especially, income rungs.

developed world The most affluent countries in the world.

developing world The more impoverished countries of the world.

collectivist cultures Societies that prize social harmony, obedience, and close family connectedness over individual achievement.

individualistic cultures Societies that promote personal achievement and independence as keys to successful adult lives.

collectivist and individualistic worldviews. Due to globalization, traditional collectivistic cultures such as China and Japan have developed more individualistic, Western worldviews. Still, there is one distinction that hasn't changed—being born female (having two X chromosomes) or being male (having an X and a Y chromosome).

The Impact of Gender

Obviously, our culture's values shape our development as boys and girls. Does a society promote gender-neutral roles or forbid females from having an education and force girls to get married at a young age? The fact that, at this moment in history, a few young people balk at labeling themselves according to the binary categories of male or female offers a compelling twenty-first-century lesson in the theoretical fluidity of gender roles. But *statistically speaking*, males and females still behave differently—and we can see these gender differences early in life.

Are boys more aggressive than girls? When we see male/female differences in motor skills, math abilities, and childhood play, are these variations mainly due to the environment (societal pressures or the way we are brought up) or to inborn, biological forces? Throughout this book, I'll examine these questions as I spell out fascinating facts about gender differences in development. To introduce this conversation, you might want to take the "Is It Boys or Girls?" quiz in Table 1.1. Keep a copy. As we travel through this semester, you can check the accuracy of your ideas.

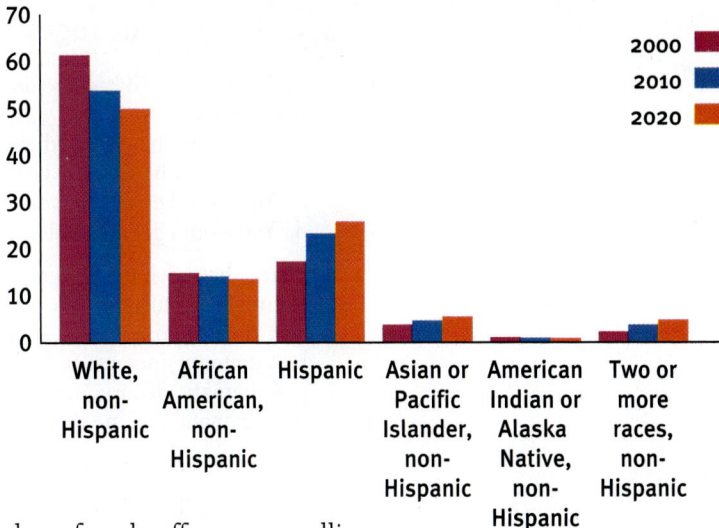

FIGURE 1.2: Racial and ethnic composition of children under age 18 in the United States by 2000, 2010, and projected for 2020 Notice that while the fraction of White children has been regularly declining since the turn of the twenty-first century, Hispanics are becoming a larger fraction of the U.S. child population.

Data from Child Trends Data Bank, 2017.

Table 1.1: Is It Boys or Girls?

1. Who are more likely to survive the hazards of prenatal development, male or female fetuses? (You will find the answer in Chapter 2.)
2. Who are more vulnerable to having enduring attachment issues after living in an institution, toddler girls or boys? (You will find the answer in Chapter 4.)
3. Who are more likely to be diagnosed with attention-deficit/hyperactivity disorder (ADHD) and autism spectrum disorder, boys or girls? (You will find answers in Chapters 5 and 6.)
4. Who are more aggressive, boys or girls? (You will find the answer in Chapter 6.)
5. Who are more likely to be diagnosed with learning disabilities in school, girls or boys? (You will find the answer in Chapter 7.)
6. Who, when they reach puberty at an earlier-than-typical age, are more at risk of developing problems, boys or girls? (You will find the answer in Chapter 8.)
7. Who are more likely to get depressed as teens, girls or boys? (You will find the answer in Chapter 9.)
8. Who gets closer to their parents as older teens, boys or girls? (You will find the answer in Chapter 9.)
9. Who benefits more from having a love relationship in their twenties—males, females, or both sexes? (You will find the answer in Chapter 10.)

Now that I've highlighted how children's development is shaped by gender, culture, and socioeconomic status—and varies throughout history—let's get to the science. After you complete this section's Tying It All Together review quiz, I will introduce the main theories, research methods, concepts, and scientific terms in this book.

Tying It All Together

1. Imagine you were born *before* the twentieth century. Which statement about your life would be *least true*?
   a. You would have a good chance of dying during childhood.
   b. You might be severely beaten or abused.
   c. You would enter the workforce right after high school.
   d. You would get married and have children at a relatively young age.

2. Name the specific demographic change that occurred during the *final third* of the twentieth century.
   a. A dramatic rise in life expectancy
   b. A dramatic increase in high school attendance
   c. A dramatic decline in the traditional two-parent married couple family
   d. A dramatic decline in family closeness

3. In a word, name the main problem with being an unmarried mother.

4. Pablo says, "I would never think of leaving my parents or living far from my brothers and sisters. A person must take care of his extended family before satisfying his own needs." Peter says, "My primary commitment is to my wife and children. A person needs, above all, to make an independent life." Pablo has a(n) _____ worldview, while Peter's worldview is more _____.

5. List and (possibly discuss with the class) the merits and the disadvantages of growing up in the 1950s versus today.

Answers to the Tying It All Together questions can be found at the end of this chapter.

Theories: Lenses for Looking at Children and Adolescents

LEARNING OUTCOMES
- Summarize the theories developmental scientists use to study childhood and adolescence.
- Describe the research strategy behavioral geneticists use.
- Explain how "nature" and "nurture" interact during development.

theory Any perspective explaining why people act the way they do. Theories allow us to predict behavior and also suggest how to intervene to improve behavior.

nature Biological or genetic causes of development.

nurture Environmental causes of development.

José's caring personality is genetic. Because Elissa has such loving parents, she is set up to be a successful adult. Sam is worried about finding his identity. If you had any of these thoughts while reading about the people in the opening chapter vignette, you were using a major theory in child development.

Theories explain what causes us to act as we do. They may allow us to predict the future. Ideally, they tell us how to improve the quality of children's lives. Theories in developmental science may offer explanations of behavior that apply to all children, or describe changes that occur at particular stages of development. This section provides a preview of both kinds of theories.

Let's begin by outlining some theories (one is actually a research discipline) that offer general explanations of behavior. I've organized these theories somewhat chronologically—based on *when* they appeared during the twentieth century—but mainly according to their position on that core issue: Is it the environment, or the wider world, that determines how we develop? Are our personalities, talents, and traits shaped mainly by biological or genetic forces? This is the famous **nature** (biology) versus **nurture** (environment) question.

Behaviorism: The Original Blockbuster "Nurture" Theory

> Give me a dozen healthy infants . . . and I'll guarantee to take any one at random and train him to be any specialist I might select—doctor, lawyer, artist, merchant-chief, and yes, even beggar man and thief.
>
> (Watson, 1930, p. 104)

So proclaimed the early-twentieth-century psychologist John Watson as he spelled out the nurture-is-all-important position of traditional behaviorism. Intoxicated by the revolution in technology and medicine I discussed in the previous section, Watson and his fellow behaviorist B. F. Skinner (1960, 1974) wanted to pioneer a new rigorous science of human behavior. These theorists argued that, since we could not measure feelings and thoughts, a true science of psychology could focus only on observable responses. Moreover, these **traditional behaviorists** believed a few general laws of learning could explain behavior from infancy through the teens.

Exploring Reinforcement

According to Skinner, the general law of learning that causes each voluntary action, from forming our first words to mastering math, is **operant conditioning**. Responses that we reward, or reinforce, are learned. Responses that are not reinforced go away, or are *extinguished*. So what accounts for Watson's beggar men and thieves, out-of-control 2-year-olds, and teenagers who get into trouble at home and school? According to Skinner, the reinforcements are operating as they should. The problem is that, instead of reinforcing positive behavior, we often reinforce the wrong things.

One excellent place to see Skinner's point is by visiting your local Walmart or restaurant. Notice how when children act up at the store, parents often buy them a toy to quiet them down. At dinner, as long as a toddler is playing quietly, adults ignore her. When she starts to hurl objects off the table, they pick her up, kiss her, and take her outside. Then they complain about their child's difficult personality, not realizing that their *own* reinforcements have produced these responses!

One of Skinner's most interesting concepts, derived from his work with pigeons, relates to *variable reinforcement schedules*. This is the type of reinforcement that typically occurs in daily life: We get reinforced unpredictably, so we keep responding, realizing that if we continue, *at some point* we will be reinforced. Readers with children will understand how difficult it is to follow the basic behavioral principle to be consistent or not let a negative variable schedule emerge. At Walmart, even though you vow, "I won't give in to bad behavior!" as your toddler's tantrums escalate, you cave in, simply to avoid other shoppers' disapproving stares ("What an out-of-control mother and bratty kid!"). Unfortunately, your child has learned, "If I keep whining, *eventually* I'll get what I want."

Reinforcement (and its opposite process, *extinction*) is a powerful force for both good and bad. It explains why a child who starts out succeeding early in elementary school (being reinforced by receiving A's) is apt to study more. If a kindergartner begins failing socially (does not get positive reinforcement from her peers), she is at risk for becoming incredibly shy or highly aggressive in third or fourth grade (see Chapter 6). If people did not reinforce you for your actions, wouldn't you withdraw or act in socially inappropriate ways?

Behaviorism makes sense of classic problems that erupt during older childhood and the teens. If classmates reinforce bullying by laughing, wouldn't that activity become normal in fifth grade (see Chapter 6)? Since peers reinforce teenagers for rebelling, wouldn't adolescents test the limits by engaging in illegal acts (see Chapter 9)? According to traditional behaviorists, the key to eliminating bullying or reducing teenage delinquency is simple: We need to reinforce the right things.

However, life is not that simple. Human beings *do* think and reason. Children do not need to be personally reinforced to learn.

This photo shows B. F. Skinner with his favorite research subject for exploring operant conditioning—the pigeon. By charting how often pigeons pecked before being reinforced by food, and varying the patterns of reinforcement, this famous behaviorist was able to tell us a good deal about how humans act.

Imagine wheeling this whining toddler through your local Walmart grocery aisle. Wouldn't you be tempted to reinforce this unpleasant behavior by silencing the child with an enticing object on the shelf?

traditional behaviorism The original behavioral worldview that focused on charting and modifying only "objective," visible behaviors.

operant conditioning Learning that determines any voluntary response. Specifically, children behave the way they do when they are reinforced for acting in a certain way.

reinforcement Behavioral term for reward.

cognitive behaviorism (social learning theory) A behavioral worldview emphasizing that children learn by watching others and that our thoughts about the reinforcers determine behavior. Cognitive behaviorists focus on charting and modifying children's thoughts.

modeling Learning by watching and imitating others.

self-efficacy According to cognitive behaviorism, an internal belief in one's competence that predicts whether children initiate activities or persist in the face of failures.

Taking a Different Perspective: Exploring Cognitions

Enter **cognitive behaviorism (social learning theory)**, launched by Albert Bandura (1977; 1986) and his colleagues in the 1970s with studies demonstrating the power of **modeling,** or learning by watching and imitating what other people do.

Because we are a social species, modeling (both imitating other people, as well as others reciprocally imitating us) is endemic in daily life. Given that modeling begins well before babies start walking, who are children most likely to *generally* model as they grow up?

Bandura (1986) finds that children model people who are nurturing, or relate to them in a caring way. (The good news here is that being a loving, hands-on parent is the best way to naturally embed your values and ideas.) Children model people whom they categorize as being similar to them. At age 2, you probably modeled anything from the vacuum cleaner to the family dog. As you traveled into your teens, you tailored your modeling selectively, based on understanding what kind of person you were.

Modeling similar people partly explains why, after children understand their gender label (girl or boy) at about age 2½, they separate into sex-segregated play groups and prefer to play with their "own group" (see Chapter 5). It accounts for why at-risk teenagers gravitate to the druggies group and then model the leader who most embodies these antisocial norms (see Chapter 9). While I will use modeling to explain behavior at several points in this book, I'll invoke another concept—also devised by Bandura—as a *genuine* foundation in the chapters to come: self-efficacy.

Self-efficacy refers to our belief in our competence, our sense that we can be successful at a given task. According to Bandura (1989, 1992, 1997), efficacy feelings determine the goals we set. They predict which activities we engage in as we travel through life. When self-efficacy is low, elementary schoolers decide not to tackle that difficult math problem. Emerging adults shy away from asking a stranger for a date. When self-efficacy is high, people not only take action, but also continue to act long after the traditional behavioral approach suggests that extinction should occur.

Let's imagine that your teenage son dreams of becoming a scientist, but gets an F on his first high school chemistry test. If his academic self-efficacy is low, he might conclude, "I'm basically not smart." He might not put forth effort on the next exam. But if he has high self-efficacy, your child will think, "I just need to work harder. I can do it. I'm *going* to get a good grade in this class!"

How do children develop low or high self-efficacy? What specific strategies stimulate efficacy feelings during elementary school and the teenage years? These are the kinds of questions we will explore throughout this book in examining Bandura's important concept.

By now, you may be impressed with behaviorism's simple, action-oriented concepts. Be consistent. Don't reinforce negative behavior. Reinforce positive things (from traditional behaviorism). Draw on the principles of modeling and stimulate efficacy feelings to help children succeed (from cognitive behaviorism).

Still, many developmentalists—even people who believe that nurture (or the environment) is important—find behaviorism unsatisfying. Aren't we made up of more than just efficacy feelings or reinforced responses? Isn't there a basic core to personality, and aren't the lessons we learn in childhood vital in shaping adult life? Notice that behaviorism doesn't address that core question: What *really* motivates us as people? To address these gaps, developmental scientists, particularly in the past, turned to the insights of that world-class genius, Sigmund Freud.

This boy is obviously not thrilled about failing his chemistry test. But if he has high self-efficacy he will think, "I just need to work harder! I can get an A next time!"

Psychoanalytic Theory: Focus on Early Childhood and Unconscious Motivations

Sigmund Freud's ideas are currently not in vogue in developmental science. However, no one can dispute the fact that Freud (1856–1939) transformed the way we think about human beings. Anytime you say, "I must have done that unconsciously" or "My problems are due to my childhood," you are quoting Freudian thought.

Freud, a Viennese Jewish physician, wrote more than 40 books and monographs in a burst of brilliance during the early twentieth century. His ideas revolutionized everything from anthropology to the arts, in addition to jump-starting the modern field of mental health. Freud's mission, however, was simple: to decode why his patients were in emotional pain.

Freud's theory is called *psychoanalytic* because it analyzes the psyche, or our inner life. By listening to his patients, Freud became convinced that our actions are dominated by feelings of which we are not aware. The roots of emotional problems lay in repressed (made unconscious) feelings from early childhood. Moreover, "mothering" during the first five years of life determines adult mental health.

Specifically, Freud posited three hypothetical structures. The *id*, present at birth, is the mass of instincts, needs, and feelings we have when we arrive in the world. During early childhood, the conscious, rational part of our personality—called the *ego*—emerges. Ego functions involve thinking, reasoning, planning, and fulfilling our id desires in realistic ways. Finally, a structure called the *superego*—the moral arm of our personality—exists in opposition to the id's desires.

According to Freud and his followers, if children have excellent parents, they will develop a strong ego, which sets them up to master the challenges of life. If parents are insensitive or their caregiving is impaired, adult behavior will be id driven, and a person's life will be out of control. The purpose of Freud's therapy, called *psychoanalysis*, was to enable his patients to become aware of the repressed early childhood experiences causing their symptoms, thereby liberating them from the tyranny of the unconscious to live rational, productive lives. (As Freud famously put it, "where *id* there was, *ego* there will be.")

In sum, according to Freud: (1) Human beings are basically irrational; (2) lifelong mental health depends on the quality of our parents' care; and (3) the roots of adult maturity are laid down during the first years of life.

By now many of you might be on a similar page as Freud. Where you are apt to part serious company with the theory relates to Freud's stages of sexuality. Freud argued that sexual feelings (which he called *libido*) are the motivation that drives human life, and he put forth the shocking idea—especially at that time—that babies are sexual human beings. As the infant develops, he argued, sexual feelings are centered on specific areas of the body called *erogenous zones*. During the first year of life, the erogenous zone is the mouth (the famous *oral stage*). Around age 2, with toilet training, sexual feelings center on elimination (the *anal stage*). Finally, around ages 3 and 4, sexual feelings shift to the genitals (the *phallic stage*). During this time, the child develops sexual fantasies relating to the parent of the opposite sex (the *Oedipus complex*), and the same-sex parent becomes a rival. Then sexuality is repressed, the child identifies with that parent, the superego is formed, and children enter *latency*—an asexual stage that lasts through elementary school.

Partly because his sexual stages seem so foreign to our thinking, we tend to reject psychoanalytic theory as outdated—an artifact of a distant era. A deeper look suggests we might be wrong. Like Freud, contemporary developmentalists believe that self-understanding—fostering children's ability to reflect on and regulate their emotions—is at the core of raising competent human beings. Like Freud, developmental scientists are passionate to trace the roots of later development to what happens

Freud, pictured here in his robust middle age, alerted us to the power of childhood experiences and unconscious motivations in shaping life.

in children's earliest months and years of life. As you read this book, perhaps you will agree that, despite its different terminology and approaches, modern child development owes a great philosophical debt to Freud. Moreover, psychoanalytic theory gave birth to that important contemporary perspective called *attachment theory*.

Attachment Theory: Focus on Nurture, Nature, and Love

British psychiatrist John Bowlby formulated **attachment theory** during the mid-twentieth century. Like Freud, Bowlby believed that children's early experiences with caregivers shape their adult life, but he focused on what he called the *attachment response*.

In observing young children separated from their mothers, Bowlby noticed that babies need to be physically close to a caregiver during the time when they are beginning to walk (Bowlby, 1969, 1973; Karen, 1998). He argued that prolonged disruptions in this biologically programmed attachment response caused serious problems in adult life. Moreover, our impulse to be close to a "significant other" is a basic human need at every age.

How does the attachment response develop? Are Bowlby and Freud right that our early attachments determine adult mental health? How can we draw on attachment theory to understand everything from toddlerhood to teenage romance? Stay tuned for answers as we explore this influential theory throughout this book.

Why did Bowlby's ideas eclipse psychoanalytic theory? A main reason was that Bowlby agreed with a late-twentieth-century shift in the way developmentalists understood human motivations. Yes, Bowlby did believe in the power of caregiving (nurture), but he firmly anchored his theory in nature (genetics). Bowlby (1969, 1973, 1980) argued that the attachment response is genetically programmed into our species to promote survival. Bowlby was an early evolutionary psychologist.

Evolutionary Psychology: Theorizing About the "Nature" of Human Similarities

Evolutionary psychologists are the mirror image of behaviorists. They look to nature, or inborn biological forces that have evolved to promote survival, to explain how children (and adults) behave. Why do pregnant women develop morning sickness just as the fetal organs are being formed, and why do newborns prefer to look at attractive faces rather than ugly ones? (That's actually true!) According to evolutionary psychologists, these reactions cannot be changed by modifying the reinforcers. They are based in the human genetic code that we all share.

Evolutionary psychology lacks the practical, action-oriented approach of behaviorism, although it does alert us to the fact that we need to pay close attention to basic human needs. Still, as we look at how far-flung topics—from childhood obesity (Chapter 6) to the timing of puberty (Chapter 8)—make sense viewed through an evolutionary psychology lens, you will realize just how influential this "look to the human genome" perspective has become in our field. What *first* convinced developmentalists that genetics is important in behavior? A simple set of research techniques.

Behavioral Genetics: Scientifically Exploring the "Nature" of Human Differences

Behavioral genetics is the name for research strategies devoted to examining the genetic contribution to the *differences* we see among human beings. How genetic is the tendency to bite our nails, develop bipolar disorders, have specific attitudes about

Bowlby believes that the intense, loving bond between this father and infant son will set the baby up for a fulfilling life.

attachment theory Theory formulated by John Bowlby centering on the crucial importance to our species' survival of being closely connected with a caregiver during early childhood.

evolutionary psychology Theory or worldview highlighting the role that inborn, species-specific behaviors play in shaping behavior.

behavioral genetics Field devoted to scientifically determining the role that hereditary forces play in determining individual differences.

life? To answer these kinds of questions, scientists typically use twin and adoption studies.

In **twin studies,** researchers typically compare identical (monozygotic) twins and fraternal (dizygotic) twins on a particular trait of interest (such as playing the oboe, obesity, and so on). Identical twins develop from the same fertilized egg (it splits soon after the one-cell stage) and are genetic clones. Fraternal twins, like any brother or sister, develop from the fertilization of two separate eggs and so, on average, share 50 percent of their genes. The idea is that if a given trait is highly influenced by genetics, identical twins should be much more alike in that quality than fraternal twins. Specifically, behavioral geneticists use a statistic called *heritability* (which ranges from 1 = totally genetic, to 0 = no genetic contribution) to summarize the extent to which a given behavior is shaped by genetic factors.

For instance, to conduct a twin study to determine the heritability of friendliness, you would select a large group of identical and fraternal twins. You would test the twin participants to measure outgoing attitudes, and then compare the strength of the relationships you found for each twin group. Let's say the identical twins' scores were incredibly similar—almost like the same person taking the tests twice—and the fraternal twins' test scores varied a great deal from one another. Your heritability statistic would be high, and you would conclude that "Friendliness is a mainly genetically determined trait."

In **adoption studies,** researchers compare adopted children with their biological and adoptive parents. Here, too, they evaluate the impact of heredity on a trait by looking at how closely these children resemble their birth parents (with whom they share only genes) and their adoptive parents (with whom they share only environments).

Twin studies of children growing up in the same family and adoption studies are fairly easy to carry out. The most powerful evidence for genetics comes from the rare **twin/adoption studies,** in which identical twins are separated in childhood and reunited in adult life. If Joe and James, who have exactly the same DNA, have similar abilities, traits, and personalities—even though they grew up in *different families*—this would be strong evidence that genetics plays a crucial role in development.

Consider, for instance, the Swedish Twin/Adoption Study of Aging. Researchers combed national registries to find identical and fraternal twins adopted into different families in that nation—where birth records of every adoptee are kept. Then they reunited these children in late middle age and gave the twins a battery of tests (Finkel & Pedersen, 2004; Kato & Pedersen, 2005).

While specific qualities varied in their heritability, you might be surprised to know that the most genetically determined quality was intelligence (Pedersen, 1996). In fact, if one twin took the standard intelligence test, statistically speaking we could predict that the other twin would have an almost identical score, despite living apart for almost an entire lifetime!

twin study Behavioral genetic research strategy, designed to determine the genetic contribution of a given trait, that involves comparing identical twins with fraternal twins (or with other people).

adoption study Behavioral genetic research strategy, designed to determine the genetic contribution to a given trait, that involves comparing adopted children with their biological and adoptive parents.

twin/adoption study Behavioral genetic research strategy that involves comparing the similarities of identical twin pairs adopted into different families, to determine the genetic contribution to a given trait.

How "genetic" are these children's friendly personalities? To answer this question, researchers compare identical twins, such as these two girls *(left)*, with fraternal twins, like this girl and boy *(right)*. If the identicals (who share exactly the same DNA) are much more similar to each other than the fraternals in their scores on friendliness tests, friendliness is defined as a highly heritable trait.

> ### HOW DO WE KNOW . . .
> ### that our nature affects our upbringing?
>
> For much of the twentieth century, developmentalists assumed that parents treated all of their children the same way. We could classify mothers as either nurturing or rejecting, caring or cold. The Swedish Twin/Adoption Study turned these basic parenting assumptions upside down (Plomin & Bergeman, 1991).
>
> Researchers asked middle-aged identical twins who had been adopted into different families as babies to rate their parents along dimensions such as caring, acceptance, and discipline styles. They were astonished to find similarities in the ratings, even though the twins were evaluating different families!
>
> What was happening? The answer, the researchers concluded, was that the genetic similarities in the twins' personalities created similar family environments. If Joe and Jim were both easy, kind, and caring, they evoked more loving parenting. If they were temperamentally difficult, they caused their adoptive parents to react in more rejecting, less nurturant ways.
>
> I vividly saw this evocative, child-shapes-parenting relationship in my own life. Because my adopted son Thomas has dyslexia, in our house we ended up doing active things like sports. Thomas didn't like to sit still for story time, so, if some psychologist had come into my home to rate how much I read to my child, I probably would have been described as a "less than optimally stimulating" parent.
>
> And now, the plot thickens. When I met Thomas's biological mother Maureen, I found out that she also has dyslexia. She's energetic and peppy. It's one thing to see the impact of nature in my son, as his mother revealed. But I can't help wondering. . . . Maureen is a very different person than I am (although we have a terrific time together—traveling and doing active things). Would Thomas have had the same kind of upbringing (at least partly) if he had grown up with his biological mother instead of me?

Behavioral genetic studies such as these have opened our eyes to the role of nature in shaping children's lives (Turkheimer, 2004). As I will describe throughout this book, scientists now know that genetic forces heavily influence many aspects of children's development.

These studies have given us tantalizing insights into nurture, too. It's tempting to assume that children growing up in the same family share the same nurture, or environment. But as you can see in the How Do We Know research box, that assumption is wrong. We inhabit different life spaces than our brothers and sisters do, even when we eat at the same dinner table and share the same room—environments that are influenced by our genes (Rowe, 2003).

The bottom line is that there is no such thing as nature *or* nurture. To understand development, scientists need to explore how nature *and* nurture combine.

Nature and Nurture Combine: Where We Are Today

Let's now lay out two basic nature-plus-nurture principles, and then introduce cutting-edge research relating to how nature and nurture interact.

Principle 1: Our Nature (Genetic Tendencies) Shapes Our Nurture (Life Experiences)

Developmentalists understand that nature and nurture are not independent entities. Children's genetic tendencies shape their wider-world experiences in two ways.

Evocative forces refer to the fact that children's inborn talents and temperamental tendencies evoke, or produce, certain responses from the world. A joyous baby elicits smiles from everyone. A toddler who is temperamentally irritable, hard

evocative forces The nature-interacts-with-nurture principle that genetic temperamental tendencies and predispositions evoke, or produce, certain responses from other people.

to handle, or has trouble sitting still is unfortunately set up to get the kind of harsh parenting she least needs to succeed. Human relationships are **bidirectional**. Just as you get grumpy when with a grumpy person, fight with your difficult neighbor, or shy away from your colleague who is paralyzingly shy, who children are as people causes others to react in specific ways, driving development for the good and the bad.

Active forces refer to the fact that children *actively select* their environments based on their genetic tendencies. A boy who is talented at reading gravitates toward devouring books and so becomes a better reader over time. His sister, who is well coordinated, may play baseball three hours a day and become a star athlete in her teenage years. Because we choose activities tailored to fit our biologically based interests and skills, minor differences in early childhood snowball—ultimately producing huge gaps in talents and traits. The high adult heritabilities in the Swedish Twin/Adoption Study for intelligence are lower in comparable behavioral genetic studies conducted during childhood (Plomin & Spinath, 2004). The reason is that, like heat-seeking missiles, our nature causes us to gravitate toward specific life experiences, so children literally become *more like themselves* genetically as they travel into adult life (Scarr, 1997).

Principle 2: We Need the Right Nurture (Life Experiences) to Fully Express Our Nature (Genetic Talents)

Developmentalists understand that even if a quality is mainly genetic, its expression can be 100 percent dependent on the outside world. Let's illustrate by returning to the high heritabilities for intelligence. If babies grow up in impoverished developing nations, having genius-level intellectual talents might be irrelevant, as there would be no chance to demonstrate these hereditary gifts.

The most fascinating demonstration of how a high-quality environment can bring out children's genetic potential relates specifically to intelligence. As you will see in Chapter 7, over the past century, scores on the standard intelligence test have been rising. The same correct items a twenty-first-century teenager needs to be ranked as "average" in intelligence would have boosted that same child into the top one-third of the population in 1950. A century ago, having the identical number of items correct would have categorized that child as gifted, in the top 2 percent of his peers (Pinker, 2011)!

What is causing this upward shift? Obviously, our "genetic" intellectual capacities can't have changed. It's just that as children have become better nourished, more educated, and more technologically adept, they perform better, especially on the kinds of abstract-reasoning items the standard intelligence test measures (see Flynn, 2007, and Chapter 7). So even when individual differences in a particular ability are "genetic," the environment makes a dramatic difference in how children perform.

This discussion brings home the fact that to promote children's potential, we need to provide the best possible environment. This is why a core goal of developmental science is to foster the correct **person–environment fit**—making the wider world bring out children's human "best."

Because this musically talented girl is choosing to spend hours playing the piano, she is likely to become even more talented as she gets older, illustrating the fact that we actively shape our environment to fit our genetic tendencies and talents.

bidirectionality The crucial principle that people affect one another, or that interpersonal influences flow in both directions.

active forces The nature-interacts-with-nurture principle that genetic temperamental tendencies and predispositions cause children to select specific environments.

person–environment fit The extent to which the environment is tailored to our biological tendencies and talents.

Hot in Developmental Science: Environment-Sensitive Genes and Epigenetically Programmed Pathways

It's a no-brainer that we need to provide a superior environment for every child. But why does one boy or girl sail through life traumas while another breaks down under the smallest stress? This question is driving the hunt for genes that make children either more or less reactive to life events (see Belsky & Pluess, 2016).

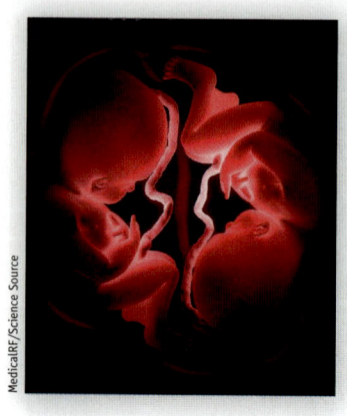

As you will learn in Chapter 8, due to an *epigenetic process*, this female fraternal twin fetus may be more insulated from developing an eating disorder by being exposed to the circulating testosterone her brother's body is giving off.

epigenetics Research field exploring how early life events alter the outer cover of our DNA, producing lifelong changes in health and behavior.

Erikson's psychosocial tasks In Erik Erikson's theory, the unique challenges children face at specific ages.

In this book, I'll be outlining findings that suggest some babies are like cactuses, set up biologically to survive in less nourishing environments; while others seem similar to fragile orchids, capable of providing gorgeous flowers but only with special care. I'll also showcase research suggesting that our genetics is altered by early life events.

Epigenetics refers to the study of how the environment—often, but not exclusively, intrauterine and early childhood experiences—alters the outer cover of our DNA, causing effects that last throughout life (see Moore, 2015). Can childhood obesity, our tendency to develop gender atypical behavior, or even the predisposition to die at a younger age be partly programmed by events during pregnancy or early infancy? Stay tuned for fascinating epigenetic hints in the chapters to come.

Emphasis on Age-Linked Theories

Now that I've highlighted this basic nature-combines-with-nurture message, it's time to explore the ideas of two psychologists who view child development as occurring in defined stages. Let's start with Erik Erikson.

Erik Erikson's Psychosocial Tasks

Erikson, born in Germany in 1904, was a psychoanalyst who parted with Freud in several crucial ways. Rather than emphasizing infant sexuality, Erikson (1963) believed that our basic human goals center on becoming an independent self and relating to others (which explains why Erikson's theory is called *psychosocial*, to distinguish it from Freud's psychosexual stages). Moreover, unlike Freud, Erikson argued that development occurs throughout life. He spelled out specific challenges we face at each life stage.

I have listed Erikson's childhood and teenage **psychosocial tasks** in Table 1.2. Each task, Erikson argued, builds on the previous one because we cannot master the issue of a later stage unless we have accomplished the developmental milestones of the previous ones.

Notice how parents take incredible joy in satisfying their baby's needs and you will understand why Erikson believed that *basic trust* (the belief that the human world is caring) is our fundamental life task in the first year of life. Erikson's second psychosocial task, *autonomy*, makes sense of the infamous "*no* stage" and "terrible twos." It tells us that we need to *celebrate* this not-so-pleasant toddler behavior as the blossoming of a separate self! Think back to elementary school, and you may realize why Erikson used the term *industry*, or learning to work—at friendships, sports, academics—as our challenge from age 6 to 12. Erikson's adolescent task, the search for *identity*, has now become a household word.

How have developmentalists expanded on Erikson's ideas about identity? Can we use Erikson's concepts of *initiative* and *industry* to highlight the unique mental

With his concept of age-related psychosocial tasks, Erik Erikson (shown here with his wife, Joan) transformed the way we think about children.

Table 1.2: Erikson's Psychosocial Stages of Childhood, Adolescence, and Emerging Adulthood

Life Stage	Primary Task
Infancy (birth to 1 year)	Basic trust versus mistrust
Toddlerhood (1 to 2 years)	Autonomy versus shame and doubt
Early childhood (3 to 6 years)	Initiative versus guilt
Middle childhood (7 to 12 years)	Industry versus inferiority
Adolescence and emerging adulthood (teens into twenties)	Identity versus role confusion
Emerging adulthood (twenties)	Intimacy versus isolation

challenges children face during preschool and elementary school? These are some topics I'll be discussing as I use Erikson's theory to help organize the scientific facts about development in the chapters to come.

Erikson offered us a beautiful roadmap for making sense of children's emotional growth. But, in terms of brilliance and transformational thinking, no theorist can equal that number one child development genius: Jean Piaget.

Piaget's Cognitive Developmental Theory

A 3-year-old tells you "Mr. Sun goes to bed because it's time for me to go to sleep." A toddler is obsessed with flushing different-sized wads of paper down the toilet and can't resist touching everything she sees. Do you ever wish you could get into the heads of young children and understand how they view the world? If so, you share the passion of the Swiss psychologist Jean Piaget.

Born in 1894, Piaget was a child prodigy himself. As the author of several dozen articles on mollusks, he was already becoming well known in biology during his teenage years (Flavell, 1963; Wadsworth, 1996). But Piaget's interests shifted to studying children when he worked in the laboratory of a psychologist named Alfred Binet, who was devising the original intelligence test. Rather than ranking children according to how much they knew, Piaget became fascinated by children's *incorrect* responses. He spent the next 60 years meticulously devising tasks to map the minds of these mysterious creatures in our midst.

Piaget believed—in his **cognitive developmental theory**—that from birth through adolescence, children progress through *qualitatively different* stages of cognitive growth (see Table 1.3). The term *qualitative* means that rather than simply knowing less or more (on a scale we can rank from 1 to 10), infants, preschoolers, elementary-school-age children, and teenagers think about the world in *completely different* ways. However, Piaget also believed that all learning occurs via a dual process called **assimilation**: We fit the world to our capacities or existing cognitive structures (which Piaget calls *schemas*). And then **accommodation** occurs; we change our thinking to fit the world (Piaget, 1971).

Let's illustrate by reflecting on your thinking while you were reading the previous section. Before reading this chapter, you probably had certain ideas about heredity and environment. In Piaget's terminology, let's call them your "heredity/environment

Jean Piaget, in his masterful studies spanning much of the twentieth century, gave us incredible insights into the way children think.

Piaget's cognitive developmental theory Jean Piaget's principle that from infancy to adolescence, children progress through four qualitatively different stages of intellectual growth.

assimilation In Jean Piaget's theory, the first step promoting mental growth, which involves fitting environmental input to current mental capacities.

accommodation In Piaget's theory, enlarging mental capacities to fit input from the wider world.

Table 1.3: Piaget's Stages of Development

Age	Name of Stage	Description
0–2	Sensorimotor	The baby manipulates objects to pin down the basics of physical reality. This stage, ending with the development of language, will be described in Chapter 3.
2–7	Preoperations	Children's perceptions are captured by their immediate appearances. "What they see is what is real." They believe, among other things, that inanimate objects are really alive and that if the appearance of a quantity of liquid changes (for instance, if it is poured from a short, wide glass into a tall, thin one), the amount actually changes. You will learn about all of these perceptions in Chapter 5.
8–12	Concrete operations	Children have a realistic understanding of the world. Their thinking is really on the same wavelength as adults'. While they can reason conceptually about concrete objects, however, they cannot think abstractly in a scientific way. You will learn about the widespread ramifications of this thinking in Chapter 6.
12+	Formal operations	Reasoning is at its pinnacle: hypothetical, scientific, flexible, fully adult. The person's full cognitive human potential has been reached. We will explore this stage in Chapter 9.

schemas." Perhaps you felt that if a trait is highly genetic, changing the environment doesn't matter; or you may have believed that genetics and environment were totally separate. While fitting (assimilating) your reading into these existing ideas, you entered a state of disequilibrium—"Hey, this contradicts what I've always believed"—and were forced to accommodate. The result was that your nature/nurture schemas became more complex and you developed a more advanced (intelligent) way of perceiving the world! Like a newborn who assimilates every new object to his small sucking schema, or a neuroscientist who incorporates each new finding into her huge knowledge base, as we assimilate each object or fact to what we already know, we must accommodate and so—inch by inch—cognitively advance.

Piaget was a great advocate of hands-on experiences. He felt that we learn by acting in the world. Rather than using an adult-centered framework, he had the revolutionary idea that we need to understand how children think *from their point of view*. Throughout this book, I hope you will adopt this hands-on, person-centered perspective to understand living from the perspective of babies, to elementary schoolers, to emerging adults.

By now, you may be overwhelmed by theories and terms. But take heart. You have the basic concepts you need for understanding this semester well in hand! Now, let's conclude by exploring a worldview that says, "Let's embrace *all* of these influences on development and explore how they interact." (For a summary of the theories, see Table 1.4.)

Table 1.4: Summary of the Major Current Theories in Child Development

Theory	Nature vs. Nurture Emphasis	Representative Questions
Traditional behaviorism	Nurture	What reinforcers are shaping this behavior?
Social learning theory/ Cognitive behaviorism	Nurture	Who is this child modeling? How can I stimulate self-efficacy?
Psychoanalytic theory	Nurture	What unconscious motives, stemming from early childhood, are motivating this person?
Attachment theory	Nature and nurture	How does the attachment response unfold in infancy? What conditions evoke this biologically programmed response?
Evolutionary theory	Nature	How might this behavior be built into the human genetic code?
Behavioral genetics	Nature	To what degree are the differences I see in children due to genetics?
Erikson's theory	Nurture	Is this baby experiencing basic trust? Where is this teenager in terms of identity?
Piaget's theory	Does not specify	How does this child understand the world? What is his thinking like?

The Ecological, Developmental Systems Approach

An influential child psychologist named Urie Bronfenbrenner (1977) was the main theorist to highlight the principle that children's behavior has *many* different causes. As you can see in Figure 1.3, Bronfenbrenner viewed each child at the center of an expanding circle of environmental influences. At the inner circle, development is shaped by the relationships between the child and people he relates to in his immediate setting, such as family, church, peers, and school. The next wider circles, that

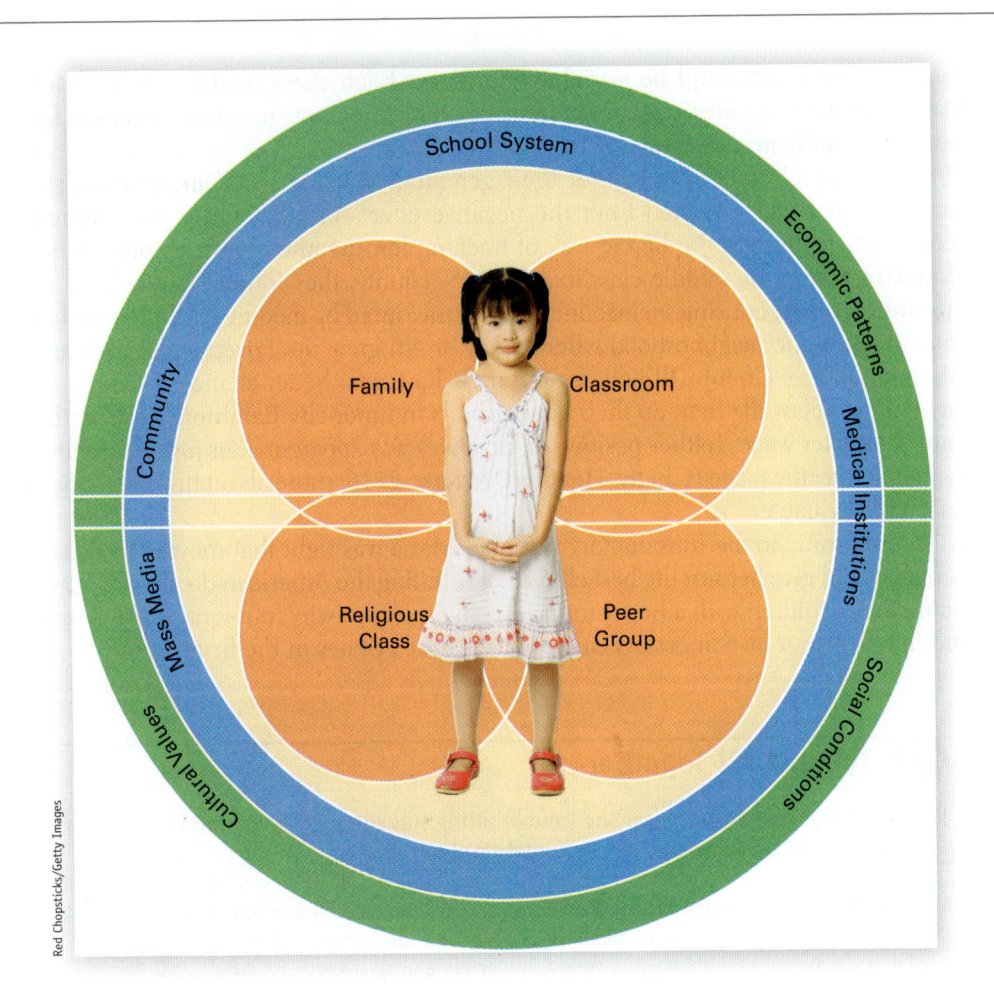

FIGURE 1.3: **Bronfenbrenner's ecological model** This set of embedded circles spells out the multiple forces that Bronfenbrenner believed shape development. First and foremost, there are the places that form the core of the child's daily life: family, church, peers, school (orange). What are the child's parents and teachers like? Who are his friends? How does that boy or girl relate at church, and behave with his siblings at home? Development also depends on the broader milieu—the media, the school system, and the community where the boy or girl lives (blue circle). At the most macro—or broadest—level, we also need to consider that child's culture, the economic and social conditions of his society (green circle), and his cohort, or the time in history in which he lives. Bottom line: Children's behavior is shaped by complex influences!

indirectly feed back to affect the child, lie in influences such as the community, and the school system itself. At the broadest levels, as I discussed earlier in the chapter, our culture, economic trends, and cohort crucially shape child development, too. Bronfenbrenner's plea to examine the total *ecology*, or life situation, of children forms the heart of a contemporary perspective called the **ecological, developmental systems approach** (Ford & Lerner, 1992; Lerner, 1998; Lerner, Dowling, & Roth, 2003). Specifically:

- **Developmental systems theorists stress the need to use many different approaches.** There are *many* valid ways of looking at behavior. Children's actions *do* have many causes. To fully understand development, we need to draw on the principles of behaviorism, attachment theory, evolutionary psychology, and Piaget. At the widest societal level, we need to look outward to children's culture and cohort. At the molecular level, we need to look inward to genes. We have to embrace the input of everyone, from nurses to neuroscientists and from anthropologists to biologists, to make sense of each child's life.

- **Developmental systems theorists emphasize the need to look at how processes interact.** As I will describe throughout this book, society (specifically communities and socioeconomic status) dramatically shape children's development because these "macro" forces determine the care parents can provide. In the same way that our body systems are in constant communication, interlocking influences converge to shape development in the real world (see Diamond, 2009).

For example, let's consider the basic marker, poverty. Growing up in poverty might affect your attachment relationships. You are less likely to get attention from your parents because they are under stress. You might not get adequate nutrition.

ecological, developmental systems approach An all-encompassing perspective on children that stresses the need to embrace a variety of approaches, and emphasizes the reality that many influences affect development.

Your neighborhood could be a frightening place. Each stress might overload your body, activating negative genetic tendencies and setting you up physiologically for emotional problems down the road.

But some children, because of their genetics, or living in a nurturing neighborhood, might be insulated from the negative effects of growing up poor. When economists performed the heroic task of tracking low-income children's probability of making it into the middle class in *every* U.S. county, they found that the odds of **upward mobility,** or rising socioeconomically (measured by income at age 26), varied depending on the neighborhood where a boy or girl grew up. Poverty-level children raised in DuPage County, Illinois, for instance, have a far better chance of constructing a middle-class life than do their counterparts in inner-city Baltimore. In fact, the impact on later wages (either positive or negative) was apparent after *just one year* of living in a specific place (Chetty, Hendren, & Katz, 2016; more about this fascinating research in Chapter 7).

So returning to the introductory vignette, María was right that moving to Shady Groves would give her son the best chance of fulfilling the American dream. And providing their children with a better future is a main reason why immigrants like María and many of your own ancestors came to the United States in the first place!

upward mobility Rising in social class and/or economic status from one's childhood.

Tying It All Together

1. Ricardo, a third grader, is having trouble sitting still and paying attention in class, so Ricardo's parents consult developmentalists about their son's problem. Pick which comments might be made by: (1) a traditional behaviorist; (2) a cognitive behaviorist; (3) a Freudian theorist; (4) an evolutionary psychologist; (5) a behavioral geneticist; (6) an Eriksonian; (7) an advocate of ecological, developmental systems approach.

    a. Ricardo has low academic self-efficacy. Let's improve his sense of competence at school.
    b. Ricardo, like other boys, is biologically programmed to run around. If the class had regular gym time, Ricardo's ability to focus in class would improve.
    c. Ricardo is being reinforced for this behavior by getting attention from the teacher and his classmates. Let's reward appropriate classroom behavior.
    d. Did you or your husband have trouble focusing in school? Perhaps your son's difficulties are hereditary.
    e. Ricardo's behavior may have many causes, from genetics to the reinforcers at school to growing up in our twenty-first-century Internet age. Let's use a variety of different approaches to help him.
    f. Ricardo is having trouble mastering the developmental task of industry. How can we promote the ability to work that is so important at this age?
    g. By refusing to pay attention in class, Ricardo may be unconsciously acting out his anger at the birth of his baby sister Heloise.

2. In the preceding question, which suggestion involves providing the right person–environment fit?

3. Dr. Kaplan, a scientist, wants to determine how being born premature might alter our genetic propensity to develop chronic disease. Dr. Kaplan is working in the field called (pick one) *outergenetics/epigenetics*.

4. Billy, a 1-year-old, mouths everything—pencils, his favorite toy, DVDs—changing his mouthing to fit the object that he is "sampling." According to Piaget, the act of mouthing everything refers to _____, whereas changing the mouthing behavior to fit the different objects refers to _____.

5. Samantha, a behaviorist, is arguing for her worldview, while Sally is pointing out behaviorism's flaws. First, take Samantha's position, arguing for the virtues of behaviorism, and then discuss some limitations of the theory.

Answers to the Tying It All Together questions can be found at the end of this chapter.

Research Methods: The Tools of the Trade

Theories give us lenses for interpreting behavior. *Research* allows us to find the scientific truth. I already touched on the research technique designed to determine the genetic contributions to children's behavior. Now let's sketch out the general research strategies that developmentalists use.

Two Standard Research Strategies: Correlations and Experiments

What impact does poverty have on children's personalities or academic success? What forces cause preschoolers to model certain people? Does a particular intervention to improve self-efficacy work? To answer any question about the impact one condition or entity (called a *variable*) can have on another, developmentalists use two different research designs: correlational studies and true experiments.

In a **correlational study**, researchers chart the relationships between the dimensions they are interested in exploring as they naturally occur. Let's say you want to test the hypothesis that parents who behave more lovingly have first graders with superior social skills. Your game plan is simple: Select a group of children by going to a class. Relate their interpersonal skills to the loving care that their parents provide.

Immediately, you will be faced with decisions related to choosing your participants. Will you explore the practices of mothers and fathers or mothers alone? Confine yourself to a middle-class group? Consider two- versus one-parent families? Look at a mix of ethnicities or not? You would need to get permission from the school system. You would need to get the parents to volunteer. Are you choosing a **representative sample**—a group that reflects the characteristics of the population about whom you want to generalize?

Then you would face your most important challenge—accurately measuring your variables. Just as a broken thermometer can't tell us if we have a fever, without adequate indices of the concepts we are measuring, we can't conclude anything at all.

With regard to the parent dimension, one possibility might be to visit parents and children and observe how they relate. This technique, called **naturalistic observation**, is appealing because it directly charts behavior as it occurs in "nature," or real life. However, this approach presents a huge practical challenge: the need to travel to each home to observe each family on many occasions. Plus, when we watch parent–child interactions, or any socially desirable activity, people try to act their best. Wouldn't you make an effort to act especially loving if a psychologist arrived at your house?

The most cost-effective strategy would be to give the parents a questionnaire with items such as: "Do you make an effort to kiss, hug, and praise your daughter? Is it important to avoid yelling at your child?" This **self-report strategy**, in which people evaluate their behavior anonymously, is the main approach researchers use with older children and adults. Still, it has biases. Do you think that people can report accurately on their activities? Isn't there a natural human tendency to magnify our positive behaviors and minimize our negative ones?

Now, turning to the child side of the question, one reasonable way to assess social skills would be to have teachers evaluate each student via a questionnaire: "Does this child make friends easily?"; "Does he relate to his peers in a mature way?" Or we could ask children to rank their classmates by showing photos: "Does Calista or Cory get a smiley face?"; "Pick your three best friends." Evaluations from expert observers, such as teachers and even peers, are often used to assess concepts such as popularity and personality during the childhood years.

LEARNING OUTCOMES

- List the main developmental science measurement techniques.
- Compare experiments and correlational studies.
- Contrast cross-sectional and longitudinal studies.
- Describe new advances in developmental science research.

correlational study
A research strategy that involves relating two or more variables.

representative sample
A group that reflects the characteristics of the overall population.

naturalistic observation
A measurement strategy that involves directly watching and coding behaviors.

self-report strategy
A measurement technique in which people report on their feelings and activities through questionnaires.

Table 1.5: Common Strategies Developmentalists Use to Measure Specific Variables (Behaviors or Concepts of Interest)

Type	Strategy	Commonly Used Ages	Pluses and Problems
Naturalistic observation	Observes behavior directly; codes actions, often by rating the behavior as either present or absent (either in real life or the lab)	Mainly with children, but can be used to evaluate parents and teachers	**Pluses:** Offers a direct, unfiltered record of behavior **Problems:** Very time intensive; people behave differently when watched
Self-reports	Questionnaires in which people report on their feelings, interests, attitudes, and thoughts	Adults and older children	**Pluses:** Easy to administer; quickly provides data **Problems:** Subject to bias if the person is reporting on undesirable activities and behaviors
Observer reports	Knowledgeable person such as a parent, teacher, or trained observer completes scales evaluating the child; sometimes peers rank the children in their class, or experts rank parents and teachers according to various traits	Typically during childhood, but again, sometimes employed to evaluate parents and teachers	**Pluses:** Offers a structured look at the person's behavior **Problems:** Observers have their own biases

Table 1.5 spells out the uses, and the pluses and minuses, of these frequently used ways of measuring concepts: naturalistic observation, self-reports, and observer evaluations.

Now, returning to our study, suppose you found a relationship (that is, a correlation) between having nurturing parents and children's interpersonal skills. Could you infer that a loving home environment *causes* children to socially flower? The answer is no!

- **With correlations, we may be mixing up the result with the cause.** Given that parent–child relationships are bidirectional, does loving parenting really *cause* superior social skills, or do socially skilled children provoke parents to act in loving ways? ("My son is such an endearing person. You want to just love him up.") This evocative chicken-or-egg argument applies to far more than child–parent interactions. Does exercise reduce teenage obesity, or are obese teens less likely to go to the gym because they are *already* overweight?

- **With correlations, there may be another variable that explains the results.** In view of our discussion of heritability, with regard to the social skills study, the immediate third force that comes to mind is genetics. Do parents who are genetically blessed with superior social skills provide a more caring home environment and genetically pass down these same positive personality traits to their sons and daughters? Would adolescents who care deeply about their weight be more likely to watch their diet, too? Given that exercise is naturally associated with other healthy acts, can we conclude that lack of exercise alone *produces* obesity?

To rule out these confounding forces, the solution is to conduct a **true experiment** (see Figure 1.4). Researchers isolate their variable of interest by manipulating that condition (called the *independent variable*), and then randomly assign people to either receive that treatment or another, *control* intervention. If we *randomly assign* people to different groups (by, say, tossing a coin), there can't be any preexisting differences between our participants that would bias our results. If the group does differ in the way we predict, we have to conclude that our intervention *caused* the particular result.

The problem is that we could never assign children to different kinds of parents! If, as Figure 1.4 suggests, developmentalists trained one group of mothers to relate in more caring ways and withheld this "intervention" from another group, the researchers would run into ethical problems. Is it fair to deprive the control group of that

true experiment The only research strategy that can determine that something causes something else; involves randomly assigning children to different treatments and then looking at the outcome.

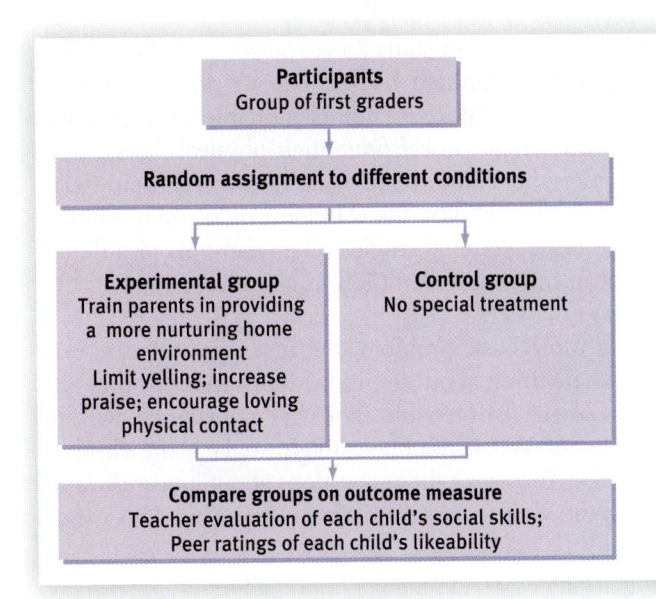

treatment? In the name of science, can we risk doing people harm? Experiments are ideal for determining what causes behavior. But to tackle the most compelling questions about children's lives, we *have* to conduct correlational research—and control as best we can for competing explanations that might bias our results.

Designs for Studying Development: Cross-Sectional and Longitudinal Studies

Experiments and correlational studies are standard, all-purpose research strategies. In studying development, however, we have a special interest: How do children change with age? To answer this question, scientists also use two research designs—cross-sectional and longitudinal studies.

Cross-Sectional Studies: Getting a One-Shot Snapshot of Groups

Because cross-sectional research is relatively easy to carry out, researchers typically use this strategy to explore changes over long periods of development (Hertzog, 1996). In a **cross-sectional study**, researchers compare *different age groups at the same time* on the trait or characteristic they are interested in, be it parenting, personality, or physical health.

Let's imagine, for instance, that, while watching a reality show, you come up with a brilliant research idea. As the show's discussions revolve around beauty and Botox, you want to see if this overload of media messages ("You must look perfect") takes a toll on children, causing them to become increasingly critical about their appearance as they travel into and through their teens.

So you get permission from different schools to give their third-, seventh-, ninth-, and eleventh-grade students a one-item questionnaire: "Rate how attractive you feel on a scale from 1 to 5." Then, as you might assume females would be more vulnerable to the media messages, you plan to analyze your data separately for girls and boys.

When psychologist Susan Harter (1999) conducted a similar cross-sectional study, notice the result, shown in Figure 1.5. Although satisfaction with physical appearance was indeed highest in third grade and then steadily declined, this was true *only* for girls!

FIGURE **1.4: How an experiment looks** By randomly assigning children to different groups and then giving an intervention (this is called the *independent variable*), we know that our treatment (nurturing parents) *caused* better social skills (this outcome is called the *dependent variable*).

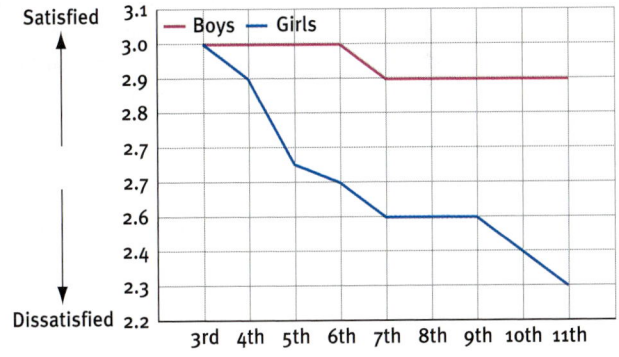

FIGURE **1.5: Satisfaction with physical appearance among boys and girls in the third through eighth grade in a U.S. study conducted in the early 1990s** Notice that, in this cross-sectional study, while older girls feel increasingly dissatisfied with their looks, boys are immune to appearance distress.

cross-sectional study
A developmental research method that involves comparing different age groups at a single time.

But wait a second . . . Harter conducted her study 25 years ago. With the current emphasis on male teens having buff, well-toned bodies, haven't adolescent male appearance pressures become more intense? Since it's now fashionable for female stars (such as Lena Dunham or Sarah Silverman) to *celebrate* their physical flaws, might contemporary female high schoolers be comfortable with having less-than-stellar looks? Would Harter's findings still apply to children traveling into adolescence today?

The bottom line is that while cross-sectional studies offer snapshots of different age groups taken at a *single* point in time, they don't tell us about real changes that occur *over years*.

Cross-sectional studies have a more basic problem. Because they measure only *group differences*, they can't reveal anything about the individual variations that give spice to life. If a particular 8-year-old girl feels terrible about her appearance, will she remain unusually miserable at age 18? What influences might make some children feel better or worse about their looks? To answer these questions about how *individual children* develop, it's vital to be on the scene to measure what is going on. This means doing longitudinal research.

Longitudinal Studies: The Gold-Standard Developmental Science Research Design

longitudinal study A developmental research strategy that involves testing the same group repeatedly over years.

In **longitudinal studies**, researchers typically select a group of children at a particular age and periodically test those boys and girls over many years (the relevant word here is *long*). So, for instance, if you were conducting a longitudinal study to test how females' feelings about their appearance change as they get older, you might select third-grade girls and retest them every few years through high school. Now you can track changes in children's feelings in the flesh. You can answer other compelling questions, too: Do parents who make a big deal out of a third-grade daughter's looks put that child at risk of having a teenage eating disorder? Or, drawing on the research tracking upward mobility described earlier in this chapter, does an exceptional third-grade teacher affect success decades later during early adult life? (The heartening answer to this last question is yes, as you will learn in Chapter 7!)

subject attrition The fact that people drop out at each testing point in longitudinal research.

Longitudinal research is tremendously exciting. But, because it demands so much time and effort, these studies are daunting to carry out. In the examples I just mentioned, imagine the hassles of finding and then testing each member of an elementary school class every few years. To account for **subject attrition**—the reality that people drop out of research—you would need to start with a huge group of children. You would not have answers to your questions for many years. For this reason, although there are hundreds of studies that cover infancy, childhood, and the teens, far fewer studies follow people from babyhood into adult life.

Longitudinal studies that track development into adulthood have their own bias. Only the most successful participants return. Imagine who would be most likely to attend your high school reunion—the people who are the high achievers or classmates who have made a mess of their lives? Given that longitudinal studies end up measuring "the best and brightest," can we generalize from this research to more representative groups?

With these cautions in mind, let's explore one remarkable study planned to measure development from babyhood to old age. More than 40 years ago, an international team of researchers descended on Dunedin, a city in New Zealand, to test more than 1,000 children born in that community over a one-year period. They gave each baby a comprehensive examination, then tested their sample thoroughly at two-year intervals during childhood and then roughly every three years after that. At each examination, they probed participants' personalities and interests, measured physical and mental health, and looked carefully at parenting practices and life events (Poulton, Moffitt, & Silva, 2015). Those infants are now middle-aged adults.

This study has provided an incredible array of findings. Can we predict adult emotional difficulties as early as age 3? Does chronic anxiety produce cellular damage as we travel through adolescence and early adult life (Shalev and others, 2014)? What teenage behaviors predict later substance abuse? (See Meier and others, 2016.)

Because they are using cutting-edge DNA technology, this landmark research is the first study to identify a constellation of genes that may promote upward mobility (Belsky and others, 2016). Plus, like other longitudinal research, the Dunedin study offers answers to those questions that preoccupy every parent: "Will my 3-year-old reader make it to Harvard?" "When should I worry about my child, and when should I *not* be concerned?"

Critiquing the Research

To summarize, when you are reading any findings in our field, keep these thoughts in mind:

- Examine the study's participants. Is the researcher choosing a representative group? From this sample, can we generalize to children at large?
- Examine the study's measures. Are they accurate? What biases might they have?
- In looking at the *many* correlational studies in this book, be attuned to the fact that their findings might be due to other forces. What competing interpretations can we come up with to explain the researcher's results?
- With cross-sectional findings, beware of making assumptions that this is the way children *really* change with age.
- Look for longitudinal studies and welcome their insights. However, understand that these studies are difficult to carry out and may be measuring atypical groups.

Emerging Research Trends

Researchers are attuned to these research issues. Today, they often use different types of measures and control for other influences that might explain their findings. A dramatic new trend is the explosion of international research, with developmentalists from nations as different as Iran and Ireland or China and Cameroon now exploring children's lives. Within just a decade, developmental science has become a truly worldwide field! Still, in addition to getting more global, scientists are getting up close and personal, too.

Quantitative research techniques—the strategies I have described in this section, using groups and statistical tests—are the main approaches that researchers use to study children. In order to make general predictions, we need to examine more than one individual and use numbers to find out the scientific "truth." But there is another small strand of research in developmental science as well.

Qualitative researchers go beyond the statistics to conduct personal interviews. Because they bring home the personal experience of development, in this book I will highlight studies quoting real-life parents and children, because stories—not numbers—best convey the magic of human life.

Some Concluding Introductory Thoughts

This discussion brings me back to the letter on page 2, and my promise to let you in on my other agendas in writing this text. Because I want to teach you to critically evaluate research, in the following pages I'll be analyzing issues with the findings

Would this 20-year-old return to be tested in a study tracking mental health that began in elementary school? If your longitudinal research systematically missed these kinds of subjects, could you conclude that children typically "get it together psychologically" as they move into adult life?

quantitative research Standard developmental science data-collection strategy that involves testing groups and using numerical scales and statistics.

qualitative research Occasional developmental science data-collection strategy that involves personal interviews.

and—in the How Do We Know features that appear in many chapters—focusing on specific tantalizing research in more depth. To bring home the personal experience of development, I've filled the chapters with quotations, and—in the Experiencing Childhood and Adolescence boxes—interviewed people myself. To bring home the principle that children's lives are continually changing, I'll be starting most chapters by setting the historical and cultural context. To emphasize the power of science to improve children's lives, I'll conclude most sections by spelling out concrete interventions that flow from the research.

This book progresses chronologically toward adulthood, stage by stage. It's designed to be read like a story, with each chapter building on concepts mentioned in the previous ones. Within each chapter and book part, I will be discussing the major aspects of development separately—physical development, cognitive development, and emotional and social development. However, I'll be continually stressing how these aspects of development connect. After all, children are not just bodies, minds, and personalities, but whole human beings!

While I want you to share my excitement in the research, please don't read this book as "the final word." Science—like children—is continually growing. Moreover, with any research finding, take the phrase "it's all statistical" to heart. Yes, developmentalists are passionate to make general predictions; but, because human beings are incredibly complex, at bottom, each child's journey is a beautiful surprise.

Now, beginning with prenatal development (Chapter 2), then infancy and toddlerhood (Chapters 3 and 4); moving on to early childhood (Chapters 5) and elementary school (Chapter 6), then looking at the wider-world contexts within which children grow (Chapter 7); and moving to adolescence (Chapters 8 and 9) and ending with a chapter devoted to emerging adulthood (Chapter 10), welcome to developmental science and the rest of this book!

Tying It All Together

1. Four developmentalists are studying whether eating excessive sugar has detrimental effects on development. To test how the amount of sugar elementary schoolers eat at breakfast relates to aggression, Alicia goes to a playground and counts the frequency of hitting on selected days. Betty randomly assigns students in a high school class into two groups; she tells one group to eat a healthy diet and another to eat candy bars, and compares their grades on tests. Calista measures the sugar consumption of toddlers and then retests the same group periodically into their twenties. David constructs a questionnaire that explores sugar consumption and gives it to parents of children of different ages. For each of the following questions, link the appropriate person's name to the correct study.
   a. Who is conducting a cross-sectional study?
   b. Who is using naturalistic observation?
   c. Who is conducting a correlational study?
   d. Who can prove that eating a lot of sugar causes problems—but is doing an unethical study?
   e. Who is going to have a problem with dropouts?
   f. Who can tell you whether toddlers who eat too many sweets continue to eat an incredible amount of sugar (compared to everyone else) as they grow up?

2. Plan a longitudinal study to test a question in child development. Describe how you would select your participants, how your study would proceed, what measures you would use, and what problems your study would have.

Answers to the Tying It All Together questions can be found at the end of this chapter.

SUMMARY

Who We Are and What We Study

Developmental science, the multidisciplinary science of child and adolescent development, is more than a century old. Scientists whose passion is working with children and teens chart normal milestones as children grow up, focus on individual differences in talents and traits, study the impact of child-rearing practices, and explore every other topic relevant to development.

Several **contexts of development** shape the experience of childhood. The most important is our **cohort,** the time in history when we travel through life. Before the twentieth century, children had more abusive lives, and many newborns did not survive. During this remarkable century, **demographic** shifts transformed childhood and we entered our modern age. Early in the twentieth century, public health miracles (such as curing previously fatal infectious diseases) meant babies routinely lived to adulthood. Education extended childhood, first during the 1930s, when high school made adolescence a defined life stage, then, in recent years, with a new in-between stage called **emerging adulthood,** in which young people put off settling down to adult commitments until their late twenties. **Fertility rates,** although they vary in different regions, have slid below replacement levels in most affluent nations today.

During the last third of the twentieth century, as the **baby boomers** reached adolescence, they upended rigid adult roles and caused a revolution in traditional marriage. Today, rather than having homemaker mothers and breadwinner dads, children are raised in a beautiful mosaic of family forms. The dramatic increase in unmarried mothers, however, means more U.S. children live in poverty than in the past. The twenty-first-century rise in **income inequalities** and **social networking sites** is altering the landscape of childhood, too.

Socioeconomic status (SES) greatly affects development. Within each nation, poverty limits children's lives starting from birth. The gaps between **developed-world** countries and **developing-world** countries are dramatic, with babies born in the most impoverished regions of the globe facing lives similar to their pre-twentieth-century counterparts.

Children's cultural and ethnic background also shapes their developing lives. Scientists distinguish between **collectivist cultures** (typically non-Western), which stress social harmony and extended-family relationships, and **individualistic cultures** (often Western), which value independence and personal achievement. Gender is another basic marker that influences development.

Theories: Lenses for Looking at Children and Adolescents

Theories offer explanations about what causes children to act the way they do. The main theories in developmental science that offer general explanations of children's behavior vary in their position on the **nature**-versus-**nurture** question. Behaviorists believe nurture is all-important. **Traditional behaviorists,** in particular B. F. Skinner, believe **operant conditioning** and **reinforcement** determine all voluntary behaviors. According to **cognitive behaviorism/social learning theory, modeling** and **self-efficacy** predicts how children act.

Sigmund Freud, in his psychoanalytic theory, believed adult personality is shaped by the way parents treat children during the first five years of life. Freud also felt that human beings are dominated by unconscious drives, that mental health depends on self-awareness, and that sexuality (different erogenous zones) drives behavior. John Bowlby's **attachment theory** draws on the psychoanalytic principle that parenting during early life (or children's attachment relationships) determines mental health, but argues that the attachment response is genetically built into our species to promote survival. **Evolutionary psychologists** adopt this nature perspective, seeing actions and traits as programmed into children's DNA. **Behavioral genetic** research—in particular, **twin studies, adoption studies,** and occasionally **twin/adoption studies**—convinced developmental scientists of the power of nature, revealing striking genetic contributions to the differences between individual human beings.

Developmental scientists today are exploring how nature *and* nurture combine. Due to **evocative** and **active forces,** children shape their environments to go along with their genetic tendencies, and human relationships are **bidirectional**—our temperamental qualities and actions influence others, just as their actions influence us. A basic developmental science challenge is to foster an appropriate **person–environment fit.** We need to match children's genetically based talents and abilities to the right environment. New research suggests that children differ genetically in how responsive they are to environmental events and that early life experiences alter our genome, producing long-lasting **epigenetic** effects.

Erik Erikson spelled out **psychosocial tasks** that children must master as they travel stage by stage, from birth to adult life. According to Jean Piaget's **cognitive developmental theory,** children progress through four qualitatively different stages of intellectual development, and all learning occurs through **assimilation** and **accommodation.**

Most developmental scientists today adopt the **ecological, developmental systems approach.** They welcome input from every theory and realize that many interacting influences shape children's growth. A prime example is **upward mobility,** which varies from child to child, depending on the neighborhood in which a person grows up.

Research Methods: The Tools of the Trade

The two main research strategies scientists use are **correlational studies,** which relate naturally occurring variations among children, and **true experiments,** in which researchers manipulate a variable (or give a specific treatment) and randomly assign participants to receive that intervention or not. With correlational studies, there are always competing possibilities for the relationships we find. While experiments do allow us to prove causes, they are often unethical and impractical. In conducting research, it's best to strive for a **representative sample,** and it's essential to take accurate measures. **Naturalistic observation, self-reports,** and observer evaluations are three common measurement strategies developmental scientists use.

The two major designs for studying development are longitudinal and cross-sectional research. **Cross-sectional studies,** which involve testing children of different ages at the same time, are easy to carry out. However, they may confuse differences between age groups with true changes that occur over time, and they can't tell us about individual differences in development.

Longitudinal studies can answer vital questions about development. However, they involve following children over years and, because of **subject attrition,** sample atypical, elite groups.

Quantitative research—studies that involve groups of participants and use statistical tests—is still the standard way we learn the scientific truth. But some developmentalists are now conducting **qualitative research**—interviewing older children and adults in depth. Child development, within just the past few years, has matured into a genuinely global field.

KEY TERMS

accommodation, p. 19
active forces, p. 17
adolescence, p. 6
adoption study, p. 15
assimilation, p. 19
attachment theory, p. 14
baby boomers, p. 7
behavioral genetics, p. 14
bidirectionality, p. 17
cognitive behaviorism (social learning theory), p. 12
cohort, p. 5
collectivist cultures, p. 8
contexts of development, p. 4
correlational study, p. 23

cross-sectional study, p. 25
demographic, p. 6
developed world, p. 8
developing world, p. 8
developmentalists (developmental scientists), p. 3
ecological, developmental systems approach, p. 21
emerging adulthood, p. 6
epigenetics, p. 18
Erikson's psychosocial tasks, p. 18
evocative forces, p. 16
evolutionary psychology, p. 14
fertility rate, p. 7

income inequality, p. 7
individualistic cultures, p. 8
longitudinal study, p. 26
modeling, p. 12
naturalistic observation, p. 23
nature, p. 10
nurture, p. 10
operant conditioning, p. 11
person–environment fit, p. 17
Piaget's cognitive developmental theory, p. 19
qualitative research, p. 27
quantitative research, p. 27
reinforcement, p. 11

representative sample, p. 23
self-efficacy, p. 12
self-report strategy, p. 23
social networking sites, p. 8
socioeconomic status (SES), p. 8
subject attrition, p. 26
theory, p. 10
traditional behaviorism, p. 11
true experiment, p. 24
twin study, p. 15
twin/adoption study, p. 15
upward mobility, p. 22

ANSWERS TO Tying It All Together QUIZZES

Setting the Context

1. c. Few people graduated from high school in the nineteenth century.
2. c. During the last third of the twentieth century, there was a dramatic decline in the traditional two-parent, married-couple family.
3. poverty
4. Pablo has a collectivist worldview, while Peter's worldview is individualistic.
5. Answers will vary.

Theories: Lenses for Looking at the Lifespan

1. (1) c; (2) a; (3) g; (4) b; (5) d; (6) f; (7) e
2. b. As Ricardo and other children need to run around, regular gym time would help to foster the best person–environment fit.
3. Dr. Kaplan is working in a field called epigenetics.
4. assimilation; accommodation
5. Samantha might argue that behaviorism is an ideal approach to children's development because it is simple, effective, and easy to carry out. Behaviorism's easily

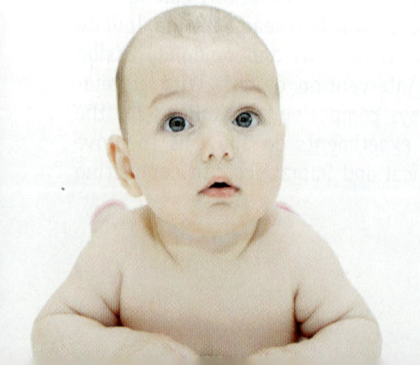

mastered, action-oriented concepts—be consistent, reinforce positive behavior, draw on principles of modeling, and stimulate efficacy feelings—can make dramatic improvements in children's behavior. Also, because behaviorism doesn't blame the child but locates problems in the learning environment, it has special appeal. Sally might argue that behaviorism's premise that nurture is all-important neglects the powerful impact of genetic forces in determining who we are. So the theory is far too limited, offering a wrongheaded view about development. We need the insights of attachment theory, evolutionary psychology, behavioral genetics, plus Piaget's and Erikson's theories to fully understand what motivates human beings.

Research Methods: The Tools of the Trade

1. a. David; b. Alicia; c. Alicia; d. Betty; e. Calista; f. Calista
2. After coming up with your hypothesis, you would need to adequately measure your concepts by choosing the appropriate tests. Your next step would be to solicit a large representative sample of a particular age group, give them these measures, and retest these people at regular intervals over an extended period of time. In addition to the investment of time and money, it would be hard to keep track of your sample and entice participants to undergo subsequent evaluations. Because the most motivated fraction of your original group will probably continue, your results will tend to reflect how the "best people" behave and change over time (not the typical person).

CONNECT ONLINE:

LaunchPad macmillan learning | Check out our videos and additional resources located at: www.macmillanlearning.com

CHAPTER 2

CHAPTER OUTLINE

Setting the Context

The First Step: Fertilization
  The Reproductive Systems
  The Process of Fertilization
  The Genetics of Fertilization

Prenatal Development
  First Two Weeks
  Week 3 to Week 8
  Principles of Prenatal Development
  Week 9 to Birth

Pregnancy
  Scanning the Trimesters
  Pregnancy Is Not a Solo Act
  What About Dads?

Threats to the Developing Baby
  Threats from Outside
  HOT IN DEVELOPMENTAL SCIENCE: The Long Shadow of Prenatal Stress
  Threats from Within
  HOW DO WE KNOW . . . About the Gene for Huntington's Disease?
  Interventions
  Infertility and New Reproductive Technologies
  INTERVENTIONS: Exploring ART

Birth
  Stage 1
  Stage 2
  Stage 3
  Threats at Birth
  Birth Options, Past and Present

The Newborn
  Tools of Discovery
  Threats to Development Just After Birth
  EXPERIENCING CHILDHOOD AND ADOLESCENCE: Marcia's Story
  A Few Final Thoughts on Resilience

Prenatal Development, Pregnancy, and Birth

It's hard to explain, Kim told me. You are two people now. When you wake up, shop, or plan meals, this other person is always with you. You are always thinking, "What will be good for the baby? What will be best for the two of us?"

Feeling the first kick—like little feathers brushing inside me—was amazing. At first I felt like I could never explain this to my husband. But Jeff is wonderful. I think he gets it. So I feel lucky. I can't imagine what this experience would be like if I didn't have a loving partner to share my joy.

Now that it's the thirtieth week and my little girl can survive, there is another shift. I'm focused on the moment she will arrive: What will it be like to hold my baby? Will she be born healthy?

The downside is the fear that she will be born with some problem. Being an older mom, it took me two years to get pregnant. Now that I've gone through those exhausting procedures and they worked (hooray!), I'd never risk having an invasive genetic test. So, you eat right and never take a drink; but there are concerns. I worry about my career. How will my boss feel about my taking maternity leave? And, of course, I worry about labor and delivery. Suppose I have some problem during birth, or my baby has a serious genetic disease?

Another downside is that, until recently, I still felt tired. Some days, I could barely make it to work. (Everything they told you about morning sickness only lasting through the first trimester is wrong—at least for me!)

But nothing equals the thrill of having my little girl inside—fantasizing about her future, watching her grow into a marvelous adult. I also adore what happens when I'm at the mall. People light up and grin, wish me good luck, or give me advice. It's like the world is watching out for me, rooting for me, cherishing me.

LEARNING OUTCOME
- List the main pregnancy concerns in earlier eras worldwide.

Setting the Context

The joy and fear Kim is experiencing seem built into our humanity. Throughout history, societies have seen pregnancy as an exciting and frightening time of life. Cultures used to make heroic efforts to keep pregnant women calm and happy. Certain groups might use good luck charms to keep evil spirits away—such as a pregnancy girdle in medieval England, a garlic-filled sack in Guatemala (Aldred, 1997; Von Raffler-Engel, 1994), or a cotton pregnancy sash in Japan (Ito & Sharts-Hopko, 2002).

In the past, societies celebrated pregnancy milestones, too. In Bulgaria, the first kick was the signal for a woman to bake bread and take it to the church. In Bali, at the seventh month, a prayer ceremony took place to recognize that there was finally a person inside whom the spirits should protect from harm (Kitzinger, 2000; Von Raffler-Engel, 1994). This chapter draws on the miracle of twenty-first-century science to explore each pregnancy concern as I chart the marvelous milestones of prenatal development, pregnancy, and birth.

In this traditional southern Indian ceremony performed at the sixth or eighth month of pregnancy, family members and friends gather around to protect the woman and fetus from "the evil eyes." Rituals such as this one are common around the world and embody our fears about this special time of life.

LEARNING OUTCOMES
- Identify the structures and process of fertilization.
- Describe what genetically happens when the sperm and ovum unite.

uterus The pear-shaped muscular organ in a woman's abdomen that houses the developing baby.

cervix The neck, or narrow lower portion, of the uterus.

fallopian tube One of a pair of slim, pipelike structures that connect the ovaries with the uterus.

ovary One of a pair of almond-shaped organs that contain a woman's ova, or eggs.

ovum An egg cell containing the genetic material contributed by the mother to the baby.

The First Step: Fertilization

Before embarking on this journey, let's focus on the starting point. What structures are involved in reproduction? What physiological process is involved in conceiving a child? What happens at the genetic level when a sperm and an egg unite to form a human being?

The Reproductive Systems

The female and male reproductive systems are shown in Figure 2.1. Notice that the female system has several parts:

- Center stage is the **uterus,** the pear-shaped muscular organ that carries the baby to term. The uterus is lined with a velvety tissue, the *endometrium*, which thickens in preparation for pregnancy and, if that event does not occur, sheds during menstruation.

- The lower section of the uterus is the **cervix.** During pregnancy, this thick uterine neck must perform an amazing feat: Be strong enough to resist the pressure of the expanding uterus; be flexible enough to open fully at birth.

- Branching from the upper ends of the uterus are the **fallopian tubes.** These slim, pipelike structures serve as conduits to the uterus.

- The feathery ends of the fallopian tubes surround the **ovaries,** the almond-shaped organs where the **ova,** the mother's egg cells, reside.

CHAPTER 2 Prenatal Development, Pregnancy, and Birth   35

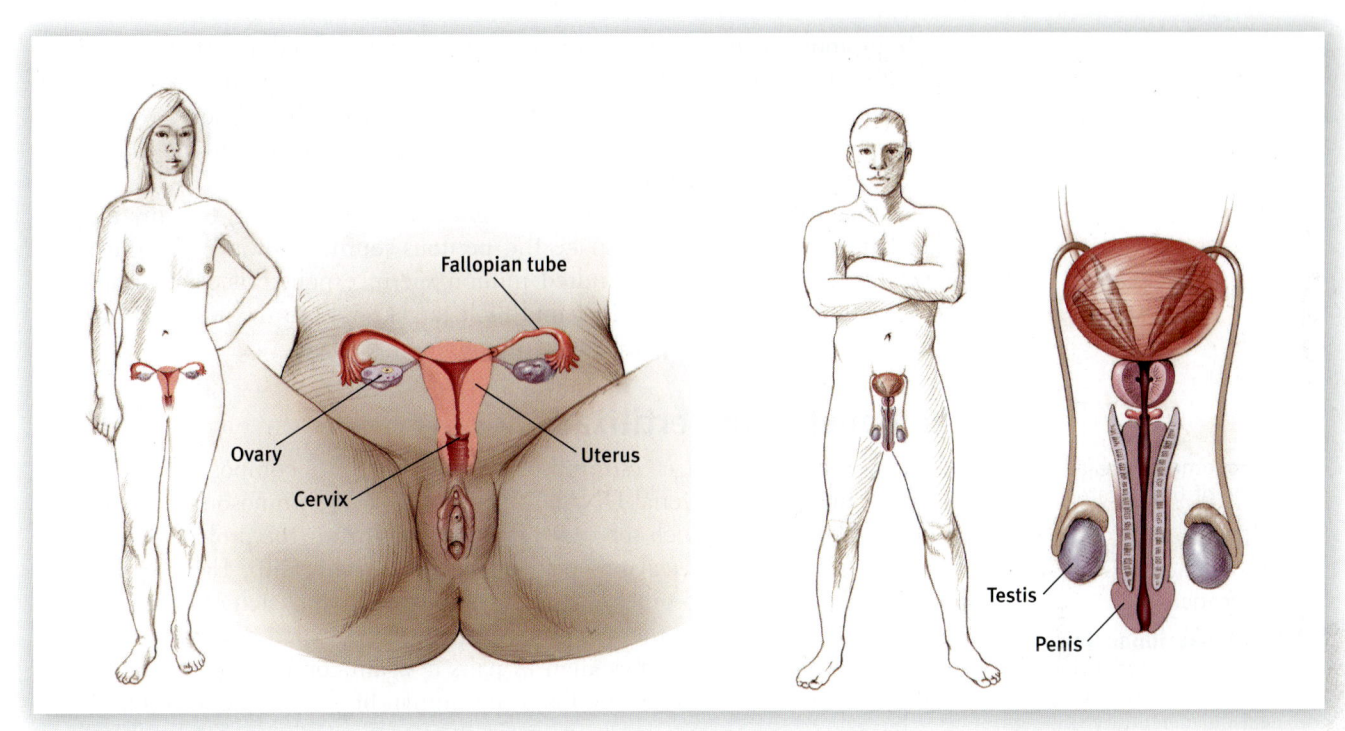

FIGURE 2.1: The female and male reproductive systems

The Process of Fertilization

The pathway that results in **fertilization**—the union of sperm and egg—begins at **ovulation**. This is the moment, typically around day 14 of a woman's cycle, when a mature ovum erupts from the ovary wall. At ovulation, a fallopian tube suctions the ovum in, and the tube begins vigorous contractions that propel the ovum on its three-day journey toward the uterus.

Now the male's contribution to forming a new life comes in. In contrast to females, whose ova are all mainly formed at birth, the **testes**—male structures comparable to the ovaries—are continually manufacturing sperm. An adult male typically produces several hundred million sperm a day. During sexual intercourse, these cells are expelled into the vagina, where a small proportion enter the uterus and wend their way up the fallopian tubes.

What happens now is a team assault. The sperm drill into the ovum, penetrating toward the center. Suddenly, one reaches the innermost part. Then the chemical composition of the ovum wall changes, shutting out the other sperm. The nuclei of the male and female cells move slowly together. When they meld into one cell, the landmark event called *fertilization* has occurred.

fertilization The union of sperm and egg.

ovulation The moment during a woman's monthly cycle when an ovum is expelled from the ovary.

testes Male organs that manufacture sperm.

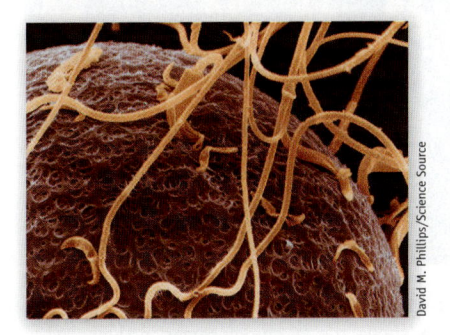

The sperm surround the ovum.

One sperm burrows in (notice the large head).

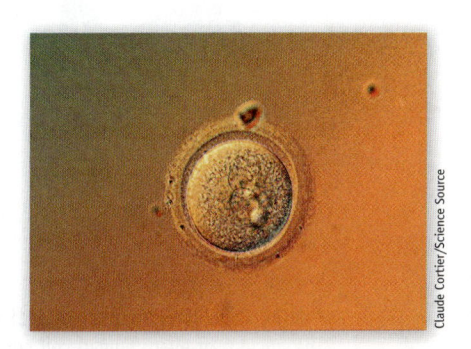

The nuclei of the two cells fuse. The watershed event called fertilization has occurred.

To promote pregnancy, it's best to have intercourse around ovulation. The ovum is receptive for about 24 hours while in the tube's outer part. Sperm take a few hours to journey from the cervix to the tube. However, sperm can live almost a week in the uterus, which means that intercourse several days prior to ovulation may also result in fertilization (Marieb, 2004).

Although the ovum emits chemical signals as to its location, the tiny tadpole-shaped travelers cannot easily make the perilous journey upward into the tubes. So, of the estimated several hundred million sperm expelled at ejaculation, only 200 to 300 reach their destination, find their target, and burrow in. What happens genetically when the sperm and egg combine?

The Genetics of Fertilization

The answer lies in looking at **chromosomes,** ropy structures composed of ladder-like strands of the genetic material **DNA.** Arrayed along each chromosome are segments of DNA called **genes,** which serve as templates for creating the proteins responsible for carrying out the physical processes of life (see Figure 2.2). Every cell in our body contains 46 chromosomes—except the sperm and ova, each of which has half this number, or 23. When the nuclei of these two cells, called *gametes,* combine at fertilization, their chromosomes align in pairs to again comprise 46. So nature has a marvelous mechanism to ensure that each human life has an identical number of chromosomes and every human being gets half of its genetic heritage from the parent of each sex.

You can see the 46 paired male chromosomes in Figure 2.3. Notice that each chromosome pair (one from our mother and one from our father) is a match, except for the sex chromosomes. The X is longer and heavier than the Y. Because each ovum carries an X chromosome, our father's contribution determines the baby's sex. If a lighter, faster-swimming, Y-carrying sperm fertilizes the ovum, we get a boy (XY). If the victor is a more resilient, slower-moving X, we get a girl (XX).

In the race to fertilization, the Y's are statistically more successful; scientists estimate that 20 percent more male than female babies are conceived. But the prenatal period is particularly hard on males. If a family member learns that she is pregnant, the odds still favor her having a boy; but because more males die in the uterus, only 5 percent more boys than girls make it to birth (Werth & Tsiaras, 2002).

chromosome A threadlike strand of DNA located in the nucleus of every cell that carries the genes, which transmit hereditary information.

DNA (deoxyribonucleic acid) The material that makes up genes, which bear our hereditary characteristics.

gene A segment of DNA that contains a chemical blueprint for manufacturing a particular protein.

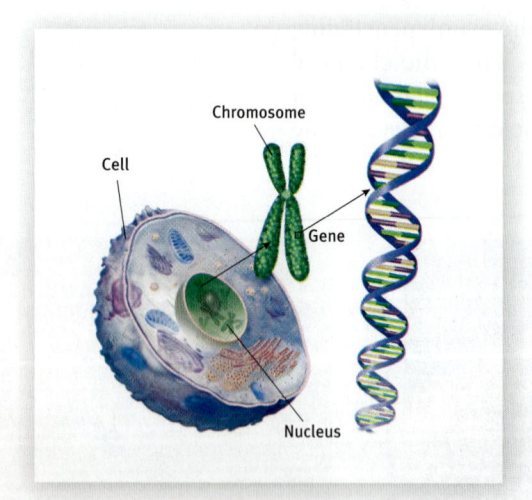

FIGURE 2.2: **The human building blocks** The nucleus of every human cell contains chromosomes, each of which is made up of two strands of DNA connected in a double helix.

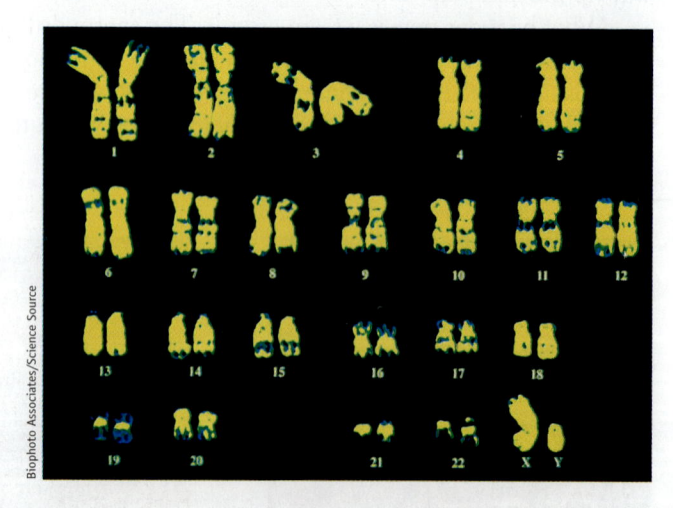

FIGURE 2.3: **A map of human chromosomes** This magnified grid, called a karyotype, shows the 46 chromosomes in their matched pairs. The final pair, with its X and Y, shows that this person is a male. Also, notice the huge size of the X chromosome compared to the Y.

And during childhood, as I will describe, males are the less hardy sex. Boys are more susceptible to developing everything from autism (see Chapter 5), to ADHD (see Chapter 6).

Tying It All Together

1. In order, list the structures involved in "getting pregnant." Choose from the following: *uterus, fallopian tubes, ovaries*. Then name the structure in which fertilization occurs.
2. The _____ house the female's genetic material, while the _____ contain the sperm. (Identify the correct names)
3. Tiffany feels certain that if she has intercourse at the right time, she will get pregnant—but asks you, "What is the right time?" Give Tiffany your answer, referring to the text discussion.
4. If a fetus has the XX chromosomal configuration, he/she is *more/less* apt to survive the prenatal journey and is *more/less* apt to be conceived.

Answers to the Tying It All Together questions can be found at the end of this chapter.

Prenatal Development

Now that we understand the starting point, let's chart prenatal development, tracing how the microscopic, fertilized ovum divides millions of times and differentiates into a living child. This miraculous transformation takes place in three stages.

LEARNING OUTCOME
- Describe the stages of prenatal development.

First Two Weeks: The Germinal Stage

The first approximately two weeks after fertilization—when the cell mass has not fully attached to the uterine wall—is called the **germinal stage** (see Figure 2.4 on page 38). Within 36 hours, the fertilized ovum, now a single cell called the **zygote**, makes its first cell division. Then the tiny cluster of cells divides every 12 to 15 hours as it wends its way down the fallopian tube. When the cells enter the uterine cavity, they differentiate into layers—some destined to form the pregnancy support structures, others the child-to-be. Now called a **blastocyst,** this ball of roughly 100 cells faces the challenge called **implantation**—embedding into the uterine wall.

The blastocyst seeks a landing site on the upper uterus. Its outer layer develops projections and burrows in. From this landing zone, blood vessels proliferate to form the **placenta**, the lifeline that passes nutrients from the mother to the developing baby. Then, the next stage of prenatal development begins: the all-important embryonic phase.

Week 3 to Week 8: The Embryonic Stage

Although the **embryonic stage** lasts roughly only six weeks, it is the most fast-paced period of development. During this time, all the major organs are constructed. By the end of this stage, what began as a clump of cells looks like a recognizable human being!

One early task is to construct the conduit responsible for all development. After the baby hooks up to the maternal bloodstream—which will nourish its growth—nutrients must reach each rapidly differentiating cell. So by the third week after fertilization, the circulatory system (our body's transport system) forms, and its pump, the heart, starts to beat.

germinal stage The first 14 days of prenatal development, from fertilization to full implantation.

zygote A fertilized ovum.

blastocyst The hollow sphere of cells formed during the germinal stage in preparation for implantation.

implantation The process in which a blastocyst becomes embedded in the uterine wall.

placenta The structure projecting from the wall of the uterus during pregnancy through which the developing baby absorbs nutrients.

embryonic stage The second stage of prenatal development, lasting from week 3 through week 8.

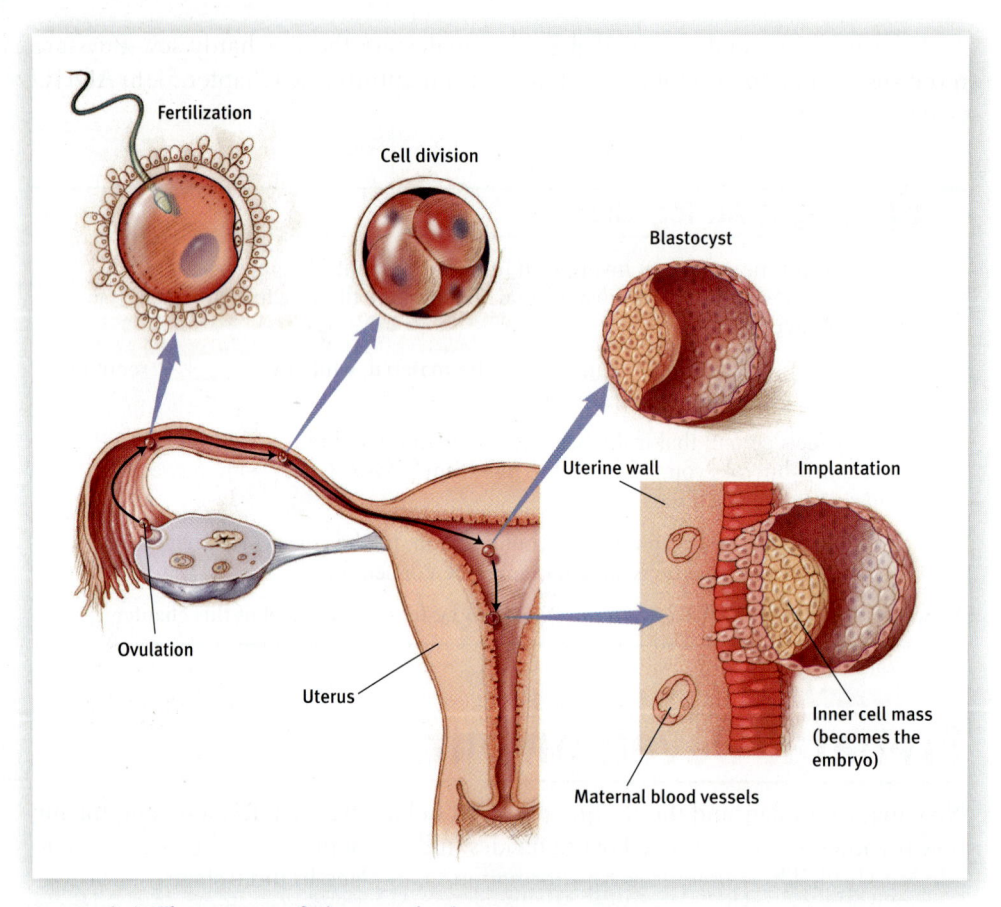

FIGURE 2.4: The events of the germinal stage The fertilized ovum divides on its trip to the uterus, then becomes a hollow ball called a blastocyst, and finally fully implants in the wall of the uterus at about 14 days after fertilization.

At the same time, the rudiments of the nervous system appear. Between 20 and 24 days after fertilization, an indentation forms along the back of the embryo and closes up to form the **neural tube.** The upper part of this cylinder becomes the brain. Its lower part forms the spinal cord. Although it is possible to "grow" new brain cells throughout life, almost all of those remarkable branching structures, called **neurons,** which cause us to think, respond, and process information, originated in neural tube cells formed during our first months in the womb.

Meanwhile, the body is developing at an astounding rate. At day 26, arm buds form; by day 28, leg swellings erupt. At day 37, rudimentary feet start to develop. By day 41, elbows, wrist curves, and the precursors of fingers can be seen. Several days later, raylike structures that will become toes emerge. By about week 8, the internal organs are in place. What started out looking like a curved stalk, then an outer-space alien, now resembles a *human* being.

Principles of Prenatal Development

In scanning the photographs of the developing embryo on the next page, can you spell out three guiding principles related to the sequence of development just described?

- Notice that from a cylindrical shape, the arms and legs grow outward and then (not unexpectedly) the fingers and toes protrude. So growth follows the **proximodistal sequence,** from the most interior (proximal) part of the body to the outer (distal) sides.

- Notice that from a huge swelling that makes the embryo look like a mammoth head, the arms emerge and the legs sprout. So development takes place according

---

neural tube A cylindrical structure that forms along the back of the embryo and develops into the brain and spinal cord.

neuron A nerve cell.

proximodistal sequence The developmental principle that growth occurs from the most interior parts of the body outward.

cephalocaudal sequence The developmental principle that growth occurs in a sequence from head to toe.

mass-to-specific sequence The developmental principle that large structures (and movements) precede increasingly detailed refinements.

CHAPTER 2 Prenatal Development, Pregnancy, and Birth   39

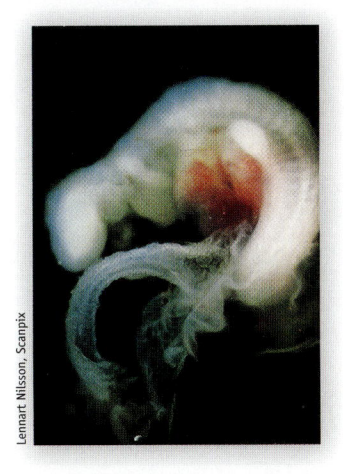

At about week 3, the embryo (the upside-down U across the top) looks like a curved stalk.

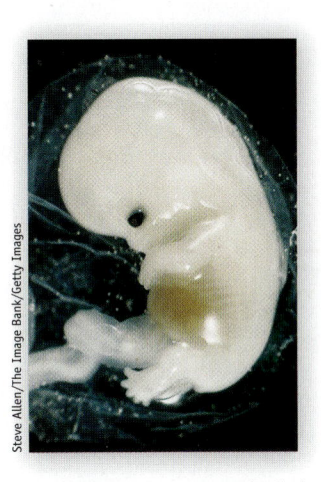

At week 4, you can see the indentations for eyes and the arms and legs beginning to sprout.

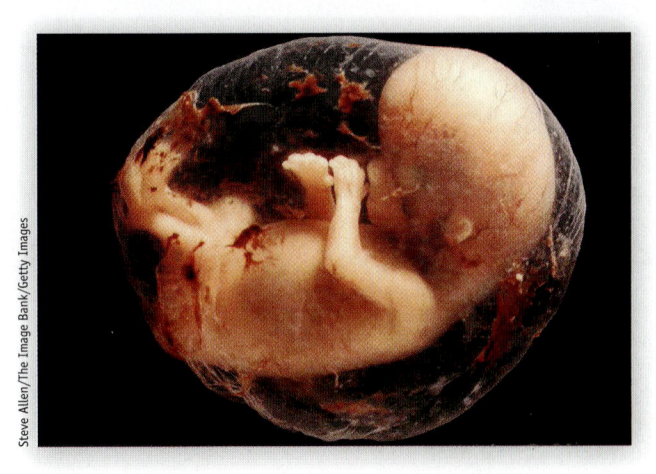

At week 9, the fetus has fingers, toes, and ears. All the major organs have developed, and the fetal stage has begun!

to the **cephalocaudal sequence,** meaning from top (*cephalo* = head) to bottom (*caudal* = tail).

- Finally, just as in constructing a sculpture, nature starts with the basic building blocks and then fills in the details. A head forms before eyes and ears; legs are constructed before feet and toes. So the **mass-to-specific sequence,** or gross (large, simple) structures before smaller (complex) refinements, is the third principle of body growth.

Keep these principles in mind. As I will describe in the next chapter, the same patterns apply to growth and motor skills *after* the baby leaves the womb.

Week 9 to Birth: The Fetal Stage

During the embryonic stage, body structures literally sprout. In the **fetal stage,** development occurs at a more leisurely pace. From the eyebrows, fingernails, and hair follicles that develop from weeks 9 to 12, to the cushion of fat that accumulates during the final weeks, it takes seven months to transform the embryo into a resilient baby ready to embrace life.

Why does our species require such a long refining period? One reason is to allow ample time for that masterpiece organ—the human brain—to form. Let's now look at this process of making a brain.

During the late embryonic stage, a mass of cells accumulates within the neural tube that will eventually produce the more than 100 billion neurons composing our brain (Stiles & Jernigan, 2010). From this zone, the neurons migrate to a region just under the top of the differentiating tube (see Figure 2.5). When the cells assemble in their "staging area," by the middle of the fetal period, they lengthen, develop branches, and interlink. This interconnecting process—responsible for every human thought and action—continues until almost our final day of life.

Figure 2.6 on page 40 shows the mushrooming brain. Notice that the brain almost doubles in size from month 4 to month 7. By now, the brain has the folded structure of an adult.

This massive growth has a profound effect. At around month 6, the fetus can hear (Crade & Lovett, 1988). By month 7, the fetus is probably able to see (Del Giudice, 2011). And by this time, with high-quality medical care, a few babies can survive.

Today, the **age of viability,** or earliest date at which a baby can be born and *possibly* live, has dropped to 22 to 23 weeks—almost halving the 38 weeks the fetus normally spends in the womb. By week 25, in affluent nations, the odds of survival are more than fifty-fifty (Lawn and others, 2011).

fetal stage The final phase of prenatal development, lasting seven months, characterized by physical refinements, massive growth, and the development of the brain.

age of viability The earliest point at which a baby can survive outside the womb.

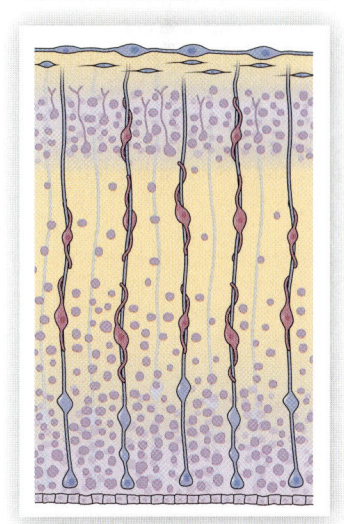

FIGURE 2.5: **Forming a brain: climbing neurons** Beginning in the earlier part of the fetal period, the neurons destined to make up the brain ascend these ladder-like filaments to reach the uppermost part of what had been the neural tube. Researchers had believed this migration was finished during mid-pregnancy, but they now realize neural migration continues well into the first year of life.

Data from Paredes and others, 2016.

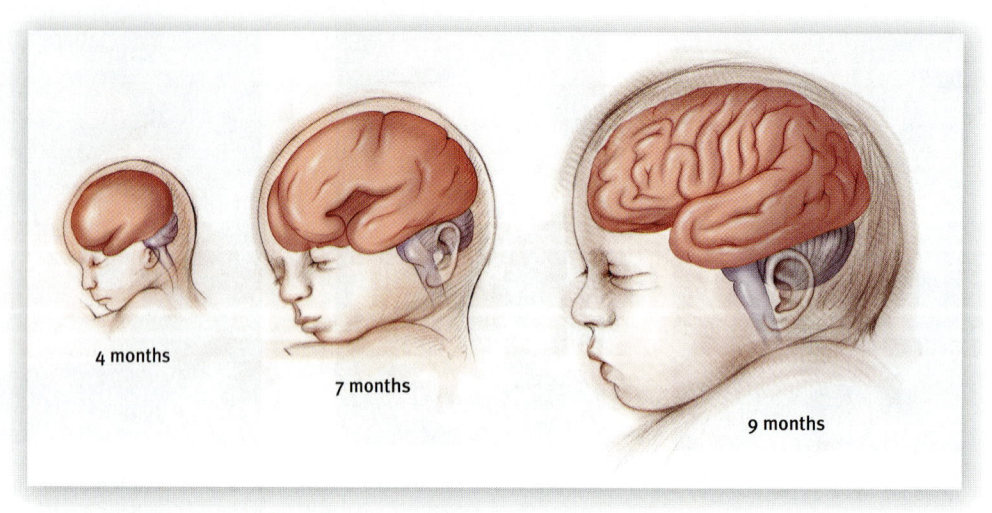

FIGURE 2.6: The expanding brain The brain grows dramatically month by month during the fetal period. During the final months, it develops its characteristic folds.

However, it is *vitally* important that the fetus stay in the uterus as long as possible. As I will describe later, being born too early (and too small) can have a lifelong impact on health.

Figure 2.7 shows the fetus during the final month of pregnancy, when its prenatal nest is cramped and birth looms on the horizon. Notice the baby's support structures: the placenta, projecting from the uterine wall, which supplies nutrients from the mother to the fetus; the **umbilical cord,** protruding from what will be the baby's bellybutton, the conduit through which nutrients flow; the **amniotic sac,** the fluid-filled chamber within which the baby floats. This encasing membrane provides insulation from infection and harm.

At this stage, parents may be running around, buying the crib or shopping for baby clothes. Middle-class couples may be marveling at the items their precious son or daughter "must have": a pacifier, a receiving blanket, a bassinet . . . and what else? What is happening during *all* nine months from the mother's—and father's—point of view?

umbilical cord The structure that attaches the placenta to the fetus, through which nutrients are passed and fetal wastes are removed.

amniotic sac A bag-shaped, fluid-filled membrane that contains and insulates the fetus.

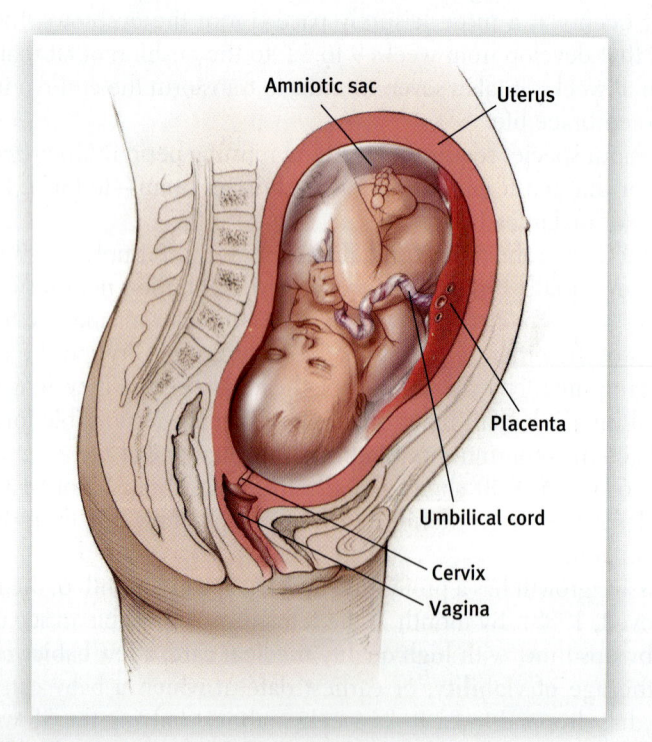

FIGURE 2.7: Poised to be born This diagram shows the fetus inside the woman's uterus late in pregnancy. Notice the placenta, amniotic sac, and umbilical cord.

Tying It All Together

1. In order, name the three stages of prenatal development. Then identify the stage in which the organs are formed.

2. A pregnant friend asks you, "How does my baby's brain develop?" Describe the process of neural migration—when it occurs, and when it is complete.

3. Match the following in utero descriptions to the correct names. (Choose from *cephalocaudal/proximodistal/mass-to-specific*.)
   a. The fingers form before the fingernails.
   b. The head forms first and the feet last.
   c. The neural tube develops and then the arms.

4. You are horrified to learn that your friend went into premature labor. Pick the minimum pregnancy age that she might be able to have a live birth: *around 12 weeks; around 22–23 weeks; around 30 weeks*.

Answers to the Tying It All Together questions can be found at the end of this chapter.

Pregnancy

The 266- to 277-day **gestation** period (or pregnancy) is divided into three segments called **trimesters,** each lasting roughly three months. (Because it is difficult to know exactly when fertilization occurs, health-care professionals date the pregnancy from the woman's last menstrual period.)

Pregnancy differs, however, from the universally patterned process of prenatal development. Despite having classic symptoms, here individual differences are the *norm*.

LEARNING OUTCOMES

- Summarize the woman's experience during each trimester of pregnancy.
- Describe how work and partner issues can impair the pregnancy experience.
- Outline the feelings of fathers-to-be.

Scanning the Trimesters

With the strong caution that the following symptoms vary—from person to person (and pregnancy to pregnancy)—let's now offer an in-the-flesh sense of how each trimester feels.

gestation The period of pregnancy.

trimester One of the 3-month-long segments into which pregnancy is divided.

First Trimester: Often Feeling Tired and Ill

After the blastocyst implants in the uterus—a few days before the woman first misses her period—pregnancy often signals its presence through unpleasant symptoms. Many women feel faint. (Yes, fainting can be a sign of pregnancy!) They may get headaches or have to urinate frequently. Like Kim in the introductory chapter vignette, they may feel incredibly tired. Their breasts become tender and painful to the touch. Therefore, many women do not need that tip-off—a missed menstrual period—to realize they are carrying a child.

Hormones, or chemicals that target certain tissues and cause them to change, trigger these symptoms. After implantation, the production of *progesterone* (literally *pro*, or "for," *gestation*)—the hormone responsible for maintaining the pregnancy—surges. The placenta produces its own unique hormone, *human chorionic gonadotropin* (HCG), thought to prevent the woman's body from rejecting the "foreign" embryo.

hormones Chemical substances released in the bloodstream that target and change organs and tissues.

Given this hormonal onslaught, the tiredness, dizziness, and headaches make sense. What about that other early pregnancy sign—morning sickness?

Morning sickness—nausea and sometimes vomiting—affects at least two out of every three women during the first trimester (Beckmann and others, 2002). This well-known symptom is not confined to the morning, however. Many women feel queasy all day. And men sometimes develop morning sickness along with their wives! This phenomenon has its own special name: *couvade* (Munroe, 2010).

But morning sickness seems senseless: Doesn't the embryo need all the nourishment it can get? Why, during the first months of pregnancy, might it be "good" to stop eating particular foods?

Consider these clues: The queasiness is at its height when the organs are forming, and, like magic, toward the end of the first trimester, it usually (but not always) disappears. Munching on bread products helps. Strong odors make many women gag. Evolutionary psychologists theorize that, before refrigeration, morning sickness prevented the mother from eating spoiled meat or toxic plants, which could be especially dangerous during the embryonic phase (Bjorklund & Pellegrini, 2002). If you have a friend struggling with morning sickness, you can give her this heartening information: Some research suggests that women with morning sickness are more likely to carry their babies to term.

This brings up that upsetting event: **miscarriage**. Roughly 1 in 10 pregnancies end in a first trimester fetal loss. For women in their late thirties, the chance of miscarrying during these weeks escalates to 1 in 5. Although early miscarriages are typically caused by problems in development incompatible with life, some women mistakenly blame themselves. When loved ones use platitudes like, "That's normal. Just try again," they minimize the grief that early miscarriage can cause (Markin, 2016).

miscarriage The naturally occurring loss of a pregnancy and death of the fetus.

Second Trimester: Feeling Much Better and Connecting Emotionally

Morning sickness, the other unpleasant symptoms, and the relatively high chance of miscarrying make the first trimester less than an unmitigated joy. During the second trimester, the magic kicks in.

By week 14, the uterus dramatically grows, often creating a need to shop for maternity clothes. The wider world may notice the woman's expanding body: "Are you pregnant?" "How wonderful!" "Take my seat." Around week 18, an event called **quickening**—a sensation like bubbles that signals the baby kicking in the womb—occurs. The woman feels viscerally connected to a growing human being.

Another landmark event that alters the emotional experience of pregnancy happens at the beginning of the third trimester, when the woman can give birth to a living child. This important late-pregnancy marker explains why some societies build in celebrations at month 6 or 7 to welcome the baby to the human community.

quickening A pregnant woman's first feeling of the fetus moving inside her body.

Third Trimester: Getting Very Large and Waiting for Birth

Look at a pregnant woman struggling up the stairs and you'll get a sense of her feelings during this final trimester: backaches (think of carrying a bowling ball); leg cramps; numbness and tingling as the uterus presses against the nerves of the lower limbs; heartburn, insomnia, and anxious anticipation as focus shifts to the birth ("When will this baby arrive?!"); irregular uterine contractions as the baby sinks into the birth canal and delivery draws very near.

Although women often do work up to the day of delivery, health-care workers advise taking time off to rest and relying on caring loved ones to help during the final months. Issues relating to working and having loving support loom large during all nine months!

Pregnancy Is Not a Solo Act

> I'm now almost five months and . . . with the right clothes I can easily hide it. By postponing making it public, . . . [my organization] will have less time to put me in this stigmatized hole of unproductive, useless, unprofessional future mom.
>
> (from a pregnant bank executive living in the Netherlands, quoted in Hennekam, 2016, p. 1776)

All the happiness I would have in seeing the heartbeat, or feeling the first kick is erased by my rocky relationship with John. If only my partner accepted this pregnancy! Now I can't focus on the baby. I'm anxious and depressed.

Some women, such as Kim in the opening vignette, are in love with motherhood. Others slog through pregnancy, anxious, ambivalent, and depressed (Brenning, Soenens, & Vansteenkiste, 2016). Now, let's focus on two forces that shape women's emotions during this landmark time.

WORK WORRIES One influence destined to erode happiness is financial concerns. Couples struggling economically and, especially, low-income single parents worry, "Can we (or I) afford this child?" But the first quotation on the previous page shows that even women in high-powered jobs have fears: "Will I be passed over for a promotion, or demoted, because my employer believes mothers can't do a good job?"

These anxieties are legitimate. **Family–work conflict,** or being pulled between the demands of caregiving and career, is a major issue for working parents (see Belsky, 2016, for a review). Even in nations such as Sweden, where both sexes get equal paid time off after birth, mothers, not fathers, most often opt to take this family leave (Duvander, 2014). In fact, there is a striking gender difference here. Because society links fatherhood with career commitment ("Supporting a family settles men down"), U.S. statistics show that married men are apt to be rewarded with a *salary raise* after their wives give birth (Killewald, 2013)!

RELATIONSHIP ISSUES The main quality that colors the emotional experience of pregnancy, however, is illustrated in the second quotation on the previous page—the relationship. Research shows that couples are emotionally tethered as they confront this life change. If one person feels unhappy about the pregnancy, the other person feels distressed, too (Canário & Figueiredo, 2016). Moreover, these shared attitudes carry over after birth. Couples who are more ambivalent about the fetus during pregnancy tend to be more stressed out during their child's first two years of life (Edwards & Hans, 2016). So, rather than being an internal event, a woman's feelings about her expanding body depend on her relationships in the world.

This woman's happiness in getting pregnant may be affected by work worries: "Will I get that promotion if my boss knows I'm having a baby? How will having a child affect my job?"

family–work conflict
A common developed-world situation, in which parents are torn between the demands of family and a career.

What About Dads?

This brings up the emotions of the traditional pregnancy partner: dads. Given the attention we lavish on pregnant women, it should come as no surprise that fathers have been relatively ignored in the research exploring this transition of life. But fathers are also bonded to their babies-to-be (Vreeswijk and others, 2014). They can feel just as devastated when a pregnancy doesn't work out. Here are some comments about miscarriage from the male point of view:

> I keep thinking that my wife is still pregnant. Where is my little girl? I was so ready to spoil her and treat her like a princess . . . but now she is gone. I don't think I'll ever be the same again.
>
> (quoted in Jaffe & Diamond, 2011, p. 218)

> I had to be strong for Kate. I had to let her cry on me and then I would . . . drive up into the hills and cry to myself. I was trying to support her even though I felt my whole life had just caved in. . . .
>
> (quoted in McCreight, 2004, p. 337)

As you can see from the above quotations, men coping with this trauma have a double burden. They may feel compelled to put aside their feelings to focus on their wives (Jaffe & Diamond, 2011; Rinehart & Kiselica, 2010). Plus, because the loss of a baby is typically seen as a "woman's issue," the wider world tends to marginalize men's pain.

These examples remind us that husbands are "pregnant" in spirit along with their wives. We should *never* thrust their feelings aside.

Returning to the beginning of the chapter, we now know that the cultural practice of pampering pregnant women makes excellent psychological sense—for both the mother *and* her child. But we need to realize that expectant fathers need cherishing, too!

Table 2.1 summarizes these points in a brief "stress during pregnancy" questionnaire. Next, we return to the baby and tackle that common fear: "Will my child be healthy?"

Table 2.1: Measuring Stress in Mothers-to-Be: A Short Section Summary Questionnaire

1. Does this woman or couple have financial troubles?
2. Is this woman concerned that being pregnant will derail her career chances?
3. Is this woman having marital problems, and does her partner want this baby?

Tying It All Together

1. Samantha just entered her second trimester. Explain how she is likely to feel for the next few months. What symptoms was Samantha apt to describe during the first trimester, after learning she was pregnant?
2. Your cousin is a high-paid executive in a marketing firm. Based on this chapter, if she gets pregnant, describe in a sentence how she may feel about revealing the news to her boss.
3. As a clinic director, you are concerned that men are often left out of the pregnancy experience. Design a few innovative interventions to make your clinic responsive to the needs of fathers-to-be.

Answers to the Tying It All Together questions can be found at the end of this chapter.

LEARNING OUTCOMES

- Name the main teratogenic threats during the first and second trimesters.
- Outline the impact of smoking, excessive alcohol, and prenatal stress on fetal development.
- Describe Down syndrome and several other single-gene disorders.
- Evaluate genetic counseling and the different prenatal diagnostic tests.
- Discuss infertility and assisted reproductive technologies.

birth defect A physical or neurological problem that occurs prenatally or at birth.

Threats to the Developing Baby

In this section, I'll explore the prenatal reasons for **birth defects,** or health problems at birth. I'll also discuss new research exploring how wider-world events while "in the womb" can potentially affect a fetus's lifelong health. In reading this catalogue of "things that can go wrong," keep these thoughts in mind: The vast majority of babies are born healthy. Many birth defects don't seriously impair a baby's ability to lead a fulfilling life. Often birth defects result from a complex nature-plus-nurture interaction. Fetal genetic vulnerabilities combine with environmental hazards in the womb. However, this section separates these conditions into two categories: toxins that flow through the placenta to impair development and genetic diseases.

Threats from Outside: Teratogens

The universal fears about the growing baby are expressed in cultural prohibitions: "Don't use scissors or your baby will have cut lips" (a cleft palate), Afghanistan; "Avoid looking at monkeys [Indonesia] or gossiping [China] or your baby will be deformed."

If you think these practices are strange, consider the standard mid-twentieth-century medical advice. Physicians routinely put U.S. women on a strict diet if they gained over 15 pounds. They encouraged mothers-to-be to smoke and drink to relax

(Von Raffler-Engel, 1994; Wertz & Wertz, 1989). Today, these pronouncements might qualify as fetal abuse! What *can* hurt the developing baby? When is damage most apt to occur?

A **teratogen** (from the Greek words *teras*, "monster," and *gen*, "creating") is the name for any substance that crosses the placenta to harm the fetus. A teratogen may be an infectious disease; a medication; a recreational drug; an environmental hazard, such as radiation or pollution; or, as you will see later, the hormones produced by a pregnant woman who is under extreme stress. Table 2.2 on page 46 describes potential teratogens in various categories.

> **teratogen** A substance that crosses the placenta and harms the fetus.

Basic Teratogenic Principles

Teratogens typically exert their damage during the **sensitive period**—the timeframe when a particular organ or system is coming "on line." For example, the infectious disease called *rubella* (German measles) often damaged a baby's heart or ears, depending on the week during the first trimester when a mother contracted the disease. The mild mosquito-borne virus, Zika, shown here, wreaks destruction during the late embryonic stage, when it prevents the immature cells from assembling in the neural tube.

> **sensitive period** The time when a body structure is most vulnerable to damage by a teratogen, typically when that organ or process is rapidly developing or coming "on line."

In general, with regard to teratogens, the following principles apply:

1. **Teratogens are most likely to cause major structural damage during the embryonic stage.** Before implantation, teratogens have an all-or-nothing impact. They either inhibit implantation and cause death, or they leave the not-yet-attached blastocyst unscathed. It is during organ formation (after implantation through week 8) that major body structures are most likely to be affected. This is why physicians advise forgoing any medications during the first trimester—that is, unless expectant mothers have a chronic disease that demands they continue their treatment (American Academy of Pediatrics [AAP], Committee on Drugs, 2000).

2. **Teratogens can affect the developing brain throughout pregnancy.** As you saw earlier, because the brain is forming during the second and third trimesters, the potential for neurological damage extends for all nine months. Typically, during the second and third trimesters, exposure to teratogens increases the risk of **developmental disorders**. This term refers to any condition that compromises normal development—from delays in reaching basic milestones, such as walking or talking, to learning problems and hyperactivity.

> **developmental disorders** Learning impairments and behavioral problems during infancy and childhood.

3. **Teratogens have a threshold level above which damage occurs.** For instance, women who drink more than four cups of coffee a day throughout pregnancy have a slightly higher risk of miscarriage; but having an occasional Diet Coke is fine (Gilbert-Barness, 2000).

4. **Teratogens exert their damage unpredictably, depending on fetal and maternal vulnerabilities.** Still, mothers-to-be metabolize toxins differently, and babies differ genetically in susceptibility. So the damaging effects of a particular teratogen can vary. On the plus side, you may know a child in your local school's gifted program whose mother drank heavily during pregnancy. On the negative side, we do not know where the teratogenic threshold lies in any particular case. Therefore, during pregnancy, it's best to err on the side of caution.

Although the damaging impact of a teratogen may surface during infancy, it can also manifest itself years later. An unfortunate example of this teratogenic time bomb took place in my own life. My mother was given a drug called diethylstilbestrol (DES) while she was pregnant with me. (DES was prescribed routinely in the 1950s

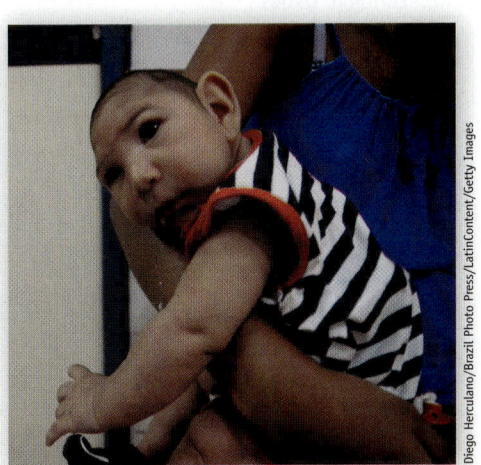

This Zika-exposed baby is a testament to the horrible damage teratogens can potentially cause during the first trimester, as he was born with the devastating condition called *microcephaly*.

Table 2.2: Examples of Known Teratogens and the Damage They Can Do

Teratogen	Consequences of Exposure
INFECTIOUS DISEASES	
Rubella (German measles)	If a pregnant woman contracts rubella during the embryonic stage, the consequences can be intellectual disability, blindness, or eye, ear, and heart abnormalities in the baby—depending on the week the virus enters the bloodstream. Luckily, women of childbearing age are now routinely immunized for this otherwise minor adult disease.
Cytomegalovirus	About 25% of babies infected with this virus develop vision or hearing loss; 10% develop neurological problems.
AIDS	HIV-infected women can transmit the virus to their babies prenatally during delivery (through the placenta) or after birth (through breast milk). Rates of transmission are much lower if infected mothers take the anti-AIDS drug AZT or if newborns are given a new drug that blocks the transmission of HIV at birth. If a mother takes these precautions, does not breastfeed, and delivers her baby by c-section (see page 60), the infection rate falls to less than 1%. While mother-to-child transmission of HIV has declined dramatically in the developed world, it remains a devastating problem in sub-Saharan Africa and other impoverished regions of the globe (AVERT, 2005).
Herpes	This familiar sexually transmitted disease can cause miscarriage, growth retardation, and eye abnormalities in affected fetuses. Doctors recommend that pregnant women with active genital herpes undergo c-sections to avoid infecting their babies during delivery.
Toxoplasmosis	This disease, caused by a parasite in raw meat and cat feces, can produce sensory and cognitive impairments in infants. Pregnant women should avoid handling raw meat and cat litter.
Zika virus	Pregnant women who contract this mild adult mosquito-borne illness during the first trimester are at high risk of miscarrying or giving birth to a baby with microcephaly (missing most of a brain). Women planning to get pregnant should avoid traveling to Zika-affected regions. Having sex with an infected partner can also transmit the virus.
MEDICATIONS	
Antibiotics	Streptomycin has been linked to hearing loss; tetracycline to stained infant tooth enamel.
Thalidomide	This drug, prescribed in the late 1950s in Europe to prevent nausea during the first trimester, prevented the baby's arms and legs from developing if taken during the embryonic period.
Anti-seizure drugs	These medications have been linked to developmental delays during infancy.
Anti-psychotic drugs	These drugs may slightly raise the risk of giving birth to a baby with heart problems.
Antidepressants	Although typically safe, third-trimester exposure to selective serotonin reuptake inhibitors and tricyclic antidepressants has been linked to temporary jitteriness, excessive crying, and eating and sleeping difficulties in newborns. Rarely, these drugs can produce seizures and dehydration in the baby, as well as miscarriage.
RECREATIONAL DRUGS	
Cocaine	This drug is linked to miscarriage, growth retardation, and learning and behavior problems.
Methamphetamine	This drug may cause miscarriage and growth retardation.
ENVIRONMENTAL TOXINS	
Radiation	Japanese children exposed to radiation from the atomic bomb during the second trimester had extremely high rates of severe intellectual disability. Miscarriages were virtually universal among pregnant women living within 5 miles of the blast. Pregnant women are also advised to avoid clinical doses of radiation such as those used in X-rays (and especially cancer treatment radiation).
Lead	Babies with high levels of lead in the umbilical cord may show impairments in cognitive functioning (Bellinger and others, 1987). Maternal exposure to lead is associated with miscarriage.
Mercury and PCBs	These pollutants are linked to learning and behavior problems.
VITAMIN DEFICIENCIES	In addition to eating a balanced diet, every woman of childbearing age should take folic acid supplements. This vitamin, part of the B complex, protects against the incomplete closure of the neural tube during the first month of development—an event that may produce *spina bifida* (paralysis in the body below the region of the spine that has not completely closed) or *anencephaly* (failure of the brain to develop—and certain death) if the gap occurs toward the top of the developing tube.

Data from Huttenlocher, 2002, and the references in this chapter.

and 1960s to prevent miscarriage.) During my early twenties, I developed cancerous cells in my cervix—and, after surgery, had three miscarriages before being blessed by adopting my son.

The Teratogenic Impact of Medicines and Recreational Drugs

The fact that some common medications are teratogenic presents dilemmas for women. Suppose you are among the estimated 1 in 10 U.S. women who enter into a pregnancy depressed (Tebeka, Le Strat, & Dubertret, 2016). You are alarmed at the research suggesting your mental state can impair your attachment to the baby (and feelings about your partner). But you also know that taking antidepressants slightly raises the risk of having a premature birth (Deligiannidis, Byatt, & Freeman, 2014; Huang and others, 2014; Jenson and others, 2013). What do you do? When it comes to medicines and pregnancy, sometimes there are no perfect choices.

With recreational drugs the choice is clear. Each substance is potentially teratogenic. So it's best to just say *no*!

Because tobacco and alcohol are woven into the fabric of daily life, let's now focus on these widely used teratogens. What *can* happen to the baby when pregnant women smoke and drink?

SMOKING Each time a pregnant woman reads the information on a cigarette pack, she is reminded that she may be doing her baby harm. Still, polls suggest that approximately 1 in 3 pregnant women—when they are young and poorly educated—smoke (Agency for Healthcare Research and Quality [AHRQ], 2014). Because this practice is such a "no, no," these surveys almost certainly underestimate the number of smoking mothers-to-be. When scientists in a national U.S. study measured blood levels of cotinine (a biological indicator of tobacco use), they discovered that roughly 1 in 4 pregnant smokers had earlier falsely reported: "Oh yes, I definitely quit!" (see Dietz and others, 2011).

The danger posed by smoking is giving birth to a smaller-than-normal, less healthy baby (Krstev and others, 2013). Nicotine constricts the mother's blood vessels, reducing blood flow to the fetus and preventing ample nutrients from reaching the child. Infants born to pregnant smokers are less able to regulate their behavior (Wiebe and others, 2015). Tobacco-exposed fetuses are more prone to develop antisocial behaviors during childhood and the teens (Huizink, 2015; Knopik and others, 2016; Liebschutz and others, 2015).

Heavy smoking (more than half a pack a day) is most poisonous for development (Huizink, 2015). And, because quitting is difficult, some women get mixed signals from health-care providers: "My doctor told me stopping would stress the baby . . . I'm continuing to smoke but not that much" (quoted in Naughton, Eborall, & Sutton, 2013, pp. 27, 28). How many cigarettes a day are dangerous? Let's keep this murky issue in mind as I turn to that other familiar teratogen: alcohol.

ALCOHOL As I mentioned earlier, it used to be standard practice to encourage pregnant women to have a nightcap to relieve stress. During the 1970s, as evidence mounted for a disorder called **fetal alcohol syndrome (FAS)**, these prescriptions were quickly revised. Whenever you hear the word *syndrome*, it is a signal that the condition has a constellation of features that are present to varying degrees. The defining qualities of fetal alcohol syndrome include a smaller-than-normal birth weight and brain; facial abnormalities (such as a flattened face); and developmental disorders ranging from serious intellectual disability to seizures and hyperactivity (Dean & Davis, 2007; May and others, 2016; Roussotte, Soderberg, & Sowell, 2010).

Women who binge-drink (have more than four drinks at a sitting), or pregnant women who regularly consume several drinks nightly, are at highest risk of giving birth to a baby with fetal alcohol syndrome. Their children, at a minimum, may be

fetal alcohol syndrome (FAS) A cluster of birth defects caused by the mother's alcohol consumption during pregnancy.

born with a less severe syndrome called *fetal alcohol spectrum disorders*, characterized by deficits in learning and impaired mental health (Wedding and others, 2007). As alcohol crosses the placenta, it causes genetic changes that impair neural growth (Hashimoto-Torii and others, 2011).

Faced with these warnings, polls in New Zealand and Australia show most women reported that they stopped using alcohol after learning they were pregnant (Parackal, Parackal, & Harraway, 2013; Pettigrew and others, 2016). Surprisingly, however, a study in the Netherlands revealed that *well-educated*, expectant mothers were likely to still drink (Pfinder and others, 2014)!

This unexpected finding may reflect cultural norms. Every U.S. public health organization recommends no alcohol during pregnancy. In Europe, having a cocktail or a glass of wine is an expected practice during meals. This may explain why European physicians disagree with their U.S. counterparts: "One drink per day can't *possibly* do the fetus harm" (Paul, 2010; Royal College of Obstetricians and Gynaecologists [RCOG], 1999).

As this woman downed her many drinks, she put her baby at risk for fetal alcohol syndrome—explaining why patrons at a bar who saw this scenario would get very upset!

Measurement Issues

Why is there *any* debate about a "safe" amount of alcohol to drink? For answers, imagine the challenges you would face as a researcher exploring the impact of tobacco or alcohol on the developing child: The need to ask thousands of pregnant women to estimate how often they indulged in these "unacceptable" behaviors and then track the children for decades, looking for problems that might appear as late as adult life. Plus, because your study is *correlational*, the difficulties you find might be due to other confounding causes. Pregnant women who drink are more likely to smoke, to be depressed, to be under stress, and to take other drugs. They could be passing down behavior problems to their sons and daughters in their genes.

Drawing on research using sophisticated techniques to control for genetics, one expert (Huizink, 2015) concludes that light smoking and drinking won't affect the fetus. But don't take this pronouncement as a green light! With a biologically at-risk baby, who knows what damage five cigarettes a day or a single glass of wine each night could do?

Hot in Developmental Science: The Long Shadow of Prenatal Stress

Giving up wine and cigarettes for the sake of the baby is doable—and many women stop using social drugs when they are having a child. Implementing the cultural advice to keep pregnant women "calm and happy" can be impossible to carry out. What happens to the fetus when pregnant women are depressed or experience traumatic stresses?

The danger is that prenatal depression and severe emotional upheavals can impair fetal growth or provoke premature labor, and so produce smaller, less healthy babies (Lin and others, 2017). In fact, in one alarming study, elevated levels of the stress hormone **cortisol**, measured in women *prior to getting pregnant*, predicted giving birth to a tinier child (Guardino & Schetter, 2013). Cortisol, transferred via the placenta to the fetus, even has a direct physiological effect, making newborns irritable during the first months of life (Baibazarova and others, 2013).

While pregnancy stresses range from poverty to abusive partners, from job concerns to experiencing a loved one's death (Class and others, 2013), the most fascinating data relates to natural disasters. Women who were pregnant during the 2011

cortisol A hormone often measured in saliva by researchers as a biological marker of stress.

earthquake in Japan had preschoolers with abnormally high rates of mental health problems (Sato and others, 2016). Months after the Red River in Fargo, North Dakota, crested in 2009, the prevalence of low-birth-weight babies in that city peaked. Women in their first trimester living close to the flood were most likely to have small newborns, suggesting again that early pregnancy is a time of maximum risk (Hilmert and others, 2016).

Being born small casts a shadow over the *whole* span of life. During World War II, in 1944, the Germans cut off the food supply to Holland, putting that nation in a semi-starvation condition for a few months. As you might imagine, miscarriages and stillbirths were far more frequent during this "Hunger Winter." But the surviving babies also had enduring scars. Midlife heart disease rates were higher if a baby had been in the womb *specifically* during the Hunger Winter (Paul, 2010). Imagine what health concerns could affect babies who were born in 2016, during the civil war in Aleppo, Syria, even if these newborns survived this human-made disaster that has stained humankind.

Imagine being this terrified refugee family escaping Aleppo, Syria, during the civil war. Horrific holocausts (and natural disasters) can have enduring consequences on development, even when a baby manages to survive.

Why might deprivation in the womb be linked to premature, age-related disease? Speculations again center on being born too small. When fetuses are deprived of nutrients and/or exposed to intense maternal stress, researchers hypothesize, the resulting impaired growth primes the baby to enter the world expecting "a state of deprivation" and to eat excessively or store fat. But while this strategy promotes survival when nutrition is scarce, it boomerangs—promoting obesity and a potentially shorter life—when a child arrives in the world in today's era of overabundant food.

Is obesity (and adult chronic disease) caused just by personal lifestyle choices or partly promoted by a poor body–environment fit at birth? These tantalizing questions are driving **fetal programming research**—studies that explore how intrauterine events may *epigenetically* change our genetic code (Belsky & Pluess, 2011).

Freud revolutionized the twentieth century by arguing that childhood experiences shape personality. Will twenty-first-century scientists trace the roots of human development to experiences in the womb?

Fetal programming research is action oriented. Ideally, interventions—such as therapy to ward off depression (Dimidjian and others, 2016) or prevent prenatal drinking (Parrish and others, 2016)—can have a long-term impact on a child's fate. With the conditions I discuss next, the problems are often more serious. They are frequently diagnosed at birth because the child's condition is "genetic." It was sealed at conception with the union of an egg and sperm.

fetal programming research New research discipline exploring the impact of traumatic pregnancy events and stress on producing low birth weight, obesity, and long-term physical problems.

Threats from Within: Chromosomal and Genetic Disorders

When a birth defect is genetic, there are two main causes. The child might have an unusual number of chromosomes, or the issue might be a faulty gene (or set of genes).

Chromosomal Problems

As we know, the normal human chromosomal complement is 46. However, sometimes a baby with a missing or extra chromosome is conceived. The vast majority of these fertilizations end in first-trimester miscarriages, as the cells cannot differentiate much past the blastocyst stage.

Still, babies can be born with an abnormal number of sex chromosomes (such as an extra X or two, an extra Y, or a single X) and survive. In this case, although the symptoms vary, the result is often learning impairments and sometimes infertility.

Down syndrome The most common chromosomal abnormality, causing intellectual disability, susceptibility to heart disease, other health problems, and distinctive physical characteristics including slanted eyes and a stocky build.

Survival is also possible when a child is born with an extra chromosome on a specific other pair. The most common example—happening in roughly 1 in every 700 births (National Down Syndrome Society [NDSS], n.d.)—produces a baby with Down syndrome.

Down syndrome typically occurs because a cell-division error, called *nondisjunction*, in the egg or sperm causes an extra chromosome or piece of that copy to adhere to chromosome pair 21. (Figure 2.3 on page 36 shows this is the smallest matching set, so the reason extra material adhering to chromosome 21 is not uniformly lethal is that this pair generally contains the fewest genes.) The child is born with 47 chromosomes instead of the normal 46.

This extra chromosome produces familiar physical features: a flat facial profile, an upward slant to the eyes, a stocky appearance, and an enlarged tongue. Babies born with Down syndrome are at high risk for having heart defects and childhood leukemia. Here, too, there is a lifespan time-bomb impact. During midlife, many adults with Down syndrome develop Alzheimer's disease (NDSS, n.d.). The most well-known problem with this familiar condition, however, is mild to moderate intellectual disability.

A century ago, Down syndrome children rarely lived to adulthood. They were shunted to institutions to live severely shortened lives. In the United States today, due to medical advances, these babies have an average life expectancy of 60 years (NDSS, n.d.). Ironically, this longevity gain can be a double-edged sword. Elderly parent caregivers may worry what will happen to their middle-aged child when they die or become physically impaired (Gath, 1993).

Knowing a Down syndrome child has a powerful effect on every person. Will this older girl become a more caring, sensitive adult through having played with this much loved younger friend?

This is not to say that every Down syndrome baby is dependent on a caregiver's help. These children can sometimes learn to read and write. They can live independently, hold down jobs, marry and have children, construct fulfilling lives. Do you know a child with Down syndrome like the toddler in this photo who is the light of her loving family and friends' lives?

Although women of any age can give birth to Down syndrome babies, the risk rises exponentially among older mothers. Over age 40, the chance of having a Down syndrome birth is 1 in 100; over age 45, it is 1 in 30 (NDSS, n.d.). The reason is that, with more time "in storage," older ova are more apt to develop chromosomal faults.

Down syndrome is typically caused by a spontaneous genetic mistake. Now let's look at a different category of genetic disorders—those passed down in the parents' DNA to potentially affect *every* child.

Genetic Disorders

Most illnesses—from cancer to heart disease to schizophrenia—are caused by complex nature-plus-nurture interactions. Several, often unknown, genes act in conjunction with murky environmental forces (Moore, 2015). A *single*, known gene causes these next disorders that often appear at birth.

single-gene disorder An illness caused by a single gene.

Single-gene disorders are passed down according to three modes of inheritance: They may be *dominant*, *recessive*, or *sex-linked*. To understand these patterns, you might want to look again at the paired arrangement of the chromosomes in Figure 2.3 (page 36) and remember that we get one copy of each gene from our mother and one from our father. Also, in understanding these illnesses, it is important to know that one member of each gene pair can be dominant. This means that the quality will always show up in real life. If both members of the gene pair are not dominant (that is, if they are recessive), the illness will manifest itself only if the child inherits two of the faulty genes.

Dominant disorders are in the first category. In this case, if one parent harbors the problem gene (and so has the illness), each child the couple gives birth to has a fifty-fifty chance of also getting ill.

Recessive disorders are in the second category. Unless a person gets two copies of the gene, one from the father and one from the mother, that child is disease free. In this case, the odds of a baby born to two carriers—that is, parents who each have one copy of that gene—having the illness are 1 in 4.

The mode of transmission for **sex-linked single-gene disorders** is more complicated. Most often, the woman is carrying a recessive (nonexpressed in real life) gene for the illness on *one* of her two X chromosomes. Since her daughters have another X from their father (who doesn't carry the illness), the female side of the family is typically disease free. Her sons, however, have a fifty-fifty chance of getting ill, depending on whether they get the normal or abnormal version of their mother's X.

Because their single X leaves them vulnerable, sex-linked disorders typically affect males. But as an intellectual exercise, you might want to figure out when females can get this condition. If you guessed that it's when the mother is a carrier (having one faulty X) and the dad has the disorder (having the gene on his single X), you are right!

Table 2.3 on page 52 visually decodes these modes of inheritance and describes a few of the best-known single-gene diseases. In scanning the first illness on the chart, Huntington's disease, imagine your emotional burden as a genetically at-risk child. People with Huntington's develop an incurable dementia in the prime of life. As a child you would probably have watched a beloved parent lose his memory and bodily functions, and then die. You would know that your odds of suffering the same fate are 1 in 2. (Although babies born with lethal dominant genetic disorders typically die before they can have children, Huntington's disease remained in the population because it, too, operates as an internal time bomb, showing up during the prime reproductive years.)

With the other illnesses in Table 2.3—programmed by recessive genes—the fears relate to bearing a child. If both you and your partner have the Tay-Sachs carrier gene, you may have seen a beloved baby die in infancy. With cystic fibrosis, your affected child would be subject to recurrent medical crises as his lungs filled up with fluid, and he would face a dramatically shortened life. Would you want to take the 1-in-4 chance of having this experience again?

The good news, as the table shows, is that the prognoses for some routinely fatal childhood single-gene disorders are no longer as dire. With hemophilia, the life-threatening episodes of bleeding can be avoided by supplying the missing blood factor through transfusions. While surviving to the teens with cystic fibrosis used to be rare, today these children can expect on average to live to their twenties and sometimes beyond (CysticFibrosis.com, n.d.). Still, with Tay-Sachs or Huntington's disease, there is *nothing* medically that can be done.

In sum, the answer to the question of whether single-gene disorders can be treated and cured is "It depends." Although people still have the faulty gene—and so are not "cured" in the traditional sense—through advances in nurture (or changing the environment), we have made remarkable progress in treating what used to be uniformly fatal diseases.

Our most dramatic progress, however, lies in **genetic testing**. Through a simple blood test, people can find out whether they carry the gene for various illnesses.

These diagnostic breakthroughs bring up difficult issues. Would you want to know whether you have the gene for Huntington's disease? The inspiring story of Nancy Wexler, the psychologist who helped discover the Huntington's gene and

---

dominant disorder An illness that a child gets by inheriting one copy of the abnormal gene that causes the disorder.

recessive disorder An illness that a child gets by inheriting two copies of the abnormal gene that causes the disorder.

sex-linked single-gene disorder An illness, carried on the mother's X chromosome, that typically leaves the female offspring unaffected but has a fifty-fifty chance of striking each male child.

genetic testing A blood test to determine whether a person carries the gene for a given genetic disorder.

Table 2.3: Some Examples of Dominant, Recessive, and Sex-Linked Single-Gene Disorders

DOMINANT DISORDERS

- **Huntington's disease (HD)** This fatal nervous system disorder is characterized by uncontrollable jerky movements and irreversible intellectual impairment (dementia). Symptoms usually appear around age 35, although the illness can occasionally erupt in childhood and in old age. There is no treatment for this disease.

RECESSIVE DISORDERS

- **Cystic fibrosis (CF)** This most common single-gene disorder in the United States is typically identified at birth by the salty character of the sweat. The child's body produces mucus that clogs the lungs and pancreas, interfering with breathing and digestion and causing repeated medical crises. As the hairlike cells in the lungs are destroyed, these vital organs degenerate and eventually cause premature death. Advances in treatment have extended the average life expectancy for people with CF to their late twenties. One in 28 U.S. Caucasians is a carrier for this disease.*

- **Sickle cell anemia** This blood disorder takes its name from the characteristic sickle shape of the red blood cells. The blood cells collapse and clump together, causing oxygen deprivation and organ damage. The symptoms of sickle cell anemia are fatigue, pain, growth retardation, ulcers, stroke, and, ultimately, a shortened life. Treatments include transfusions and medications for infection and pain. One in 10 African Americans is a carrier of this disease.*

- **Tay-Sachs disease** In this universally fatal infant nervous system disorder, the child appears healthy at birth, but then fatty material accumulates in the neurons and, at 6 months, symptoms such as blindness, intellectual disability, and paralysis occur and the baby dies. Tay-Sachs is found most often among Jewish people of Eastern European ancestry. An estimated 1 in 25 U.S. Jews is a carrier.†

SEX-LINKED DISORDERS

- **Hemophilia** These blood-clotting disorders typically affect males. The most serious forms of hemophilia (A and B) produce severe episodes of uncontrolled joint bleeding and pain. In the past, these episodes often resulted in death during childhood. Today, with transfusions of the missing clotting factors, affected children can have a fairly normal life expectancy.

*Sickle cell anemia may have remained in the population because having the trait (one copy of the gene) conferred an evolutionary advantage: It protected against malaria in Africa. Scientists also speculate that the cystic fibrosis trait may have conferred immunity to typhoid fever.

†Due to a vigorous public awareness program in the Jewish community, potential carriers are routinely screened and the rate of Tay-Sachs disease has declined dramatically.

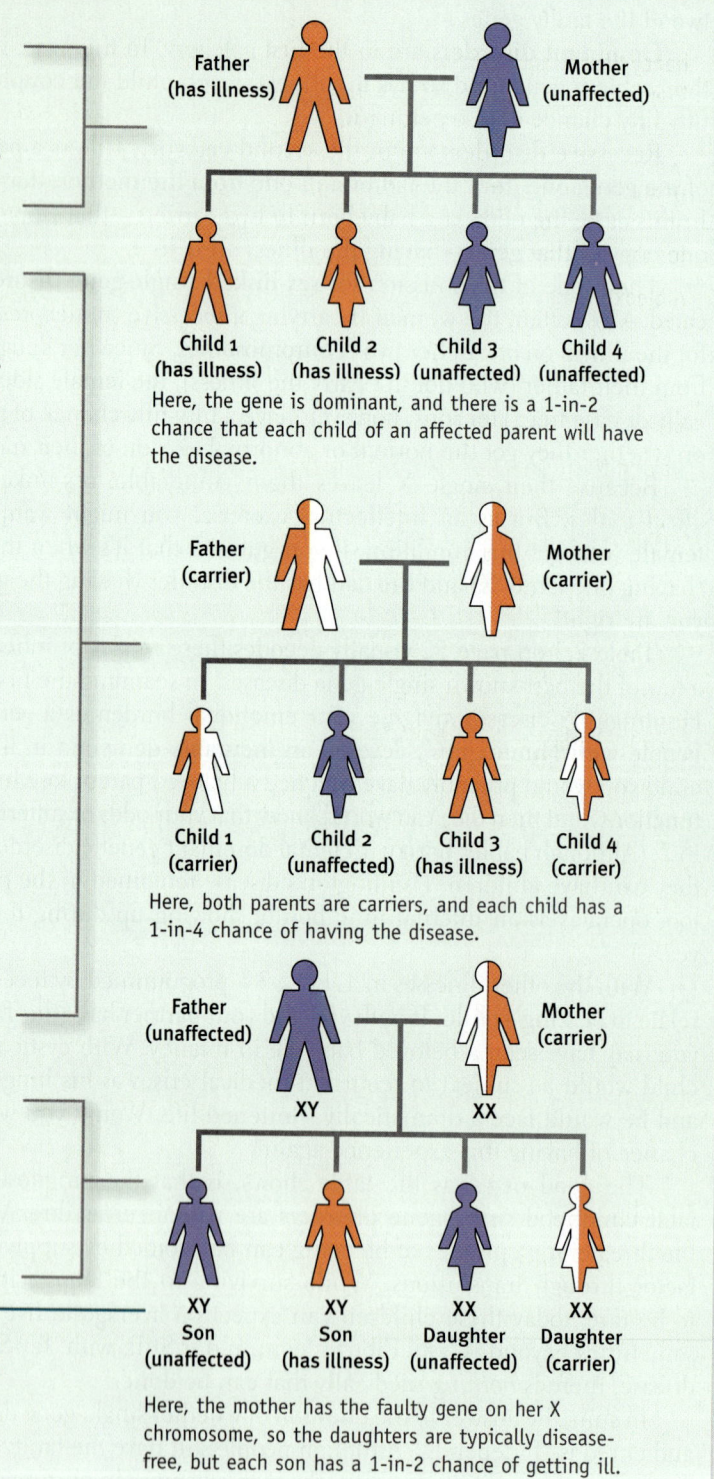

Pedigree 1 (Dominant): Father (has illness) × Mother (unaffected) → Child 1 (has illness), Child 2 (has illness), Child 3 (unaffected), Child 4 (unaffected). Here, the gene is dominant, and there is a 1-in-2 chance that each child of an affected parent will have the disease.

Pedigree 2 (Recessive): Father (carrier) × Mother (carrier) → Child 1 (carrier), Child 2 (unaffected), Child 3 (has illness), Child 4 (carrier). Here, both parents are carriers, and each child has a 1-in-4 chance of having the disease.

Pedigree 3 (Sex-Linked): Father (unaffected) XY × Mother (carrier) XX → Son XY (unaffected), Son XY (has illness), Daughter XX (unaffected), Daughter XX (carrier). Here, the mother has the faulty gene on her X chromosome, so the daughters are typically disease-free, but each son has a 1-in-2 chance of getting ill.

---

whose mother died of the disease, is instructive here (see the How Do We Know box). While Nancy will not say whether she has been tested, her sister Alice refused to be screened because she felt not knowing was better for her emotionally than the anguish of living with a positive result.

HOW DO WE KNOW . . .
about the gene for Huntington's disease?

Nancy Wexler and her sister got the devastating news from their physician father, Milton: "Your mother has Huntington's disease. She will die of dementia in a horrible way. As a dominant single-gene disorder, your chance of getting ill is fifty-fifty. There is nothing we can do [see Table 2.3]. But that doesn't mean we are going to give up." In 1969, Milton Wexler established the Hereditary Disease Foundation, surrounded himself with scientists, and put his young daughter, Nancy, a clinical psychologist, in charge. The hunt was on for the Huntington's gene.

A breakthrough came in 1979, when Nancy learned that the world's largest group of people with Huntington's lived in a small, inbred community in Venezuela—descendants of a woman who harbored the gene mutation that caused the disease. After building a pedigree of 18,000 family members, collecting blood samples from thousands more, and carefully analyzing the DNA for differences, the researchers hit pay dirt. They isolated the Huntington's gene.

Having this diagnostic marker is the first step to eventually finding a cure. So far the cure is elusive, but the hunt continues. Nancy still serves as the head of the foundation, vigorously advocating for research on the illness that killed her mother. She works as a professor in Columbia University's Neurology and Psychiatry Department. But every year, she comes back to the village in Venezuela to counsel and just visit with her families—her relatives in blood.

Interventions

The advantages of genetic testing are clearer when the issue relates to having a child. Let's imagine that you and your spouse know you are carriers of the cystic fibrosis gene. If you are contemplating having children, what should you do?

Sorting Out the Options: Genetic Counseling

Your first step would be to consult a **genetic counselor**, a professional skilled in both genetics and counseling, to help you think through your choices. In addition to laying out the odds of having an affected child, genetic counselors describe advances in treatment. For example, they inform couples who are carriers for cystic fibrosis about biological strategies on the horizon, such as gene therapy. They also highlight the interpersonal and economic costs of having a child with this disease. They explore the ambiguities of making this difficult decision in simple terms (Werner-Lin, McCoyd, & Bernhardt, 2016). But they are trained never to offer advice. Their goal is to permit couples to make a *mutual decision* on their own.

Now, suppose that armed with this information, you and your partner go ahead and conceive. Let's scan the major tests that are available to every woman carrying a child.

Tools of Discovery: Prenatal Tests

Blood tests performed during the first trimester can detect (with reasonable accuracy) various chromosomal conditions, such as Down syndrome. Brain scans (MRIs) offer a vivid prenatal window on the developing brain (Jokhi & Whitby, 2011). The standard fetal diagnostic test has been a staple for over 40 years: the **ultrasound.**

genetic counselor A professional who counsels parents-to-be about their children's risk of developing genetic disorders and about available treatments.

ultrasound In pregnancy, an image of the fetus in the womb that helps to date the pregnancy, assess the fetus's growth, and identify abnormalities.

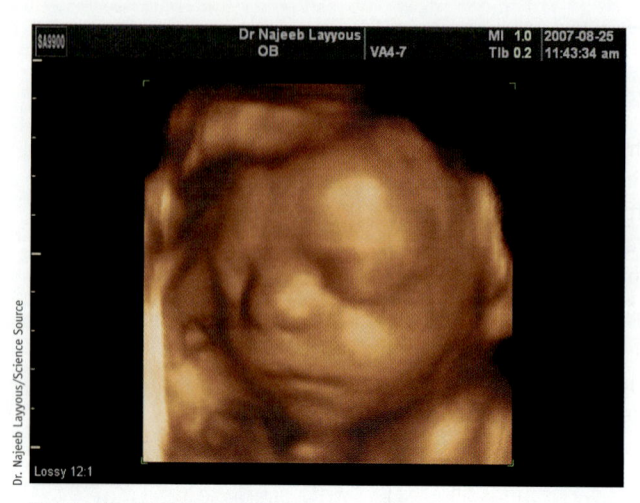

Due to the miracles of 3D ultrasound technology, when women visit their health-care provider, they can clearly see their baby's face. As they peer through this "window on the womb," doctors can get vital information about the health of this 26-week-old fetus, too.

chorionic villus sampling (CVS) A relatively risky first-trimester pregnancy test for fetal genetic disorders.

amniocentesis A second-trimester procedure that involves inserting a syringe into a woman's uterus to extract a sample of amniotic fluid, which is tested for genetic and chromosomal conditions.

Ultrasounds, which now provide a clear image of the fetus (see the accompanying photo), are used to date the pregnancy and assess in utero growth, in addition to revealing physical abnormalities. By making the baby visually real, ultrasound visits have become emotional landmarks on the pregnancy journey itself (Paul, 2010). Imagine the thrill of getting this vivid photo of your baby months before she is born!

Pregnant women embrace ultrasound technology and noninvasive genetic tests (Verweij and others, 2013). They tend to be more wary of the procedures described next, because those require entering the womb.

During the first trimester, **chorionic villus sampling (CVS)** can diagnose a variety of chromosomal and genetic conditions. A physician inserts a catheter into the woman's abdomen or vagina and withdraws a piece of the developing placenta for analysis. Knowing early on is the advantage of CVS; however, this test can be slightly dangerous, as it carries a risk of miscarriage and limb impairments (Karni, Leshno, & Rapaport, 2014).

During the second trimester, a safer test, called **amniocentesis**, can determine the fetus's fate. The doctor inserts a syringe into the woman's uterus and extracts a sample of amniotic fluid. The cells can reveal a host of genetic and chromosomal conditions, as well as the fetus's sex.

Amniocentesis is planned for a gestational age (typically week 14) when there is enough fluid to safely siphon out. However, it also carries a small chance of infection and miscarriage, depending on the skill of the doctor performing the test (Karni, Leshno & Rapaport, 2014). Moreover, when the results arrive, a woman is well into her second trimester; and, as of this writing (2017), in some U.S. states, it is illegal to terminate a pregnancy after 20 weeks.

Will the political pressure to reverse *Roe v. Wade* make these procedures illegal in the United States? Not necessarily. Even some high-risk mothers (women in their late thirties or forties) who would never consider abortion might want to know in advance whether their baby has a genetic disease.

Yes, a diagnosis of serious fetal problems transforms pregnancy joy into pain (Fonseca, Nazaré, & Canavarro, 2014). But knowledge confers power. If you were pregnant and at high risk of having a child with some genetic disorder, would you decide to undergo these tests?

The summary timeline spanning these pages outlines these procedures and charts the landmark events of prenatal development and pregnancy. I cannot emphasize

TIMELINE: Prenatal Development, Pregnancy, Prenatal Threats, Tools of Discovery

	Germinal stage (weeks 1 and 2)	Embryonic stage (weeks 3–8)	Fetal stage (weeks 9–38)
PRENATAL DEVELOPMENT	Zygote → blastocyst, which implants in uterus.	All major organs and structures form.	Massive growth and refinements; brain develops; live birth is possible at 22–24 weeks.
THREATS	At fertilization: chromosomal and single-gene diseases.	Teratogens can cause basic structural abnormalities.	Teratogens can impair growth, affect the brain, and so cause developmental disorders. They can also produce miscarriage or premature labor.

strongly enough that giving birth to a baby with serious birth defects is rare. That is not true, however, of the topic I turn to now—problems conceiving a child.

Infertility and New Reproductive Technologies

I feel incomplete and useless . . . all the other blessings are valueless unless you can have a child.

(from Nadia, a 35-year-old Pakistani woman, quoted in an interview in Batool & de Visser, 2016, p. 184)

According to Psalm 127:3, "Children are a heritage unto the Lord and the fruit of his womb is His Reward." So why didn't I get this gift? I asked myself over and over if I was being punished.

(quoted in Ferland & Caron, 2013, p. 183)

The idea that being unable to give birth renders females useless (the often used, evocative word here is *barren*) begins in *Genesis*. When biblical patriarch Abraham's beloved wife Sarah couldn't get pregnant, he felt compelled to "procreate" with a substitute wife.

Infertility—the inability to conceive a child after a year of unprotected intercourse—is far from rare, affecting an estimated 1 in 5 couples. These rates have been rising, due to sexually transmitted diseases (in the developing world) and the fact that so many developed-world women today delay childbearing to their mid-thirties and beyond (Petraglia, Serour, & Chapron, 2013).

While infertility can affect women (and men) of every age, just as with miscarriage and Down syndrome—as we know from the standard phrase, "the ticking of the biological clock"—getting pregnant is far more difficult at older ages. Within the first six months of trying, roughly 3 out of 4 women in their twenties conceives. At age 40, only 1 out of 5 achieves that goal (Turkington & Alper, 2001). Because of their more complicated anatomy, we often assume infertility is usually a "female" problem. Not so! Male issues—which can vary from low sperm motility to varicose veins in the testicles—are *equally* likely to be involved (Turkington & Alper, 2001).

As the quotes at the beginning of this section suggest, infertility is apt to hit women hardest (Teskereci & Oncel, 2013). But males also feel pressured to prove their manhood by fathering a child (here, the revealing word is *impotent*). In one Danish questionnaire study, almost 1 in 3 patients at a male fertility clinic confessed that their condition affected their sense of masculinity and self-esteem (Mikkelsen, Madsen, & Humaidan, 2013).

In the Middle East, women coping with fertility problems may worry about being shunned by their family: Will my husband abandon me (Behboodi-Moghamdam and others, 2013)? Will my in-laws kick me out of the house (see Batool & de Visser, 2016)?

In every nation, infertility isolates couples from relationships. Imagine going to dinner parties and needing to listen quietly as everyone at the table bonds around the joys and trials of having kids.

> **infertility** The inability to conceive after a year of unprotected sex. (Includes the inability to carry a child to term.)

	First trimester (month 1–month 3)	**Second trimester (month 4–month 6)**	**Third trimester (month 7–month 9)**
PREGNANCY	Morning sickness, tiredness, and other unpleasant symptoms may occur; miscarriage is a worry.	Woman looks pregnant. Quickening occurs (around week 18). Mother can feel intensely bonded to baby.	Woman gets very large and anxiously waits for birth.
TOOLS OF DISCOVERY	Ultrasound Blood tests Chorionic villus sampling (CVS) (around week 10)	Ultrasound Amniocentesis (around week 15)	Ultrasound

Then there are the painful reminders of what you are missing from life: "Going out shopping, everyone seems to be pregnant"; "Whenever I listen to the news of newborns around me, I can't just sleep . . ." (as reported in Batool & de Visser, 2016).

What helps people cope? Again, the key is having a collaborative, supportive mate (Darwiche and others, 2013; Ying & Loke, 2016), someone who loves you as *a person*, not a baby-making machine.

> When I told him (my second husband) when we were dating that I could not have children, he said, "If god wanted me to have kids, he would have made me fall in love with a woman who could have them."
>
> (quoted in Ferland & Caron, 2013, p. 186)

Today, having a caring collaborator is very important for any couple, gay or straight, as science offers so many options to help fulfill the quest to have a (partly) biological child.

INTERVENTIONS: Exploring ART

For females, there are treatments to attack every problem on the reproductive chain (see the illustration in Figure 2.8) — from fertility drugs to stimulate ovulation, to hormonal supplements to foster implantation; from surgery to help clean out the uterus and the fallopian tubes, to artificial insemination (inserting the sperm into the woman's uterus through a syringe). Males may take medications or undergo surgery to increase the quality and motility of the sperm. Then there is that ultimate approach: **assisted reproductive technology (ART)**.

Assisted reproductive technology refers to any strategy in which the egg is fertilized outside the womb. The most widely used ART procedure is **in vitro fertilization (IVF)**. After the woman is given fertility drugs (which stimulate multiple ovulations), her eggs are harvested and placed in a laboratory dish, along with the partner's sperm, to be fertilized. A few days later, the fertilized eggs are inserted into the uterus. Then, the couple anxiously waits to find out if the cells have implanted in the uterine wall.

In vitro fertilization, initially developed to bypass blocked fallopian tubes, has spawned amazing variations. A sperm may be injected directly into the ovum if it cannot penetrate the surface on its own. The woman may use a donor egg — one from another woman — in order to conceive. Or, she may go to a sperm bank to utilize a donor sperm. The fertilized eggs may be inserted into a "carrier womb" — a surrogate mother, who carries the couple's genetic offspring to term. If both partners are female, one person may donate her eggs (be the genetic parent) while the other carries the

assisted reproductive technology (ART) Any infertility treatment in which the egg is fertilized outside the womb.

in vitro fertilization An infertility treatment in which conception occurs outside the womb.

FIGURE 2.8: **Some possible missteps on the path to reproduction** In this diagram, you can see some problems that may cause infertility in women. You can also use it to review the ovulation-to-implantation sequence.

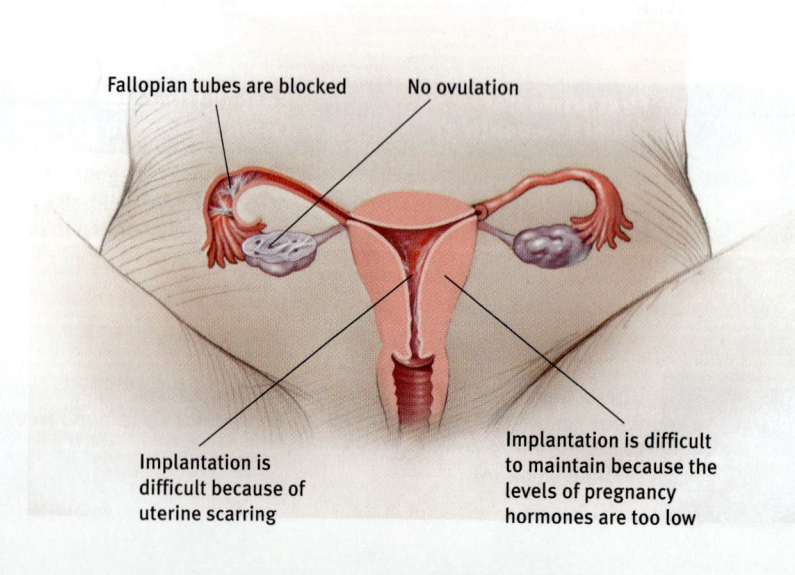

- Fallopian tubes are blocked
- No ovulation
- Implantation is difficult because of uterine scarring
- Implantation is difficult to maintain because the levels of pregnancy hormones are too low

baby (be the gestational mother) (Roache, 2016). If the same sex couples are male, they search for a surrogate to carry their biological child.

In addition to the painful procedures—taking hormones, harvesting the eggs, waiting anxiously to see whether one or two will take—ART can be very expensive, especially when added "pregnancy players" are involved. As the cost of soliciting a donor egg can be as high as $30,000, and fees to the donor vary from $5,000 to $15,000, an investment can top $40,000—and that's *before* each roughly $12,000 round of treatment even begins! (See Jaffe & Diamond, 2011.)

The outcome is dicey. According to 2014 U.S. data, the odds of a woman under age 35 getting pregnant after a round of in vitro treatments was roughly fifty-fifty. Over age 43, success rates per cycle slid down to less than 1 in 10 (CDC, 2010a).

Critics emphasize the headaches (and heartaches) involved in ART; the pain, the cost, the high chance of miscarrying if many eggs take (often to counter this risk, doctors engage in a procedure gently named "fetal reduction"); the virtual certainty of having fragile, small babies when several conceptions come to term (Gentile, 2014); the issues attached to third-party arrangements ("Should I meet my egg or sperm donor?" "Do I tell my child this person exists?") (Johnson, 2013).

These criticisms ignore the life-changing blessing ART provides: "I could never have accomplished all of this myself," gushed one grateful Taiwanese woman. Another said: "I no longer felt pitiful. . . . My child represents the continuation of my life" (quoted in Lin, Tsai, & Lai, 2013, p. 194).

Now let's look at what happens when these wished-for pregnancies—or any pregnancies—reach the final step: exploring the miracle of birth.

Tying It All Together

1. Teratogen A caused limb malformations. Teratogen B caused developmental disorders. Teratogen A wreaked its damage during the _____ stage of prenatal development and was taken during the _____ trimester of pregnancy, while teratogen B probably did its damage during the _____ stage and was taken during the _____ trimester.

2. Seto's and Brandon's mothers each contracted rubella (German measles) during different weeks in their first trimester of pregnancy. Seto has heart problems; Brandon has hearing problems. Which teratogenic principle is illustrated here?

3. Monique is planning to become pregnant and asks her physician if it will be okay for her to have a glass of wine with dinner each night. What would her doctor answer if Monique lived in the United States? What might the doctor say if Monique lived in France?

4. Imagine that in 2018, a tornado hits Nashville, Tennessee. Based on the fetal programming research, which *two* predictions might you make about babies who were in utero during that time?
   a. They might be at higher risk of being born small.
   b. They might be at higher risk of developing premature heart disease.
   c. They might be at higher risk of being very thin throughout life.

5. Latasha gives birth to a child with Down syndrome, while Jennifer gives birth to a child with cystic fibrosis. Which woman should be more worried about having another child with that condition, and why?

6. To a friend who is thinking of choosing between chorionic villus sampling (CVS) and amniocentesis, mention the advantages and disadvantages of each procedure.

7. After years of unsuccessful fertility treatments, Jennifer and Brad are considering ART. First describe some pros and cons of this procedure. According to the text, what force is most critical in determining how well Jennifer has been coping with her troubles getting pregnant?

Answers to the Tying It All Together questions can be found at the end of this chapter.

LEARNING OUTCOMES
- List the three stages of birth.
- Contrast natural childbirth and c-sections.

Birth

During the last weeks of pregnancy, the fetus's head drops lower into the uterus. At their weekly visits to the health-care provider, women, such as Kim in the opening chapter vignette, may be told, "It should be any minute now." The uterus begins to contract as it prepares for birth. The cervix thins out and softens under the weight of the child. Anticipation builds . . . and then—she waits!

> I am 39 weeks and desperate for some sign that labor is near, but so far NOTHING—no softening of the cervix, no contractions, and the baby has not dropped—the idea of two more weeks makes me want to SCREAM!!!

What sets off labor? One hypothesis is that the trigger is a hormonal signal that the fetus sends to the mother's brain. Once it's officially under way, labor proceeds through three stages.

Stage 1: Dilation and Effacement

This first stage of labor is the most arduous. The thick cervix, which has held in the expanding fetus for so long, has finished its job. Now it must *efface*, or thin out, and *dilate*, or widen from a tiny gap about the size of a dime to the width of a coffee mug or a medium-sized bowl of soup. This transformation is accomplished by *contractions*—muscular, wavelike batterings against the uterine floor. The uterus is far stronger than a boxer's biceps. Even at the beginning of labor, the contractions put about 30 pounds of pressure on the cervix to expand to its cuplike shape.

The contractions start out slowly, perhaps 20 to 30 minutes apart. They become more frequent and painful as the cervix more rapidly opens up. Sweating, nausea, and intense pain can accompany the final phase, as the closely spaced contractions reach a crescendo, and the baby is poised for the miracle of birth (see Figure 2.9).

Stage 2: Birth

The fetus descends through the uterus and enters the vagina, or birth canal. Then, as the baby's scalp appears (an event called *crowning*), parents get their first exciting glimpse of this new life. The shoulders rotate; the baby slowly slithers out, to be captured and cradled as it enters the world. The prenatal journey has ended; the journey of life is about to begin.

Stage 3: The Expulsion of the Placenta

In the ecstasy of the birth, the final event is almost unnoticed. The placenta and other supporting structures must be pushed out. Fully expelling these materials is essential to avoid infection and to help the uterus return to its pre-pregnant state.

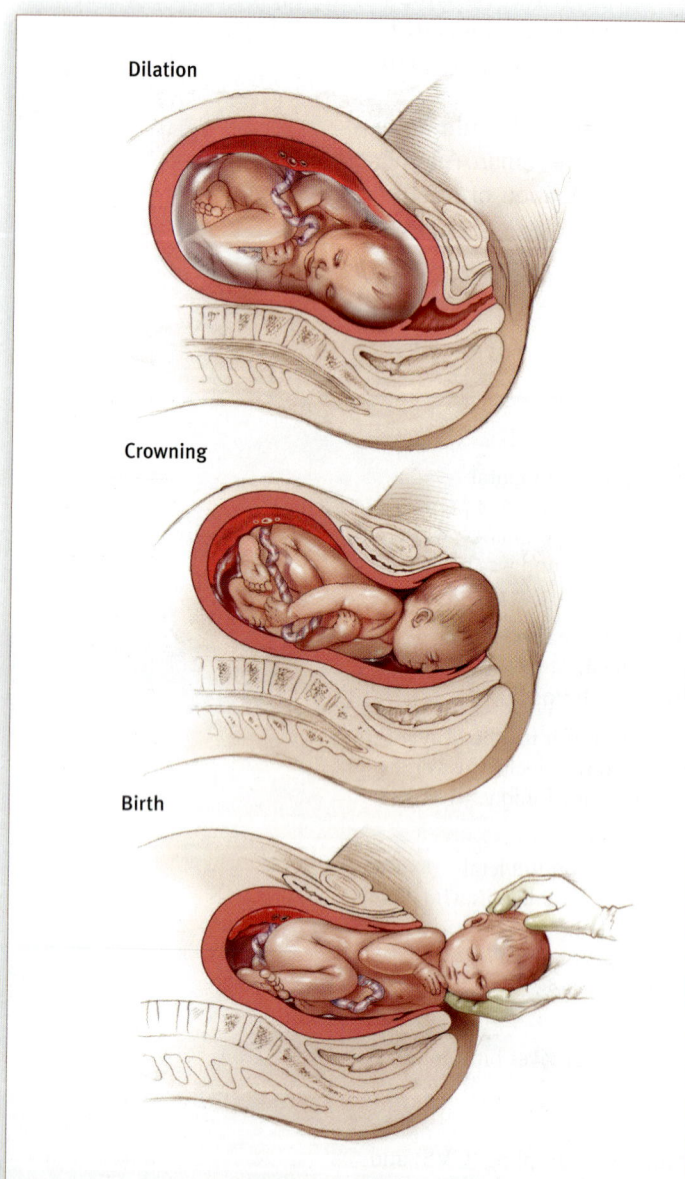

FIGURE 2.9: **Labor and childbirth** In the first stage of labor, the cervix dilates; in the second stage, the baby's head emerges and the baby is born.

Threats at Birth

Just as with pregnancy, a variety of missteps may happen during this landmark passage into life: problems with the contraction mechanism; the inability of the cervix to fully dilate; deviations from the normal head-down position as the fetus descends and positions itself for birth (this atypical positioning, with feet, buttocks, or knees first, is called a *breech birth*); difficulties stemming from the position of the placenta or the umbilical cord as the baby makes its way into the world. Today, these in-transit troubles are easily surmounted through obstetrical techniques. This was not the case in the past, however.

Birth Options, Past and Present

For most of human history, pregnancy was a grim nine-month march to an uncertain end (Kitzinger, 2000; Wertz & Wertz, 1989). The eighteenth-century New England preacher Cotton Mather captured the emotions of his era when, on learning that a parish woman was pregnant, he thundered, "Your death has entered into you!" Not only were there the hazards involved in getting the baby to emerge, but a raging infection called childbed fever could also set in and kill a new mother (and her child) within days.

Women had only one another or lay midwives to rely on during this frightening time. So birth was a social event. Friends and relatives flocked around, perhaps traveling miles to offer comfort when the woman's due date drew near. Doctors were of little help, because they could not view the female anatomy directly. In fact, due to their clumsiness (using primitive forceps to yank the baby out) and their tendency to spread childbed fever by failing to wash their hands, eighteenth- and nineteenth-century doctors often made the situation worse (Wertz & Wertz, 1989).

Techniques gradually improved toward the end of the nineteenth century, but few wealthy women dared enter hospitals to deliver, as these institutions were hotbeds of contagious disease. Then, with the early-twentieth-century conquest of many infectious diseases, it became fashionable for affluent middle-class women to have a "modern" hospital birth. By the late 1930s, the science of obstetrics gained the upper hand, fetal mortality plummeted, and birth became genuinely safe (Leavitt, 1986). By the turn of this century, in the developed world, this conquest was virtually complete. In 1997, there were only 329 pregnancy-related maternal deaths in the United States (Miniño and others, 2002).

This watershed medical victory was accompanied by discontent. The natural process of birth had become an impersonal event. Women protested the assembly-line hospital procedures and objected to being strapped down and sedated in order to give birth. They eagerly devoured books describing the new Lamaze technique, which taught controlled breathing, allowed partner involvement, and promised undrugged births. During the women's movement of the 1960s and early 1970s, the natural-childbirth movement arrived.

Natural Childbirth

Natural childbirth, a vague label for returning the birth experience to its "true" natural state, is now embedded in the labor and birth choices available to women today. To avoid the hospital experience, some women choose to deliver in homelike birthing centers. They may use certified midwives rather than doctors and draw on the help of a *doula*, a nonmedical pregnancy and labor coach. Women who are committed to the most natural experience may give birth in their own homes. (Table 2.4 on the next page describes some natural birth options, as well as some commonly used medical procedures.)

This classic nineteenth-century illustration shows just why early doctors were clueless about how to help pregnant women. They could not view the relevant body parts!

natural childbirth Labor and birth without medical interventions.

Table 2.4: The Major Players and Interventions in Labor and Birth

NATURAL-BIRTH PROVIDERS AND OPTIONS

Certified midwife: Certified by the American College of Nurse Midwives, this health-care professional is trained to handle *low-risk* deliveries, with obstetrical backup should complications arise.
- *Plus:* Offers a birth experience with fewer medical interventions and more humanistic care.
- *Minus:* If the delivery suddenly becomes high risk, an obstetrician may be needed on the scene.

Doula: Mirroring the "old-style" female experience, this person provides loving emotional and physical support during labor, offering massage and help in breathing and relaxation, but not performing actual health-care tasks, such as vaginal exams. (Doulas have no medical training.)
- *Plus:* Provides caring support from an advocate.
- *Minus:* Drives up the birth expense.

Lamaze method: Developed by the French physician Ferdinand Lamaze, this popular method prepares women for childbirth by teaching pain management through relaxation and breathing exercises.
- *Plus:* Offers a shared experience with a partner (who acts as the coach) and the sense of approaching the birth experience with greater control.
- *Minus:* Doesn't necessarily work for pain control "as advertised"!

Bradley method: Developed by Robert Bradley in the 1940s, this technique is designed for women interested in having a completely natural, nonmedicated birth. It stresses good diet and exercise, partner coaching, and deep relaxation.
- *Plus:* Tailored for women firmly committed to forgoing any medical interventions.
- *Minus:* May set women up for disappointment if things don't go as planned and they need those interventions.

MEDICAL INTERVENTIONS

Episiotomy: The cutting of the perineum or vagina to widen that opening and allow the fetus to emerge (not recommended unless there is a problem delivery).*
- *Plus:* May prevent a fistula, a vaginal tear into the rectal opening, which produces chronic incontinence and pain.
- *Minus:* May increase the risk of infection after delivery and hinder healing.

Epidural: This most popular type of anesthesia used during labor involves injecting a painkilling medication into a small space outside the spinal cord to numb the woman's body below the waist. Epidurals are now used during the active stage of labor—effectively dulling much of the pain—and during c-sections, so that the woman is awake to see her child during the first moments after birth.
- *Plus:* Combines optimum pain control with awareness; because the dose can be varied, the woman can see everything, and she has enough feeling to push during vaginal deliveries.
- *Minus:* Can slow the progress of labor in vaginal deliveries, can result in headaches, and is subject to errors if the needle is improperly inserted. Concerns also center on the fact that the newborn may emerge "groggy."

Electronic fetal monitor: This device is used to monitor the fetus's heart rate and alert the doctor to distress. With an external monitor, the woman wears two belts around her abdomen. With an internal monitor, an electrode is inserted through the cervix to record the baby's heart rate through the fetal scalp.
- *Plus:* Shown to be useful in high-risk pregnancies.
- *Minus:* Can give false readings, leading to a premature c-section. Also, its superiority over the lower-tech method of listening to the baby's heartbeat with a stethoscope has not been demonstrated.

C-section: The doctor makes an incision in the abdominal wall and the uterus and removes the fetus manually.
- *Plus:* Is life-saving to the mother and baby when a vaginal delivery cannot occur (as when the baby is too big to emerge or the placenta is obstructing the cervix). Also is needed when the mother has certain health problems or when the fetus is in serious distress.
- *Minus:* As a surgical procedure, it is more expensive than vaginal delivery and can lead to more discomfort after birth.

*Late-twentieth-century research has suggested that the once-common U.S. practice of routinely performing episiotomies had no advantages and actually hindered recovery from birth. Therefore, in recent decades, the episiotomy rate in the United States has declined.

At the medical end of the spectrum, as Table 2.4 shows, lies the arsenal of physician interventions designed to promote a less painful and safer birth. Let's now pause for a minute to look at the last procedure in the table: the cesarean section.

The Cesarean Section

A **cesarean section** (or **c-section**), in which a surgeon makes incisions in the woman's abdominal wall and enters the uterus to remove the baby manually, is the final solution for labor and delivery problems. This operation exploded in popularity during the 1970s. By 2015, c-sections accounted for an amazing 1 in 3 U.S. deliveries (CDC, 2016). In Shanghai, China, where the former one-child policy made women frantic to have a

cesarean section (c-section) Delivering a baby surgically by extracting the fetus through incisions in the woman's abdominal wall.

perfect child, the percentage tops 1 in 2 (Hellerstein, Feldman, & Duan, 2016).

C-sections may be planned because the physician knows in advance that there are dangers in a vaginal birth. But, as in China, it's now fashionable in many countries for some affluent women to choose this operation. Women opt for c-sections because they mistakenly assume this procedure is more hassle-free and safer (in fact, as with any surgery, this delivery method is more dangerous than a natural birth).

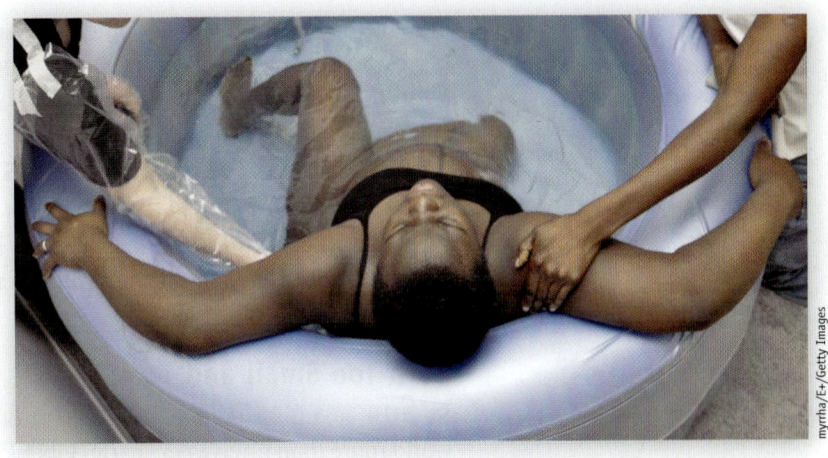

Many of these procedures, however, are provoked by problems once labor has begun. What fraction of emergency c-sections is due to doctors' fears of legal liability ("I might get sued unless I get this baby out")? We don't know. What we do know is that the best-laid birth plans may not work out, and some women can feel upset if they had counted on having a child "the natural way":

Today, women have a variety of birth choices in the developed world. The woman in this photo is having a water birth.

> "I sort of feel like I failed in the birthing arena," said one Australian woman. . . . "Logically, I knew that the c-section was necessary, but somehow I think if I was slim . . . and had not eaten as much ice cream that would not have happened."
>
> (quoted in Malacrida & Boulton, 2014, p. 18)

While some affluent women may bemoan their c-sections, the real tragedy is the horrifying lack of access to routine medical interventions in the least-developed regions of the world. Every day almost 900 women in impoverished regions of the world die of preventable pregnancy-related causes, such as postpartum hemorrhage, infections, or other complications that would prompt an immediate c-section in developed nations (World Health Organization [WHO], 2016). So let's keep in mind that billions of developing-world mothers-to-be still approach birth with a more basic concern than their Western counterparts. Their worries are not, "Should I *choose* a c-section?" It's not, "What birth method should I use?" Unfortunately, all too often, it's still: "Will I survive my baby's birth?" (Lester, Benfield, & Fathalla, 2010; Potts, Prata, & Sahin-Hodoglugil, 2010).

Tying It All Together

1. Melissa says that her contractions are coming every 10 minutes now. Sonia has just seen her baby's scalp emerge. In which stages of labor are Melissa and Sonia?
2. To a friend interested in having the most natural birth possible, spell out some of these options.
3. C-sections may sometimes be *overused/underused* in the developed world; but life-saving medical interventions are *underutilized/overutilized* in poor areas of the globe.

Answers to the Tying It All Together questions can be found at the end of this chapter.

The Newborn

Now that we have examined how the baby arrives in the world, let's focus on that tiny arrival. What happens after the baby is born? What dangers do babies face after birth?

Tools of Discovery: Testing Newborns

The first step after the newborn enters the world is to evaluate its health in the delivery room with a checklist. The child's heart rate, muscle tone, respiration, reflex response, and color are rated on a scale of 0 to 2 at one minute and then again at five minutes

LEARNING OUTCOMES
- Describe the Apgar scale and the potential consequence(s) of low birth weight.
- Outline trends in infant mortality in the developed and developing worlds.

Apgar scale A quick test used to assess a just-delivered baby's condition by measuring heart rate, muscle tone, respiration, reflex response, and color.

after birth. On this checklist called the **Apgar scale**, newborns with five-minute Apgar scores over 7 are usually in excellent shape. However, if the score stays below 7, the child must be monitored or resuscitated and kept in the hospital for awhile.

Threats to Development Just After Birth

After their babies have been checked out medically, most mothers and fathers eagerly take their robust, full-term baby home. But other parents hover at the hospital and anxiously wait. The reason, most often, is that their child has arrived in the world too small and/or too soon.

Born Too Small and Too Soon

In 2010, about 15 million babies were born *preterm*, or premature—they entered the world more than three weeks early (Chang and others, 2013). In the United States, about 1 in every 11 babies is categorized as **low birth weight (LBW)**. They arrive in the world weighing less than 5½ pounds. Babies can be designated as low birth weight because they either arrived before their due date or did not grow sufficiently in the womb.

low birth weight (LBW) A weight at birth of less than 5½ pounds.

Earlier in this chapter, I highlighted smoking and maternal stress as risk factors for going into labor early and/or having a low-birth-weight baby. But uncontrollable influences—such as an infection that prematurely ruptures the amniotic sac, or a cervix that cannot withstand the pressure of the growing fetus's weight—also can cause this too-early or excessively small arrival into life.

You might assume that prematurity has declined in tandem with our pregnancy medical advances. Not so! Ironically, the same cutting-edge procedures discussed earlier, such as c-sections on demand and ART, boost the probability of a baby leaving the womb early and being more frail (Chang and others, 2013).

Many early arrivals are fine. The vulnerable newborns are the 1.4 percent classified as **very low birth weight (VLBW)**, who weigh less than 3¼ pounds. When these infants are delivered, often *very* prematurely, they are immediately rushed to a major medical center to enter a special hospital unit for frail newborns—the **neonatal intensive care unit**.

very low birth weight (VLBW) A weight at birth of less than 3¼ pounds.

neonatal intensive care unit (NICU) A special hospital unit that treats at-risk newborns, such as low-birth-weight and very-low-birth-weight babies.

> At 24 weeks my water broke, and I was put in the hospital and given drugs. I hung on, and then, at week 26, gave birth. Peter was sent by ambulance to Children's Hospital. When I first saw my son, he had needles in every point of his body and was wrapped in plastic to keep his skin from drying out. Peter's intestines had a hole in them, and the doctor had to perform an emergency operation. But Peter made it! . . . Now it's four months later, and my husband and I are about to bring our miracle baby home.

Peter was lucky. He escaped the fate of the more than 1 million babies who die each year as a consequence of being very premature (Chang and others, 2013). Is this survival story purchased at the price of a life of pain? Enduring health problems are a serious risk with newborns such as Peter, born too soon and excessively small. Study after study suggests low birth weight can compromise brain development (Rose and others, 2014; Yang and others, 2014). It can limit intellectual and social skills throughout childhood (Murray and others, 2014) and the adolescent years (Healy and others, 2013; Saigal and others, 2016; Yang and others, 2014)—in addition, as you know, to possibly promoting overweight and early age-related disease. And what about the costs? Astronomical sums are required to keep frail babies such as Peter alive—expenses that can bankrupt families and are often borne by society as a whole (Caplan, Blank, & Merrick, 1992).

When a child is born at the cusp of viability—at around 22 weeks—doctors, not infrequently, refuse to vigorously intervene (Duffy & Reynolds, 2011; Ramsay & Santella, 2011). But survival rates vary, depending on the individual baby and—very important—that child's access to high-quality care (Sjörs, 2010). Plus, due to dramatic neonatal advances occurring

This baby has an excellent Apgar score. Notice his healthy, robust appearance.

Experiencing Childhood and Adolescence: Marcia's Story

The service elevator at Peck Hall takes forever to get there, then moves in extra-slow motion up to the third floor. If, as sometimes happens, it's out of service, you are out of luck. It's about a 30-minute drive from my dorm in the motorized wheelchair, including the ramps. When it rains, there's the muck—slowing you up—keeping you wet. So I try to leave at least an hour to get to class.

My goal is to be at least five minutes early so I don't disrupt everything as I move the chair, back and forth, back and forth, to be positioned right in front. Because my bad eye wanders to the side, you may not think I can read the board. That's no problem, although it takes me weeks to get through a chapter in your book! The CP [cerebral palsy], as you know, affects my vocal cords, making it hard to get a sentence out. But I won't be ashamed. I am determined to participate in class. I have my note-taker. I have my hearing amplifier turned up to catch every sound. My mind is on full alert. I'm set to go.

I usually can take about two courses each semester—sometimes one. I'm careful to screen my teachers to make sure they will work with me. I'm almost 30 and still only a junior, but I'm determined to get my degree. I'd like to be a counselor and work with CP kids. I know all about it—the troubles, the physical pain, what people are like.

I'm not sure exactly what week I was born, but it wasn't really all that early; maybe two months at the most. My problem was being incredibly small. They think my mom might have gotten an infection that caused me to be born weighing less than one pound. The doctors were sure I'd never make it. But I proved everyone wrong. Once I got out of the ICU and, at about eight months, went into convulsions, and then had a stroke, everyone thought that would be the end again. They were wrong. I want to keep proving them wrong as long as I live.

I've had tons of physical therapy, and a few surgeries; so I can get up from a chair and walk around a room. But it took me until about age five to begin to speak or take my first step. The worst time of my life was elementary school—the kids who make fun of you; call you a freak. In high school, and especially here at MTSU, things are much better. I've made close friends, both in the disability community and outside. Actually, I'm a well-known figure, especially since I've been here so long! Everyone on campus greets me with a smile as I scoot around.

In my future? I'd love to get married and adopt a kid. OK, I know that's going to be hard. Because of my speech problem, I know you're thinking it's going to be hard to be a counselor, too. But I'm determined to keep trying, and take every day as a blessing. Life is very special. I've always been living on borrowed time.

---

during the 1980s, many more small babies are now living to adulthood unimpaired (Baron & Rey-Casserly, 2010). I have vividly seen these statistics in operation when, in recent years, a student proudly informed our class: "I weighed less than 2 pounds at birth" or "I was born at the twenty-sixth week of life."

Even when they do have disabilities, these tiny babies can have a full life. Listen to my former student Marcia, whose 15-ounce body at birth would have easily fit in the palm of your hand—and whom no doctor believed was capable of surviving. Marcia, as the Experiencing Childhood box describes, is partially deaf, blind in one eye, and suffers from the disorder cerebral palsy. She was born with the sensory impairments that, as research shows, predict tiny babies will almost certainly have enduring difficulties functioning in the world (Saigal and others, 2016). But rarely have I met someone so upbeat, joyous, and fully engaged in life.

The Unthinkable: Infant Mortality

In the developed world, prematurity is the primary cause of **infant mortality**—the term for deaths occurring within the first year of life. The good news is that in affluent nations, infant mortality is at an historic low (see Figure 2.10 on the next page). The bad news is the dismal standing of the United States compared to many other industrialized countries. Why does the United States rank a humiliating fifty-sixth in this basic marker of a society's health (Central Intelligence Agency [CIA], 2017)? The main cause lies in income inequalities, stress, poor health practices, and limited access to high-quality prenatal care.

infant mortality Death during the first year of life.

This baby weighing less than one pound was incredibly lucky to make it out of the womb alive—but she is at high risk for having enduring problems as she travels through life.

FIGURE 2.10: Deaths of infants under 1 year of age per 1,000 live births in selected countries (estimated data for 2016)
Infant mortality rates vary tremendously around the globe. Notice the huge disparities between affluent and least-developed countries. Also notice that the United States has more than twice the infant mortality rate of Norway and Japan.

Data from Central Intelligence Agency, 2017.

The socioeconomic link to pregnancy and birth problems is particularly troubling. In every affluent nation—but especially the United States—poverty puts women at higher risk of delivering prematurely or having their baby die before age 1. So, sadly, I must end this chapter on a downbeat note. At this moment in history, our wealthiest nations are falling short of "cherishing" each woman during this landmark journey of life.

A Few Final Thoughts on Resilience

But I also can't leave you with the downbeat impression that what happens during pregnancy is destiny. Yes, researchers now believe events in utero play a role in how we develop. But a basic message of this book is that human beings are resilient. A quality environment matters greatly in shaping our life path. As discussed in Chapter 1, the environment can even epigenetically change our DNA (Moore, 2015).

Now that we are on the topic of DNA and genetics, I feel compelled to highlight a personal point, as an adoptive mom. In this chapter, you learned about the feelings of attachment (or mother–child bond) that often begin before birth. But I can assure you that to bond with a baby, you don't need to personally carry that child inside or share the same set of genes. So, just a reminder for later chapters when we scan the beautiful mosaic of families on our landscape today: The bottom-line blessing is being a parent, not being pregnant. Parenting is far different from personally giving birth!

The next two chapters turn directly to the joys of babyhood, as we catch up with Kim and her daughter Elissa, and track development during the first two years of life.

Families come in many forms, and the love you have for *all* your adopted children is no different than if you personally gave birth. Take it from me as an adoptive mom!

Tying It All Together

1. Baby David gets a two-minute Apgar score of 8; at five minutes, his score is 9. What does this mean?

2. Rates of premature births have *risen/declined* due to ART, and low birth weight *always causes serious problems/can produce problems/has no effects* on later development.

3. Bill says, "Pregnancy and birth are very safe today." George says, "Hey, you are very wrong!" Who is right?
    a. Bill, because worldwide maternal mortality is now very low.
    b. George, because birth is still unsafe around the world.
    c. Both are partly correct: Birth is typically very safe in the developed world, but maternal and infant mortality remains unacceptably high in the poorest regions of the globe.

4. Sally brags about the U.S. infant mortality rate, while Samantha is horrified by it. First make Sally's case and then Samantha's, referring to the chapter points.

5. You want to set up a program to reduce prematurity and neonatal mortality among low-income women. List some steps that you might take.

Answers to the Tying It All Together questions can be found at the end of this chapter.

SUMMARY

The First Step: Fertilization

Every culture cherishes pregnant women. Some build in rituals to announce the baby after a certain point during pregnancy, and many use charms to ward off fetal harm. Pregnancy is a time of intense mixed emotions—joyous expectations coupled with uneasy fears.

The female reproductive system includes the **uterus** and its neck, the **cervix**; the **fallopian tubes**; and the **ovaries**, housing the **ova**. To promote **fertilization**, the optimum time for intercourse is when the egg is released. **Hormones** program **ovulation** and all of the events of pregnancy. At intercourse, hundreds of millions of sperm, produced in the **testes**, are ejaculated, but only a small fraction make their way to the fallopian tubes to reach the ovum. When the single victorious sperm penetrates the ovum, the two 23 **chromosome** pairs (composed of **DNA**, segmented into **genes**) unite to regain the normal complement of 46 that form our body's cells.

Prenatal Development

During the first stage of pregnancy, the two-week-long **germinal stage**, the rapidly dividing **zygote** travels to the uterus, becomes a **blastocyst**, and faces the next challenge—**implantation**. The second stage of pregnancy, the **embryonic stage**, begins after implantation and ends around week 8. During this intense six-week period, the **neural tube** forms and all the major body structures are created, according to the **proximodistal, cephalocaudal,** and **mass-to-specific** principles of development.

During the third stage of pregnancy, the **fetal stage**, development is slower paced. The hallmarks of this stage are enormous body growth and construction of the brain as the **neurons** migrate to the top of the tube and differentiate. Another defining landmark of this seven-month phase occurs around week 22, when the fetus can possibly be **viable**, that is, survive outside the womb if born.

Pregnancy

The nine months of **gestation**, or pregnancy, are divided into **trimesters**. The first trimester is often characterized by unpleasant symptoms, such as morning sickness, and a relatively high risk of **miscarriage**. The landmarks of the second trimester are looking clearly pregnant, experiencing **quickening**, and often feeling intensely emotionally connected to the child. During the third trimester, the woman's uterus gets very large, and she anxiously awaits the birth.

A woman's feelings about being pregnant can be affected by career concerns, and **family–work conflict** is common when working mothers (and fathers) have a child. The most critical force affecting the emotional quality of pregnancy, however, is having a supportive partner. Dads, the neglected pregnancy partners, also feel bonded to their babies.

Threats to the Developing Baby

Rarely, babies are born with a **birth defect**. One possible cause is **teratogens**, toxins from the outside that exert their damage during the **sensitive period** for the development of a particular body part. In general, the embryonic stage is the time of greatest vulnerability, although toxins can affect the developing brain during the second and third trimesters also, producing **developmental disorders**. While there is typically a threshold level beyond which damage can occur, teratogens have unpredictable effects. Damage may not show up until decades later.

Any recreational drug is potentially teratogenic. Smoking during pregnancy is a risk factor for having a smaller-than-optimal-size baby. Drinking excessively during pregnancy can produce **fetal alcohol syndrome,** or *fetal alcohol spectrum disorder.* Because it raises **cortisol** levels, depression and intense stress during pregnancy can produce premature labor and lead to smaller-than-normal babies. **Fetal programming research** suggests that natural (or human-made) disasters can have enduring epigenetic effects, because being born small may prime babies for obesity and premature, age-related chronic diseases.

The second major cause of prenatal problems is genuinely "genetic"—chromosomal problems and single-gene diseases. **Down syndrome** is one of the few disorders in which babies born with an abnormal number of chromosomes survive. Although Down syndrome, caused by having an extra chromosome on pair 21, produces intellectual disability and other health problems, babies with this condition do live fulfilling lives.

With **single-gene disorders,** a specific gene passed down from one's parents causes the disease. In **dominant disorders,** a person who harbors a single copy of the gene gets ill, and each child born to this couple (one of whom has the disease) has a fifty-fifty chance of developing the condition. If the disorder is **recessive**, both parents carry a single copy of the "problem gene" that is not expressed in real life, but they have a 1-in-4 chance of giving birth to a child with that disease (that is, a son or daughter with two copies of the gene). With **sex-linked disorders,** the problem gene is recessive and lies on the X chromosome. If a mother carries a single copy of the gene, her daughters are spared (because they have two Xs), but each male baby has a fifty-fifty risk of getting the disease. Through advances in genetic testing, couples (and individuals) can find out if they harbor the genes for many diseases. **Genetic testing** poses difficult issues with regard to whether people want to find out if they have incurable adult-onset diseases.

Couples at high risk for having a baby with a single-gene disorder (or any couple) may undergo **genetic counseling** to decide whether they should try to have a child. During pregnancy, tests, including the **ultrasound,** and more invasive procedures such as **chorionic villus sampling** (during the first trimester) and **amniocentesis** (during the second trimester) allow us to determine the baby's genetic fate.

Infertility can be emotionally traumatic and socially isolating, especially for women because of their historic imperative to bear children. Problems getting pregnant are far from rare today, especially at older ages. The most radical intervention, **assisted reproductive technologies (ART),** such as **in vitro fertilization (IVF),** in which the egg is fertilized outside of the womb, is emotionally and physically demanding, costly, and offers no guarantee of having a baby. However, this landmark procedure has given couples who could never have conceived the chance to have a biological child.

Birth

Labor and birth consist of three stages. During the first stage of labor, contractions cause the cervix to efface and fully dilate. During the second stage, birth, the baby emerges. During the third stage, the **placenta** and supporting structures are expelled.

For most of history, childbirth was life-threatening to both the mother and the child. During the first third of the twentieth century, birth became much safer. This victory set the stage for the later-twentieth-century **natural childbirth** movement. Today, women in the developed world can choose from a variety of birth options, including **cesarean sections.** Impoverished, developing-world women do not have this kind of access or luxury of choices. Their main concern is surviving the baby's birth.

The Newborn

After birth, the **Apgar scale** and other tests are used to assess the baby's health. While most babies are healthy, **low birth weight** can compromise development. **Very-low-birth-weight** infants are most apt to have enduring problems and need careful monitoring in the **neonatal intensive care unit** during their early weeks or months of life.

Infant mortality is a serious concern in the developing world. While rates of infant mortality are generally very low in developed-world countries, the United States has a comparatively dismal standing compared to other affluent countries on this basic health parameter. Even though the environment in the womb (stress during pregnancy) can affect the baby, providing a high-quality environment shapes development throughout childhood (and adult life).

KEY TERMS

age of viability, p. 39
amniocentesis, p. 54
amniotic sac, p. 40
Apgar scale, p. 62
assisted reproductive technology (ART), p. 56
birth defect, p. 44
blastocyst, p. 37
cephalocaudal sequence, p. 39
cervix, p. 34
cesarean section (c-section), p. 60
chorionic villus sampling (CVS), p. 54
chromosome, p. 36
cortisol, p. 48
developmental disorders, p. 45
DNA (deoxyribonucleic acid), p. 36
dominant disorder, p. 51
Down syndrome, p. 50
embryonic stage, p. 37
fallopian tube, p. 34
family–work conflict, p. 43
fertilization, p. 35
fetal alcohol syndrome (FAS), p. 47
fetal programming research, p. 49
fetal stage, p. 39
gene, p. 36
genetic counselor, p. 53
genetic testing, p. 51
germinal stage, p. 37
gestation, p. 41
hormones, p. 41
implantation, p. 37
in vitro fertilization (IVF), p. 56
infant mortality, p. 63
infertility, p. 55
low birth weight (LBW), p. 62
mass-to-specific sequence, p. 39
miscarriage, p. 42
natural childbirth, p. 59
neonatal intensive care unit (NICU), p. 62
neural tube, p. 38
neuron, p. 38
ovary, p. 34
ovulation, p. 35
ovum, p. 34
placenta, p. 37
proximodistal sequence, p. 38
quickening, p. 42
recessive disorder, p. 51
sensitive period, p. 45
sex-linked single-gene disorder, p. 51
single-gene disorder, p. 50
teratogen, p. 45
testes, p. 35
trimester, p. 41
ultrasound, p. 53
umbilical cord, p. 40
uterus, p. 34
very low birth weight (VLBW), p. 62
zygote, p. 37

ANSWERS TO Tying It All Together QUIZZES

The First Step: Fertilization

1. ovaries, fallopian tubes, uterus; fertilization occurs in the fallopian tubes
2. ovaries for female; testes for male
3. Tell Tiffany that the best time to have intercourse is around the time of ovulation.
4. *She* is *more* apt to survive and *less* apt to be conceived.

Prenatal Development

1. germinal; embryonic; fetal. Organs are formed during the embryonic stage.
2. From the neural tube, a mass of cells differentiates during the late embryonic phase. During the next few months, the cells ascend to the top of the neural tube, completing their migration by week 25. In the final months of pregnancy,

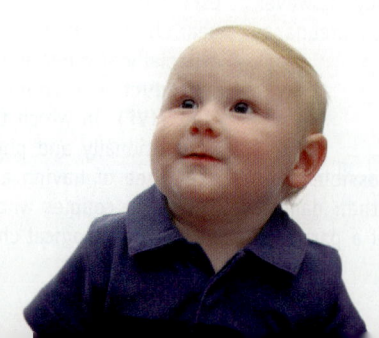

the neurons elongate and begin to assume their mature structure.

3. (a) mass-to-specific (b) cephalocaudal (c) proximodistal
4. around 22–23 weeks

Pregnancy

1. In this second trimester, she will feel better physically and perhaps experience an intense sense of emotional connectedness when she feels the baby move. During the first trimester she may have been very tired, perhaps felt faint, and had morning sickness.
2. Your cousin may be reluctant to tell her employer she is pregnant because she worries that the news may negatively affect her career.
3. You may come up with a host of interesting possibilities. Here are a few of mine: Include fathers in all pregnancy and birth educational materials the clinic provides; strongly encourage men to be present during prenatal exams; alert female patients about the need to be sensitive to their partners; set up a clinic-sponsored support group for fathers-to-be.

Threats to the Developing Baby

1. Teratogen A most likely caused damage during the *embryonic stage* of development and was taken during the *first trimester* of pregnancy. Teratogen B probably did its damage during the *fetal stage* and was taken during the *second or third trimesters*.
2. Teratogens exert damage during the sensitive period for the development of a particular organ.
3. A doctor in the United States would advocate no alcohol, while a physician in France might say a glass of wine is fine.
4. a and b. They might be at higher risk of being born small and of developing premature heart disease.
5. Jennifer. Down syndrome is typically caused by an unlikely, random event. With cystic fibrosis, that single-gene recessive disorder, the mom (in this case, Jennifer) has a 1-in-4 chance of giving birth to another child with that disease.
6. Tell your friend that the plus of chorionic villus sampling is finding out a child's genetic fate in the first trimester. However, this procedure is more dangerous, carrying a slight risk of limb malformations and, possibly, miscarriage. Amniocentesis is much safer and can show a fuller complement of genetic disorders but must be performed in the second trimester. And in some U.S. states, should a woman decide to terminate the pregnancy at this point, it may be illegal.
7. *Cons:* ART is expensive, requires effort, and causes physical symptoms, and the chance per cycle of getting pregnant is small—especially for older women. *Pros:* ART gives women (and men) who could never have a biological child a chance to have a baby who is genetically theirs! The best predictor of Jennifer's coping well is having a supportive spouse.

Birth

1. Melissa is in stage 1, effacement and dilation of the cervix. Sonia is in stage 2, birth.
2. "You might want to forgo any labor medications, and/or give birth in a birthing center under a midwife's (and doula's) care. Look into new options such as water births, and, if you are especially daring, consider giving birth at home."
3. C-sections may sometimes be *overused* in the developed world. But they are seriously *underutilized* in poor areas of the globe.

The Newborn

1. Baby David is in excellent health.
2. Rates of premature births *have risen* due to ART; and low birth weight *can produce problems* in later development.
3. c. While birth is very safe in the developed world, maternal and infant mortality is a serious problem in the least-developed countries.
4. Sally: The United States—like other developed countries—has made tremendous strides in conquering infant mortality. Samantha: The fact that the United States has higher infant mortality rates than other developed countries is incredibly distressing.
5. You can come up with your own suggestions. Here are mine: Increase the number of nurse-practitioners and obstetrician-gynecologists in poor urban and rural areas. Provide monetary incentives to health-care providers to treat low-income women. Offer special "healthy baby" educational programs at schools, community centers, and local churches. Make it easier for low-wage workers to see a health-care provider by providing incentives to employers. Set up volunteer programs to visit isolated pregnant single mothers. Target nutrition programs to low-income mothers-to-be.

CONNECT ONLINE:

LaunchPad macmillan learning | Check out our videos and additional resources located at: www.macmillanlearning.com

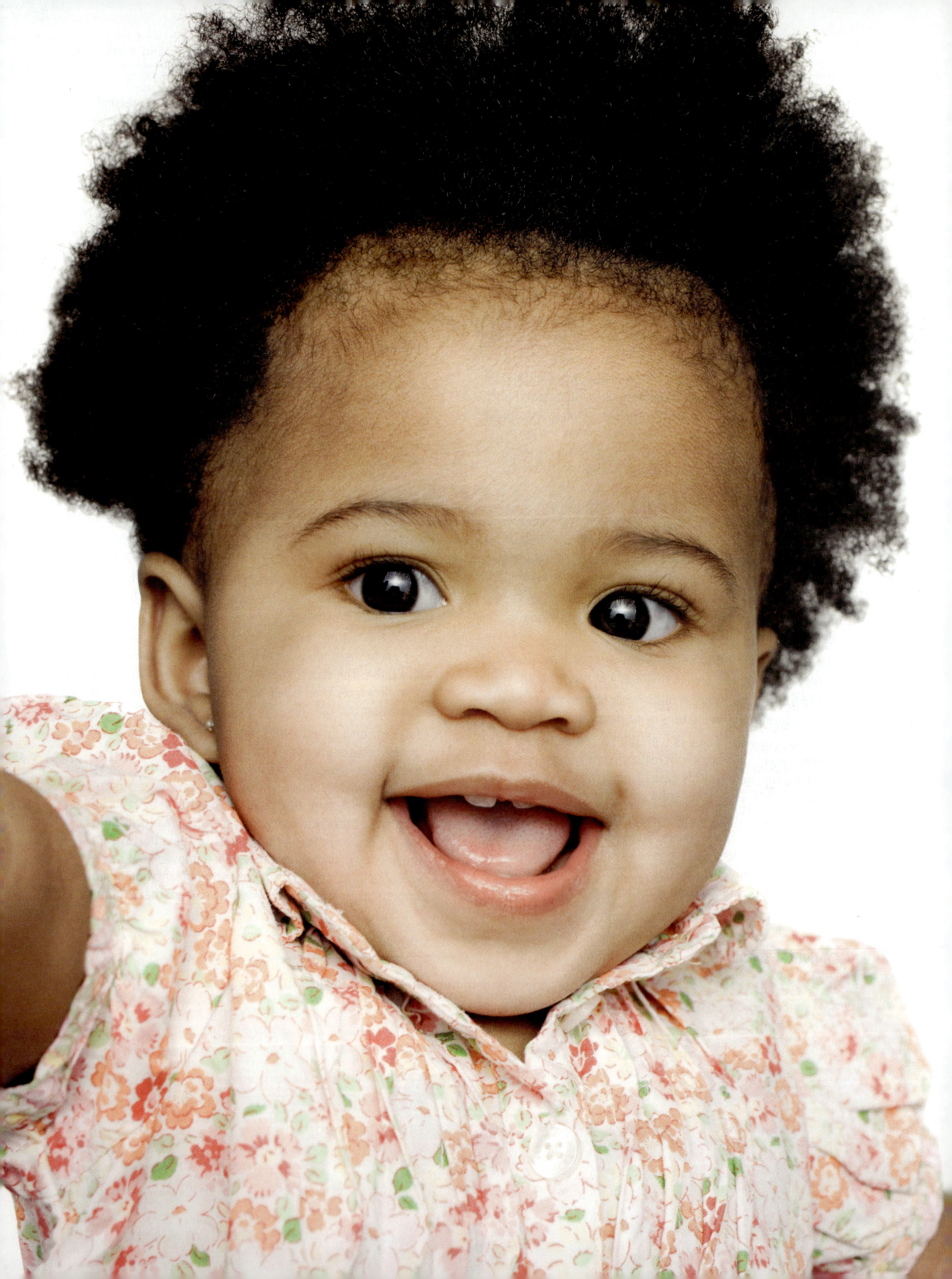

Infancy and Toddlerhood

This two-chapter part is devoted to infancy and toddlerhood. How does a helpless newborn become a walking, talking, loving child?

Chapter 3—**Physical and Cognitive Development in Infants and Toddlers** starts by offering an overview of brain development, then explores those basic newborn states: feeding, crying, and sleeping. Next, I chart sensory and motor development: What do babies see? How do newborns develop from lying helplessly to being able to walk? What can caregivers do to keep babies safe as they travel into the world? Finally, I'll offer an overview of infants' blossoming cognition and their first steps toward language, the capacity that allows us to enter the human community.

Chapter 4—**Emotional and Social Development in Infants and Toddlers** looks at what makes us human: our relationships. First, I'll explore the attachment bond between caregiver and child, then examine poverty and day care. The final part of this chapter focuses on toddlerhood—from age 1 to 2½. Toddlers are intensely attached to their caregivers and passionate to be independent. During this watershed age, when children are walking and beginning to talk, we first learn the rules of the human world.

Application to Developing Lives Parenting Simulation: *Babies and Toddlers*

Below is a list of questions you will answer in the Babies and Toddlers simulation module. As you answer these questions, consider the impact your choice will have on the physical, cognitive, and social and emotional development of your child.

Physical
- Will you get your baby vaccinated?
- Will you breast-feed your baby? If so, for how long?
- What kind of foods will you feed your baby during the first year?
- How will you encourage motor development?
- How does your baby's height and weight compare to national norms?

Cognitive
- What kind of activities are you going to expose your baby to (music class, reading, educational videos)?
- What kind of activities will you do to promote language development?
- What stage of Piaget's cognitive stages of development is your child in?

Social and Emotional
- How will you soothe your baby when he or she is crying?
- Can you identify your baby's temperament?
- Can you identify your baby's attachment style?
- What kind of discipline will you use with your child?

CHAPTER 3

CHAPTER OUTLINE

Setting the Context
The Expanding Brain
Neural Pruning and Brain Plasticity

Basic Newborn States
Eating
EXPERIENCING CHILDHOOD: A Passion to Eradicate Malnutrition: A Career in Public Health
Crying
INTERVENTIONS: What Quiets a Young Baby?
Sleeping
INTERVENTIONS: What Helps a Baby Self-Soothe?
To Co-Sleep or Not to Co-Sleep?
HOT IN DEVELOPMENTAL SCIENCE: SIDS

Sensory and Motor Development
What Do Newborns See?
Expanding Body Size
Mastering Motor Milestones
INTERVENTIONS: Baby-Proofing, the First Person–Environment Fit

Cognition
Piaget's Sensorimotor Stage
Critiquing Piaget
Tackling the Core of What Makes Us Human: Infant Social Cognition

Language: The Endpoint of Infancy
Nature, Nurture, and the Passion to Learn Language
Tracking Emerging Language

Physical and Cognitive Development in Infants and Toddlers

In Chapter 2, I talked to Kim at the beginning of the third trimester, anxiously waiting for her child's birth. Now, let's pay her a visit and meet Elissa, her baby girl.

She's been here for 5 months and 10 days, and I feel like she's been here forever. For me, it was love at first sight and, of course, the same for Jeff. But the thrill is watching a wonderful person emerge day by day. Take what's happening now. At first, she couldn't care less, but a month ago, it was like, "Wow, there's a world out there!" See that baby seat? Elissa can make the colored buttons flash by moving her legs. When I put her in it, she bats her legs like crazy. She can't get enough of the lights and sounds. Now that she is finally able to reach, notice her hunger to grab for everything and the way she looks at your face—like she can get into your soul. Sometimes, I think she understands what I'm feeling . . . but I know she must be way too young for this.

Elissa doesn't cry much—nothing like other babies during the first three months. Actually, I was worried. I asked the doctor whether there was something wrong. Crying is vital to communicating what you need! The same is true of sleeping. I'm almost embarrassed to tell you that I have the only baby in history who has been regularly giving her mother a good night's sleep since she was 2 months old.

Breast-feeding is indescribable. It feels like I am literally making her grow. But, here I also was concerned. Could I do this? What helped me persevere through the painful first week was my supportive husband—and most important, the fact that my boss gave me paid time off from work. I feel sad for my friend, Nora, who had to abandon this incredible experience when she needed to go back to her job right after her son's birth.

Pick her up. Feel what it's like to hold her—how she melts into you. But notice how she squirms to get away. It's as if she is saying, "Mom, my agenda is to get moving into the world." I plan to YouTube every step now that she's traveling into life.

At 5 months of age, Elissa has reached a milestone. She is poised to physically encounter life. This chapter charts the transformation from lying helplessly to moving into the world and the other amazing physical and cognitive changes that occur during infancy and toddlerhood—that remarkable first two years of life.

To set the context, I'll first spell out some brain changes (and principles) that program development. Then, I'll chart those basic newborn states—eating, crying, and sleeping—and track babies' emerging vision and motor skills. The final sections of this chapter tour cognition and language, the capacity that makes our species unique.

Left: Kiyoko Fukuda/a.collectionRF/amana images RF/Getty Images

PART II Infancy and Toddlerhood

LEARNING OUTCOME
- Define synaptogenesis, neural pruning, myelination, and brain plasticity.

What does this young baby see and understand about the tremendous loving object he is facing? That is the mystery we will be exploring in this chapter.

cerebral cortex The outer, folded mantle of the brain, responsible for thinking, reasoning, perceiving, and all conscious responses.

axon A long nerve fiber that usually conducts impulses away from the cell body of a neuron.

dendrite A branching fiber that receives information and conducts impulses toward the cell body of a neuron.

synapse The gap between the dendrites of one neuron and the axon of another, over which impulses flow.

synaptogenesis Forming of connections between neurons at the synapses. This process, responsible for all perceptions, actions, and thoughts, is most intense during infancy and childhood but continues throughout life.

myelination Formation of a fatty layer encasing the axons of neurons. This process, which speeds the transmission of neural impulses, continues from birth to early adulthood.

Setting the Context

What causes the remarkable changes—from seeing to walking to speaking—that unfold during infancy and toddlerhood? Answers come from scanning development in that masterpiece structure—the human brain.

The Expanding Brain

The **cerebral cortex,** the outer, furrowed mantle of the brain, is the site of every conscious perception, action, and thought. With a surface area 10 times larger than the monkey's and 1,000 times larger than the rat's, the cortex is what makes human beings different from any other species on earth.

Because of our immense cortex, humans are also unique in the amount of brain growth that occurs outside the womb. During the first four years of life, brain volume quadruples (Stiles & Jernigan, 2010). It takes more than two decades for the brain to fully mature. Actually, the cortex only starts taking over behavior a few months *after* birth.

During the fetal period and first year of life, the cells composing the brain migrate to the top of the neural tube (Paredes and others, 2016). When they reach this staging area, they explode into their mature form. The cells form long **axons**—fibers that conduct impulses away from the cell body. They sprout **dendrites**—treelike, branching ends. As the dendrites proliferate at junctions, or **synapses,** the axons and dendrites interconnect (see Figure 3.1).

Synaptogenesis, the process of making myriad connections, programs every skill—from Elissa's vigorous push-ups to composing symphonies or solving problems in math. Another critical transformation is called **myelination:** The axons form a fatty layer around their core. Just as a stream of water prevents us from painfully bumping down a water park slide, the myelin sheath is the lubricant that permits the neural impulses to speedily flow. This insulating layer may also determine which cells thrive (Stiles & Jernigan, 2010).

Synaptogenesis and myelination occur at different rates in specific brain areas (Dean and others, 2014). In the visual cortex, the part of the brain responsible for interpreting visual stimuli, the axons are myelinated by about age 1. In the frontal lobes, the brain region involved in reasoning, the myelin sheath is still forming into our twenties.

This makes sense. Seeing is a skill we need soon after birth. Visual abilities, as you will learn in this chapter, develop rapidly during our first year of life. But we won't need the skills to compose symphonies, do higher math, or competently make our way in the world until we become adults. So there are parallels between our unfolding abilities and the way our brain matures.

Neural Pruning and Brain Plasticity

So far, you might imagine that more neural connections equal superior skills. Not so! Neural loss is critical to development, too. Following a phase of lavishly producing synapses, each cortical region undergoes synaptic pruning and neural death. This shedding timetable also reflects our expanding abilities. It begins around age 1 in the visual cortex. It starts during late childhood in the frontal lobes. Just as weeding is critical to sculpting a beautiful garden, we need to get rid of the unnecessary neurons to permit the essential cells to flower.

Why does the brain undergo this frantic overproduction, followed by cutting back? Clues come from research suggesting that during infancy, synaptic connections progressively strengthen in more distant areas of the brain (Damaraju and others, 2014). Perhaps having an oversupply of connections allows us to "recruit" from this wider pool and redirect these extra neurons to perform other functions, should we have a major sensory deficit or brain insult early in life (Fox, Levitt, & Nelson, 2010; Stiles & Jernigan, 2010). Actually, our cortex is malleable, or **plastic** (able to be changed), particularly during infancy and the childhood years.

Using brain scans, which measure the brain's energy consumption, researchers find that among people blind from birth, activity in the visual cortex is intense while reading Braille and localizing sounds in space. This suggests that, without environmental stimulation from the eye, the neurons programmed for vision are captured, or taken over, to strengthen hearing and touch (Collignon and others, 2011; Fox, Levitt, & Nelson, 2010).

A similar process occurs with language, normally represented in the left hemisphere of the brain. If an infant has a left-hemisphere stroke, with intense verbal stimulation the right hemisphere takes over, and language develops normally (Rowe and others, 2009). Compare this to what happens when a person has a left-hemisphere stroke after language is located firmly in its appropriate places. The result can be devastating—a permanent loss in understanding speech or forming words.

So, brain plasticity highlights the basic nature-combines-with-nurture principle that governs human life. Yes, the blueprint for our cortex is laid out at conception. But environmental stimulation is vital in strengthening specific neural networks and determining which connections will be pruned (Fox, Levitt, & Nelson, 2010). Before the pruning phase, the brain is particularly malleable—permitting us to grow a somewhat different garden should disaster strike. Still, as synaptogenesis is a lifelong process, we continue to grow, to learn, to develop intellectually from age 1 to age 101.

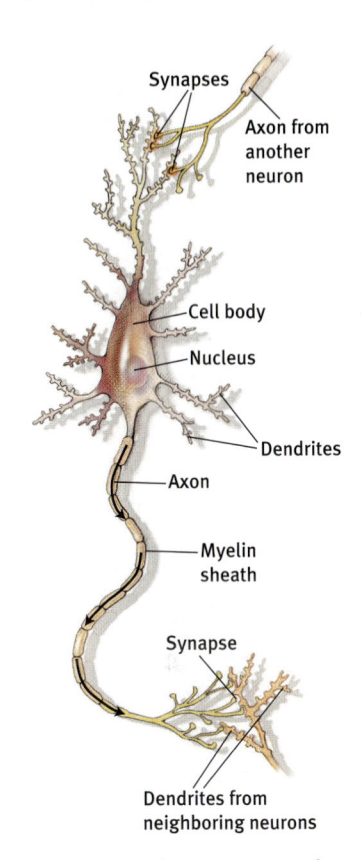

FIGURE 3.1: The neuron and synapses Here is an illustration of the remarkable structure that programs every developing skill, perception, and thought. Notice the dendrites receiving information at the synapses and how impulses flow down the long axon to connect up with the dendrites of the adjoining cells.

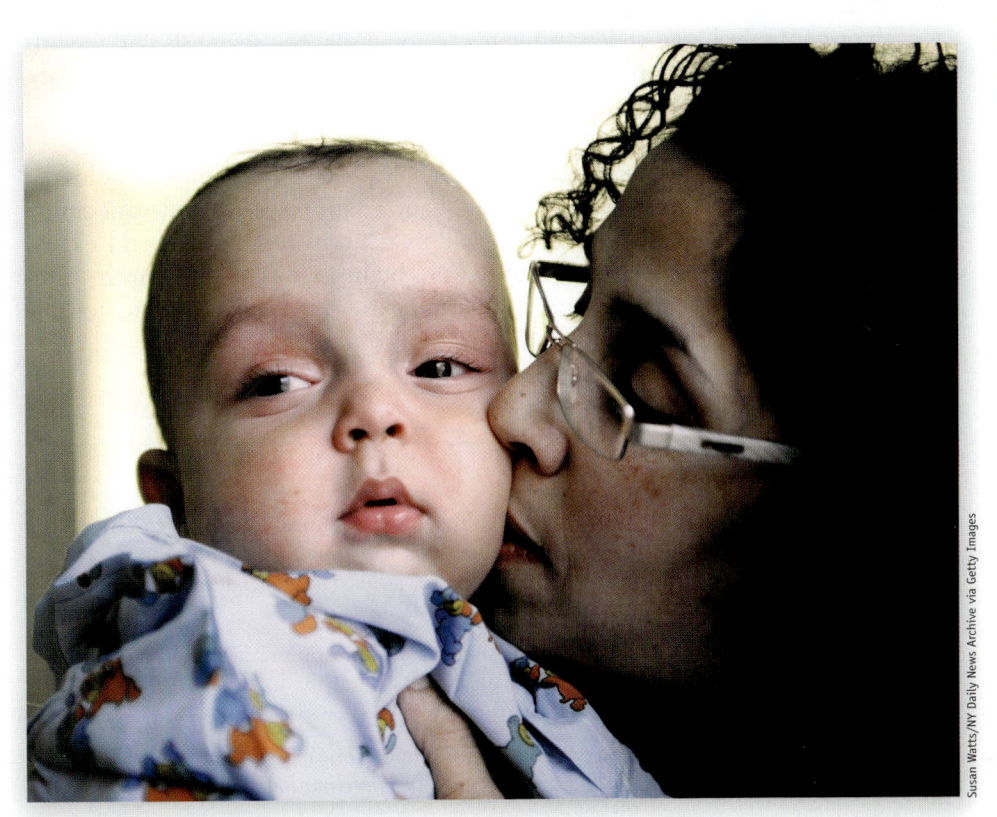

This resilient baby has survived major surgeries in which large sections of his brain had to be removed. Remarkably—because the cortex is so *plastic* at this age—he is expected to be left with few, if any, impairments.

plastic Malleable, or capable of being changed (refers to neural or cognitive development).

Table 3.1: Brain-Busting Facts to Wrap Your Head Around

- Our adult brain is composed of more than 1 billion neurons and, via synaptogenesis, makes roughly 60 trillion neural connections.

- As preschoolers, we have roughly double the number of synapses we have as adults—because, as our brain develops, roughly 40 percent of our synapses are ultimately pruned (see the text). So, ironically, the overall cortical thinning during elementary school and adolescence is a symptom of brain maturation.

- Specific abilities, such as language, that scientists had believed were localized in one part of the cortex are dependent on many brain regions. Moreover, the cortical indicators of "being advanced" in an ability shift in puzzling ways as a child gets older. For instance, while rapid myelination in the left frontal lobe predicts language abilities at age 1, by age 4 this relationship reverses, with linguistically advanced preschoolers showing more myelin in the right frontal lobe. Although there is a steeper-than-normal loss in cortical thickness when children show rapid IQ declines, boys and girls whose intelligence scores rise show no special cortical changes.

- Boys' brains, on average, are 10 percent larger than girls' brains, even during childhood, when both sexes are roughly the same size, body-wise.

- The most amazing finding relates to the surprising, dramatic variability in brain size from child to child. Two normal 10-year-old boys might have a twofold difference in brain volume, without having any difference in intellectual abilities!

Information from Dean and others, 2014; Giedd and others, 2010; Stiles & Jernigan, 2010.

Table 3.1 offers additional fascinating facts about neurons, synaptogenesis, and the pruning phase. Notice from the last item that, in the same way as the houses in your subdivision look different—although they may have had the same original plan (as each owner took charge of decorating his personal space)—scientists find remarkable variability in the brains of *normally* developing girls and boys (Giedd and others, 2010). And why should these variations be a surprise, given the diversity of interests and talents we develop in life!

Now keeping in mind the basic brain principles—(1) development unfolds "in its own neurological time" (you can't teach a baby a skill before the relevant part of the brain comes on-line); (2) stimulation sculpts neurons (our wider-world experiences physically change our brain); and (3) the brain is still "under construction" (and shaped by those same experiences) for as long as we live—let's explore how the expanding cortex works magic during the first years of life.

Tying It All Together

1. Cortez and Ashley are arguing about what makes our brain unique. Cortez says it's the size of our cortex. Ashley says it's the fact that we "grow" most of our brain after birth and that the cortex continues to mature for at least two decades. Who is right—Cortez, Ashley, or both students?

2. Latisha tells you that the myelin sheath speeds neural impulses and the more synaptic connections, the higher the level of development. Is Latisha totally correct? If not, describe how she is wrong.

3. When babies have a stroke, they may end up (choose one) *more/less* impaired than they would be as adults, due to brain (choose one) *myelination/plasticity*.

4. Which neural process is occurring in babies, mothers, and grandmas alike? (Choose one) *myelination/synaptogenesis*

Answers to the Tying It All Together questions can be found at the end of this chapter.

Basic Newborn States

Visit a newborn and you will see simple activities: She eats, she cries, she sleeps. In this section, I'll spotlight each state.

Eating: The Basis of Living

Eating patterns undergo amazing changes during the first two years of life. Let's scan these transformations and then discuss nutritional topics that loom large in the first years of life.

Developmental Changes: From Newborn Reflexes to 2-Year-Old Food Cautions

Newborns seem to be eating even when sleeping—a fact vividly brought home to me by the loud smacking that erupted from my son's bassinet. The reason is that babies are born with a powerful **sucking reflex**—they suck virtually all the time. Newborns also are born with a **rooting reflex.** If *anything* touches their cheek, they turn their head in that direction and suck.

Reflexes are automatic activities. Because they do not depend on the cortex, they are not under conscious control. It is easy to see why the sucking and rooting reflexes are vital to surviving after we exit the womb. If newborns had to learn to suck, they might starve before mastering that skill. Without the rooting reflex, babies would have trouble finding the breast.

Sucking and rooting have clear functions. What about the other infant reflexes shown in Figure 3.2? Do you think the grasping reflex may have helped newborns survive during hunter-gatherer times? Can you think of why newborns, when adults stand them on a table, take little steps (the stepping reflex)? Whatever their value, these reflexes, and a few others, must be present at birth. They must disappear as the cortex grows.

As the cortex matures, voluntary processes replace these newborn reflexes. By month 4 or 5, babies no longer suck continually. Their sucking is governed by *operant conditioning*. When the breast draws near, they suck in anticipation of that delicious reinforcer: "Mealtime has arrived!" Still, Sigmund Freud named infancy the oral stage for good reason: During the first years of life, the theme is "Everything in the mouth."

This impulse to taste everything leads to scary moments as children crawl and walk. There is nothing like the sickening sensation of seeing a baby put a forgotten pin in his mouth or taste your possibly poisonous plant. My personal heart-stopping experience occurred when my son was almost 2. I'll never forget the frantic race to the emergency room after Thomas toddled in to joyously share a treasure, an open vial of pills!

LEARNING OUTCOMES

- Identify the purpose of newborn reflexes.
- Name two issues that limit breast-feeding.
- Describe the prevalence of undernutrition and food insecurity.
- List techniques to quiet a crying baby.
- Outline infant sleep changes and offer a strategy to promote baby sleep.
- Describe sudden infant death syndrome (SIDS).

sucking reflex The automatic, spontaneous sucking movements newborns produce, especially when anything touches their lips.

rooting reflex Newborns' automatic response to a touch on the cheek, involving turning toward that location and beginning to suck.

reflex A response or action that is automatic and programmed by noncortical brain centers.

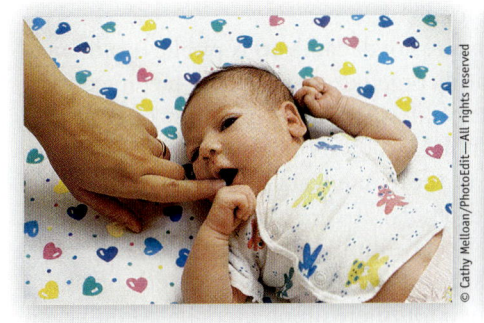

Rooting Whenever something touches their cheek, newborns turn their head in that direction and make sucking movements.

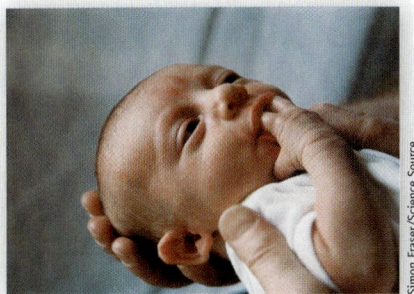

Sucking Newborns are programmed to suck, especially when something enters their mouth.

Grasping Newborns automatically vigorously grasp anything that touches the palm of their hand. If the baby's brain is developing normally, each of these reflexes is present at birth and gradually disappears after the first few months of life.

FIGURE 3.2: Some newborn reflexes In addition to the reflexes illustrated here, other newborn reflexes include the Babinski reflex (stroke a baby's foot and her toes turn outward), the stepping reflex (place a baby's feet on a hard surface and she takes small steps), and the swimming reflex (if placed under water, newborns can hold their breath and make swimming motions).

Luckily, a mechanism may protect toddlers from sampling every potentially lethal substance during their first travels into the world. Between ages 1½ and 2, children can revert to eating a few familiar foods, such as peanut butter sandwiches and apple juice. Evolutionary psychologists believe that, like morning sickness, this behavior is adaptive. Sticking to foods they know reduces the risk of children poisoning themselves when they begin to walk (Bjorklund & Pellegrini, 2002). Because this *2-year-old food caution* gives caregivers headaches, we need to reassure frantic parents: Picky eating can be *normal* during the second year of life (as long as a child eats a reasonable amount of food).

What is the best diet during a baby's first months? When is not having enough food a widespread problem? These questions bring up breast-feeding and global malnutrition.

Breast Milk: Nature's First Food

For most of human history, as I discussed in Chapter 1, babies faced perils right after birth. Infectious diseases and impure food and water ensured that many newborns did not survive beyond age 1 (Gordon, 2015). Before the early-twentieth-century public-health miracles, breast-feeding—for as long as possible—was a life-saving act (Preston, 1991).

Breast-feeding is a life-saver in poor nations today. In Southern Africa—Zambia, Zimbabwe, and Swaziland—mothers who nurse (without offering other liquids or foods) increase their infants' survival odds (Motsa, Ibisomi, & Odimegwu, 2016). In the developed world, exclusive breast-feeding is linked to widespread benefits, from making toddlers more resistant to the flu (McNiel, Labbok, & Abrahams, 2010) to accelerating myelin formation (Deoni and others, 2013) to producing 1-year-olds who are less reactive to stress (Beijers, Riksen-Walraven, & de Weerth, 2013). In one sophisticated longitudinal study, women who nursed for longer had kindergarteners with fewer disruptive behaviors—such as aggression and tantrums—if these children were genetically at-risk (Jackson, 2016).

But these findings involve correlations. And just because a relationship exists between two variables does not mean one *causes* the other. The research exploring breast milk's benefits does not control for maternal motivation (Sulaiman, Liamputtong, & Amir, 2016). In the study just mentioned, wouldn't a woman's passion to breast-feed a "fussy" infant suggest that she is generally a more committed mother (Chong and others, 2016)? Perhaps this intense commitment to caregiving mutes a child's temperamental tendency to misbehave.

The "correlation-is-not-causation" issue is especially problematic because, in the developed world, breast-feeding is *strongly* linked to social class. Women who nurse for months tend to be well-educated and affluent (Dennis and others, 2013). They spend more time in hands-on infant care (Smith & Ellwood, 2011). Is it really breast *milk* that promotes health, or the extra love that goes along with providing this natural food?

Despite these issues, for decades every public health organization has vigorously urged exclusive breast-feeding during the first six months of life (American Academy of Pediatrics [AAP], 2005; UNICEF, 2009). But, from Asia (Sulaiman and others, 2016) to the United States (Chong and others, 2016; Johnson and others, 2016), most new mothers don't follow this advice. Even in hunter-gatherer societies such as the Amazonian Tsimani, where 8 in 10 women still nurse their toddlers, women routinely supplement breast milk with other foods (Martin and others, 2016). Why?

This woman has the luxury of nursing her infant for months because she is affluent and doesn't need to return to work full-time after giving birth.

Work Demands

One reason for abandoning the breast-feeding advice—particularly in the United States—is the need to work (Flower and others, 2008; Vaughn and others, 2010). Women with paid-for maternity leave nurse their babies for longer (Mirkovic, Perrine, & Scanlon, 2016); work conflict dampens down the motivation to persist (Chong and others, 2016). In one striking comparison, U.S. mothers who returned to work full-time within three months after a child's birth breast-fed their babies an average 15 weeks *less* than their counterparts with part-time jobs (Lubold, 2016).

Imagine being a restaurant server or supermarket clerk who needs to work 40 or 50 hours per week to make ends meet (Guendelman and others, 2009). Would you have time to nurse your baby, no matter what the experts advised?

Physical Pain

But even when a woman has the luxury of breast-feeding for months, she can be let down by her body. This "natural" activity can be painful to carry out (Martin and others, 2016; Brown, Rance, & Bennett, 2016). As one new mother reported: "I never realized . . . that I would be reduced to tears every time I fed" (Sheehan, Schmied, & Barclay, 2013, p. 23). Another woman, forced to abandon the breast because of pain, anguished: "I felt so horrible . . . that I couldn't do this for my child" (quoted in Andrews & Knaak, 2013, p. 95).

Yes, exclusive breast-feeding for as long as possible is vital in nations where water and food are still impure (such as in Africa). But, because so many contemporary women cannot follow the six-month advice, it seems unfair to make mothers feel guilty when things don't work out. And rather than a person's milk delivery method, what's *really* important is the way a mother bonds with her child.

Malnutrition: A Serious Developing-World Concern

Breast-feeding gives *every* newborn a chance to thrive. However, there comes a time—at around 6 months of age—when babies need solid food. That's when the horrifying developing-world inequalities, described in the Experiencing Childhood box, hit (Caulfield and others, 2006).

Experiencing Childhood: A Passion to Eradicate Malnutrition: A Career in Public Health

What is it like to battle malnutrition in the developing world? Listen to Richard Douglass describe his career:

I grew up on the South Side of Chicago—my radius was maybe 4 or 5 blocks in either direction. Then, I spent my junior year in college in Ethiopia, and it changed my life. I lived across the street from the hospital, and every morning I saw a flood of people standing in line. They would wait all day . . . , and eventually a cart would come and take away the dead. When I saw the lack of doctors, I realized I needed to get my master's and Ph.D. in public health.

In public health we focus on primary prevention, how to prevent diseases and save thousands of people from getting ill. My interest was in helping to eradicate Kwashiorkor in Ghana. What the name literally means is "the disease that happens when the second child is born." The first child is taken off the breast too soon and given a porridge that doesn't have amino acids, and so the musculature and the diaphragm break down. You get a bloated look (swollen stomach), and then you die. If a child does survive, he ends up stunted, and so looks maybe 5 years younger.

Once someone gets the disease, you can save their life. But it's a 36-month rehabilitation that requires taking that child to the clinic for treatment every week. In Ghana it can mean traveling a dozen miles by foot. So a single mom with two or three kids is going to drop out of the program as soon as the child starts to look healthy. Because of male urban migration, the African family is in peril. If a family has a grandmother or great-auntie, the child can make it because this woman can take care of the children. So the presence of a grandma saves kids' lives.

Most malnutrition shows up after wars. In Ghana there is tons of food. So it's a problem of ignorance, not poverty. The issue is partly cultural. First, among some groups, the men eat, then women, then older children, then the babies get what is left. So the meat is gone, the fish is gone, and then you just have that porridge. We have been trying to impose a cultural norm that everyone sits around the dining table for meals, thereby ensuring that all the children get to eat. The other issue is just pure public health education—teaching families "just because your child looks fat doesn't mean that he is healthy."

I feel better on African soil than anywhere else. With poor people in the developing world who are used to being exploited, they are willing to write you off in a heartbeat if you give them a reason; but if you make a promise and follow through, then you are part of their lives. I keep going back to my college experience in Ethiopia . . . watching those people standing at the hospital, waiting to die. Making a difference for them is the reason why I was born.

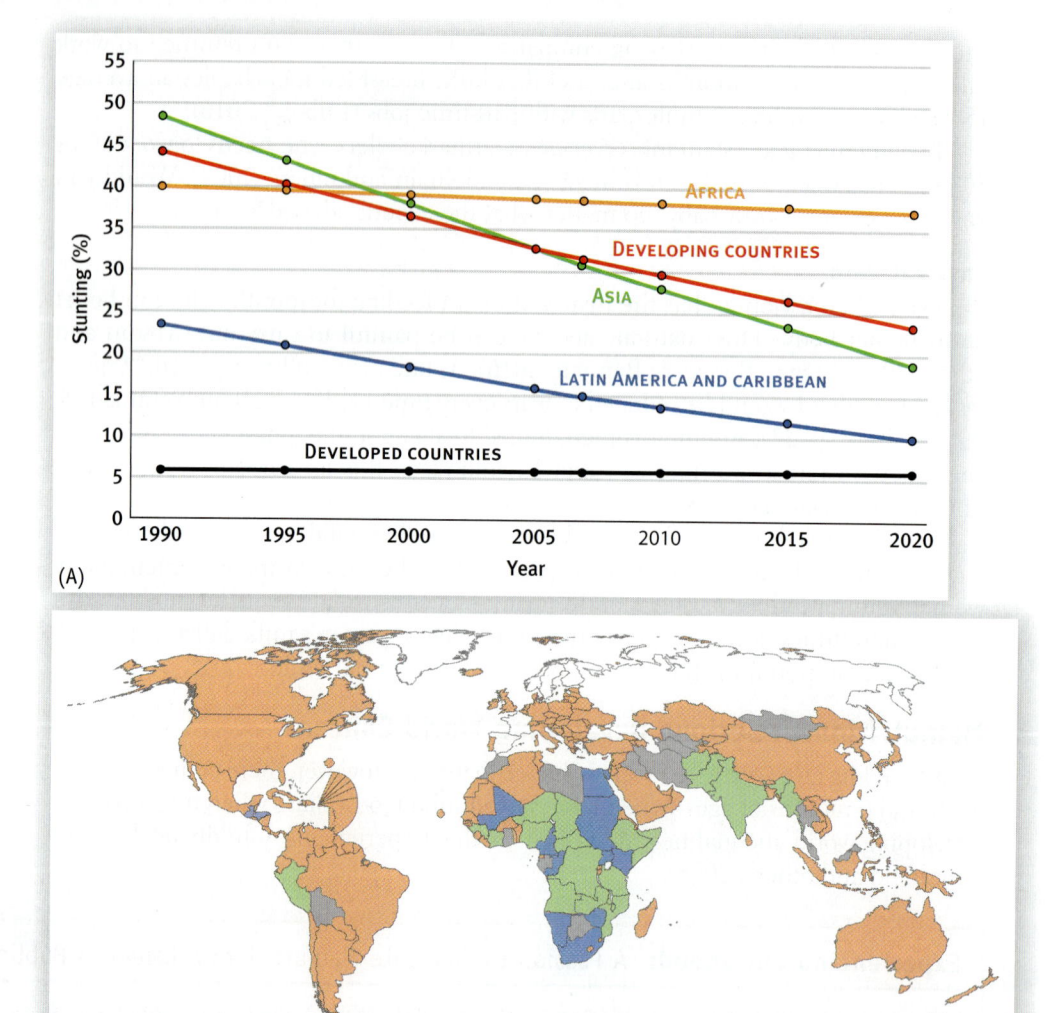

FIGURE 3.3: **(A) Trends in stunting in different world regions, 1990–2020 (B) Stunting prevalence in different world regions today** The good news is that stunting has dramatically declined in Asia, Latin America, and the Caribbean (see chart A), although, as you can see on the map (B), this sign of severe malnutrition is still unacceptably high in Africa, Southeast Asia, and South Central Asia.
Data from de Onis, Blössner, & Borghi, 2012.

undernutrition A chronic lack of adequate food.

stunting Excessively short stature in a child, caused by chronic lack of adequate nutrition.

micronutrient deficiency Chronically inadequate level of a specific nutrient important to development and disease prevention, such as vitamin A, zinc, and/or iron.

food insecurity According to U.S. Department of Agriculture surveys, the number of households that report needing to serve unbalanced meals, worrying about not having enough food at the end of the month, or having to go hungry due to lack of money (latter is *severe food insecurity*).

How many young children suffer from **undernutrition,** having a serious lack of adequate food? For answers, epidemiologists measure **stunting,** the percentage of children under age 5 in a given region who rank below the fifth percentile in height, according to the norms for their age. This very short stature is a symptom of *chronic* inadequate nutrition, which compromises every aspect of development and activity of life (Abubakar and others, 2010; UNICEF, 2009).

The good news is that, as Figure 3.3A shows, stunting rates have dramatically declined in Asia, Latin America, and the Caribbean. The tragedy, as you can see in Figure 3.3B, is that in sub-Saharan Africa and South Asia, malnutrition still affects an alarming 2 in 5 girls and boys. In the developing world, **micronutrient deficiencies**—inadequate levels of nutrients such as iron, zinc, or vitamin A—are rampant. Disorders, such as Kwashiorkor (described in the Experiencing Childhood box on the previous page), can even strike when there is ample food.

How many young children are stunted or chronically hungry in the United States? In 2015, more than 1 in 6 (17 percent) of U.S. households with children was **food insecure.** Caregivers reported not having the money to provide a balanced

> **Table 3.2:** Major U.S. Federal Nutrition Programs Serving Young Children[†]
>
> **Food Stamp Program (now called SNAP, Supplemental Nutrition Assistance Program):** This mainstay federal nutrition program provides electronic cards that participants can use like a debit card to buy food. Families with young children make up the majority of food stamp recipients.
>
> **Special Supplemental Nutrition Program for Women, Infants, and Children (WIC):** This federally funded grant program is specifically for low-income pregnant women and mothers with children under age 5. WIC offers a monthly package of supplements tailored to the family's unique nutritional needs (such as infant formula and baby cereals) plus nutrition education and breast-feeding support.
>
> **Child and Adult Care Food Program (CACFP):** This program reimburses child-care facilities, day-care providers, after-school programs, and providers of various adult services for the cost of serving high-quality meals. Surveys show that children in participating programs have higher intakes of key nutrients and eat fewer servings of fats and sweets than those who attend facilities that do not participate.
>
> Information from U.S. Department of Agriculture, Food and Nutrition Service, 2014.
> [†]This information was correct as of 2017; however, as the new Congress may cut funding for these services, the status of some programs may have changed by the time you are reading this book.

diet, or being worried that their funds for food might run out. About 1 in 11 families reported *severe food insecurity*. They sometimes went hungry due to lack of money.

While rates of U.S. food insecurity vary—from more than 1 in 3 families in an impoverished Mississippi County, to under 1 in 25 in an affluent Virginia suburb—as of this writing (2017), low-income children have access to the nutrition-related entitlement programs described in Table 3.2 (Hunger and Poverty Facts and Statistics, 2016). So—at least for now—in the United States, this developing-world scourge is rare.

Crying: The First Communication Signal

At 2 months, when Jason cried, I was clueless. I picked him up, rocked him, and kept a pacifier glued to his mouth; I called my mother, the doctor, even my local pharmacist, for advice. Since it put Jason to sleep, my husband and I took car rides at three in the morning—the only people on the road were teenagers and other new parents like us. Now that my little love is 10 months old, I know why he is crying, and those lonely countryside tours are long gone.

Crying, that vital way we communicate our feelings, reaches its lifetime peak at around one month after birth (St. James-Roberts, 2007). However, a distinctive change in crying occurs at about month 4. As the cortex blossoms, crying rates decline, and babies use this communication to express their needs.

It's tempting to think of crying as a negative state. However, because crying is as vital to survival as sucking, when babies cry too little, this can signal a neurological problem (Zeskind & Lester, 2001). When babies cry, we pick them up, rock them, and give them loving care. So, up to a point, crying cements the infant–parent bond.

Still, there is a limit. When a baby cries continually, she may have that bane of early infancy—**colic**. Despite what some "friends" (unhelpfully) tell new mothers, it's a myth that inept parents produce colicky babies. Colic is caused by an immature nervous system. After they exit the cozy womb, some babies get unusually distressed when bombarded by stimuli, such as being handled or fed (St. James-Roberts, 2007). So we need to back off from blaming stressed-out caregivers for this biological problem of early infant life.

Imagine having a baby with colic. You feel helpless. You cannot do anything to quiet the baby down. There are few things more damaging to parental self-efficacy than an infant's out-of-control crying (Keefe and others, 2006).

The good news is that colic is short-lived. Most parents find that around month 4, their baby suddenly becomes a new, pleasant person overnight. For this reason, there is only cause for concern when a baby cries excessively *after* this age (Schmid and others, 2010).

colic A baby's frantic, continual crying during the first three months of life; caused by an immature nervous system.

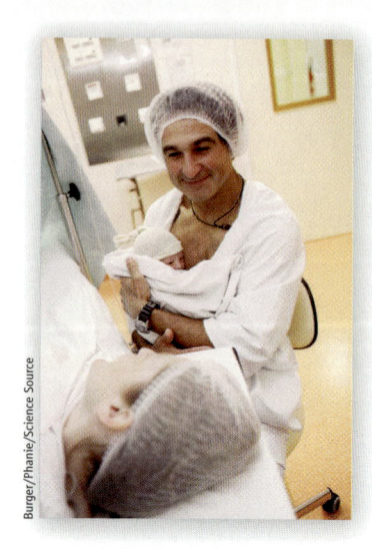

Because it promotes intense skin-to-skin bonding, kangaroo care is an effective baby-calming technique.

skin-to-skin contact An effective calming strategy that involves holding a young infant next to a caregiver's body.

kangaroo care Carrying a young baby in a sling close to the caregiver's body. This technique is most useful for soothing an infant.

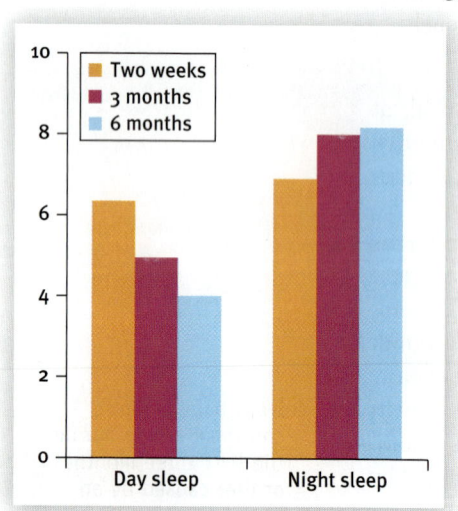

FIGURE 3.4: Mean number of hours babies sleep during the day and night, at 2 weeks, 3 months, and 6 months of age This chart shows that particularly during the first three months of life, babies shift their cycle to mainly nighttime slumber (but unfortunately, infants continue to wake up several times each night).
Data from Figueiredo and others, 2016.

INTERVENTIONS: What Quiets a Young Baby?

What calms a crying newborn? The familiar answer: Pick up the baby, hold her, rock her, feed her, provide a pacifier or anything that satisfies the need to suck.

Skin-to-skin contact, holding a baby close, has a clear physiological effect. It reduces newborn's levels of the stress hormone *cortisol* (Beijers, Cillessen, & Zijlmans, 2016). The best real-world evidence comes from the !Kung San hunter-gatherers of Botswana. In this culture, where mothers strap infants to their chests and feed them on demand, the frequency of colic is dramatically reduced.

Kangaroo care, using a baby sling, can even help premature infants grow (World Health Organization [WHO], 2003b). In one experiment, developmentalists had mothers with babies in an intensive care unit carry their infants in baby slings for one hour each day. At 6 months of age, compared to a group given standard care, the kangaroo-care babies scored higher on developmental tests. Their parents were rated as providing a more nurturing home environment, too (Feldman & Eidelman, 2003).

Imagine having your newborn whisked away to spend weeks with strangers. Now, think of being able to caress his tiny body, the sense of self-efficacy that would flow from helping him thrive. So it makes sense that any cuddling intervention can have an impact on the baby and the parent–child bond.

Another baby-calming strategy is infant massage. From helping premature infants gain weight to treating toddler (and adult) sleep problems, massage enhances well-being from the beginning to the end of life (Field, Diego, & Hernandez-Reif, 2007, 2011).

We all know the power of a cuddle or a relaxing massage to soothe our troubles. Can holding and stroking in early infancy *generally* insulate children against stress? Consider this study with rats.

Because rodent mothers (like humans) differ in the "hands-on" contact they give their babies, researchers classified rats who had just given birth into one of three groups: high licking and grooming, average licking and grooming, and low licking and grooming. As adults, the lavishly licked and groomed rats reacted in a more placid way when exposed to stress (Menard & Hakvoort, 2007). We need to be cautious about generalizing this finding to humans. Advocating for the !Kung San approach to caregiving might be asking too much of modern moms. Still, the implication is clear: During the first months of life (or, for as long as you can), keep touching and loving 'em up!

Cuddles calm us from day 1 to age 101. However, as children get older, the reasons for their crying undergo fascinating changes. The long car ride that magically quieted a 2-month-old evokes agony in a toddler who cannot stand to be confined. First, it's swaddling, then watching a mobile, then seeing Mom enter the room that has the power to soothe. In preschool, it's monsters that cause wailing; during elementary school and teenager-hood, it's failing or being rejected by our social group. As emerging adults, we weep for a lost job or love. Our crying shows just where we are emotionally as we travel from babyhood until adult life!

Sleeping: The Main Newborn State

If crying is a crucial baby (and adult) communication signal, sleep is the quintessential newborn state. Visit a relative who has recently given birth. Will her baby be crying or eating? No, she is almost certain to be asleep. Two-week-old babies typically sleep for almost 14 hours out of a 24-hour day (Figueiredo and others, 2016, see Figure 3.4). And there is a reason for the saying, "She sleeps like a baby." Perhaps because it mirrors the whooshing sound in the womb, noise helps newborns zone out. The problem for parents is that babies wake up and start wailing, like clockwork, every 3 to 4 hours.

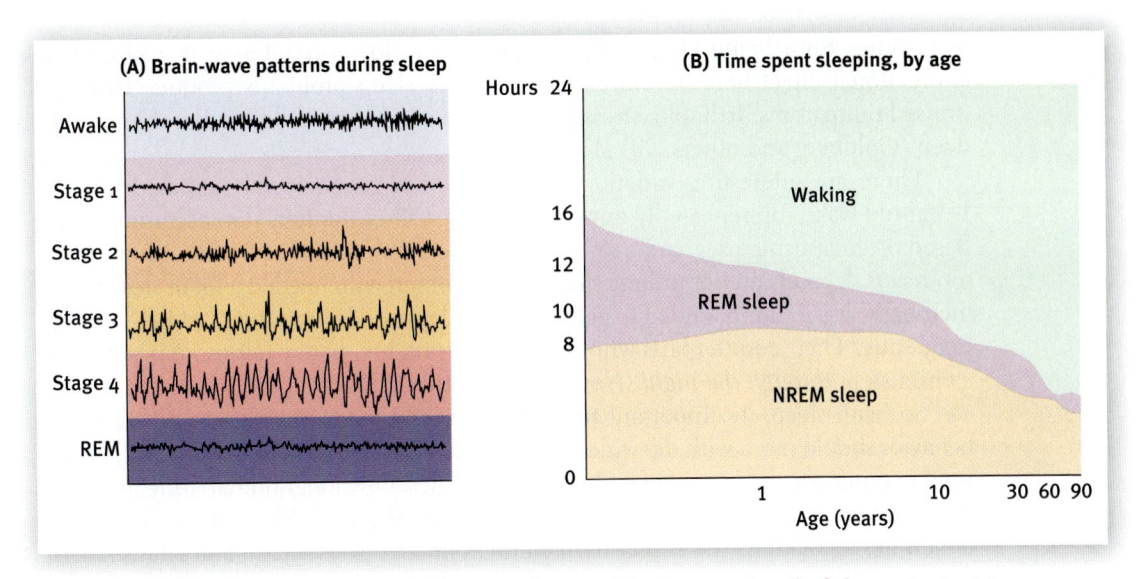

FIGURE 3.5: Sleep brain waves and lifespan changes in sleep and wakefulness In chart A, you can see the EEG patterns associated with the four stages of sleep that first appear during adolescence. After we fall asleep, our brain waves get progressively slower (these are the four stages of non-REM sleep) and then we enter the REM phase during which dreaming is intense. Now, notice in chart B the time young babies spend in REM. As REM sleep helps consolidate memory, is the incredible time babies spend in this phase crucial to absorbing the overwhelming amount of information that must be mastered during the first years of life?
Data from Roffwarg, Muzio, & Dement, 1966.

Developmental Changes: From Signaling to Self-Soothing to Shifts in REM Sleep

During the first year of life, infant sleep patterns adapt to the human world. Within the first three months of life, as Figure 3.4 shows, sleep shifts toward nighttime hours. Then, by about 6 months of age, there is a milestone. The typical baby sleeps for 6 hours a night. At age 1, the typical pattern is roughly 12 hours of sleep a night, with an additional morning and afternoon nap. During year 2, the caretaker's morning respite to do housework or rest is regretfully lost, as children give up the morning nap. Finally, by late preschool, sleep often (although not always) occurs only at night (Anders, Goodlin-Jones, & Zelenko, 1998).

In addition to its duration and on-again/off-again pattern, infant sleep differs physiologically from our adult pattern. When we fall asleep, we descend through four stages, involving progressively slower brain-wave frequencies, and then cycle back to **REM sleep**—a phase of rapid eye movement, when dreaming is intense and our brain-wave frequencies look virtually identical to when we are in the lightest sleep stage (see Figure 3.5). When infants fall asleep, they immediately enter REM and spend most of their time in this state. It is not until adolescence that we undergo the adult sleep cycle, with four distinct stages (Anders, Goodlin-Jones, & Zelenko, 1998).

Although parents are thrilled to say, "My child is sleeping through the night," this statement is false. Babies *never* sleep continuously through the night. However, by about 6 months of age, many have the skill to become **self-soothing**. They put themselves back to sleep when they wake up (Goodlin-Jones and others, 2001).

Imagine being a new parent. Your first challenge is to get your baby to develop the skill of nighttime self-soothing. Around age 1, because your child is now put into the crib while still awake, there may be issues getting your baby to *go* to sleep. During preschool and elementary school, the sleep problem shifts again. Now, it concerns getting the child *into* bed: "Mommy, can't I stay up later? Do I *have* to turn off the lights?"

Although it may make them cranky, parents expect to be sleep-deprived with a young baby; but once a child has passed the 5- or 6-month milestone, parents get agitated if an infant has never permitted them a full night's sleep. Parents expect sleep problems when their child is ill or under stress, but not the zombielike irritability

> **REM sleep** The phase of sleep involving rapid eye movements, when the EEG looks almost like it does during waking. REM sleep decreases as infants mature.
>
> **self-soothing** Children's ability, usually beginning at about 6 months of age, to put themselves back to sleep when they wake up during the night.

that comes from being chronically sleep-deprived for years. There is a poisonous bidirectional effect here: Children with chronic sleep problems produce irritable, stressed-out parents. Irritable, stressed-out parents produce childhood problems with sleep (Goldberg and others, 2013).

There are interesting variations. Some women get unusually agitated when a 1-year-old wakes up repeatedly during the night. Other mothers don't seem to mind. Based on measuring pregnant mothers' sleep, researchers discovered that how a person reacts depends on her unique sleep style. Women who needed a lot of sleep while their baby was in utero tended to get unusually depressed when their toddler woke up frequently. Their counterparts who slept less during pregnancy felt more upset when a child slept *through the night* (Newland and others, 2016)!

So, with sleep, it's important to have the right *person–environment fit*—a baby's behavior should mesh with the wider world (in this case, the parent world). Still, I don't want to minimize the impact of enduring sleep issues. One longitudinal study suggested chronic sleep problems that continue into preschool put children at risk for having difficulties regulating their emotions in elementary school (Williams and others, 2016).

INTERVENTIONS: What Helps a Baby Self-Soothe?

Returning to infancy, what should parents do when their baby signals (cries out) from the crib? At one end of the continuum stand the behaviorists: "Don't reinforce crying by responding—and be consistent. Never go in and comfort the baby lest you let a variable reinforcement schedule unfold, and the child will cry longer." At the other pole, we have John Bowlby with his emphasis on the attachment bond, or Erik Erikson with his concept of *basic trust* (see Table 3.3). During the first year of life, both Bowlby and Erikson imply that caregivers should sensitively respond when an infant cries. These contrasting points of view evoke passions among parents, too:

> I feel the basic lesson parents need to teach children is how to be independent, not to let your child rule your life, give him time to figure things out on his own, and not be attended to with every whimper.

> I am going with my instincts and trying to be a good, caring mommy. Putting a baby in his crib to "cry it out" seems cruel. There is no such thing as spoiling an infant!

Where do you stand on this "Teach 'em" versus "Give unconditional love" controversy? Given that in a young baby the cortex has not fully come on-line, the behavioral "teach 'em not to cry" doesn't work during early infancy (Douglas & Hill, 2013; Stremler and others, 2013). But, by about month 7 or 8, it may be better

Table 3.3: Erikson's Psychosocial Stages of Childhood, Adolescence, and Emerging Adulthood

Life Stage	Primary Task
Infancy (birth to 1 year)	**Basic trust versus mistrust**
Toddlerhood (1 to 2 years)	Autonomy versus shame and doubt
Early childhood (3 to 6 years)	Initiative versus guilt
Middle childhood (7 to 12 years)	Industry versus inferiority
Adolescence and emerging adulthood (teens into twenties)	Identity versus role confusion
Emerging adulthood (twenties)	Intimacy versus isolation

According to Erikson, in the first year of life, our mission is to feel confident that the human world will lovingly satisfy our needs. Basic trust is the foundation for the challenges we face at every life stage.

to hang back, as babies who are quickly picked up may have more trouble learning to self-soothe (St. James-Roberts, 2007). So, if parents care vitally about getting a good night's sleep, it's best not to react to every nighttime whimper—but only when an infant approaches age 1 and can "learn" to get to sleep on her own.

Vigorous "settling activities"—carrying a child around at bedtime, making a big deal of an infant's getting to sleep—are correlated with sleep difficulties at age 5 (Sheridan and others, 2013). Therefore, new parents might metaphorically err on the side of letting sleeping dogs lie, meaning not make excessive efforts to quiet the child. Still, this doesn't mean don't get involved!

Research suggests that parents who use gentle, sensitive, and loving bedtime routines tend to have babies with fewer sleep problems (Teti and others, 2010). When caregivers spend ample time gently lulling infants to sleep, bedtime cortisol levels slide down (Philbrook & Teti, 2016). So, rather than any specific sleep strategy, the real key to promoting infant sleep is to put a child to bed with love.

And notice that when you feel disconnected from loved ones, you too may have trouble sleeping. To sleep soundly at *any age*, we need to feel cushioned by love.

By lovingly preparing his baby for bed, this man is helping ensure a better night's sleep for *both* father and child. He also may be fostering basic trust—according to Erikson, the foundation for having a good life.

The principle that love cushions sleep raises that controversial issue: Should parents have a baby regularly sleep with them in their bed?

To Co-Sleep or Not to Co-Sleep?

How do you feel about **co-sleeping**, or sharing a bed with a child? In the past, experts in our individualistic society strongly cautioned against co-sleeping (see Ferber, 1985). Behaviorists warned that bed sharing could produce "excessive dependency." Freudian theorists implied that co-sleeping might place a child at risk for sexual abuse. To ward off these evils, the standard practice was to place an infant's crib in a separate room.

In collectivist cultures, this solo sleep arrangement would qualify as infant abuse! (See Latz, Wolf, & Lozoff, 1999; Yang & Hahn, 2002.) Japanese parents, for instance, often separate to give each child a sleeping partner, because they believe co-sleeping is crucial to babies developing into caring, loving adults (Kitahara, 1989).

Who is right? As the research about co-sleeping is inconclusive (see Belsky, 2016, for a review), the key, again, is to arrange the right person–environment fit—that is, do what works best for you, but with this caution: In families where bed sharing is not part of the traditional culture, continual co-sleeping may be a symptom of marital distress. In one rural Pennsylvania survey, mothers who reported that they always had their babies share the family bed were more apt to report unhappy marriages, to (erroneously) see their babies as frequently waking up at night, and, ironically, were less emotionally available to their infants at bedtime than a comparison group whose babies slept alone (Teti and others, 2016).

What do U.S. parents do? National polls show most couples adopt a midway approach: They usually room share, but not bed share. They follow the professional advice that the best way to promote breast-feeding (and possibly guard against SIDS) is *not* to isolate infants in a separate room (Smith and others, 2016). What is *sudden infant death syndrome (SIDS)*?

co-sleeping The standard custom, in collectivist cultures, of having a child and parent share a bed.

sudden infant death syndrome (SIDS) The unexplained death of an apparently healthy infant, often while sleeping, during the first year of life.

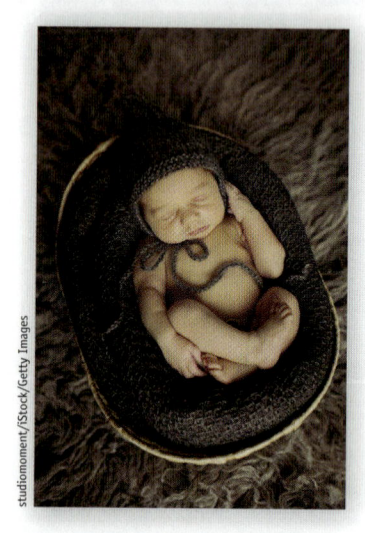

This portable sleeping basket is user friendly around the world, but in the Maori culture, it qualifies as culture friendly, too.

Hot in Developmental Science: SIDS

Sudden infant death syndrome (SIDS) refers to the unexplained death of an apparently healthy infant, often while sleeping, during the first months of life. Although it strikes only about 1 in 1,000 U.S. babies, SIDS is a top-ranking cause of infant mortality in the developed world (Karns, 2001).

What causes SIDS? In autopsying infants who died during the peak risk zone for SIDS (about 1 to 10 months), researchers targeted abnormalities in a particular region of the brain. Specifically, SIDS infants had either too many or too few neurons in a section of the brain stem involved in coordinating tongue movements and maintaining the airway when we inhale (Lavezzi and others, 2010). SIDS has been linked to pathologies in the part of the brain stem producing cerebrospinal fluid, too (Lavezzi and others, 2013).

But even if SIDS is caused by biological pre-birth problems, this tragedy can have post-birth environmental causes. In particular, SIDS is linked to infants being inadvertently smothered, by being placed face down in a "fluffy" crib. During the early 1990s, this evidence prompted the American Academy of Pediatrics to urge parents to put infants to sleep on their backs. The "Back to Sleep" campaign worked, because from 1992 to 1997, there was a 43 percent reduction in SIDS deaths in the United States (Gore & DuBois, 1998).

Still, because placing babies on their backs requires that infants sleep separately in a crib, the "Back to Sleep" public health message contradicts the strong pro co-sleeping culture among non-Western groups. To circumvent this barrier, New Zealand scientists devised a strategy to permit Maori mothers to follow their traditional sleeping style and minimize the SIDS risk. They encouraged these women to return to another old-style practice—weaving a baby sleeping-basket. By placing this basket on parents' beds, co-sleeping has now become scientifically "correct" (Ball & Volpe, 2013)!

Table 3.4 offers a section summary in the form of practical tips for caregivers dealing with infants' eating, crying, and sleeping. Now it's time to move on to sensory development and moving into the world.

Table 3.4: Infants' Basic States: Summary Tips for Caregivers (and Others)

Eating

- Don't worry about continual newborn sucking and rooting. These are normal reflexes, and they disappear after the first months of life.
- As the baby becomes mobile, be alert to the child's tendency to put everything into the mouth and baby-proof the home (see the next section's discussion).
- Try to breast-feed, but if you need to work full-time or if nursing is too painful, don't berate yourself. The main benchmark of good motherhood is providing a child with loving care.
- Employers should make efforts to support nursing in the workplace. To really promote breast-feeding, *society* should offer mothers universal paid family leave!
- After the child is weaned, provide a balanced diet. But don't get frantic if a toddler limits her intake to a few "favorite foods" at around age 1½—this pickiness is normal and temporary.

Crying

- Appreciate that crying is crucial—it's the way babies communicate their needs—and realize that this behavior is at its peak during the first months of life. The frequency of crying declines and the reasons why a child is crying become clearer after early infancy.
- If a baby has colic, hang in there. This condition typically ends at month 4. Moreover, understand that colic has nothing to do with insensitive mothering.

- During the day, carry a young infant around in a "baby sling" as much as possible. In addition, employ infant massage to soothe the baby.

Sleeping
- Expect to be sleep-deprived for the first few months, until the typical infant learns to self-soothe; meanwhile, take regular naps. After that, expect periodic sleep problems and understand that children will give up their daytime nap at around age 2.
- After about 6 to 8 months of age, to promote self-soothing, don't pick up a sleeping infant at the first whimper. But the choice is really up to you—as the best way to promote sleep is to put a baby to bed with love.
- Co-sleeping is a personal decision; but the safest policy may be to room share, yet not routinely to have a baby sleep in a family bed.
- For sleep troubles occurring regularly into preschool, seek professional help.

Tying It All Together

1. You're a nurse in the obstetrics ward, and new parents often ask you why their babies turn their heads toward anything that touches their cheek and then suck. You say (pick two): *This is called the rooting reflex; This behavior is programmed by the lower brain centers to automatically occur at birth and disappear as the brain matures; This is a sign of early intelligence.*

2. Elaine tells you that breast-feeding is more difficult than medical authorities suggest. Make her argument, drawing on the points in this section.

3. Your sister and her husband are under enormous stress because of their 1-month-old's crying. Based on this section, give your relatives advice for soothing their child.

4. Jorge tells you that he's thrilled because last night his 6-month-old finally slept through the night. Is Jorge's child *ahead of schedule, behind schedule,* or *on time* for this milestone? Is Jorge right in saying, "My child is sleeping *through* the night"?

5. Poll your classmates, asking them if they believe in co-sleeping and whether they would immediately go in to quiet a crying infant. Do you find any differences in their answers by ethnicity, by gender, or by age?

Answers to the Tying It All Together questions can be found at the end of this chapter.

Sensory and Motor Development

Sleeping, eating, and crying are easy to observe; but suppose you could time-travel back to your first days of life. What would you experience through your senses?

One sense is operational before we leave the womb. Using ultrasound, researchers can see startle reactions in fetuses in response to noise, showing that rudimentary hearing capacities exist before birth. As I mentioned in the previous chapter, the basics of vision may also be in place by about the seventh month of fetal life.

Table 3.5 on page 86 lists other interesting facts about newborn senses. Now, let's focus on vision because the research in this area is so extensive, the findings are so astonishing, and the studies devised to get into babies' heads are so brilliantly planned.

What Do Newborns See?

Imagine you are a researcher who wants to figure out what a newborn can see. What do you do? You put the baby into an apparatus, present images, and watch his eyes move. Specifically, researchers use the **preferential-looking paradigm**—the principle

LEARNING OUTCOMES
- Explain how scientists find out what infants can see.
- Describe the face perception findings and the purpose of the visual cliff study.
- Name three core principles of motor development.
- Trace how motor development unfolds and its impact on caregivers.

preferential-looking paradigm A research technique to explore early infant sensory capacities and cognition, drawing on the principle that we are attracted to novelty and prefer to look at new things.

Table 3.5: Some Interesting Facts About Other Newborn Senses

Hearing: Fetuses can discriminate different tones in the womb (Lecanuet and others, 2000). Newborns prefer women's voices, as they are selectively sensitive to higher-pitched tones. At less than 1 week of age, babies recognize their mother's voice (DeCasper & Fifer, 1980). By 1 month of age, they tune in to infant-directed speech (described on page 98) communications tailored to them.

Smell: Newborns prefer the odor of breast milk to that of amniotic fluid (Marlier, Schaal, & Soussignan, 1998). Plus, smelling breast milk has a soothing effect; newborns cry more vigorously when facing a scentless breast (one covered with a transparent film) (Doucet and others, 2007).

Taste: Newborns are sensitive to basic tastes. When they taste a bitter, sour, or salty substance, they stop sucking and wrinkle their faces. They suck more avidly on a sweet solution, although they will stop if the substance grows too sweet. Having babies suck a sweet solution before a painful experience, such as an injection, reduces agitation and so is a helpful pain-management technique (Fernandez and others, 2003; Gibbins & Stevens, 2001).

---

habituation The predictable loss of interest that develops once a stimulus becomes familiar; used to explore infant sensory capacities and thinking.

that human beings are attracted to novelty and look selectively at new things. They draw on a process called **habituation**—the fact that we naturally lose interest in a new object after some time.

You can notice preferential looking and habituation in operation right now in your life. If you see or hear something new, you look up with interest. After a minute, you habituate and return to reading this book.

By showing newborns small- and large-striped patterns and measuring preferential looking, researchers find that at birth the ability to see clearly at distances is very poor. With a visual acuity score of roughly 20/400 (versus our ideal adult 20/20), a newborn would qualify as legally blind in many states (Kellman & Banks, 1998). But because the visual cortex matures quickly, vision improves rapidly, and by about age 1, infants see just like adults.

What visual capacities *do* we have at birth? A century ago, the first American psychologist, William James, described the inner life of the newborn as "one buzzing, blooming confusion." Studies exploring **face perception** (making sense of human faces) offer scientific data about the truth of James's ideas.

face-perception studies Research using preferential looking and habituation to explore what very young babies know about faces.

Focusing on Faces

Actually, when babies emerge from the womb, they selectively attend to the social world. When presented with the paired stimuli in Figure 3.6, newborns spend more time looking at the face pattern than at the scrambled pattern. They follow that facelike stimulus longer when it is moved from side to side (Farroni, Massaccesi, & Simion, 2002; Slater and others, 2010).

Newborns can make amazing distinctions. They prefer to look at a photo of their mother compared to one of a stranger (Bushnell, 1998). They also gravitate toward attractive-looking people!

Researchers selected photos of attractive and unattractive women, then took infants from the maternity ward and measured preferential looking. Babies looked at the attractive faces for significantly longer—61 percent of the time (Slater and others, 2010). Unhappily, our tendency to prefer people based on their looks seems somewhat biologically built in. (In case you are interested, more symmetrical faces tend to be rated as better-looking.)

Face preferences sharpen over time. Two-month-old infants preferentially look at speaking faces (those that move or make sounds) versus still faces (Bahrick and others, 2016). When researchers show photos of entrancing colored objects, 4-month-old babies gravitate to these visually captivating images rather than scanning a drabber face. But, no matter how exciting the competing stimulus, 8-month-olds prefer to gaze at a face (Kwon and others, 2016).

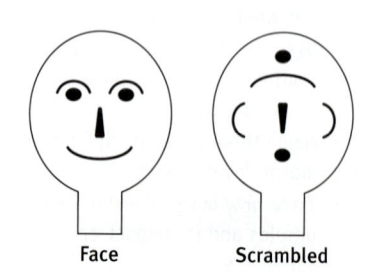

Face   Scrambled

FIGURE 3.6: Babies prefer faces When shown these illustrations, newborns looked most at the facelike drawing. Might the fact that infants are biologically programmed to selectively look at faces be built into evolution to help ensure that adults give babies loving care?

At around the same age, an important lifelong pattern locks in. Infants selectively look at photos showing fearful expressions (versus happy or angry faces) (Grossman & Jessen, 2017). This **fear bias**—or hypersensitivity to facial expressions of fear, as you will learn in the next chapter—seems built into our species to keep us safe from harm.

A related, selective perception has not-so-nice effects. At approximately 9 months of age, infants around the world become less sensitive to facial differences in other ethnic groups (Kobayashi and others, 2016).

In a classic study demonstrating this visual narrowing, researchers tested European American babies at different points during the first year of life for their ability to discriminate between different faces within their own racial group and those belonging to other ethnicities (African American, Middle Eastern, and Chinese). While the 3-month-olds preferentially looked at "new faces" of every ethnicity, showing they could see the differences between individuals in each group, by 9 months of age, the babies could only discriminate between faces of their own ethnicity.

Why did this skill disappear? The cause, as you may have guessed, is cortical pruning—the fact that unneeded synapses in our visual system atrophy, or are lost (Slater and others, 2010). So if you have wondered why other races look more alike (compared to your own ethnic group, of course!), it's a misperception. You learned not to see these differences during your first year of life!

Is Prejudice Partly Prewired?

This tantalizing research suggests that spending our first years of life in a racially homogenous environment might promote prejudice because the resulting neural atrophy could blunt our ability to decode the emotions of other ethnic groups. Amazingly, in testing U.S. teens adopted from Eastern European or Asian orphanages (places where infants are only exposed to caregivers of their ethnicity), scientists discovered that this was true. The longer a child lived in an orphanage, the less sensitive that adolescent was at picking up facial expressions of people from other races. Moreover, brain scans showed an unusual spike in the amygdala (our brain's fear center) when these young people viewed "foreign" faces. Therefore, simply being born in a multicultural city, such as New York or Chicago, might make us more tolerant because that experience prewires us *visually* to be more sensitive to the feelings of other races (Telzer and others, 2013)!

The main conclusion, however, is that William James was wrong. Newborns don't experience the world as a "blooming, buzzing confusion." We arrive in life with built-in antennae to tune into the human world. But visual skills change as we mature, in sometimes surprising ways.

Now let's trace another visual capacity as it comes on-line—the ability to see and become frightened of heights.

Seeing Depth and Fearing Heights

Imagine you are a researcher facing a conundrum: How can I find out when babies develop **depth perception**—the ability to "see" variations in heights—without causing them harm? Elinor Gibson's ingenious solution was to develop an apparatus called the **visual cliff**. As Figure 3.7 shows, Gibson and her colleague placed infants on one end of a table with a checkerboard pattern while their mothers stood at the opposite end (Gibson & Walk, 1960). At the table's midpoint, the checkerboard design moved from table to floor level, so it appeared to the babies that if they crawled beyond that point, they would fall. Even when parents encouraged their children to venture beyond what appeared to be the drop-off, 8-month-old babies refused to move—showing that depth perception fully comes on-line, but only when infants begin to crawl.

While we might think this adorable 8-month-old child would be entranced by these paintings, her attention is apt to be riveted on the human (facial) scene.

fear bias The human tendency to be hypersensitive to fearful facial cues that, by alerting us to danger, may prevent us from getting injured or killed.

depth perception The ability to see (and fear) heights.

visual cliff A table that appears to "end" in a drop-off at its midpoint; used to test infant depth perception.

FIGURE 3.7: **The visual cliff** Even though his mother is on the other side, this 8-month-old child gets anxious about venturing beyond what looks like the drop-off point in the table—demonstrating that by this age babies have depth perception.

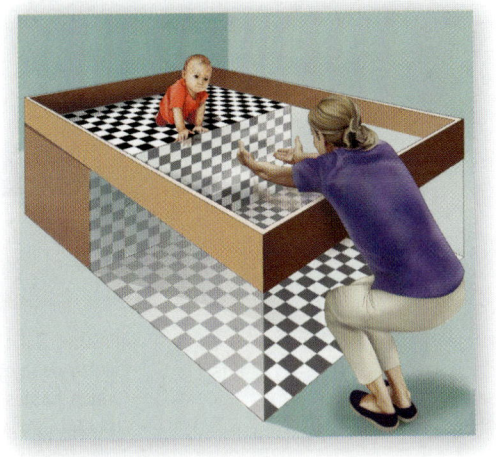

In sum, the sick feeling we have when leaning over a balcony—"Wow, I'd better avoid falling into that space below"—emerged when we started moving into the world and needed that fear to protect us from getting hurt. How does mobility unfold?

Expanding Body Size

Our brain may expand dramatically after birth. Still, it's outpaced by the blossoming of the envelope in which we live. Our bodies grow to 21 times their newborn size by the time we reach adulthood (Slater, 2001). This growth is most dramatic during infancy, slows down during childhood, and speeds up again during the preadolescent years. Still, looking at overall height and weight statistics is not that revealing. This body sculpting occurs in a definite way.

Imagine taking time-lapse photographs of a baby's head from birth to adulthood and comparing your photos to snapshots of the body. While you would not see much change in the size and shape of the head, the body would elongate and thin out. Newborns start out with tiny "frog" legs timed to slowly straighten out by about month 6. Then comes the stocky, bowlegged toddler, followed by the slimmer child of kindergarten and elementary school. So during childhood, growth follows the same principle as inside the womb: Development, as Figure 3.8 suggests, proceeds according to the *cephalocaudal sequence*—from the head to the feet.

Now think of Mickey Mouse, Big Bird, and Elmo. They, too, have relatively large heads and small bodies. Might our favorite cartoon characters be enticing because they mimic the proportions of a baby? Did the deliciously rounded infant shape evolve to seduce adults into giving babies special care?

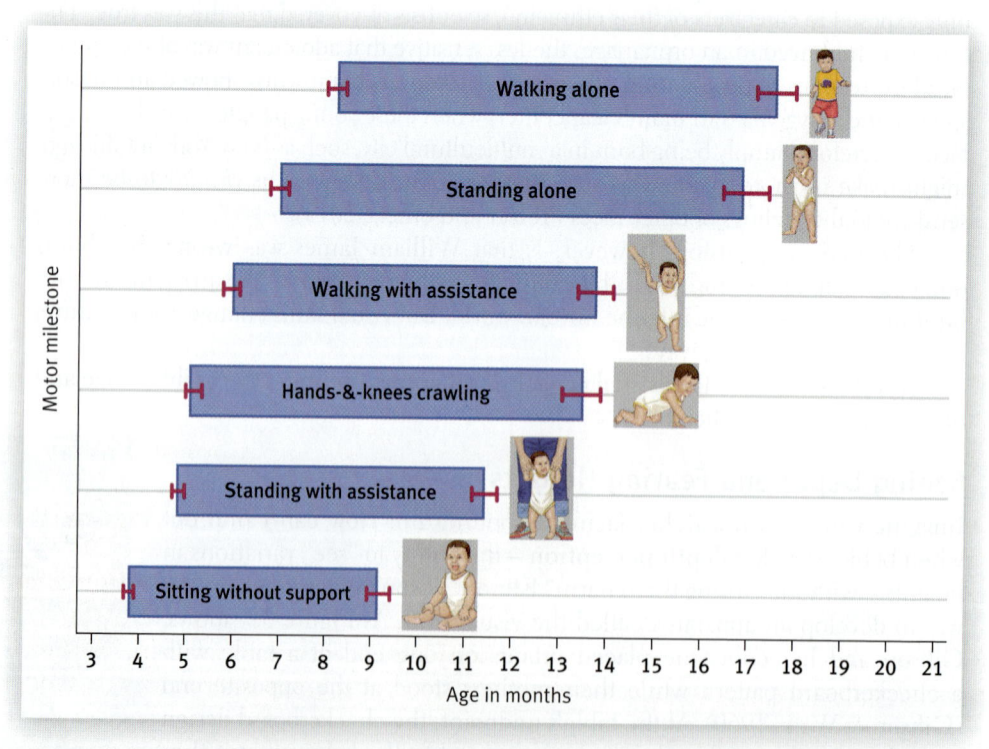

FIGURE 3.8: Approximate age ranges for reaching five motor milestones Notice how motor development follows the cephalocaudal principle, and the remarkable age gaps in the times at which babies *normally* reach each skill.
Data from World Health Organization, 2006.

Mastering Motor Milestones

Actually, all three growth principles spelled out in the previous chapter—*cephalocaudal, proximodistal,* and *mass-to-specific*—apply to infant *motor milestones*, the exciting progression of physical abilities during the first year of life. First, babies lift their head, then pivot their upper body, then sit up without support, and finally stand (the cephalocaudal sequence). Infants have control of their shoulders before they can make their arms and fingers obey their commands (proximodistal sequence, from interior to outer parts).

But the most important principle in programming motor abilities throughout childhood is the *mass-to-specific* sequence (large before small and detailed). From the wobbly first step at age 1 to the home run out of the ballpark during the teenage years—as the neurons myelinate—big, uncoordinated movements are honed and perfected as children grow.

At 8 or 10 months of age, getting around is a challenge that babies approach in creative, unique ways.

Variations (and Joys) Related to Infant Mobility

Charting these milestones does not speak to the joy of witnessing them unfold—that landmark moment when your daughter masters turning over, after those practice "push-ups," or first connects with the bottle, grasps it, and awkwardly moves it to her mouth. I'll never forget when my son, after what seemed like years of cruising around holding onto the furniture, finally ventured (so gingerly) out into the air, flung up his hands, and, *yes, yes,* took his ecstatic first step!

The charts don't mention the hilarious glitches that happen when a skill is emerging—the first days of "creeping," when a baby can only move backward and you find him huddled in the corner in pursuit of objects that get farther way. Or when a child first pulls herself to a standing position in the crib, and her triumphant expression changes to bewilderment: "Whoops, now tell me, Mom, *how do I get down?*"

Actually, rather than viewing motor development in static stages, researchers stress the variability and ingenuity of babies' passion to get moving into life (Adolph, 2008). Consider the creeping or belly-crawling stage. Some babies scoot; others hunch over or launch themselves forward from their knees, roll from side to side, or scrape along with a cheek on the floor (Adolph & Berger, 2006). And can I *really* say that there was a day when my son mastered walking? When walking, or any other major motor skill, first occurs, children do not make steady progress (Adolph & Berger, 2006). They may take their first solo step on Monday and then revert to crawling for a week or so before trying, oh so tentatively, to tackle toddling again.

But suppose a child is behind schedule. Let's say your son is almost 15 months old and has yet to take his first solo step. And what about the fantasies that set in when an infant is ahead? "Only 8 months old, and he's walking. Perhaps my baby is special—a genius!"

What typically happens is that, within weeks, the worries become a memory and the fantasies about the future are shown to be completely wrong. Except in the case of children who have developmental disorders, the rate at which babies master motor milestones has no relation to their later intelligence. Since different regions of the cortex develop at different times, why should our walking or grasping-an-object timetable predict development in a complex function such as grasping the point of this book?

But even if a baby's early locomotion (physically getting around) does not mean he will end up an Einstein, each motor achievement provokes other advances.

Motor Milestones Have Widespread Effects

Consider, for instance, that landmark event: reaching. Because it allows babies to physically make contact with the world, the urge to grasp objects propels sitting, as a child will tolerate plopping over in her hunger to touch everything she can (Harbourne and others, 2013).

Now consider how crawling changes the parent–child bond (Campos and others, 2000). When infants crawl, parents see their children as more independent—people with a mind of their own. Many say this is the first time they discipline their child. So as babies get mobile, our basic child-rearing agenda emerges: Children's mission is to explore the world. Adults' job, for the next two decades, lies in limiting exploration—as well as giving love.

INTERVENTIONS: Baby-Proofing, the First Person–Environment Fit

Motor development presents perils. Now safety issues become a concern. How can caretakers encourage these emerging skills and protect children from getting hurt? The answer is to strive for the right person–environment fit—that is, to **baby-proof** the house.

Get on the floor and look at life from the perspective of the child. Cover electrical outlets and put dangerous cleaning substances on the top shelf. Unplug countertop appliances. Take small objects off tables. Perhaps pad the furniture corners, too. The challenge is to anticipate possible dangers and stay one step ahead. There will come a day when that child can pry out those outlet covers or ascend to the top of the cleanser-laden cabinet. Unfortunately, those exciting motor milestones have a downside, too!

baby-proofing Making the home safe for a newly mobile infant.

Tying It All Together

1. Your 3-month-old perks up when you start the vacuum cleaner, and then after a moment, loses interest. You are using a kind of _____ paradigm; and the scientific term for when your baby loses interest is _____.
2. Tania says, "Visual capacities improve dramatically during the first year of life." Thomas replies, "No, in some ways our vision gets worse." Who is correct: Tania, Thomas, or both students? Why?
3. One implication of the face perception studies is that the roots of adult prejudice begin (choose one) *at birth/during the second 6 months of life/after age 2*.
4. If Alicia's 8-month-old daughter is participating in a visual cliff study, when she approaches the drop-off, she should (choose one): *crawl over it/be frightened*.
5. What steps would you take to baby-proof the room you are sitting in right now?

Answers to the Tying It All Together questions can be found at the end of this chapter.

LEARNING OUTCOMES
- Describe the purpose of Piaget's sensorimotor stage.
- Outline the development of objective permanence.
- List two critiques of Piaget's theory.
- Explain some findings relating to social cognition.

Cognition

Why *do* infants have an incredible hunger to explore, to reach, to touch, to get into every cleanser-laden cabinet and remove outlet plugs? For the same reason that, if you landed on a different planet, you would need to get the basics of reality down.

Imagine stepping out onto Mars. You would roam the new environment, exploring the rocks and the sand. While exercising your *walking schema*, or habitual way of physically navigating, you would need to make drastic changes. On Mars, with its minimal gravity, when you took your normal earthling stride, you would probably bounce up 20 feet. Just like a newly crawling infant, you would have to accommodate, and in the process reach a higher mental equilibrium, or a better understanding of

Table 3.6: Piaget's Stages: Focus on Infancy

Age (years)	Name of Stage	Description
0–2	Sensorimotor	The baby manipulates objects to pin down the basics of physical reality. This stage ends with the development of language.
2–7	Preoperations	Children's perceptions are captured by their immediate appearances. "What they see is what is real." They believe, among other things, that inanimate objects are really alive and that if a liquid looks visually different (for example, if it is poured from a short, wide glass into a tall, thin one), the amount actually becomes different.
8–12	Concrete operations	Children have a realistic understanding of the world. Their thinking is on the same wavelength as that of adults. While they can reason conceptually about concrete objects, however, they cannot think abstractly in a scientific way.
12+	Formal operations	Reasoning is at its pinnacle: hypothetical, scientific, flexible, fully adult. Children's full cognitive potential is reached.

life. Moreover, as a scientist, you would not be satisfied to perform each movement only once. The way to pin down the physics of this planet would be to repeat each action over and over again. Now you have the basic principles of Jean Piaget's **sensorimotor stage** (see Table 3.6).

Piaget's Sensorimotor Stage

Specifically, Piaget believed that during our first two years on this planet, our mission is to make sense of physical reality by exploring the world through our senses. Just as in the earlier Mars example, as infants *assimilate*, or fit the outer world to what they are capable of doing, they *accommodate* and so gradually mentally advance.

Let's take the "everything into the mouth" schema that figures so prominently during the first year of life. As babies mouth each new object—or, in Piaget's words, assimilate everything to their mouthing schema—they realize that objects have different characteristics. Some are soft or prickly. Others taste terrible or great. Through continual assimilation and accommodation, by age 2, babies make a dramatic mental leap—from relying on reflexes to reasoning and using symbolic thought.

Circular Reactions: Habits That Pin Down Reality

By observing his own children, Piaget discovered that driving all these advances were what he called **circular reactions**—habits, or action-oriented schemas, the child repeats again and again.

From the newborn reflexes, during months 1 to 4, **primary circular reactions** develop. These are repetitive actions centered on the child's body. A thumb randomly makes contact with his mouth, and a 2-month-old removes that interesting object, observes it, and moves it in and out. Waving her legs captivates a 3-month-old for hours.

At approximately 4 months of age, **secondary circular reactions** appear. As the cortex blossoms and the child begins to reach, action-oriented schemas become centered on the *outside* world. Here is how Piaget described his daughter Lucienne's first secondary circular reactions:

> Lucienne at 0:4 [4 months] is lying in her bassinet. I hang a doll over her feet which . . . sets in motion the schema of shakes. Her feet reach the doll . . . and give it a violent movement which Lucienne surveys with delight. . . . After the first shakes, Lucienne makes slow foot movements as though to grasp and explore. . . . When she tries to kick the doll, and misses . . . she begins again very slowly until she succeeds [without looking at her feet].
> (Piaget, 1950, p. 159 [as cited in Flavell, 1963, p. 103])

sensorimotor stage Piaget's first stage of cognitive development, lasting from birth to age 2, when babies' agenda is to pin down the basics of physical reality.

circular reactions In Piaget's framework, repetitive action-oriented schemas (or habits) characteristic of babies during the sensorimotor stage.

primary circular reactions In Piaget's framework, the first infant habits during the sensorimotor stage, centered on the body.

secondary circular reactions In Piaget's framework, habits of the sensorimotor stage lasting from about 4 months of age to the baby's first birthday, centered on exploring the external world.

During the next few months, secondary circular reactions become better coordinated. By about 8 months of age, babies can simultaneously employ two circular reactions, using both grasping and kicking together to explore the world.

Then, around a baby's first birthday, **tertiary circular reactions** appear. Now, the child is not constrained by stereotyped schemas. He can operate like a real scientist, flexibly changing his behavior to make sense of the world. A toddler becomes captivated by the toilet, throwing toys and different types of paper into the bowl. At dinner, he gleefully spits his food out at varying velocities and hurls his bottle off the high chair in different directions to see where it lands.

How important are circular reactions in infancy? Spend time with a young baby, as she bats at her mobile or joyously pinwheels her legs. Try to prevent a 1-year-old from hurling plates from a high chair, flushing money down the toilet, or inserting bits of cookie into a USB slot. Then you will understand: Infancy is all about the insatiable drive to repeat interesting acts. (See Table 3.7 for a recap of the circular reactions, as well as a look at the sensorimotor substages.)

Piaget's concept of circular reactions offers a new perspective on those obsessions that drive adults crazy during what researchers call the **little-scientist phase** (and parents call the "getting into everything" phase). This is the time, around age 1, when the child begins experimenting with objects in a way that mimics how a scientist behaves: "Let me try this, then that, and see what happens." The reason you can't derail a 1-year-old from putting oatmeal into the computer, or

tertiary circular reactions In Piaget's framework, "little-scientist" activities of the sensorimotor stage, beginning around age 1, involving flexibly exploring the properties of objects.

little-scientist phase The time around age 1 when babies use tertiary circular reactions to actively explore the properties of objects, experimenting with them like scientists.

Table 3.7: The Circular Reactions: A Summary Table (with a Look at Piaget's Sensorimotor Substages)

PRIMARY CIRCULAR REACTIONS: 1–4 MONTHS

Description: Repetitive habits center around the child's own body.

Examples: Sucking toes; sucking thumb.

SECONDARY CIRCULAR REACTIONS: 4 MONTHS–1 YEAR

Description: Child "wakes up to wider world." Habits center on environmental objects.

Examples: Grabbing for toys; batting mobiles; pushing one's body to activate the lights and sounds on a swing.

Substages: From 4 to 8 months, children use single secondary circular reactions such as those above; from 8 to 12 months, they employ two circular reactions in concert to attain a goal (that is, they may grab a toy in each hand, bat a mobile back and forth, coordinate the motions of toys).

TERTIARY CIRCULAR REACTIONS: 1–2 YEARS

Description: Child flexibly explores the properties of objects, like a "little scientist."

Examples: Exploring the various dimensions of a toy; throwing a bottle off the high chair in different directions; putting different kinds of food in the computer; flushing dollars down the toilet.

Substages: From 12 to 18 months, the child experiments with concrete objects; from 18 to 24 months, his little-scientist behavior transcends what is observable and involves using symbols to stand for something else. (I'll be describing the many advances ushered in by this ability to reason symbolically in later chapters.)

clogging the toilet with your hard-earned wages (making a plumber a parent's new best friend) is that circular reactions allow infants to pin down the basic properties of the world.

Why do *specific* circular reactions, such as flushing dollar bills down the toilet, become irresistible during the little-scientist phase? This question brings me to Piaget's ideas about how babies progress from reflexes to the ability to think.

Tracking Early Thinking

How do we know when infants think? According to Piaget, one hallmark of thinking is deferred imitation—repeating an action that the baby witnessed at an earlier time. When Piaget saw Lucienne, at 16 months of age, mimic a tantrum she had seen another child have days earlier, he realized she had the mental skills to keep that image in her mind, mull it over, and translate it into action on her own. Another sign of reasoning is make-believe play. To pretend you are cleaning the house or talking on the phone like Mommy, babies must realize that something *signifies*, or stands for, something else.

But the most important sign of emerging reasoning is **means–end behavior**— when the child is able to perform a separate, or different, action to get to a goal. Pushing the toilet lever to make the water swirl down, manipulating a switch to turn on the light, screwing open a bottle to extract the juice—all are examples of "doing something different" to reach a particular end.

If you have access to a 1-year-old, you might try to construct your own means–end task. First, show the child something she wants, such as a cookie or a toy. Then, put the object in a place where the baby must perform a different action to get the treat. For instance, you might put the cookie in a clear container and cover the top with Saran Wrap. Will the baby ineffectively bang the side of the container, or will she figure out the *different* step (removing the cover) essential to retrieving what she wants? If you conduct your test by putting the cookie in an opaque container, the baby must have another basic understanding: She must realize that—although she doesn't see it—the cookie still exists.

Object Permanence: Believing in a Stable World

Object permanence refers to knowing that objects exist when we no longer see them—a perception that is, obviously, fundamental to our sense of living in a stable world. Suppose you felt that this book disappeared when you averted your eyes or that your house rematerialized out of nothing when you entered your driveway. Piaget believed that object permanence is not inborn. This perception develops gradually throughout the sensorimotor stage.

Piaget's observations suggested that during early infancy, life is a series of disappearing pictures. If an enticing image, such as her mother, passed her line of sight, Lucienne would stare at the place from which the image had vanished as if it would reappear out of thin air. (The relevant phrase here is "out of sight, out of mind.") Then, around month 5, when the *secondary circular reactions* are first flowering, there was a milestone. An object dropped out of sight and Lucienne leaned over to look for it, suggesting that she knew it existed independently of her gaze. Still, this sense of a stable object was fragile. The baby quickly abandoned her search after Piaget covered that object with his hand.

Hunting for objects under covers becomes an absorbing game as children approach age 1. Still, around 9 or 10 months of age, children make a surprising mistake called the **A-not-B error**: Put an object in full view of a baby into one out-of-sight

> **means–end behavior** In Piaget's framework, performing a different action to get to a goal— an ability that emerges in the sensorimotor stage as babies approach age 1.
>
> **object permanence** In Piaget's framework, the understanding that objects continue to exist even when we can no longer see them, which gradually emerges during the sensorimotor stage.
>
> **A-not-B error** In Piaget's framework, a classic mistake made by infants in the sensorimotor stage, whereby babies approaching age 1 go back to the original hiding place to look for an object even though they have seen it get hidden in a second place.

A minute ago, this 4-month-old girl was delightedly grabbing this little dog, but when this barrier blocked her vision, it was "out of sight, out of mind." If you have access to a young baby, can you perform this test to track the beginning of object permanence?

location, have the baby get it, and then move it to another place while the child is watching, and she will look for it in the initial place!

See if you can perform this classic test if you have access to a 10-month-old: Place an object, such as a toy, under a piece of paper (A). Then have the baby find it in that place a few times. Next, remove the toy as the infant watches and put it under a *different* piece of paper (B). What happens? Even though the child saw you put the toy in the new location, he will probably look under the A paper again, as if it had migrated unseen to its original place!

By their first birthday, children seem to master the basic principle. Move an object to a new hiding place and they look for it in the correct location. However, as Piaget found when he used this strategy but *covered* the object with his hand, object permanence does not fully emerge until children are almost 2 years old.

Emerging object permanence explains many puzzles about development. Why does peek-a-boo become a favorite activity at around 8 months? The reason is that a child now thinks there is *probably* still someone behind those hands, but doesn't know for sure.

Emerging object permanence offers a wonderful perspective on why younger babies are so laid back when you remove an interesting object, but then become possessive by their second year of life. Those toddler tantrums do not signal a new, awful personality trait called "the terrible twos." They simply show that children are smarter. They now have the cognitive skills to know that objects still exist when you take them away.

Finally, the concept of object permanence, or fascination with disappearing objects, plus means–end behavior makes sense of a 1-year-old's passion to flush dollar bills down the toilet or the compulsion to stick bits of cookie in a USB port. What could be more tantalizing during the little-scientist phase than taking a new action to get to a goal and causing things to disappear and possibly reappear? It also explains why you can't go wrong if you buy your toddler nephew a pop-up toy.

But during the first year of life, there is no need to arrive with any toy. Buy a toy for an infant and he will push it aside to play with the box. Your niece probably prefers fiddling with the TV remote to any object from Toys R Us. Toys only become interesting once we realize that they are different from real life. So a desire for dolls or action figures—or for anything that requires make-believe play—shows that a child is making the transition from the sensorimotor period to symbolic thought. With the concepts of circular reactions, emerging object permanence, and means–end behavior, Piaget masterfully made sense of the puzzling passions of infant life!

Critiquing Piaget

Piaget's insights transformed the way psychologists think about childhood. Research confirms the fact that children are, at heart, little scientists. The passion to decode the world is built into being human from our first months of life (Gopnik, 2010). However, Piaget's timing was seriously off. Piaget's trouble was that he had to rely on babies' actions (for instance, taking covers off hidden objects) to figure out what they knew. He did not have creative strategies, like preferential looking and habituation, to decode what babies understand before they can physically respond. Using these techniques, researchers realized that young infants know far more about life than this master theorist ever believed (Baillargeon, Scott, & Bian, 2016). Specifically, scientists now understand that:

- **Infants grasp the basics of physical reality well before age 1.** To demonstrate this point, developmentalist Renée Baillargeon (1993) presented young babies with physically impossible events, such as showing a traveling rabbit puppet that never appeared in a gap it had to pass through to reach its place on the other side (illustrated in Figure 3.9A). Even 5-month-olds looked astonished when they saw these impossible events. You could almost hear them thinking, "I know that's not the way objects should behave."

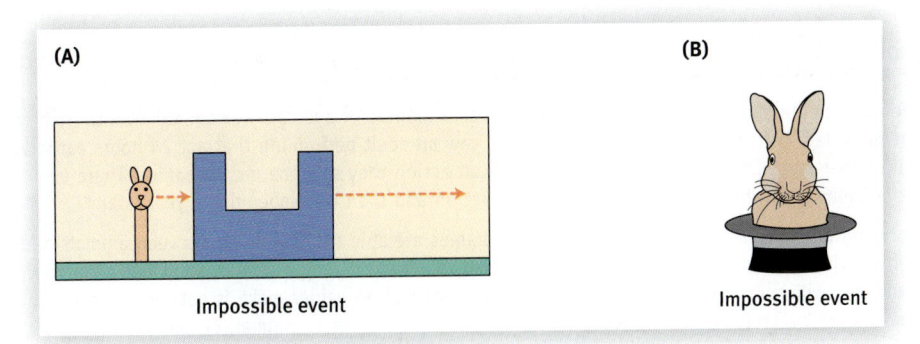

FIGURE 3.9: Two impossible events At about 5 months of age, babies were surprised by the physically impossible sequence in part A—but they did not look surprised by the event in part B until about age 1. The bottom line: Infants understand the physical world far earlier than Piaget believed, but this knowledge occurs gradually.
Information from Baillargeon, 1993; Baillargeon & DeVos, 1991; Baillargeon & Graber, 1987.

- **Infants' understanding of physical reality develops gradually.** For instance, while Baillargeon discovered that the impossible event of the traveling rabbit in the figure provoked astonishment around month 5, other research shows it takes until age 1 for babies to master fundamental realities, such as the fact that you cannot take a large rabbit out of a little container (shown in Figure 3.9B). (As an aside, that explains why "magic" suddenly becomes interesting around age 2 or 3.) Therefore, rather than viewing development in huge qualitative stages, contemporary researchers decode step by step how cognition *gradually* emerges.

Information-processing researchers use the metaphor of a computer with separate processing steps to decode children's (and adults') intellectual skills. For instance, instead of seeing means–end behavior as a capacity that suddenly emerges at age 1, a psychologist using this approach would isolate the talents involved in this milestone—memory, attention, the ability to inhibit one's immediate perceptions—and chart how each skill develops over time.

Table 3.8 on the next page showcases insights about babies' memories and mathematical capacities, derived from using this gradual, specific approach. In Chapter 6, I will describe how information-processing perspectives shed light on memory and thinking during elementary school. Now, it's time to tackle another question: What do babies understand about human minds?

> **information-processing approach** A perspective on understanding cognition that divides thinking into specific steps and component processes, much like a computer.
>
> **social cognition** Any skill related to understanding feelings and negotiating interpersonal interactions.

For this 1-year-old, pushing the buttons on the TV remote is utterly captivating. Information-processing researchers want to understand what specific skills made this boy capable of achieving this miraculous means–end feat.

Tackling the Core of What Makes Us Human: Infant Social Cognition

Social cognition refers to any skill related to managing and decoding people's emotions, and getting along with other human beings. One hallmark of being human is that we are always making inferences about people's feelings and goals, based on their actions. ("He's running, so he must be late"; "She slammed the door in my face, so she must be angry.") When do these judgments first occur? Piaget would say not before age 2 (or much later) because infants in the sensorimotor period can't think conceptually. Here, too, Piaget was incorrect. Babies make sophisticated judgments about intentions at an incredibly young age (Baillargeon, Scott, & Bian, 2016).

Table 3.8: Infant Memory and Conceptual Abilities: Some Interesting Findings

Memory: Researchers find that babies as young as 9 months of age can "remember" events from the previous day. Infants will push a button if they saw an adult performing that act 24 hours earlier. In another study, most 10-month-olds imitated an action they saw one month earlier. There even have been cases where babies this age saw an action and then remembered it a *year* later.*

Forming categories: By 7 to 9 months of age, babies are able to distinguish between animals and vehicles. They will feed an animal or put it to bed, but even if they watch an adult put a car to bed, they will not model her action. So the first classification babies make is between something that moves by itself or cannot move on its own. (Is it alive, like an animal, or inanimate?) Then, categorization abilities get more refined depending on familiarity. For example, 11-month-old infants can often distinguish between dogs and cats but not among dogs, rabbits, and fish.

Understanding numbers: By about 5 months of age, infants can make differentiations between different numbers—for instance, after seeing three dots on a screen, they will look preferentially at a subsequent screen showing four dots. Infants also have an implicit understanding of addition and subtraction. If they see someone add one doll to another, or take away a doll from a set, they look surprised when they see an image on a screen showing the incorrect number of dolls.

Information from Mandler, 2007.
*Because memory is central to cognition, a preverbal baby's skill in this area predicts the rapidity of language development and scores on intelligence tests.

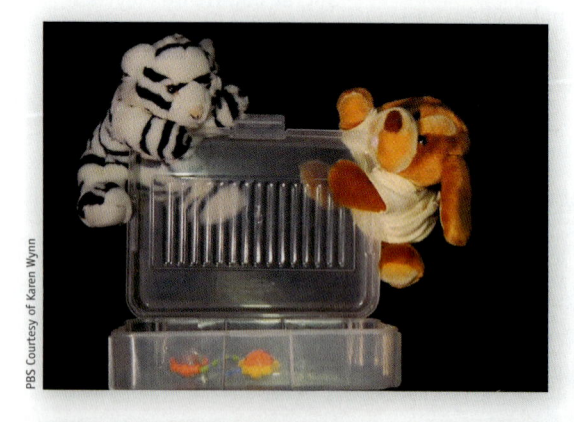

After seeing this video sequence of events, even infants under 6 months of age preferentially reached for the "nice" tiger rather than the "mean" dog—showing that the fundamental human *social-cognitive* awareness that "he's acting mean or nice" emerges at a remarkably young age.

In one classic example, researchers first showed infants a video of a puppet or stuffed animal helping another puppet complete a challenging task (the nice puppet). In the next scene, another puppet hindered the stuffed animal from reaching his goal (the mean puppet). Then the experimenter offered the baby both puppets. And guess what? By the time they could reach (at about month 5), most infants grasped the "nice" stuffed animal rather than the puppet that acted "mean" (Hamlin & Wynn, 2011; Hamlin, 2013b).

This remarkable finding suggests we clue into motivations such as "She's not nice!" months before we begin to speak (Hamlin, 2013b). More astonishing, 8-month-old babies can make adult-like judgments about intentions. They preferentially reach for a stuffed animal that tries to help a puppet but fails. Here the reasoning may be: "He is a good guy. Even though he didn't succeed, he tried" (Hamlin, 2013a). Notice that these infants have intuitively mastered modern legal concepts we use in assessing criminal intent. Our system must determine: Was this an accident or did he mean it? He should only be punished if he *meant* to do harm.

But I cannot leave you with the sense that our species is primed to be mini-biblical King Solomons, behaving in a wise, ethical way. Some not-so-appealing human tendencies also erupt before age 1.

Using a similar procedure, the same research group found that 8-month-olds reach for a puppet they previously viewed hindering (acting mean) to another puppet if they view that puppet as different from themselves (Hamlin, 2013b; Hamlin and others, 2013). The principle here seems to be: "The enemy of my enemy is my friend." Or put more graphically: "I *like* people who are mean to people who are different than me." (In the next chapter, you will learn that a fear of anyone different—meaning, not a baby's primary caregiver—kicks in at exactly 8 months of age!)

In sum, during their second six months on this planet, babies can decode intentions—inferring underlying motivations from the way people behave. This mind-reading talent paves the way for that related human milestone: language, communicating our thoughts through words.

Tying It All Together

1. You are working at a child-care center, and you notice Darien repeatedly opening and closing a cabinet door. Then Jai comes over and pulls open the door. You decide to latch it. Jai—undeterred—pulls on the door and, when it doesn't open, begins jiggling the latch. And then he looks up, very pleased, as he manages to figure out how to open the latch. Finally, you give up and decide to play a game with Sam. You hide a stuffed bear in a toy box while Sam watches. Then Sam throws open the lid of the box and scoops out the bear. Link the appropriate Piagetian term to each child's behavior: *circular reaction; object permanence; means–end behavior.*

2. Jose, while an avid Piaget fan, has to admit that in important ways, this master theorist was wrong. Jose can legitimately make which two criticisms? (1) Cognition develops gradually, not in stages; (2) Infants understand human motivations; (3) Babies understand the basic properties of objects at birth.

3. Baby Sara watches her big brother hit the dog. Based on the research in this section, Sara might first understand her brother is being "mean" (choose one) *months before/at/months after age 1.*

Answers to the Tying It All Together questions can be found at the end of this chapter.

Language: The Endpoint of Infancy

Piaget believed that language signals the end of the sensorimotor period because this ability requires understanding that a symbol stands for something else. True, in order to master language, you must grasp the idea that the abstract word-symbol *textbook* refers to what you are reading now. But the miracle of language is that we string together words in novel, understandable ways. What causes us to master this feat, and how does language evolve?

LEARNING OUTCOMES
- Define the language acquisition device (LAD).
- List the stages of language development.
- Describe the function and features of infant directed speech (IDS).

Nature, Nurture, and the Passion to Learn Language

The essential property of language is elasticity. How can I come up with this new sentence, and why can you understand its meaning, although you have never seen it before? Why does every language have a **grammar**, with nouns, verbs, and rules for organizing words into sentences? According to the linguist Noam Chomsky, the reason is that humans are biologically programmed to make "language," via what he labeled the **language acquisition device (LAD).**

Chomsky developed his nature-oriented concept of a uniquely human LAD in reaction to the behaviorist B. F. Skinner's nurture-oriented proposition that we learn to speak through being reinforced for producing specific words (for instance, Skinner argued that we learn to say "I want cookie" by being rewarded for producing those sounds by getting that treat). This pronouncement was another example of the traditional behaviorist principle that "all actions are driven by reinforcement" run amok (see Chapter 1). It defies common sense to suggest that we can generate billions of new sentences by having people reinforce us for every word!

Still, Skinner is correct in one respect. I speak English instead of Mandarin Chinese because I grew up in New York City, not Beijing. So the way our genetic program for making language gets expressed depends on our environment. Again, nature plus nurture work together to explain every activity of life.

Currently, developmentalists adopt a **social-interactionist perspective** on this core skill. They focus on the motivations that propel language (Hoff-Ginsberg, 1997). Babies are passionate to communicate. Adults are passionate to help babies learn to talk. How does the infant passion to communicate evolve?

grammar The rules and word-arranging systems that every human language employs to communicate meaning.

language acquisition device (LAD) Chomsky's term for a hypothetical brain structure that enables our species to learn and produce language.

social-interactionist perspective An approach to language development that emphasizes its social function, specifically that babies and adults have a mutual passion to communicate.

Table 3.9: Language Milestones from Birth to Age 2*

Age	Language Characteristic
2–4 months	*Cooing:* First sounds growing out of reflexes Example: "ooooh"
5–11 months	*Babbling:* Alternate vowel–consonant sounds Examples: "ba-ba-ba," "da-da-da"
12 months	*Holophrases:* First one-word sentences Example: "ja" ("I want juice.")
18 months–2 years	*Telegraphic speech:* Two-word combinations, often accompanied by an explosion in vocabulary Example: "Me juice"

*Babies vary a good deal in the ages at which they begin to combine words.

Tracking Emerging Language

The pathway to producing language occurs in stages. Out of the reflexive crying of the newborn period comes *cooing* ("oooh" sounds) at about month 4. At around month 6, delightful vocal circular reactions called **babbling** emerge. Babbles are alternating consonant and vowel sounds, such as "da da da," that infants playfully repeat with variations of intonation and pitch.

The first word emerges out of the babble at around 11 months, although that exact landmark is difficult to define. There is little more reinforcing to paternal pride than when your 8-month-old genius repeats your name. But when does "da da da" really refer to Dad? In the first, **holophrase** stage of true speech, one word, accompanied by gestures, says it all. When your son says "ja" and points to the kitchen, you know he wants juice . . . or was it a jelly sandwich, or was he referring to his sister Jane?

Children accumulate their first 50 or so words, centering on the important items in their world (people, toys, and food), slowly (Nelson, 1974). Then, typically between ages 1½ and 2, there is a vocabulary explosion as the child begins to combine words. Because children pare down communication to its essentials, just like an old-style telegram ("Me juice"; "Mommy, no"), this first word-combining stage is called **telegraphic speech.** Table 3.9 summarizes these language landmarks and offers examples and the approximate time each milestone occurs.

Just as with the other infant achievements described in this chapter, developmentalists are passionate to trace language to its roots. It turns out that newborns are pre-wired to gravitate to the sounds of living things—as they suck longer when reinforced by hearing monkey and/or human vocalizations (versus pure tones). By 3 months of age, preferences get more selective. Now babies perk up *only* when they hear human speech (Vouloumanos and others, 2010).

By 8 months of age (notice the similarity to the visual-system atrophy research described earlier in this chapter), infants—like adults—lose their ability to hear sound tones in languages not their own (Gervain & Mehler, 2010). Simultaneously, a remarkable sharpening occurs. When language starts to explode, toddlers can hear the difference between similar sounds like "bih" and "dih" and link them to objects after *hearing this connection just once!*

Caregivers promote these achievements by continually talking to babies. Around the world, they train infants in language by using *infant-directed speech.* **Infant-directed speech (IDS)** (what you and I call *baby talk*) uses simple words, exaggerated tones, elongated vowels, and has a higher pitch than we use in speaking to adults (Hoff-Ginsberg, 1997). Although IDS sounds ridiculous ("Mooommy taaaaking baaaaby ooooout!" "Moommy looooves baaaaby!"), infants perk up when they hear this conversational style (Santesso, Schmidt, & Trainor, 2007). So we naturally use infant-directed speech with babies, just as we are compelled to pick up and rock a

---

babbling The alternating vowel and consonant sounds that babies repeat with variations of intonation and pitch and that precede the first words.

holophrase First clear evidence of language, when babies use a single word to communicate a sentence or complete thought.

telegraphic speech First stage of combining words in which a toddler pares down a sentence to its essential words.

infant-directed speech (IDS) The simplified, exaggerated, high-pitched tones that adults and children use to speak to infants that function to help teach language.

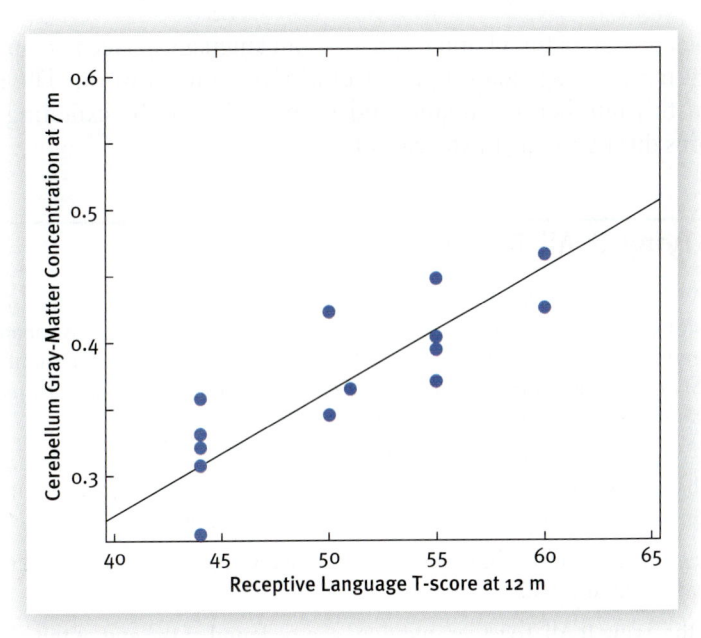

FIGURE 3.10: The relationship between gray matter (synaptogenesis) concentration in the cerebellum at 7 months of age and language comprehension at a child's first birthday This chart shows a close correlation between the quantity, or amount, of synaptogenesis in this particular brain region and a child's ability to understand language at age 1. The surprise is that this part of the brain—the cerebellum—does not qualify as a "higher brain center," as it programs balance and coordination.
Data from Deniz Can, Richards, & Kuhl, 2013.

child when she cries. Does IDS really help promote emerging language? The answer is yes.

Babies identify individual words better when they are uttered in exaggerated IDS tones (Thiessen, Hill, & Saffran, 2005). When adults are learning a new language, they benefit from the slow, repetitive IDS style. Therefore, rather than being just for babies, IDS is a strategy that teaches language across the board (Ratner, 2013). In fact, notice that when you are teaching a person *any* new skill you, too, are apt to automatically use IDS.

The close link between brain development at 7 months of age and children's speech understanding at age 1, shown in Figure 3.10, suggests that the neurological roots of language appear months before this capacity emerges (Deniz Can, Richards, & Kuhl, 2013; see also Dean and others, 2014). One surprising, observable sign of soon-to-emerge language is pointing with the right hand. Babies who demonstrate this pointing preference at an early age (let's say around 10 months of age) have larger later vocabularies because right-hand pointing is a general tip-off showing that the left-brain language centers are coming on-line (Mumford & Kita, 2016).

But even though our unique language timetable is genetically programmed (meaning due to biological differences), parents who use more IDS communications have babies who speak at a younger age (Ratner, 2013).

IDS is different from other talk. You don't hear this speech style on TV, at the dinner table, or on videos designed to produce 8-month-old Einsteins. IDS kicks in *only* when we communicate with babies one on one. So, if parents are passionate to accelerate language, investing millions in learning tools seems a distant second best to spending time *talking* to a child (Ratner, 2013).

Consistently pointing with her right hand points to the fact that this adorable 8-month-old may have a world-class vocabulary at age 2 or 3.

A basic message of this chapter is that—from language to face perception to social cognition—our main agenda is to connect with the human world. The next chapter focuses on this number-one infant (and human) agenda by exploring attachment relationships during the first two years of life.

Tying It All Together

1. (a) "We learn to speak by getting reinforced for saying what we want." (b) "We are biologically programmed to learn language." (c) "Babies are passionate to communicate." Identify the theoretical perspective reflected in statements (a), (b), and (c): *Skinner's operant conditioning perspective; Chomsky's language acquisition device; a social-interactionist perspective on language.*

2. Baby Ginny is 4 months old; baby Jamal is about 7 months old; baby Sam is 1 year old; baby David is 2 years old. Identify each child's probable language stage by choosing from the following items: *babbling; cooing; telegraphic speech; holophrases.*

3. A friend makes fun of adults who use baby talk. Given the information in this section, is her teasing justified?

Answers to the Tying It All Together questions can be found at the end of this chapter.

SUMMARY

Setting the Context

Because our large **cerebral cortex** develops mainly after birth, during the first two years of life, the brain mushrooms. **Axons** elongate and develop a fatty cover called myelin. **Dendrites** sprout branches and at **synapses** link up with other cells. **Synaptogenesis** and **myelination** program every ability and human skill. Although the brain matures for decades, we do not simply "develop more synapses." Each region undergoes rapid synaptogenesis, followed by pruning (or cutting back). Before pruning, the brain is particularly **plastic**, allowing us to compensate for early brain insults—but synaptogenesis and learning occur throughout life.

Basic Newborn States

Eating patterns undergo dramatic changes during infancy. We emerge from the womb with **sucking** and **rooting reflexes**, which jump-start eating, as well as other **reflexes**, which disappear after the early months of life. Although the "everything into the mouth" phase of infancy can make life scary for caregivers, a 2-year-old's food caution can protect toddlers from poisoning themselves.

Breast-feeding is vital to survival in regions of the world without clean water and food. Although the link between nursing and infant health in developed nations can often be explained by confounding forces, such as greater maternal commitment and high social class, every public health organization advocates exclusive breast-feeding for the first 6 months of life. Most women, however, don't follow this advice. Breast-feeding is difficult when women need to work full-time or find nursing physically painful. The benchmark of being a good mother is unrelated to offering the breast; it's providing love.

Undernutrition, in particular **stunting** and **micronutrient deficiencies,** affect a significant fraction of young children in impoverished areas of the world. Although families with children in the United States may suffer from **food insecurity,** stunting is rare in the United States, thanks to government entitlement programs.

Crying is at its height during early infancy, and declines around month 4 as the cortex develops. **Colic,** excessive crying that disappears after early infancy, is basically a biological problem. Strategies for quieting babies include rocking, **skin-to-skin** contact, and massage. **Kangaroo care** helps at-risk premature babies grow.

Sleep is the basic newborn state, and from the 14-hour, waking-every-few hours newborn pattern, babies gradually adjust to sleeping through the night. **REM sleep** lessens and shifts to the end of the cycle. Babies, however, really do not ever sleep through the night. At about 6 months, many learn **self-soothing,** the ability to put themselves back to sleep when they wake up. The decision about whether to "let a baby cry it out" or respond immediately at night is personal, because the best way to foster sleep is to provide a caring bedtime routine. **Co-sleeping**—the norm in collectivist cultures—is controversial; and U.S. parents today typically room share, rather than share a bed.

Sudden infant death syndrome (SIDS)—when a young baby stops breathing, often at night, and dies—is a main cause of developed-world infant mortality. Although SIDS may be caused by impairments in the developing fetal brain, it tends to occur most often when babies sleep facedown. Therefore, a late-twentieth-century SIDS campaign urging parents to put babies to sleep on their backs (not stomachs) has been effective, although delivering this message is difficult in cultures that prize co-sleeping.

Sensory and Motor Development

The **preferential-looking paradigm** (exploring what objects babies look at) and **habituation** (the fact that we get less interested in looking at objects that are no longer "new") are used to determine what very young babies can see. Although at birth visual acuity is poor, it improves very rapidly. **Face-perception studies** show that newborns look at facelike stimuli, recognize their mothers, and even prefer good-looking people from the first weeks of life. At the same time as infants get more adept at reading facial cues and develop a **fear bias**, neural pruning causes babies to become less able to see facial variations in people of other races and ethnic groups. Sadly, this loss of sensitivity may promote prejudice against people outside of our ethnic group. **Depth perception** studies using the **visual cliff** show that babies get frightened of heights around the time they begin to crawl.

Infants' bodies lengthen and thin out as they grow. The cephalocaudal, proximodistal, and mass-to-specific principles apply to how the body changes and to emerging infant motor milestones. Although they do progress through stages when getting to walking, babies show incredible creativity and variability when they first attain various skills. Earlier-than-normal motor development does not predict advanced cognition; but as babies get more mobile, parents need to discipline their children and **baby-proof** their home.

Cognition

During Piaget's **sensorimotor stage,** babies master the basics of physical reality through their senses and begin to symbolize and think. **Circular reactions** (habits the baby repeats) help babies pin down the basics of the physical world. **Primary circular reactions**—body-centered habits, such as sucking one's toes—emerge first. **Secondary circular reactions,** habits centered on making interesting external stimuli last (for example, batting mobiles), begin around month 4. **Tertiary circular reactions,** also called **"little-scientist"** activities—like spitting food at different velocities just to see where the oatmeal lands—are the hallmark of the toddler years. A major advance in reasoning that occurs around age 1 is **means–end behavior**—understanding the need to do something different to achieve a goal.

Piaget's most compelling concept is **object permanence**—knowing that objects exist when you no longer see them. According to Piaget, this understanding develops gradually during the first years of life. When this knowledge is developing, infants make the **A-not-B error,** looking for an object in the place where they first found it, even if it has been hidden in another location before their eyes.

Using preferential looking, and watching babies' expressions of surprise at impossible events, researchers now know that babies understand physical reality far earlier than Piaget believed. Because Piaget's stage model also does not fit the gradual way cognition unfolds, contemporary developmentalists may adopt an **information-processing approach,** breaking thinking into separate components and steps. Scientists studying **social cognition** find that babies understand people's motivations (and prefer people, based on judging their inner intentions) remarkably early in life.

Language: The Endpoint of Infancy

Language, specifically our use of **grammar** and our ability to form infinitely different sentences, sets us apart from any other animal. Although B. F. Skinner believed that we learn to speak through being reinforced, the more logical explanation is Chomsky's idea that we have a biologically built-in **language acquisition device (LAD). Social-interactionists** focus on the mutual passion of babies and adults to communicate.

First, babies coo, then **babble**, then use one-word **holophrases,** and finally, at age 1½ or 2, progress to two-word combinations called **telegraphic speech.** Caregivers naturally use **infant-directed speech** (IDS; exaggerated intonations and simpler phrases) when they talk to babies. Talking to babies in **IDS** is better than any baby-genius tape in promoting this vital human skill.

KEY TERMS

A-not-B error, p. 93
axon, p. 72
babbling, p. 98
baby-proofing, p. 90
cerebral cortex, p. 72
circular reactions, p. 91
colic, p. 79
co-sleeping, p. 83
dendrite, p. 72
depth perception, p. 87
face-perception studies, p. 86
fear bias, p. 87
food insecurity, p. 78
grammar, p. 97
habituation, p. 86
holophrase, p. 98
infant-directed speech (IDS), p. 98
information-processing approach, p. 95
kangaroo care, p. 80
language acquisition device (LAD), p. 97
little-scientist phase, p. 92
means–end behavior, p. 93
micronutrient deficiency, p. 78
myelination, p. 72
object permanence, p. 93
plastic, p. 73
preferential-looking paradigm, p. 85
primary circular reactions, p. 91
reflex, p. 75
REM sleep, p. 81
rooting reflex, p. 75
secondary circular reactions, p. 91
self-soothing, p. 81
sensorimotor stage, p. 91
skin-to-skin contact, p. 80
social cognition, p. 95
social-interactionist perspective, p. 97
stunting, p. 78
sucking reflex, p. 75
sudden infant death syndrome (SIDS), p. 84
synapse, p. 72
synaptogenesis, p. 72
telegraphic speech, p. 98
tertiary circular reactions, p. 92
undernutrition, p. 78
visual cliff, p. 87

ANSWERS TO Tying It All Together QUIZZES

Setting the Context

1. Both Cortez and Ashley are right. We are unique in our massive cerebral cortex, in growing most of our brain outside of the womb, and in the fact that the human cortex does not reach its adult form for more than two decades.

2. Latisha is only partly right. Synaptic loss and neural pruning are essential to fostering babies' emerging abilities.

3. When babies have a stroke, they may end up *less* impaired than during adulthood, due to *brain plasticity*.

4. *Synaptogenesis* is occurring in babies, mothers, and grandmas alike. *Myelination* (or formation of the myelin sheath) ends by the mid-twenties.

Basic Newborn States

1. You need to pick the first two statements: The rooting reflex is programmed by the low brain centers to appear at birth and then go away as the cortex matures. Its appearance is definitely *not* a sign of early intelligence.

2. Elaine should say that breast-feeding is difficult if women need to work full-time. It also can be physically painful. This explains why many women don't follow the professional advice.

3. Tell your relatives to carry the child around in a baby sling (kangaroo care). Also, perhaps make heavy use of a pacifier and employ baby massage.

4. Jorge's child is right on schedule, but he's wrong to say his child is sleeping through the night. The baby has simply learned to self-soothe.

5. The answers here will depend on the class.

Sensory and Motor Development

1. You are using a kind of *preferential-looking* paradigm; the scientific term for when your baby loses interest is *habituation*.

2. Both Tania and Thomas are right. In support of Tania's "dramatic improvement" position, babies develop a remarkable sensitivity to facial nuances (such as their preference for good-looking people and the fear bias) early in life. Thomas is also correct that in some ways vision gets worse during infancy. He should mention the fact that by 9 months of age we have "unlearned" the ability to become as sensitive to facial distinctions in people of other ethnic groups.

3. The roots of adult prejudice may begin *during the second 6 months of life*.

4. The child should *be frightened* of the cliff.
5. Your answers might include installing electrical outlet covers; putting sharp, poisonous, and breakable objects out of a baby's reach; carpeting hard floor surfaces; padding furniture corners; installing latches on cabinet doors; and so on.

Cognition

1. Circular reaction = Darien; means–end behavior = Jai; object permanence = Sam.
2. Cognition develops gradually rather than in distinct stages; infants understand human motivations.
3. Baby Sara should pick up this idea *months before* age 1.

Language: The Endpoint of Infancy

1. (a) The idea that we learn language by getting reinforced reflects Skinner's operant conditioning perspective; (b) Chomsky hypothesized that we are biologically programmed to acquire language; (c) the social-interactionist perspective emphasizes the fact that babies and adults have a passion to communicate.
2. Baby Ginny is cooing; baby Jamal is babbling; baby Sam is speaking in holophrases (one-word stage); and baby David is using telegraphic speech.
3. No, your friend is wrong! Baby talk—or in developmental science terms, infant-directed speech (IDS)—helps promote early language.

CONNECT ONLINE:

LaunchPad macmillan learning | Check out our videos and additional resources located at: www.macmillanlearning.com

CHAPTER 4

CHAPTER OUTLINE

Attachment: The Basic Life Bond

Setting the Context

Exploring the Attachment Response

Is Infant Attachment Universal?

Does Infant Attachment Predict Later Relationships and Mental Health?

Exploring the Genetics of Attachment Stability and Change

HOT IN DEVELOPMENTAL SCIENCE: Experiencing Early Life's Worst Deprivation

Wrapping Up Attachment

Settings for Development

The Impact of Poverty in the United States

INTERVENTIONS: Giving Disadvantaged Children an Intellectual and Social Boost

The Impact of Child Care

INTERVENTIONS: Choosing Child Care

Toddlerhood: Age of Autonomy and Shame and Doubt

Socialization

HOW DO WE KNOW . . . That Shy and Exuberant Children Differ Dramatically in Self-Control?

Being Exuberant and Being Shy

INTERVENTIONS: Providing the Right Temperament–Socialization Fit

Some Concluding Thoughts: Giving Is Built into Being Human, Too

Emotional and Social Development in Infants and Toddlers

We've talked to Kim during pregnancy and visited when Elissa was a young baby. Now let's catch up with mother and daughter when Elissa is 15 months old.

Elissa had her first birthday in December. She's such a happy baby, but now if you take something away, it's like, "Why did you do that?" Pick her up. First everything is fine, and then she squirms and her arms go out toward me. She's busy walking, busy exploring, but she's always got an eye on me. When I make a motion to leave, she stops and races near. Elissa has a stronger connection to her dad now, because Jeff watches the baby some afternoons . . . but when she's tired or sick, it's still Mom.

It was difficult to go back to work. You hear terrible things about day care, stories of babies being neglected. I finally decided to send Elissa to a neighbor who watches a few toddlers in her home. I hated how my baby screamed the first week when I dropped her off. But it's obvious that she's happy now. Every morning she runs smiling to Ms. Marie's arms.

It's bittersweet to see my baby separating from me, running into the world, becoming her own person. The clashes are more frequent now that I'm turning up the discipline, expecting more from my "big girl." But mainly it's hard to be apart. I think about Elissa 50 million times a day. I speed home to see her. I can't wait to glimpse her glowing face in the window, how she jumps up, and we run to kiss and cuddle again.

Imagine being Kim, with your child the center of your life. Imagine being Elissa, wanting to be independent but needing your mother close. In this chapter, I'll focus on **attachment**, the powerful bond of love between caregiver and child.

My discussion of attachment starts a conversation that continues throughout this book. After exploring this core relationship, I'll turn to the wider world, first examining how that basic marker, socioeconomic status (SES), affects young children's development, then spotlighting day care, the setting where so many developed-world babies spend their days. The last section of this chapter focuses on the emotional challenges of **toddlerhood,** the famous time lasting roughly from age 1 to 2½ years. (Your tip-off that a child is a toddler is that endearing "toddling" gait that characterizes the second year of life.)

attachment The powerful bond of love between a caregiver and child (or between any two people).

toddlerhood The important transitional stage after babyhood, from roughly age 1 year to 2½.

Attachment: The Basic Life Bond

LEARNING OUTCOMES

- Describe how psychologists learned that attachment is crucial.
- List the attachment milestones.
- Contrast secure attachment and insecure attachments.
- Name three forces affecting the attachment dance.
- Evaluate the genetics of attachment stability and change.
- Examine the effects of institutionalization.

Perhaps you remember being intensely in love. You may be in that wonderful state right now. You cannot stop fantasizing about your significant other. Your moves blend with your partner's. You connect in a unique way. Knowing that this person is there gives you confidence. Your world depends on having your lover close. Now you know how Elissa feels about her mother and the powerful emotions that flow from Kim to her child.

Setting the Context: How Developmentalists (Slowly) Got Attached to Attachment

During much of the twentieth century, U.S. psychologists seemed indifferent to this intense connection. At a time when psychology was dominated by behaviorism, studying love seemed unscientific. Behaviorists suggested that babies wanted to be close to their mothers because this "maternal reinforcement stimulus" provided food. Worse yet, the early behaviorist John Watson seemed *hostile* to mother love:

> When I hear a mother say "bless its little heart" when it falls down, I . . . have to walk a block or two to let off steam. . . . Can't she train herself to substitute a kindly word . . . for . . . the coddling? . . . Can't she learn to keep away from the child a large part of the day?
> (Watson, 1928/1972, pp. 82–83)

And then he made this memorable statement:

> I sometimes wish that we could live in a community of homes [where] . . . we could have the babies fed and bathed each week by a different nurse. (!)
> (Watson, 1928/1972, pp. 82–83)

European psychoanalysts felt differently. They believed that attachment was crucial to infant life.

Consider a heart-rending mid-twentieth-century film that featured babies living in orphanages (Blum, 2002; Karen, 1998). In these sterile, pristine institutions, behaviorists would predict that infants should thrive. So why did babies lie listless on cots—unable to eat, withering away?

Now consider that ethologists—the forerunners of today's evolutionary psychologists—noticed that *every* species had a biologically programmed attachment response (or drive to be physically close to their mothers) that appeared at a specific point soon after birth. When the famous ethologist Konrad Lorenz (1935) arranged to become a group of newly hatched goslings' attachment-eliciting stimulus, Lorenz became the adored Pied Piper the geese tried to follow to the ends of the earth.

However, it took a rebellious psychologist named Harry Harlow to convince U.S. psychologists that the behaviorist meal-dispenser model of mother love was wrong. In a classic study, Harlow (1958) separated newborn monkeys from their mothers and raised them in a cage with a wire-mesh "mother" (which offered food from a milk bottle attached to its chest) and a cloth "mother" (which was soft and provided contact comfort). The babies stayed glued to the cloth mother, making occasional trips to eat from the wire mom. In stressful situations, they scurried to the cloth mother for comfort. Love won, hands down, over getting fed!

Moreover, as adults, the motherless monkeys were unable to have sex; they were frightened of their peers. After being artificially inseminated and giving birth, the females became uncaring, abusive parents. One mauled her baby so badly that it later died (Harlow and others, 1966; C. M. Harlow, 1986).

In Harlow's landmark study, baby monkeys clung to the cloth-covered "mother" (which provided contact comfort) as they leaned over to feed from the wire-mesh "mother"—vividly refuting the behaviorist idea that infants become "attached" to the reinforcing stimulus that feeds them.

Then, in the late 1960s, John Bowlby put the evidence together—the orphanage findings, Lorenz's ethological studies, Harlow's research, his own clinical work with children who had been separated from their mothers during World War II (Hinde, 2005). In landmark books, Bowlby (1969, 1973, 1980) argued that there is no such thing as "excessive mother love." Having a **primary attachment figure** is crucial to development. It is essential to living fully at any age. By the final decades of the twentieth century, attachment moved to the front burner in developmental science. It remains front and center today.

> **primary attachment figure** The closest person in a child's or adult's life.

Exploring the Attachment Response

Bowlby (1969, 1973) made his case for the crucial value of attachment based on evolutionary theory. Like other species, he argued, human beings have a critical period when the attachment response "comes out." As with Lorenz's geese, attachment is built into our genetics to allow us to survive. Although the attachment response is programmed to emerge during our first two years of life, **proximity-seeking behavior**—our need to make contact with an attachment figure—is activated when our survival is threatened at *any* age.

Bowlby believed that threats to survival come in two categories. First, they may be activated by our internal state. When a toddler clings only to her mom, you know she must be tired. When you have a fever or the flu, you immediately text your "significant other."

Second, they are evoked by wider-world dangers. During preschool, a huge dog caused us to run into our parents' arms. As adults, a professor's nasty comment or a humiliating work experience provokes a frantic call to our primary attachment figure, be it our spouse, father, or best friend.

Although we all need to touch base with our significant others when we feel threatened, older children can be separated from their attachment figures for some time. During infancy and toddlerhood, simply being physically apart causes distress. Now, let's trace how attachment unfolds.

> **proximity-seeking behavior** Acting to maintain physical contact or to be close to an attachment figure.
>
> **preattachment phase** The first phase of John Bowlby's developmental attachment sequence, during the first three months of life, when infants show no visible signs of attachment.
>
> **social smile** The first real smile, occurring at about 2 months of age.
>
> **attachment in the making** Second phase of Bowlby's attachment sequence, when, from 4 to 7 months of age, babies slightly prefer the primary caregiver.

Attachment Milestones

Bowlby believed that, during their first three months of life, babies are in the **preattachment phase**. Remember that during this reflex-dominated time, infants have yet to wake up to the world. However, at around 2 months of age, a milestone occurs called the **social smile**. Bowlby believed that this first smile does not show true attachment. Because it pops up in response to any human face, it is an automatic reflex that evokes care from adults.

Still, a baby's eagerly awaited first smile can be an incredible experience for a parent. Suddenly, your relationship with your child is on a different plane. Now, I have a confession to make: During my first two months as a new mother, I was worried, as I did not feel anything for this beautiful child I had waited so long to adopt. I date Thomas's first endearing smile as the defining event in my lifelong attachment romance.

At roughly 4 months old, infants enter a transitional period, called **attachment in the making**. At this time, Piaget's environment-focused secondary circular reactions are unfolding. The cortex is coming on-line. Babies may show a slight preference for their primary caregiver. But still, a 4- or 5-month-old is the ultimate party person, thrilled to be cuddled by anyone—from Grandma, to a neighbor, to a stranger at the mall.

By about 7 or 8 months of age, this changes. As I discussed in Chapter 3, babies can hunt for covered objects—showing that they have the cognitive skills to miss their caregivers. Now that they can crawl, or walk holding

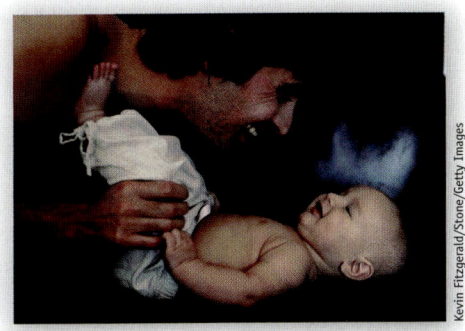

A baby's first social smile, which appears at the sight of any face at about 2 to 3 months of age, is biologically programmed to delight adults and charm them into providing love and care.

onto furniture, children can get hurt. The stage is set for **clear-cut** (or **focused**) **attachment**—the beginning of the full-blown attachment response.

Separation anxiety signals this milestone. When a baby is about 7 or 8 months old, she suddenly gets uncomfortable if a caregiver leaves the room. Then, **stranger anxiety** appears. A child gets agitated when any unfamiliar person picks her up. So, as children approach age 1, the universal friendliness of early infancy is gone. While they may still joyously gurgle at the world from their caregiver's arms, it's normal for babies to forbid any "stranger"—a nice day-care worker or even a loving Grandma who flies in for a visit—to invade their space.

Between ages 1 and 2, the distress reaches a peak. A toddler clings and cries when Mom or Dad makes a motion to leave. It's as if an invisible string connects the caregiver and the child. In a classic study at a playground, 1-year-olds played within a certain distance from their mothers. Interestingly, this zone of optimum comfort (about 200 feet) was identical for both the parent and the child (Anderson, 1972).

To see these changes, pick up a young baby (such as a 4-month-old) and an older infant (perhaps a 10-month-old) and compare their reactions. Then, observe 1-year-olds at a park. Can you measure this attachment zone of comfort? Do you notice the busy, exploring toddlers periodically checking back to make sure a caregiver is there?

Social referencing, the scientific term for this regular checking-back, helps alert toddlers to which situations are dangerous and which are safe. ("Should I climb up this slide, Mommy?" "Does Daddy think this object is OK to explore?"). It explains why 8-month-old infants suddenly become sensitive to fearful faces (see Chapter 3). Our lifelong human *fear bias* is exquisitely timed to kick in when we first move into the world.

When does the need to be *physically* close to a caregiver go away? Although the marker is hazy, clear-cut attachment tapers off at about age 3. Children still care just as much about their primary caregiver. But now, according to Bowlby, they have the skills to carry a **working model,** or internal representation, of this number-one person in their minds (Bretherton, 2005).

The bottom-line is that our human critical period for attachment unfolds during our most vulnerable time of life—when babies first become mobile and are most in danger of getting hurt. Moreover, what compensates parents for the frustrations of having a Piagetian "little scientist" is enormous gratification. Just when a toddler keeps messing up the house and saying "No!" parents know that their child's world revolves only around them.

Do children differ in the way they express this priceless connection? If so, what might these differences imply about the infant–parent bond?

Attachment Styles

Mary Ainsworth, Bowlby's colleague, answered these questions by devising a classic test of attachment—the **Strange Situation** (Ainsworth, 1967; Ainsworth and others, 1978).

The Strange Situation procedure begins when a mother and a 1-year-old enter a room full of toys. After the child has time to explore, an unfamiliar adult enters the room. Then the mother leaves the baby alone with the stranger and, a few minutes later, returns to comfort the child. Next, everyone leaves the baby alone in the room, and finally the mother returns (see Figure 4.1). By observing the child's reactions to these separations and reunions through a one-way mirror, developmentalists categorize infants as either *securely* or *insecurely attached*.

A few weeks ago, this 7-month-old boy would have happily gone to his neighbor. But everything changes during the phase of clear-cut attachment when stranger anxiety emerges.

clear-cut (focused) attachment Critical attachment phase, from 7 months through toddlerhood, defined by the need to have a primary caregiver nearby.

separation anxiety When a baby gets upset as a primary caregiver departs.

stranger anxiety Beginning at about age 7 months, when a baby grows wary of people other than a caregiver.

social referencing A baby's monitoring a caregiver for cues as to how to behave.

working model In Bowlby's theory, the mental representation of a caregiver that enables children over age 3 to be physically apart from the caregiver.

Strange Situation Procedure to measure attachment at age 1, involving separations and reunions with a caregiver.

In kindergarten, this child can say goodbye with minimal separation anxiety because she is in the working-model phase of attachment.

Securely attached children use their mother as a secure base, or anchor, to explore the toys. When she leaves, they may or may not become highly distressed. Most important, when she returns, their eyes light up with joy. Their close relationship is apparent in the way they melt into their mothers' arms. **Insecurely attached** children react in one of three ways:

- **Avoidant** infants rarely show much emotion—positive or negative—when their attachment figure leaves and returns. They seem wooden, disengaged, without much feeling at all.

- Babies with an **anxious-ambivalent attachment** are at the opposite end of the spectrum—clingy, nervous, too frightened to explore the toys. Frantic when their attachment figure leaves, they are inconsolable when a parent comes back.

- Children showing a **disorganized attachment** behave in a bizarre manner. They freeze, run around erratically, or even look frightened when the caregiver returns.

Developmentalists point out that insecure attachments do not show a weakness in the *underlying* connection. Avoidant infants are just as bonded to their caregivers as babies who are categorized as secure. Anxious-ambivalent infants are not more closely attached even though they show intense separation distress. To take an analogy from adult life, when a person who cares deeply about you pretends to be indifferent, is this individual less in love? Is a lover who can't let his partner out of sight more attached than a person who allows his significant other to have an independent life? Unless they endure the grossly abnormal rearing conditions described later in this section, *every infant* is closely attached (Zeanah, Berlin, & Boris, 2011). Figure 4.2 on page 110 offers a visual summary of the different attachment styles.

> **secure attachment** Ideal attachment response when a child responds with joy at being reunited with a primary caregiver.
>
> **insecure attachment** Deviation from the normally joyful response of being reunited with a primary caregiver, signaling problems in the caregiver–child relationship.
>
> **avoidant attachment** An insecure attachment style characterized by a child's indifference to a primary caregiver at being reunited after separation.
>
> **anxious-ambivalent attachment** An insecure attachment style characterized by a child's intense distress when reunited with a primary caregiver after separation.
>
> **disorganized attachment** An insecure attachment style characterized by responses such as freezing or fear when a child is reunited with the primary caregiver in the Strange Situation.

FIGURE 4.1: The Strange Situation The classic Strange Situation, involving separations and reunions from a caregiver, can tell us whether this 1-year-old girl is securely or insecurely attached.

Secure Attachment: The child is thrilled to see the caregiver.

Avoidant Attachment: The child is unresponsive to the caregiver.

Anxious-Ambivalent Attachment: The child cannot be calmed by the caregiver.

Disorganized Attachment: The child seems frightened and behaves bizarrely when the caregiver arrives.

FIGURE 4.2: Secure and insecure attachments: A summary photo series

The Attachment Dance

Look at a baby and a caregiver and it is almost as if you are seeing a dance. The partners are alert to each other's signals. They know when to come on stronger and when to back off. They are absorbed and captivated, oblivious to the world. This blissful **synchrony,** or sense of being emotionally in tune, is what makes the infant–mother relationship our model for romantic love. Ainsworth and Bowlby believed that the parent's "dancing potential," or sensitivity to a baby's signals, produces secure attachments (Ainsworth and others, 1978). Were they correct?

The Caregiver

Decades of studies suggest that the answer is yes. From Peru to Peoria, sensitive caregivers have babies who are securely attached (Posada and others, 2016). Parents who misread their baby's signals or are rejecting, disengaged, or depressed are more apt to have infants who are categorized as insecure (see Behrens, Parker, & Haltigan, 2011; and Zeanah, Berlin, & Boris, 2011 for a review).

Moreover, an infant's attachment category, to some degree, mirrors that of his mom. Women who describe happy childhoods tend to have securely attached babies. Mothers who report dysfunctional early lives are more likely to have insecure 1-year-olds (Behrens, Haltigan, & Bahm, 2016; Verhage and others, 2016). With the caution that this correlation could be due to shared genetics, there is some intergenerational continuity to the attachment dance.

However, there can also be a tantalizing mismatch in infant–caregiver congruence (Behrens, Haltigan, & Bahm, 2016)—which suggests that some women, despite having unhappy childhoods, step up to the plate and offer their babies loving care. On the negative side, you may know a world-class caregiver with an insecurely attached child. The reason is that the attachment dance has *two partners*.

synchrony The reciprocal aspect of the attachment relationship, with a caregiver and infant responding emotionally to each other in a sensitive, exquisitely attuned way.

The blissful rapture, the sense of being totally engrossed with each other, is the reason why developmentalists use the word *synchrony* to describe parent–infant attachment.

The Child

Listen to a mother comparing her babies ("Sara was fussy; Matthew is easier to soothe") and you will realize that not all infants have the same dancing talent. The reason is that babies differ in **temperament**—characteristic, inborn behavioral styles of approaching the world.

In a pioneering study, developmentalists classified middle-class babies into three temperamental styles: *Easy* babies had rhythmic eating and sleeping patterns; they were happy and easily soothed. More wary babies were labeled *slow to warm up*. One in 10 infants were ranked as *difficult*—hypersensitive, unusually agitated, reactive to every sight and sound (Thomas & Chess, 1977; Thomas, Chess, & Birch, 1968). Here is an example:

> Everything bothers my 5-month-old little girl—a bright light, a rough blanket, a sudden noise—even, I'm ashamed to admit, sometimes my touch. I thought colic went away by month 3. I'm getting discouraged and depressed.

Think back to the stressful Strange Situation. Can you see why some developmentalists argue that temperamental reactivity, rather than the quality of caregiving, determines a child's attachment status at age 1? (See, for example, Kagan, 1984.)

Does a baby's biology (nature) evoke insensitive caregiving and then insecure infant attachments? As you might imagine—given the *bidirectional* nature of relationships—the answer is yes. Temperamentally fussy babies (infants who rarely smile and get agitated when adults pick them up) provoke less loving caregiving, especially when mothers are anxious and depressed (Nolvi and others, 2016). To use an analogy from real-life dancing, imagine waltzing with a partner who couldn't keep time with the music, or think of a time you tried to soothe a person who was too upset to relate. Even a world-class dancer, or someone with exceptional social skills, would feel inept.

The Caregiver's Other Significant Others

To continue the analogy, the attachment waltz has additional partners. As I discussed in Chapter 2, a woman's attachment to her baby depends in part on her partner's bonding style. If a couple has marital problems, or a caregiver's significant other feels ambivalent about the child, it's hard to relate to an infant in a loving way (Cowan, Cowan, & Mehta, 2009; Moss and others, 2005). For single parents, having other caring attachments—with family members, friends, and neighbors—is also crucial to providing sensitive care (see Chapter 7). A basic message of this book is that no parent is an island. The dance of attachment depends on having a supportive wider world.

Table 4.1 summarizes these messages in a questionnaire showing the different forces that predict caregiver-to-baby bonding. My discussion shows that by viewing mothers as solely responsible for promoting secure attachments, Bowlby and Ainsworth were taking an excessively limited view. What about the general theory? Is attachment to a primary caregiver universal? Do infants in different countries fall into the same categories of secure and insecure?

---

temperament A person's characteristic, inborn style of dealing with the world.

Imagine the frustration of caring for this temperamentally frazzled baby—an infant who responded to every sight and sound with a frantic wail. Is it fair to blame this child's attachment issues on a parent's care?

Table 4.1: Predicting Caregiver-to-Baby Bonding: Four Section Summary Questions

1. Did this person have a happy childhood?
2. Is this baby temperamentally easy?
3. For couples: Is this relationship loving and are both partners excited about having a child?
4. For single parents: Does this caregiver have other close attachments?

Is Infant Attachment Universal?

From Chicago to Capetown, from Naples to New York, Bowlby's and Ainsworth's attachment ideas get high marks (van IJzendoorn & Sagi, 1999). Babies around the world get attached to a primary caregiver at roughly the same age. As Figure 4.3 shows, the percentages of infants categorized as secure in different countries are remarkably similar—roughly 60 to 70 percent (Sroufe, 2000; Tomlinson, Cooper, & Murray, 2005).

The most amazing validation of attachment theory comes from the Efé, a communal hunter-gatherer people living in Africa. Efé newborns nurse from any lactating woman, even when their own parent is around. They are dressed and cared for by the whole community. But Efé babies still develop a primary attachment to their mothers at the typical age! (See van IJzendoorn & Sagi, 1999.)

So far you might be thinking that during the phase of clear-cut attachment, babies are connected to one person. You would be incorrect. A toddler may be attached to her father and day-care provider, as well as her mom. And, just as you and I connect differently with each "significant other," a baby can be securely attached to his father and insecurely attached to his mother.

Interestingly, when babies are upset, they run to the person who spends the most time with them even if they are insecurely attached to that adult. So the *amount* of hands-on caregiving, not its quality, evokes the biologically programmed, security-seeking response (Umemura and others, 2013). The good news is that if a child is securely attached *to one person*, then that may be all that matters for his life.

In a heartening longitudinal study, 15-month-olds labeled as "double insecure" (insecurely attached to both parents) were prone to have behavior problems in third grade. But children who were securely attached to only one parent were insulated

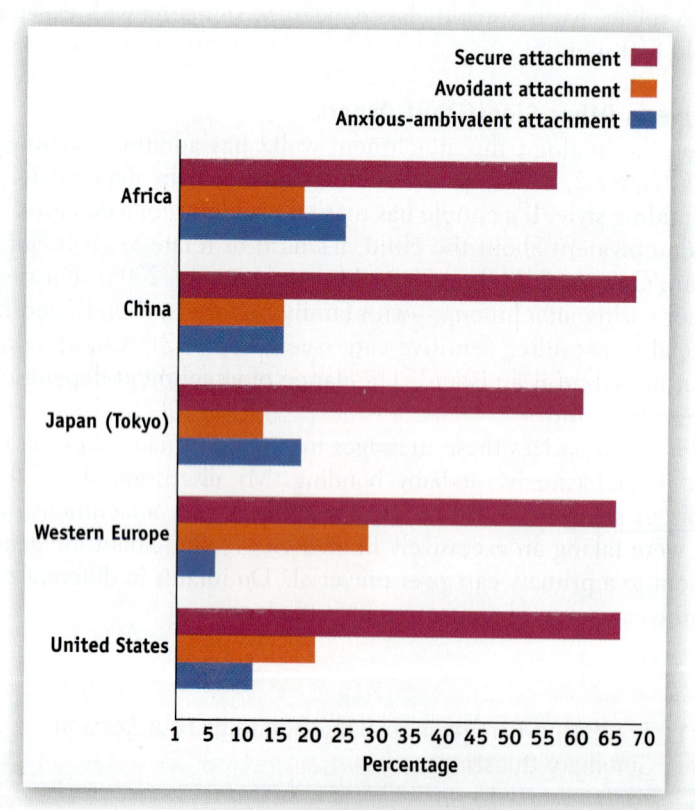

FIGURE 4.3: Snapshots of attachment security (and insecurity) around the world
Around the world, roughly 60 to 70 percent of 1-year-olds are classified as securely attached—although there are interesting differences in the percentages of babies falling into the different insecure categories.
Data from van IJzendoorn & Sagi, 1999, p. 729.

from poor mental health (Kochanska & Kim, 2013). Therefore, having *one* nurturing figure during infancy—a father, a grandma, an aunt—may be all we need to protect us from problems down the road. How *does* infant attachment relate to problems down the road?

Does Infant Attachment Predict Later Relationships and Mental Health?

Bowlby's argument, in his working-model concept, is that our attachment relationships during infancy determine how we relate to other people and feel about ourselves (Bretherton, 2005). A baby who acts avoidant with his parents will be aloof with his friends and teachers. An anxious-ambivalent infant will behave in a needy way in her relationships. A secure baby is set up to succeed socially.

Again, decades of research support Bowlby's prediction. Securely attached babies are more socially competent (McElwain and others, 2011; Rispoli and others, 2013). Insecure attachment foreshadows trouble managing one's emotions and interpersonal difficulties later on (Kochanska and others, 2010; Pasco Fearon and others, 2010; von der Lippe and others, 2010).

The most potent predictor of problems is the disorganized attachment style. This erratic, confused infant response is a risk factor for "acting-out issues" (aggression, disobedience, trouble controlling one's behavior) as children travel through elementary school (Bohlin and others, 2012; Pasco Fearon & Belsky, 2011).

However, the operative phrase here is *risk factor*. Programs that train mothers to be responsive caregivers can block the pathway from infant disorganized attachment to disruptive preschool behaviors (Mountain, Cahill, & Thorpe, 2017). Longitudinal studies that measure attachment at age 1 and then track babies into adulthood suggest that, while there normally is continuity, sensitive, loving relationships—at *every stage of childhood*—can transform a baby's "attachment status" from insecure to secure. Unfortunately, however, even the most blissful babyhood does not inoculate children from attachment traumas later on (Pinquart, Feubner, & Ahnert, 2013; Zayas and others, 2011).

Consider a boy named Tony who, in one major infant-to-adult attachment study, was categorized as securely attached at age 1. In preschool and early elementary school, Tony was popular, self-assured, and still securely attached; but as a teenager, he suffered devastating attachment blows. First, his parents went through a difficult divorce. Then his mother was killed in a car accident and his father moved to another state, leaving Tony with his aunt. It should come as no surprise that as an angry, depressed adolescent, Tony was classified as insecurely attached. But by age 26, Tony recovered. He met a wonderful woman and became a father. His status slowly returned to secure (Sroufe and others, 2005).

It seems logical that life experiences would change our attachment relationships for the better or the worse. But research—involving the "love hormone" oxytocin—suggests genetics is also involved.

Because this hands-on dad is caring for his infant son full time, he will be the loving attachment figure this young baby runs to during the toddler years.

Exploring the Genetics of Attachment Stability and Change

Oxytocin is known as the attachment hormone because this chemical elicits bonding, caregiving, and nurturing in other mammals and human beings (Rilling, 2013). When researchers in the infant-to-adult attachment study explored variations in a gene involved in producing oxytocin, they found that young people, like Tony, who changed in attachment status, showed one variant of this particular gene. Others, with a less environment-responsive genetic profile, were apt to stay stable in attachment from age 1. Therefore, some children seem genetically immune to less sensitive

oxytocin The hormone whose production is centrally involved in bonding, nurturing, and caregiving behaviors in our species and other mammals.

caregiving. Others vitally need a nurturing environment to thrive. (Stay tuned for more about environment-responsive infants later in this chapter.)

The bottom-line theme of *all* these studies, however, is that Bowlby was wrong. We are not destined to have lifelong problems if we suffered from inadequate caregiving early in life. But what if a baby has experienced not just poor caregiving, but *no* caregiving at all?

Hot in Developmental Science: Experiencing Early Life's Worst Deprivation

"When I . . . walked into the . . . building (in 1990)," said a British school teacher . . . "what I saw was beyond belief . . . babies lay three and four to a bed, given no attention. . . . There were no medicines or washing facilities, . . . physical and sexual abuse were rife. . . . I particularly remember . . . the basement. There were kids there who hadn't seen natural light in years."

(McGeown, 2005, para. 4)

This scene was not from some horror movie. It was real. This woman had entered a Romanian orphanage, the bitter legacy of the dictator Ceausescu's decision to forbid contraception, which caused a flood of unwanted babies that destitute parents dumped on the state.

When the Iron Curtain fell and revealed these grisly Eastern European scenes, British and American families rushed in to adopt these children. But then parents began to report distressing symptoms—sons and daughters who displayed a strange, indiscriminate friendliness (see Kreppner and others, 2011). These responses did not qualify as insecure attachment. They showed a complete lack of *any* attachment response.

Which institution-reared babies are apt to show these deficits? Can children recover from this deprivation, and is there an age at which help comes too late? Studies tracking the Romanian babies, as well as children adopted from orphanages in China and Russia, offer the following tantalizing conclusions (Julian, 2013).

First, babies adopted from the most negligent, worst-off institutions—such as in Romania—are most at risk for problems. In these places, damage is evident if adoption occurs after 6 months of age. In orphanages, like those in Russia that are classified as "socially depriving" but that satisfy infants' basic health needs, the cutoff point for having deficits is close to 18 months. Therefore, just as Bowlby would predict, the zone of attachment (7–18 months) is a sensitive period for receiving caregiving. But there is also a **dose–response effect**—meaning that the intensity (dose) of deprivation predicts the impact on (response of) a given child. The risk of having enduring problems depends on the length of time a child stays in an orphanage (Almas and others, 2016) and the care that institution provides (McCall and others, 2016).

What are these children's symptoms? A classic sign of this "institutionalization syndrome" is the indiscriminate friendliness I just described (this condition is called *reactive attachment disorder*). Another is deficits in children's ability to focus their attention (McLaughlin and others, 2010; Wiik and others, 2011) because lack of stimulation delays the maturation of the brain (McLaughlin and others, 2010).

Interestingly, boys are more vulnerable than girls to persistent attachment problems (McLaughlin and others, 2012). While a massive catch-up growth often occurs after moving to a new, loving home (Sheridan and others, 2013), the negative intellectual effects of institutional care linger into the adolescent years (Almas and others, 2016; see Figure 4.4). By exploring these grossly abnormal, worst-case scenarios, developmentalists are learning vital information about resilience, brain plasticity, and its limits in human beings.

dose–response effect Term referring to the fact that the amount (dose) of a substance, in this case the depth and length of deprivation, determines its probable effect or impact on the person. (In the orphanage studies, the "response" is subsequent emotional and/or cognitive problems.)

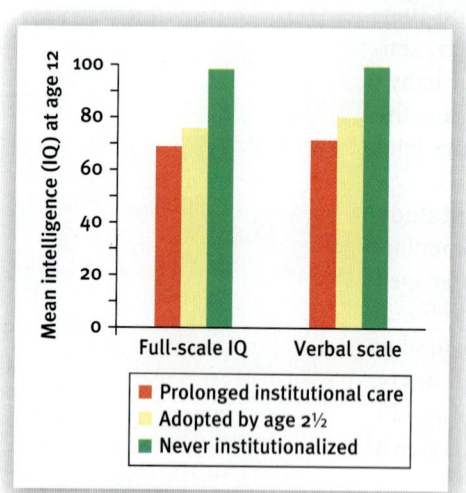

FIGURE 4.4: Dose–response impact of institutional care on later intelligence Notice that intelligence test scores are higher when Romanian orphanage infants are adopted into foster families before the end of toddlerhood (yellow versus red bars). But compared to being raised outside of an orphanage (green bar), spending any time in an institution still has marked, enduring, negative effects on cognition.
Data from Almas and others, 2016.

CHAPTER 4 Emotional and Social Development in Infants and Toddlers

Wrapping Up Attachment

To summarize, the quality of attachment during infancy lays the foundation for healthy development in a variety of life realms. Still, attachment capacities (and human brains) are malleable, and negative paths can be altered, as long as the deprivation is not too profound and the wider world provides special help. How does the wider world affect development during infancy and beyond? To explore this question, let's now look at two important social contexts of early childhood: poverty and day care.

Tying It All Together

1. List an example of "proximity-seeking in distress" in your own life within the past few months.

2. Muriel is 1 month old, Janine is 5 months old, Ted is 1 year old, and Tania is age 4. List each child's phase of attachment.

3. Match the term to the correct definition: (1) social referencing; (2) working model; (3) synchrony; (4) Strange Situation.
    a. A researcher measures a child's attachment at age 1 after several separations and reunions with the mother.
    b. A toddler keeps looking back at the parent while exploring at a playground.
    c. An elementary school child keeps an image of her parent in mind to calm herself at school.
    d. A mother and baby relate to each other as if they are totally in tune.

4. Your cousin is the primary caregiver of her 1-year-old son. On a recent visit to her house, you notice that the baby shows no emotion when his mother leaves the room and—more important—seems indifferent when she returns. How might you classify this child's attachment style?

5. Manuel is arguing for the validity of attachment theory as spelled out by Bowlby and Ainsworth. Manuel should say (pick one, neither, or both): *Infants around the world get attached to a primary caregiver at roughly the same age/a child's attachment status at age 1 never changes.*

6. Jasmine is adopting a 2-year-old from an orphanage in Haiti. List a few issues Jasmine might have to deal with, and then give Jasmine a piece of good attachment news.

Answers to the Tying It All Together questions can be found at the end of this chapter.

Settings for Development

What is the impact of living in poverty on children? And what about that crucial place where many young children spend their time—day care?

LEARNING OUTCOMES

- Discuss early-childhood poverty in the United States.
- Explore preschools and day care, making reference to what caregivers should look for in choosing a specific setting for a child.

The Impact of Poverty in the United States

In Chapter 3, I examined the devastating physical and emotional effects of early-childhood poverty in developing nations. Now let's turn to research in the United States. What fraction of young U.S. children live in poverty? How does being poor during the earliest years of life affect later well-being?

How Common Is Early-Childhood Poverty?

As Figure 4.5 on page 116 shows, in 2014, almost 1 in 4 U.S. children under age 6 lived below the poverty line. If we include boys and girls in "low-income" families (those earning within 2 times the official poverty cutoff), the statistic is close to 1 in 2 (Jiang, Ekono, & Skinner, 2016)! Moreover, for the past 40 years, young children

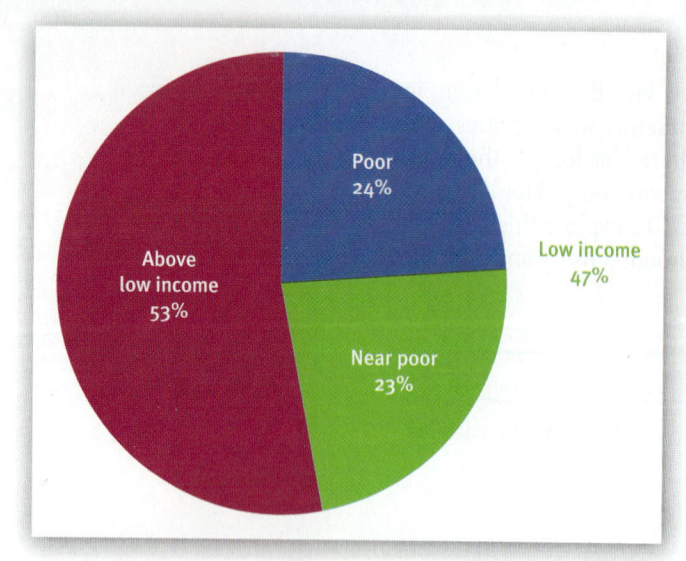

FIGURE 4.5: Percentage of U.S. children under 6 years old with different family incomes This astonishing chart shows just how widespread economic disadvantage is among young U.S. children.

Data from Jiang, Ekono, & Skinner, 2016.

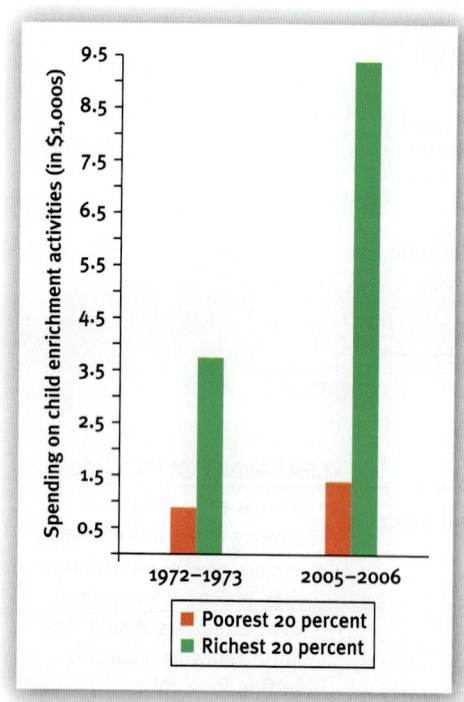

FIGURE 4.6: Family enrichment expenditures for children in the poorest 20 percent (red bars) and richest 20 percent (green bars) of U.S. families in 1972–1973 and 2005–2006 Low-income U.S. parents spend far less money on child enrichment activities, such as books and learning toys, than the richest 20 percent of families—an expenditure gap that has increased threefold since the early 1970s.

Data from Duncan, Magnuson, & Votruba-Drzal, 2017.

have been more likely to live in poverty than every other U.S. age group (except women over 85) (Economic Policy Institute, 2011).

One cause is single motherhood. Imagine how difficult life is as a woman raising a baby alone. You need to work long hours, pay for child care, and still have enough money to feed and clothe your family. Now imagine how difficult it would be for *any* person to perform this feat with a job that pays less than $12 an hour. In 2013, more than 1 in 4 U.S. men age 25–34 had salaries below this amount. So it's no wonder that economic disadvantage is often the price of starting families during the very time young people are supposed to marry and give birth.

How Does Early-Childhood Poverty Affect Later Development?

Unfortunately, poverty affects children's physiology. Low-income toddlers and preschoolers have elevated levels of the stress hormone cortisol (Evans & Kim, 2013). One longitudinal study, measuring maternal salivary cortisol at different points during an infant's first two years of life, showed impoverished mothers also had high levels of this biological indicator of stress (Finegood and others, 2017).

Imagine arriving home exhausted from a low-wage job, or being unemployed, *food insecure*, and on the brink of getting evicted because you can't pay the rent. How would you deal with the kind of stressed-out, irritable infant discussed in the preceding section (Paulussen-Hoogeboom and others, 2007)? Although money cannot buy loving parents, it can buy any mother the economic luxury to relate sensitively to a child.

Poverty's most poisonous impact is on education. Being poor during the first four years of life dramatically lowers the odds of graduating from high school (Duncan, Magnuson, & Votruba-Drzal, 2017). With poverty and education, there is a clear dose–response effect: The depth of deprivation and its timing (during the earliest years of life) matter most. Why is poverty, before *entering* kindergarten, particularly detrimental to academic success?

Figure 4.6 offers one vivid answer. Low-income parents can't provide their infants and toddlers with the brain-stimulating activities that are the birthright of being born affluent in the contemporary United States: infant cognitive tools, baby gym visits, regular trips to museums. Moreover, notice that this gap in family "enrichment expenditures" has widened over the past 40 years. Technology combined with accelerating income inequalities means today's disadvantaged boys and girls face daunting intellectual hurdles even before they enter the classroom doors.

What amplifies these impediments is living in crowded, dilapidated housing (Leventhal & Newman, 2010) and perhaps having to move repeatedly (Miller, Sadegh-Nobari, & Lillie-Blanton, 2011)—chaotic conditions tailor-made to impair early childhood focusing skills (Blair, 2017; Hendry, Jones, & Charman, 2016). And if families live in high-crime neighborhoods, parents may be frightened to take their sons and daughters outside because the street is apt to be a dangerous place (Anakwenze & Zuberi, 2013).

Unfortunately, the cognitive impact of this chaos is evident before children even walk. When researchers explored how well 6-month-olds tracked visual stimuli, low-SES babies performed worse than the average child that age (Clearfield & Jedd, 2013).

Luckily, in wealthy world regions, low-income parents have government programs designed to help.

INTERVENTIONS: Giving Disadvantaged Children an Intellectual and Social Boost

In the United States, the main government-sponsored early-childhood program is **Head Start**. This famous mainstay program, first established in 1965 by Lyndon Johnson as part of his "Great Society" effort to reduce poverty, has the goal of offering the kind of learning experiences to make poverty-level preschoolers as ready for kindergarten as their middle-class peers.

Early Head Start extends this help to infants and toddlers. This federal program trains parents to be more effective caregivers, supporting low-income pregnant women by providing home visits and other services (Phillips & Lowenstein, 2011).

Do these interventions work? The answer *can be* yes. Programs that train poverty-level mothers to respond sensitively to their babies help promote secure attachment (Mountain, Cahill, & Thorpe, 2016). High-quality **preschools** (teaching-oriented programs that typically begin at age 3) make a difference in *every* child's life (Lee, 2016; Miller, Sadegh-Nobari, & Lillie-Blanton, 2011; Pölkki & Vornanen, 2016; Votruba-Drzal and others, 2013).

Day care (group settings for infants and toddlers) can be a lifeline for babies and toddlers who live in disorganized, chaotic homes (Berry and others, 2014; Phillips & Lowenstein, 2011). In one fascinating dose–response finding, researchers discovered that the more hours per week *poverty-level* 1-year-olds spent in day care, the lower their average cortisol rates (Berry, Blair, & Granger, 2016).

The problem is that here, too, money matters—especially in the United States. While social welfare states like Finland offer every child uniformly high-quality care, even as of early 2016, Head Start was seriously underfunded (Barnett & Friedman-Krauss, 2016). Because Head Start's budget depends on congressional approval, we don't know this classic U.S. program's future fate. Moreover, no one-shot intervention during early childhood can erase the impact of attending substandard elementary schools or being raised in a dysfunctional neighborhood where it is virtually impossible to construct a middle-class life (Chetty & Hendren, 2016; much more about this topic in Chapter 7).

But I can't end this discussion by leaving you with the stereotypical impression that *every* impoverished child's home life is deficient, or that *all* low-income neighborhoods blunt children's ability to learn. History is rife with examples of famous artists, scientists, and transformative public figures who grew up in families who could barely make ends meet—people who credit their parents for making them the successful people they became.

In one study, researchers found that if caregivers were securely attached to their own parents and had optimistic attitudes about life, they could put aside their problems and offer their children the ultimate in tender loving care (Kochanska and others, 2007). As a student of mine commented, "I don't see my family in your description of poverty. My mom is my hero. We grew up poor, but in terms of parenting, we were very rich."

> **Head Start** A federal program offering high-quality day care at a center and other services to help preschoolers aged 3 to 5 from low-income families prepare for school.
>
> **Early Head Start** A federal program that provides counseling and other services to low-income parents and children under age 3.
>
> **preschool** A teaching-oriented group setting for children aged 3 to 5.
>
> **day care** Less academically oriented group programs serving young children, most often infants and toddlers.

The Impact of Child Care

For affluent readers, this discussion of poverty can feel distant from your life. Child care affects every family, from millionaires to middle-class urban mothers and fathers to the rural poor. Almost 3 in 5 mothers in the United States returns to work during a baby's first year of life (U.S. Department of Labor Statistics, Fertility, 2017). Unlike in European nations, where free child care is a national birthright, in the United States, with average costs well over $1,000 per month, the expense of sending one child to day care is daunting, even to couples who are middle class. When we combine

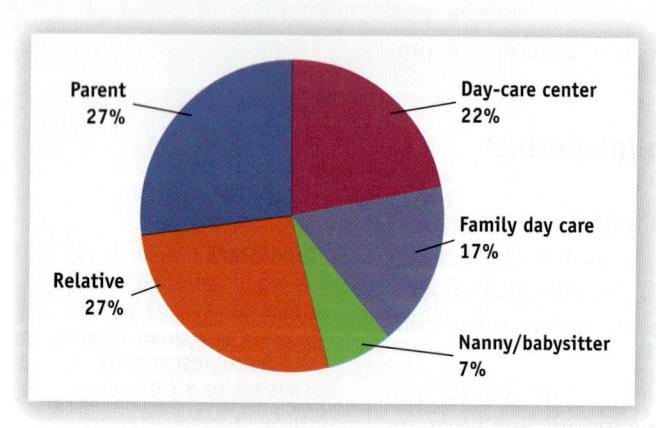

FIGURE 4.7: Day-care arrangements for infants and toddlers with employed mothers, late 1990s Notice that, by the end of the twentieth century, while most infants and toddlers with working mothers were cared for by other family members, 1 in 5 attended licensed day-care centers.
Data from Shonkoff & Phillips, 2000, p. 304.

Pie chart values: Parent 27%, Day-care center 22%, Family day care 17%, Nanny/babysitter 7%, Relative 27%.

family day care A day-care arrangement in which a neighbor or relative cares for a small number of children in his or her home for a fee.

day-care center A day-care arrangement in which a large number of children are cared for at a licensed facility by paid providers.

these economic concerns ("This is taking up a huge chunk of my paycheck!") with anxieties about "leaving my baby with strangers," it makes sense that many new U.S. parents struggle to keep child care in the family. They may rely on grandma or juggle work schedules so that one spouse is always home (Phillips & Lowenstein, 2011).

People who use paid caregivers have several options. Well-off families often hire a nanny or babysitter. Parents who want a less expensive option often turn to **family day care**, in which a neighbor or local parent cares for a small group of children in her home.

The big change on the child-care landscape has been the dramatic increase in licensed **day-care centers**—larger settings that cater to children of different ages. By the late twentieth century, roughly 1 in 2 U.S. preschoolers attended these facilities. The comparable figure for infants and toddlers was more than 1 in 5 (see Figure 4.7).

Child Care and Development

Imagine you are the mother of a U.S. infant and must return to work. You probably have heard the media messages that link full-time day care with less than adequate mothering. So you are guilty, and perhaps feel compelled to explain your decision to disapproving family and friends (Fothergill, 2013). You may wonder, "Will my child be securely attached if I see her only a few hours a day?" You certainly worry about the quality of care your child would receive: "Will my baby get enough attention at the local day-care center?" "Am I *really* harming my child?"

To answer these kinds of questions, in 1989, developmentalists began the National Institute of Child Health and Human Development (NICHD) Study of Early Child Care. They selected more than 1,000 newborns in 10 regions of the United States and tracked the lives of these children, measuring everything from attachment to academic abilities, from mental health to mothers' caregiving skills. They looked at the hours each child spent in day care, and assessed the quality of each setting. The NICHD newborns are being followed as they travel into adult life (Vandell and others, 2010).

The good news is that putting a baby in day care does not weaken the attachment bond. Most infants attending day care are securely attached to their parents. The important force that promotes attachment is the *quality* of the dance—whether a parent is a sensitive caregiver—not whether she works (Nomaguchi and DeMaris, 2013; Phillips & Lowenstein, 2011). Moreover, what happens at home is the crucial influence affecting how young children develop, outweighing long hours spent in day care during the first years of life (Belsky and others, 2007b; Stein and others, 2013).

However, when we look at *just* the impact of spending those long hours, the findings are less upbeat. In contrast to the research with poverty-level infants, middle-class toddlers show *elevated* cortisol levels when they attend full-time day care (Berry, Blair, & Granger, 2016). Even worse, the NICHD follow-ups suggested that long hours spent in day care, beginning early in life, predict children's having a slightly higher risk of "acting-out issues" as late as in their teens (Vandell and others, 2010; see also Coley and others, 2013).

These results do not offer comfort to the millions of parents with babies who rely heavily on day care. Luckily, the correlations are weak (Vandell and others, 2010). Day care's negative effects apply mainly to children who attend large centers, not smaller family day care (Coley and others, 2013; Groeneveld and others, 2010).

What is the trouble with day-care centers? For hints, let's scan the general state of child care in the United States.

Exploring Child-Care Quality in the United States

Visit several facilities and you will immediately see that U.S. day care varies dramatically in quality. In some places, babies are warehoused and ignored. In others, every child is nurtured and loved.

The essence of quality day care again boils down to the dance—that is, the attachment relationship between caretakers and the children. Children develop intense attachments to their day-care providers. If a particular caregiver is sensitive, a child in her care tends to be securely attached (Ahnert, Pinquart, & Lamb, 2006; De Schipper, Tavecchio, & van IJzendoorn, 2008).

Child-care providers and parents agree: To be effective in this job, you need to be patient, caring, empathic, and child-centered (Berthelsen & Brownlee, 2007; Virmani & Ontai, 2010). You also need to work in a setting where you can relate to children in a one-to-one way. To demonstrate this point, researchers videotaped teachers at 64 Dutch preschools, either playing with three children or with five. Teachers acted more empathic in the three-child group. They were more likely to criticize and get angry with the group of five (De Schipper, Riksen-Walraven, & Geurts, 2006). These differences in teachers' tone and style were especially pronounced with younger children (the 3-year-olds). So group size matters; and the lower the child–teacher ratio, the better—especially earlier in life.

What other aspects of a program should parents look for, particularly with toddlers and 3-year-olds? The same qualities we crave from our government, or workplace, or this class. We want to know exactly what to expect.

Excellent child-care facilities feature predictable, comforting routines: Children arrive and put their belongings in their own cubby; then play time, snack time, and rest time occur in a fixed sequence each day. Caregivers offer comfort through the *way* they interact (La Paro & Gloeckler, 2016). They stimulate children cognitively and socially. They balance consistent rules with lots of love (much more about this ideal child-rearing approach in Chapter 7).

It's also important for boys and girls to feel confident that a familiar person is providing care (Harrist, Thompson, & Norris, 2007). Forming an attachment takes time. Therefore, children are more apt to be securely attached to a caregiver when that person has been there a longer time (Ahnert, Pinquart, & Lamb, 2006).

However, partly because of the abysmal pay (in the United States, it's often close to the minimum wage), day-care workers are apt to quit. Surveys in Canada (Royer & Moreau, 2016) and Finland (Pölkki & Virnanen, 2016) show that most people in this field love their jobs. But no matter how much someone adores young children, that person must have enough money to survive. One U.S. comparison suggested that when teachers reported having *minimally adequate* wages and paid time-off, toddlers in that particular class were happier and better behaved (King and others, 2016).

Day-care providers also need to have the freedom to make their own choices about what activities to use and how to arrange the class day. In the Canadian survey I just mentioned, teachers cited work autonomy as the job feature most vital to their well-being.

In sum, now we know why day-care centers are at risk of providing inadequate care. Their culprit is lack of autonomy and less consistent care. Family day cares typically feature one stable caregiver who has considerable personal freedom (since the person is watching the children in her home). In large facilities, where directors or corporate bosses plan the day, staff is more apt to come and go (Ahnert, Pinquart,

How will these male day-care workers feel about working at a nontraditional job? As the text shows, keys lie in whether they don't feel overwhelmed by caring for too many children, have enough money to meet their needs, and can use their creativity to arrange this class the way they want.

& Lamb, 2006; Gerber, Whitebrook, & Weinstein, 2007; Groeneveld and others, 2010). Yes, children attending family day care are vulnerable because there is less oversight about what happens during the day. But, ideally, this more intimate setting can provide the nurturing, stable security very young children need.

INTERVENTIONS: Choosing Child Care

Given these findings, what should parents do? The take-home message is not "avoid a day-care center," but rather "choose the best possible place." Look for low staff turnover; a predictable daily routine; caregivers who offer stimulation, empathy, and clear rules. Make sure that the staff members feel happy about their workplace as well.

Finally, here, too, consider a child's biology. While attending low-quality day cares are harmful for infants and toddlers with an environment-responsive genetic profile, these same children may flourish if a program is top notch (Belsky & Pluess, 2013). So, as we learn more about genetics, making blanket generalizations—such as "day care is bad (or good)"—may not be appropriate. It depends on the quality of the program, a child's home environment, and, now, the biology of a given child.

Table 4.2 draws on these messages in a checklist. And if you are a U.S. parent who relies heavily on day care, keep those guilty thoughts at bay. Your child may blossom at a high-quality day care. Moreover, *your* responsiveness matters most. You are your child's major teacher and the main force in making your child secure.

Now that we have examined attachment, poverty, and day care, it's time to turn to the topic I have been implicitly talking about all along—toddlerhood.

Table 4.2: Choosing a Day-Care Center: A Checklist

Overall Considerations

- Consider the caregiver(s). Are they nurturing? Do they feel that despite the low pay, they have enough money to live and the freedom to do what they want? Do they adore young children and especially enjoy working at *this place*?

- Ask about stability, or staff turnover. Have caregivers left in the last few months? Can infants have the same care provider when they move to the toddler room?

- Look for a low caregiver-to-baby ratio (and a small group of children overall). The ideal is one caregiver to every two or three babies.

- Look at the daily routine. Does a structured ritual flow through each day? Are activities clearly laid out, and do caregivers follow these plans? Do teachers stimulate cognition and behave in loving and predictable ways? (For toddlers and 3-year-olds it's also vital to have safe, age-appropriate play materials, such as blocks and books, as well as a dress-up corner, areas for painting near sinks, and places for children to congregate for group activities.)

Additional Suggestions

- For infants and toddlers in full-time care, limit exposure by having a child take occasional vacations or build in special time with the child every day.

- Consider the home environment. If a toddler's family life is chaotic or she lives in a dangerous neighborhood, it's better to spend the entire day at a stable, nurturing place.

- Consider a child's temperament. The kind of genetically responsive (highly environment-sensitive) babies I discussed earlier have special trouble coping with less than optimal care; but these same toddlers may flourish in a high-quality setting.

- And finally, for society: *Pay child-care workers decently and make day care more affordable for U.S. parents, too!*

Background information from the researchers cited in this section.

Tying It All Together

1. Hugo is telling your class which low-SES children are at highest risk of not graduating from high school. Pick the statement he should *not* make: *These children are poor during elementary school; these children are poor during the first four years of life.*

2. Nancy is anxious about her decision to put her 6-month-old in day care. Give a "good news" statement to ease Nancy's mind, and then be honest and give some "not such good news" statements about day care.

3. Imagine you are interviewing for a job at a local day-care center. What questions should you ask the director to better ensure that you will be satisfied at work?

Answers to the Tying It All Together questions can be found at the end of this chapter.

Toddlerhood: Age of Autonomy and Shame and Doubt

LEARNING OUTCOMES
- Outline the emotional challenges of toddlerhood.
- Contrast exuberant and inhibited toddlers, and child-rearing strategies for each temperament.
- Summarize the caregiving advice in this section.

Imagine time-traveling back to when you were a toddler. Everything is entrancing—a bubble bath, the dishwasher soap box, the dirt and bugs in your backyard. You are just cracking the language barrier and thrilled to finally travel on your own two feet. Passionate to sail into life, you are also intensely connected to that number-one adult in your life. So, during our second year on this planet, the twin agendas that make us human first emerge: We need to be closely connected, and we want to be free, autonomous selves. This is why Erik Erikson (1950) used the descriptive word **autonomy** to describe children's challenge as they emerge from the cocoon of babyhood (see Table 4.3).

Autonomy involves everything from the thrill a 2-year-old feels when forming his first sentences, to the delight children have in dressing themselves. But it also involves those not-so-pleasant meltdowns we associate with the "terrible twos." In one study, while 1 in 3 parents labeled their child as having behavior problems that were "off the charts" (Schellinger & Talmi, 2013), this feeling may be a misperception. As you can see in Figure 4.8 on the next page, difficulties "listening" and angry outbursts (Barry & Kochanska, 2010) are *normal* during that magic age when children's passion is to explore the world (recall Piaget's little scientist behaviors).

Erikson used the words *shame* and *doubt* to refer to the situation in which a toddler's drive for autonomy is not fulfilled. But feeling shameful and doubtful is also vital to shedding babyhood and entering the human world. During their first year of life, infants show joy, fear, and anger. At age 2, more complicated, uniquely human emotions emerge: pride and shame. The appearance of these **self-conscious emotions** is a milestone—showing that a child is becoming aware of having a self. The gift (and

autonomy Erikson's second psychosocial task, when toddlers confront the challenge of understanding that they are separate individuals.

self-conscious emotions Feelings of pride, shame, or guilt, which first emerge around age 2 and show the capacity to reflect on the self.

Table 4.3: Erikson's Psychosocial Stages of Childhood, Adolescence, and Emerging Adulthood

Life Stage	Primary Task
Infancy (birth to 1 year)	Basic trust versus mistrust
Toddlerhood (1 to 2 years)	**Autonomy versus shame and doubt**
Early childhood (3 to 6 years)	Initiative versus guilt
Middle childhood (7 to 12 years)	Industry versus inferiority
Adolescence and emerging adulthood (teens into twenties)	Identity versus role confusion
Emerging adulthood (twenties)	Intimacy versus isolation

sometimes curse) of being human is that we are capable of self-reflection, able to get outside of our heads and observe our actions from an outsider's point of view. Children show signs of this uniquely human quality between ages 2 and 3, when they feel ashamed or are clearly proud of their actions for the first time (Kagan, 1984).

Socialization: The Challenge for 2-Year-Olds

Shame and pride are vital in another respect. They are essential to **socialization**—being taught to live in the human community.

When does the U.S. socialization pressure *heat up*? For answers, developmentalists surveyed middle-class parents about the rules they set for their 14-month-olds and when the children just turned 2 (Smetana, Kochanska, & Chuang, 2000). While rules for younger toddlers centered on safety issues ("Stay away from the stove!"), by age 2, parents were telling their children to "share," "sit at the table," and "don't disobey, bite, or hit." Therefore, we expect children to begin to act "like adults" around their second birthdays. No wonder 2-year-olds are infamous for those tantrums called the "terrible twos"!

Figure 4.8 illustrates just how difficult it is for toddlers to control themselves and to follow socialization rules when their parents are around. When can children follow unwanted directions when a parent *isn't* in the room? To answer this question related to early *conscience*—the ability to adopt internal standards for our behavior, or have that little voice inside us that says, "Even though I want to do this, it's wrong"—researchers devised an interesting procedure. Accompanied by their mothers, children enter a laboratory full of toys. Next, the parent gives an unwelcome instruction—telling the child either to clean up the toys or not to touch another easily reachable set of enticing toys. Then the mother leaves the room, and researchers watch the child through a one-way mirror.

Not unexpectedly, children's ability to "listen to a parent in their head" and stop doing what they want improves dramatically from age 2 to age 4 (Kochanska, Coy, & Murray, 2001). Who is better or worse at this feat of self-control?

As you might expect, the marked differences in self-control we see in young children have genetic roots (Gartstein and others, 2013; Wang & Saudino, 2013). Some of us are biologically better able to resist temptation at any age! Parenting matters, too. Caregivers who label a toddler's emotions ("You are really upset about that!") can help coach children to manage disappointment without immediately lashing out (Scrimgeour, Davis, &

socialization How children are taught to behave in socially appropriate ways.

This toddler has reached a human milestone: She can feel shame, which shows that she is aware that she has a separate self.

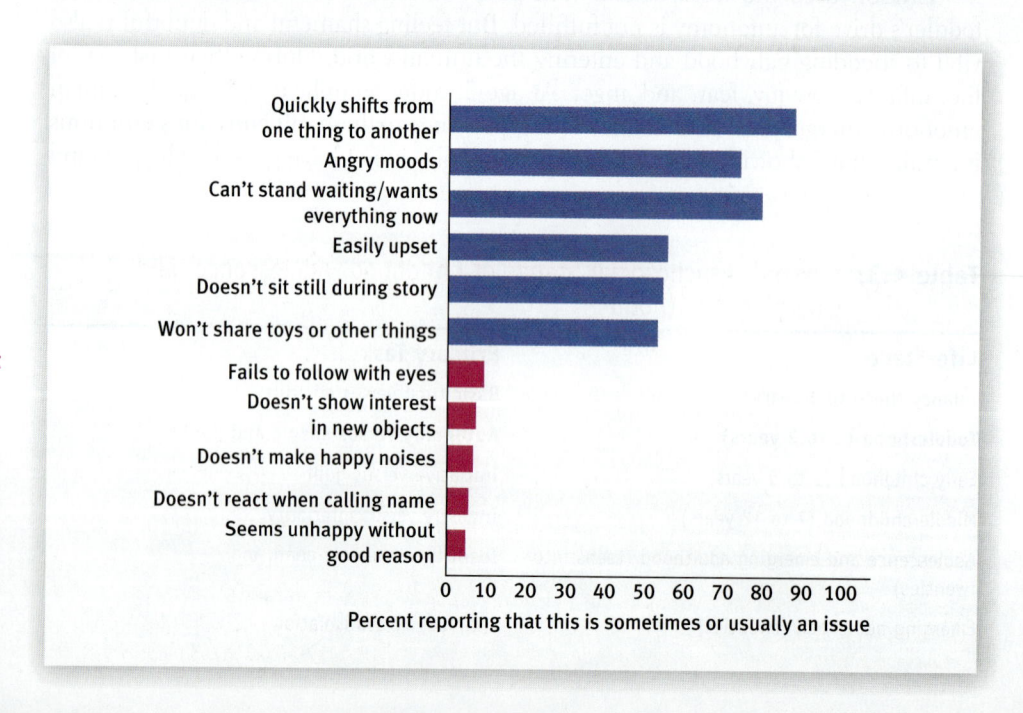

FIGURE 4.8: Rates of specific difficult behaviors, based on a survey of Dutch parents of 6,491 toddlers
Notice that most parents say their toddlers don't listen, have temper tantrums, and refuse to sit still or share—but the unusual troubling behaviors in red are warning signs of real problems.
Data from Beernick, Swinkels, & Buitelaar, 2007.

Buss, 2016). While mothers excel at this gentle coaching, a father's warmth weighs heavily in socializing children at older ages (Lickenbrock and others, 2013; Schueler & Prinz, 2013). So Dad's influence—at least in traditional two-parent families—is important, but mainly when children move beyond the clear-cut attachment zone.

What temperamental traits provoke early compliance? The answer comes as no surprise. Fearful toddlers are more obedient (Aksan & Kochanska, 2004; see also the How Do We Know box). Exuberant, joyful, fearless, intrepid toddler-explorers are especially hard to socialize! (See Kochanska & Knaack, 2003.)

HOW DO WE KNOW . . .
that shy and exuberant children differ dramatically in self-control?

How do researchers measure toddler temperaments? How do they test later self-control? Their first step is to design situations tailored to elicit fear, anger, and joy and then observe how toddlers act.

In the fear-eliciting "treatment," a child enters a room filled with frightening toy objects, such as a dinosaur with huge teeth or a black box covered with spider webs. The experimenter asks that boy or girl to perform a mildly risky act, such as putting a hand into the box. To measure anger, the researchers restrain a child in a car seat and then rate how frustrated the toddler gets. To tap into exuberance, the researchers entertain a child with a set of funny puppets. Will the toddler respond with gales of laughter or be more reserved?

Several years later, the researchers set up a situation provoking noncompliance by asking the same child, now age 4, to perform an impossible task (such as throwing Velcro balls at a target from a long distance without looking) to get a prize. Then they leave the room and watch through a one-way mirror to see if the boy or girl will cheat.

Toddlers at the high end of the fearless, joyous, and angry continuum show less "morality" at age 4. Without the strong inhibition of fear, their exuberant impulses to "get closer" are difficult to dampen down. So they succumb to temptation, sneak closer, and look directly at the target as they hurl the balls (Kochanska & Knaack, 2003).

Being Exuberant and Being Shy

Adam [was a vigorous, happy baby who] began walking at 9 months. From then on, it seemed as though he could never stop.

(10 months) Adam . . . refuses to be carried anywhere. . . . He trips over objects, falls down, bumps himself.

(12 months) The word *osside* appears. . . . Adam stands by the door, banging at it and repeating this magic word again and again.

(19 months) Adam begins attending a toddler group. . . . The first day, Adam climbs to the highest rung of the climbing structure and falls down. . . . The second day, Adam upturns a heavy wooden bench. . . . The fourth day, the teacher [devastates Adam's mother] when she says, "I think Adam is not ready for this."

(13 months) [Erin begins to talk in sentences the same week as she takes her first steps.] . . . Rather suddenly, Erin becomes quite shy. . . . She cries when her mother leaves the room, and insists on following her everywhere.

(15 months) Erin and her parents go to the birthday party of a little friend. . . . For the first half-hour, Erin stays very close to her mother, intermittently hiding her face on her mother's skirt.

(18 months) Erin's mother takes her to a toddlers' gym. Erin watches the children . . . with a "tight little face." . . . Her mother berates herself for raising such a timid child.

(Lieberman, 1993, pp. 83–87, 104–105)

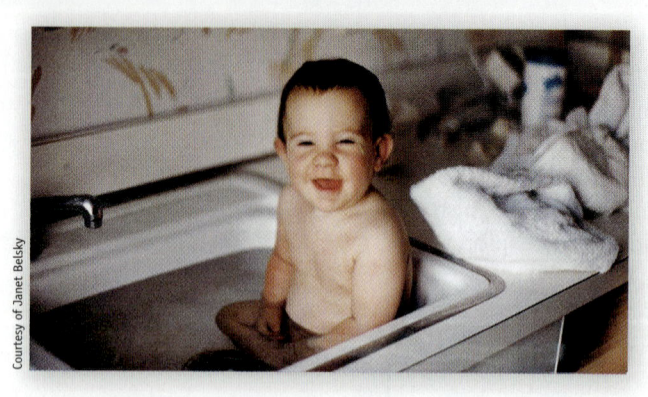

My exuberant son—shown enjoying a sink bath at 9 months of age—began to have problems at 18 months, when his strong, joyous temperament collided with the need to "please sit still and listen, Thomas!"

Observe 1-year-olds and you will immediately pick out the Erins and the Adams. Some children are wary and shy. Others are whirlwinds of activity, constantly in motion, bouncing off the walls. I remember my own first toddler group at the local Y, when—just like Adam's mother—I first realized how different my exuberant son was from the other children his age. After enduring the horrified expressions of the other mothers as Thomas whirled gleefully around the room while everyone else sat obediently for a snack, I came home and cried. How was I to know that the qualities that made my outgoing, joyous, vital baby so charismatic during his first year of life might go along with his being so difficult to tame?

Psychologist Jerome Kagan carried out classic longitudinal studies following toddlers with shy temperaments. Kagan (1994; see also Degnan, Almas, & Fox, 2010) classifies about 1 in 5 middle-class European American toddlers as inhibited. Although they are comfortable in familiar situations, these 1-year-olds, like Erin, get nervous when confronted with anything new. Inhibited 13-month-olds shy away from approaching a toy robot, a clown, or an unfamiliar person. They take time to venture out in the Strange Situation, get agitated when the stranger enters, and cry bitterly when their parent leaves the room.

Intense shyness is also moderately "genetic" (Smith and others, 2012), and we can see clues to this temperament early in life. At 4 months of age, inhibited toddlers excessively fret and cry (Marysko and others, 2010; Moehler and others, 2008). At month 8 or 9, they have special trouble ignoring distracting stimuli such as flashing lights or background noise. Their attention wanders to any off-topic, irrelevant, unpleasant event (Pérez-Edgar and others, 2010a).

Inhibited toddlers tend to be fearful throughout childhood (Degnan, Almas, & Fox, 2010). They overfocus on threatening stimuli in their teens (Pérez-Edgar and others, 2010a). Using brain scans, Kagan's research team found that his inhibited toddlers, as young adults, showed more activity in the part of the brain that codes negative emotions when shown a stranger's face on a screen (Schwartz and others, 2003). So for all of you formerly very shy people (your author included) who think you have shed that childhood wariness, you still carry your physiology inside.

Still, if you think you have come a long way in conquering your *overpowering* childhood shyness, you are probably correct. Many anxious toddlers (and exuberant explorers) get less inhibited as they move into elementary school and their teens (Degnan, Almas, & Fox, 2010; Pérez-Edgar and others, 2010b).

INTERVENTIONS: Providing the Right Temperament–Socialization Fit

Faced with a temperamentally timid toddler such as Erin or an exuberant explorer like Adam or Thomas, what can parents do?

Socializing a Shy Baby

In dealing with fearful children, parents' impulse is to back off ("Erin is emotionally fragile, so I won't pressure her to go to day care or clean up her toys"). This "treat 'em like glass" approach is apt to backfire, provoking more wariness down the road (Natsuaki and others, 2013). With shy children, be caring but provide a gentle push. Exposing a shy toddler to *supportive* new social situations—such as family day care—helps teach that child to cope.

Raising a Rambunctious Toddler

When fearless explorers can't stop bouncing off the walls, it's natural for adults to get flooded with anxiety (Lorber, Mitnick, & Slep, 2016). Many parents resort to a harsh discipline strategy called **power assertion**—yelling, screaming, and hitting. Another response is to give up, abandoning any attempt to discipline a child.

power assertion An ineffective socialization strategy that involves yelling, screaming, or hitting a child.

Both reactions are counterproductive. Relying on power assertion alone strongly predicts behavior problems down the road (Brotman and others, 2009; Kochanska & Knaack, 2003; Leve and others, 2010). Disengaging from discipline robs the child of the tools to modify his behavior. Plus, it conveys the message, "You are out of control and there is nothing I can do."

While in interviews, mothers give screaming and hitting low marks; when these same people are observed interacting with their misbehaving toddlers, they often automatically resort to power assertion techniques (Passini, Pihet, & Favez, 2014). When dealing with toddler defiance, what kind of discipline works best?

The answer brings me to a fascinating study tracking the usefulness of different child-rearing strategies when toddlers act up (Larzelere & Knowles, 2015). If 2-year-olds whine, reasoning and emotion coaching are most effective. But for disruptive behavior, such as hitting or biting, the best response is to set firm limits, such as immediately putting the child in time-out.

The ultimate all-purpose socializer, however, is a secure attachment (Kochanska & Kim, 2013). As my husband insightfully commented, "Punishment doesn't matter much to Thomas. What he does, he does for your love."

Table 4.4 offers a summary of this discussion, listing these different toddler temperaments, their infant precursors, their pluses and potential later dangers, and lessons for socializing each kind of child. Now let's look at some general temperament-sensitive lessons for raising every child.

An Overall Strategy for Temperamentally Friendly Childrearing

In the classic study, discussed earlier, in which developmentalists classified babies as easy, slow-to-warm-up, or difficult, researchers found that difficult infants were more likely to have problems with their teachers and peers (Thomas & Chess, 1977; Thomas, Chess, & Birch, 1968). However, some children learned to compensate for their biology and to shine. The key, the researchers discovered, lay in a parenting

Table 4.4: Exuberant and Inhibited Toddler Temperaments: A Summary

Inhibited, Shy Toddler

- **Developmental precursor:** Responds with intense arousal to external stimulation in infancy.
- **Plus:** Easily socialized; shows early signs of conscience; not a discipline problem.
- **Minus:** Shy, fearful temperament can persist into adulthood, making social encounters painful.
- **Child-rearing advice:** Don't overprotect the child. Expose the baby to unfamiliar people and supportive new situations.

Exuberant Toddler

- **Developmental precursor:** Emotionally intense but unafraid of new stimuli.
- **Plus:** Joyous; fearless; outgoing; adventurous.
- **Minus:** Less easily socialized; potential problems with conscience development; at higher risk for later "acting-out" behavior problems.
- **Child-rearing advice:** While calm reasoning works best to quell whining, employ time-outs for defiant behavior. But, above all, use lots of love.

goodness of fit An ideal parenting strategy that involves arranging children's environments to suit their temperaments, minimizing their vulnerabilities and accentuating their strengths.

strategy they labeled **goodness of fit**. Parents who carefully arranged their children's lives to minimize their vulnerabilities and accentuate their strengths had infants who later did well.

Understanding that their child was overwhelmed by stimuli, these parents kept the environment calm. They may have offered a quiet environment for studying and encouraged their child to do activities that took advantage of his talents. They went overboard to provide a placid, nurturing, low-stress milieu.

Here, too, emerging genetic studies suggest these parents were right. Again, researchers find that children are genetically predisposed to be highly responsive or relatively immune to environmental events (Ellis and others, 2011a). In typical settings, highly reactive babies may be categorized as difficult because they are wired to react negatively to changes. These same infants, however, may flourish when the environment is exceptionally calm (for review, see Belsky & Pluess, 2009). In fact, in one study, when environment-responsive children were put in a nurturing, placid environment, they performed *better* than their laid-back peers (Obradović, Burt, & Masten, 2010)!

The lesson again is that making assumptions about the enduring quality of infant attachment, seeing full-time day care as a universal stress, or, in this case, labeling a baby (or person) as "difficult" or "easy" is not appropriate. With the right person–environment fit, what looks like a liability might be a gift!

Some Concluding Thoughts: Giving Is Built into Being Human, Too

In this section, I've been emphasizing how confrontation comes on strongly during our second year on this planet. But I cannot leave you with the impression that angry independence is the sum-total of toddlers' emotional lives.

Two-year-olds will step in to help a researcher retrieve an out-of-reach object; they comfort that person when she bangs her finger and says, "Ouch!" (Dunfield & Kuhlmeier, 2013; Hepach, Vaish, & Tomasello, 2013; Thompson & Newton, 2013). Eighteen-month-olds even perform sharing acts that go beyond our adult norm, giving some of their own stickers to an experimenter when that person has acted selfishly in a previous trial (Sebastián-Enesco, Hernández-Lloreda, & Colmenares, 2013).

The fact that toddlers naturally take joy in giving suggests that giving is built into being human.

This impulse to help, comfort, and share, which blossoms during toddlerhood, appears in cultures worldwide (House and others, 2013). And doing good makes young children feel good. Toddlers look happier after giving a treat to another person than when they get that treat for themselves. They seem especially joyous when engaging in costly giving—giving up something they *wanted to get* (Aknin, Hamlin, & Dunn, 2012). So the principle that it feels better to give than to receive doesn't need to be vigorously instilled in us at a mosque, synagogue, or church. Caring is also baked into humanity, beginning before age 2 (Hepach, Vaisch, & Tomasello, 2013)!

How does sharing and kindness evolve during childhood, and how do infants' attachments to parents spread to peers? What happens to babies who are shy or exuberant, difficult or easy, as they journey into elementary school? Stay tuned for answers to these questions (and many more) as we enter the childhood years.

Tying It All Together

1. If Amanda is 2½, which prediction is FALSE? *Amanda wants to be independent, yet is closely attached./Amanda can possibly feel shame./Amanda's parents haven't begun to discipline her.*

2. To a colleague who confides that he's worried about his timid toddler, what comforting words can you offer?

3. Think back to your own childhood: Did you fit into either the shy or exuberant temperamental type? How did your parents cope with your personality style?

Answers to the Tying It All Together questions can be found at the end of this chapter.

SUMMARY

Attachment: The Basic Life Bond

For much of the twentieth century, behaviorists minimized the mother–child bond. European psychoanalysts such as John Bowlby were finding, however, that attachment was a basic human need. Harlow's primate studies convinced U.S. developmentalists of the importance of **attachment**, and Bowlby transformed developmental science by arguing that having a loving **primary attachment figure** is biologically built into our species, and crucial to development. Although threatening situations evoke **proximity-seeking behavior** at any age—during **toddlerhood**—just being physically apart from an attachment figure elicits distress.

According to Bowlby, life begins with a 3-month-long **preattachment phase**, characterized by the first **social smile**. After an intermediate phase called **attachment in the making**, at about 7 months of age, the landmark phase of **clear-cut attachment** begins, signaled by **separation anxiety** and **stranger anxiety**. During this period spanning toddlerhood, children need their caregiver to be physically close, and they rely on **social referencing** to monitor their behavior. After age 3, children can tolerate separations, as they develop an internal **working model** of their caregiver—which they carry into life.

To explore individual differences in attachment, Mary Ainsworth devised the **Strange Situation**. Using this test, which involves separations and reunions, developmentalists categorize 1-year-olds as **securely** or **insecurely attached**. Securely attached 1-year-olds use their primary attachment figure as a secure base for exploration and are delighted when she returns. **Avoidant** infants seem indifferent. **Anxious-ambivalent** children are overly frantic and inconsolable. Children with a **disorganized attachment** react in an erratic way and may show fear when their parent reenters the room.

Caregiver–child interactions are characterized by a beautiful **synchrony,** or attachment dance. Although a baby's attachment style can sometimes mirror the caregiver's own working model of attachment, attachment is also affected by the child's **temperament** and depends on the caregiver's other close relationships as well.

Cross-cultural studies support the idea that attachment to a primary caregiver is universal, with similar percentages of babies in various countries classified as securely attached. When distressed, babies run to the caregiver who spends the most time with them, but infants can be attached to several people, and having a secure attachment to only one caregiver may be all that infants need for optimal development.

As Bowlby predicted in his working-model concept, securely attached babies have superior mental health. Infants with insecure attachments (especially disorganized attachments) are at risk for later problems. However, the good-news/bad-news finding is that, when the caregiving environment changes, attachment security can change for the better or worse. A gene related to **oxytocin** production may make children more or less vulnerable to variations in caregiver sensitivity. Babies exposed to the worst-case attachment situation, living in an orphanage with virtually no caregiving, experience a **dose–response effect.** Although the risk of having enduring problems sets in during the "attachment zone," the risk of lifelong impairments depends on the depth of the deprivation and the age at which a child leaves that institution.

Settings for Development

Early-childhood poverty—widespread in the United States—affects children's physical health. It compromises caregiver sensitivity and—most important—has long-term effects on school success. **Head Start** and **Early Head Start** programs help impoverished young children in the United States. Poverty-level babies and toddlers benefit from full-time **day care. Preschool** has positive effects for every child. Despite their many daily challenges, low-income parents who are upbeat about life can give their children exceptional care.

It is common for parents to go back to work during a baby's first year of life, but due to the expense of day care and anxieties about leaving their baby with strangers, parents in the United States ideally prefer to keep infant care in the family. Paid child-care options include nannies (for affluent parents), **family day care** (in which a person cares for a small number of children in her home), and larger **day-care centers.**

The NICHD Study of Early Child Care showed that the best predictor of being securely attached at age 1 is having a sensitive parent. But middle-class children who attend day-care centers full time (versus family care) have elevated cortisol levels and a slightly higher risk of acting out as teens.

In choosing day care, search for loving teachers, low child-to-caregiver ratios, care-provider stability, and a predictable daily structure. Find out if the staff feels a sense of autonomy and believes their salary meets their basic needs. Because day-care workers are so poorly paid in the United States, staff turnover is a serious problem. This issue, plus the lack of freedom at larger, more institutional places, may explain why day-care centers can be problematic. Babies who are genetically prone to be environment-responsive are especially vulnerable to low-quality day care.

Toddlerhood: Age of Autonomy and Shame and Doubt

Erikson's **autonomy** captures the essence of toddlerhood, the landmark age when we shed babyhood, first observe the self, and enter the human world. **Self-conscious emotions** such as pride and shame emerge and are crucial to **socialization,** which begins in earnest at around age 2. Difficulties with focusing and obeying are normal during toddlerhood, but at this age, children differ in their ability to control themselves. Temperamentally fearful children show earlier signs of "conscience." Exuberant, active toddlers are especially hard to socialize.

As young babies, shy toddlers react with intense motor activity to stimuli. They are more inhibited in elementary school and adolescence and show neurological signs of social wariness as young adults. Still (with sensitive parenting), many shy toddlers and fearless explorers lose these extreme tendencies as they grow older.

To help an inhibited baby, don't overprotect the child. With exuberant toddlers, **power assertion** is a serious danger. For acts of defiance, like hitting, it is vital to set limits, as long as parents use discipline along with lots of love. Parents should promote **goodness of fit**—tailoring the environment to a child's temperament. Giving, helping, and sharing—not just confrontation—are built into toddlerhood, too.

KEY TERMS

anxious-ambivalent attachment, p. 109
attachment, p. 105
attachment in the making, p. 107
autonomy, p. 121
avoidant attachment, p. 109
clear-cut (focused) attachment, p. 108
day care, p. 117
day-care center, p. 118

disorganized attachment, p. 109
dose–response effect, p. 114
Early Head Start, p. 117
family day care, p. 118
goodness of fit, p. 126
Head Start, p. 117
insecure attachment, p. 109
oxytocin, p. 113
power assertion, p. 124

preattachment phase, p. 107
preschool, p. 117
primary attachment figure, p. 107
proximity-seeking behavior, p. 107
secure attachment, p. 109
self-conscious emotions, p. 121
separation anxiety, p. 108

social referencing, p. 108
social smile, p. 107
socialization, p. 122
Strange Situation, p. 108
stranger anxiety, p. 108
synchrony, p. 110
temperament, p. 111
toddlerhood, p. 105
working model, p. 108

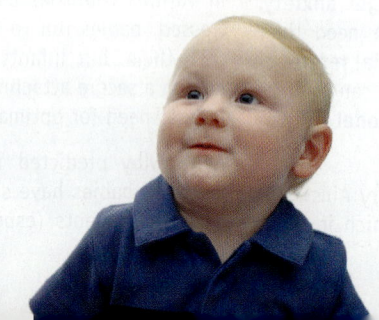

ANSWERS TO Tying It All Together QUIZZES

Attachment: The Basic Life Bond

1. Your responses will differ, but any example you give, such as "I called Mom when that terrible thing happened at work," should show that under stress your impulse is to immediately contact your attachment figure.
2. Muriel = preattachment; Janine = attachment in the making; Ted = clear-cut attachment: Tania = working model.
3. (1) b; (2) c; (3) d; (4) a
4. The child has an avoidant attachment.
5. Manuel should say: Infants around the world get attached to a primary caregiver at roughly the same age.
6. Caution Jasmine that her baby may have difficulties focusing and may show indiscriminate friendliness; if she is adopting a boy, her child may have special trouble in developing a secure attachment. However, tell Jasmine that these problems can be muted with loving care.

Settings for Development

1. Children are at highest risk when their families are poor *during their first four years of life*.
2. The good news is that Nancy's parenting is the main force in determining her child's attachment (and emotional health). The bad news is that some day-care centers leave much to be desired, and long hours spent in these centers provoke spikes in cortisol levels, as well as a slightly elevated risk of later acting-out issues.
3. To supplement the critical question of how much the job pays, ask whether there is paid time off for planning the curricula, sick leave, and vacation days. Does this position encourage professional development time (attendance at conferences)? What are my chances for promotion? Will I have freedom to structure the day? How many babies and toddlers will be in the group (the fewer, the better)? If caring for infants, can I move up to the toddler room? How many staff members have left in the past few months? (This is a good clue as to how user-friendly this work place is.) Then linger and make your own observations by visiting different rooms and questioning staff members about their jobs.

Toddlerhood: Age of Autonomy *and* Shame *and* Doubt

1. Parents typically discipline their 2-year-olds (last alternative is wrong).
2. You might tell him that most children grow out of their shyness, even if they do not completely shed this temperamental tendency. But stress the advantages of being shy: His baby will be easier to socialize and may have a stronger conscience.
3. These answers will be totally your own.

CONNECT ONLINE:

LaunchPad macmillan learning | Check out our videos and additional resources located at: www.macmillanlearning.com

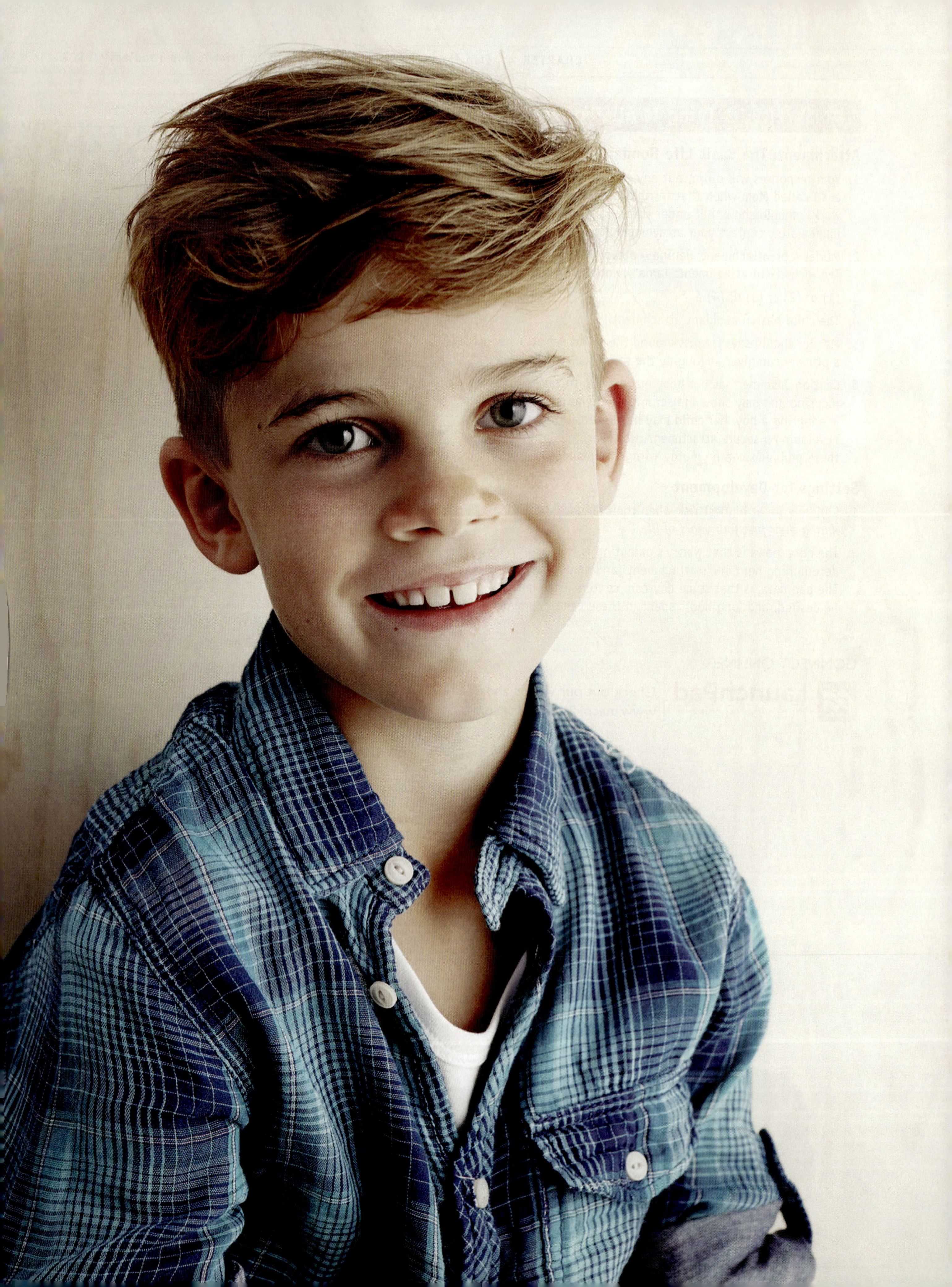

Childhood

In this three-chapter book part, the first two chapters trace children's development in stages. The final chapter explores the settings within which children develop: home, school, and community.

Chapter 5—**Early Childhood** focuses on preschool and kindergarten (ages 3 to 6). I'll explore young children's unfolding physical skills. Then, the heart of this chapter—cognition—decodes the strange ways preschoolers think, offers a framework for teaching, and shows how language develops. Next, I'll trace how children learn they have an enduring self and decode other people's mental states. The final section enters the world of preschool play and describes those conditions defined by the inability to relate to the human world: autism spectrum disorders.

Chapter 6—**Middle Childhood** turns to elementary school (ages 7 to 12). After spelling out why two world-class psychologists target middle childhood as the first adult-like life stage, I'll describe the brain changes that make elementary school-aged children's thinking unique, and explore issues relating to health and motor skills. Then, I'll examine cognition and emotional states, tracking self-awareness (and self-esteem), caring acts, and aggression. The final part explores friendships and popularity, then examines bullying.

Chapter 7—**Settings for Development: Home, School, and Community** first tackles children's family lives. Is there an ideal way of parenting? Why do some children thrive in spite of dysfunctional early lives? What is the impact of spanking, child abuse, and divorce on the child? You will learn about intelligence tests, what makes schools successful, and how teachers can make every child eager to learn. Throughout this chapter, I'll be highlighting the important role neighborhoods play in determining children's success.

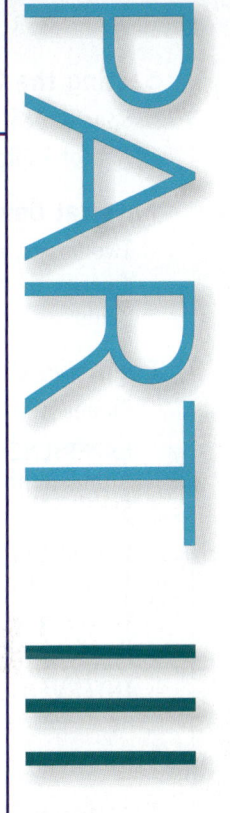

Application to Developing Lives Parenting Simulation: Early and Middle Childhood

In the *Early Childhood* and *Middle Childhood* modules of *Developing Lives*, you will consider the impact your choices will have on the physical, cognitive, and social and emotional development of your child.

Early Childhood & Middle Childhood modules

Physical	Cognitive	Social and Emotional
• What kinds of food will your child eat?	• What is your child's Piagetian stage?	• What social environment will you place your child in?
• How much physical activity will you encourage?	• What kind of education will you choose?	• How will you discipline your child?
• Will you regulate your child's TV or video game time?	• Will you put your child in tutoring if needed?	• Will you eat meals as a family or have a different routine?

Left: sanneberg/Shutterstock

CHAPTER 5

CHAPTER OUTLINE

Setting the Context
Special "Mind Reading" Talents
Age of Exploration

Physical Development
Two Types of Motor Talents
Threats to Preschool Physical Skills

Cognitive Development
Piaget's Preoperational Stage

EXPERIENCING CHILDHOOD: Animism and the Power of Stephen King

INTERVENTIONS: Using Piaget's Ideas at Home and at Work

Vygotsky's Zone of Proximal Development

INTERVENTIONS: Becoming an Effective Scaffolder

Language

Emotional Development
Constructing Our Personal Past
Making Sense of Other People's Minds

INTERVENTIONS: Stimulating Theory of Mind

Social Development
Play: The Work of Early Childhood
Girls' and Boys' Play Worlds

HOW DO WE KNOW . . . That Pink Gives Girls Permission to Act Like Boys?

HOT IN DEVELOPMENTAL SCIENCE: Autism Spectrum Disorders

Early Childhood

As the 3-year-olds drift in to Learning Preschool, Ms. Angela fills me in:

"First, we have free play. Then, read a story. At 10:30, we have snack and go outside. We focus on stretching the children's capacities, but don't expect too much—no academics at this age. The goal is to get them to master the basics for school and life: listen; take turns; share; be respectful; talk about feelings; don't yell (use your inside voice). The room is arranged into activity centers to give the children plenty of room to explore."

At the kitchen center, Kanesha is pretending to scrub pots. "What is your name?" I ask. "You know!" says Kanesha, looking at me as if I'm totally dumb. Kanesha gives me a plate: "Let's have psghetti and Nadia makeacake." We are having a wonderful time talking as she loads me up with plastic food. The problem is that we aren't communicating. Who is Nadia, that great cook?

Then two girls and a boy run from the doll corner and things begin to escalate: "We are mommies and daddies. Our Barbies need food!" Sara and Tania grab plastic vegetables off the table; Mark commandeers Kanesha's pot. Then, Ms. Angela runs in: "What are you supposed to do?" The kids chant, "Listen; take turns; share," and everyone starts giggling and gives Kanesha hugs.

I move to the crafts table. "Hey!" Moriah yells as José cuts his sheet into pieces, "José has more than me!" Moriah is making beautiful circles with paste. José tries to copy her but can only make random lines. These children are so different in their physical abilities, even though they are the same age. But—oh no—here come the children from the kitchen corner, and things get out of control again! Luckily, it's story time.

Ms. Angela reads a book about a bear who takes honey from the community cave when no one is around. "What is Little Bear feeling?" she asks. One boy says, "Hungry!" Another says, "Sad." Then José proudly informs the class, "He's happy and scared because he is being bad." But—just when I conclude José is a psychological genius—Ms. Angela follows up: "When the bears return, will they know it's him?" José and everyone yell, "Yes!"

At the activity centers, the girls are already separating from the boys. During outdoor play, however, I notice (a bit sadly) that José abandons Moriah as the boys joyously wrestle and compete to jump as far as they can. As the wind starts gusting, everyone gets excited and these gender differences disappear: "Let's catch Mister Wind. . . . He ran away again!" And now (whew!) it's time for lunch and rest.

These 3-year-olds have amazing skills. They can cut, climb, and jump, follow directions (a bit), and tell me about their lives. But they are clearly on a different wavelength in the way they think about life. Why was the class certain that the other animals would know who took the honey even though no one saw the offending bear? Why was Kanesha sure I *had* to know her name and why did Moriah assume José had more paper when he cut his sheet into pieces? What makes pretending compelling during preschool, and why do girls and boys separate into same-sex groups? This chapter offers answers as we immerse ourselves in the magical stage called **early childhood** (ages 3 to 6).

early childhood
The first phase of childhood, lasting from age 3 through kindergarten, or about age 6.

Left: © Corbis RF/Age Fotostock

LEARNING OUTCOMES

- Describe what makes humanity special.
- Contrast Erikson's early-childhood and middle-childhood tasks.

middle childhood The second phase of childhood, comprising the ages from roughly 7 to 12 years.

Imagine that these chimps could *really* share what insights they were having and understand what is in each other's minds. Wouldn't they be the species who has transformed the world?

initiative Erik Erikson's term for the early childhood psychosocial task that involves exuberantly testing skills.

industry Erik Erikson's term for the middle childhood psychosocial task involving bending to adult reality and needing to work for what we want.

Setting the Context

To introduce this special age, let's first step back. What makes human beings unique? What makes early childhood different from the next stage of development, called **middle childhood** (ages 7 to 12)?

Special "Mind Reading" Talents

The monkeys in this photo are clearly enjoying life (Poirier & Smith, 1974). But why did this species stay in the savanna while human beings had the talent to construct cities and negotiate cyberspace?

The reason, according to evolutionary theorists, is that humans have a unique capacity—the complex ability to reflect on our actions and read each other's minds. Monkeys do possess basic mindreading skills (see Buttelmann, Call, & Tomasello, 2009), yet because they lack language capacities, our primate cousins can't share each other's thoughts to transform the world. ("Oh, now I understand what you were trying to do. Let's work together to improve on that.")

In this chapter, you will learn how, during early childhood, the *social cognitive skills* that define humanity lock in. I'll also explain why early childhood is special compared to older ages. That master theorist, Erik Erikson, best captured the essential quality defining this unique stage of life.

Age of Exploration

Erikson, as you can see from Table 5.1, labeled the early childhood psychosocial task as **initiative**. From risking racing a tricycle in the street to scaling the school monkey bars, Erikson believed that our mission during preschool is to confidently exercise our bodies and minds.

In middle childhood (beginning approximately at age 7), this agenda shifts. Now our challenge is to develop **industry**, as we understand that succeeding in the world requires work. Therefore, the in-between interlude, when we have mastered walking and talking but haven't yet entered elementary school, is a time of vigorously testing our talents before we must bend to reality and curb our basic desires. Exploration (and initiative) is a vital prelude to confronting the demands of adult life.

Table 5.1: Erikson's Psychosocial Stages of Childhood, Adolescence, and Emerging Adulthood

Life Stage	Primary Task
Infancy (birth to 1 year)	Basic trust versus mistrust
Toddlerhood (1 to 2 years)	Autonomy versus shame and doubt
Early childhood (3 to 6 years)	**Initiative versus guilt**
Middle childhood (7 to 12 years)	Industry versus inferiority
Adolescence and emerging adulthood (teens into twenties)	Identity versus role confusion
Emerging adulthood (twenties)	Intimacy versus isolation

In Erikson's framework, during early childhood our agenda is to take the initiative to expand our skills.

Exuberantly taking off on your tricycle versus listening to the teacher and making sure you have finished your homework shows why early childhood is a magical time before we enter the adult world and must work.

Beginning with physical development, then moving to cognitive development, emotional development, and finally to play—the work of childhood—let's now track this age of exploration in the flesh.

Tying It All Together

1. In a sentence, explain what makes human beings different from other species.
2. When Steven played with his 4-year-old and 8-year-old sons, he realized that while the younger child was passionate to run, his older son was careful to follow the rules of the game. Use Erikson's distinction between initiative and industry to explain this difference between Steven's two sons.
3. Drawing on Erikson's preschool task, pick the stage of life most similar to early childhood.

Answers to the Tying It All Together questions can be found at the end of this chapter.

Physical Development

Compare preschoolers to older children and you will immediately see the *cephalocaudal principle* of physical growth discussed in Chapters 2 and 3. Three-year-olds have large heads and squat, rounded bodies. As children get older, their limbs lengthen and their bodies thin out. Because they grow at similar rates, boys and girls are roughly the same size until they reach the preadolescent years.

LEARNING OUTCOMES
- Describe physical development.
- Name two types of motor skills.
- Outline threats to preschool physical skills.

The tip-off about the ages of the children in these two photographs relates to the *cephalocaudal principle* of development. We know that the children in the left photo are preschoolers because they have squat shapes and relatively large heads, whereas the longer bodies in the right photo are typical of the middle childhood years.

Table 5.2: Selected Motor Skill Milestones: Progression from Age 2 to Age 6

At age 2	At age 4
Picks up small objects with thumb and forefinger, feeds self with spoon	Cuts paper, approximates circle
Walks unassisted, usually by 12 months	Walks down stairs, alternating feet
Rolls a ball or flings it awkwardly	Catches and controls a large bounced ball across the body

At age 5	At age 6
Prints name	Copies two short words
Walks without holding on to railing	Hops on each foot for 1 meter but still holds railing
Tosses ball overhand with bent elbows	Catches and controls a 10-inch ball in both hands with arms in front of body

gross motor skills Physical abilities that involve large muscle movements, such as running and jumping.

fine motor skills Physical abilities that involve small, coordinated movements, such as drawing and writing one's name.

Now visit a playground to see the *mass-to-specific* principle—the progression from clumsy to sure, swift movements from ages 2 to 6. Toddlers have trouble grasping markers; at age 6, they draw bodies and faces. Two-year-olds are just mastering spearing food; in first grade, they hurl balls down the alley and sometimes hit bowling pins. You can see the changes from mass to specific in a few skills from ages 2 to 6 in Table 5.2.

Two Types of Motor Talents

Developmentalists divide physical skills into two categories. **Gross motor skills** refer to large muscle movements, such as running, climbing, and hopping. **Fine motor skills** involve small, coordinated movements, such as drawing faces and writing one's name.

The stereotype that boys are better at gross motor abilities and girls at fine motor tasks is true—although often the differences are small. The largest sex difference in sports-related abilities occurs in throwing speed. During preschool, boys can typically hurl a ball much faster and farther than girls can (Geary, 1998; Thomas & French, 1985). Does this mean that girls can't compete with boys on teams? Not necessarily. The boys probably will be faster pitchers and more powerful hitters. But the female talent at connecting with the ball, which involves fine motor coordination, may even things out.

Imagine that a preschooler has exceptional physical abilities. Will that child be advanced at school? The answer is yes, provided we look at complex fine motor skills. Researchers asked 5-year-olds to copy images and then reproduce designs displayed on another page. Performance on this more difficult test (involving fine motor coordination and judging spatial dimensions) strongly predicted elementary school math and writing skills (Carlson, Rowe, & Curby, 2013; see also the next chapter).

This study suggests that, to improve their academic abilities, we might train young children to reproduce images. The problem is that pressuring (forcing) preschoolers to perform physical (and intellectual) tasks can be counterproductive. During early childhood, we should provide activities—such as cutting paper or scaling the monkey bars—that boys and girls naturally enjoy (Zaichkowsky & Larson, 1995). Allow young children to exercise their talents, but don't push, and provide the right person–environment fit.

These boys—being generally advanced in their gross motor skills—may be the victors when they compete with girls in this potato sack race. But this girl's exceptional fine motor talents set her up to do well in school.

Threats to Preschool Physical Skills

Now that we've scanned what normally happens, let's examine two forces that can limit children's growth and motor skills.

Lack of Outdoor Play

Anyone who is middle-aged or older can immediately identify one influence limiting physical initiative. When I was in preschool, children spent their days running outside. Today, a range of forces converge to limit the free-form physical explorations that have always defined early childhood, from adult anxieties ("If I let my child go to the park, he may be abducted or hurt") to living in dangerous neighborhoods ("With all that violence, I would never let my daughter out of the house") to the pressure to focus on academics at an early age ("Wouldn't my son be learning more by staying indoors and playing with that new computer device I just bought from Amazon?").

Today, the Internet coupled with tempting high-tech educational toys lure parents away from letting children play outdoors. In one longitudinal study, researchers measured mothers' use of "screen time" by asking how many hours per day pregnant women watched TV or spent on-line. Then they looked at their children's outdoor play during the first five years of life. As you might imagine, more parent screen time predicted less preschool time outdoors (Xu and others, 2016).

Learning tools can stimulate vital school-related skills, such as teaching children to ignore distracting information and focus their attention (Axelsson, Andersson, & Gulz, 2016). But wouldn't running around outside be equally effective at training children's minds? In one preschool study, children who engaged in "exercise play" (physically playing outside) were rated more well-liked by their peers (Lindsey, 2014).

Imagine buying this device, guaranteed to propel your child into a kindergarten star. How would you like your child spending his time?

Lack of Food

A telling example highlighting the social function of play relates to the problem discussed in Chapter 3: *undernutrition*. In addition to causing stunting, undernutrition impairs gross and fine motor skills because it compromises the development of our bones, muscles, and brain. Most important, when children don't have sufficient food, they are too tired to engage with the world.

During the 1980s, researchers observed how undernourished children in rural Nepal maximized their growth by cutting down on play (Anderson & Mitchell, 1984). Play, as you will learn later in this chapter, does more than exercise our bodies; it is crucial in promoting children's ability to compromise and understand other people's points of view. Therefore, it's important to understand that what happens physically during the first years of life affects all aspects of thinking—a topic I turn to now.

Tying It All Together

1. Jessica has terrific gross motor skills but trouble with fine motor skills. Select the two sports from this list that Jessica would be most likely to excel at: *long-distance running, tennis, water ballet, the high jump, bowling.*

2. Drawing on this section, which strategy would be *least helpful* in stimulating physical development during early childhood?
   a. Enrolling 4-year-olds in sports
   b. Encouraging pregnant women to reduce their Internet time
   c. Providing low-cost, safe spaces in the community for children to play (such as free local Y's)
   d. Ensuring that young children have enough food

Answers to the Tying It All Together questions can be found at the end of this chapter.

LEARNING OUTCOMES

- Describe Piaget's preoperational stage, referring to specific terms and concepts.
- Compare Vygotsky's and Piaget's theories.
- Describe Vygotsky's ideas about language.
- Outline how language develops, making reference to its specific properties.

preoperational thinking In Piaget's theory, the type of cognition characteristic of children aged 2 to 7, marked by an inability to step back from one's immediate perceptions and think conceptually.

concrete operational thinking In Piaget's framework, the type of cognition characteristic of children aged 8 to 11, marked by the ability to reason about the world in logical, adult ways.

conservation tasks Piagetian tasks that involve changing the shape of substances to see whether children can go beyond the way that substance visually appears to understand that the amount remains the same.

Cognitive Development

How *does* a young child's cognition unfold? The genius who decoded this question (no surprise) was Jean Piaget.

Piaget's Preoperational Stage

As discussed in Chapter 1, Piaget believed that through assimilation (fitting new information into their existing cognitive structures) and accommodation (changing those cognitive slots to fit input from the world), children undergo qualitatively different stages of cognitive growth. In Chapter 3, I discussed Piaget's sensorimotor stage. Now, it's time to tackle Piaget's next stage: preoperations (see Table 5.3).

Just as with Erikson's stages, we can best understand preoperations in conjunction with Piaget's next stage of cognitive growth. **Preoperational thinking** is defined by what young children are missing—the ability to step back from their immediate perceptions. **Concrete operational thinking** is defined by what older children possess: the ability to reason about the world in a logical, adult-like way.

When children leave infancy and enter the stage of preoperational thought, they have made tremendous mental strides. Still, their thinking seems on a different planet from that of adults. The problem is that preoperational children are unable to look beyond the way objects immediately appear. By about age 7 or 8 (during elementary school), children can mentally transcend what first catches their eye. They have entered the concrete operational stage.

Taking the World at Face Value

You saw vivid examples of this "from another planet" thinking in the chapter-opening vignette. Now let's enter the minds of young children and explore how they reason about physical substances and the social world.

Strange Ideas About Substances

The fact that preoperational children are locked into immediate appearances is illustrated by Piaget's (1965) famous **conservation tasks**. In Piaget's terminology, *conservation* refers to knowing that the amount of a given substance remains identical despite changes in its shape or form.

Table 5.3: Piaget's Stages: Focus on Childhood

Age (years)	Name of Stage	Description
0–2	Sensorimotor	The baby manipulates objects to pin down the basics of physical reality. This stage ends with the development of language.
2–7	Preoperations	Children's perceptions are captured by their immediate appearances: "What they see is what is real." They believe, among other things, that inanimate objects are really alive and that if the appearance of a quantity of liquid changes (for example, if it is poured from a short, wide glass into a tall, thin one), the amount of liquid itself changes.
8–12	Concrete operations	Children have a realistic understanding of the world. Their thinking is really on the same wavelength as that of adults. While they can reason conceptually about concrete objects, however, they cannot think abstractly in a scientific way.
12+	Formal operations	Reasoning is at its pinnacle: hypothetical, scientific, flexible, fully adult. Our full cognitive human potential has been reached.

In the conservation-of-mass task, an adult gives a child a round ball of clay and asks that boy or girl to make another ball "just as big and heavy." Then she reshapes the ball to look like a pancake and asks, "Is there still the same amount now?" In the conservation-of-liquid task, the procedure is similar: present a child with identical glasses containing equal amounts of liquid. Make sure the child agrees, "Yes, they have the same amount of juice [or water]." Then pour the liquid into a tall, thin glass while the child watches and ask, "Is there more or less juice now, or is there the same amount?"

Typically, when children under age 7 are asked this final question, they give a peculiar answer: "Now there is more clay" or "The tall glass has more juice." Why? "Because now the pancake is bigger" or "The juice is taller." Then, after adults remold the clay into a ball or pour the liquid into the original glass, the children report: "Now it's the same again." The logical conflict in their statements doesn't bother them at all. Figure 5.1 illustrates these procedures, as well as additional Piagetian conservation tasks to perform with children you know.

Why can't young children conserve? One issue is that children don't grasp a concept called **reversibility**. This is the idea that an operation (or procedure) can be repeated in the opposite direction. Adults accept the fact that we can change substances, such as our hairstyle or our house decorations, and then reverse things to their original state. Young children lack this fundamental *schema*, or cognitive structure, for understanding the world.

> **reversibility** In Piaget's conservation tasks, the concrete operational child's knowledge that a specific change in the way a given substance looks can be reversed.

Type of conservation	Initial step and question	Transformation and next question	Preoperational child's answer
Number	Two equal rows of pennies. "Are these two rows the same?" (Yes.)	Increase spacing of pennies in one line. "Now is the amount of money the same?"	"No, the longer row has more."
Mass	Two equal balls of clay. "Do these two balls have the same amount of clay?" (Yes.)	Squeeze one ball into a long pancake shape. "Now is the amount of clay the same?"	"No, the long, thin one has more clay."
Volume or liquid	Two glasses of the same size with liquid. "Do these glasses have the same amount of juice?" (Yes.)	Pour one into a taller, narrower glass. "Now do these glasses have the same amount of juice?"	"No, the taller glass has more juice."
Matter*	Two identical cubes of sugar. "Do these cubes have the same amount of sugar?" (Yes.)	Dissolve one cube in a glass of water. "Now is there the same amount of sugar?"	"No, because you made one piece of sugar disappear."

*That is, the idea that a substance such as sugar is "still there" even though it seems to have disappeared (by dissolving).

FIGURE 5.1: Four Piagetian conservation tasks Can you perform these tasks with a child you know?

centering In Piaget's conservation tasks, the preoperational child's tendency to fix on the most visually striking feature of a substance and not take into account other dimensions.

decentering In Piaget's conservation tasks, the concrete operational child's ability to look at several dimensions of an object or substance.

class inclusion The understanding that a general category can encompass several subordinate elements.

identity constancy In Piaget's theory, the preoperational child's inability to grasp that a person's core "self" stays the same despite changes in external appearance.

A second problem lies in a perceptual style that Piaget calls **centering**. Young children interpret things according to what first catches their eye, rather than taking in the entire visual array. In the conservation-of-liquid task, children become captivated by the liquid's height. They don't notice that the width of the original glass makes up for the other container's increased height.

In concrete operations, children **decenter**. They can step back from a substance's immediate appearance and understand that an increase in one dimension makes up for a loss in the other one.

Centering—or fixating on immediate impressions—impairs **class inclusion**. This is the knowledge that a category can comprise subordinate elements. For example, spread 20 Skittles® and a few gummy bears in a dish and ask a 3-year-old: "Would you rather have the Skittles or the candy?" and she is almost certain to say, "The Skittles," even when you have determined beforehand that both types of candy have equal appeal. She gets mesmerized by the number of Skittles and does not notice that "candy" is the label for both.

This tendency to focus on immediate appearances explains why, in the opening chapter vignette, Moriah believed that José had more paper when he cut his sheet into sections. Her attention was captured by the spread-out pieces, and she believed that now there must be more paper than before.

The same idea that "bigger" automatically equals "more" extends to every aspect of preoperational thought. Ask a 3-year-old if he wants a nickel or a dime, and he will choose the first option. (This is a great source of pleasure to older siblings asked to equally share their funds.) Perhaps because greater height means "older" in their own lives, children even believe that a taller person has been on earth for a longer time:

I was substitute teaching with a group of kindergarten children—at the time I was about 22—and when I met a student's mother, she was shocked. "When I asked Ben about you," she said, "he told me you were much older than his regular teacher." This teacher was in her mid- to late fifties and looked it. However, then we figured out the difference. This woman was barely 5 feet tall, and I am 6 feet 2!

Peculiar Perceptions About People

Young children's idea that "what catches my eye right now is real" explains why a 3-year-old thinks her mommy becomes a princess when she dresses up for Halloween, or cries after visiting the beauty salon, because she is sure her short haircut has transformed her into a boy. It makes sense of why a favorite strategy of older sisters and brothers (to torture younger siblings) is to put on a mask and see the child run in horror from the room. As these examples show, young children lack **identity constancy**. They don't realize that people remain their essential selves despite changes in the way they visually appear.

I got insights into this identity constancy deficit at my son's 5th birthday party, when I hired a "gorilla" to entertain the guests (some developmental psychologist!). As the hairy 6-foot figure rang the doorbell, mass hysteria ensued—requiring the gorilla to take off his head. After the children calmed down, and the gorilla put on his head again to enact his skit, guess what? Pure hysteria again!

Why did that huge animal cause pandemonium? The reason is that the children believed that the gorilla, even though a costumed figure, was alive.

When this 4-year-old's dad puts on a mask, he suddenly becomes a scary monster because she has not grasped the principle of identity constancy.

This 4-year-old boy's animistic thinking causes him to believe that his bear is going to enjoy the ride he is about to provide.

> **Experiencing Childhood:** Animism and the Power of Stephen King
>
> *There was one shadow that would constantly cast itself on my bedroom wall. It looked just like a giant creeping towards me with a big knife in his hand.*
>
> *I used to believe that Satan lived in my basement. The light switch was at the bottom of the steps, and whenever I switched off the light it was a mad dash to the top. I was so scared that Satan was going to stab my feet with knives.*
>
> *Boy, do I remember the doll that sat on the top of my dresser. I called it "Chatty Kathy." This doll came to life every night. She would stare at me, no matter where I went.*
>
> *My mother used to take me when she went to clean house for Mrs. Handler, a rich lady. Mrs. Handler had this huge, shiny black grand piano, and I thought it came alive when I was not looking at it. It was so enormous, dark, and quiet. I remember pressing one of the bass keys, which sounded really deep and loud and it terrified me.*
>
> *I remember being scared that there was something alive under my bed. I must tell you I sometimes still get scared that someone is under my bed and that they are going to grab me by my ankles. I don't think I will ever grow out of this, as I am 26.*
>
> Can you relate to any of these childhood memories collected from my students? Perhaps your enemy was that evil creature lurking in your basement; the scary stuffed animal on your dresser; a huge object (with teeth) such as that piano; or your local garbage truck.
>
> Now you know where that master storyteller Stephen King gets his ideas. King's genius is that he taps into the preoperational thoughts that we have papered over, though not very well, as adults. When we read King's tale of a toy animal that clapped cymbals to signal someone's imminent death, or about Christine, the car with a mind of its own, or about the laundry-pressing machine that loved human blood—these stories fall on familiar childhood ground. Don't you still get a bit anxious when you enter a dark basement? Even today, at night, do you ever have an uneasy feeling that some strange monster might be lurking beneath your bed?

Animism refers to the problem young children have in sorting out what is alive. Specifically, preschoolers see inanimate objects—such as dolls or costumed figures—as having consciousness, too. Turn to the chapter-opening vignette to see examples of animistic thinking—for instance, the hungry Barbies or the wind that ran away. Now think back to when you were age 5 or 6. Do you remember being afraid the escalator might suck you in? Or perhaps you recall believing, as in the Experiencing Childhood box, that your dolls came alive at night.

Listen to young children talking about nature, and you'll hear delightful examples of animism: "The sun gets sleepy when I sleep." "The moon likes to follow me in the car." The practice of assigning human motivations to natural phenomena is not something we grow out of as adults. Think of the Greek thunder god Zeus, or the ancient Druids who worshiped the spirits that lived within trees. Throughout history, humans have regularly used animism to make sense of a frightening world.

A related concept is called **artificialism.** Young children believe that human beings make nature. Here is an example of this "daddy power" from Piaget's 3-year-old daughter, Laurent:

> L was in bed in the evening and it was still light: "Put the light out please" . . . (I switched the electric light off.) "It isn't dark"—"But I can't put the light out outside" . . . "Yes you can, you can make it dark." . . . "How?" . . . "You must turn it out very hard. It'll be dark and there will be little lights everywhere (stars)."
>
> (Piaget, 1951/1962, p. 248)

Animism and artificialism perfectly illustrate Piaget's concept of assimilation. The child knows that she is alive and so applies her "alive" schema to every object. Watching adults perform heroic physical feats, such as turning off lights, a 3-year-old generalizes the same "big people control things" schema to the universe. Imagine being a young child taking a family vacation. After visiting that gleaming construction called Las Vegas, wouldn't it make sense that people carved out the Grand Canyon and the Rocky Mountains, too?

The sun and moon examples illustrate another aspect of preoperational thought. According to Piaget, young children believe that they are the literal center of the

animism In Piaget's theory, the preoperational child's belief that inanimate objects are alive.

artificialism In Piaget's theory, the preoperational child's belief that human beings make everything in nature.

egocentrism In Piaget's theory, the preoperational child's inability to understand that other people have different points of view from one's own.

universe, the pivot around which everything else revolves. Their worldview is defined by **egocentrism**—the inability to understand that other people have different points of view.

By *egocentrism*, Piaget does not mean that young children are vain or uncaring—although they will tell you they are the smartest people on earth and the heavenly bodies are at their beck and call. There is nothing more loving than a 3-year-old offering a favorite "blankee" if he sees you upset. The child is egocentric, however, because he assumes that what comforts *him* will automatically comfort you.

You can see delightful examples of egocentrism when talking with a young child. Have you ever had a 3-year-old discuss an experience at school without providing any background information, as if you *automatically* knew her teacher and the rest of the class?

Piaget views egocentrism as a perfect example of centering in the human world. Young children are unable to decenter from their own mental processes. They don't realize that what is in their mind is not in everyone else's awareness, too.

Getting on the Adult Wavelength

Piaget discovered that the transition away from preoperations happens gradually. First, children are preoperational in every area. Then, between ages 5 and 7, their thinking gets less static, or "thaws out" (Flavell, 1963). In the conservation-of-liquid task, for instance, a 6-year-old might first say the taller glass had more liquid, but then, after seeing the liquid poured back into a wide glass, becomes unsure: "Is it bigger or not?" She has reached the tipping point where she is poised to reason on a higher cognitive plane.

By age 8, the child has reached this higher-level, concrete operational state: "Even though the second glass is taller, the first is wider" (showing decentering); "You can pour the liquid right back into the short glass and it would look the same" (illustrating reversibility). Now, she doesn't realize that she ever thought differently: "Are you silly? Of course it's the same!"

Piaget found that specific conservations appear at different ages. First, children master conservation of number and then mass and liquid. They may not figure out the most difficult conservations until age 11 or 12. Imagine the challenge of understanding the last task in Figure 5.1 (see page 139)—realizing that when sugar is dissolved in water and seems to disappear, it still exists, but in a different molecular form.

Still, according to Piaget, age 7 or 8 is a landmark for looking beyond immediate appearances, for understanding categories, for decentering in the physical and social worlds, for abandoning the tooth fairy and the idea that our stuffed animals are alive, and for entering the mental planet of adults.

Table 5.4 shows examples of different preoperational ideas. Now test yourself by seeing if you can classify each statement in Piagetian terms.

Table 5.4: Can You Identify the Type of Preoperational Thought from These Real-World Examples?

Here are your possible choices: (a) no identity constancy, (b) animism, (c) artificialism, (d) egocentrism, (e) no conservation, and (f) inability to use classification.

____ 1.	Heidi was watching her father fix lunch. After he cut her sandwich into quarters, Heidi said, "Oh, Daddy, I only wanted you to cut it in two pieces. I'm not hungry enough to eat four!" (Bjorklund & Bjorklund, 1992, p. 168).
____ 2.	My 2-year-old son and I were taking our yearly trip to visit Grandma in Florida. As the plane took off and gained altitude, Thomas looked out the window and said with a delighted grin, "Mommy, TOYS!"
____ 3.	Melanie watched as her father, a professional clown, put on his clown outfit and then began applying his makeup. Before he could finish, Melanie suddenly ran screaming from the room, terrified of the strange clown.
____ 4.	Your child can't understand that he could live in his town and in his state at the same time. He tells you angrily, "I live in Newark, not New Jersey."
____ 5.	As you cross the George Washington Bridge over the Hudson River to New Jersey, your child asks, "Did the same people who built the bridge also make the river?"

Answers: 1. (e) 2. (d) 3. (a) 4. (f) 5. (c)

INTERVENTIONS: Using Piaget's Ideas at Home and at Work

Piaget's concepts provide marvelous insights into young children's minds. For teachers, the theory explains why you need the same-sized cups at a kindergarten lunch table or an argument will erupt, even if you poured each drink from identical cans. Nurses understand that rationally explaining a medical procedure to a 4-year-old is less effective than providing a magic doll to help the child cope.

The theory makes sense of why organizing baseball is impossible with 4- or 5-year-olds. Grasping the rules of games requires abstract conceptualization—skills that preoperational children do not possess. It tells us why young children are terrified of the dark and scary amusement park clowns. So for parents who are uneasy about playing into children's fantasies when they provide "anti-monster spray" to calm bedtime fears, one justification is that, according to Piaget, when a child is ready, she naturally grows out of these ideas.

Piaget's concepts explain the power of pretending (more about this later) and the lure of that favorite childhood holiday, Halloween. When a 4-year-old child dresses up as Batman, he is grappling with understanding that you can look different, yet remain your essential self. The theory accounts for why fourth graders become captivated with soccer and can be avid collectors of baseball cards. Now that they understand rules and categories, concrete operational children are passionate to exercise their conceptual and classification skills.

The theory explains why "real school," the academic part, begins at about age 7. Before middle childhood, we don't have the intellectual tools to understand reversibility, a concept critical to mathematics (if 2 plus 4 is 6, then 6 minus 4 must equal 2). Even empathizing with the teacher's agenda is a concrete operational skill.

The fact that age 8 is a coming-of-age marker is represented in the classic movie *Home Alone*. The plot of this film would be unthinkable if its hero were 5, or even 6. If the star were 11, the movie would not be as interesting because, by this age, a child could competently take care of himself. Age 8 is when we make the transition to being "home alone." It is the time when we shift from worrying about imaginary threats such as monsters, to grappling with the realistic dangers we face during life.

Children take great pride in collecting, classifying, and trading items like Yu-Gi-Oh cards because they have reached concrete operations and are practicing their new skills.

Evaluating Piaget

Piaget clearly transformed our ideas about young children. Still, in important areas, Piaget was incorrect.

I described a major problem with Piaget's theory in Chapter 3: just as he minimized what babies know, Piaget overstated young children's egocentrism. If babies can decode intentions, the awareness that we live in "different heads" must dawn on children at a far younger age than 8! (Much more about this mindreading ability soon.)

We might also disagree with Piaget that children abandon animism by age 7 or 8. Maybe he was giving us too *much* credit here. Do you have a good luck charm that keeps the plane from crashing, or a place you go for comfort where you can hear the trees whispering to you?

Children worldwide do learn to conserve (Dasen, 1977, 1984). But because nature interacts with nurture, the ages at which they master specific conservation tasks vary from place to place. An example comes from a village in Mexico, where weaving is the main occupation. Young children in this collectivist culture grasp conservation tasks involving spatial concepts earlier than age 7 or 8 because they have so much hands-on training in this skill (Maynard & Greenfield, 2003). This brings up the dimension Piaget's theory leaves out: how teaching promotes cognitive growth.

Because this girl growing up in Mexico gets so much practice at weaving, we might expect her to grasp concrete operational conservation tasks related to spatial concepts at a relatively early age.

zone of proximal development (ZPD) In Vygotsky's theory, the gap between a child's ability to solve a problem totally on his own and his potential knowledge if taught by a more accomplished person.

scaffolding The process of teaching new skills by entering a child's zone of proximal development and tailoring one's efforts to that person's competence level.

Vygotsky's Zone of Proximal Development

Piaget implies that we can't convince preschoolers that their dolls are not alive or that the width of one glass makes up for the height of the other. Children naturally grow out of those ideas while manipulating objects on their own. The Russian psychologist Lev Vygotsky (1962, 1978) had a different perspective: People propel mental growth.

Vygotsky was born in the same year as Piaget. He showed as much brilliance at a young age, but—unlike Piaget, who lived to a ripe old age—he died of tuberculosis in his late thirties. Still, Vygotsky's writings have given him towering status in developmental science. One reason is that Vygotsky was an educator. He believed that adults make children mentally advance.

Vygotsky theorized that learning takes place within the **zone of proximal development (ZPD)**, which he defined as the difference between what the child can do by himself and his level of "potential development as determined through problem solving under adult guidance or in collaboration with more capable peers" (Vygotsky, 1978, p. 86; also, see the diagram in Figure 5.2). Teachers must tailor their instruction to a child's proximal zone. Then, as that child becomes more competent, adults should slowly back off and allow the student more responsibility for directing learning on his own. This sensitive pacing has a special name: **scaffolding** (Wood, Bruner, & Ross, 1976).

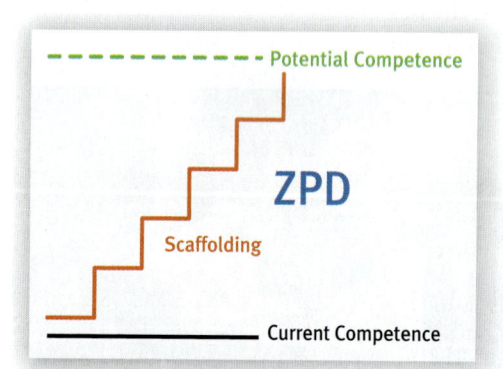

I gave an illustration of scaffolding in the Chapter 3 discussion of infant-directed speech (IDS). IDS, or baby talk, permits caregivers to penetrate a young child's zone of proximal development for language and so scaffolds emerging speech. In the opening vignette, you saw Ms. Angela draw on Vygotsky's ideas when she articulated the practices good teachers adopt: Encourage students to stretch their capacities, but operate within their proximal zones. Now let's explore scaffolding in operation as a mother teaches her 5-year-old daughter how to play her first board game, Chutes and Ladders:

> Tiffany threw the dice, then looked up at her mother. Her mother said, "How many is that?" Tiffany shrugged her shoulders. Her mother said, "Count them," but Tiffany just sat and stared. Her mother counted the dots aloud, and then said to her daughter, "Now you count them," which Tiffany did. This was repeated for the next five turns. Tiffany waited for her mother to count the dots. On her sixth move, however, Tiffany counted the dots on the dice on her own after her mother's request. . . . Eventually, Tiffany threw the dice and counted the dots herself and continued to do so, practicing counting and moving the pieces on both her own and her mother's turns.
>
> (Bjorklund & Rosenblum, 2001)

FIGURE 5.2: Vygotsky's zone of proximal development These lines illustrate the ZPD—the gap between a child's current and potential intellectual ability. If a teacher sensitively teaches within this zone and employs scaffolding (see stepwise lines)—providing support, then backing off when help is no longer needed—students will reach their full intellectual potential.

Notice that this mother was a superb scaffolder. By pacing her interventions to Tiffany's capacities, she paved the way for her child to master the game. But this process did not just flow from parent to child. Tiffany was also teaching her mother how to respond. Just as your professor is gaining new insights into children while teaching this class—or at this minute, as I struggle to write this page, I'm learning to better connect with Vygotsky's ideas—education is a *bidirectional*, mind-expanding duet (Scrimsher & Tudge, 2003).

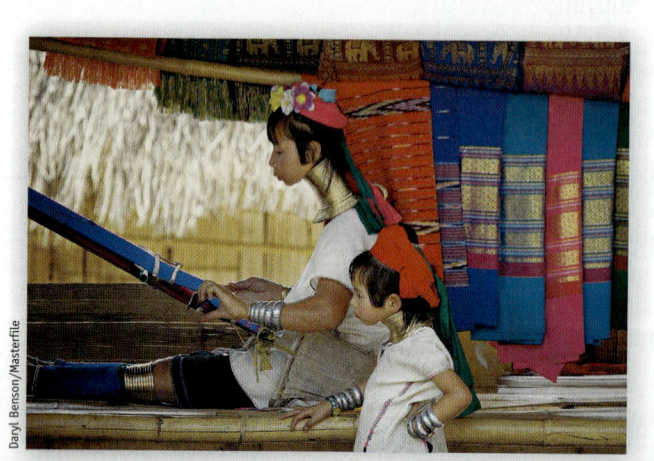

In our culture, we have definite ideas about good scaffolders: They actively instruct but are sensitive to a child's responses. However, in collectivist societies, such as among the Mayans living in Mexico's Yucatán Peninsula, children listen. They watch adults. They are not explicitly taught the skills for adult life (Rogoff and others, 2003). So the qualities our culture sees as vital to socializing children are not necessarily part of the ideology of good parenting around the globe.

This young girl in Thailand is learning to weave just by observing her mother—a strategy that we might find unusual in our teaching-oriented culture.

INTERVENTIONS: Becoming an Effective Scaffolder

In our teaching-oriented society, what do superior scaffolders do? Let's list a few techniques:

- They foster a secure attachment, as nurturing, responsive interactions are a basic foundation for learning (Laible, 2004).
- They break a larger cognitive challenge, such as learning Chutes and Ladders, into manageable steps (Berk & Winsler, 1999).
- They continue helping until the child has fully mastered the concept before moving on, as Tiffany's mother did earlier.

Table 5.5 compares Vygotsky's and Piaget's ideas and summarizes these world-class geniuses' backgrounds (Vianna & Stetsenko, 2006). Although often described in opposing terms, these theories form an ideal pair. Piaget gave us insights into the structure of childhood cognition. Vygotsky offered us an engine to transform children's lives.

Table 5.5: Vygotskian (left) and Piagetian (right) Perspectives on Life and Learning

Biography	Russian, Jewish, communist (reached teenage years during the Russian Revolution), believed in Marx	Swiss, middle-class family
Basic interests	Education, literature, literary criticism, biology, mollusks	Wanted to know how to stimulate thinking. Wanted to trace the evolution of thought in stages
Overall orientation	Look at interpersonal processes and the role of society in cognition	Look for universal developmental processes
Basic ideas	1. We develop intellectually through social interactions. 2. Development is a collaborative endeavor. 3. People cause cognitive growth.	1. We develop intellectually through physically acting on the world. 2. Development takes place on our own inner timetable. 3. When we are internally ready, we reach a higher level of cognitive development.
Implications for education	Instruction is critical to development. Teachers should sensitively intervene within each child's zone of proximal development.	Provide ample materials to let children explore and learn on their own.

Language

So far, I have been discussing the mental milestones in this chapter as if they occurred in a vacuum. But language, that uniquely human cognitive skill, is the motor that helps scaffold everything we learn. Vygotsky (1978) actually put speaking front and center in children's ability to think.

Inner Speech

According to Vygotsky, thinking happens when the words a child hears from parents and other scaffolders migrate inward to become talk directed at the self. Using the earlier Chutes and Ladders example, after listening to her mother say "Count them" a number of times, Tiffany learned the game by repeating "Count them" to herself. Thinking, according to Vygotsky, is really **inner speech.**

Support for this idea comes from listening to young children as they monitor their actions. A 3-year-old might say, "Don't touch!" as she moves near the stove; or reminds herself to be "a good girl" at preschool that day (Manfra & Winsler, 2006). We adults sometimes behave the same way. If something is *really important*—and if no one is listening—have you ever reminded yourself "Be sure to do X, Y, and Z" out loud?

Developing Speech

How does language *itself* unfold? Actually, during early childhood, language does more than unfold. It explodes.

By our second birthday, we are beginning to put together words (see Chapter 3). By kindergarten, we basically have adult language nailed down. Considering the challenges involved in mastering language, this achievement is remarkable. To speak like adults, children must articulate word sounds. They must string units of meaning together in sentences. They must produce sentences that are grammatically correct. They must understand the meanings of words.

The word sounds of language are called **phonemes.** When infants begin to speak, they produce single phonemes—for instance, they call their bottle *ba*. They repeat sounds that seem similar, such as calling their bottle *baba*, when they cannot form the next syllable of the word. By age 3, while children have made tremendous strides in producing phonemes, they still—as you saw in the chapter-opening vignette—have trouble pronouncing multisyllabic words (like *psghetti*). Then, early in elementary school, these articulation problems disappear—but not completely. Have you ever had a problem pronouncing a difficult word that you silently read on a page?

The meaning units of language are called **morphemes** (for example, the word *boys* has two units of meaning: *boy* and the plural suffix *-s*). As children get older, their average number of morphemes per sentence—called their **mean length of utterance (MLU)**—expands. A 2-year-old's telegraphic utterance of "Me juice" (2 MLUs) grows to "Me want juice" (3 MLUs) and then, at age 4, to "Please give me the juice" (5 MLUS). Also around age 3 or 4, children are fascinated by producing long, jumbled-together sentences strung together by *and* ("Give me juice and crackers and milk and cookies and . . .").

This brings up the steps to mastering grammar, or **syntax.** What's interesting here are the classic mistakes that young children make. As parents are well aware, one of the first words that children utter is *no*. First, children add this word to the beginning of a sentence ("No eat cheese" or "No go inside"). Then, they move the negative term inside the sentence, next to the main verb ("I no sing" or "He no do it"). A question starts out as a declarative sentence with a rising intonation: "I have a drink, Daddy?" Then it, too, is replaced by the correct word order: "Can I have a drink, Daddy?" Children typically produce grammatically correct sentences by the time they enter school.

The most amazing changes occur in **semantics**—understanding word meanings. Here, children go from three- or four-word vocabularies at age 1 to knowing about 10,000 words by age 6! (See Slobin, 1972; Smith, 1926.) While we have the other core abilities under our belts by the end of early childhood, our vocabularies continue to grow from age 2 to 102.

One mistake young children make while learning language is called **overregularization.** At approximately age 3 or 4, they adopt general rules for plurals or past tenses even to exceptions. A preschooler will say *runned, goed, teached, sawed, mouses, feets,* and *cup of sugars* rather than using the correct irregular form (Berko, 1958).

According to Vygotsky, by talking to her image in the mirror "out loud," this girl is learning to monitor her behavior. Have you ever done the same thing when no one was watching?

inner speech In Vygotsky's theory, the way in which human beings learn to regulate their behavior and master cognitive challenges, through silently repeating information or talking to themselves.

phoneme The sound units that convey meaning in a given language—for example, in English, the *c* sound of *cat* and the *b* sound of *bat*.

morpheme The smallest unit of meaning in a particular language—for example, *boys* contains two morphemes: *boy* and the plural suffix *-s*.

mean length of utterance (MLU) The average number of morphemes per sentence.

syntax The system of grammatical rules in a particular language.

semantics The meaning system of a language—that is, what the words stand for.

overregularization An error in early language development, in which young children apply the rules for plurals and past tenses even to exceptions, so irregular forms sound like regular forms.

Table 5.6: Challenges on the Language Pathway: A Summary Table

Type of Challenge	Description	Example
Phonemes	Has trouble forming sounds	*Baba, psghetti*
Morphemes	Uses few meaning units per sentence	*Me go home*
Syntax (grammar)	Makes mistakes in applying rules for forming sentences	*Me come out*
Semantics	Has problems understanding word meanings	*Calls the family dog a horsey*
Overregularization	Puts irregular pasts and plurals into regular forms	*Foots; runned*
Over/underextension	Applies verbal labels too broadly/narrowly	*Calls every old man grandpa; tells another child he can't have a grandpa because grandpa is the name for his grandfather alone*

Another error lies in children's semantic mistakes. Also around age 3, children may use **overextensions**—extending a verbal label too broadly. In Piaget's terminology, they assimilate the word *horsey* to all four-legged creatures, such as dogs, cats, and lions in the zoo. Or they use **underextensions**—making name categories too narrow. A 3-year-old may insist that only her own pet is a dog and all the other neighborhood dogs must be called something else. As children get older, through continual assimilation and accommodation, they sort out these glitches.

Table 5.6 summarizes these challenges. Now you might want to have a conversation with a 3- or 4-year-old child. Can you pick out examples of overregularization, overextensions or underextensions, problems with syntax (grammar), or difficulties pronouncing phonemes (word sounds)? Can you figure out the child's MLU?

overextension An error in early language development in which young children apply verbal labels too broadly.

underextension An error in early language development in which young children apply verbal labels too narrowly.

Tying It All Together

1. While with your 3-year-old nephew Mark, you observe many examples of preoperational thought. Give the Piagetian label—egocentrism, animism, no conservation, artificialism, identity constancy—for each of the following:
    a. Mark tells you that the tree in the garden is watching him.
    b. When you stub your toe, Mark gives you his stuffed animal.
    c. Mark explains that his daddy made the sun.
    d. Mark says, "There's more now," when you pour juice from a wide carton into a skinny glass.
    e. Mark tells you that his sister turned into a princess yesterday when she put on a costume.

2. In a sentence, explain the basic mental difference between an 8-year-old in the concrete operational stage and a preoperational 4-year-old.

3. Four-year-old Christopher knows the alphabet and is sounding out words in books. Drawing on Vygotsky's theory, Chris's parents should (choose one): *buy alphabet books, because their son will easily recognize each word; buy "easy-to-read" books just above their son's skill level; challenge Chris by getting him books with complicated stories.*

4. Your 3-year-old cousin is talking out loud and making comments such as "Put the big piece here," while constructing a puzzle. What would Vygotsky say about this behavior?

5. You are listening to a preschooler named Joshua. Pick out the examples of overregularization and overextension from the following comments:
    a. When offered a piece of cheese, Joshua said, "I no eat cheese."
    b. Seeing a dog run away, Joshua said, "The doggie runned away."
    c. Taken to a petting zoo, Joshua pointed excitedly at a goat and said, "Horsey!"

Answers to the Tying It All Together questions can be found at the end of this chapter.

Emotional Development

LEARNING OUTCOMES
- Explain autobiographical memory.
- Outline theory of mind, mentioning its importance and variations from child to child.

Language makes us capable of the uniquely human talents described at the beginning of this chapter. We are the only species that reflects on our past (Fivush, 2011). The essence of being human is that we effortlessly transport ourselves into each other's heads, decoding what people are thinking from their own point of view. How do children learn to articulate their past experiences? When do we *fully* grasp that other people's perspectives are different from our own?

Constructing Our Personal Past

Autobiographical memories refer to reflecting on our life histories: from our earliest memories at age 3 or 4 to that incredible experience at work last week. Children's understanding that they have a personal autobiography is scaffolded through a specific kind of talk. Caregivers reminisce with young children: "Remember going on a train to visit Grandma?" "What did we do at the beach last week?" These *past-talk conversations* are teaching a lesson: "You have a past and future. You are an enduring self."

Past-talk conversations typically begin with parents doing the "remembering" when toddlers begin to speak (Harley & Reese, 1999). Then, during preschool, children become partners in these mutual stories and, at age 4 or 5, initiate past-talk conversations on their own (Nelson & Fivush, 2004). Listen to this vivid autobiographical memory produced by a 6-year-old:

INTERVIEWER: Can you tell me about the ballet recital?

CHILD: It was driving me crazy.

INTERVIEWER: Really?

CHILD: Yes, I was so scared because I didn't know any of the people and I couldn't see mom and dad. They were way on top of the audience. . . . Ummm, we were on a slippery surface and we all did "Where the Wild Things Are" and we . . . Mine had horns sticking out of it . . . And I had baggy pants.

(Nelson & Fivush, 2004)

As this girl reaches adolescence, she will link these memories to each other and construct a timeline of her life (Chen, McAnally, & Reese, 2013; Habermas, Negele, & Mayer, 2010). By about age 16, she will use these events to reflect on her enduring personality ("This is the kind of person I am, as shown by how I felt at age 4 or 5 or 9"). Then she will have achieved that Eriksonian milestone—an *identity* to carry through life (more about this topic in Chapter 10).

Caregivers can help stimulate autobiographical memory by sensitively asking questions about exciting experiences they shared with their child (Valentino and others, 2014). ("Wasn't the circus amazing? What did you like best?") By highlighting specific ways of thinking, past-talk conversations help scaffold the values a given society holds dear (Alea & Wang, 2015). But lecturing doesn't work. Parents must engage preschoolers in a loving, mutual, give-and-take talk (Salmon & Reese, 2015). Autobiographical memories are apt to be richer when children are securely attached (McDonnell and others, 2016). Therefore, the quality of these memories offers clues into a person's early life.

In one study, 8-year-olds with depressed mothers produced overly general autobiographical memories ("I went to the circus") rather than recalling specifics ("I remember how I went to the circus, and I'll never forget the cotton candy and lions") (Woody, Burkhouse, & Gibb, 2015). Traumatic childhood experiences produce stunted personal autobiographies, too (Salmon & Reese, 2015).

The most chilling example of this autobiographical memory failure (what Freud might call *repression*) occurred with children who were removed from an abusive home. If a boy or girl was insecurely attached, that child either made false statements about what took place that day or denied remembering anything about the traumatic event (Melinder and others, 2013).

autobiographical memories Recollections of events and experiences that make up one's life history.

When they get home, this mother can help her daughter construct her "personal autobiography" by starting a dialogue about their wonderful day at the beach.

The take-home message is that our personal autobiography (or full sense of self) is scaffolded through loving caregiver–child interactions. Relationships—as Vygotsky believed—teach us to be an independent self.

And at the same time as they understand their pasts, children begin to fully grasp that other people live in a different mental space.

Making Sense of Other People's Minds

Listen to 3-year-olds having a conversation, and it's as if you're hearing separate monologues, like mental ships passing in the night. Around age 4 or 5, children relate in a *give-and-take* way. They have reached that landmark called **theory of mind**, the understanding that other people have perspectives different from their own. Developmentalists use a creative procedure to demonstrate this milestone—*the false-belief task*.

With a friend and a young child, see if you can perform the classic theory-of-mind task illustrated on the next page in Figure 5.3 (Wimmer & Perner, 1983). Hide a toy somewhere (location A) while the child and your friend watch. Then have your friend leave the room. Once she is gone, move the toy to another hiding place (location B). Next, ask the child where *your friend* will look for the toy when she returns. If the child is under age 4, he will typically answer the second hiding place (location B), even though your friend could not know the toy has been moved. It's as if the child doesn't grasp the fact that what *he* observed can't be in your friend's head, too.

> **theory of mind**
> Children's first cognitive understanding, which appears at about age 4, that other people have different beliefs and perspectives from their own.

What Happens When Children Have a Theory of Mind?

Having a theory of mind is not only vital to having a real conversation, it is crucial to convincing someone to do what you say. Researchers asked children to persuade a puppet to do something aversive, such as eat broccoli or brush its teeth. Even controlling for verbal abilities, the number of arguments a given boy or girl made was linked to advanced theory of mind (Slaughter, Peterson, & Moore, 2013).

Theory of mind is essential to understanding that people may not have your best interests at heart. One developmentalist had children play a game with "Mean Monkey," a puppet the experimenter controlled (Peskin, 1992). Beforehand, the researcher had asked the children which sticker they wanted. Then, she had Mean Monkey pick each child's favorite choice. Most 4-year-olds figured out how to play the game and told Mean Monkey the opposite of what they wanted. Three-year-olds never caught on. They always pointed to their favorite sticker and got the "yucky" one instead.

A student brought home the real-world message of this research. She commented that her 4-year-old nephew had reached the stage where he was lying. Three-year-olds do impulsively tell lies. For example, after peeking at a forbidden toy while adults watched through a one-way mirror, many later report: "I did not look!" (See Ma and others, 2015.) But when children have a theory of mind, their lies become more strategic and sophisticated. So having the talent to lie effectively is a crucial life skill! (See Evans, Xu, & Lee, 2011.)

The false-belief studies, conducted during the last decades of the twentieth century, convinced developmentalists that Piaget's ideas about preoperational egocentrism were wrong. Although theory-of-mind abilities (and, of course, lying talents!) mature during elementary school (Hughes & Devine, 2015; Wang and others, 2016) and into adulthood, even as young as preschool, children clearly grasp the principle that other people live in different heads.

Individual Differences in Theory of Mind

Boys and girls around the world typically pass false-belief tasks at around age 4 or 5. But perhaps because parents in nations such as Iran and China strongly socialize obedience, children in these collectivist cultures take longer to grasp the idea that people have conflicting opinions than do Western 4-year-olds (Shahaeian and others, 2011; see also Table 5.7 on page 151 for some fascinating neural findings related to theory of mind and the collectivist/individualistic distinction).

FIGURE 5.3: The false-belief task In this classic test for *theory of mind*, children under age 4 are likely to say that Ms. X will look for the toy under the bed, even though Ms. X could not possibly know the toy was moved to this new location.
Data from Wimmer & Perner, 1983.

(1) Another adult and a young child watch while you hide a toy in a place like a desk drawer.

(2) The other adult [Ms. X] leaves the room.

(3) You hide the toy under the bed and then ask the child, "Where will Ms. X look for the toy?"

Conversely, because they have extensive hands-on experience colliding (that is, arguing) with opposing sibling perspectives—"Hey, I want that toy!" "No, I do!"—Western preschoolers who have older brothers and sisters tend to pass theory-of-mind tasks at somewhat earlier ages than only children do (McAlister & Peterson, 2013).

Bilingual preschoolers—because they must sensitively switch languages—and boys and girls with superior language skills also reach this social milestone earlier than the typical child (Adi-Japha, Berberich-Artzi, & Libnawi, 2010; Chertkow and others, 2010; Hughes & Devine, 2015). Preschoolers' ability to control themselves is particularly

Table 5.7: Brain-Imaging Theory-of-Mind and Autobiographical-Memory Findings to Wrap Your Head Around

Reflecting on the self and others' mental states is a frontal-lobe activity involving slightly different brain regions: When Westerners are asked to recall autobiographical memories, a brain region called the *medial frontal cortex* lights up. When given theory-of-mind–type tasks, a slightly different area of the medial frontal cortex is activated. Therefore, thinking about ourselves and decoding other people's emotions involves distinctive (but closely aligned) brain areas.

Interesting cultural variation: This classic neural separation, however, does not exist when Chinese adults think about themselves and their mothers. More astonishing, thinking about yourself and family members activates either the same or more separate brain regions, depending on whether you have a collectivist (interdependent) or individualistic (self-oriented) worldview.

Interesting variation from person to person: When you judge the mental state of someone you view as similar, such as a good friend, a closely aligned brain region lights up as when you are asked to reflect on yourself (as if you are drawing on your feelings about how you would respond in interpreting this person's feelings). But, inferring the mental states of dissimilar others—people you view as very different—activates truly separate brain areas. Research also suggests that when people are asked to imagine the feelings of disliked out-group members (for example, a Palestinian is told to empathize with the perspective of a Jewish-Israeli West Bank settler), this instruction elicits reduced activity in the "social" brain!

Conclusion: Our attitudes about the self in relationship to other human beings are mirrored in the physical architecture of our brain.

Information from Abu-Akel & Shamay-Tsoory, 2011; Heatherton, 2011; Oddo and others, 2010; Rabin and others, 2010.

strongly related to mastering false-belief tasks (Carlson, Claxton, & Moses, 2016; Duh and others, 2016; Wang and others, 2016; more about this basic talent in the next chapter). Being early (or late) in developing theory of mind, in turn, has real-world effects.

In reviewing 20 studies, researchers found that children (especially girls) with superior theory-of-mind skills were more popular during preschool and early elementary school. Moreover, this advantage stayed stable with age, which suggests that the talent of understanding other people's mental states is an asset we carry through childhood and the adult years (Slaughter, Peterson, & Moore, 2013).

Theory-of-mind abilities are linked to sharing and helping—especially during elementary school (Imuta and others, 2016). Again, advanced theory of mind is more linked to behaving in a caring way for girls (Kuhnert and others, 2017).

The most poignant example of critical social importance about theory of mind involves friendships. Even controlling for age, language skills, and popularity, researchers found that 5-year-old boys and girls with poor theory-of-mind abilities were more likely to travel friendless from kindergarten to second grade (Fink and others, 2015).

One reason that these best friends connected may be that both have a theory of mind.

INTERVENTIONS: Stimulating Theory of Mind

Given its bedrock importance for relationships, here are some strategies adults can use to enhance children's theory of mind (Mori & Cigala, 2016):

- Continually train preschoolers in perspective-taking by pointing out other people's feelings, as Ms. Angela did throughout the chapter-opening vignette.

- When reading stories to young children, discuss what each protagonist is feeling. In one study, when researchers used this strategy at a preschool serving low-income children, the group trained in being alert to mental states showed better theory-of-mind abilities two months later when compared to children offered traditional story time (Tompkins, 2015).

- Embed false-belief tasks into games. For instance, leave a room and have the child hide a toy in a new place, then return and look for that toy where you think it should be. Open a chocolate box that is full of pencils, and then ask children to predict what an unfamiliar person will expect to find when she looks inside.

- Encourage dramatic play. Have children dress up in costumes and pretend.

Actually, dressing up in costumes and pretending does not need to be taught. As I will describe next, pretending is *basic* to the early childhood years.

Tying It All Together

1. Andrew said to Madison, his 3-year-old son, "Remember when we went to Grandma and Grandpa's last year? . . . It was your birthday, and what did Grandma make for you?" This _____ conversation will help scaffold Madison's _____.

2. Pick the statement that would *not* signify that a child has developed a full-fledged theory of mind:
   a. He's having a give-and-take conversation with you.
   b. He realizes that if you weren't there, you can't know what's gone on—and tries to explain what happened while you were absent.
   c. When he has done something he shouldn't do, he is likely to lie convincingly.
   d. He's learning to read.

3. What popular preschool game is implicitly tailored to teach theory of mind?

Answers to the Tying It All Together questions can be found at the end of this chapter.

Social Development

LEARNING OUTCOMES
- List the different play types.
- Outline the development and functions that pretending serves.
- Describe the characteristics and causes of gender-segregated play.
- List the symptoms, prevalence, and treatments for autism spectrum disorders.

Think back to your hours pretending to be a superhero or supermodel, or playing with battleships and Barbies with your friends. Why is pretend play a core preschool passion, and why do boys and girls play in different ways?

Play: The Work of Early Childhood

Developmentalists divide young children's play (the non-sports-oriented kind) into different categories. **Exercise play** involves the running and chasing behavior you saw in the opening vignette. **Rough-and-tumble play** refers to the excited shoving and wrestling that is most apparent with boys.

Actually, rough-and-tumble play is classically male behavior. Boys (but not girls) who engage in rough-and-tumble play *with their own sex* are especially popular with their peers (Lindsey, 2014). Rough-and-tumble play, evolutionary psychologists believe, is biologically built into being male (Bjorklund & Pellegrini, 2002; Flanders and others, 2013; Pellegrini, 2006).

Pretending

Fantasy play, or *pretending*, is different. Here, the child takes a stance apart from reality and makes up a scene, often with a toy or other prop. While fantasy play also can be intensely physical, this "as if" quality makes it unique. Children must pretend to be pirates or superheroes as they wrestle and chase.

THE DEVELOPMENT AND DECLINE OF PRETENDING Research suggests that the roots of pretending emerge in later infancy, and mothers scaffold this skill. In a classic study, developmentalists watched 1-year-olds with their mothers at home. Although toddlers often initiated a fantasy episode, they needed a parent to expand on the scene (Dunn, Wooding, & Hermann, 1977). For example, a child would pretend to make a phone call, and his mother would pick up the real phone and say, "Hello, this is Mommy. Should I come home now?"

Rough-and-tumble play is not only tremendously exciting, but it seems to be genetically built into being "male."

At about age 3, children transfer pretending with mothers to pretending with peers. **Collaborative pretend play,** or fantasizing *together* with another child, gets going at about age 4 (Smolucha & Smolucha, 1998). Because they must work together to develop the scene, collaboratively pretending shows that preschoolers have a theory of mind. (You need to understand that your fellow playwright has a different script in his head.) Collaboratively pretending, in turn, helps teach young children to make better sense of other people's minds (Nicolopoulou and others, 2010).

Anyone with a child can see these changes firsthand. When a 2-year-old has his "best friend" over, they play in parallel orbits—if things go well. More likely, a titanic battle erupts, as each child exerts autonomy and initiative by attempting to gain possession of the toys. By age 4, children can play *together*. At age 5, they can often pretend together for hours—with only a few world-class fights that are usually resolved.

Although fantasy play can continue into early adolescence, when children reach concrete operations, their interest shifts to structured games (Bjorklund & Pellegrini, 2002). At age 3, a child pretends to bake in the kitchen corner; at 9, he wants to bake a cake. At age 4, you ran around playing pirates; at 9, you tried to hit the ball like the Pittsburgh Pirates do.

THE PURPOSES OF PRETENDING Interestingly, around the world, when children pretend, their play has similar plots. Let's eavesdrop at a U.S. preschool:

BOY 2: I don't want to be a kitty anymore.

GIRL: You are a husband?

BOY 2: Yeah.

BOYS 1 AND 2: Husbands, husbands! *(Yell and run around the playhouse)*

GIRL: Hold it, Bill, I can't have two husbands.

BOYS 1 AND 2: Two husbands! Two husbands!

GIRL: We gonna marry ourselves, right?

(Corsaro, 1985, pp. 102–104)

Why do young children play "family," and assume the "correct" roles when they play mommy and daddy? For answers, let's turn to the insights of that genius, Lev Vygotsky, again.

Play allows children to practice adult roles. Vygotsky (1978) believed that pretending allows children to rehearse being adults. The reason girls pretend to be mommy and baby is that women are the main child-care providers around the world. Boys play soldiers because this activity offers built-in training for the wars they face as adults (Pellegrini & Smith, 2005).

Play allows children a sense of control. As the following preschool conversation suggests, pretending has a deeper psychological function, too:

GIRL 1: Yeah, and let's pretend when Mommy's out until later.

GIRL 2: Ooooh. Well, I'm not the boss around here, though. 'Cause mommies are the bosses.

GIRL 1: *(Doubtfully)* But maybe we won't know how to punish.

GIRL 2: I will. I'll put my hand up and spank. That's what my mom does.

GIRL 1: My mom does too.

(Corsaro, 1985, p. 96)

For these 4-year-old girls (aka women who have dressed up to go to a party), their collaborative pretend play is teaching them vital theory-of-mind skills.

exercise play Running and chasing play that exercises children's physical skills.

rough-and-tumble play Play that involves shoving, wrestling, and hitting, but in which no actual harm is intended; especially characteristic of boys.

fantasy play Pretend play in which a child makes up a scene, often with a toy or other prop.

collaborative pretend play Fantasy play in which children work together to develop and act out scenes.

While reading the preceding chapters, you may have been thinking that the supposedly carefree early childhood years are hardly free of stress. We expect 3- and 4-year-olds to "sit still," "share," and use their "inside voice" at the same age when, Erikson believes, their mission is to passionately explore life. We discipline preschoolers when they don't have the concrete operational talents to make sense of abstract adult rules. Vygotsky (1978) believed that, confronted by these continual frustrations, young children enter "an illusory role" in which they take control. In play, *you* can be the spanking mommy or the queen of the castle, even when you are small and sometimes feel like a slave.

To penetrate the inner world of preschool fantasy play, sociologist William Corsaro (1985, 1997) went undercover, entering a nursery school as a member of the class. (No problem. The children welcomed their new playmate, whom they called Big Bill, as a clumsy, enlarged version of themselves.) As Vygotsky would predict, Corsaro found that preschool play plots often centered on mastering upsetting events. There were separation/reunion scenarios ("Help! I'm lost in the forest." "I'll find you.") and danger/rescue plots ("Get in the house. It's gonna be a rainstorm!"). Sometimes, play scenarios centered on that ultimate frightening event, death:

Imagine that, like the supersized preschooler shown here (Professor William Corsaro), you could spend years going down slides, playing family, and bonding with 3- and 4-year-olds—and then get professional recognition for your academic work. What an incredible career!

CHILD 1: We are dead, we are dead! Help, we are dead! (*Puts animals on their sides*)

CHILD 2: You can't talk if you are dead.

CHILD 1: Oh, well, Leah's talked when she was dead, so mine have to talk when they are dead. Help, help, we are dead!

(Corsaro, 1985 p. 204)

Notice that these themes are basic to Disney movies and fairy tales. From *Finding Nemo*, *Bambi*, and *The Lion King* to—my personal favorite—*Dumbo*, there is nothing more heart-wrenching than being separated from your parent. From the greedy old witch in *Hansel and Gretel* to the jealous queen in *Sleeping Beauty*, no scenario is as sweet as triumphing over evil and possible death.

Play furthers our understanding of social norms. Corsaro (1985) found that death was a touchy play topic. When children proposed these plots, their partners might try to change the script. This relates to Vygotsky's third insight about play: Although children's play looks unstructured, it has clear boundaries and rules. Plots involving dead animals waking up make children uncomfortable because they violate the conditions of life. Children get especially uneasy when a play partner proposes scenarios with gory themes, such as cutting off people's heads (Dunn & Hughes, 2001). Therefore, play teaches children how to act and how not to behave. Wouldn't you want to retreat if someone showed an intense interest in decapitation while having a conversation with you?

The idea that play teaches social norms brings me to that basic childhood play rule—girls and boys behave in different ways.

Girls' and Boys' Play Worlds

[Some] girls, all about five . . . years old, are looking through department store catalogues, . . . concentrating on what they call "girls' stuff" and referring to some of the other items as "yucky boys' stuff." . . . Shirley points to a picture of a couch . . . "All we want is the pretty stuff," says Ruth. Peggy now announces, "If you come to my birthday, every girl in the school is invited. I'm going to put a sign up that says, 'No boys allowed!'"

"Oh good, good, good," says Vickie. "I hate boys."

(Corsaro, 1997, p. 155)

gender-segregated play
Play in which boys and girls associate only with members of their own sex—typical of childhood.

Does this conversation bring back memories of being age 5 or 6? How does **gender-segregated play** develop? What are the differences in boy versus girl play, and what causes the sexes to separate into these different camps?

Exploring the Separate Societies

Visit a playground and observe children of different ages. Notice that toddlers show few signs of gender-segregated play. In preschool, children start to play in sex-segregated groups (Martin & Ruble, 2010). By approximately age 5 or 6, gender-segregated play is solidly entrenched, although boys and girls may *occasionally* play in mixed groups (Fabes, Martin, & Hanish, 2003). Still, with friendships, there is a total split: Boys are almost always best friends with boys and girls with girls (Maccoby, 1998).

Now, go back to the playground and look at the *way* boys and girls relate. Do you notice that boy and girl play differs in the following ways?

BOYS EXCITEDLY RUN AROUND; GIRLS CALMLY TALK Boys' play is more rambunctious. Even during physical games such as tag, girls play together in calmer, more subdued ways (Maccoby, 1998; Pellegrini, 2006). The difference in activity levels is striking if you have the pleasure of witnessing one gender playing with the other gender's toys. In one memorable episode, after my 4-year-old son and a friend invaded a girl's stash of dolls, they gleefully ran around the house bashing Barbie into Barbie and using their booty as swords.

BOYS COMPETE IN GROUPS; GIRLS PLAY COLLABORATIVELY, ONE-ON-ONE Their exuberant, rough-and-tumble play explains why boys tend to take over preschool playgrounds, running and yelling, filling most of the physical space. Another difference lies in playgroup *size*. Boys get together in packs. Girls play in smaller, more intimate groups (Maccoby, 1990, 1998; Ruble, Martin, & Berenbaum, 2006).

Boys and girls also differ in the *way* they relate. Boys try to establish dominance and compete to be the best. This competitive versus cooperative style spills over into children's talk. Girl-to-girl collaborative play really sounds collaborative ("I'll be the doctor, OK?"). Boys give each other bossy commands like "I'm doing the operation. Lie down, now!" (see Maccoby, 1998). Girl-to-girl fantasy play involves nurturing themes. Boys prefer the warrior, superhero mode.

The stereotypic quality of girls' fantasy play came as a shock when I spent three days playing with a visiting 5-year-old niece. We devoted day 1 to setting up a beauty shop, complete with nail polishes and shampoos. We had a table for massages and a makeover section featuring every cosmetic I owned. Then we opened for business with our relatives and (of course!)—by charging for our services—made money for toys. We spent the last day playing with a "pool party" Barbie combo my niece selected at Walmart that afternoon.

Boys' and girls' different play interests show why the kindergartners in the vignette at the beginning of this section came to hate those "yucky" boys. Another reason why girls turn off to the opposite sex is the unpleasant reception they get from the other camp. Researchers observing at a preschool found that, while active girls played with the boys early in the year, they eventually were rejected and forced to play with their own sex (Pellegrini and others, 2007). Therefore, boys first erect the barriers: "No girls allowed!" Moreover, the gender barriers are *generally* more rigid for males.

BOYS LIVE IN A MORE EXCLUSIONARY, SEPARATE WORLD My niece did choose to buy Barbies, but she also plays with trucks. She loves chasing and competing at jumping and running, not just doing her nails. So, even though they may dislike the opposite sex, girls cross the divide. Boys avoid that chasm—refusing to venture down the Barbie aisle or consider buying a toy labeled "girl." Therefore, boys live in a more roped-off gender world (Boyle, Marshall, & Robeson, 2003).

A visit to this first grade lunchroom vividly brings home the fact that by middle childhood, gender segregation is entrenched.

Now, you might be interested to know what happened during my final day pretending with the pool party toys. After my niece said, "Aunt Janet, let's pretend we are the popular girls," our Barbies tried on fancy dresses ("What shall I wear, Jane?") in preparation for a pool party, where the dolls met up to discuss—*guess what*—shopping and where they did their nails!

What Causes Gender-Stereotyped Play?

Why do children, such as my niece, play in gender-stereotyped ways? Answers come from exploring three forces: biology (nature), socialization (nurture), and cognitions (thoughts).

A BIOLOGICAL UNDERPINNING Ample evidence suggests that gender-segregated play is biologically built in. Children around the world form separate play societies (Maccoby, 1998). Troops of juvenile rhesus monkeys behave *exactly* like human children. The males segregate into their own groups and engage in rough-and-tumble play (Pellegrini, 2006). Grooming activities similar to my niece's beauty-shop behaviors are prominent among young female monkeys, too (Bjorklund & Pellegrini, 2002; Suomi, 2004).

Actually, male gender-typed play is tied to hormone levels during the first months of life. Researchers looked at the naturally occurring amount of salivary testosterone in 3-month-old boys and girls (females also produce this classic male sex hormone). Remarkably, both sexes with high concentrations of testosterone displayed more male play behaviors at age 2 (Saenz & Alexander, 2013).

Moreover, female fetuses exposed to high levels of prenatal testosterone show more masculine interests as teens and emerging adults (Udry, 2000)! After taking maternal blood samples during the second trimester—the time when the neurons are being formed (see Chapter 2)—one developmentalist tracked these women's daughters for the next two decades.

Females exposed to elevated prenatal testosterone, he discovered, were more interested in traditionally male occupations, such as engineering, than were their lower-hormone-level counterparts. They were also less likely to wear makeup, and in their twenties, they showed more stereotypically male interests (such as race-car driving). Therefore, in utero testosterone seems to epigenetically affect children's DNA, programming a more "feminized" or "masculinized" brain.

THE AMPLIFYING EFFECT OF SOCIALIZATION The wider world helps biology along. From the images in preschool coloring books (Fitzpatrick & McPherson, 2010) to the messages beamed out in television sitcoms (Collins, 2011; Paek, Nelson, & Vilela, 2011); from traditional parental gender-role attitudes (Halpern & Perry-Jenkins, 2016) to the color pink that screams "Just for girls" (see the How Do We Know box)—everything brings home the message: Males and females act in different ways.

Peers play a powerful role in this programming. When they play in mixed-gender groups, children act in less gender-stereotyped ways (Fabes and others, 2003): With girls, boys tone down their rough-and-tumble activities; girls are less apt to play quietly with dolls when they are pretending with boys. Therefore, splitting into separate play societies trains children to behave in ways typical of their own sex (Martin & Fabes, 2001).

Same-sex playmates reinforce one another for selecting gender-stereotyped activities ("Let's play with dolls." "Great!"). They model each other as they play together in "gentle" or "rough" ways. The pressure to toe the gender line is promoted by strong social sanctions. Children reject classmates who behave in "gender atypical ways" (such as girls who hit and especially boys who play with dolls) (Lee & Troop-Gordon, 2011; Smith, Rose, & Schwartz-Mette, 2010). In fact, in the study I mentioned earlier, while preschool boys who engaged in rough-and-tumble play with their own sex

HOW DO WE KNOW...
that pink gives girls permission to act like boys?

While I was writing this chapter, the 2017 Women's March erupted around the globe. Witnessing the sea of pink-hued hats, I wondered: What power does the color pink have in women's lives? This research offered fascinating cues (Weisgram, Fulcher, & Dinella, 2014).

In two creative studies exploring the impact of color in gender toy preferences, developmentalists seated preschool boys and girls at tables featuring a variety of toys. The first study featured classic boy toys (such as guns and fighter jets) in traditionally masculine colors (like gray and black), as well as male-type toys painted in that classic female hue, pink. In a second study, the psychologists labeled unfamiliar objects, such as a nutcracker, as toys designed for either "boys" or "girls," and then painted these objects in either traditional or opposite-gender hues.

Boys, they discovered, gravitated to toys designated for "boys" no matter their color. But if an object for boys was painted in pink, girls decided it was fine to play with that toy. Therefore, *pink* may give girls a green light to enjoy boy pleasures, such as fighter jets and guns, because that color signals, "That's okay for my sex."

This research suggests that pink becomes a defining symbol of womanhood during our earliest years of life. Moreover, donning this color during adulthood, I believe, may allow women to both embrace their gender identity and rebel at the same time. Wearing pink gives women full latitude to fight just like men!

Wearing pink boxing gloves may permit this woman to excel at her offbeat profession and prove her femininity at the same time.

---

were especially popular, the class disliked children who used this play style with girls (Lindsey, 2014).

THE IMPACT OF COGNITIONS A cognitive process reinforces these external messages. According to **gender schema theory** (Bem, 1981; Martin & Dinella, 2002), once children understand their category (girl or boy), they selectively attend to the activities of their own sex.

When do we first grasp our gender label and start this lifelong practice of modeling our group? The answer is at about age 2½, right after we begin to talk (Martin & Ruble, 2010)! Although they may not learn the real difference until much later (unless they have an opposite-sex sibling they can see naked!), 3-year-olds can tell you that girls have long hair and cry a lot, whereas boys fight and play with trucks. At about age 5, when they are mastering the similar concept of identity constancy (the knowledge that your essential self doesn't change when you dress up in a gorilla costume), children grasp the idea that once you start out as a boy or girl, you stay that way for life (Kohlberg, 1966). However, mistakes are common. I once heard my 5-year-old nephew ask my husband, "Was that jewelry from when you were a girl?"

In sum, my niece's beauty-shop activities had a biological basis, although a steady stream of reinforcements from adults and playmates accelerated this process almost from birth. Identifying herself as "a girl," and then spending hours modeling the women in her life, promoted classically "feminine" sex role behavior, too.

Throughout this chapter, I've been emphasizing how the ability to reflect on one's feelings and experiences, and to understand other people's perspectives, is fundamental

gender schema theory
Explanation for gender-stereotyped behavior that emphasizes the role of cognitions; specifically, the idea that once children know their own gender label (girl or boy), they selectively watch and model their own sex.

Children spend hours modeling their own sex, demonstrating why gender schema theory (the idea that "I am a boy" or "I am a girl") also encourages behaving in gender-stereotyped ways.

to humanity. Therefore, it seems appropriate to conclude by describing the familiar condition when these basic human skills don't fully lock in—autism spectrum disorders.

Hot in Developmental Science: Autism Spectrum Disorders

Autism spectrum disorders (ASDs) are syndromes that center on deficits in self-awareness and theory of mind—the inability to have normal back-and-forth conversations, to share feelings, and to connect with adults and friends. To qualify for this diagnosis, according to the most recent *Diagnostic and Statistical Manual* (*DSM*-5), these severe social impairments need to be accompanied by restricted, stereotyped, repetitive behavior: rocking, flipping objects, being hypersensitive to sensory input, preferring the nonhuman world (American Psychiatric Association, 2013).

Autism spectrum disorders, often diagnosed in preschool, typically persist and therefore rob children of having a fulfilling life. Poor social referencing (or no social referencing) (DeQuinzio and others, 2016) and delayed language (Kover, Edmunds, & Weismer, 2016) foreshadow this condition. Because autism has no cure, deteriorated thinking (Rosenthal and others, 2013) is an unfortunate path this disorder can take during the adult years.

The good news is that autism is still fairly rare, currently affecting roughly 1 in every 68 children in the United States (Ramsey and others, 2016). The problem is the alarming increase in this diagnosis over the past two decades. (See Figure 5.4 for an example from Denmark.) ASDs are several times more common in boys than girls (Volkmar and others, 2014).

What causes these devastating brain conditions? The fact that autism may run in families leads scientists to believe that this condition often has genetic causes (Fischbach and others, 2016). A puzzling array of environmental risk factors have been linked to this disorder, from air pollution (Volk and others, 2013) to maternal abusive relationships (Roberts and others, 2013); from prenatal medication use (Christensen and others, 2013) to—very important—being born extremely premature (Verhaeghe and others, 2016). Given its strong tie to prematurity and birth problems, it's no surprise that older parents are at higher risk of having a child with this condition. But astonishingly, one study traced the risk back a generation—to the advanced age of the granddad (see Frans and others, 2013)!

At this point, it's critical to set the record straight. Despite what some parents (and adults) still believe, vaccines do *not* cause autism (Fischbach and others, 2016). The initial small study suggesting this link was resoundingly discredited as methodologically flawed. Multiple careful and subsequent studies conducted over the past decade confirm that there is *no link* between autism spectrum disorders and vaccines (see Centers for Disease Control and Prevention, 2017).

Moreover, when parents succumb to misplaced fears and decide not to vaccinate their babies and toddlers, this practice puts *every* child at risk—because it exposes the whole population to illnesses such as measles, which vaccines now prevent. As I spelled out in Chapter 1, vaccinations qualify as a landmark twentieth-century medical magic bullet that helped vanquish child mortality and extend our lifespan well into the adult years. If we want to "blame" modern medicine for the recent rise in autism, the most reasonable culprit would be the (also landmark) advances in saving very tiny, at-risk babies, as described in Chapter 2.

When a child is diagnosed with an autism spectrum disorder, what are the possible treatments? The classic intervention, developed about 40 years ago, involves operant conditioning. Children receive services from different professionals, while their parents get training in reinforcing adaptive behavior (Scahill and others, 2016). The interesting finding that having older siblings reduces the intensity of a child's social problems (Ben-Itzchak, Zukerman, & Zachor, 2016) suggests that school-based peer interventions can also be effective (Chang & Locke, 2016). And although

---

autism spectrum disorders (ASDs) Conditions characterized by persistent, severe, widespread social and conversational deficits; lack of interest in people and their feelings; and repetitive, restricted behavior patterns, such as rocking, ritualized behavior, hypersensitivity to sensory input, and a fixation on inanimate objects. A core characteristic of these disorders is impairments in theory of mind.

At the 2017 March for Science in San Francisco, people were passionate to point out the medical advances we take for granted today—in particular, the fact that vaccinations have wiped out many life-threatening childhood diseases, such as polio.

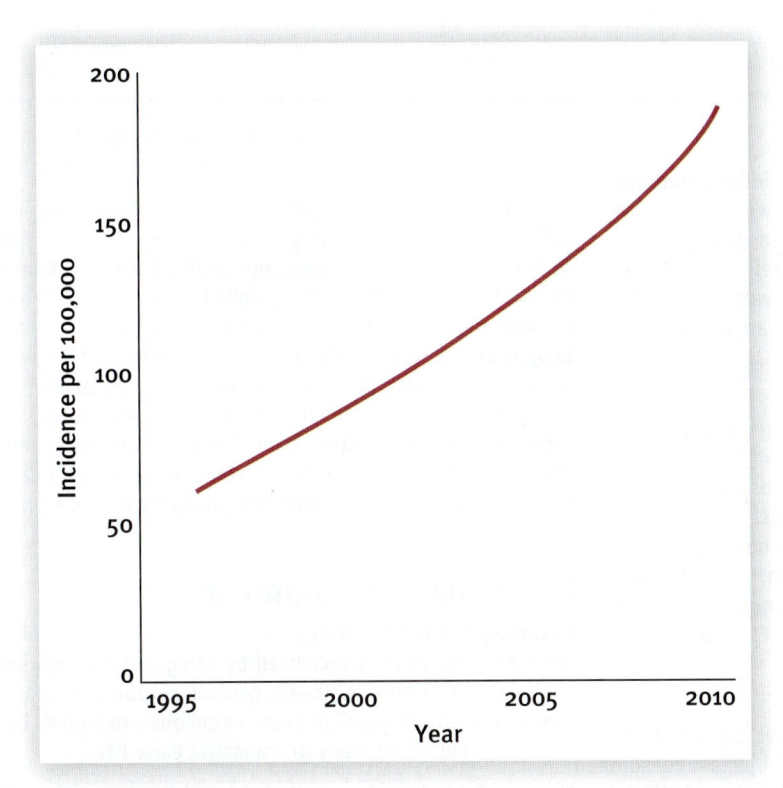

FIGURE 5.4: **Time trends of autism spectrum diagnoses among children aged 4–6 in Denmark, 1995–2010** This chart vividly shows the rise in autism spectrum diagnoses among young children over the early twenty-first century in one representative Western nation (Denmark). Is this alarming increase partly due to the massive media attention focused on this condition? We do not know. But autism rates vary from place to place (Ramsey and others, 2016) partly because this condition is hard to distinguish from other developmental disorders, making illness statistics less than fully accurate (Hedley and others, 2016).
Data from Jensen, Steinhausen, & Lauritson, 2014.

medications don't touch the core symptoms, they can mute the emotional storms emblematic of this disorder, too.

Autism is a poster child for what happens when our uniquely human ability to understand other people's mental states is blocked. In the next chapter, I'll describe how children fully make sense of the adult world during that watershed age called middle childhood.

Tying It All Together

1. When Melanie and Miranda play, they love to make up pretend scenes together. Are these two girls likely to be about age 2, age 5, or age 9?

2. In watching 4-year-olds at a playground, which two observations are you likely to make?
    a. The boys are playing in larger groups.
    b. Both girls and boys love rough-and-tumble play.
    c. The girls are quieter and they are doing more negotiating.

3. Who may be more receptive to playing with toys of the other sex, 4-year-old Sara or 4-year-old Sam?

4. Mark argues that gender-typed behavior is biologically built in, whereas Martha believes that the environment shapes this behavior. Drawing on this chapter, make Mark's and then Martha's case.

5. Autism spectrum disorders are becoming *more/less* prevalent, and scientists have *evidence/no evidence* that these disorders are caused by vaccines.

Answers to the Tying It All Together questions can be found at the end of this chapter.

SUMMARY

Setting the Context

Childhood comprises two phases—**early** and **middle childhood.** During early childhood, we learn to decode other people's mental states, the talent that makes humanity special. At this age, Erikson believed, children's mission is **initiative,** exploring their emerging skills. During the elementary school years, our task is **industry,** the need to inhibit our desires and start to work.

Physical Development

Physical growth slows down after infancy. Girls and boys are roughly the same height during preschool and much of elementary school. Boys are a bit more competent at **gross motor skills.** Girls are slightly superior in **fine motor skills.** Although fine motor skills in preschool predict elementary school success, we need to be careful not to push young children. Computers and learning toys may discourage exercising outside. Undernutrition impairs development by making children too tired to play.

Cognitive Development

Piaget's preoperational stage lasts from about ages 3 to 7. **Preoperational thinkers** focus on the way objects and substances (and people) immediately appear. **Concrete operational thinkers** can step back from their visual perceptions and reason on a more conceptual plane. In Piaget's **conservation tasks,** preoperational children believe that when the shape of a substance has changed, the amount of it has changed. One reason is that young children lack the concept of **reversibility,** the understanding that an operation can be performed in the opposite direction. Another reason is that children **center** on what first captures their eye and cannot **decenter,** or focus on several dimensions at one time. Centering also affects **class inclusion** (understanding overarching categories). Preoperational children believe that if something *looks* bigger visually, it equals "more."

Preoperational children lack **identity constancy**—they don't understand that people are "the same" in spite of changes to their external appearance. Children's thinking is characterized by **animism** (the idea that inanimate objects are alive) and by **artificialism** (the belief that everything in nature was made by humans). They are **egocentric,** unable to understand that other people have different perspectives from their own. Although Piaget's ideas offer a wealth of insights into children's thinking, this premier theorist underestimated what young children know. Children in every culture do progress from preoperational to concrete operational thinking—but the learning demands of the particular society affect the ages at which specific conservations are attained.

Lev Vygotsky, with his concept of the **zone of proximal development,** suggested that learning occurs when adults tailor instruction to a child's capacities and then use **scaffolding** to gradually promote independent performance. Education, according to Vygotsky, is a collaborative, bidirectional learning experience.

Language makes every other childhood skill possible. Vygotsky believed that we learn everything through using **inner speech.** During early childhood, language abilities expand dramatically. **Phonemic** (sound articulation) abilities improve. As the number of **morphemes** in children's sentences increases, their **mean length of utterance (MLU)** expands. **Syntax,** or knowledge of grammatical rules, improves. **Semantic** understanding (vocabulary) shoots up. Common language mistakes young children make include **overregularization** (using regular forms for irregular verbs and nouns), **overextension** (applying word categories too broadly), and **underextension** (applying word categories too narrowly).

Emotional Development

Autobiographical memories, or the child's understanding of having a personal past, is socialized by caregivers through sensitive past-talk conversations. Overly general autobiographical memories (or not recalling salient events from one's past) may be a sign of having had an unhappy or traumatic early life.

Theory of mind, our knowledge that other people have different perspectives from our own, is measured by the false-belief task. While children around the world typically pass this milestone at about age 4 or 5, a variety of forces affect this critical skill. Because it has widespread positive social effects, strategies have been developed to promote theory of mind.

Social Development

Play, that defining activity of early childhood, comprises **exercise play** and **rough-and-tumble play** (play fighting and wrestling typical of boys). **Fantasy play** is jump-started by mothers when children are around age 1. The emergence of **collaborative play** at about age 4 signals that children can play together with peers. After reaching a peak in preschool, during concrete operations, pretending declines. Pretending may help children practice adult roles, offer young children a sense of control, and teach boys and girls appropriate social norms.

Gender-segregated play unfolds during preschool, when children begin to play mainly with their own sex. Boy-to-boy play is rambunctious, while girls play together in quiet, collaborative ways. Boys compete in groups; girls play one-to-one. Boys' play is more excluding of girls. Gender-stereotyped play seems to have a biological basis, as shown by the fact that high testosterone levels in utero and during babies' early months promote stereotypically male behaviors. In addition to being biologically built in, typical gender behavior is socialized by adults and by peers when children play together in same-sex groups. According to **gender**

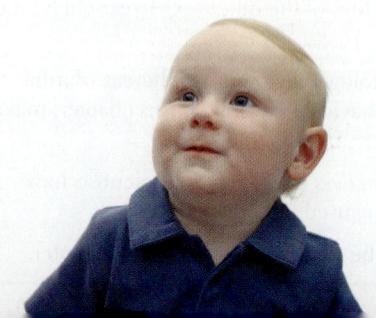

schema theory, once children understand that they are a boy or a girl, they attend to and model behaviors of their own sex.

Autism spectrum disorders (ASDs) are characterized by severely impaired social skills and abnormal, repetitive behaviors. These incurable conditions, which wreak havoc on development, are rising in prevalence and may have multiple causes—but research has proved that vaccination is definitely not one of them.

KEY TERMS

animism, p. 141
artificialism, p. 141
autism spectrum disorders (ASDs), p. 158
autobiographical memories, p. 148
centering, p. 140
class inclusion, p. 140
collaborative pretend play, p. 153
concrete operational thinking, p. 138
conservation tasks, p. 138
decentering, p. 140
early childhood, p. 133
egocentrism, p. 142
exercise play, p. 152
fantasy play, p. 152
fine motor skills, p. 136
gender schema theory, p. 157
gender-segregated play, p. 154
gross motor skills, p. 136
identity constancy, p. 140
industry, p. 134
initiative, p. 134
inner speech, p. 146
mean length of utterance (MLU), p. 146
middle childhood, p. 134
morpheme, p. 146
overextension, p. 147
overregularization, p. 146
phoneme, p. 146
preoperational thinking, p. 138
reversibility, p. 139
rough-and-tumble play, p. 152
scaffolding, p. 144
semantics, p. 146
syntax, p. 146
theory of mind, p. 149
underextension, p. 147
zone of proximal development (ZPD), p. 144

ANSWERS TO Tying It All Together QUIZZES

Setting the Context

1. Our mindreading ability is what makes us different from other animals.
2. Steven's younger son is showing initiative by pushing his body. His older son is displaying industry by carefully obeying the rules.
3. Adolescence is the other age of exploration.

Physical Development

1. Long-distance running and the high jump would be ideal for Jessica, as these sports heavily tap into gross motor skills.
2. a. Based on the principle that we should not push preschoolers, enrolling 4-year-olds in sports would be counterproductive.

Cognitive Development

1. (a) animism; (b) egocentrism; (c) artificialism; (d) can't conserve; (e) (no) identity constancy
2. Children in concrete operations can step back from their current perceptions and think conceptually, whereas preoperational children can't go beyond how things immediately appear.
3. Buy Chris easy-to-read books that are just above his skill level.
4. Vygotsky would say it's normal—the way children learn to think through their actions and control their behavior.

5. (b) = overregularization; (c) = overextension

Emotional Development

1. This *past-talk* conversation will help stimulate Madison's *autobiographical memory*.
2. d
3. Hide and seek implicitly teaches theory of mind.

Social Development

1. The girls are about age 5.
2. a and c (Girls don't typically engage in rough-and-tumble play.)
3. Sara (The gender toy-line is more permeable for girls.)
4. Mark's evidence for biology: Girls and boys worldwide and young monkeys play (and behave) in gender-defined ways. Female testosterone levels, early in development, predict having more male occupational interests. Martha's case for the environment: Gender-defined behavior is drummed in from the media and parents and is solidified during preschool by children playing in same-sex groups. Pink permits girls to act like boys!
5. Autism spectrum disorders (ASDs) are becoming *more* prevalent, and scientists have *no* evidence they are caused by vaccines.

CONNECT ONLINE:

LaunchPad macmillan learning

Check out our videos and additional resources located at: www.macmillanlearning.com

CHAPTER 6

CHAPTER OUTLINE

Setting the Context

Physical Development
Brain Development: Slow-Growing Frontal Lobes
Motor Skills, Obesity, and Health

Cognitive Development
An Information-Processing Perspective on Intellectual Growth

INTERVENTIONS: Using Information-Processing Theory at Home and at Work

HOT IN DEVELOPMENTAL SCIENCE: Attention-Deficit/Hyperactivity Disorder

INTERVENTIONS: Helping Children with ADHD

Emotional Development
Observing and Evaluating the Self

INTERVENTIONS: Promoting Realistic Self-Esteem

Doing Good: Morality and Prosocial Behavior

INTERVENTIONS: Socializing Moral Children

Doing Harm: Aggression

INTERVENTIONS: Taming Excessive Aggression

Social Development
Friendships: The Proving Ground for Relationships

Popularity: Rising in the Peer Ranks

Bullying: Moral Disengagement in Action

EXPERIENCING CHILDHOOD: Middle-Aged Reflections on My Middle-Childhood Victimization

INTERVENTIONS: Attacking Bullying and Helping Rejected Children

Middle Childhood

Ten-year-old José has a new best friend, Matt. The boys bonded over their love of soccer and their passion for chess. Although this offbeat obsession kept them far from the popular kids' group, their take-charge kindness has made them the go-to people when the class gets out of control. A perfect example happened last week when the fifth-grade boys decided to physically (!) play tag using a video game.

When he saw the kids jostling, filling up the recess area with joyous noise, Saul ran over and asked, "Can I play?"

Several kids closed ranks, jeering, "No fat kids allowed!"

Then Adam pushed in, as usual, disrupting the game, hogging the device the kids had renamed "the ball." A few minutes later, an anxious child named Jimmy worked up the guts to timidly enter the group.

"Get out!" erupted Adam, "You wuss. You girl!"

Adam bopped Jimmy over the head, did his standard imitation of Saul's lumbering walk and—as usual—a few boys smirked. Jimmy started to cry and began to slink away. But suddenly, José intervened.

"Cool it, guys," he said. "Man, are you all right? Come join us."

José comforted Jimmy and managed to tell the other boys to lay off Saul ("Hey guys, that's mean!"), while Matt did his best to keep Adam from disrupting the game. All of this earned these two good-guy heroes exuberant fist pumps from the teacher and the rest of the class!

Why are some children, such as José and Matt, unusually caring, while others, like Adam, are impulsive, aggressive, and rude? Why do social hierarchies blossom during late elementary school, and what makes bullying compelling at this age? What makes children bond as friends, and which mental skills allow some 10-year-olds, such as José and Matt, to master complex strategy games, such as chess? This chapter answers these questions and others, as we enter **middle childhood,** that landmark stage from approximately ages 7 to 12.

To introduce our discussion, let's first briefly summarize why both Piaget and Erikson view middle childhood as the tipping point when we first grasp "the adult world."

middle childhood The second phase of childhood, comprising the ages from roughly 7 to 12 years.

LEARNING OUTCOME
- Explain what makes middle childhood unique by referring to Piaget's and Erikson's theories.

Setting the Context

As I mentioned in the last chapter, Piaget believed that young children are tethered to their immediate perceptions. At age 7 or 8, we transcend appearances and think abstractly for the first time. Piaget offered a scientific explanation for why the Jesuits labeled year 7 as the age of "reason." During concrete operations (see Table 6.1), we first think logically about life.

Then Erikson fleshed out the implications of this mental advance. During middle childhood, we realize that succeeding in life requires *industry* (see Table 6.2). We need to control our impulses and work for what we want.

Table 6.1: Piaget's Stages: Focus on Childhood

Age (years)	Name of stage	Description
0–2	Sensorimotor	The baby manipulates objects to pin down the basics of physical reality. This stage ends with the development of language.
2–7	Preoperations	Children's perceptions are captured by their immediate appearances: "What they see is what is real." They believe, among other things, that inanimate objects are really alive and that if the appearance of a quantity of liquid changes (for example, if it is poured from a short, wide glass into a tall, thin one), the amount of liquid itself changes.
8–12	Concrete operations	**Children have a realistic understanding of the world. Their thinking is really on the same wavelength as that of adults. While they can reason conceptually about concrete objects, however, they cannot think abstractly in a scientific way.**
12+	Formal operations	Reasoning is at its pinnacle: hypothetical, scientific, flexible, fully adult. Our full cognitive human potential has been reached.

Table 6.2: Erikson's Psychosocial Stages of Childhood, Adolescence, and Emerging Adulthood

Life Stage	Primary Task
Infancy (birth to 1 year)	Basic trust versus mistrust
Toddlerhood (1 to 2 years)	Autonomy versus shame and doubt
Early childhood (3 to 6 years)	Initiative versus guilt
Middle childhood (7 to 12 years)	**Industry versus inferiority**
Adolescence and emerging adulthood (teens into twenties)	Identity versus role confusion
Emerging adulthood (twenties)	Intimacy versus isolation

In Erikson's framework, during elementary school, our task is to work for what we want.

Tying It All Together

1. Drawing on Erikson's and Piaget's theories, name the qualities that make middle childhood (and human beings) special.

Answers to the Tying It All Together quizzes can be found at the end of this chapter.

Physical Development

Reaching Piaget's and Erikson's middle childhood landmarks depends on that human masterpiece structure, the frontal lobes.

Brain Development: Slow-Growing Frontal Lobes

In contrast to other species, our huge *cerebral cortex* actually takes more than two full decades to mature. The *myelin sheath*—the fatty neural cover—grows into our twenties. *Synaptogenesis* (making billions of connections between neurons) is on an extended blossoming and pruning timetable, too, especially in the brain region responsible for thinking through our actions and managing our emotions—the **frontal lobes**.

Figure 6.1, which compares the size of our cortex to that of other species, shows the huge frontal lobes at the top of the brain. During early childhood, the neurons in the visual and motor cortices are in their pruning phase, which explains why vision develops rapidly and why children master basic physical milestones, such as walking, at a young age. However, the frontal lobes are only beginning their synaptic blossoming when we start toddling around. Pruning in this part of the brain begins at about age 9.

Frontal lobe pruning explains why we have such high expectations for children during late elementary school. We expect fifth graders to grasp complex games such as chess, take responsibility for finishing their homework, and get along with their peers. These adult-like talents are accompanied by expanding motor skills.

Motor Skills, Obesity, and Health

In Chapter 5, I implied that lack of outdoor exercise might prevent preschoolers from fully developing their physical skills. Now let's delve into cutting-edge research relating to this issue during the middle childhood years.

Actually, studies from Britain to Germany and from Ireland to the United States confirm that today's elementary school children are less proficient physically than in the past (Burns and others, 2015; Gaul & Issartel, 2016; Lubans and others, 2010;

LEARNING OUTCOMES

- Outline how the frontal lobes develop.
- Describe recent changes in elementary motor skills.
- Explain what adults can do to promote children's physical development.
- List some facts about childhood obesity.

frontal lobes The area at the front uppermost part of the brain, responsible for reasoning and planning our actions.

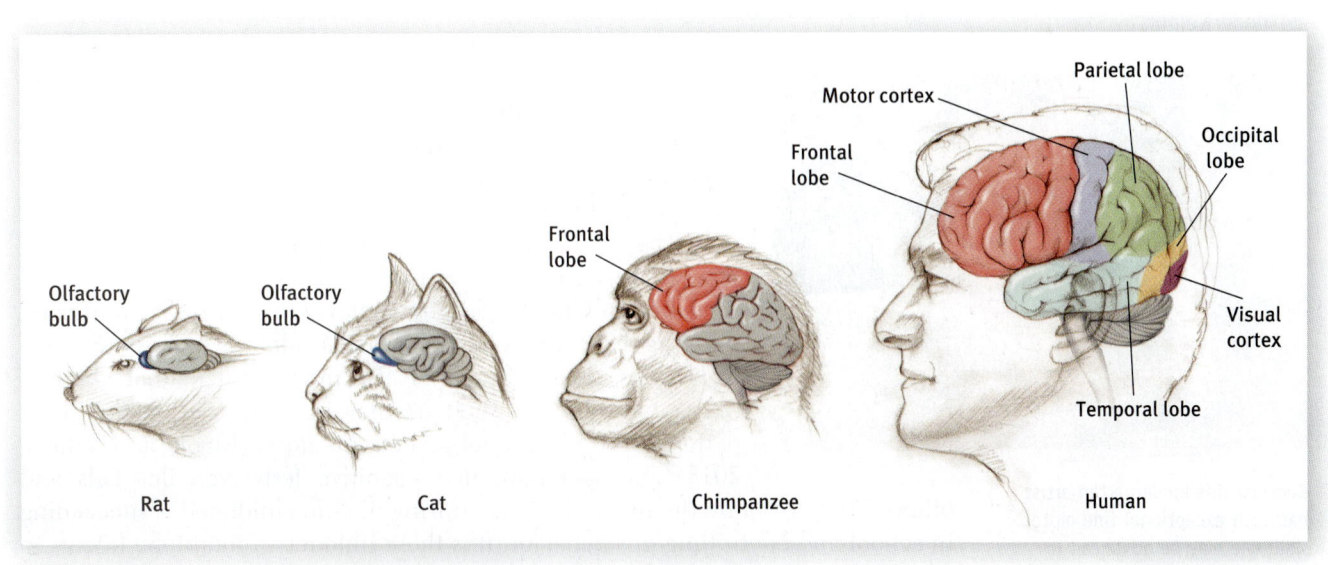

FIGURE 6.1: The human cortex and that of some other species Notice the size of our cortex in comparison to other species. Our mammoth frontal lobes make humanity unlike any other animal on earth.

This scene would be typical just a few decades ago. Today, bike riding with friends in elementary school is becoming more rare.

childhood obesity A body mass index at or above the 95th percentile compared to the U.S. norms established for children in the 1970s.

body mass index (BMI) The ratio of a person's weight to height; the main indicator of overweight or underweight.

Because this kindergarten artist has such exceptional fine motor skills, he may be advanced in school.

Vandorpe and others, 2011). Yes, boys and girls do become stronger and more coordinated as they travel from first to sixth grade. But average scores on standard motor-skill tests are lower today than in previous cohorts, particularly as children advance to older grades.

The logical reason for this loss, as I suggested in the last chapter, is that children no longer regularly play outside (Lubans and others, 2010). When I was 7 or 8, after school I biked for hours around my town pretending to be a cowgirl (that's true!). In one recent German study, less than 1 in 2 second graders spent at least four days per week engaging in this kind of vigorous physical exercise (either indoors or outdoors) for a *single* hour (Kobel and others, 2015).

However, there are dramatic differences from child to child. Perhaps because peers and adults reinforce boys and girls who are skilled at "object control" ("Wow! This child is terrific at hitting or catching balls; let's have her on the team"), preschoolers with superior motor talents tend to be more physically active during middle childhood (Henrique and others, 2016). Skill at catching and throwing balls at age 10 predicts exercising more in high school (Barnett and others, 2009). But, interestingly, the correlation between physical coordination and fitness (aerobic exercise) decreases as children travel into their teens (Haga, Gísladóttír, & Sigmundsson, 2015). And when we see joggers sprinting up the street, it's evident that adults can be exceptionally physically fit, without having much motor finesse!

Physically active parents have daughters and sons with better motor skills (Kobel and others, 2015), as we intuitively understand when we see 8- or 10-year-olds regularly shooting baskets or riding bikes with their moms and dads. Not being a micromanaging parent matters a good deal (Bradley and others, 2011). In one Danish survey, if mothers agreed with questionnaire items such as "I keep total tabs on my child's activities," elementary schoolers were apt to live more sedentary lives (Janssen, 2015). Therefore, to produce physically skilled children, caregivers should encourage outdoor activities but not micromanage or hover over a child.

Longitudinal studies suggest that sports-oriented children tend to be more active as adults (Smith and others, 2015); but you may know a sedentary family member who became fit after falling in love with ballroom dancing or running marathons at age 30 or 55. Unfortunately, change is more difficult when struggling with **childhood obesity**. As early as preschool, having a high **body mass index (BMI)** sets children up to battle weight problems for life. (Check out Table 6.3 for some stereotypes and interesting facts about this important health condition.)

Obesity, as the stereotypes table suggests, has clear negative emotional effects. But is it really important for children to have good elementary school motor skills?

If boys and girls are developing normally, the answer is no. Although studies vary (see Lopes and others, 2013), as I suggested in Chapter 5, gross motor skills such as running and jumping have no relationship to academic success (Stöckel & Hughes, 2016). But, as I also mentioned in that chapter, fine motor talents, such as drawing skills, do predict later performance on school-related memory (Rigoli and others, 2013) and speed-oriented cognitive tests (van der Fels and others 2015). Because the main challenge during middle childhood is succeeding in school and controlling our behavior, it is these uniquely frontal-lobe talents to which I now turn.

Table 6.3: Stereotypes and Research Facts About Child Obesity

Stereotype #1: Children become obese because they eat excessively and don't exercise.

Answer: *False.* The tendency to be overweight is epigenetically programmed, and a child's fate is shaped amazingly early in life. Excessive weight gain during the first year of life strongly predicts later obesity.

Stereotype #2: Parents are responsible for child obesity, because they overfeed their daughters and sons.

Answer: *It's complicated.* Pushing food on infants can unleash the epigenetic tendency to put on pounds, but parental feeding practices are less important in promoting child overweight at older ages.

Stereotype #3: School-based anti-obesity programs that measure children's BMI and inform families about this condition are effective.

Answer: *False.* These well-intended interventions are apt to backfire, making overweight children and their parents anxious and heightening children's strong tendency to stigmatize obese classmates.

Stereotype #4: Obese children tend to be bullied and suffer from psychological problems.

Answer: *True, with interesting exceptions.* Unfortunately, peers are apt to reject overweight classmates as early as preschool, and bullying, depression, and suicide are more common among obese teens. But in the African American community and in nations such as Korea, overweight children are less apt to be stigmatized.

Stereotype #5: Childhood obesity is increasing.

Answer: *False!* Child obesity rates escalated dramatically during the 1980s and rose more slowly until about a decade ago. Since about 2012, the good news is that the prevalence of this health problem has declined, particularly in preschool children.

Information from Barrera and others, 2016; Cheung and others, 2016; Faguy, 2016; Kim, Yun, & Kim, 2016; Nmyanzi, 2016; Puhl & Latner, 2007; Taveras, 2016; Vanderloo & Mandich, 2013.

Tying It All Together

1. When Steven played hide-and-seek with his 4-year-old nephew, he realized that while Ethan could run well, the child was having trouble not betraying his hiding place and understanding the rules of the game. The reason is that Ethan's _____ cortex is on an earlier developmental timetable than his _____ lobes.

2. Imagine transporting yourself to the 1950s and watching fourth graders in your neighborhood. Which observation is *false*?
    a. Children were better coordinated than they are today.
    b. Children were more physically active than they are today.
    c. Parents spent more time monitoring children's outdoor play than they do today.

3. Excellent motor skills are *crucially important/not very important* in adult fitness, and preschool *gross motor skills/fine motor skills* predict children's later academic abilities.

4. Obesity can be easily cured by diet and exercise. (*true/false*)

Answers to the Tying It All Together quizzes can be found at the end of this chapter.

Cognitive Development

As I discussed in Chapter 5, Piaget and Vygotsky gave us terrific insights into how children think. But neither theorist explained *why* industry locks in. What skills are involved in managing our behavior and working for what we want? Parents might want to know if they can trust a 6-year-old to take care of a dog. Teachers might want tips for helping third graders memorize spelling words, or need strategies to intervene with students who have trouble sitting still in class. To get this information, everyone would gravitate toward the *information-processing approach*.

LEARNING OUTCOMES

- Outline the information-processing perspective on memory.
- List three examples of executive functions.
- Describe ADHD's features, causes, and treatments.

An Information-Processing Perspective on Intellectual Growth

Information-processing theorists, as I described in Chapter 3, divide thinking into steps. Let's illustrate this approach by examining memory, the basis of all thought.

Making Sense of Memory

Information-processing theorists believe that to become "a memory," information passes through different stages. First, we hold stimuli arriving from the outside world briefly in a sensory store. Then, features that we notice enter the most important store, called *working memory*.

Working memory is where the "cognitive action" takes place. Here, we keep information in awareness and act to either process it or discard it. Working memory is made up of limited-capacity holding bins and an "executive processor," which allows us to mentally process material for permanent storage (Baddeley, 1992; Best & Miller, 2010).

To get a real-life example of the fleeting quality of working memory, you might try to challenge yourself to remember an address without relying on your smartphone. If you keep that information in your mind, notice that you are apt to succeed at this mental feat. But if you are interrupted by a text, the information evaporates. In fact, for adults, working memory bin capacity is roughly the size of a city and local street address: seven chunks of information.

Researchers find that working memory bin size dramatically enlarges during early elementary school (Cowan, 2016). The executive processor continues to mature well into the teens (Linares, Bajo, & Pelegrina, 2016). These achievements may explain why children reach concrete operations at roughly age 7 or 8 (Case, 1999). Now, children have the memory capacities to step back from their first impressions and remember that what they saw previously (for example, a wider glass in the conservation-of-liquid task) compensates for what they are seeing right now (a taller glass).

Expanding working memory explains why theory-of-mind capacities blossom during elementary school. In order to effortlessly relate to people or to lie effectively (Alloway and others, 2015), children must switch back and forth mentally from their own perspective to another person's point of view. Actually, working memory and theory of mind are both facets of a basic self-control skill critical to children succeeding in life.

Exploring Executive Functions

Executive functions is a broad term that refers to every frontal lobe feat of self-control. Here are three school-related examples that show just how dramatically this talent at the core of being human blossoms as children travel into fourth and fifth grade.

Older Children Rehearse Information

Rehearsal is a major way we learn. We repeat material to embed it in memory. In a classic study, developmentalists had kindergarteners and fifth graders memorize objects (such as a cat or a desk) pictured on cards (Flavell, Beach, & Chinsky, 1966). Prior to the testing, the researchers watched the children's lips to see if they were repeating the names of the objects to themselves. Eighty-five percent of the fifth graders used rehearsal; only 10 percent of the kindergarteners did. So, one reason why older children are superior learners is that they understand that they need to rehearse.

Older Children Underst and How to Selectively Attend

The ability to manage our awareness to focus on just what we need to know is called **selective attention.** In a classic study, researchers presented boys and girls of different ages with cards. On the top half of each card was an animal photo; on the bottom half was a picture of some household item (see Figure 6.2). The children were instructed to remember only the animals.

---

working memory In information-processing theory, the limited-capacity gateway system, containing all the material that we can keep in awareness at a single time. The material in this system is either processed for more permanent storage or lost.

executive functions Abilities that allow us to plan and direct our thinking and control our immediate impulses.

rehearsal A learning strategy in which people repeat information to embed it in memory.

selective attention A learning strategy in which people manage their awareness so as to attend only to what is relevant and to filter out unneeded information.

FIGURE 6.2: **A selective attention study** In this study measuring selective attention, children were asked only to memorize the animals on the top half of the cards. Then researchers looked for age differences in the children's memory for the irrelevant household items.

As you might expect, older children were better at recalling the animal names. But when asked to remember the household items, both age groups performed equally well—suggesting that young children clog their memory bin space with irrelevant information (Bjorklund, 2005) because they cannot selectively attend as well.

Older Children Are Superior at Inhibition

To measure differences in inhibition, researchers ask children to perform some action that contradicts their immediate tendencies, such as saying, "Press a button as fast as you can each time you see an animal on the screen, but don't respond when you see a dog" (Pnevmatikos & Trikkaliotis, 2013). This "go, don't go" challenge is exemplified by the classic kindergarten game Simon Says.

Actually, fostering inhibition—that is, not doing what we feel like doing—is a continual *socialization* goal. From completing your assignments for this class rather than partying, to resisting the urge to check Facebook while you are reading this very page, inhibiting our responses can often be difficult even for most adults.

The childhood game of Simon Says is far from all fun and games—it's tailored to train executive functions by giving children practice in the vital skill of inhibiting their immediate responses.

INTERVENTIONS: Using Information-Processing Theory at Home and at Work

So, returning to the beginning of this section, parents will need to regularly remind a 6-year-old child to feed the dog. Teachers *cannot* assume that third graders will automatically understand how to memorize spelling words. Scaffolding study skills (such as the need to rehearse) or teaching selective attention strategies (such as underlining important words for a test) should be an integral part of education in elementary school. And for everyone else, understand that while, over time, children's executive functions greatly improve, controlling and inhibiting our behavior takes effort *throughout* life. (See Table 6.4 on the next page for some information-processing tips to use with children.)

Now let's look at the insights information-processing theory offers for understanding and helping children with that well-known condition, attention-deficit/hyperactivity disorder, or ADHD.

Table 6.4: Information-Processing Guidelines for Teachers and Parents

General Principle for Younger (and Some Older) Children

Don't expect boys and girls to remember, without prompting, regular chores such as feeding a pet.

Expect most children to have a good deal of trouble in situations that involve inhibiting a strong "prepotent impulse"—such as not touching desirable toys, following unpleasant rules, or doing homework.

Throughout Middle Childhood

1. Actively teach the child study skills (such as rehearsing information) and selective attention strategies (such as underlining important points) for tests.
2. Scaffold organizational strategies for school and life. For example, get the child to use a notebook for each class assignment and keep important objects, such as pencils, in a specific place.
3. Expect situations that involve multiple tasks (such as getting ready for school) and activities that involve *ongoing* inhibition (such as refraining from watching TV before finishing homework) to be especially problematic. Build in a clear structure for mastering these difficult executive-functioning tasks: "At 8 or 9 P.M., it's time to get everything ready for school." "Homework must be completed by dinnertime, or immediately after you get home from school."
4. To promote selective attention (and inhibition), have a child do her homework, or any task that involves concentration, in a room away from tempting distractions such as the TV or Internet.

Hot in Developmental Science: Attention-Deficit/Hyperactivity Disorder

attention-deficit/hyperactivity disorder (ADHD) The most common childhood learning disorder in the United States, disproportionately affecting boys; characterized by inattention and hyperactivity at home and at school.

Attention-deficit/hyperactivity disorder (ADHD)—defined by inattentiveness and hyperactivity/distractibility—is the most widely diagnosed childhood disorder in the United States, affecting roughly 1 in 10 children (CDC Attention deficit hyperactivity disorder, n.d.). While ADHD may sometimes be diagnosed in preschool, because sitting still and focusing are vital during elementary school, this label is typically applied to boys and girls during middle childhood. Actually, at every age, boys are several times more likely than girls to receive this label (CDC Attention deficit hyperactivity disorder, n.d.).

ADHD follows a bewildering array of paths: from first appearing in preschool to erupting during adulthood; from persisting for decades to fading after months (Sonuga-Barke & Halperin, 2010). Twin and adoption studies confirm that ADHD has primarily genetic causes (Thapar & Cooper, 2016). Epigenetic forces are also involved, from being exposed to prenatal maternal smoking to being born premature (Owens & Hinshaw, 2013; see Chapter 2).

Some scientists feel ADHD is caused by the delayed maturation of the frontal lobes. Others speculate that impairments in lower brain centers are to blame (Berger and others, 2013; Hoogman and others, 2013; Wang and others, 2013). Everyone agrees that ADHD is tied to a lower-than-normal output of dopamine, the neurotransmitter that modulates sensitivity to rewards (Silvetti and others, 2014).

The hallmark of ADHD, however, is executive function deficits (Halperin & Healey, 2011). These children have problems with working memory (Alderson and others, 2013) and especially inhibition (Barkley, 1998). When told, "Don't touch the toys," boys and girls diagnosed with ADHD have special trouble resisting this impulse.

These children have difficulties with selective attention. Researchers asked elementary schoolers to memorize a series of words. Some words were more valuable to remember (worth more points), and others less. Boys and girls with ADHD memorized an equal number of words as a comparison group; but like the younger children I described in the previous section, they got lower scores because they clogged their memory bins with less valuable words (Castel and others, 2010).

As you might imagine, performing tasks under time pressure, such as getting ready for school by 7:00 A.M., presents immense problems for boys and girls with ADHD. These children have more trouble estimating time (Gooch, Snowling, & Hulme, 2011). Moreover, perhaps because of their dopamine deficit, they seem less affected by punishments and rewards (Stark and others, 2011). So yelling or threatening simply may not work.

These issues explain why school is so problematic for boys and girls with ADHD. Working memory is critical to performing academic tasks. Focusing on a teacher demands inhibitory and selective attention skills. Taking tests can involve exceptional time-management talents, too.

Because the same difficulties with inhibition and time management spill over into problems at home, children with ADHD are more apt to be bullied by their siblings (Peasgood and others, 2016) and view their parents as over-controlling (Molina & Musich, 2015). Frustrated caregivers tend to resort to power-assertion disciplinary techniques (Wymbs & Pelham, 2010). They lash out at a 9-year-old who seems incapable of getting his things in order. They scream at, hit, and punish a daughter who can't "just sit still." Therefore, due to an evocative process, boys and girls with ADHD are least likely to get the sensitive parenting that they need. Their executive-function problems cause these children to routinely fail with their peers (Normand and others, 2013; Staikova and others, 2013). Given these dangers, what should caring adults do?

INTERVENTIONS: Helping Children with ADHD

The well-known treatment for ADHD is psycho-stimulant medications (Barkley & Murphy, 2006; Wender and others, 2011), often supplemented by parent (and sometimes teacher) training. Intervening with at-risk parents may be vital because, when adults have ADHD, their affected children tend to develop this condition at younger ages (Breaux, Brown, & Harvey, 2016).

Parent training often involves teaching caregivers to effectively use time outs and consistently reward appropriate behaviors (Ryan-Krause, 2011; Young & Amarasinghe, 2010). It's important not to pressure sons and daughters to complete demanding, time-based tasks. Children themselves may get practice in relaxing their minds via an EEG (which offers feedback about our brain waves) (Janssen and others, 2016).

Apart from consulting a health-care worker, what else should adults do? Because children with ADHD learn better in noisy environments, to help a fifth grader focus on homework, provide "white" background noise (Baijot and others, 2016). Give frequent small reinforcers for good behavior, rather than waiting for a big prize (10 minutes on the computer later today works better than promising a family trip to Disney World next month) (Scheres, Tontsch, & Thoeny, 2013). As exercise mutes the impulse to uncontrollably run around, adults should build more physical activity into the day (Messler, Holmberg, & Sperlich, 2016). Presenting learning tasks in a gaming format is also especially beneficial for children with ADHD (Forster and others, 2014).

Students have told me that getting absorbed in games or sports was the treatment that "cured" a sibling's ADHD. Traditional, medication-oriented experts are listening (see Halperin & Healey, 2011). Scientists point out that medicines, even when they work, can have upsetting side effects. Once a person stops the treatment, symptoms sometimes return (Graham and others, 2011; Sonuga-Barke & Halperin, 2010). Might exercise, or even providing time for playing games, help mend a child's brain?

As of this writing (2017), scientists are poised to find physiological answers to these questions. A large-scale neuroimaging study is exploring brain changes as children with this condition travel from age 10 thorough the adolescent years (Silk and others, 2016).

But perhaps some brains don't need mending. ADHD symptoms appear on a continuum (Bell, 2011; Larsson and others, 2012). Where should we *really* put the cutoff point between normal childhood inattentiveness and a diagnosed "disease"?

Parent training will ideally help mothers and fathers feel more in control (and be far less angry and impatient) when dealing with this child who has ADHD.

Although he may regularly tune out in class, this boy clearly has no problem being riveted to this game. Therefore, it makes sense that providing high-intensity academics-related video games may help cure wandering school minds.

The dramatic early-twenty-first-century U.S. rise in the prevalence of ADHD (CDC, 2010b) is troubling. So is the male tilt to this diagnosis, as boys are more physically active than girls. Without denying that ADHD causes considerable heartache, what role might a poor elementary school child–environment fit play in this "disorder" at this moment in history?

So far I have been focusing on executive functions as they relate to school success. In the rest of this chapter, I'll turn to the emotional and the social sides of life.

> ### Tying It All Together
>
> 1. Observe a 6-year-old for a day and list specific examples of failures in inhibition and selective attention.
> 2. Laura's son has been diagnosed with ADHD. Based on this section, list some environmental strategies she might use to help her child.
> 3. Ted argues that ADHD is being overdiagnosed. Make Ted's case, referring to the information in this section.
>
> Answers to the Tying It All Together quizzes can be found at the end of this chapter.

LEARNING OUTCOMES

- Contrast internalizing and externalizing tendencies.
- Outline changes in self-awareness and self-esteem as children get older.
- Point out the perils of having excessively high or low self-esteem.
- Explain what promotes prosocial acts, referring to shame, guilt, induction, and moral disengagement.
- Compare the different types of aggression.
- List the two-step pathway to producing a highly aggressive child.

emotion regulation The capacity to manage one's emotional state.

externalizing tendencies A personality style that involves acting on one's immediate impulses and behaving disruptively and aggressively.

internalizing tendencies A personality style that involves intense fear, social inhibition, and often depression.

self-awareness The capacity to observe our abilities and actions from an outside frame of reference and to reflect on our inner state.

Emotional Development

Think of the overwhelming executive-function relationship challenges elementary school boys and girls face every single day. Children need to cool down their rage when they get a failing grade or are rejected by their peers. They must manage their terror and approach a scary teacher, or regularly work up the courage to join the daunting kind of social group I described in the introductory vignette. **Emotion regulation** is the term developmentalists use for the skills involved in controlling our feelings so that they don't get in the way of a productive life.

Children with **externalizing tendencies** have special trouble with this challenge. Like Adam in the chapter-opening vignette (or boys and girls with ADHD), they act on their immediate emotions and often behave disruptively and aggressively. Perhaps you know a child who bursts into every scene, fighting, bossing people around, wreaking havoc with his classmates and adults.

Children with **internalizing tendencies** have the opposite problem. Like Jimmy in the introductory vignette, they hang back in social situations. They are timid and self-conscious, frightened and depressed.

The beauty of being human is that we vary in our temperamental tendencies—to be shy or active, boisterous or reserved. But having serious trouble *controlling* one's aggression or anxiety puts children at a disadvantage around the world (Chen & Santo, 2016; Fu and others, 2016).

In Chapter 4, I discussed the temperaments that put toddlers at risk for having these emotion regulation issues—being exuberant or inhibited. Now, let's look at how these temperamental tendencies affect older children's emotional lives, beginning with their perceptions of themselves.

Observing and Evaluating the Self

How does **self-awareness**, or our perceptions about ourselves, change during middle childhood? To answer this question, Susan Harter (1999) asked children of different ages to describe themselves. Here are examples of the responses she found:

> I am 3 years old and I live in a big house. . . . I have blue eyes and a kitty that is orange. . . . I love my dog Skipper. . . . I'm always happy. I have brown hair. . . . I'm really strong.

I'm in fourth grade, and I'm pretty popular. . . . That's because I'm nice to people . . . , although if I get into a bad mood I sometimes say something that can be a little mean. At school I'm feeling pretty smart in . . . Language Arts and Social Studies. . . . But I'm feeling pretty dumb in Math and Science. . . .

(Harter, 1999, pp. 37, 48)

Notice that the 3-year-old talks about herself in terms of external facts. The fourth grader's descriptions are internal and psychological, anchored in her feelings, abilities, and traits. The 3-year-old describes herself in unrealistic, positive ways as "always happy." The fourth grader lists her deficiencies and strengths in different areas of life. Moreover, while the younger child talks about herself as if she were living in a bubble, the older child focuses on how she measures up to her classmates. So Harter believes that when children reach concrete operations, they realistically evaluate their abilities and decide whether they like or dislike the person they see. **Self-esteem**—the tendency to feel good or bad about ourselves—first becomes a *major issue* in elementary school.

Actually, worldwide, self-esteem tends to decline during early elementary school (Frey & Ruble, 1985, 1990; Super & Harkness, 2003). A mother may sadly notice this change when her 8-year-old daughter starts to make comments such as, "I am not pretty" or "I can't do math." ("What happened to that self-confident child who used to feel she was the most beautiful, intelligent kid in the world?") Caring teachers struggle with the same comparisons, the fact that their fourth graders are exquisitely sensitive to who is popular, which classmates are getting A's, and who needs special academic help.

Therefore, to expand on Erikson's theory, the price of entering the real world is both industry *and* inferiority. In fact, inferiority ("I'm jealous because he is better than me!") helps *propel* industry ("I need to work hard so I can be better than him!").

But luckily, most children avoid just feeling inferior, because reaching concrete operations produces another change. Notice how the fourth grader quoted above compares her abilities in different areas such as personality and school. So, as they get older, children's self-esteem doesn't hinge on one quality. Even if they are not doing well in a certain area, they take comfort in the places where they shine.

According to Harter, children draw on five areas to determine their self-esteem: *scholastic competence* (academic talents); *behavioral conduct* (obedience or being "good"); *athletic skills* (performance at sports); *peer likeability* (popularity); and *physical appearance* (looks). As you might expect, children who view themselves as failing in several competence realms often report low self-esteem. However, to really understand a given child's self-esteem, we need to know the priority that boy or girl puts on doing well in a particular area of life.

To understand this point, take a minute to rate yourself in your people skills, politeness or good manners, intellectual abilities, looks, and physical abilities. If you label yourself as "not so good" in an area you don't care about (for me, it would be motor skills), it won't make a dent in your self-esteem. If you care deeply about some skill where you feel deficient, you would get pretty depressed.

This discounting ("It doesn't matter if I'm not a scholar; I have great relationship skills") lets us gain self-esteem from the areas in which we excel. The problem is that children with externalizing issues take this discounting to an extreme—minimizing their problems in *essential* areas of life.

Two Kinds of Self-Esteem Distortions

Normally, we base our self-esteem on signals from the outside world: "Am I succeeding or not doing so well?" However, when children with externalizing problems *are* failing—for instance, being rejected in school—they may deny reality (Lynch and others, 2016) and impulsively blame others, to preserve their unrealistically high self-worth (Woltering & Shi, 2016). Perhaps you know an adult whose anger gets him into continual trouble but who copes by taking the position, "I'm wonderful. It's their fault." Because this person seems impervious to his flaws and has difficulty regulating his emotions, he cannot change his behavior and so ensures that he continues to fail.

self-esteem Evaluating oneself as either "good" or "bad" as a result of comparing the self to other people.

According to Susan Harter, even when children are failing in other areas of life, they can sometimes derive their self-esteem from the skills in which they shine. Do you think this girl can use this science prize to feel good about herself, even if she understands that she is not very popular with the other kids?

learned helplessness
A state that develops when a person feels incapable of affecting the outcome of events, and so gives up without trying.

Children with internalizing tendencies have the opposite problem. Their intense anxiety may cause them to read failure into benign events ("My teacher hates me because she looked at me the wrong way") (see Chen & Santo, 2016). They are at risk of developing **learned helplessness** (Abramson, Seligman, & Teasdale, 1978), feeling that they are powerless to affect their fate. They give up at the starting gate, assuming, "I'm going to fail, so why even try?"

So children with externalizing and internalizing tendencies face a similar danger—but for different reasons. When boys and girls minimize their difficulties or assume they are incompetent, they cut off the chance of working to change their behavior and ensure that they *will* fail.

Table 6.5 summarizes these self-esteem problems and their real-world consequences. Then, Table 6.6 offers a checklist, based on Harter's five dimensions, for evaluating yourself. Are there areas where you gloss over your deficiencies? Do you have pockets of learned helplessness that prevent you from living a full life?

Table 6.5: Externalizing and Internalizing Problems, Self-Esteem Distortions, and Consequences— A Summary Table

Description	Self-Esteem Distortion	Consequence
Children with externalizing problems act out "emotions," are impulsive, and are often aggressive.	May ignore real problems and have unrealistically high self-esteem.	Continue to fail because they don't see the need to improve.
Children with internalizing problems are intensely fearful.	Can read failure into everything and have overly low self-esteem.	Continue to fail because they decide that they cannot succeed and stop working.

Table 6.6: Identifying Your Self-Esteem Distortions: A Checklist Using Harter's Five Domains

You have externalizing issues if you regularly have thoughts like these:

1. **Academics**: "When I get poor grades, it's because my teachers don't give good tests or teach well"; "I have very little to learn from other people"; "I'm smarter than practically everyone else I know."
2. **Physical skills**: "When I play baseball, soccer, etc., and my team doesn't win, it's my teammates' fault, not mine"; "I believe it's OK to take physical risks, such as not wearing a seatbelt or running miles in the hot sun, because I know I won't get hurt"; "It's all statistics, so I shouldn't be concerned about smoking four packs a day or about drinking a six-pack of beer every night."
3. **Relationships**: "When I have trouble at work or with my family, it's typically my co-workers' or family's fault"; "My son (or mate, friend, mother) is the one causing the conflict between us."
4. **Physical appearance**: "I don't think I have to work to improve my appearance because I'm basically gorgeous."
5. **Conduct**: "I should be able to come to work late (or turn in papers after the end of the semester, talk in class, etc.)"; "Other people are too uptight. I have a right to behave any way I want to."

Diagnosis: You are purchasing high self-esteem at the price of denying reality. Try to look at the impact of your actions more realistically and take steps to change.

You have internalizing issues if you regularly have thoughts like these:

1. **Academics**: "I'm basically stupid"; "I can't do well on tests"; "My memory is poor"; "I'm bound to fail at science"; "I'm too dumb to get through college"; "I'll never be smart enough to get ahead in my career."
2. **Physical skills**: "I can't play basketball (or some other sport) because I'm uncoordinated or too slow"; "I'll never have the willpower to exercise regularly (or stick to a diet, stop smoking, stop drinking, or stop taking drugs)."
3. **Relationships**: "I don't have any people skills"; "I'm doomed to fail in my love life"; "I can't be a good mother (or spouse or friend)."
4. **Physical appearance**: "I'm basically unattractive"; "People are born either good-looking or not, and I fall into the *not* category"; "There is nothing I can do to improve my looks."
5. **Conduct**: "I'm incapable of being on time (or getting jobs done or stopping talking in class)"; "I can't change my tendency to rub people the wrong way."

Diagnosis: Your excessively low self-esteem is inhibiting your ability to succeed. Work on reducing your helpless and hopeless attitudes and try for change.

INTERVENTIONS: **Promoting Realistic Self-Esteem**

This discussion shows why school programs focused *just* on raising self-esteem—those devoted to instilling the message, "You are a terrific kid"—are missing the boat (Baumeister and others, 2003; Swann, Chang-Schneider, & McClarty, 2007). True self-esteem is derived from industry—working for a goal. Therefore, when children are having trouble in a vital life domain, it's important to (1) enhance *self-efficacy*, or the feeling that "I can succeed if I work" (Miller & Daniel, 2007) and (2) promote *realistic* perceptions about the self. How might caring adults carry out this two-pronged approach?

Enhancing Self-Efficacy

As developmentalist Carol Dweck has demonstrated, one key to enhancing academic self-efficacy is to praise children for effort ("You are trying so hard!"), rather than making comments about basic ability ("You are incredibly smart!"). In her studies, elementary schoolers who were praised for being "very intelligent" after successfully completing problems later had *lower* self-efficacy. They were afraid to tackle other challenging tasks ("I'd better not try this or everyone might learn I'm dumb!") (Molden & Dweck, 2006; Mueller & Dweck, 1998).

Emphasizing effort is vital because, during concrete operations, children begin to categorize themselves according to fixed labels ("I'm the dumb kid" or "the poor kid in class"). Another downside of the concrete operational passion for categorizing everything described in Chapter 5 is succumbing to rigid racial or gender stereotypes, such as believing that women or African Americans can't do science or math.

But, when adults praise elementary schoolers for effort and show inspiring movies such as *Hidden Figures* (the untold story of how female African American scientists boosted the U.S. space program to success), they are implicitly teaching children the lesson: "You are not defined by a fixed criterion such as your gender or the color of your skin." Therefore, instilling the efficacious message that "working matters" *both* prevents prejudice and preserves self-esteem!

By complimenting her child for being such a hard worker, this mother is socializing her son not to succumb to negative stereotypes like "Black kids can't be scientists."

Encouraging Accurate Perceptions

Still, if a child—like Jimmy in the chapter-opening vignette—has internalizing tendencies, efficacy-enhancing interventions may not be enough. These children feel they are failing when they are not. Therefore, adults must continually provide accurate feedback: "The class doesn't hate you. Notice that Matt and José wanted you in the game." And, if an elementary schooler with externalizing tendencies discounts his failures at the price of preserving unrealistic self-esteem, gently point out reality, too (Thomaes, Stegge, & Olthof, 2007). Using the example of Adam in the vignette, you might say, "The kids don't like you when you barge in and take over those games, but I *know* you can control yourself if you try!"

So, returning to the beginning of this section, school programs (and adults) that value each child as a person, as well as foster self-efficacy ("You can succeed if you work hard"), promote *true* self-esteem (Miller & Daniel, 2007).

Doing Good: Morality and Prosocial Behavior

On September 11, 2001, the nation was riveted by the heroism of the firefighters who ran into the World Trade Center, risking almost certain death. We marveled at the "ordinary people" working in the Twin Towers, whose response to this emergency was to help others get out first.

What qualities made hundreds of New York City firefighters run into the burning Twin Towers on September 11, 2001, knowing that they might be facing death? This is the kind of question that developmentalists who study prosocial behavior want to answer.

prosocial behavior Sharing, helping, and caring actions.

empathy Feeling the exact emotion that another person is experiencing.

sympathy A state necessary for acting prosocially, involving feeling upset *for* a person who needs help.

Prosocial behavior is the term developmentalists use to describe such amazing acts of self-sacrifice, as well as the minor acts of helping, comforting, and sharing that we perform during daily life. Do we have to be taught to reach out in a caring way?

The answer is no. As I discussed in Chapters 3 and 4, the impulse to be prosocial and ethical blossoms during our first two years of life.

Individual and Gender Variations

However, as you saw in the vignette at the beginning of this chapter, children differ in this natural human propensity to be ethical and kind. Developmentalists visited preschool classrooms and looked at spontaneous sharing, the coming-from-the-heart giving that is different from being ordered to "Share!" When they tested these children in elementary school, during adolescence, and in emerging adulthood, the 3-year-olds who shared most readily were more prosocial at every age (Eisenberg and others, 2014). So, if your 8-year-old niece seems unusually generous (especially at cost to herself), she may grow up to be an unusually prosocial adult.

What about your 8-year-old nephew? Are females generally more prosocial than males? Studies suggest that girls are far more likely than boys to reach out and comfort a classmate who is being bullied (boys tend to actively confront the bully) (Duffy and others, 2016; Mulvey & Killen, 2016; Reijntjes and others, 2016). Females are more physiologically attuned to others' distress than males (Groen and others, 2013). The problem is that being sensitive to another person's emotional pain may not result in *acting* in a prosocial way.

Decoding Prosocial Behavior in a Deeper Way

Empathy is the term developmentalists use for directly feeling another person's emotions. For example, your daughter gets intensely anxious when she hears a teacher berating her best friend. She is overcome with horror when she sees a video of the Twin Towers crashing down.

Sympathy is the more muted feeling that we experience *for* another human being. Your daughter feels terrible *for* her friend. Her heart goes out to the people who lost their lives on 9/11, but she isn't overwhelmed with distress. Developmentalists believe that sympathy, rather than empathy, is related to behaving in a prosocial way (Eisenberg, 1992, 2003).

The reason is that experiencing another person's distress can provoke a variety of reactions, from being immobilized with fear to behaving in a far-from-caring way. We can vividly see this point when, out of embarrassment, we witness children (and even some adults) laugh hysterically as someone spills a lunchroom tray. So to be prosocial, children need to mute their empathic feelings into a sympathetic response (Eisenberg, 1992).

Actually, during middle childhood, acting prosocially requires sophisticated information-processing skills. Children must know *when* to be generous, which explains why 2-year-olds share with everyone, but, around age 5, we become selective, reaching out to people who are kind to us (Paulus & Moore, 2014). Older children also tailor their prosocial behavior to whether they can *effectively* offer aid. Preoperational preschoolers automatically offer you their blankee when you are upset, because they are egocentric and assume that everything that comforts them will comfort you. However, just as I would not run into a flaming building because I'm not a firefighter, the reasons elementary school children report for not acting prosocial are that they don't have the skills to help (Denham, 1998; Eisenberg & Fabes, 1998).

Returning to gender differences, this suggests we take a more nuanced approach to the idea that females are more (or less) prosocial than males. Yes, girls qualify as more prosocial if we measure comforting someone in pain. Boys, as you saw in the opening vignette, may be more prosocial in their competence realm. They are more apt to stand up to a bully and take prosocial charge of a group. After all, that's what being a gentleman-in-training is all about!

So, do children get more prosocial with age? Unfortunately, the answer is no. During elementary school, other motivations override this basic caring sense (Visconti, Ladd, & Kochenderfer-Ladd, 2015). In one study exploring reactions to stories, while preschoolers were likely to say that a character who searched for prizes should "share things equally," with a helper, 8-year-olds tailored their giving to whether the other person had earned the gift. "If he was lazy, there is no reason to share" (Rizzo and others, 2016).

Therefore, the lifelong process of justifying uncaring actions locks in as children get older and grasp the complexities of the adult world: "Refugees are not like us—so we shouldn't let them into the United States"; "I refuse to give money to street people, because if human beings weren't lazy, everyone could succeed" (more about these serious limitations to self-efficacy in the next chapter). Given the universal human tendency to succumb to what Albert Bandura calls **moral disengagement** (rationalizing amoral, uncaring acts), what can adults do to promote moral behavior in a child?

INTERVENTIONS: Socializing Moral Children

Provide the right socialization climate. Foster a secure, loving attachment (Pastorelli and others, 2016). Continually remind a boy or girl about fundamental ethical principles ("Hurting other people is wrong"). (See Visconti, Ladd, & Kochenderfer-Ladd, 2015.) Be attuned to children's caring acts and attribute that behavior to their personality—for instance, by saying, "You really are a caring person for doing that" instead of "That was a nice thing you did" (Eisenberg, 2003).

In a fascinating study, when researchers asked 8-year-olds to recall a time they acted in a generous way, their later behavior became more prosocial (Tasimi & Young, 2016). It was as if they mentally reminded themselves: "I remember how great I felt when I did that helpful thing. I *want* to feel that way again!"

Many studies of prosocial behavior focus on a socialization technique called **induction** (Hoffman, 1994, 2001). Caregivers who use induction point out the ethical issues when a child has performed a hurtful act. Now, imagine that classic situation when your 8-year-old daughter has invited everyone in class but Sara to her birthday party. Instead of punishing your child—or giving that other classic response, "Kids will be kids"—here's what you should say: "It's hurtful to leave Sara out. Think of how terrible she must feel!"

Induction has several virtues: It offers children concrete feedback about exactly what they did wrong and moves them off of focusing on their own punishment ("Now, I'm really going to get it!") to the *other* child's distress ("Oh, gosh, she must feel hurt"). Induction also allows for reparations, the chance to make amends. Induction works because it stimulates guilt.

Guilt and Prosocial Acts

Think back to an event during childhood when you felt terrible about yourself. Perhaps it was the day you were caught cheating and sent to the principal. What you may remember was feeling so ashamed. Developmentalists, however, distinguish between feeling ashamed and experiencing guilt. **Shame** is the primitive feeling we have when we are *personally* humiliated. **Guilt** is the more sophisticated emotion we experience when we have violated a personal moral standard or hurt another human being.

I believe that Erikson may have been alluding to this maturity difference when he labeled "shame" as the emotion we experience as toddlers, and reserved "guilt" for the feeling that arises during preschool, when our drive to master the world causes other people distress. While shame and guilt are both "self-conscious" emotions, they have opposing effects. Shame causes us to withdraw from people, to slink away, and

---

moral disengagement Rationalizing moral or ethical lapses by invoking justifications, such as "He deserved that."

induction The ideal discipline style for socializing prosocial behavior, which involves getting a child who has behaved hurtfully to empathize with the pain he has caused the other person.

shame A feeling of being personally humiliated.

guilt Feeling upset about having caused harm to a person or about having violated one's internal standard of behavior.

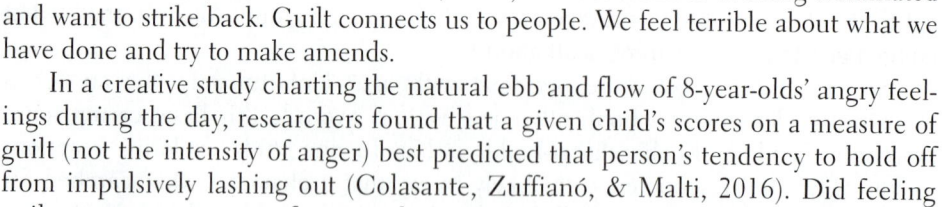

crawl into a hole (Thomaes and others, 2007). We feel furious at being humiliated and want to strike back. Guilt connects us to people. We feel terrible about what we have done and try to make amends.

In a creative study charting the natural ebb and flow of 8-year-olds' angry feelings during the day, researchers found that a given child's scores on a measure of guilt (not the intensity of anger) best predicted that person's tendency to hold off from impulsively lashing out (Colasante, Zuffianó, & Malti, 2016). Did feeling guilty ever prevent you from retaliating when someone behaved insensitively? Did apologizing for acting insensitively ever make you feel closer to someone you love?

Table 6.7 summarizes these section messages in four tips. Now that we have analyzed what makes us act morally (the angel side of personality), let's enter humanity's darker side, aggression.

When parents use shame to discipline, a child's impulse is to get furious. But by pointing out how disappointed she is in her "good girl," this mother can induce guilt—and so ultimately have a more prosocial child.

aggression Any hostile or destructive act.

Table 6.7: How to Produce Prosocial Children: A Summary Table

- Praise a child effusively when she is being generous, and label her as a caring person. Give her many chances to act prosocially, and keep reminding her of situations when she acted in a caring way.
- When the child has hurt another person, clearly point out the moral issue and alert him to how the other person must feel.
- Avoid teasing and shaming. When the child has done something wrong, tell her you are disappointed and give her a chance to make amends.
- As moral disengagement tends to flare up during concrete operations, when children define certain people or groups as "less worthy," repeatedly emphasize basic moral precepts, such as the need to "help strangers" and "treat everyone with respect"—*and accompany these mantras by modeling these principles in your own life!*

Doing Harm: Aggression

Aggression refers to acts designed to cause harm, from shaming to shoving, from gossiping to starting wars. It should come as no surprise that physical aggression reaches its life peak at around age 2½ (Dodge, Coie, & Lynam, 2006; van Aken and others, 2008). Imagine being a toddler continually ordered by giants to do impossible things, such as sitting still. Because being frustrated provokes aggression, it makes perfect sense that hitting and having tantrums are normal during the "terrible twos."

As children get older and become skilled at regulating their emotions, rates of open aggression (yelling or hitting) dramatically decline (Dishion & Tipsord, 2011). During middle childhood, the reasons for aggression change. Preschool fights center on objects, such as toys. When children have a full-fledged sense of self-esteem, they strike out because they are wounded as human beings (Coie & Dodge, 1998). How do researchers categorize aggressive acts?

Types of Aggression

One way developmentalists classify aggression is by its motive. **Proactive aggression** refers to hurtful behavior that we initiate to achieve a goal. Johnny kicks José to gain possession of the block pile. Sally spreads a rumor about Moriah to replace her as Sara's best friend. **Reactive aggression** occurs in response to being hurt, threatened, or deprived. José, infuriated at Johnny, kicks him back.

Its self-determined nature gives proactive aggression a "cooler" emotional tone. When we behave aggressively to get something, we plan our behavior. We feel a sense of self-efficacy as we carry out the act. Reactive aggression involves white-hot,

proactive aggression A hostile or destructive act initiated to achieve a goal.

reactive aggression A hostile or destructive act carried out in response to being frustrated or hurt.

disorganized rage. When you hear that your best friend has betrayed you, or even have a minor frustrating experience such as being caught in traffic, you get furious and blindly lash out (Deater-Deckard and others, 2010).

This feeling is normal. According to a classic theory called the *frustration-aggression hypothesis*, when human beings are thwarted, we are biologically primed to strike back.

In addition to its motive—proactive or reactive—developmentalists distinguish between different *forms* of aggression. Hitting and yelling are direct forms of aggression. A more devious type of aggression is **relational aggression,** acts designed to hurt relationships. Not inviting Sara to a birthday party, spreading rumors, or tattling on a disliked classmate all qualify as relationally aggressive acts.

Because it targets self-esteem and involves more sophisticated social skills, relational aggression follows a different developmental path than openly aggressive acts. Just as rates of open aggression are declining during middle childhood, relational aggression rises. In fact, the overabundance of relational aggression during late elementary school and early adolescence (another intensely frustrating time) may explain why we label these ages as the "meanest" times of life.

Most of us assume relational aggression is more common in girls. But in research, this "obvious" relationship isn't always found. Yes, overt aggression is severely sanctioned in females, so girls make relational aggression their major mode (Ostrov & Godleski, 2010; Smith, Rose, & Schwartz-Mette, 2010). But as spreading rumors and talking trash about competitors is vital to dethroning adversaries and climbing the social ranks, one study showed that teenage boys were just as relationally aggressive as teenage girls (Mayeux & Cillessen, 2008)!

Table 6.8 summarizes the different types of aggression and gives examples from childhood and adult life. While scanning the table, notice that we all behave in

> **relational aggression** A hostile or destructive act designed to cause harm to a person's relationships.

Excluding someone from your group is a classic sign of *relational aggression*—which really gets going in middle childhood. Can you remember being the target of the behavior shown here when you were in fourth or fifth grade?

Table 6.8: Aggression: A Summary of the Types

What Motivated the Behavior?

Proactive aggression: Acts that are actively instigated to achieve a goal.

Examples: "I'll hit Tommy so I can get his toys"; "I'll cut off that car so I can get ahead of him"; "I want my boss's job, so I'll spread a rumor that he is having an affair."

Characteristics: Emotionally cool and more carefully planned.

Reactive aggression: Acts that occur in response to being frustrated or hurt.

Examples: "Jimmy took my toy, so I'm going to hit him"; "That guy shoved me to take my place in line, so I'm going to punch him out."

Characteristics: Furious, disorganized, impulsive response.

What Was Its Form?

Direct aggression: Everyone can see it.

Examples: Telling your boyfriend you hate his guts; beating up someone; screaming at your mother; having a tantrum; bopping a playmate over the head with a toy.

Characteristics: Peaks at about age 2 or 3; declines as children get older; more common in boys than in girls, especially physical aggression.

Relational aggression: Carried out indirectly, through damaging or destroying the victim's relationships.

Examples: "Sara got a better grade than me, so I'm going to tell the teacher that she cheated"; "Let's tell everyone not to let Sara play in our group"; "I want Sara's job, so I'll spread a rumor that she is stealing money from the company"; "I'm going to tell my best friend that her husband is cheating on her because I want to break up their marriage."

Characteristics: Occurs mainly during elementary school and may be at its peak during adolescence, although—as we all know—it's common *throughout* adulthood.

every aggressive way. Also, aggression is not "bad." Proactive aggression, particularly the relational kind, helps children climb the social ranks (more about this in the next section). Without reactive aggression (fighting back when attacked), our species would never survive. Still, this disorganized, rage-filled aggression doesn't work. Excessive reactive aggression *ensures* that children are apt to have problems getting along with people during life (White, Jarrett, & Ollendick, 2013).

Understanding Highly Aggressive Children

You just saw that, during elementary school, boys and girls typically get less physically aggressive. However, a percentage of children remain unusually aggressive. These boys and girls are labeled with externalizing disorders defined by high rates of aggression. They are classified as defiant, antisocial kids.

The Pathway to Producing Problematic Aggression

Longitudinal studies suggest that there may be a poisonous two-step, nature-plus-nurture pathway to being labeled as a highly aggressive child.

STEP 1: THE TODDLER'S EXUBERANT (OR DIFFICULT) TEMPERAMENT EVOKES HARSH DISCIPLINE When toddlers are impulsive and fearless, caregivers often react by using *power-assertion*. They shame, scream, and hit: "Shut up! You are impossible. You'll get a beating from mom." But physically punishing a "difficult" toddler is apt to induce more rage (as I will describe in the next chapter's discussion of spanking); so, unfortunately, the very children who most need loving parenting often get the harshest, most punitive care.

STEP 2: THE CHILD IS REJECTED BY TEACHERS AND PEERS IN SCHOOL Typically, the transition to being an "antisocial child" occurs during the transition to middle childhood. As impulsive, by now clearly aggressive, children travel outside the family, they get rejected by their classmates. Being socially excluded is a powerful stress that provokes reactive aggression (Ettekal and Ladd, 2015). Moreover, because these children *generally* may have executive function deficits (Cooley & Fite, 2016), during elementary school they are apt to start failing their classes (Romano and others, 2010). This amplifies the frustration ("I'm not making it in any area of life!") and compounds their tendency to lash out ("It's their fault, not mine!").

hostile attributional bias The tendency of highly aggressive children to see motives and actions as threatening when they are actually benign.

A Hostile Worldview

As I just implied, reactive-aggressive children also think differently in social situations. They may have a **hostile attributional bias** (Crick & Dodge, 1996). They see threat in benign social cues. A boy gets accidentally bumped at the lunch table, and he sees a deliberate provocation. A girl decides that you are her enemy when you look at her the wrong way. So the child's behavior provokes a more hostile world.

To summarize, let's enter the mind of a reactive-aggressive child, such as Adam in the chapter-opening vignette. During early childhood, your fearless temperament continually got you into trouble with your parents. You have been harshly disciplined for years. In school, your classmates shun you. So you never have a chance to interact with other children and improve your emotion regulation skills. In fact, your hostile attributional bias makes perfect sense. You are living in a "sea of negativity" (Jenson and others, 2004). And yes, the world *is* out to do you in!

This boy who has been shunned by other children for his disruptive behavior in elementary school may respond by developing a hostile attributional bias, unrealistically feeling that his classmates are all against him.

INTERVENTIONS: Taming Excessive Aggression

When an older child has an externalizing disorder, how should parents act? Avoid the punitive, shaming discipline style that exacerbates hostile attributional biases as boys travel into their teens (Yaros, Lochman, & Wells, 2015). Vigorously socialize prosocial behavior using the strategies in Table 6.7 (page 178). Understand that the same sensation-seeking, risk-taking propensities that promote excessive childhood aggression can be potential life assets. In an amazing decades-long study, when researchers measured temperament during infancy and then looked at a person's personality during adulthood, the *one* quality that predicted being highly competent at age 40 was having been fearless during the first year of life (Blatney, Jelinek, & Osecka, 2007). So, with the right person–environment fit, a "difficult-to-tame" child may become a prosocial hero, like the firefighters on 9/11.

Why are peer relationships so vital during middle childhood, and how exactly do older children relate? This brings me to the final topic in this chapter—relationships.

Tying It All Together

1. You interviewed a 4-year-old and a fourth grader for your class project in child development, but mixed up your interview notes. Which statement was made by the 4-year-old?
   a. "My friend Megan is better at math than me."
   b. "Sometimes I get mad at my friends, but maybe it's because I'm too stubborn."
   c. "I have a cat named Kit, and I'm the smartest girl in the world."

2. Identify which of the following boys has internalizing or externalizing tendencies. Then, for one of these children, design an intervention using principles spelled out in this section: Ramon sees himself as wonderful, but he is having serious trouble getting along with his teachers and the other kids; Jared is a great student, but when he gets a B instead of an A, he decides that he's "dumb" and gets too depressed to work.

3. Carl, a fourth grader, is faced with the dilemma of whether to stand up for a bullied classmate. Which consideration does *not* predict he will reach out?
   a. Carl has the skills to help.
   b. Carl believes that the child deserves his help.
   c. Carl is incredibly sensitive to other people's emotions.

4. A teacher wants to intervene with a student who has been teasing a classmate. Identify which statement is guilt-producing, which is shame-producing, and which involves the use of induction. Then name which response(s) would promote prosocial behavior.
   a. "Think of how bad Johnny must feel."
   b. "If that's how you act, you can sit by yourself. You're not nice enough to be with the other kids."
   c. "I'm disappointed in you. You are usually such a good kid."

5. Alyssa wants to replace Brianna as Chloe's best friend, so she spreads horrible rumors about Brianna. Brianna overhears Alyssa dissing her and starts slapping Alyssa. Of the four types of aggression discussed in this section—*direct, proactive, reactive, relational*—which two describe Alyssa's behavior, and which two fit Brianna's actions?

6. Mario feels that everyone in the fifth grade is out to get him. What is the label for Mario's worldview?

Answers to the Tying It All Together quizzes can be found at the end of this chapter.

What was this incredibly brave prosocial soldier really like at age 1 or 2? Probably a fearless handful!

Social Development

What childhood talents foster peer success? Answers come from examining that core childhood relationship called friendship. Why do children choose specific friends, and what benefits do elementary school friendships provide?

Friendships: The Proving Ground for Relationships

The essence of friendship is similarity (Poulin & Chan, 2010). Children gravitate toward people who are "like them" in interests and activities (Dishion & Tipsord, 2011). In preschool, an active child will tend to make friends with a classmate who

LEARNING OUTCOMES
- Outline the different features of friendship and popularity.
- Explain which qualities make children "unpopular."
- Describe why some rejected children can succeed in adult life.
- Summarize the bullying research.

likes to run around. In the vignette at the beginning of this chapter, José and Matt probably connected around their love of chess.

But, since they are in concrete operations, José and Matt probably gravitated toward each other for deeper reasons, such as shared morals ("I like José because we think the same way about what's right") (McDonald and others, 2014; Spencer and others, 2013), and especially loyalty ("I can trust José to stand up for me") (Hartup & Stevens, 1997; Newcomb & Bagwell, 1995). Listen to these fifth graders describing their best friend:

> He is my very best friend because he tells me things and I tell him things.
>
> Jessica has problems at home and with her religion and when something happens she always comes to me and talks about it. We've been through a lot together.
>
> (quoted in Rose & Asher, 2000, p. 49)

These quotations would resonate with the ideas of personality theorist Harry Stack Sullivan. Sullivan (1953) believed that a chum (or best friend) fulfills the developmental need for self-validation and intimacy that emerges at around age 9. Sullivan also felt that best friends serve as a vital training ground for adult romance.

Although they don't realize it, these fifth-grade best buddies bonding over their secrets and plans may be training each other in the skills to be happily married for life!

The Protecting and Teaching Functions of Friends

In addition to teaching us how to behave in adult love relationships, friends stimulate children's personal development in two important ways.

Friends Protect and Enhance the Developing Self

Perhaps you noticed this protective function in the quotation above in which the fifth grader spoke about how she helped her best friend when she had problems at home. In one fascinating study, although elementary schoolers who were bullied normally experienced cortisol spikes at school, a victimized boy or girl who had a best friend showed no change in this basic barometer of stress (Peters and others, 2011). Close friends can also mute children's genetic tendency toward developing depression (Reindl, Gniewosz, & Reinders, 2016) or help reduce the symptoms of ADHD (Becker, Fite, and others, 2013).

Friends Teach Us to Manage Our Emotions and Handle Conflicts

Friends offer on-the-job training in being our "best" (that is, prosocial) self. Your parents will love you no matter what you do, but the love of a friend is contingent. So, to keep a friendship, children must dampen down their immediate impulses and use their emotion regulation talents to yield to the other person's needs (Bukowski, 2001; Denham and others, 2003).

This is not to say that friends are always positive influences. They can bring out a child's worst self by encouraging relational aggression ("We are best friends, so Sara can't play with us") and dangerous behavior ("Let's walk together on these scary railroad tracks"). Best friends can promote an "us-against-them" mentality and promote a shared, hostile attributional worldview ("It's their fault you are getting into trouble. Only I can protect you from the outside world") (Spencer and others, 2013; more about these dark sides of friendship in Chapter 9). However, in general, Sullivan may be right: Friends do teach us how to relate as adults.

Popularity: Rising in the Peer Ranks

Friendship involves collaborating with a single person in a one-to-one way. Popularity involves competition. Children aggressively strive for dominance as they struggle to climb the social totem pole.

Although children differ in social status in preschool, we now understand why "Who is popular?" becomes an absorbing question during later elementary school.

Entering concrete operations makes children highly sensitive to making social comparisons. Moreover, during adulthood, popularity fades into the background because we select our own social circles. Children must make it on a daily basis in a classroom full of random peers.

Who Is Popular and Who Is Unpopular?

How do children vary in popularity during the socially stressful later elementary school years? Here are the categories researchers find when they ask third, fourth, or fifth graders to list the two or three classmates they like most and dislike most:

- *Popular children* are frequently named in the most-liked category and never appear in the disliked group. They stand out as being really liked by everyone.

- *Average children* receive a few most-liked and perhaps one or two disliked nominations. They rank around the middle range of class status.

- *Rejected children* land in the disliked category often and never appear in the preferred list. They stand out among their classmates in a negative way.

What qualities make children popular? What gets elementary schoolers rejected by their peers?

Decoding Popularity

In elementary school, popular children are often friendly, outgoing, prosocial, and kind (Mayberry & Espelage, 2007). However, starting as early as third grade, popularity can also be linked to high levels of relational aggression (Ostrov and others, 2013; Rodkin & Roisman, 2010).

Figure 6.3, based on a study conducted in an inner city school, illustrates this unfortunate truth. Notice that relationally aggressive third to fifth graders were more apt to be rated as popular class leaders. But notice that the association between this poisonous kind of aggression and popularity was stronger for girls—which explains why we see relational aggression as mainly a female activity. Relational aggression earns females more social mileage than males.

Relational aggression is especially effective at propelling popularity during preadolescence, when rebellion is in flower and social status often becomes children's primary goal (Caravita & Cillessen, 2012; more about this change in Chapter 9). The good news is that the study described in Table 6.8 on the next page shows that being "popular" is different from being personally liked.

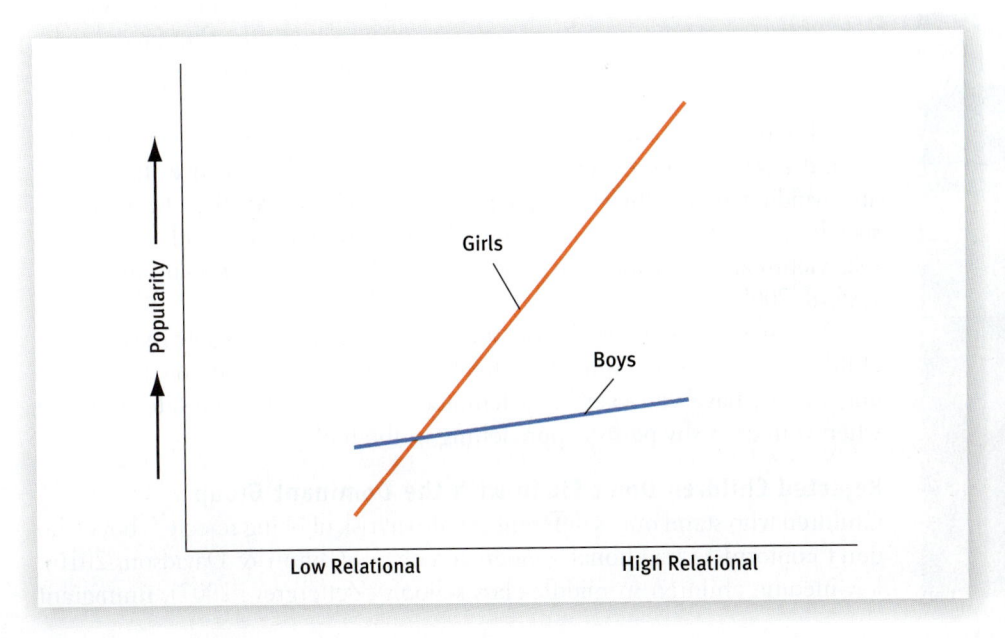

FIGURE 6.3: How relational aggression related to popularity among 227 elementary schoolers attending a low-income, urban school In this city school, being relationally aggressive "worked" to make children—both males and females—more popular; but this type of aggression was far, far more often effective at promoting popularity among girls.
Data from Waasdorp and others, 2013, p. 269.

Table 6.8: Social Goals in Fifth Grade and How They Relate to Peer Preferences a Year Later

1. I like it when I learn new ways to make a friend.
2. I try to figure out what makes for a good friend.
3. I try to get to know other kids better.
4. It's important to me that the other kids think I'm popular.
5. I want to be friendly with the popular kids.
6. It's important to me to have cool friends.
7. It's important to me that I don't embarrass myself around my friends.
8. When I am around other kids, I mostly just try not to goof up.
9. I try to avoid doing things that make me look foolish around other kids.

Researchers asked 980 fifth graders to fill out these questionnaire items and then charted their social rankings over the next year. Boys and girls who checked the yellow items were more likely to ascend the classroom social hierarchy (that was their goal); but children who checked the blue items were increasingly preferred as friends. Unfortunately, however, agreeing with the red items predicted that children would be increasingly disliked during the next year.

Information from Rodkin and others, 2013.

When researchers asked fifth graders questions such as those in the table above and then tracked their later social status, boys and girls whose agenda was being popular (those agreeing with the yellow items) did rise in the social ranks. But in sixth grade, the class preferred people with the blue agendas—children with prosocial goals. So reaching out in a caring way is important at every age if we look at what really matters: being liked as a human being.

Now let's focus on the fifth graders who checked the red items—children terrified about socially goofing up. This socially anxious group became more unpopular over time (Rodkin and others, 2013). Who exactly do peers reject?

Rejected Children Have Externalizing (and Often Internalizing) Problems

Actually, the traits that universally land a child into the rejected category are externalizing issues. Classmates shun boys and girls (like Adam in the chapter-opening vignette) who make reactive aggression a major life mode. Children with internalizing disorders may or may not be rejected. However, a child who is *socially anxious*—such as Jimmy in the introductory vignette or the fifth graders who agreed with the red items on the table—is apt to be avoided as early as first grade (Degnan, Almas, & Fox, 2010).

Moreover, a poisonous nature-evokes-nurture interaction sets in when a child enters school extremely socially shy. As children realize that people are avoiding them, their shyness gets more intense. So they become less socially competent—and increasingly likely to be rejected (and, as you will see, victimized)—as they advance from grade to grade (Booth-LaForce & Oxford, 2008).

A bidirectional process is also occurring. The child's anxiety makes other children nervous and want to retreat. In response to your own awkward encounters, have you ever been tempted to walk in the opposite direction when you saw a shy person approaching in the hall?

Rejected Children Don't Fit in with the Dominant Group

Children who stand out as different are also at risk of being rejected: boys who don't conform to traditional gender stereotypes (Braun & Davidson, 2016), low-income children in middle-class schools (Zettergren, 2007), immigrant

This child's behavior is tailor-made to set him up for being rejected in third grade, as he is violating the rigid elementary school gender norms.

children in ethnically homogenous societies (Strohmeier, Kärnä, & Salmivalli, 2010)—any child whom classmates label as "different," "weird," or "not like us."

Exploring the Fate of the Rejected

Is childhood rejection a prelude to poor adult mental health? The answer is sometimes. Highly physically aggressive children are at risk for getting into trouble—at home, in school, and with the law—during adolescence and in their adult years (also more about this pathway in Chapter 9). Being friendless during childhood predicts having psychological problems as a young adult (Sakyi and others, 2016).

Still, because some qualities (such as conformity and being mean) that gain children social mileage do not translate well into adult life, being rejected for being different can have surprising benefits. Consider an awkward little girl named Eleanor Roosevelt who was rejected at age 8 but ended her life as a worldwide role model for women (and all human beings). To understand the fleeting quality of childhood peer status, you might organize a reunion of your fifth- or sixth-grade class. You might be surprised at how many unpopular classmates flowered during their high school or their college years.

Bullying: Moral Disengagement in Action

> You can get bullied because you are weak or annoying or because you are different. Kids with big ears get bullied. Dorks get bullied. . . . Teacher's pet gets bullied. If you say the right answer in class too many times, you can get bullied.
>
> (quoted in Guerra, Williams, & Sadek, 2011, p. 306)

Children who are different can triumph in the proving ground of life. This is not the case on the proving ground of the playground. As you just read, being different, weak, socially awkward, or even "too good" provokes **bullying**—being teased, made fun of, and verbally or physically abused by one's peers.

As I have implied, it's normal for children to be bullied as they strive for status. But the roughly 10 to 20 percent of children subject to chronic harassment fall into two categories. The first (less common) type are **bully-victims**. These children are highly aggressive boys and girls who bully, get harassed, then bully again in an escalating cycle of pain (Deater-Deckard and others, 2010; Waasdorp, Bradshaw, &, Duong, 2011). The classic victim, however, has internalizing issues (Crawford & Manassis, 2011). These children are anxious, shy, low on the social hierarchy, and unlikely to fight back (Cook and others, 2010; Degnan and others, 2010; Scholte, Sentse, & Granic, 2010; also, see my personal confession in the Experiencing Childhood box on the next page).

Home used to be a refuge for children who were being harassed at school. Not anymore! Social media, texting, and the Internet have made bullying a 24/7 concern.

Cyberbullying, aggressive behavior carried out via electronic media, is potentially more toxic than traditional bullying in several respects. Broadcasting demeaning comments on Instagram and Facebook ensures having a large, amorphous audience that multiplies the victim's distress. Sending a text anonymously can be scarier than confronting the person face to face. ("Who hates me this much?"; "Perhaps it's someone I trusted as a friend?") (See Sticca & Perren, 2013.)

Moreover, the temptation to bully on-line is easy emotionally, as it removes inner controls. Children can lash out free from immediate consequences (Runions, 2013), without experiencing the sympathy (and guilt) linked to seeing a victim's pained face.

Cyberbullying's ease, its relentless presence, and scary public nature explain why teens see this behavior as worse than traditional bullying (Bonanno & Hymel, 2013; Sticca & Perren, 2013). Still, the same motives propel each type of harassment: Kids bully for revenge (as reactive aggression, or to get back at someone). Kids bully for recreation (it's exciting and fun). Kids bully because this activity offers social rewards, or reinforcement from one's peers (Runions, 2013).

Although she didn't fit in with her snobbish, patrician childhood group, by standing up for racial equality and pressuring her husband (the U.S. president) to admit Jewish refugees during the Holocaust, Eleanor Roosevelt, our post–World War II ambassador to the United Nations, became the social conscience of a nation.

bullying A situation in which one or more children (or adults) harass or target a specific child for systematic abuse.

bully-victims Exceptionally aggressive children (with externalizing disorders) who repeatedly bully and get victimized.

cyberbullying Systematic harassment conducted through electronic media.

> **Experiencing Childhood:** Middle-Aged Reflections on My Middle-Childhood Victimization
>
> It was a hot August afternoon when the birthday present arrived. As usual, I was playing alone that day, maybe reading or engaging in a favorite pastime, fantasizing that I was a princess while sitting in a backyard tree. The gift, addressed to Janet Kaplan, was beautifully wrapped—huge but surprisingly light. This is amazing! I must be special! Someone had gone to such trouble for me! When I opened the first box, I saw another carefully wrapped box, and then another, smaller box, and yet another, smaller one inside. Finally, surrounded by ribbons and wrapping paper, I eagerly got to the last box and saw a tiny matchbox—which contained a small burnt match.
>
> Around that time, the doorbell rang, and Cathy, then Ruth, then Carol, bounded up. "Your mother called to tell us she was giving you a surprise birthday party. We had to come over right away and be sure to wear our best dresses!" But their excitement turned to disgust when they learned that no party had been arranged. My 9th birthday was really in mid-September—more than a month away. It turned out that Nancy and Marion—the two most popular girls in class—had masterminded this relational aggression plot directed against me.
>
> Why was I selected as the victim among the other third-grade girls? I had never hurt Nancy or Marion. In fact, in confessing their role, they admitted to some puzzlement: "We really don't dislike Janet at all." Researching this chapter has offered me insights into the reasons for this 60-year-old wound.
>
> Although I did have friends, I was fairly low in the classroom hierarchy. Not only was I shy, but I was that unusual girl—a child who genuinely preferred to play alone. But most important, I was the perfect victim. I have always disliked competitive status situations. When taunted or teased, I don't fight back.
>
> As an older woman, I still dislike status hierarchies and social snobberies. I'm not a group (or party) person. I far prefer talking one-to-one. I am happy to spend hours alone. Today, I consider these attributes a plus (after all, having no problem sitting by myself for many thousands of hours was a prime skill that allowed me to write this textbook!), but they caused me anguish in middle childhood. In fact, when I'm in status-oriented peer situations even today—as a widowed older woman—I still find myself occasionally getting teased by the group!
>
> P.S. I can honestly tell you that what happened to me in third grade is irrelevant to my life. I can't help wondering, though. Suppose, as would be likely today, my classmates had been invited to my so-called birthday via social media: "Janet is having a party, and she is inviting X, Y, and Z." Could being targeted through this humiliating, public venue have caused more enduring emotional scars?

Actually, bullying—of any kind—often demands an appreciative audience. One person (or a few people) does the harassing, while everyone else eggs on the perpetrator by laughing, posting similar comments on-line, or passively standing by.

Therefore, children are less apt to bully when their classmates don't condone this behavior. Conversely, when the class norm supports relational aggression, elementary schoolers get more aggressive over time (Rohlf, Busching, & Krahé, 2016). In this situation, everyone is apt to bully regardless of whether or not they see this behavior as morally wrong (Scholte and others, 2010; Werner & Hill, 2010).

The fact that the nicest boys and girls bully when the atmospheric conditions are right (Mulvey & Killen, 2016) explains why programs to attack bullying focus on changing the peer-group norms.

INTERVENTIONS: Attacking Bullying and Helping Rejected Children

In the Olweus Bully Prevention Program, administrators plan a school assembly to discuss bullying early in the year. Then they form a bullying-prevention committee composed of children from each grade. Teachers and students are on high alert for bullying in their classes. The goal is to develop a schoolwide norm to not tolerate peer abuse (Olweus, Limber, & Mihalic, 1999).

Do the many bullying-prevention programs now in operation work? The answer is: "Yes, to some extent" (Espelage & De La Rue, 2013). But, because bullying or relational aggression is such an effective way to gain status, this phenomenon, present at every age, is a bit like bad weather—not in our power to totally control.

That's why I'd like to end this section by commenting on the classic recipients of this unfortunate, universal human activity—children who are socially shy. How can we help these boys and girls succeed?

In following a group of shy 5-year-olds, researchers found that a child who developed friendships in kindergarten or first grade became less socially anxious over time (Gazelle & Ladd, 2003). So, to help a temperamentally anxious child, parents should connect their son or daughter with a playmate who might become a close friend. Friendships, again, are the gateway to well-being in elementary school (and life).

How do children choose friends in the teenage years? How do we change physically and emotionally as puberty unfolds? Stay tuned for Part IV of this book.

Tying It All Together

1. Best friends in elementary school (pick false statement): *Support each other/have similar values/encourage prosocial behavior.*
2. Describe in a sentence the core difference between being well liked and being popular.
3. Which child is *not* at risk of being rejected in late elementary school?
   a. Miguel, a shy boy
   b. Mathew, who likes to play with girls' toys
   c. Nicholas, who lashes out in rage at other kids
   d. Elaine, who is relationally aggressive

Answers to the Tying It All Together quizzes can be found at the end of this chapter.

SUMMARY

Setting the Context

Piaget and Erikson view **middle childhood** as the life stage when we first become adult. Concrete operations allow children to go beyond their immediate impressions and think abstractly. During middle childhood, we learn that the key to success lies in industry, managing our impulses, and working for what we want.

Physical Development

All the achievements of middle childhood are made possible by our mammoth, slow-growing **frontal lobes**. During this life stage, motor skills expand; but, because children no longer play outside, the average elementary schoolchild today is less physically competent than in the past. Children who are well coordinated tend to be more physically active. Parents can stimulate motor skills by sharing physical activities and not micromanaging their daughters and sons. Being fit is not dependent on being well coordinated as we travel into adult life, and only fine motor skills predict academic success. But, having a high preschool **BMI** predicts lifetime weight struggles, and **childhood obesity** sets boys and girls up for a more difficult life.

Cognitive Development

Information-processing theory allows us to understand how industry locks in. In this perspective, material is processed through **working memory** in order to be recalled at a subsequent time. As children get older, working memory bin capacity dramatically expands, which explains why children reach concrete operations at age 7 or 8. Our ability to keep other people's perspectives in mind explains why theory-of-mind capacities improve through adolescence.

Executive functions—the ability to think through our actions and manage our cognitions—dramatically improve during middle childhood. Children become adept at **rehearsal, selective attention,** and inhibiting their immediate responses. The research on executive functions provides a wealth of insights that parents and teachers can use in real life.

Attention-deficit/hyperactivity disorder (ADHD), the most common childhood disorder in the United States causes widespread problems at home and school. This condition, usually diagnosed in elementary school (more often among boys), can have many pathways and causes. Treatments involve medication, training for parents and children, providing white noise, exercise, and high-intensity games. The dramatic rise in contemporary Western ADHD diagnoses could be partly a product of a poor child-environment fit.

Emotional Development

Emotion regulation, the ability to manage and control our feelings, is crucial to having a successful life. Children with

externalizing tendencies often "act out" their emotions and behave aggressively. Children with **internalizing tendencies** have problems managing intense fear. Both temperamental tendencies, at their extreme, cause problems during childhood.

Self-awareness changes dramatically as children move into middle childhood. Concrete operational children think about themselves in psychological terms, accurately scan their abilities, and evaluate themselves in comparison with peers. These realistic self-perceptions explain why **self-esteem** normally declines during elementary school. Relationships, academics, behavior, sports, and looks are the five areas from which elementary schoolchildren derive their self-esteem.

Children with externalizing tendencies minimize their difficulties with other people and may have unrealistically high self-esteem. Children with internalizing tendencies may develop **learned helplessness,** the feeling that they are incapable of doing well. Because both attitudes keep children from improving their behavior, the key to helping *every* child is to enhance self-efficacy and promote realistic views of the self.

Prosocial behaviors and morality seem built into our human biology but differ from child to child. There also is consistency, with prosocial preschoolers tending to be prosocial later on. Girls are more apt to comfort victimized children, but females are not necessarily more prosocial than males. Each gender acts prosocially in its own distinctive way.

Behaving prosocially involves transforming one's **empathy** (directly experiencing another's feelings) into **sympathy** (feeling for another person), having the executive function talents to decide when to be prosocial, and feeling able to effectively provide aid. Unfortunately, during elementary school, other considerations—such as "Does this person deserve my help?"—promote **moral disengagement,** and so inhibit some prosocial acts. To encourage morality, define the child as "a good person," allow her to remember the joy of giving, and use **induction** (get a child who has behaved hurtfully to understand the other person's feelings). Induction helps stimulate prosocial behavior because it induces **guilt.** Child-rearing techniques involving **shame** (personal humiliation) backfire, making children angry and less likely to behave in prosocial ways.

Aggression, or hurtful behavior, is also basic to being human. Rates of overt aggression (hitting, yelling) decline as children get older and are replaced by less openly aggressive acts. **Proactive aggression** is hurtful behavior we initiate. **Reactive aggression** occurs in response to being frustrated or hurt. Relational aggression refers to aggression designed to damage social relationships. **Relational aggression** increases during late elementary school and middle school and is present in girls and boys. High levels of reactive aggression provoke problems in children's relationships.

A two-step pathway may produce a highly aggressive child. When toddlers are very active (exuberant) and have trouble regulating their emotions, caregivers respond harshly and punitively—causing anger and aggression. Then, during school, the child's "bad" behavior provokes social rejection, which leads to more reactive aggression. Highly aggressive children may have a **hostile attributional bias.** This "the world is out to get me" outlook is understandable because aggressive children may have been living in a rejecting environment since their earliest years. To help highly aggressive elementary schoolers, avoid harsh punishment and cultivate morality. Understand that acting-out, risk-taking girls and boys can flourish if they find the right environment as adults.

Social Development

Friendships, those close one-to-one relationships, become vital during elementary school. In childhood (and adulthood), we select friends who are similar to ourselves and look for qualities such as loyalty and having similar moral worldviews. Friends provide emotional support and teach children how to have fulfilling love relationships during adult life.

Popularity is different from friendships because this activity involves competing to rise in the peer ranks. While relational aggression helps children climb the popularity totem pole, being kind causes children to be well-liked by their peers. Rejected children are disliked—either because of serious externalizing or internalizing problems, or because they are different from the group. Although unpopular, friendless children are at risk for later emotional problems, children who are rejected for being different may excel as adults.

Children who are unpopular—either aggressive **bully-victims** or, more typically, shy, anxious children—are vulnerable to chronic **bullying.** The anonymous, 24/7 public nature of **cyberbullying** makes this behavior more toxic than face-to-face harassment. Because bullying depends on peer reinforcement, school bully prevention programs try to change class norms favoring relational aggression. To help socially anxious children, connect timid kindergarteners with a friend. Understand that friendships, not social status, matter most during the childhood years.

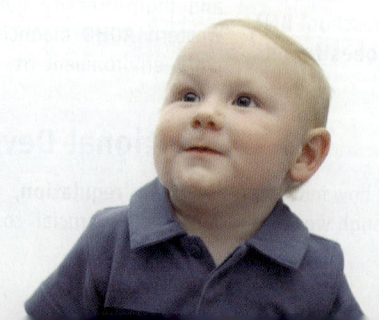

KEY TERMS

aggression, p. 178
attention-deficit/hyperactivity disorder (ADHD), p. 170
body mass index (BMI), p. 166
bullying, p. 185
bully-victims, p. 185
childhood obesity, p. 166
cyberbullying, p. 185
emotion regulation, p. 172
empathy, p. 176
executive functions, p. 168
externalizing tendencies, p. 172
frontal lobes, p. 165
guilt, p. 177
hostile attributional bias, p. 180
induction, p. 177
internalizing tendencies, p. 172
learned helplessness, p. 174
middle childhood, p. 163
moral disengagement, p. 177
proactive aggression, p. 178
prosocial behavior, p. 176
reactive aggression, p. 178
rehearsal, p. 168
relational aggression, p. 179
selective attention, p. 168
self-awareness, p. 172
self-esteem, p. 173
shame, p. 177
sympathy, p. 176
working memory, p. 168

ANSWERS TO Tying It All Together QUIZZES

Setting the Context

1. Our ability to transcend immediate appearances and control our emotions to work for a goal make middle childhood (and humanity) special.

Physical Development

1. Ethan's *motor* cortex is on an earlier developmental timetable than his *frontal lobes*.
2. c (Parents used to be less micromanaging or heavily involved.)
3. Excellent motor skills are *not very important* to adult fitness and preschool; *fine motor* skills predict children's later academic abilities.
4. False; it's difficult to cure childhood obesity by diet and exercise.

Cognitive Development

1. Answers are up to the students, but examples should center on not being able to focus on something that requires careful attention, and reacting impulsively when a child should be able to inhibit her responses.
2. Don't put your son in demanding situations that involve time management. When he studies, provide "white" background noise. Use small immediate reinforcers, such as prizes for good behavior that day. Get your son involved in sports or playing exciting games. Avoid power assertion (yelling and screaming), and go out of your way to provide lots of love.
3. Ted might mention the fact that boys are more often diagnosed with this disorder and that exercise mutes the symptoms of this condition. Each phenomenon suggests that, rather than being an internal, biological "problem," ADHD results from a poor childhood–environment fit.

Emotional Development

1. c (This child has clearly not left the preoperational bubble.)
2. Ramon = externalizing tendencies. Jared = internalizing tendencies. *Suggested intervention for Ramon:* Point out his realistic problems ("You are having trouble in X, Y, Z areas."), but cushion criticisms with plenty of love. *Suggested intervention for Jared:* Continually point out reality ("No one can always get A's. In fact, you are a fabulous student."). Get Jared to identify his "hopeless and helpless" ways of thinking, and train him to substitute more accurate perceptions.
3. c (Being intensely sensitive to others' emotions does not predict behaving prosocially.)
4. a = induction; good for promoting prosocial behavior; b = shame; bad strategy; and c = guilt; good for promoting prosocial behavior.
5. Alyssa = proactive, relational; Brianna = direct, reactive.
6. Mario has a hostile attributional bias.

Social Development

1. The final choice is incorrect as best friends can encourage negative behavior.
2. Being popular demands being aggressive and competitive—qualities that may not make children be well-liked by peers.
3. d (Unfortunately, relationally aggressive children can be popular.)

CONNECT ONLINE:

LaunchPad macmillan learning | Check out our videos and additional resources located at: www.macmillanlearning.com

CHAPTER 7

CHAPTER OUTLINE

Setting the Context

Home

Parenting Styles

INTERVENTIONS: Lessons for Thinking About Parents

How Much Do Parents Matter?

HOT IN DEVELOPMENTAL SCIENCE: Resilient Children

INTERVENTIONS: Lessons for Readers Who Are Parents

Spanking

Child Abuse

INTERVENTIONS: Taking Action Against Child Abuse

Divorce

School

Unequal at the Starting Gate

Intelligence and IQ Tests

EXPERIENCING CHILDHOOD: From Dyslexic Child to College Professor Adult

INTERVENTIONS: Lessons for Schools

Classroom Learning

HOT IN DEVELOPMENTAL SCIENCE: Communities Matter in Children's Success

Settings for Development: Home, School, and Community

José's parents migrated from Honduras to Las Vegas when he was a baby. Leaving their close, extended family was painful, but they knew their child would not have a future in their dangerous town.

At first, life was going well. They easily got green cards. Manuel joined the Culinary Workers' Union. María trained as a Spanish language computer tech. Liberated from the horrifying conditions in her country, where parents had to confine their children to the house to keep them safe, María was thrilled to lavish love on her child. Lavishing love was easy because José was such a sunny, talented boy. At age 5, José could put together puzzles that would stump children twice his age. He was picking up English beautifully, even though his parents, who spoke only Spanish at home, could not help him with school.

Then, when José was 6, Manuel was laid off. He started to drink. He came home late to regularly yell at his wife. María fell into a depression, agonizing over whether to break her family apart. After she had that difficult conversation—"Dad and I will be living separately"—her sweet boy cried for months. This painful talk couldn't have been more poorly planned. The next day, José was tested for the gifted program at school.

José's fluid reasoning score was off the charts. But growing up in a Spanish-speaking family was a handicap. José didn't make the gifted cutoff, because his verbal comprehension score was below the mean.

Now, three years later, life is going well. María found a job that allowed her to find a small (affordable!) apartment in the best school district in the state. José is returning to his old, delightful self. María sings the praises of her son's fifth-grade teacher for appreciating José's gifts and emphasizing collaboration in class. She adores her new, caring community and is grateful for the fact that shared custody is working because (to her shock) Manuel has become a loving, hands-on dad. The thorn in María's side is Grandma—or, to be exact, José's attitude toward Grandma. Having her mother in the house is a godsend. José doesn't have to stay home alone when María works 70-hour weeks. But José feels ashamed to bring his friends home to see that "old world" lady. He wants to be a regular American boy. The downside of seeing your baby blossom in this country is watching your heritage fade.

How do children, such as José, react after their parents get divorced? Given that we must succeed in the world, how important are the lessons we learn from our parents as opposed to our peers? What was that test José took, and what strategies can teachers use to make every child eager to learn? What role does the neighborhood play in children's success? Now we tackle these questions, and others, as I explore the settings within which children develop: home, school, and community.

While my discussion focuses on children around the world, in this chapter, I'll pay special attention to boys and girls, such as José, whose families differ from the traditional two-parent, middle-class, European American norm. So let's begin by scanning the tapestry of families in the twenty-first-century United States.

Left: Julia Sjöberg/Folio Images/Alamy Stock Photo

Setting the Context

LEARNING OUTCOMES
- Identify which type of U.S. family is most likely to be poor.
- Outline some immigration statistics.

Today, the *traditional nuclear family*—heterosexual married couples with biological children—has dwindled to less than half of U.S. households. Another 20 percent are *blended families*—spouses divorced and remarried—so children have stepparents and, often, stepsiblings. One and a half million never-married couples are raising children; two million boys and girls have gay or bisexual parents. Grandparents are bringing up a growing number of children (1.3 million), too (see Healthychildren.org, n.d.).

The most important distinction relates to the 1 in 4 U.S. children living in single-parent families (see Figure 7.1A). With an alarming *2 out of 3* one-parent households classified as low income, most people raising children alone in the United States can barely make ends meet (see Figure 7.1B).

On a brighter note, twenty-first-century Western children are being raised in the first truly global world. How long have you lived in Chicago or Cleveland, Canada or Sweden? Where were you born, and why did your parents move? (See Table 7.1 for interesting statistics relating to our world on the move.)

First generation immigrant grandmothers, such as this woman who is helping raise her grandchild, show that strong, loving families take many forms. What is this grandma doing right? This is the question we will explore in this next section.

FIGURE 7.1: Living arrangements of children in U.S. families Chart A shows that the two-parent married couple family is still the most common one. Chart B shows the huge disparity in the proportion of two-parent families versus single parents earning less than $40,000 per year, the estimated earnings cutoff permitting a family of four to financially survive.
Data from HealthyChildren.org, n.d.; Yang, Granja, & Koball, 2017.

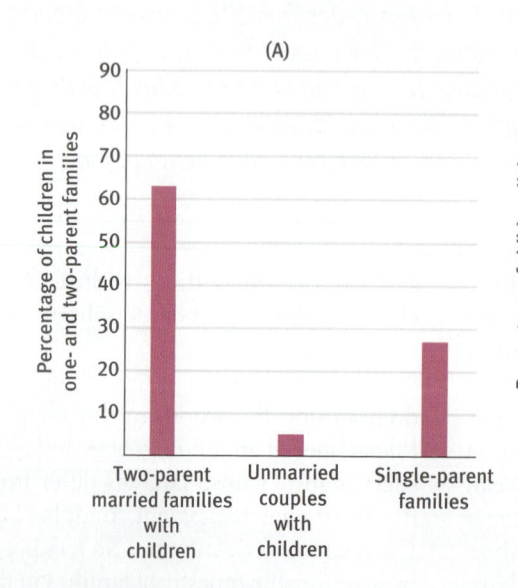

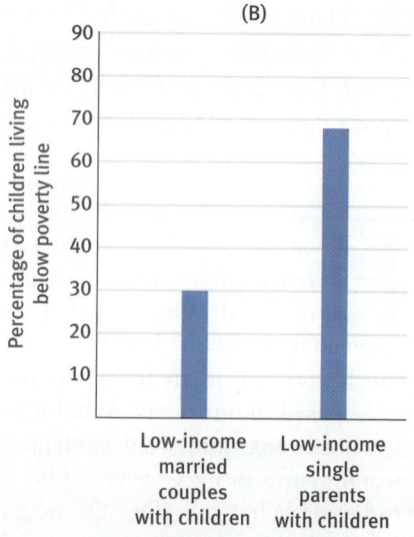

Table 7.1 A New World on the Move

- As of 2015, 1 in 30 people worldwide (a whopping 245 million adults!) lived outside of their nation of birth—a number that ballooned by more than 100 million people since the turn of this century.
- Luxemburg (42 percent), Israel (33 percent), and Switzerland (28 percent) rank as the top three nations in the percentage of foreign-born residents. But in absolute numbers, the United States still remains "a nation of immigrants." In 2015, 47 million people—almost 1 in 5 U.S. adults—were born in another country.
- With 60 million refugees at that time, 2015–2016 marked an historic march of humanity fleeing persecution. About 1.1 people from the Middle East sought protection in Germany. In the United States, however, contrary to popular opinion, most refugees were not flooding in from the war-torn Middle East. They arrived from gang-ridden Central American nations, such as El Salvador, Honduras, and Guatemala.
- The *vast majority* of immigrants are not seeking refuge from oppression. They move in search of an economically secure future for themselves and their children, the classic reason why human beings migrated in the past!

Information from Bornstein, 2017.

Home

Can children thrive in every family? The answer is yes. The key lies in what parents do. We already know that parents need to promote a secure attachment and be sensitive to a child's temperamental needs. Is there a discipline style that works best? In landmark studies conducted a half century ago, developmentalist Diana Baumrind (1971) decided yes.

Parenting Styles

Think of a parent you admire. What is that mother or father doing right? Now think of parents who you feel are not fulfilling this job. Where are they falling short? Most likely, your list will center on two functions. Are these people nurturing? Do they provide discipline or rules? By classifying parents on these two dimensions—being caring and child-centered, and giving "structure"—Baumrind (1971) spelled out the following **parenting styles**:

- **Authoritative parents** rank high on nurturing and setting limits. They set clear standards but also provide some freedom and lots of love. In this house, there are specific bed and homework times. However, if a daughter wants to watch a favorite TV program, these parents might relax the rule that homework must be finished before dinner. They could let a son extend his regular 9:00 P.M. bedtime for a special event. Although authoritative parents firmly believe in structure, they understand that rules don't take precedence over human needs.
- **Authoritarian parents** are more inflexible. Their child-rearing motto is, "Do just what I say." In these families, rules are not negotiable. While authoritarian parents may love their children deeply, their child-rearing style can seem uncaring and cold.
- **Permissive parents** are at the opposite end of the spectrum from authoritarian parents. Their parenting mantra is, "Provide total freedom and unconditional love." In these households, there are no set bedtimes and no homework demands. Here, the child-rearing principle is that children's wishes rule.
- **Rejecting-neglecting parents** are the worst of both worlds—low on structure and on love. In these families, children are neglected, ignored, and emotionally abandoned. They are left to raise themselves (see Figure 7.2 on the next page for a recap).

LEARNING OUTCOMES

- Evaluate Baumrind's ideas.
- Identify resilient children's qualities.
- Outline collective efficacy issues for immigrant children.
- Contrast different ideas about the importance of parents.
- Summarize the research on corporal punishment, child abuse, and divorce.

parenting style In Diana Baumrind's framework, how parents align on love and discipline.

authoritative parents In the parenting-styles framework, the best child-rearing style, when parents provide ample love and family rules.

authoritarian parents In the parenting-styles framework, when parents provide many rules but rank low on love.

permissive parents In the parenting-styles framework, when parents provide few rules but lots of love.

rejecting-neglecting parents In the parenting-styles framework, the worst child-rearing approach, when parents provide little discipline or love.

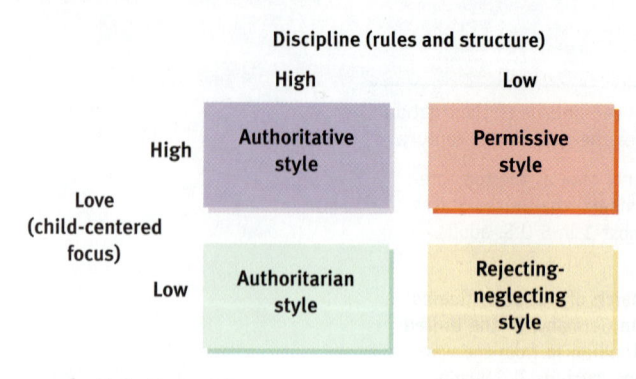

FIGURE 7.2: Parenting styles: A summary diagram
Information from Baumrind, 1971.

In relating the first three discipline studies to children's behavior (the fourth was added later), Baumrind found that children with authoritative parents were more academically successful, well-adjusted, and kind. Hundreds of studies worldwide have confirmed this finding. In a recent global example, "balanced parental discipline" (that is, love plus structure) was correlated with prosocial behavior among children living in Colombia, Italy, Jordan, Kenya, the Philippines, Thailand, and the United States (Pastorelli and others, 2016).

Decoding Parenting in a Deeper Way

These studies offer a beautiful blueprint for the right way to raise children: Provide clear rules and lots of love. However, if you classify your parents along these dimensions, you may find problems. Perhaps one parent was permissive and another authoritarian. Or maybe your families' rules randomly varied from authoritative to permissive over time.

One study suggested that the worst situation for a teenager's mental health occurred when families had inconsistent rules (Dwairy, 2010). Imagine how frustrated you would be if your parents sometimes came down very hard on you and, in other *similar situations*, seemed not to care!

But aren't there times when parenting styles should vary, that is, situations when children *need* a more authoritarian or permissive approach? These questions bring me to two classic critiques of Baumrind's parenting styles.

Critique 1: Parenting Styles Can Vary from Child to Child

Perhaps your parents came down harder on a brother or sister because that sibling needed more discipline, while your personality flourished with a permissive style. As I described earlier in this book, good parents *should* vary their childrearing, depending on the unique personality of a specific child.

Unfortunately, however, as I also stressed in earlier chapters, when children are "high maintenance" (difficult to raise), due to an evocative process, parenting styles may change for the worse. A mother might become excessively controlling (authoritarian) when her child has a chronic illness (Pinquart, 2013). She might yell, scream, and wall herself off emotionally from a son or daughter with ADHD.

So, again, parenting is far more bidirectional and child-evoked than Baumrind assumes. Does an authoritarian (or permissive) parenting style *ever* work best?

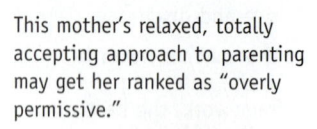

This mother's relaxed, totally accepting approach to parenting may get her ranked as "overly permissive."

Critique 2: Parenting Styles Can Vary Depending on One's Society

Critics point out that Baumrind's styles perspective reflects a Western middle-class perspective on childrearing. But new immigrants from Mexico who tend to avoid spanking their children (Lee & Altschul, 2015) may regard this parenting technique as too harsh (much more about spanking soon). Conversely, in collectivist cultures such as China, child-centered parenting may seem too lax.

This point was spelled out in a controversial book called *The Battle Hymn of The Tiger Mother* (2011). Amy Chua, a second-generation Chinese American parent, argued that, in contrast to our laid-back democratic style, more traditional Asian, rule-oriented "no back talk" childrearing was the best way to produce a Harvard-bound, high-achieving child (see Chua, 2011; Lui & Rollock, 2013).

Do Asian-heritage U.S. parents *typically* adopt a more authoritarian parenting style? Unless they are recent immigrants, the answer is no (Choi and others, 2013; Kim, Wang, and others, 2013).

If we want children to excel at school, should parents adopt Chua's rule-oriented child-rearing advice? Not really. From Japan (Uji and others, 2014) to Turkey (Cenk & Demir, 2016), from Indonesia (Abubakar and others, 2015) to Palestine (Alt, 2016), *authoritative parenting* is linked to academic achievement (and overall well-being).

In the past, adults were forced to act authoritarian because life was so dangerous (see Chapter 1). Even today, parents living in war-torn nations reluctantly report using authoritarian child-rearing techniques. As one mother in violence-wracked El Salvador anguished: ". . . I do not let my son go outside. . . . I think we have become overprotective against our will" (Rojas-Flores and others, 2013, p. 278). But in twenty-first-century Western nations, authoritarian parenting is a symptom of feeling less socially competent (Egeli & Rinaldi, 2016) and more stressed-out in the parenting role (Nomaguchi & House, 2013).

INTERVENTIONS: Lessons for Thinking About Parents

How can you use these insights to think about parents in a more empathic way?

- Understand that parenting styles don't operate in a vacuum. They vary depending on a family's unique life situation and child.

- Realize that while withdrawing emotionally is understandable when a child is "difficult," authoritarian parenting is not the best way to raise a child unless a family lives in a dangerous neighborhood or part of the world.

- Celebrate the fact that today we have the luxury to be child-centered, in the sense of listening empathically to our daughters and sons. Although specific discipline practices differ, most parents in our world village agree: "Give children limits, but above all offer lots of love!"

Table 7.2 gives you a chance to step back and list your own parenting priorities. Let's now consider that philosophical question: Is parenting critically important to how children turn out?

Table 7.2: Checklist for Identifying Your Parenting Priorities

Rank the following goals in order of their importance to you, from 1 (for highest priority) to 8 (for lowest priority). It's OK to use the same number twice if two goals are equally important to you.

_____ Producing an obedient, well-behaved child

_____ Producing a caring, prosocial child

_____ Producing an independent, self-sufficient child

_____ Producing a child who is extremely close to you

_____ Producing an intelligent, creative thinker

_____ Producing a well-rounded child

_____ Producing a happy, emotionally secure child

_____ Producing a spiritual (religious) child

What do your rankings reveal about the qualities you most admire in human beings?

How Much Do Parents Matter?

The most inspiring place to start is with those world-class role models who had terrible childhoods but succeeded brilliantly as adults.

Hot in Developmental Science: Resilient Children

His aristocratic parents spent their time gallivanting around Europe; they never appeared at the nursery doors. At age 7, he was wrenched from the only person who loved him—his nanny—and shipped off to boarding school. Insolent, angry, refusing to obey orders or sit still, he was regularly beaten by the headmaster and teased by the other boys. Although gifted at writing, he was incapable of rote memorization; he couldn't pass a test. When he graduated at the bottom of his boarding school class, his father informed him that he would never amount to anything. His name was Winston Churchill. He was the man who stood up to Hitler and carried England to victory in World War II.

Churchill's upbringing was a recipe for disaster. He had neglectful parents, behavior problems, and was a failure at school. But this dismal childhood produced the leader who saved the modern world.

Resilient children, like Churchill or Abraham Lincoln (in the photo), confront terrible conditions such as parental abuse, poverty, and war and go on to construct successful, loving lives. What qualities allow these children to thrive?

Developmentalists find that resilient children often have a special talent, such as Churchill's gift for writing, or Lincoln's towering intellect. They are adept at regulating their emotions. They have a high sense of self-efficacy and an optimistic worldview (Grych, Hamby, & Banyard, 2015). They possess a strong faith or sense of meaning in life (Wright & Masten, 2005).

Being resilient depends on inner resources—having good executive functions and intellectual and social skills. But the number of wider-world traumas matters (Panter-Brick and others, 2015). If you are exposed to a series of tragedies—for instance, your parents getting divorced after experiencing a disaster such as a hurricane—it's more difficult to preserve your efficacy feelings or rebound to construct a happy life (Becker-Blease, Turner, & Finkelhor, 2010; Kronenberg and others, 2010).

Most important, children who succeed against incredible odds typically have at least one close, caring relationship with a parent or another adult (such as Churchill's nanny). Like a plant that thrives in the desert, resilient children have the internal resources to extract love from their parched environment. But they cannot survive without any water at all.

The same qualities apply to immigrant children facing **acculturation,** the challenge of adapting to a different culture. But here, a family's fit to the new society looms large. Can this girl balance the need to preserve her cultural identity while embracing the norms of this new nation (Telzer and others, 2016)? Is this boy moving to a place that welcomes families from his region of the world (Bornstein, 2017; Pieloch, McCollough, & Marks, 2016)?

We marvel at the stamina of children who travel thousands of miles from war-torn nations and thrive. Might these survivors have resilience-promoting genes? As I mentioned in Chapter 4, some scientists believe a genetic profile may set certain newborns up to be relatively immune to stressful life events, but that this same "immunity" gene-form is a liability when the wider world is nurturing and calm. So, yes, some babies may arrive in this world biologically blessed to weather the biblical upheavals of human life.

Abandoned by his father at age 9 and raised in a Kentucky shack without any chance to attend school, Abraham Lincoln grew up to become our most beloved president and perhaps the greatest man of the nineteenth century. What made this resilient child thrive? The answer: towering intellectual gifts, a remarkable drive to learn, optimism, self-efficacy, and a world-class talent for understanding human motivations and connecting with people in a caring, prosocial way.

resilient children Children who rebound from serious early life traumas to construct successful adult lives.

acculturation Among immigrants, the tendency to become similar to the mainstream culture after time spent living in a new society.

Will these children succeed in their new home? In addition to having the classic attributes linked to resilience, it depends on whether their new community is a welcoming place and—very importantly—if they are genetically resistant to stress.

Making the Case That Parents Don't Matter

What matters more in how children develop, their parents or their genes? Twin and adoption studies, as I mentioned in Chapter 1, come down firmly on the "it's mainly genetic" side. Faced with this nature-oriented behavioral-genetic research message, one developmentalist famously concluded that it doesn't matter if you were raised in your particular family or the one down the street. Given adequate parenting, and a decent environment, children grow up to express their genetic fate (see Scarr, 1997; Scarr & Deater-Deckard, 1997).

Psychologist Judith Harris provided the most interesting twist on this "parents don't matter" argument. Harris (1995, 1998, 2002, 2006) believes that the environment has a dramatic impact on our development; but, rather than parents, our peer group socializes us to become adults.

Harris begins by taking aim at the principle underlying attachment theory—that the lessons we learn from our parents transfer to our other relationships. Learning, Harris believes, is context-specific. We cannot use the same *working model* with our mother and with the classroom bully, since we would never survive. Furthermore, because we live our lives in the wider world, she argues, the messages we absorb from the culture of our contemporaries must take precedence over the lessons we are taught at home.

Any parent can relate to Harris's peer-power principle when witnessing her 3-year-old pick up every bad habit from his preschool classmates. I outlined a chilling example of a similar group influence in the last chapter when I described how aggressive middle-school norms can evoke bullying in the "nicest kids."

An equally compelling argument lies in the pivotal role *adult peers*—meaning, the community—play in shaping children's lives. As I will emphasize throughout this chapter, parents become better caregivers—and children are more apt to thrive—in neighborhoods defined by high **collective efficacy**, places where community ties are close and neighbors bond around shared prosocial norms. To paraphrase that familiar African proverb: "It takes a village to raise children and successful parents, too!"

These arguments about the importance of genetics and living in caring communities alert us to the fact that when we see children acting out, we cannot leap to the assumption that "it's just the parents' fault." As Bronfenbrenner's ecological developmental systems theory predicts, many influences—from peer groups, to schools, to

collective efficacy Communities defined by strong cohesion, a commitment to neighbor-to-neighbor helping, and shared prosocial values among residents.

Look at these exuberant boys, passionate to fit in with their friends. Then ask yourself whether these children are acting the same way they were taught to behave at home. Suddenly, doesn't Judith Harris's theory that "peer groups shape development" make a good deal of sense?

neighborhoods, to living in a particular nation—affect how children behave. But you may be thinking that the idea that parents are *not* important goes way too far.

Many experts agree. For children to realize their genetic potential, parents should provide the best possible environment (Ceci and others, 1997; Kagan, 1998; Maccoby, 2002). In fact, even in the most efficacious community, when children are biologically vulnerable, superior parenting is required.

Making the Case for Superior Parenting

Imagine, for instance, that your daughter is temperamentally "difficult." You know from reading this book that you may be tempted to disengage emotionally from your child. You understand that adopting this less responsive parenting style can make the situation worse. So you inhibit your use of *power assertion*. You provide lots of love. You arrange the environment to minimize your child's vulnerabilities and highlight her strengths.

Actually, when a child is biologically reactive, sensitive caregiving can make a critical difference. From the studies mentioned in Chapter 3, showing that loving touch helps premature infants grow, to my suggestions for raising fearful or exuberant kids (discussed in Chapters 4 and 6), the message is the same: With vulnerable children, outstanding parenting matters most.

So let's celebrate the fact that resilient children can flower in the face of difficult life conditions. But when a baby needs special nurturing, high-quality nurturing is required.

INTERVENTIONS: Lessons for Readers Who Are Parents

Now let's summarize by offering some concrete parenting advice.

There are no firm guidelines about how to be an effective parent—except to show lots of love, set consistent rules, and adapt your discipline to your unique child. You will face special challenges if you live in a dangerous environment or have a son or daughter who is "harder to raise" (where you may have to work harder to stay loving and attached). Your power is limited at best.

Try to see this message as liberating. Children cannot be massaged into having an idealized adult life. Your child's future does not totally depend on you. Focus on the quality of your relationship, and enjoy these wonderful years. And if your son or daughter is having difficulties, draw inspiration from Winston Churchill's history. Predictions from childhood to adult life can be hazy. Your struggling child may grow up to save the world!

Now that I've covered the general territory, let's turn to specifics. First, I'll examine the controversy surrounding spanking and then focus on the worst type of parenting, child abuse. Finally, I'll explore that common family event, divorce.

Spanking

corporal punishment The use of physical force to discipline a child.

Poll friends and family about **corporal punishment**—any discipline technique that involves physical measures such as spanking—and you are likely to get strong reactions. Some people adhere to the biblical principle, "Spare the rod and spoil the child." They may blame the decline in spanking for every social problem. Others blame corporal punishment for *creating* those social problems. They believe that parents who rely on "hitting" are implicitly teaching children that it is OK to respond in a violent way. To put these positions into perspective, let's take a tour of the total turnaround in corporal punishment attitudes in recent times.

Before the twentieth century, corporal punishment was standard practice. Flogging was routine in prisons (Gould & Pate, 2010), the military, and other places (Pinker, 2011). In the United States, it was legal for men to "physically chastise" their wives (Knox, 2010). Today, in Western democracies, these practices are universally condemned.

In fact, 24 nations—from Spain to Sweden or Croatia to Costa Rica—have passed laws banning child corporal punishment. Organizations from the American Academy of Pediatrics to the United Nations to the Methodist Church have also put forth resolutions that call spanking "inhumane" (Knox, 2010).

The United States is a dramatic exception. Although spanking is illegal at schools and day-care centers in most states, any U.S. senator proposing a bill to ban this behavior would be severely condemned. Not only is our individualistic society wary about the government intruding into parental "freedom," but *many* U.S. parents do spank their daughters and sons (Barkin and others, 2007).

Still, with surveys showing that only 1 in 10 parents admit they "often spank," corporal punishment is not the preferred U.S. discipline mode. Today, the most frequent punishments parents report are removal of privileges and, to a lesser extent, getting sent to one's room (Barkin and others, 2007).

Who in the United States is most likely to spank? Corporal punishment is widely accepted in the African American community (Burchinal, Skinner, & Reznick, 2010; Lorber, O'Leary, & Smith Slep, 2011). As one Black woman reported: "I would rather me discipline them than (the police)" (Taylor, Hamvas, & Paris, 2011, p. 65). As you might imagine from the "spare the rod, spoil the child" injunction, people who believe this biblical pronouncement is literally true are apt to use this disciplinary technique (Rodriguez & Henderson, 2010).

Adults who were spanked as children see more value in this child-rearing approach (Simons & Wurtele, 2010). (In my classes, I often hear students report: "I was spanked and it helped; so I plan to do the same with my kids.") But if you feel that physical punishment got out of hand when you were a child, you are probably passionate about never hitting your own daughter or son (Gagne and others, 2007).

What do experts advise? Today, an overwhelming number of psychologists believe that spanking is *never* appropriate (Gershoff & Grogan-Kaylor, 2016). Hitting, as I mentioned earlier, models violence. Yes, spanking may produce immediate compliance. But it impairs prosocial behavior because it gets children to only focus on themselves (Andero & Stewart, 2002; Benjet & Kazdin, 2003; Knox, 2010).

A few mainstream developmentalists, such as Diana Baumrind, have a (slightly) different view (Baumrind, Larzelere, & Cowan, 2002). They believe that if we rule out corporal punishment completely, caregivers may resort to more damaging, shaming practices such as saying, "I hate you. You will never amount to anything." But even these psychologists have clear limits as to how and when physical discipline might be used:

- Never hit an infant. *Babies can't control their behavior. They don't know what they are doing wrong.* For a preschooler, a few light swats on the bottom can be a last resort disciplinary technique if a child is engaging in dangerous activities—such as running into the street—that need to be immediately stopped (Larzelere & Kuhn, 2005).

- This action, however, must be accompanied by a verbal explanation ("What you did was wrong because . . ."). Spanking should only be considered if other approaches fail.

The issue is that, with more than a hundred studies linking corporal punishment to mental health problems (see Gershoff & Grogan-Kaylor, 2016), we need to firmly dispel the misconception that spanking produces well-disciplined, obedient children. Because corporal punishment is rampant in neighborhoods low in collective efficacy, where daily life is frustrating and dangerous, its best to intervene by making communities more caring (Ma, 2016).

Frequent spanking promotes the very behavior it is supposed to cure. To take one example, researchers found that parents who believed strongly in spanking had sons and daughters who said that during disagreements with a playmate, hitting that other child was fine (Simons & Wurtele, 2010). Worse yet, what starts out as a "normal" spanking can escalate as a parent "gets into it," the child cries more, and soon we have that worst-case scenario: child abuse.

Child Abuse

Child maltreatment—the term for actions that endanger children's physical or emotional well-being—comprises four categories. *Physical abuse* refers to bodily injury that leaves bruises. It encompasses everything from overzealous spanking to battering that may lead to a child's death. *Neglect* refers to caregivers' failure to provide adequate supervision and care. It might mean abandoning the child, not providing sufficient food, or failing to enroll a son or daughter in school. *Emotional abuse* refers to shaming, terrorizing, or exploiting a child. *Sexual abuse* covers the spectrum from rape and incest to fondling and exhibitionistic acts.

Everyone can identify serious forms of maltreatment; but there is a gray zone as to what activities cross the line (Cicchetti, 2016). Does every spanking that leaves bruises qualify as physical abuse? If a mother leaves her toddler in an 8-year-old sibling's care, is she neglectful? Are parents who walk around naked in the house guilty of sexual abuse? Emotional abuse is inherently murky to define, although this form of maltreatment may be the most common of all (Foster and others, 2010).

This labeling issue partly explains why maltreatment statistics vary, depending on who we ask. In one global summary (involving an incredible 150 studies and 10 million participants), scientists estimated that roughly 3 of 1,000 children worldwide were physically maltreated, using informants' (that is, other people's) reports. In polling adults themselves, the rates were 10 times higher (Stoltenborgh and others, 2013). In one study in Canada, a shocking 1 in 4 people reported being maltreated as a child (MacMillan and others, 2013).

Obviously, far more people will report that they were abused than the "objective" abuse-rate figures indicate. But, although some adults may err on the side of over-reporting (saying "I was abused" because they are chronically angry with their parents), reports to authorities probably qualify as the iceberg's tiny tip (Greenfield, 2010). Why is maltreatment still swept under the rug in our day and age? Before answering this question, let's look at what provokes this parenting pathology and probe its effects.

Exploring the Risk Factors

As ecological, developmental systems theory predicts, several categories of influence can spark child abuse (Wolfe, 2011).

Parents' Personality Problems Are Important
People who maltreat their children tend to suffer from psychological disorders such as depression and externalizing problems such as substance abuse (Plant, Donohue, & Holland, 2016). They may have hostile attributional biases (McCarthy & Lumley, 2012), assuming that a toddler is "bad" when she engages in benign activities like running around.

Life Stress Accompanied by Social Isolation Can Be Crucial
Abusive parents are often young and poorly educated (Cicchetti, 2016). They tend to be coping with an overload of upsetting life events, from domestic violence to severe poverty (Annerbäck, Svedin, & Gustafsson, 2010). They feel cut off from caring social contacts. Again, feeling isolated in neighborhoods low in collective efficacy can be the match that causes child abuse to flare up (Barnhart & Maguire-Jack, 2016).

Children's Vulnerabilities Play a Role
A child who is emotionally fragile can fan this fire—a baby who cries excessively (Reijneveld and others, 2004), has a medical problem (Svensson, Bornehag, & Janson, 2011), or is premature (Sieswerda-Hoogendoorn and others, 2013). Therefore, in a

---

child maltreatment Any act that seriously endangers a child's physical or emotional well-being.

A loving family life—and particularly, a caring relationship with one's spouse—can break the intergenerational cycle of abuse.

terrible irony, the very children that most need unusually loving care are apt to provoke an out-of-control caregiver's wrath. The fact that abusive parents may target just one child was brought home to me when I was working as a clinical psychologist at a city hospital in New York. A mother was referred for treatment for abusing her "spiteful" 10-year-old, although she never harmed his "sweet" 3-year-old brother. So disturbances in the attachment relationship are a core ingredient in the poisonous recipe for producing a battered child.

Exploring the Consequences

Maltreated children tend to suffer from internalizing and externalizing problems. They may have impaired theory of mind abilities and get rejected by their peers (Cicchetti, 2016). Just as with the orphanage-reared babies discussed earlier, neuroimaging studies suggest child maltreatment may compromise the developing brain (Ahn and others, 2016).

Because traumatic childhood experiences prime the body to *epigenetically* break down (Danese & Baldwin, 2016), children who are maltreated have more physical problems during adult life (Cicchetti, 2016). They are at risk of getting embroiled in abusive love relationships (McCloskey, 2013); and yes, abused children are at higher risk of maltreating their own daughters and sons.

Still, most abused children become decent caring parents. Some are passionate to go in the opposite direction (Berlin, Appleyard, & Dodge, 2011). As one woman described: "I made a vow to protect my children. . . . It was almost like a mantra, that I'm never going to strike [my child]" (quoted in Hall, 2011, p. 38).

Adults who break the cycle of abuse tend to have good intellectual and coping skills (Hengartner and others, 2013). They are fortunate to have the DNA profile that I alluded to earlier, which makes them genetically more resistant to stress (Banducci and others, 2014). Having a loving marriage also offers potent insulation from repeating the trauma of abuse (Jaffee and others, 2013).

INTERVENTIONS: Taking Action Against Child Abuse

What should you do if you suspect child abuse? The law requires teachers, social workers, and health-care professionals to report the situation to child protective services. Children in imminent danger are removed from the home, and the cases are referred to juvenile court. Judges do not have the power to punish abusive parents, but they can place the children in foster care and limit or terminate parental rights.

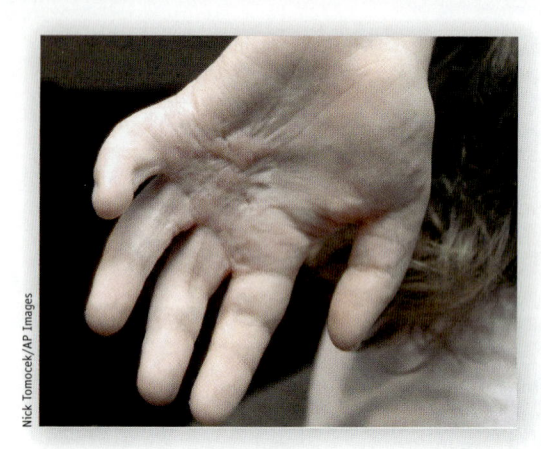

Imagine you are a teacher who sees these suspicious burns on a student's hands. You know that unusual injuries like this can signal child abuse, but you aren't absolutely sure. Would you immediately report the situation to the authorities? Would you talk to the parents first? What exactly would you do?

In one Chinese survey, teenagers mentioned that having neighbors who spoke up helped prevent them from being physically abused (Cheung, 2016). But, even in the most efficacious neighborhood, adults have powerful temptations not to intervene. If you make a false report, you risk ruining a family's life. "Are those burns a sign of child abuse or a normal accident?" "If I do report the situation, will the authorities take action?"

This last fear seems justified. In one Swedish study, even in the face of accusations of severe abuse, only 1 percent of the cases actually went to trial (Otterman, Lainpelto, & Lindblad, 2013). This is unfortunate, because when parents have a history of abuse, the situation can get worse. In one study that tracked at-risk families, the home environment deteriorated from preschool to kindergarten, with mothers doing more yelling and hitting over time, especially with their sons (Haskett, Neupert, & Okado, 2014).

Divorce

Although it still occurs too often, child abuse is no longer common in this day and age (see Pinker, 2011). However, since the late-twentieth-century lifestyle revolution, children are more apt to face another unwelcome family change: divorce. How does divorce affect children, and what can adults do to help?

Let's start with the bad news. Studies worldwide comparing children of divorce with their counterparts in intact, married families show these boys and girls are at a disadvantage—academically, socially, and in terms of mental health (Al Gharaibeh, 2015; Lamela and others, 2016). One reason may be economic (see Weaver & Schofield, 2015). Divorce can propel a mother-headed household into poverty, even though that family had previously been middle class (Schramm and others, 2013; see also Figure 7.1A on page 192).

The good news is that children normally adjust to this life transition well, as long as their parents are authoritative and the divorce is fairly conflict free (Weaver & Schofield, 2015). Still, I don't want to minimize the guilt people feel when making this choice. One Israeli woman described a fairly common scenario when she lamented that for months her daughter's conversations started with the anxious phrase, "Soon, when Dad will come back home" (quoted in Cohen, Leichtentritt, & Volpin, 2014, p. 37).

In this qualitative study exploring the feelings of newly divorced Israeli mothers, women said their main agenda was to minimize their children's pain. So they struggled to put aside their vengeful feelings and not bad-mouth their former spouses. One mother helped her child cope with his father's painful absence by making it into a shared game: "I laugh. I tell him, 'OK you miss daddy. But where is he?' And he says, 'Far, far away'" (quoted in Cohen, Leichtentritt, & Volpin, 2014, p. 39).

Others vowed to avoid mentioning the gritty details: "I don't want to hurt him," said a woman named Trina. "I won't tell them that his father pointed a gun at his mother" (quoted in Cohen, Leichtentritt, & Volpin, 2014, p. 37).

parental alienation The practice among divorced parents of bad-mouthing a former spouse, with the goal of turning a child against that person.

This is not to say that **parental alienation**—poisoning children against ex-partners—is rare. Even years after separating, some people can't resist demonizing the other parent, especially after an acrimonious divorce (see van Lawick & Visser, 2015).

The temptation to engage in *relational aggression* (enlisting children against a former spouse) brings up issues related to custody and visitation. When the divorce is bitter (or labeled "high conflict"), should a child frequently see both a mother and father?

For almost the entire twentieth century, mothers were routinely given custody, based on the psychoanalytic principle that women are inherently superior nurturers—a practice that unfairly limited fathers from being fully involved in their children's lives. Today, Western nations have rectified this situation by passing laws encouraging joint custody (see Lavadera, Caravelli, & Togliatti, 2013). Spouses don't have to split living arrangements 50-50. But even though the child lives mostly with a

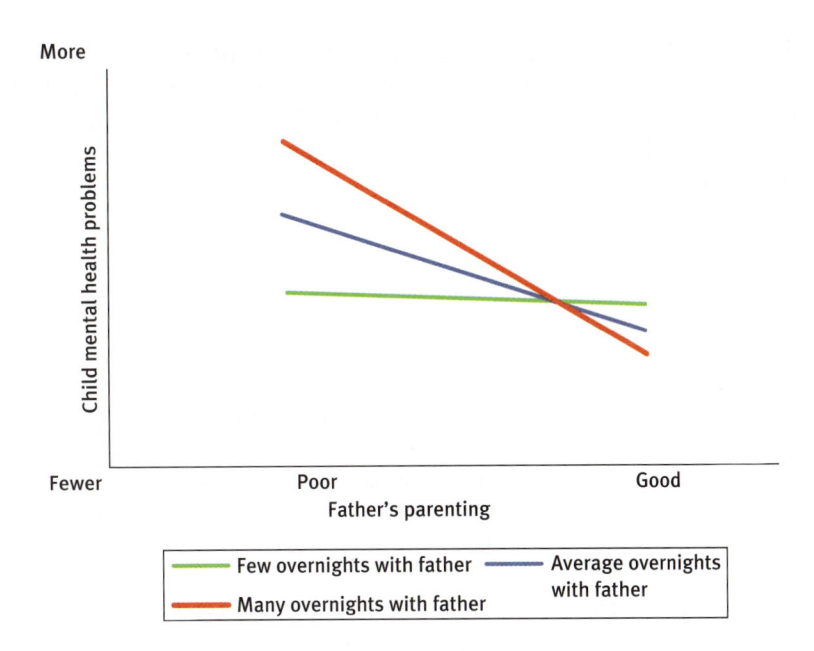

FIGURE 7.3: **Child mental health problems as a function of father's parenting and whether the child spent many or few overnights at that parent's house** Notice from the red line that staying over often at a divorced dad's house is good for children, *if* that man is a good parent. But frequent overnights with a father who has poor parenting skills are clearly detrimental to children's mental health.

Data from Sandler, Wheeler, & Braver, 2013.

mother (or father), when parents share custody, the other partner can see a son or daughter any time.

Does shared custody help children cope? The answer hinges on the quality of care the other partner provides (Lamela and others, 2016). As the study summarized in Figure 7.3 illustrates, while more overnights with a dad who was a good parent promoted adjustment, when children spent time with an inadequate father, post-divorce child emotional problems escalated (Sandler, Wheeler, & Braver, 2013).

So with custody and visitation, we need to take a person-centered, ecological, developmental systems approach. Go for shared custody in the abstract, but if an ex-spouse is antisocial or the partners continually bad-mouth each other, limit access to mainly one caregiver to protect the child (see DeGarmo, 2010; Lessard and others, 2010).

After a divorce, it's normal for childrearing to get more disorganized, as parents cope with their upsetting feelings. But one study showed that it's important to guard against being too permissive, as having firm rules prevents children from acting out during this difficult time (Stallman & Ohan, 2016). The bottom line, however, is that what really matters is the ongoing parenting style. Children should spend their time with the parent (or parents) who parent the best (Weaver & Schofield, 2015).

Should older children be able to choose which custody arrangement they prefer? One study, comparing standard divorce mediation with approaches centered more on child wishes, suggested yes (Ballard and others, 2013).

Still, in another poll of divorced parents and their teens, everyone recoiled at the idea of putting *total* decision making on a child's shoulders (Cashmore & Parkinson, 2008). Imagine forcing a son or daughter to admit, "I prefer to live with Mom (or Dad)." And consider the coercion that might ensue from the parent side. During one semester's divorce discussion, a student poignantly described this scenario when she informed the class: "My daughter told the judge she wanted to live with her father, and then, years later said, 'Mom, I wanted you, but I was afraid to say so because I was frightened of Dad.'"

Do you think this girl should be testifying in court about whether to live with her Mom or Dad? Clearly, there are serious minuses here.

At this point, some readers might be thinking that unhappy couples should bite the bullet and stay together for the sake of their children. If the marriage is full of conflict, think again. As another student explained during this divorce discussion, "Because the atmosphere at home was terrible, I felt much happier after my parents divorced."

Table 7.3 summarizes these points in a parenting-related divorce questionnaire and offers tips for succeeding at stepparenting, that new common family form. Now let's turn to that other setting within which children develop—school.

Table 7.3: Parenting Questions and Stepparenting Advice Relating to Divorce

Parenting Questions

1. Do the ex-spouses continually bad-mouth each other? (Parental alienation is poisonous for children.)
2. Does the child see the ex-spouse frequently? (Joint custody is great, but only if the other partner is a good parent.)
3. Does the child have input into custody decisions? (This can be positive, as long as the total decision-making burden doesn't fall on children.)
4. After the divorce, do the parent(s) set consistent rules? (Authoritative post-divorce childrearing is the main force that predicts how well children cope!)

Stepparenting Advice

1. Go slow in disciplining your new family. Understand that children naturally feel that their real parent is their "original" mom and/or dad.
2. Realize that, with authoritative parenting, attachments lock in over time. One study showed that children were more apt to view their stepdad as their "real" father the longer he lived in the house.
3. Strive for harmony in your childrearing. Agreeing on parenting styles is doubly important when raising a family the second time around!

Information from Kinniburgh-White, Cartwright, & Seymour, 2010; Kalmijn, 2013; and the references in this section.

Tying It All Together

1. Montana's parents set firm rules but value their children's input about family decisions. Pablo's parents have rules for everything and tolerate no *ifs*, *ands*, or *buts*. Sara's parents don't really have rules—at their house, it's always playtime. Which parenting style is being used by Montana's parents? By Pablo's parents? By Sara's parents?

2. Ahmid and his family moved to your town from a refugee relocation center in the Middle East. Based on this chapter, spell out some qualities that predict whether this traumatized child may be resilient, and summarize your community's main goal.

3. Melissa's son Jared, now in elementary school, was premature and has a difficult temperament. What might Judith Harris advise about fostering this child's development, and what might this chapter recommend?

4. Your sister is concerned about a friend who uses corporal punishment with her baby and her 4-year-old. She asks what the experts say. Pick which two statements developmentalists might make.

    a. Never spank children of any age.
    b. Mild spanking is OK for the infant.
    c. Corporal punishment is linked to some mental health problems.
    d. If the child has a difficult temperament, corporal punishment might help.

5. Ms. Johnson is worried about an 8-year-old who meanders around the neighborhood at all hours of the night. Yesterday, she saw burn marks on the child's arms. Describe how Ms. Johnson might feel about reporting this situation to the police, and what might happen if she accuses the parent of neglect.

6. Imagine you are a family court judge deciding to award joint custody. In a phrase, explain your main criterion for awarding unlimited overnights with a particular divorced dad.

Answers to the Tying It All Together questions can be found at the end of this chapter.

School

What was the test that José (in the chapter-opening vignette) took, and what does intelligence really mean? What makes for good teaching and superior schools? Before tackling these school-related topics, let's step back and, again, explore the impact of that basic marker—poverty—on young children's cognitive skills.

Unequal at the Starting Gate

Chapter 4 described the oversized negative impact early-childhood poverty has on high school success. Figure 7.4 reveals that devastation by offering sobering concrete statistics relating to an entering U.S. kindergarten class (Lee & Burkam, 2002). Disadvantaged children begin school *several years behind* their affluent counterparts on tests of reading readiness and math (see also Duncan, Magnuson, & Vortuba-Drzal, 2017).

You would think that when children start a race miles behind, they would get special help catching up. The reality, of course, is the reverse. From class size to the quality of teacher training, U.S. kindergartens serving poor children rank at the bottom of the educational heap.

Let's keep these mammoth disparities in school quality favoring affluent children in mind as we explore the controversial topic of intelligence tests.

Intelligence and IQ Tests

What does it mean to be intelligent? Ask people on the street this question, and they will probably mention both academic and "real life" skills (Sternberg, 2007; Sternberg, Grigorenko, & Kidd, 2005).

Traditional intelligence tests—called **intelligence quotient** (or **IQ**) tests—measure *only* academic abilities. These tests differ from **achievement tests**, the yearly evaluations children take to measure knowledge in various subjects. IQ tests are designed to predict general academic *potential*, or a child's ability to master any school-related task. Do the tests measure mainly genetic capacities and have any relevance beyond school? To approach these hot-button issues, let's examine the intelligence test that children typically take today: the WISC.

Examining the WISC

The **WISC (Wechsler Intelligence Scale for Children)**, now in its fifth revision, was devised by David Wechsler and is the current standard intelligence test. As you can see in Table 7.4 on the next page, the WISC samples a child's performance in five basic areas. This means that, in addition to giving the child a single overall score, testers can look in a more detailed way at particular skills (see Cormier, Kennedy, & Aquilina, 2016).

Achievement tests are given to groups. The WISC is administered individually by a trained psychologist in about an hour of testing and concludes with a written report. If the child scores at the 50th percentile for his age group, his IQ is defined as 100. If that child's IQ is 130, he ranks at roughly the 98th percentile, or in the top 2 percent of children his age. If a child's score is 70, he is at the opposite end of the distribution, performing in the lowest 2 percent of children that age. This score distribution looks like a bell-shaped curve.

When do children take this test? The answer, most often, is during elementary school when there is a question about a child's classroom performance. School personnel then use the IQ score as one component of a multifaceted assessment—which

LEARNING OUTCOMES

- Describe the WISC and how psychologists use this test.
- Explore the controversial meaning of IQ.
- Contrast Sternberg and Gardner's ideas.
- Describe successful schools.
- Outline intrinsic motivation.

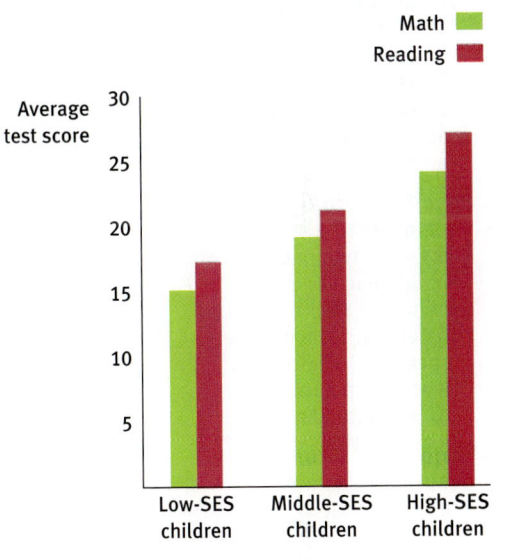

FIGURE 7.4: Socioeconomic status and kindergartners' scores on tests of readiness for reading and math As children's socioeconomic status rises, so do average scores on tests of math and reading readiness. Notice the dramatic differences between low-income and affluent children.
Data from Lee & Burkam, 2002.

intelligence quotient (IQ) Measure designed to evaluate a child's overall cognitive ability, or general aptitude for mastering academic work.

achievement tests Measures that evaluate a child's knowledge in specific school-related areas.

WISC (Wechsler Intelligence Scale for Children) The standard intelligence test used in childhood, consisting of different subtests.

Table 7.4: The WISC-5 A Subtest Sampler

Subtest	Sample (simulated) Item
Verbal Comprehension Index	
Similarities (analogies)	Cat is to kitten as dog is to _____.
Vocabulary (defining words)	What is a table?
Fluid Reasoning Index	
Picture completion	Pick out what is missing in this picture.
Block design	Arrange these blocks to look like the photograph on the card within a time limit.
Processing Speed Index	
Coding	Using the key above, put each symbol in the correct space below.
Working Memory Index	
Digit span	Repeat these numbers forward. Now repeat these numbers backward.

intellectual disability The label for significantly impaired cognitive functioning, measured by deficits in behavior accompanied by having an IQ of 70 or below.

specific learning disorder The label for any impairment in language or any deficit related to listening, thinking, speaking, reading, writing, spelling, or understanding mathematics.

dyslexia A learning disorder that is characterized by reading difficulties, lack of fluency, and poor word recognition that is often genetic in origin.

gifted The label for superior intellectual functioning characterized by an IQ score of 130 or above, showing that a child ranks in the top 2 percent of his age group.

includes achievement test scores, teachers' ratings, and parents' input—to determine whether a boy or girl needs special help (Sattler, 2001). If a child's low score (below 70) and other behaviors warrant this designation, she may be classified as **intellectually disabled**. If a child's IQ is far higher than would be expected, compared to her performance on achievement tests, she is classified with a **specific learning disorder**, an umbrella term for any impairment in language or difficulties related to listening (such as ADHD), thinking, speaking, reading, spelling, or math.

Although children with learning disabilities often score in the average range on IQ tests, they have trouble with schoolwork. Many times, they have a debilitating impairment called **dyslexia** that undercuts every academic skill. Dyslexia, a catchall term that refers to any reading disorder, may have multiple causes (see Table 7.5). What's important is that, despite having good instruction and doing well on tests of intelligence, a dyslexic child is struggling to read (Shaywitz, Morris, & Shaywitz, 2008).

My son, for instance, has dyslexia, and our experience shows just how important having a measure of general intelligence can be. Because Thomas was falling behind in the third grade, my husband and I arranged to have our son tested. Thomas was defined as having a learning disability because his IQ score was above average, but his achievement scores were well below the norm for his grade. Although we were aware of our son's reading problems, the testing was vital in easing our anxieties. Thomas—just as we thought—was capable intellectually. Now we just had to get our son through school with his sense of self-efficacy intact!

Often, teachers and parents urge testing for a happier reason: They want to confirm that a child is intellectually advanced. If the child's IQ exceeds a certain number (typically 130), she is labeled as **gifted** (see Figure 7.5) and is eligible for

FIGURE 7.5: The bell curve snapshot of the gifted As the bell curve illustrates, more than 2 out of 3 test takers have WISC scores clustering within 15 points of 100 (the 50th percentile). At an IQ of 130 or above, the child's score is gifted because that boy or girl performed at about the top 2 percent of all test takers that age.

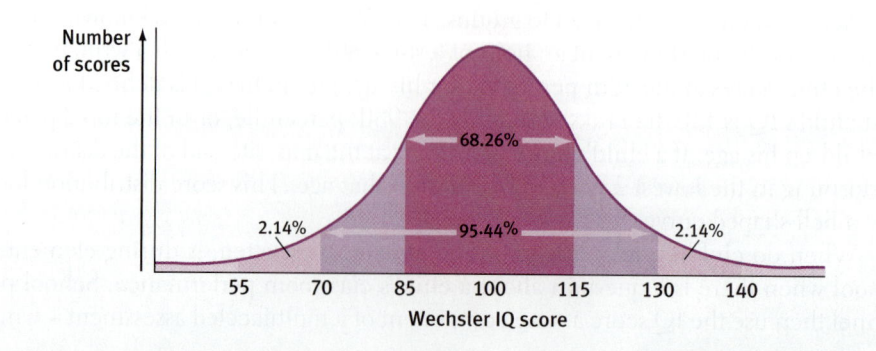

Table 7.5: Some Interesting Facts About Dyslexia

- Reading difficulties are shockingly prevalent among U.S. children. According to one survey, more than 1 in 4 high school seniors were reading below the most basic levels. The figures were higher for fourth graders—over 1 in 3 had trouble grasping the basic points of a passage designed for their grade.
- Specific learning disabilities (including dyslexia) are a mainly male diagnosis—affecting roughly 3 times as many boys as girls worldwide.
- Dyslexia is inherited and "genetic" in origin. However, the condition has several genetic variants, and, as I mentioned in the text, difficulty in learning to read can be due to different causes.
- Late-appearing language (entering the word-combining phase of speech at an older-than-typical age, such as close to age 2½ [see Chapter 3]) and especially phonemic deficits (the inability to differentiate sounds [see Chapter 5]) are early predictors of dyslexia.
- Dyslexia can sometimes be diagnosed in the preschool pre-reading years by combining behavioral tests with brain scans. At-risk children can even be identified during their first weeks after birth—by looking at the pattern of their brain waves evoked by different sounds.
- Although many boys and girls with dyslexia eventually learn to read, this condition persists to some extent into adulthood. Early interventions—involving intensive instruction in teaching at-risk kindergartners and first graders to identify phonemes—can be effective, but special help may be needed throughout elementary school.
- Children with dyslexia unfortunately perform more poorly on general tests of executive functions. They are at higher risk of developing other mental health problems, such as depression and anxiety disorders. About 15 to 50 percent also have ADHD.

Information from Beneventi and others, 2010; Gooch, Snowling, & Hulme, 2011; Henry, Messer, & Nash, 2012; Hensler and others, 2010; Kraft and others, 2016; Landerl & Moll, 2010; Leppänen and others, 2010; Panicker & Chelliah, 2016; Shao and others, 2016; Shaywitz and others, 2008.

reliability In measurement terminology, a basic criterion for a test's accuracy that scores must be fairly similar when a person takes the same test more than once.

validity In measurement terminology, a basic criterion for a test's accuracy involving whether that measure reflects the real-world quality it is supposed to measure.

special programs. In U.S. public schools, the law mandates intelligence testing before children can be assigned to a gifted program or remedial class (Canter, 1997; Sattler, 2001).

Table 7.5 offers a fact sheet about dyslexia. The Experiencing Childhood box on page 208 provides a firsthand view of what it is like to triumph over this debilitating condition. Now that we have explored the measure and when it is used, let's turn to what the scores mean.

Decoding the Meaning of the IQ Test

The first question we need to grapple with in looking at the meaning of the test relates to a measurement criterion called **reliability.** When people take a test that is thought to measure a basic trait (such as IQ) more than once, their results should not vary. Imagine that your IQ score randomly shifted from gifted to average, year by year. Clearly, this test score would not tell us anything about a stable attribute called intelligence.

The good news is that, by elementary school, IQ test performance does typically remain stable (Ryan, Glass, & Bartels, 2010). In one amazing study, people's scores remained fairly similar when they first took the test in childhood and then were retested more than a half-century later (see Deary and others, 2000). Still, among individual children, IQ can change. Scores are most likely to shift when children have undergone life stresses.

This research tells us that we should never evaluate a child's IQ during a family crisis such as divorce. But being reliable is only the first requirement. The test must be **valid.** This means it must predict what it is supposed to be measuring. Is the WISC a valid test?

When this second grader takes the WISC, her IQ is apt to be reliable, staying roughly the same at older ages, unless she undergoes severe stress. But what does this score mean? Stay tuned as I tackle this fascinating issue relating to validity, right below the Experiencing Childhood box on the next page!

> **Experiencing Childhood: From Dyslexic Child to College Professor Adult**
>
> Aimee Holt, a colleague of mine who teaches our school's psychology students, is beautiful and intelligent, the kind of golden girl you might imagine would have been a great childhood success. When I sat down to chat with Aimee about her struggles with dyslexia and other learning disabilities, I found first impressions can be very misleading.
>
> *In first grade, the teachers at school said I was mentally retarded. I didn't notice the sounds that went along with letters. I walked into walls and fell down a lot. My parents refused to put me in a special school and finally got me accepted at a private school, contingent on getting a good deal of help. I spent my elementary school years being tutored for an hour before school, an hour afterwards, and all summer.*
>
> *Socially, elementary school was a nightmare. . . . I remember kids laughing at me, calling me stupid. There was a small group of people that I was friendly with, but we were all misfits. One of my closest friends had an inoperable brain tumor. Because of my problems coordinating my vision with my motor skills, I couldn't participate in normal activities, such as sports or dance. By seventh grade, after years of working every day with my wonderful reading teacher, I was reading at almost grade level.*
>
> *Then when we moved to Tennessee in my freshman year of high school, I felt like a new person. Nobody knew that I had learning difficulties. We moved to a rural community, so I got to be a top student, because I'd had the same classes in my Dallas private school the year before. In the tenth and eleventh grades, I was making A's and B's. I got a scholarship to college, where I was a straight-A student (with a GPA of 3.9).*
>
> *My mom is the reason I've done well. She always believed in me, always felt I could make it; she never gave up. Plus, as I mentioned, I had an exceptional reading teacher. My goal was always to be an elementary school teacher, but, after teaching for years and realizing that a lot of the kids in my classes were not being accurately diagnosed, I decided to go to graduate school to get my Ph.D.*
>
> *Today, in addition to teaching, I do private tutoring with children like me. First, I get kids to identify word sounds (phonemes) because children with dyslexia have a problem decoding the specific sounds of words. I'll have the children identify how many sounds they hear in a word. . . .*
>
> *"Which sounds rhyme, which don't?" . . . "If I change the word from cat to hat, what sound changes?" Most children naturally pick up on these reading cues. Kids with dyslexia need to have these skills directly taught.*
>
> *Many children I tutor are in fourth or even sixth grade and have had years of feeling like a failure. They develop an attitude of "Why try? I'm going to fail anyway." I can tell them that I've been there and that they can succeed. So I work on academic self-efficacy—teaching them to put forth effort. Most of these kids are intelligent, but as they progress through school, their IQ drops because they are not being exposed to written material at their grade level. I try to get them to stay in the regular classroom, with modifications such as books on tape and oral testing, to prevent that false drop in their knowledge base. I was so fortunate—with a wonderful mother, an exceptional reading teacher, getting the help I needed at exactly the right time—that I feel my mission is to give something back.*

If our predictor is academic performance, the answer is yes. A child who gets an IQ score of 130 will tend to perform well in the gifted class. A child whose IQ is 80 will probably need remedial help. But now we turn to the controversial question: Does the test measure genetic learning potential or biological smarts?

Are the Tests a Good Measure of Genetic Gifts?

When evaluating children living in poverty (or boys and girls growing up in non-English-speaking families), logic tells us that the answer is *definitely* no. Look back at the items on the WISC verbal comprehension scale (Table 7.4 on page 206), and you will immediately see that if parents stimulate a child's vocabulary, she will be at a test-taking advantage. If, as I documented in Chapter 4, a family doesn't have the funds to buy preschoolers advanced learning toys, children will be handicapped on each part of the test.

Evidence that the environment weighs heavily in IQ comes from the fascinating fact that over the past century, IQ test scores have risen dramatically around the world (see Chapter 1)—a phenomenon called the **Flynn effect** (named for its discoverer James Flynn). More years of education have made twenty-first-century children and

Flynn effect Remarkable rise in overall performance on IQ tests that has been occurring around the world over the past century.

adults far better abstract thinkers than their parents and grandparents were at the same age (Must, Must, & Mikk, 2016). Incredibly, Flynn (2007) calculates that the average-scoring child taking the WISC in 1900 would rank as "mentally deficient" using today's IQ norms!

We now have compelling research showing that being poor *itself* artificially depresses test scores. For low-income children, the IQ score mainly reflects environmental forces. For upper-middle-class children, the test score is reflective of genetic gifts (Turkheimer and others, 2003). So if an elementary schooler comes from a poverty-level family and attends a low-quality school, then yes, his IQ predicts his current school performance. But that score can't reflect *true intellectual potential* unless the child has been exposed to the incredible learning advantages upper-middle-class life provides.

Now, imagine that you are an upper-middle-class child. You were regularly read to, visited museums, and attended the best schools. Your IQ score is only 95 or 100. Is your intellectual potential limited for life?

Do IQ Scores Predict Real-World Performance?

One student who approached me after this class lecture and proudly admitted that his IQ was 140 was not thinking of school learning. He assumed that his score measured a basic "smartness" that carried over to every life activity. In measurement terminology, this student would agree with Charles Spearman. Spearman believed that IQ test scores reflect a general underlying, all-encompassing intelligence factor called **g**.

Psychologists debate the existence of g. Many strongly believe that the IQ test *generally* predicts intellectual capacities. They argue that we can use the IQ as a summary measure of a person's cognitive potential for all life tasks (Herrnstein & Murray, 1994; Rushton & Jensen, 2005). Others believe that people have unique intellectual talents. There is no one-dimensional quality called g (Eisner, 2004; Schlinger, 2003; Sternberg, 2007). These critics believe it is inappropriate to rank people on a continuum from highly intelligent to not very smart (Gould, 1981; Sternberg, Grigorenko, & Kidd, 2005).

Tantalizing evidence for g lies in the fact that people differ in the speed with which they process information (Brody, 2006; Rushton & Jensen, 2005). Intelligence test scores also correlate with various indicators of life success, such as occupational status. However, the problem is that the gateway to high-status professions, such as law and medicine, is school performance, which is what the tests predict (Sternberg, 1997; Sternberg, Grigorenko, & Bundy, 2001).

One problem with believing that IQ tests offer a *total* X-ray into intellectual capacities is that people may carry around their test-score ranking as an inner wound. A psychologist supervisor once confessed to me that he was really not that intelligent because his IQ was only 105. He devalued the criterion his IQ was supposed to predict—his years of real-life success—by accepting what, in his case, was an invalid score!

A high test score can produce its own problems. Suppose the student who told me his IQ was 140 decided he was so intelligent he didn't have to open a book in my class. He might be in for a nasty surprise when he found out that what *really* matters is your ability to work. Or that student might worry, "I'd better not try in Dr. Belsky's class because, if I do put forth effort and *don't* get an A, I will discover that my astronomical IQ score was wrong." (As I suggested in Chapter 6, this type of interpretation isn't rare; as studies show that telling elementary schoolers they "are basically smart" makes them afraid to tackle challenging academic tasks.)

Even the firmest advocate of g would admit that people have specific intellectual talents. Some of us are marvelous mechanically yet miserable at math, wonderful socially but hopeless at taking tests.

> **g** Charles Spearman's term for a general intelligence factor that he claimed underlies all cognitive activities.

Toward a Broader View of Intelligence

Because real-world intelligence involves such different abilities, perhaps we should go beyond the skills the IQ test measures and explore those talents in a truly broad way. Psychologists Robert Sternberg and Howard Gardner have devoted their careers to offering this broader view of what it means to be smart.

Sternberg's Successful Intelligence

Robert Sternberg (1984, 1996, 1997) has been a man on a mission. In hundreds of publications, this psychologist transformed the way we think about intelligence. Sternberg's passion comes from the heart. He began school with a problem himself:

> As an elementary school student, I failed miserably on the IQ tests. . . . Just the sight of the school psychologist coming into the classroom to give . . . an IQ test sent me into a wild panic attack. . . . You don't need to be a genius to figure out what happens next. My teachers in the elementary school grades certainly didn't expect much from me. . . . So I gave them what they expected. . . . Were the teachers disappointed? Not on your life. They were happy that I was giving them what they expected.
>
> (Sternberg, 1997, pp. 17–18)

Sternberg believes that traditional intelligence tests do damage in school. As I implied earlier, the relationship between IQ scores and schooling is somewhat bidirectional. Children who attend inferior schools or who miss months of classroom work due to illness perform more poorly on intelligence tests (Sternberg, 1997). Worse yet, Sternberg argues, when schools assign children to lower-track, less demanding classes based on their low test scores, the students' IQs gradually decline year by year.

Most importantly, Sternberg (1984) believes that conventional intelligence tests are too limited. Although they do measure one type of intelligence, they do not cover the whole terrain.

IQ tests, according to Sternberg, measure **analytic intelligence.** They test how well people can solve academic problems. They do not measure **creative intelligence,** the ability to "think outside the box" or to formulate problems in new ways. Nor do they measure a third type of intelligence called **practical intelligence,** common sense, or "street smarts."

Brazilian street children who make their living selling flowers show impressive levels of practical intelligence. They understand how to handle money in the real world. However, they do very poorly on measures of traditional IQ (Sternberg, 1984, 1997). Others, such as Winston Churchill, can be terrible scholars but flower after they leave their academic careers. Then there are people who excel at IQ test taking and traditional schooling but fail abysmally in the real world. Sternberg argues that to be **successfully intelligent** in life requires a balance of all three types of intelligence. (As a postscript, Sternberg later added a fourth type of intellectual gift—that rare attribute called *wisdom*; see Sternberg, 2010.)

---

analytic intelligence In Robert Sternberg's framework on successful intelligence, the facet of intelligence involved in performing well on academic problems.

creative intelligence In Robert Sternberg's framework on successful intelligence, the facet of intelligence involved in producing novel ideas or innovative work.

practical intelligence In Robert Sternberg's framework on successful intelligence, the facet of intelligence involved in knowing how to act competently in real-world situations.

successful intelligence In Robert Sternberg's framework, the optimal form of cognition, which involves striking the right balance of analytic, creative, and practical intelligence.

Being a math whiz (*analytic intelligence*) demands different skills from deftly snagging this fish (*practical intelligence*). That's why Robert Sternberg believes that IQ tests, which mainly measure school-type analytic skills, do not tap into many of the abilities that make people successful in the real world.

Gardner's Multiple Intelligences

Howard Gardner (1998) did not have Sternberg's problem with intelligence tests:

> As a child, I was a good student and a good test taker . . . but . . . music . . . and the arts were important parts of my life. Therefore, when I asked myself what optimal human development is, I became more convinced that [we] had to . . . broaden the definition of intelligence to include these activities, too.
>
> (Gardner, 1998, p. 3)

Gardner is not passionately opposed to standard intelligence tests. Still, he believes that using the single IQ score is less informative than measuring children's unique gifts. (Gardner's motto is: "Ask not how *intelligent* you are, but *how* are you intelligent?") According to his **multiple intelligences theory**, human abilities come in eight, and possibly nine, distinctive forms (Gardner, 2004; Gardner & Moran, 2006).

In addition to the verbal and mathematical skills measured by traditional IQ tests, people may be gifted in *interpersonal intelligence*, or understanding other people. Their talents may lie in *intrapersonal intelligence*, the skill of understanding oneself. They may be gifted in *spatial intelligence*, grasping where objects are arranged in space. (You might rely on a friend who is gifted in spatial intelligence to beautifully arrange the furniture in your house.) Some people have high levels of *musical intelligence, kinesthetic intelligence* (the ability to use the body well), or *naturalist intelligence* (a gift for dealing with animals or plants and trees). There may even be an *existential (spiritual) intelligence*, too.

Evaluating the Theories

These perspectives on intelligence are exciting. Some readers may be thinking, "I'm gifted in practical or musical intelligence. I knew there was more to being smart than school success!" But let's use our practical intelligence to critique these approaches. Why did Gardner select these particular eight abilities and not others (Barnett, Ceci, & Williams, 2006; White, 2006)? Yes, parents may marvel at a 6-year-old's creative or kinesthetic intelligence, but it is analytic intelligence that will get this child into the school gifted program, not his artistic productions or how well his body moves (Eisner, 2004).

We can also criticize Sternberg's ideas. Is there a creative or practical intelligence apart from a particular field? Adopting the idea that there is a single "creative" intelligence might lead to the conclusion that Michelangelo would be a talented musician or that Mozart could beautifully paint the Sistine Chapel.

The bottom line is that neither Gardner nor Sternberg has developed replacements for our current IQ test. But this does not matter. Their mission is to transform the way schools teach (Gardner & Moran, 2006; Sternberg, 2010).

INTERVENTIONS: Lessons for Schools

Gardner's theory has been embraced by teachers who understand that intelligence involves more than traditional academic skills. However, to implement his ideas requires revolutionizing the way we structure education. Therefore, the main use of multiple intelligences theory has been in helping "nontraditional learners" succeed (Schirduan & Case, 2004). Here is how Mark, a dyslexic teenager, describes his use of spatial intelligence to cope with the maze of facts in history:

> I'll picture things; for example, if we are studying the French revolution . . . Louis the 16th . . . I'll have a picture of him in my mind [and I'll visualize] the castle and peasants to help me learn.
>
> (quoted in Schirduan & Case, 2004, p. 93)

Being a world-class gymnast (*kinesthetic intelligence*) doesn't necessarily mean that you will also shine in reading or math. That's why Howard Gardner believes that schools need to broaden their focus to teach to the different kinds of intelligences that we all possess.

multiple intelligences theory In Howard Gardner's perspective on intelligence, the principle that there are eight separate kinds of intelligence—verbal, mathematical, interpersonal, intrapersonal, spatial, musical, kinesthetic, naturalist—plus a possible ninth type, called spiritual intelligence.

Sternberg, being an experimentalist, has put his theory through rigorous tests. Does instruction tailored to each type of intelligence produce better achievement than teaching in the traditional way? Unfortunately, when Sternberg's research team carried out a massive intervention trial—assigning 7,702 fourth graders in 223 classrooms to either be taught according to his theory or using several typical approaches—the outcome was inconsistent (Sternberg and others, 2014). So, while the concept of successful intelligence is intuitively appealing, it's not clear that Sternberg's ideas merit changing the way classrooms operate. How *do* classrooms operate?

Classroom Learning

The diversity of intelligences, cultures, and educational experiences at home is matched by the diversity of American schools. There are small rural schools and large urban schools, public and private schools, traditional schools where students wear uniforms and schools that teach according to Gardner's intelligences. There are single-sex schools, charter schools, religious schools, magnet schools that cater to gifted students, and alternative schools for children with behavior problems or learning disabilities.

Can students thrive in every school? The answer is yes, provided schools have an intense commitment to student learning and teachers can excite students to learn. The rest of this chapter focuses on these challenges.

Examining Successful Schools

What qualities make a school successful? Insights come from surveying public elementary schools that are beating the odds. These schools, while serving high fractions of economically disadvantaged children, have students who are thriving.

In the Vista School, located on a Native American reservation, virtually all the children are eligible for a free lunch. However, Vista consistently boasts dramatic improvements on statewide reading and math tests. According to Ms. Thompson, the principal, "Our job is not to make excuses for students, but just to give them every possible opportunity. At Vista, teachers refuse to dumb down the curriculum. We offer tons of high-level conceptual work" (quoted in Borko and others, 2003, p. 177).

At Beacon Elementary School, in Washington State, 2 out of every 3 students exceed state-mandated writing standards despite coming from impoverished backgrounds. Here, Susie Murphy, the principal, comments: "You can . . . say, these kids are poor. You just need to love them. Or you can [say] . . . the best way to love them is to give them an education so they can make choices in their life" (quoted in Borko and others, 2003, p. 186). Beacon teachers, she continues, "are here . . . by choice. They are committed to proving that kids who live in poverty can learn every bit as well as other kids" (p. 192). At Beacon, the teachers' goal is to challenge all their students.

In addition to attending a well-maintained school, having a genuinely inclusive mix of students is another defining feature of schools that "beat the odds."

The school builds in opportunities for teachers to share ideas: "We have mini-workshops in geometry, or problem solving. Our whole staff talks about the general focus and where math is going" (p. 194).

Committed teachers, professional collaboration, and a mission to "deliver for *all* our kids" explains why a rural Florida elementary school, serving mainly low-income children, boosted the test scores of its most struggling students in a single year. Rather than isolating boys and girls with "learning differences," this school embedded every child into academic life. Before instituting their focus on inclusiveness, only 1 in 3 at-risk children ranked as proficient in math and language arts. At the year's end, these rates shot upward—to roughly 2 in 3 students.

As Ms. Richards, the principal, explained: "We've got to . . . meet all [kids'] needs. . . . That's how we started . . . to make . . . everyone successful." A special education teacher named Ms. Wood summed up this school's teaching strategy best when she said, "We have ongoing conversations about challenging students . . . at our school . . . the meat of the curriculum is presented to everyone" (adapted from McLeskey, Waldron, & Redd, 2014, p. 63).

To summarize, successful schools set high standards. Teachers believe that every child can benefit from challenging, conceptual work. These schools excel in collective efficacy, reaching out to nurture each member of the teaching community. In Baumrind's parenting-styles framework, these schools are authoritative in their approach.

Now that we have the outlines for what is effective, let's tackle the challenge every teacher faces: getting students eager to learn.

Producing Eager Learners

But to go to school in a summer morn,

O! it drives all joy away;

Under a cruel eye outworn,

The little ones spend the day

In sighing and dismay.

—William Blake, from "The Schoolboy" (1794)

Jean Piaget believed that the hunger to learn is more important than food or drink. Why, then, do children over the centuries lament, "I hate school"? The reason is that learning loses its joy when it becomes a requirement instead of an activity we choose to engage in for ourselves.

The Problem: An Erosion of Intrinsic Motivation

Developmentalists divide motivation into two categories. **Intrinsic motivation** refers to self-generated actions, those that arise from our inner desires. When Piaget described our hunger to learn, he was referring to intrinsic motivation. **Extrinsic motivation** refers to activities that we undertake in order to get external reinforcers, such as praise or pay or a good grade.

Unfortunately, the learning activity you are currently engaged in falls into the extrinsic category. You know you will be tested on what you are reading. Worse yet, if you pick up this book for an intrinsic reason—because you wanted to learn about child development—the fact that you might be graded would likely cause your basic interest to fade.

Numerous studies show that when adults give external reinforcers for activities that are intrinsically motivating, children are less likely to want to perform those activities for themselves (Patall, Cooper, & Robinson, 2008; Stipek, 1996). In one classic example, researchers selected preschoolers who were intrinsically interested in art. When they gave a "good player" award (an outside reinforcer) for the art projects, the children later showed a dramatic decline in their interest in doing art for fun (Lepper, Greene, & Nisbett, 1973). This research makes sense of the question you may have wondered about: "Why, after taking that literature class, am I less interested in reading on my own?"

Young children enter kindergarten brimming with intrinsic motivation. When does this love affair with school turn sour? Think back to your childhood, and you will realize that enchantment wanes during early elementary school, when teachers provide those external reinforcers—grades (Stipek, 1997). Moreover, during first or second grade, classroom learning often becomes abstract and removed from life. Rote activities, like filling in worksheets and memorizing multiplication tables, have replaced the creative hands-on projects of kindergarten. So ironically, school may be

intrinsic motivation The drive to act based on the pleasure of taking that action in itself, not for an external reinforcer or reward.

extrinsic motivation The drive to take an action because that activity offers external reinforcers such as praise, money, or a good grade.

Compare the activities of this kindergarten class of little scientists with rote learning and grades, and you will immediately understand why by about age 8, many children begin to say, "I hate school."

the very setting where Piaget's little-scientist activities are *least* likely to occur.

Then, as children enter concrete operations—at around age 8—and begin comparing their performance to that of their peers, this competitive orientation further erodes intrinsic motivation (Dweck, 1986; Self-Brown & Mathews, 2003). The focus shifts from "I want to improve for myself" to "I want to do *better* than my friends."

In sum, several forces explain why many children dislike school. School involves extrinsic reinforcers (grades). School learning, because it often involves rote memorization, is not intrinsically interesting. In school, children cannot set their own learning goals. Their performance is judged by how they measure up to the rest of the class.

Therefore, it is no wonder that studies in Western nations document an alarming decline in intrinsic motivation as children travel through school (Katz, Kaplan, & Gueta, 2010; Spinath & Steinmayr, 2008). Susan Harter (1981) asked children to choose between two statements: "Some kids work really hard to get good grades" (referring to extrinsic motivation) or "Some kids work really hard because they like to learn new things" (measuring intrinsic motives). When she gave these alternatives to hundreds of California public school children, intrinsic motivation declined from third to ninth grade.

Still, external reinforcers can be vital hooks that get us intrinsically involved. Have you ever reluctantly taken a required class (perhaps even this course in child development) and found yourself captivated by the subject? Given that extrinsically motivating activities are basic to school and life, how can we make them work best?

The Solution: Making Extrinsic Learning Part of Us

To answer this question, Edward Deci and Richard Ryan (1985, 2000) make the point that we engage in some types of extrinsic learning unwillingly: "I have to take that terrible anatomy course because it is a requirement for graduation." We enthusiastically embrace other extrinsic tasks, which may not be inherently interesting, because we identify with their larger goal: "I want to memorize every bone of the body because that information is vital to my nursing career." In the first situation, the learning activity is irrelevant. In the second, the task has become intrinsic because it is connected to our inner self. Therefore, the key to transforming school learning from a chore into a pleasure is to make extrinsic learning relate to children's goals and desires.

The most boring tasks take on an intrinsic aura when they speak to children's passions. Imagine, for instance, how a first grader's motivation to sound out words might change if a teacher, knowing that student was captivated by dinosaurs, gave that boy the job of sounding out dinosaur names. Deci and Ryan believe that learning becomes intrinsic when it satisfies our basic need for relatedness (attachment). Finally, extrinsic tasks take on an intrinsic feeling when they foster autonomy, or offer us choices about how to do our work (Patall, Cooper, & Robinson, 2008; Ryan and others, 2006).

Studies around the globe suggest that when teachers and parents take away children's autonomy—by controlling, criticizing, or micromanaging learning tasks—they erode intrinsic motivation (see Jang, Reeve, & Deci, 2010; Soenens & Vansteenkiste, 2010). We can see this principle in our own lives. By continually denigrating our work, or hovering over every move, a controlling supervisor has the uncanny ability to turn us off to the most intrinsically interesting job.

Our need for autonomy explains why, as I suggested in the section on successful schools, assigning high-level conceptual learning tasks can be effective with every child. Conversely, the poisonous effects of taking away autonomy suggests why the U.S. practice of forcing teachers to follow a rigid set of learning requirements erodes satisfaction in this field ("I can't teach the way I want. I have to teach to the end-of-year tests, or I'll get fired").

But in a national experiment, when certain school districts gave staff the chance to *choose* between several new programs and provided *clear data* about their effectiveness, teachers did willingly embrace these options—and, after 4 years, students made impressive gains on standard reading tests (Slavin and others, 2013). Therefore, providing autonomy (giving choices) and fostering relevance (pointing out the importance of an activity to that person's goals) benefits *both* students and teachers!

Table 7.6 summarizes these messages for teachers: Focus on relevance, enhance relatedness, and provide autonomy. The table also pulls together other teaching tips based on Gardner's and Sternberg's perspectives on intelligence, our look at what makes schools successful, and research that shows how emphasizing collaborative learning can mute the uptick in bullying described in Chapter 6 (Choi, Johnson, & Johnson, 2011). Now let's conclude by tackling that interesting question: Can an exceptional elementary school teacher change students' lives?

Table 7.6: Lessons for Teachers: A Recap of This Chapter's Insights

Parenting Questions

1. **Foster relevance.** For instance, in teaching reading, tailor the assigned books to fit the children's passions. And entice students to learn to read in other ways, such as energizing first and second graders by telling them they will be able to break a code used all over the world, just like a detective!
2. **Foster relatedness.** Develop a secure, loving attachment with every student. Continually tell each child how proud you are when that boy or girl tries hard or succeeds.
3. **Foster autonomy.** As much as possible, allow your students to select among several equivalent assignments (such as choosing which specific books to read). Don't give time limits, such as "It's 9:30 and this has to be done by 10:00," and don't hover, take over tasks, or make negative comments. Stand by to provide information and careful scaffolding (see Chapter 5) when students ask. Build in assignments that allow high-level thinking, such as writing essays instead of rote work such as copying sentences or filling out worksheets.

Teaching Tips Based on Gardner's and Sternberg's Theories

1. Offer balanced assignments that capitalize on students' different kinds of intelligence—creative work such as essays; practical-intelligence activities such as calculating numbers to make change at a store; single-answer analytic tasks (using Sternberg's framework); and classroom time devoted to music, dance, art, and caring for plants (capitalizing on Gardner's ideas).
2. Explicitly teach students to use their different intelligences in mastering classroom work.

Additional Teaching Tips

1. Don't rely on IQ test scores in assessing the abilities of low-income and ethnic-minority students; this number says little about children's true academic potential.
2. Avoid praising children for being "brilliant." Compliment them for hard work.
3. Go beyond academics to teach children interpersonal skills.
4. Strive for excellence. Expect all students to succeed.
5. Foster collaborative work. Grade competition is not only tailor-made to reduce intrinsic motivation, but it may also be a reason why relational aggression becomes rampant in later elementary school.
6. Minimize students' tendency to make grade-oriented comparisons (such as who got A's, B's, C's, and so on) by continually emphasizing that what matters is personal improvement.

Think back to your favorite teacher. Perhaps it was the talented woman who transformed a hated math class into a magical journey, or a middle-school teacher who believed in your gifts, even though you were struggling in class. You always felt this person made an enduring difference in your life. Now scientific data shows you were right!

In meticulous studies, economist Raz Chetty and his colleagues (Chetty, Friedman, & Rockoff, 2014) tracked the performance of two million students enrolled in an urban elementary school district as the children traveled into their twenties.

The researchers identified what they called *value-added teachers*—educators whose students showed elevated bumps on end-of-year state tests, compared to the typical teacher a child would have in that grade. The economists were amazed to find that students who were taught by a value-added teacher for *one year* were more likely to attend college and less prone to have babies as teens. They earned more money than their classmates during emerging adulthood, too. Based on tax data at age 28, the researchers calculated that each student's boost in lifetime earnings as a result of having this exceptional teacher for a *single year* was roughly $40,000.

We talk about good educators being worth their weight in gold. This study shows that cliché is literally true. According to Chetty's calculations, a single value-added teacher can boost an entire class's lifetime earnings by over half a million dollars!

This beloved public school teacher may do far more than simply boost her students' scores on end-of-year achievement tests. She could help propel these third graders into a middle-class life.

Hot in Developmental Science: Communities Matter in Children's Success

Throughout this chapter—from discussing the power of peers to living in neighborhoods high in collective efficacy to attending high-quality schools—I've been making the case that where children grow up makes a difference in their lives. Again, Raz Chetty's landmark research brings that message home.

Chetty's research team (Chetty & Hendren, 2017) calculated the odds of upward mobility—that is, rising in social status—for children growing up in *every county* in the United States. Even given equal family income, living in a "better community" made it more likely for poor children to make it into the middle class.

What is a "better community"? One answer comes as no surprise: Communities that promote upward mobility have less concentrated poverty, more high-ranked schools, a higher percentage of two-parent families, and less crime. But these places also stand out as special in far less obvious ways. In counties fostering upward mobility, income inequality is less dramatic—that is, there isn't such a huge gap between rich and poor. Moreover, in these communities, poor children's economic strides don't come at the expense of their relatively affluent peers. In upwardly mobile counties, Chetty's calculations showed, children whose families ranked at the 75th percentile of the income distribution rose in social status (though not as much).

Does decent housing cost more in these communities? Not necessarily. For instance, at that time in the New York City area, the researchers found that children being raised in Hudson County, New Jersey, had far higher rates of upward mobility than their age-mates in the New York City boroughs of Queens or the Bronx, even though the median rents in these areas were roughly the same.

Does moving to a better area during early childhood matter most? Here, the answer is yes. In fact, if families relocate to an upwardly mobile community when their children are young, and remain through high school, their sons and daughters benefit greatly. Twenty years spent in DuPage County, Illinois (ranked highest in upward mobility), versus low-ranked Baltimore, Maryland, statistically increased a given poverty-level child's annual income by one-third. Moreover, the researchers found that staying in deprived low-mobility communities was especially toxic for boys.

I believe the message here is that the U.S. mantra that, given sufficient industry, every poor child can succeed is incorrect. Having an efficacy-promoting *environment* is critically important in allowing talented, disadvantaged children to construct a middle-class life. And rather than retreating to isolated, gated communities, affluent parents might want to pay attention to this research, too. Healthy communities thrive on economic diversity. Income inequalities hinder everyone—both the rich and the poor.

In Chapter 9, I will vividly demonstrate exactly why low-efficacy communities—neighborhoods blighted by concentrated poverty—are so toxic for boys when I discuss teenage gangs. Then, in Chapter 10, I'll explore how the rise in income inequalities may be limiting the life chances of this cohort of U.S. emerging adults.

Tying It All Together

1. If Devin, from an upper-middle-class family, and Adam, from a low-income family, are starting kindergarten, predict which statement is most accurate:
   a. Both children will perform equally well on school readiness tests, but Adam will fall behind because he is likely to attend a poor-quality kindergarten.
   b. Devin will outperform Adam on school readiness tests, and the gap will probably widen because Adam will attend a poor-quality kindergarten.

2. Malik hasn't been doing well in school, and his achievement test scores have consistently been well below average for his grade. On the WISC, Malik gets an IQ score of 115. What is your conclusion?

3. You are telling a friend about the deficiencies of relying on a child's IQ score. Pick *two* arguments you might make.
   a. The tests are not reliable; children's scores typically change a lot during the elementary school years.
   b. The tests are not valid predictors of school performance.
   c. As people have different abilities, a single IQ score may not tell us much about a child's unique gifts.
   d. As poor children are at a disadvantage in taking the test, you should not use the IQ scores as an index of "genetic school-related talents" for low-income children.

4. Josh doesn't do well in reading or math, but he excels in music and dance, and he gets along with all kinds of children. According to Sternberg's theory of successful intelligence, Josh is not good in _____, but he is skilled in _____ and _____. According to Gardner's theory of _____, Josh is strong in which intelligences?

5. A school principal asks for tips to help her students with learning difficulties. Based on this section, you should advise (pick one): *making the material simple/putting these children together in a special class/providing high-level creative work and embedding these children in the life of the school.*

6. (a) Define intrinsic and extrinsic motivation. (b) Give an example of a task in your life right now being driven by each kind of motivation. (c) Based on your reading, can you come up with ways to make these unpleasant extrinsic tasks feel more intrinsic?

7. Your friend wants to move out of her dangerous Chicago neighborhood. But she is afraid that if she relocates to an economically diverse section of the city, her daughter will be classified as "the poor kid in the neighborhood," and be rejected by her classmates. Based on Chetty's research, what should you advise?

Answers to the Tying It All Together questions can be found at the end of this chapter.

SUMMARY

Home

Families vary, from never-divorced two-parent couples to blended families, from gay-parent families to unmarried couples or grandparents raising a child. The main distinction is that mother-headed families are far more likely to live in poverty than their two-parent counterparts. Today, developed-world children are growing up in the first genuinely global village. Children can thrive in any kind of family, depending on the care parents provide.

According to Diana Baumrind's **parenting styles** approach, based on setting rules and nurturing, parents are classified as **authoritative, authoritarian, permissive,** or **rejecting-neglecting.** Although child-rearing approaches do vary in families, with at-risk children evoking poorer parenting, even Asian-heritage families, while often seen as authoritarian, also adopt a child-centered authoritative style. Today, being authoritarian, while necessary in dangerous environments, is a symptom of parenting distress.

Resilient children, boys and girls who do well in the face of traumatic life experiences, tend to have good executive functions; possess special talents; have one close, secure attachment; and are not faced with an overload of life blows. For immigrant children facing **acculturation,** it's important to have a welcoming community. A specific genetic profile may offer some remarkable survivor children resilience in the face of stress.

Behavioral-genetic researchers argue that children grow up to fulfill their genetic destiny, and adequate parenting is all that is necessary. Judith Harris believes that peer groups—not parents—are the main socializers in children's lives. Evidence for Harris's theory comes from the fact that in communities high in **collective efficacy,** both children and parents thrive. Exceptional parenting, however, is crucial when children are biologically and socially at risk. Parents need to be flexible, tailoring their childrearing to the environment and to their children's needs. They should also relax and enjoy these fleeting years.

Attitudes about **corporal punishment** have changed dramatically, with many nations now outlawing spanking. The United States is an outlier because, although spanking is not preferred, many U.S. parents do occasionally use this discipline. Hundreds of studies show corporal punishment is detrimental to children's well-being.

Child maltreatment—physical abuse, neglect, emotional abuse, or sexual abuse—can sometimes be hard to classify. Maltreatment statistics differ, depending on whether we ask adults to reflect on their childhoods or consider observers' reports. Parents' personality problems, severe life stress, low community support, and having an at-risk child are the main factors that can provoke abuse. Abused children often have problems that can persist into adult life. Although teachers and health-care professionals are required to report suspected abuse, it is difficult for people to speak up, and authorities often do not follow through on reports. So, unfortunately, the prevalence of reported child abuse underestimates the magnitude of this problem today.

Children of divorce are at risk for negative life outcomes, but most boys and girls adapt well to this common childhood event. Parents feel guilty when they divorce, and struggle not to bad-mouth an ex-spouse. Keys to making divorce less traumatic lie in minimizing **parental alienation,** giving children some say in custody arrangements, and promoting high-quality parenting. Shared custody is a common arrangement today, but it works well only if both partners are good parents.

School

Many children from low-income families enter kindergarten well behind their affluent counterparts in basic academic skills. These inequalities at the starting gate are magnified by the fact that poor children are likely to attend the poorest-quality kindergartens.

Achievement tests measure a child's knowledge. **Intelligence quotient (IQ)** tests measure a child's basic potential to succeed at school. The **Wechsler Intelligence Scale for Children (WISC)** the main childhood IQ test, has specific parts, and is given individually to a child. If the IQ score is below 70—and if other indicators warrant this designation—a child may be labeled as **intellectually disabled.** If the child's score is much higher than his performance on achievement tests, he is classified as having a **specific learning disorder** such as **dyslexia.** If a child's IQ score is at or above 130, she is considered **gifted** and is eligible to be placed in an accelerated class.

IQ scores satisfy the measurement criterion called **reliability,** meaning that people tend to get roughly the same score if they take the test more than once. However, stressful life experiences can artificially lower a child's score. The test is also **valid** if our benchmark is predicting school performance. Some psychologists believe that the test score reflects a single quality called **g** that predicts success in every area of life; others feel that intelligence involves multiple abilities and that it is inappropriate to rank people as intelligent or not based on a single IQ score. The remarkable **Flynn effect** (an increase in test performance over the last century due to improved environments) suggests that, for disadvantaged children, the IQ score does not accurately reflect a person's genetic gifts.

Robert Sternberg and Howard Gardner argue that we need to expand our measures of intelligence beyond traditional tests. Sternberg believes that there are three types of intelligence: **analytic intelligence** (academic abilities), **creative intelligence,** and **practical intelligence** (real-world abilities, or "street smarts"). **Successful intelligence** requires having a good balance among these three skills. Gardner, in his **multiple intelligences theory,** describes eight (or possibly nine) types of intelligences. Although neither of these psychologists has developed alternatives to conventional IQ tests, their ideas can lead to rethinking the way we teach.

Schools that serve disadvantaged students who flower academically share a mission to have every child succeed. They provide a challenging academic environment and assume that each student can do well at high-level work. Teachers support and mentor one another at these high collective-efficacy schools.

Why do many children dislike school? The reason is that classroom learning is based on **extrinsic motivation** (external reinforcers such as grades), which impairs **intrinsic motivation** (the desire to learn for the sake of learning). School learning is inherently less interesting because it often involves rote memorization. Being evaluated in comparison to the class also limits a child's interest in learning for learning's sake. Studies show a disturbing decline in intrinsic motivation as children progress through elementary school.

Teachers (and parents) can make extrinsic learning tasks more intrinsic by offering class material relevant to children's interests, fostering relatedness (or a close attachment), and giving students choices about how to do their work. Stimulating intrinsic motivation by offering more autonomy (providing choices) helps motivate teachers to adopt new effective teaching strategies. Rigorous statistical studies confirm that good teachers make an enduring difference in students' lives. Studies tracking upward mobility in every U.S. county show that the child's community matters, too. Being raised in an economically diverse community, with less income inequalities, benefits disadvantaged children and their relatively affluent counterparts.

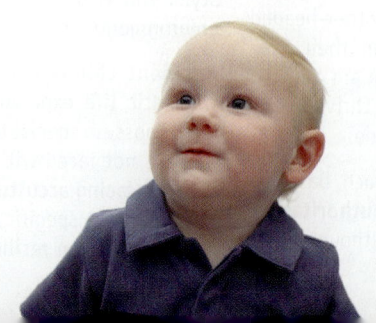

KEY TERMS

acculturation, p. 196
achievement tests, p. 205
analytic intelligence, p. 210
authoritarian parents, p. 193
authoritative parents, p. 193
child maltreatment, p. 200
collective efficacy, p. 197
corporal punishment, p. 198
creative intelligence, p. 210
dyslexia, p. 206
extrinsic motivation, p. 213
Flynn effect, p. 208
g, p. 209
gifted, p. 206
intellectual disability, p. 206
intelligence quotient (IQ), p. 205
intrinsic motivation, p. 213
multiple intelligences theory, p. 211
parental alienation, p. 202
parenting style, p. 193
permissive parents, p. 193
practical intelligence, p. 210
rejecting-neglecting parents, p. 193
reliability, p. 207
resilient children, p. 196
specific learning disorder, p. 206
successful intelligence, p. 210
validity, p. 207
WISC (Wechsler Intelligence Scale for Children), p. 205

ANSWERS TO Tying It All Together QUIZZES

Home

1. Montana's parents = authoritative. Pablo's parents = authoritarian. Sara's parents = permissive.
2. Ahmid is more apt to be resilient if he has good social and intellectual skills, an optimistic worldview, at least one close secure attachment, and the right genetic profile. The goal of your community should be to go out of your way to warmly welcome this child and his family.
3. Judith Harris's advice: Get your son in the best possible peer group. This chapter's recommendation: Provide exceptionally sensitive parenting.
4. a and c
5. Ms. Johnson might feel torn about reporting her observations because she is worried about making false accusations. Even if she does make a report, there is a good chance authorities will not investigate the situation.
6. The main criterion for awarding joint custody—or unlimited visits—should be whether the father is a good parent.

School

1. b
2. Malik has a learning disability.
3. c and d
4. Analytic intelligence; creative intelligence and practical intelligence; multiple intelligences; Josh's strengths are in musical, kinesthetic, and interpersonal intelligence.
5. You should advise giving these children high-level creative work and embed them in the life of the school.
6. (a) Intrinsic motivation is self-generated—we work at something simply because it gives us joy. Extrinsic motivation refers to activities propelled by external reinforcers like grades. (b) Ask yourself: Am I doing this because I love it or only because this activity results in an external reward? (c) 1. Make disliked, extrinsic tasks relevant to a larger personal goal. ("Cleaning the house will help me become a more organized person. Plus, it's great exercise, so I'll become healthier.") 2. Increase your sense of autonomy or feeling of having choices around this activity. ("I'll do my housecleaning at the time of day that feels least burdensome while I listen to my favorite CD.") 3. Enhance attachments. ("If my significant other comes home to a clean house, she'll feel wonderful!")
7. Go for it!

CONNECT ONLINE:

LaunchPad macmillan learning | Check out our videos and additional resources located at: www.macmillanlearning.com

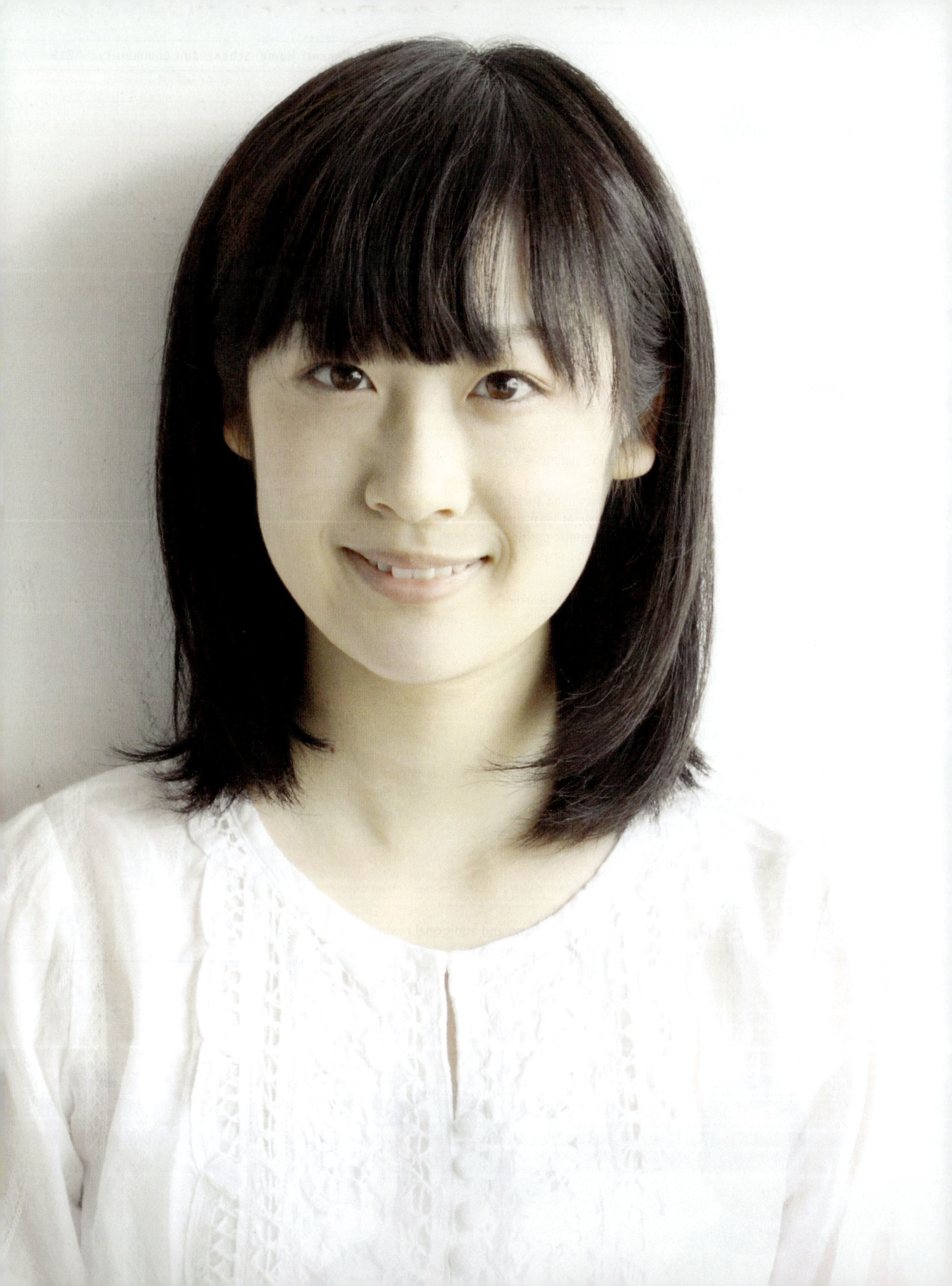

Adolescence

PART IV

This two-chapter part devoted to adolescence progresses somewhat chronologically from puberty through the late teens.

Chapter 8—**Physical Development in Adolescents** covers puberty, that early teenage total body change. It also focuses on two other body-oriented topics: body image (and eating disorders) and adolescent sexuality.

Chapter 9—**Cognitive, Emotional, and Social Development in Adolescents** examines teenage minds and relationships. How do adolescents reason? Are teenagers more socially sensitive or emotionally disturbed than adults? What can parents, schools, and society do to help? How do adolescents separate from their parents and connect with peers?

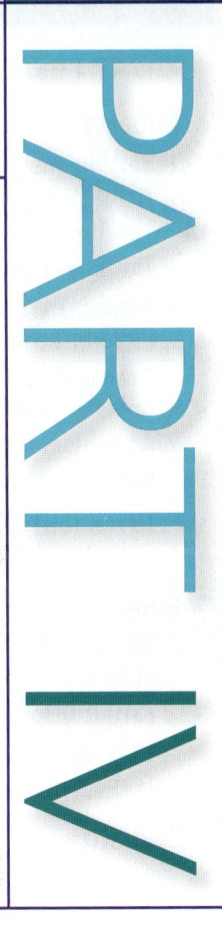

Application to Developing Lives Parenting Simulation: *Adolescence*

Below is a list of questions you will answer in the Adolescence simulation module. As you answer these questions, consider the impact your choice will have on the physical, cognitive, and social and emotional development of your adolescent.

Physical

- Will your child experiment with smoking, drinking, or drugs during adolescence?
- How will you respond if you learn your child is experimenting with drugs?
- How will you encourage your child to spend his or her free time after school (sports, part-time job)?

Cognitive

- What stage of Piaget's cognitive stages of development is your child in?
- What kind of path do you see your teenager pursuing after high school (college, military, work program)?

Social and Emotional

- How will you respond if your child is struggling to fit in with peers?
- How often do you think you and your teenager will have conflicts?
- How social will your child be during his or her teen years?
- How much privacy will you grant your teenager?
- How will you respond when your teenager starts dating?

Left: Indeed/Getty Images

CHAPTER 8

CHAPTER OUTLINE

Puberty
Setting the Context: Culture, History, and Puberty
The Hormonal Programmers
The Physical Changes
HOW DO WE KNOW . . . How Puberty Progresses?
Individual Differences in Puberty Timetables
An Insider's View of Puberty
Wrapping Up Puberty
INTERVENTIONS: Minimizing Puberty Distress

Body Image Issues
The Differing Body Concerns of Girls and Boys
Eating Disorders
INTERVENTIONS: Improving Teenagers' Body Image

Sexuality
Exploring Sexual Desire
Who Is Having Intercourse?
Who Are Teens Having Intercourse With?
HOT IN DEVELOPMENTAL SCIENCE: Is There Still a Sexual Double Standard?
Wrapping Up Sexuality: Contemporary Trends
INTERVENTIONS: Toward Teenager-Friendly Sex Education

Physical Development in Adolescents

Samantha and her twin brother, Sam, were so much alike—in their physical features, their personalities, their academic talents. Except for the sex difference, they seemed like identical twins. Then, when Samantha was 10, she started to tower over Sam and the rest of the fifth-grade class.

Yes, there were downsides to developing first—needing to hide behind a locker when you dressed for gym; not having anyone to talk to when you got your period at age 10; being teased about your big, strange body. But what fun! Once a neglected, pudgy elementary school child, by sixth grade, Samantha was hanging out with the popular eighth-grade boys. At age 12, she was smoking and drinking. By 14, she regularly defied her helpless parents and often left the house at 2 A.M.

Samantha's parents were frantic, but their daughter couldn't have cared less. Everything else was irrelevant compared to exploring being an adult. It took a life-changing service learning trip and a pregnancy scare to get Samantha back on track. Samantha had abandoned Sara, her best friend since first grade, for her new "mature" friends. But when the two girls got close again on that memorable trip, Sara's calming influence woke Samantha up. Samantha credits comments like, "Why would you ruin your future by having unprotected sex?" with saving her life. Plus, Samantha's lifelong competition with her brother helped refocus her thoughts. Although Sam was also an early developer, when he shot up to 6 feet in the spring of seventh grade, he became stellar at sports and also a social star.

Now that Samantha is 33, married, and expecting her first child, it's interesting for the twins and Sara to get together and really talk (for the first time) about their early teens. Sam remembers getting much stronger and his first incredible feelings of being in love. Samantha recalls being excited about her changing body, but obsessively worrying about being too fat. Then, there is Sara, who says middle school was no problem because she didn't menstruate until age 14. Everyone goes through puberty, but why does everyone react in different ways?

Why did Samantha have trouble as an early-maturing girl, while Sam and Sara sailed through **puberty**? What is this landmark physical process of becoming adult *really* like? This chapter explores this question in depth, then tackles body image and sex. As you read the following pages, think back to when you were 10 or 12 or 14. How did you feel about your body during puberty? When did you begin dating and fantasizing about having sex?

puberty The hormonal and physical changes by which children become sexually mature human beings and reach their adult height.

LEARNING OUTCOMES

- Describe the secular trend.
- List the hormonal and physical changes of puberty.
- Outline gender and individual differences in puberty.
- Contrast the causes and consequences of maturing early in girls and boys.

Puberty

Compare photos of yourself in late elementary school and high school to get a vivid sense of how puberty physically catapults us into adulthood. From the size of our thighs to the shape of our nose, we become a different-looking person in under five years. Today, puberty is a pre-teen and early adolescent change (Archibald, Graber, & Brooks-Gunn, 2003; Herting & Sowell, 2017). Today, as you saw with Samantha, who started menstruating at age 10 and has just gotten pregnant at age 32, the gap between being physically able to have children and actually having children can be more than twice as long as infancy and childhood combined.

This lack of person–environment fit, when our body is passionately saying "have sex" while society is telling teenagers to "say no" to intercourse, explains why adolescent sexuality provokes such anxiety among Western adults. Our concerns are recent. They are a product of living in the contemporary developed world.

These photographs of fourth graders and high school juniors offer a vivid visual reminder of the total body transformation of puberty.

Setting the Context: Culture, History, and Puberty

As my sisters and I went about doing our daily chores, we choked on the dust stirred up by the herd of cattle and goats that had just arrived in our compound. . . . These animals were my bride wealth, negotiated by my parents and the family of the man who had been chosen as my husband. . . . I am considered to be a woman, so I am ready to marry, have children, and assume adult privileges and responsibilities. My name is Telelia ole Mariani. I am 14 years old.

(quoted in Wilson, Ngige, & Trollinger, 2003, p. 95)

Throughout history, and even now in some impoverished world regions (as the quotation above suggests), puberty was a young person's signal to get married and give birth (Schlegel, 1995; Schlegel & Barry, 1991). Today, society must downplay the body changes because sexuality (and parenthood) isn't supposed to happen for years. In other cultures, people could celebrate children's blossoming bodies in a coming-of-age ceremony called the *puberty rite*.

Celebrating Puberty

Puberty rites were emotional events, carefully choreographed to teach adult gender roles. Often, children were removed from their families and forced to perform stressful tasks. There was anxiety ("Can I really do this thing?") and feelings of awe and self-efficacy, as the young person returned to joyfully enter the community as an adult (Feixa, 2011; Weisfeld, 1997).

puberty rite A "coming of age" ritual held in traditional cultures to celebrate children's transition to adulthood.

In one Amazonian tribe, for instance, after proving their manhood by killing a large animal, boys would metaphorically "die"—by drinking a hallucinogen and spending time in isolation to "be born again" as adults. Among the Masai of Africa, young males had to stoically endure a painful circumcision, then master military maneuvers before proudly returning home to take wives (Feixa, 2011).

For girls, **menarche**, or first menstruation, was the signal for celebrating the entrance into womanhood. In the traditional Navajo Kinaalda ceremony, for instance, girls in their first or second menstrual cycle, guided by a female mentor, would perform the running ritual, pushing their bodies to sprint for miles. (Imagine your motivation to train for this event when your culture told you that the quality of your run symbolized how long you would live!) The female role model massaged the girl's body, painted her face, and supervised her as she prepared a huge corn cake (a symbol of fertility) to be served to the community during a joyous, all-night singalong. The Navajo believe that when females begin menstruating, they possess special spiritual powers, so everyone would gather around for the girl's blessings as they give her a new adult name.

Today, however, many girls reach menarche at age 10 or even 9. At that age—in *any* society—could people be ready for adult life? The answer is no. In the past, we reached puberty at an older age.

The Declining Age of Puberty

This fascinating decline, called the **secular trend in puberty**, is illustrated in Figure 8.1. In the 1860s, the average age of menarche in northern Europe was over 17 (Tanner, 1978). In the 1960s, in the developed world, it dropped to under age 13 (Parent and others, 2003). Then, after a pause, about 20 years ago, the menarche marker began to slide downward again (Lee & Styne, 2013).

A century ago, many girls could not get pregnant until their late teens. Today, many girls can have babies *before* their teenage years!

Researchers typically use menarche as their benchmark for charting the secular trend because it is an obvious sign of being able to have a child. The male signal of fertility, **spermarche**, or first ejaculation of live sperm, is a hidden event.

In addition, because it reflects better nutrition, in the same way as with stunting (discussed in Chapter 3), we can use the secular trend in puberty as an index of a nation's economic development. In the United States, African American girls begin to menstruate at close to age 12. In impoverished African countries, such as Senegal, the comparable menarche age is over 16 (Parent and others, 2003)!

This photo shows South African boys returning from an "initiation school" to welcome their entry into adulthood. As is classic, in this culture the puberty ritual involves separation from one's family and symbolically being "reborn" as a man.

menarche A girl's first menstruation.

secular trend in puberty A decline in the average age at which children reach puberty.

spermarche A boy's first ejaculation of live sperm.

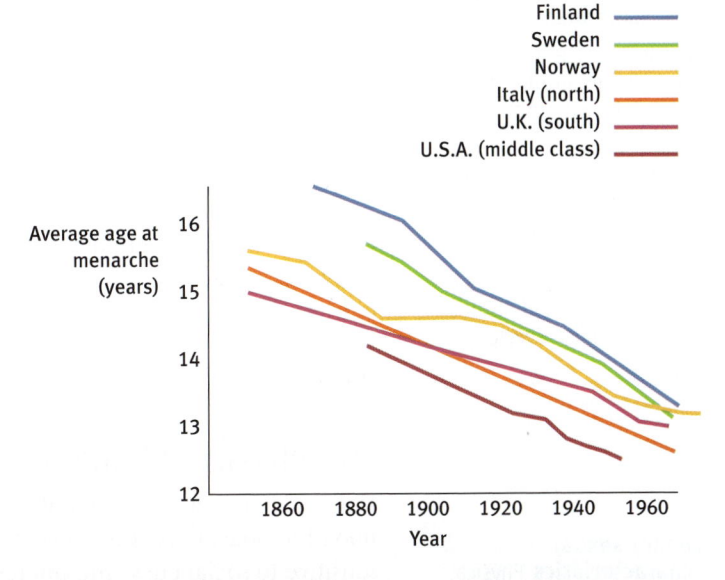

FIGURE 8.1: The secular trend in puberty Notice that the average age of menarche dramatically declined in developed countries during the first half of the twentieth century. Why is this decline continuing? Stay tuned for surprising answers later in this chapter.

Data from Tanner 1978, p. 103.

For this rural, 15-year-old Vietnamese boy, reaching puberty means it's time to assume his adult responsibilities as a fisherman. The reason he now has the strength and stamina to wield this heavy net is that the all-important hormonal system programming the body changes of manhood (the HPG axis) has fully kicked in.

adrenal androgens Hormones produced by the adrenal glands that program puberty.

HPG axis The main hormonal system that programs puberty; it involves a triggering hypothalamic hormone that causes the pituitary to secrete its hormones, which in turn cause the ovaries and testes to develop and secrete the hormones that produce the major body changes.

gonads The sex organs—the ovaries in girls and the testes in boys.

testosterone The hormone responsible for maturation of the male reproductive organs and other signs of puberty in men, and for hair and skin changes and sexual desire in both sexes.

primary sexual characteristics Physical changes of puberty that directly involve the reproductive organs, such as growth of the penis and onset of menstruation.

Given that nutrition is critical, what *exactly* sets puberty off? For answers, let's focus on the hormonal systems that program the physical changes.

The Hormonal Programmers

Puberty is programmed by two command centers. One system, located in the adrenal glands at the top of the kidneys, begins to release its hormones at about ages 6 to 8, several years before children show observable signs of puberty. The **adrenal androgens,** whose output increases to reach a peak in the early twenties, eventually produce (among other events) pubic hair development, skin changes, body odor, and, as you will read later in this chapter, our first feelings of sexual desire (Herting & Sowell, 2017).

About two years later, the most important command center kicks in. Called the **HPG axis**—because it involves the hypothalamus (in the brain), the pituitary (a gland at the base of the brain), and the **gonads** (the *ovaries* and the *testes*)—this system produces the major body changes (Plant, 2015).

As you can see in Figure 8.2, puberty is set off by a three-phase chain reaction. At about age 9 or 10, pulsating bursts of the hypothalamic hormone stimulate the pituitary gland to step up production of its hormones. This causes the ovaries and testes to secrete several closely related compounds called estrogens and the hormone called **testosterone** (Herting & Sowell, 2017).

As the blood concentrations of estrogens and testosterone float upward, these hormones unleash a physical transformation. Estrogens produce females' changing shape by causing the hips to widen and the uterus and breasts to enlarge. They set in motion the cycle of reproduction, stimulating the ovaries to produce eggs. Testosterone causes the penis to lengthen, promotes the growth of facial and body hair, and is responsible for a dramatic increase in muscle mass and other internal masculine changes.

Boys and girls *both* produce estrogens and testosterone. Testosterone and the adrenal androgens are responsible for sexual arousal in females and males. However, women produce mainly estrogens. The concentration of testosterone is roughly 8 times higher in boys after puberty than it is in girls; in fact, this classic "male" hormone is responsible for *all* the physical changes in boys.

Now, to return to our earlier question: What primes the triggering hypothalamic hormone? As Figure 8.2 illustrates, many forces help unleash the pulsating hypothalamic bursts—from genetics to exposure to light; from possible chemicals in our water and food to environmental stress (more about this fascinating force later). A threshold level of a hormone called *leptin,* tied to body fat, is essential. This explains why undernutrition delays puberty and why obesity might push the timer to a younger age (more about this later). These primers, in turn, unleash a cascade of body changes.

The Physical Changes

Puberty causes a total *psychological* and physical transformation. As the hormones flood the body, they affect specific brain regions, making teenagers more emotional, sensitive to social cues, and interested in taking risks (as you will read in Chapter 9). Scientists divide the physical changes into three categories:

- **Primary sexual characteristics** refer to the body changes directly involved in reproduction. The growth of the penis and menstruation are examples of primary sexual characteristics.

- **Secondary sexual characteristics** is the label for the hundreds of other changes that accompany puberty, such as breast development, the growth of pubic hair, voice changes, and alterations in the person's skin.

- The **growth spurt** merits its own special category. At puberty—as should come as no surprise—there is a dramatic increase in height and weight.

Health-care workers use a standard scale to plot the growth of the child's main secondary sexual characteristics in stages (see the How Do We Know box on page 228). Now let's offer a motion picture of all of the changes, first in girls and then in boys.

For Girls

The most dramatic early sign of puberty in girls is the growth spurt. First, girls' growth picks up speed, accelerates, and then begins to decrease (Herting & Sowell, 2017). During a visit to my 11-year-old niece, I got a vivid sense of this "peak velocity" phase of growth. Six months earlier, I had towered over her. Now, she insisted on standing back-to-back to demonstrate: "Look, Aunt Janet, I'm taller than you!"

About six months after the growth spurt begins, breasts and pubic hair become visible. On average, girls' breasts take about four years to grow to their adult form (Tanner, 1955, 1978).

Menarche typically occurs in the middle to final stages of breast and pubic hair development, when girls' growth is winding down (Lee & Styne, 2013; Peper & Dahl, 2013). So you can tell your 12-year-old niece, who has just begun to menstruate, that, while her breasts are still "works in progress," she is probably about as tall today as she will be as an adult.

When they reach menarche, can girls get pregnant? Yes, but there is often a window of infertility until the system fully gears up. Does puberty unfold in the same way for every girl? The answer is no. Because the hormonal signals are complex, in some girls, pubic hair development (programmed by the adrenal androgens) is underway before the breasts begin to enlarge. Occasionally, a girl does grow much taller after she begins to menstruate.

The most fascinating variability relates to the *rate* of change. Some children are developmental "tortoises." Their progression through puberty is slow-paced. Others are "hares." They speed through the body changes. For instance, while breast development takes *an average* of four years, the entire process—from start to finish—can range from less than two to an incredible nine! (See Mendle and others, 2010.)

These external changes are accompanied by internal upheavals. During puberty, the uterus grows, the vagina lengthens, and the hips develop a cushion of fat. The vocal cords get longer, the heart gets bigger, and the red blood cells

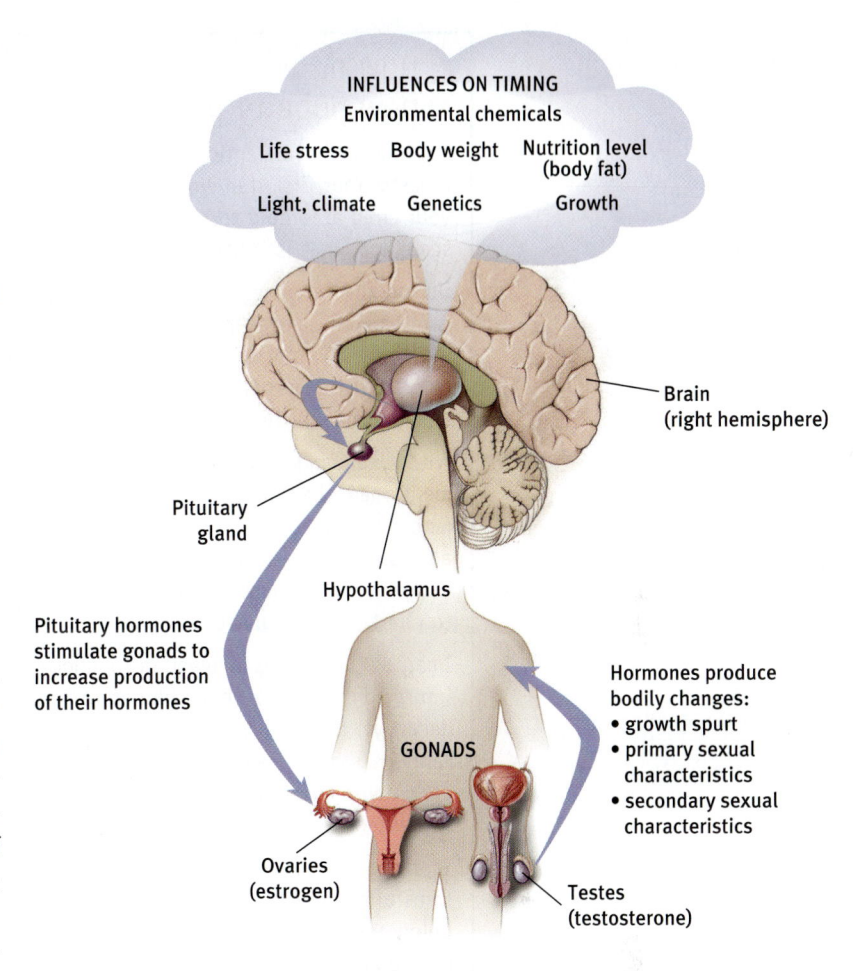

FIGURE 8.2: The HPG axis: The three-phase hormonal sequence that triggers puberty As you can see here, in response to various genetic and environmental influences, the hypothalamus releases a hormone that stimulates the pituitary gland to produce its own hormones, which cause the ovaries in girls and the testes in boys to grow and secrete estrogens and testosterone, producing the physical changes of puberty.

secondary sexual characteristics Physical changes of puberty not directly involved in reproduction, such as female breast development and male facial hair.

growth spurt A dramatic increase in height and weight that occurs during puberty.

HOW DO WE KNOW...
how puberty progresses?

Imagine being a frantic parent concerned that your 8-year-old daughter is developing breasts. Your first step would be to visit your pediatrician, who would probably evaluate your child according to Tanner's five pubertal stages. What are the origins of this classic scale and what is it like? (See Roberts, 2016.)

During the early twentieth century, as the new science of pediatrics flourished, health-care workers needed benchmarks for evaluating their patients. Was a particular boy or girl growing normally? What exactly does growing "normally" mean? Then, during the late 1940s, James Tanner came to the rescue with landmark research tracking physical development in the flesh.

With a colleague, Tanner entered a London orphanage and began a mammoth study (as I mentioned when discussing Bowlby's research in Chapter 4, British orphanages were common during this era). The researchers photographed and measured children's bodies from ages 3 to 5 years, and then every 3 months during puberty. These meticulous assessments, converted into atlases, remain the gold standard that health-care workers use worldwide to chart pubertal growth.

Imagine the hurdles involved in conducting this research today. Now, caregivers must give informed consent for their children to be tested. It defies modern standards of ethics (and decency!) to have strangers regularly measure (and photograph) pre-teens' private parts. Tanner's sample—all white, probably somewhat malnourished, and perhaps subject to early abuse—was totally unrepresentative. But his stages remain the beacon that allowed adolescent research (and practice) to blossom for the past 50 years.

Tanner didn't formulate world-class theories. Still, his decades of dogged scientific work transformed our thinking about teenagers almost as much as Piaget's or Erikson's ideas. Below you can see how health-care workers would classify this 8-year-old girl's breast development, according to Tanner's five stages.

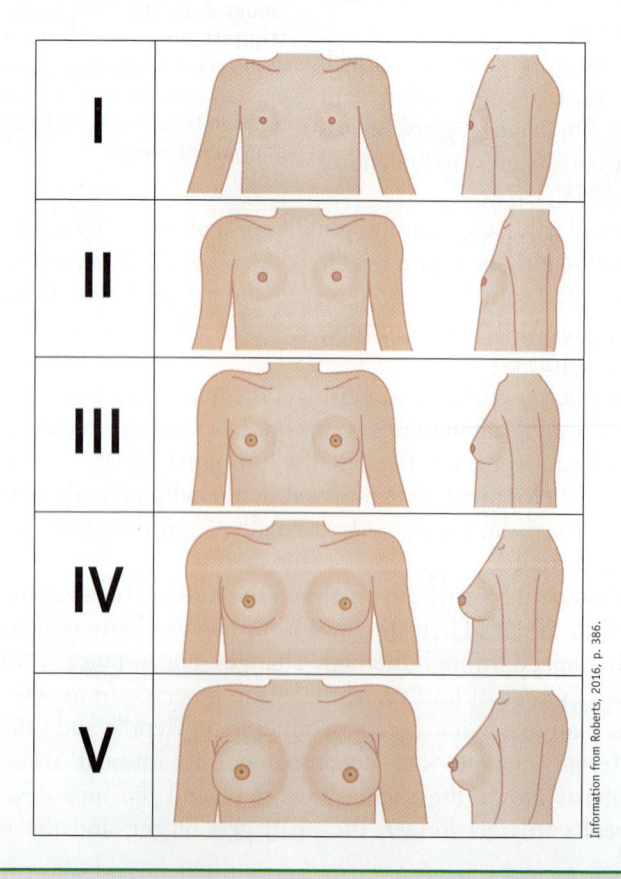

Information from Roberts, 2016, p. 386.

carry more oxygen. So, after puberty, girls become much stronger (Archibald, Graber, & Brooks-Gunn, 2003). The increases in strength, stamina, height, and weight are astonishing in boys.

For Boys

In boys, health-care workers also track the growth of the penis, testicles, and pubic hair by five Tanner stages. However, because these organs of reproduction begin developing first, boys still look like children to the outside world for a year or two after their bodies start changing. Voice deepening, the development of body hair, and that other visible sign of being a man—the need to shave—all take place after the growth of the testes and penis is underway (Tanner, 1978). Now, let's pause to look at the most obvious signals that a boy is becoming a man—the mammoth alterations in body size, shape, and strength.

In Chapter 5, I mentioned that elementary school boys and girls are roughly the same size. Then, during the puberty growth spurt, males shoot up an incredible average of 8 inches, compared to 4 inches for girls (Tanner, 1978). Boys also become far stronger than the other sex.

One cause is the tremendous increase in muscle mass. Another lies in the dramatic cardiovascular changes. At puberty, boys' hearts increase in weight by more than one-third. In particular, notice in Figure 8.3 that, compared to females, after puberty, males have many more red blood cells and a much greater capacity for carrying oxygen in their blood. The visible signs of these changes are a big chest, wide shoulders, and a muscular frame. The real-world consequence is that after puberty, males get a boost in gross motor skills that give them an edge in everything from soccer to sprinting and from cycling to carrying heavy loads.

Do you know any seventh- or eighth-grade boys? If so, you might notice that growth during puberty takes place in the opposite pattern to the one that occurs earlier in life. Rather than following the *cephalocaudal* and *proximodistal* sequences (from the head downward and from the middle of the body outward), at puberty, the person's hands, feet, and legs grow first. While this happens for both sexes, these changes are especially obvious in boys because their growth is so dramatic.

Their long legs and large feet explain why, in their early teens, boys look gawky. Add to that the crackly voice produced by the growing larynx, the wispy look of beginning

Because the landmark change of shaving occurs fairly late in the sequence of puberty, we can be sure that this 14-year-old boy has been looking like a man, for some time, in ways we can't see.

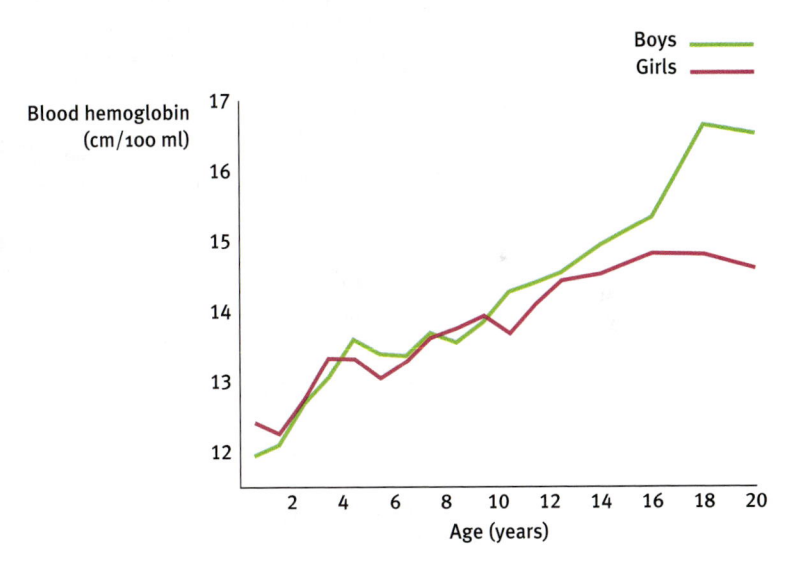

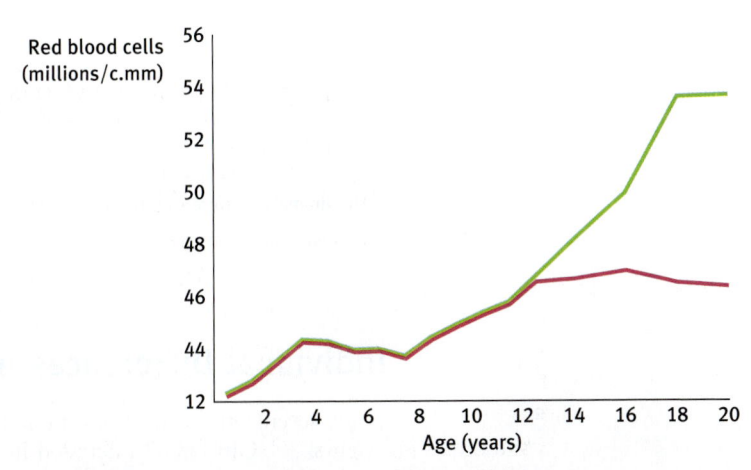

FIGURE 8.3: Changes in blood hemoglobin and red blood cells during puberty in males and females At puberty, increases in hemoglobin and in the number of red blood cells cause children of both sexes to get far stronger. But notice that these changes are more pronounced in boys than in girls.

Data from Tanner, 1955, p. 103.

facial hair, and the fact that during puberty a boy's nose and ears grow before the rest of his face catches up. Plus, the increased activity of the sweat glands and enlarged pores leads to that familiar condition that produces such emotional agony: acne. Although girls also suffer from acne, boys are more vulnerable to this problem because testosterone, which males produce in abundance, produces changes in the hair and skin.

Are Boys on a Later Timetable? A Bit

Visit a middle school and you will be struck by the fact that boys, on average, appear to reach puberty two years later than girls. But appearances can be deceiving. In girls, as I mentioned earlier, the externally visible signs of puberty, such as the growth spurt and breast development, take place toward the beginning of the sequence. For boys, the hidden development—growth of the testes—occurs first (Huddleston & Ge, 2003; Lee & Styne, 2013).

If we look at the *real* sign of fertility, the gender differences are not far apart. In one study, boys reported that spermarche occurred at roughly age 13, only about six months later than the average age of menarche (Stein & Reiser, 1994).

Figure 8.4 graphically summarizes some of these changes. Now, let's explore the numbers inside the chart. Why do children undergo puberty at such different ages?

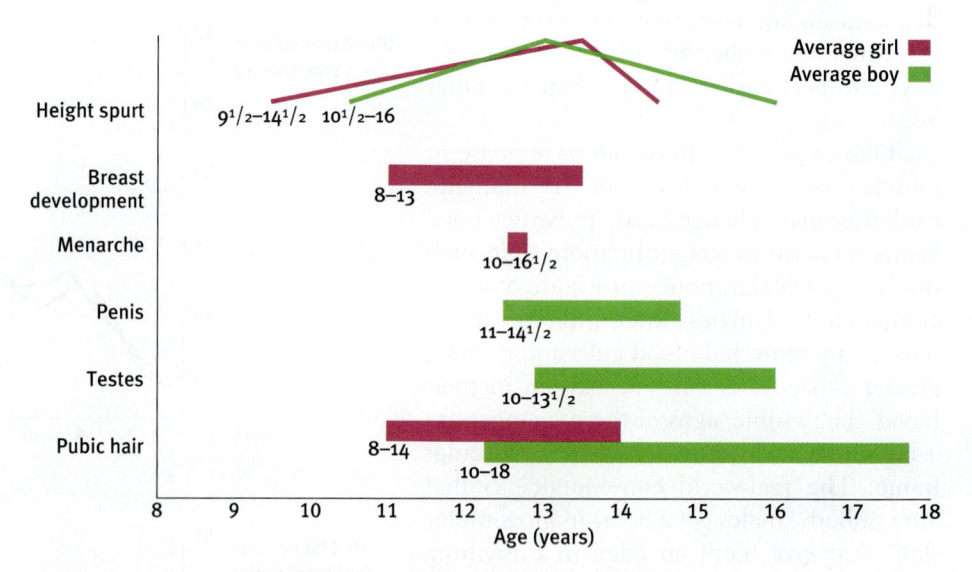

FIGURE 8.4: **The sequence of some major events of puberty** This chart shows the ages at which some important changes of puberty occur in the average boy and girl. The numbers below each change show the range of ages at which that event begins. Notice that girls are on a slightly earlier timetable than boys, that boys' height spurt occurs at a later point in their development, and the dramatic differences from child to child in pubertal timing.

Data from Tanner, 1978, pp. 23, 29.

Individual Differences in Puberty Timetables

> I'm seventeen already. But I still look like a kid. I get teased a lot, especially by the other guys. . . . Girls aren't interested in me, either, because most of them are taller than I am. When will I grow up?
>
> (adapted from an online chat room)

The gender difference in puberty timetables can cause anxiety. As an early-maturing girl, I vividly remember slumping to avoid the humiliation of having my partner's head encounter my chest in sixth-grade dancing class! But nature's cruelest blow may relate to the individual differences in timing. Why is there a five-year difference in puberty timetables between children living in the same environment? (See Parent and others, 2003.)

Not unexpectedly, genetics is important. Identical twins go through puberty at roughly the same ages (Lee & Styne, 2013; Silventoinen and others, 2008). Asian Americans tend to be slightly behind other U.S. children in puberty timetables (Sun and others, 2002). African American and Hispanic boys and girls are ahead of other North American groups (Lee & Styne, 2013; Rosenfield, Lipton, & Drum, 2009).

But remember that in impoverished African countries—where children are poorly nourished—girls begin to menstruate, on average, as late as age 16. During the past 30 years, obesity rates in the United States skyrocketed among African American elementary school girls and boys (Boonpleng and others, 2013). Given that body fat is intimately involved, and the secular trend has picked up steam, does being overweight predict when a boy or girl physically matures?

Look at female middle school friends—such as these girls getting ready for a dance—and you will be struck by the differences in puberty timetables. As the text shows, a variety of forces predict why children mature earlier or later than their peers.

Overweight and Early Puberty (It's All About Girls)

The answer is yes—if we consider female children *only*. Controlling for other forces, having a high BMI (body mass index) during elementary school does predict entering puberty earlier for girls (Lee & Styne, 2013; Rosenfield, Lipton, & Drum, 2009). Even more interestingly, rapid weight gain in the *first nine months of life* is strongly linked to menstruating at a younger age! (See Walvoord, 2010.)

This finding dovetails with the research I presented in Table 6.3 (page 167), suggesting that our overweight path is set in motion early in life. Now—in addition to foreshadowing later obesity—we know that weight gain during infancy may predict early puberty, too.

Interestingly, for boys the data is inconsistent. Some studies show obese boys mature early; others suggest these children develop later than their peers (see Lee & Styne, 2013).

Now let's turn to a more astonishing environmental influence predicting puberty, specifically in girls—the quality of a child's family life.

In Table 6.3, I suggested that overfeeding this adorable 8-month-old girl might program lifelong overweight. Now we know that excessive weight gain during infancy can have another negative epigenetic effect—priming this baby to reach puberty at an early age.

Family Stress and Early Puberty (Again, It's About Girls)

Drawing on an *evolutionary psychology perspective*, some developmentalists argue that when family stress is intense, a physiological mechanism kicks in to accelerate puberty and free a child from an inhospitable nest. Just as stress in the womb "instructs" the baby to store fat (as the fetal programming hypothesis described in Chapter 2 suggests), an unhappy childhood signals the body to expect a short life and pushes adult fertility to a younger age (Belsky and others, 2015).

I must emphasize that genetics is the most important force predicting a child's puberty timetable (the age when that person's parents developed). But, if a girl is temperamentally vulnerable, *controlling for every other influence* (genetics, body weight, and so on), her family life makes its small, tantalizing contribution (Ellis and others, 2011b). Early-maturing girls are more apt to grow up in mother-headed households (Graber, Nichols, & Brooks-Gunn, 2010; Neberich and others, 2010) and report intense childhood stress (Allison & Hyde, 2013; Ellis, 2004). In one longitudinal study, mothers' use of *power-assertive* discipline during preschool—yelling, shaming, rejecting—was associated with earlier menstruation (Belsky and others, 2007a;

Belsky, Houts, & Pasco Fearon, 2010). Even prenatal maternal stress may promote early menarche because, when women experience emotional upheavals during their pregnancies, these traumas can produce depression and so provoke more uncaring childrearing during a daughter's infant years (Belsky and others, 2015).

Why—specifically in girls—is the hypothalamic timer sensitive to body weight and family stress? We do not know. But these surprising findings emphasize the ecological/developmental systems message: *Many* influences—from genetics to gender, from physiology to parenting to everything else—affect how children grow.

Table 8.1 summarizes these points by spelling out questions that can predict a girl's chance of reaching puberty at a younger-than-average age. If you were an early maturer, how many—if any—of these forces applied to you?

Now that I've described the physical process, let's look at how children feel about three classic signs of puberty—breast development, menstruation, and first ejaculation. Then we'll explore the mental health impact of reaching puberty relatively early or late.

Table 8.1: Predicting a Girl's Chances of Early Puberty: Some Questions

1. Did this girl's parents reach puberty early?
2. Is this girl African American?
3. Is this girl overweight? Did she gain weight rapidly during her first year of life?
4. Has this girl's family life been stressful and unhappy? Were her caregivers angry and depressed during that child's first years of life?

An Insider's View of Puberty

Think back to how you felt about your body during puberty. You probably remember having mixed emotions: fear, pride, embarrassment, excitement. If a researcher asked you to describe your inner state, would you want to talk about how you *really* felt? The reluctance of pre-teens to discuss what is happening ("Yuck! Just don't go there!") explains why, to study reactions to puberty, psychologists often ask adults to remember this time of life. Or they may use indirect measures, such as having children tell stories about pictures, to reveal their inner concerns.

The Breasts

In a classic study, researchers used this indirect strategy to explore how girls feel in relation to their parents while undergoing that most visible sign of becoming a woman—breast development (Brooks-Gunn and others, 1994). They asked a group of girls to tell a story about the characters in a drawing that showed an adult female (the mother) taking a bra out of a shopping bag while an adolescent girl and an adult male (the father) watched. While girls often viewed mothers as being excited and happy, they typically described the teenager as humiliated by her father's presence in the room. Moreover, girls in the middle of puberty told the most negative stories about fathers, suggesting that body embarrassment is at its height while children are undergoing the physical changes.

Because society strongly values this symbol of being a woman (and our contemporary culture sees bigger as better!), other research suggests that U.S. girls feel proud of their developing breasts (Brooks-Gunn & Warren, 1988). However, among girls in ballet schools, where there are strong pressures

Imagine how these girls auditioning at a premier ballet academy in New York City will feel when they develop breasts and perhaps find that their womanly body shape interrupts their career dreams—and you will understand why children's reactions to puberty depend on their unique environment.

to look prepubescent, breast development evokes distress (Brooks-Gunn & Warren, 1985). The principle that children's reactions to puberty depend on messages from the wider world holds true for menstruation, too.

Menstruation

Imagine being a Navajo girl and feeling that when you menstruate, you have entered a special spiritual state. Compare this with the less-than-glowing portrait most cultures paint about "that time of the month" (Brooks-Gunn & Ruble, 1982; Costos, Ackerman, & Paradis, 2002). From the advertisements for pills strong enough to handle even menstrual pain to its classic description as "the curse," it is no wonder that in the past girls approached this milestone with dread (Brooks-Gunn & Ruble, 1982).

Luckily, upper-middle-class mothers are trying to change these cultural scripts. When researchers asked 18- to 20-year-old students at Oregon State University to write about their "first period experiences," 3 out of 4 women recalled their moms as being thrilled ("She treated me like a princess"). One person wrote that the day after she told her mother, "I saw an expensive box of chocolates and a card addressed to me. It said 'Congrats on becoming a woman'" (quoted in Lee, 2008, p. 1332).

These positive responses matter. In one research summary, while low-income women in the United States recalled frequently feeling "gross, smelly and disgusting" at menarche (Herbert and others, 2016), about half of all middle-class young women described getting their period as "no big deal."

First Ejaculation

Daughters must confide in their mothers about menarche because this event demands specific coping techniques. Spermarche, in contrast, does not require instructions from the outside world. Who talks to male adolescents about first ejaculation, and how do teenagers feel about their signal of becoming a man? Read these memories from some 18-year-olds (Stein & Reiser, 1994):

> I woke up the next morning and my sheets were pasty. . . . After you wake up your mind is kind of happy and then you realize: "Oh my God, this is my wet dream!"
> (quoted in Stein & Reiser, 1994, p. 380)

> My mom, she knew I had them. It was all over my sheets and bedspread and stuff, but she didn't say anything, didn't tease me and stuff. She never asked if I wanted to talk about it—I'm glad. I never could have said anything to my mom.
> (quoted in Stein & Reiser, 1994, p. 377)

Most of these boys reported that they needed to be secretive. They didn't want to let *anyone* know. And notice from the second quotation—as you saw earlier with fathers and pre-teen girls—that boys also view their changing bodies as especially embarrassing around the parent of the opposite sex.

Is this tendency for children to hide the symptoms of puberty around the parent of the other gender programmed into evolution to help teenagers emotionally separate from their families? We do not know. We do have massive information, however, on the *emotional* impact of being early or late.

Maturing Early Can Be a Problem for Girls

Imagine being an early-maturing girl. How would you feel if you looked like an adult while everyone else in your classes still looked like a child? Now imagine being a late maturer and thinking, "What's wrong with my body? Will I *ever* grow up?"

Actually, the timing of development matters, but again the results differ for boys and girls. Early-maturing boys are more prone to abuse substances, particularly if these teens are low in impulse control (Castellanos-Ryan and others, 2013). They are at risk getting depressed if they have prior personality problems and an unhappy family life (Benoit, Lacourse, & Claes, 2013). But because males become so much stronger

While early-maturing girls may be prone to get into trouble, for these manlike seventh-grade boys, developing earlier can be a social plus, as they are right on time for the average girl in this class.

during puberty (and therefore are better at sports) and early-maturing boys are more in synch with the average girl, reaching puberty early boosts boys' popularity and self-esteem (Li and others, 2013).

Unfortunately, the research is consistently downbeat for the other sex: *Hundreds of studies suggest that early-maturing girls can have widespread difficulties during their adolescent years.*

Early-Maturing Girls Are at Risk of Developing Externalizing Problems

Because we choose friends who are "like us," early-maturing girls may gravitate toward becoming friends with older girls and boys. So, around the world, they tend to get involved in "adult activities" such as smoking, drinking, and taking drugs at younger ages (Ren, Guo, & Chen, 2015). Maturing early heightens the tendency—described in the next chapter—for teens to make dangerous, impulsive decisions with their peers (Kretsch & Harden, 2014).

Because they are so busy testing the limits, one classic longitudinal Swedish study showed, early-maturing girls tended to get worse grades than their classmates in the sixth and seventh grades (Simmons & Blyth, 1987). By their twenties, these girls were several times less likely to have graduated from high school than their later-developing peers (Stattin & Magnusson, 1990).

The main danger, of course, is having unprotected sex. Because they may not have the cognitive abilities to resist this social pressure and often have older boyfriends, early-maturing girls are more likely to have intercourse at a younger age (Graber, Nichols, & Brooks-Gunn, 2010). They are less apt to use contraception, making them more vulnerable to becoming pregnant as teens (Allison & Hyde, 2013). Imagine being a sixth- or seventh-grade girl thrilled to be pursued by the high school boys. Would you have the presence of mind to say no?

Early-Maturing Girls Are at Risk of Getting Anxious and Depressed

As if this were not enough, early-maturing girls, especially in affluent environments, are more likely to experience bouts of low self-worth (Mendle and others, 2016). In fourth or fifth grade, these girls are at risk of being bullied because they look so different from the other children in class (Allison & Hyde, 2013). Now, compound this with the shame attached to *generally* having a larger body size. Not only are early-maturing girls apt to be heavier during elementary school, but they also end up shorter and stockier because their height spurt occurs at an earlier point in their development (Adair, 2008; Must and others, 2005). Late-maturing girls are more prone to fit the tall ultra-slim model shape. Reaching puberty early sets girls up for having a poor body image and becoming depressed.

So far, I've been painting a dismal portrait of early-maturing girls. But, as with any aspect of development, it's important to look at the *whole* context of a person's life. Early maturation may not pose body-image problems in ethnic groups that have a healthier, more inclusive idea about the ideal female body (more about this later).

Most important, these negative effects happen mainly when there are other risk factors in a child's life. For example, if a girl is exposed to harsh parenting (Deardorff and others, 2013), then yes, early maturation can be the straw that breaks the camel's back (Lynne-Landsman, Graber, & Andrews, 2010). But if that child has authoritative parents (Ren and others, 2015), strong religious values—and doesn't gravitate to older "at-risk" friends—her puberty timetable will not matter (Stattin & Magnusson, 1990).

The dangers linked with maturing early also seem dependent on the nation in which a girl grows up. In one interesting international comparison, while early-maturing Swedish girls were more prone to get into trouble than late maturers, this was not true in Slovakia (see Figure 8.5). The reason, these researchers argue, is that

Scandinavia is a permissive society that accepts adolescent sex, whereas Slovakia severely restricts these activities (Skoog and others, 2013). So, again, a structured, highly protective community can cushion a girl (or any child) from acting on the potentially harmful behavioral messages her body gives off.

This brings us to that critical setting: school. In classic studies, developmentalists found that early-maturing girls had special problems after moving to a large middle school versus staying in a smaller K–8 school (Simmons & Blyth, 1987). Therefore, based on this research, psychologists argued that it is a bad idea to compound the stressful changes of puberty by forcing pre-teens to change schools (see Eccles & Roeser, 2003).

But, because some middle schools offer superior nurturing (Farmer and others, 2011), it's important to go beyond a school's structure and ask more basic questions: Is this an authoritative environment (see Chapter 7)? Does this class have caring peer norms (see Chapter 6)? Moreover, imagine being locked into the calcified status hierarchies that can solidify, based on spending your whole childhood with the same group of peers. The advantage of middle school is that it offers you (and everyone else) a liberating new start!

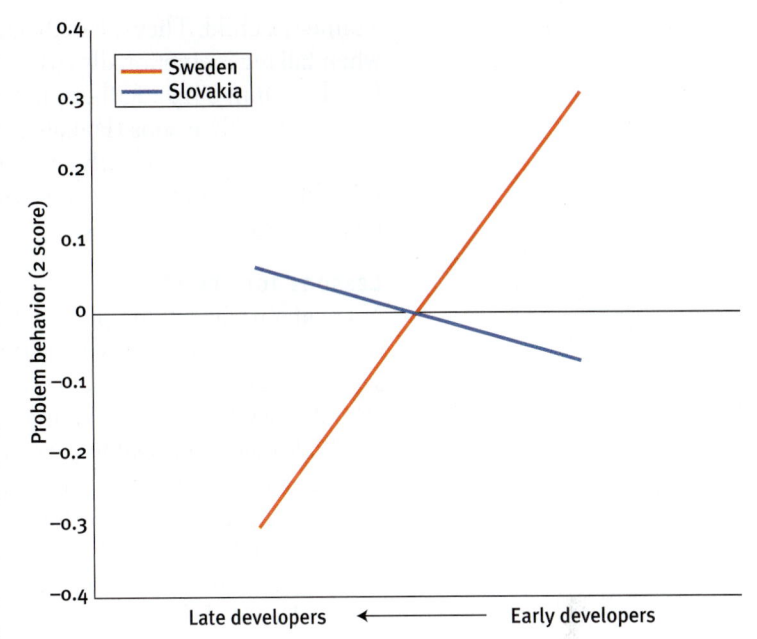

FIGURE 8.5: The interaction between culture and pubertal timing in predicting girls' problem behavior in Sweden (red line) and Slovakia (blue line) Notice that in sexually permissive Sweden, maturing early has a huge impact on a girl's risk of getting into trouble (with drugs, ignoring curfews, being truant at school, and so on); but a girl's puberty timetable has comparatively little impact on her behavior if that child lives in Slovakia.

Data from Skoog and others, 2013.

Wrapping Up Puberty

Now let's summarize all these research messages:

- **Children's reactions to puberty depend on the environment in which they physically mature.** Negative feelings are more likely to occur when society looks down on a given sign of development (as with menstruation) or when the physical changes are not valued in a person's particular group (as with breast development in ballerinas). Living in a sexually permissive society or being in a non-nurturing school during puberty magnifies the stress of body changes.

- **With early-maturing girls, we should take special steps to arrange the right body–environment fit.** Having an adult body at a young age is dangerous for girls, but only when the changes happen in a high-risk milieu. Therefore, when a girl reaches puberty early, it's important for parents to closely monitor her activities (see Ren and others, 2015).

- **Communication about puberty should be improved—especially for boys.** While a few contemporary mothers may be doing a fine job discussing menstruation with their daughters, boys, in particular, seem to enter puberty without much guidance about what to expect (Omar, McElderry, & Zakharia, 2003).

INTERVENTIONS: Minimizing Puberty Distress

Given these findings, what are the lessons for parents? What changes should society make?

Lessons for Parents

It's tempting for parents to avoid discussing puberty because children are so sensitive about their changing bodies (see Elliot, 2012; Hyde and others, 2013). This reluctance is a mistake. Developmentalists urge parents to discuss what is happening with a same-sex child. They advise beginning these discussions when the child is at an age when talking is emotionally easier, before the changes take place (Graber, Nichols, & Brooks-Gunn, 2010). Fathers, in particular, need to make special efforts to talk about puberty with their sons (Paikoff & Brooks-Gunn, 1991).

Finally, parents of early-maturing daughters should try to get their child involved in positive activities, especially with friends the same age and, if possible, carefully pick the best school or class.

Lessons for Society

No matter what a child's puberty timetable, the implicit message of this section is that schools matter *tremendously* at this gateway-to-adulthood age. Rather than viewing sixth or seventh grade as relatively unimportant (compared to, say, high school), caring schools are vital to setting young teens on the right path.

It also seems critical to provide adequate puberty education. Think back to what you wanted to know about your changing body ("My breasts don't look right"; "My penis has a strange shape"), and you will realize that offering a few fifth-grade health lectures is not enough. The good news is that, in recent years, Western nations have developed innovative school sex-education programs (American Teens' Sources of Sexual Health Education, 2017). But, since discussing sex is controversial (more about this inflammatory issue later), a declining fraction of U.S. middle schools even mention puberty (Lindberg, Maddow-Zimet, & Boonstra, 2016). Sex education is apt to begin in high school, after many children have finished developing (Centers for Disease Control and Prevention, 2015). (That's like locking the barn door after the horses have been stolen!)

UNESCO has global guidelines aimed at teaching young children (aged 5 to 8) to respect their bodies. But, with the exception of a few European nations, schools routinely ignore this document—offering "too little too late" alarmist-oriented talk focused on pubertal damage control: "Don't get pregnant," "Avoid STIs" (Goldman & Coleman, 2013). Suppose our culture *celebrated* puberty, as the Navajo do? Perhaps we might really celebrate every body size.

Tying It All Together

1. In contrast to earlier times, give the main reason why our culture can't celebrate puberty today.

2. You notice that your 11-year-old cousin is starting to look more like a young woman. (a) Outline the three-phase hormonal sequence that is setting off the physical changes. (b) Name the three classes of hormones involved in puberty.

3. Kendra has recently begun to menstruate. Calista has just shot up in height. Carl is developing facial hair. Statistically speaking, which child is at the beginning of puberty?

4. Brianna, an overweight second grader, has harsh, rejecting parents. Based on this chapter, you might predict that Brianna should enter puberty *earlier/later* than her peers.

5. Based simply on knowing a child's puberty timetable, spell out who is most at risk of getting into trouble (for example, with drugs or having unprotected sex) as a teen.

6. You are on a committee charged with developing programs to help children cope emotionally with puberty. What recommendations might you make?

Answers to the Tying It All Together questions can be found at the end of this chapter.

Body Image Issues

What do you daydream about?

Being skinny.

—Amanda (quoted in Martin, 1996, p. 36)

Puberty is a time of intense physical preoccupations, and there is hardly a teenager who isn't concerned about some body part. How important is it for young people to be *generally* satisfied with how they look?

Consider this finding: Susan Harter (1999) explored how feeling competent in each of her five "self-worth" dimensions—scholastic abilities, conduct, athletic skills, peer likeability, and appearance (discussed in Chapter 6)—related to teenagers' overall self-esteem. She found that being happy about one's looks outweighed *anything else* in determining whether adolescents generally felt good about themselves.

This finding is not just true of teenagers in the United States. It appears in surveys conducted in many countries among people at various stages of life. If we are happy with the way we look, we are likely to be happy with who we are as human beings.

Feeling physically appealing is important to everyone (Mellor and others, 2010). But, in a late-twentieth-century study, Harter found that, beginning in elementary school, girls in particular get increasingly distressed with their looks (see Figure 1.5 on page 25). One reason for this gender difference comes as no surprise—the intense cultural pressure for females to be thin.

The Differing Body Concerns of Girls and Boys

The distorting impact of the **thin ideal**, or pressure to be abnormally thin, was graphically suggested in an Irish survey. The researchers found that 3 out of 4 female teens with average BMIs felt they were too fat (Lawler & Nixon, 2011). More alarming, 2 out of 5, of the *underweight* girls in this poll also wanted to shed pounds (Lawler & Nixon, 2011). While some boys in this study (those who were genuinely heavy, for instance) also worried about their weight, males tend to want to build up their muscles—and are at risk of spending excessive hours at the gym laboring to increase their body mass (Parent & Moradi, 2011; Smolak & Stein, 2010).

Body concerns are apt to take over children's lives at puberty because, during early adolescence, social sensitivities reach a peak (more about this in the next chapter). But new research suggests that the uniquely female weight obsession may

LEARNING OUTCOMES

- List several influences promoting teenage body distress.
- Contrast the different eating disorders.
- Evaluate eating disorder treatments.

thin ideal Media-driven cultural idea that females need to be abnormally thin.

When did our culture develop the idea that women should be unrealistically thin? Historians trace this change to the 1970s, when extremely slim actresses like Audrey Hepburn became our cultural ideal. More recently, as shown in the second photo, similar body pressures have infected the other sex, causing pubescent boys to struggle for the muscular male shape that is our contemporary cultural ideal.

actually have pre-birth epigenetic roots. One group of scientists discovered that mothers exposed to intense stress during pregnancy were likely to have daughters with eating issues (Steigler & Thaler, 2016). In perhaps the most provocative study, scientists found that female twin pairs were more apt to develop unhealthy dieting practices at puberty than fraternal twin girls whose other twin was male. This fascinating finding suggests that testosterone (given off by the male twin's body) may dampen down a *biological* tendency for girls to become weight obsessed during their pubertal years (Culbert and others, 2013).

Still, even if the signal to "be supersensitive to weight" has biological roots, outer-world pressures prime the pump: Pre-teens love to tease one another about weight ("Ha, ha, you are getting fat!") (Compian, Gowen, & Hayward, 2004; Jackson & Chen, 2008; Lawler & Nixon, 2011). As you will see soon, this teasing can activate unhealthy dieting practices that wreak havoc on vulnerable children's lives (Douglas & Varnado-Sullivan, 2016).

A primary culprit is the media, for its regular drumbeat advocating the female thin ideal. As early as preschool, one study showed, girls have internalized the message, "You need to be thin" (Harriger and others, 2010). Digitally altered images beamed from TV, the Internet, and magazines set body-size standards that are often impossible to attain (López-Guimerà and others, 2010). It's no wonder, then, that simply hours spent watching media, predicts body dissatisfaction in both ballet dancers and nonphysically active girls (Nerini, 2015).

Still, some children are less susceptible to the media messages. In Albert Bandura's social learning framework, for instance, African American and Latino girls should be more insulated from the thin ideal because their role models, such as Beyoncé, demonstrate that beauty comes in ample sizes. As one young African American woman in an interview study explained: "I feel like . . . for the woman of color . . . the look is like thick thighs, you know, fat butt . . . [men] like, like want you to have meat on your body" (quoted in Hesse-Biber and others, 2010, p. 704).

Does this mean that, unless they are obese, Latino and African American teens don't worry about their weight? Unfortunately, if an ethnic minority girl identifies with the mainstream Western thin ideal, she is just as likely to develop eating disorders as any other teen (Sabik, Cole, & Ward, 2010). What *exactly* are eating disorders like?

Eating Disorders

In the morning I'll have a black coffee. At noon I have a mix of shredded lettuce, carrots and cabbage. At around dinnertime I have 9 mini whole-wheat crackers. On a bad day I may have . . . with my (morning) black coffee an egg white, . . .
(adapted from Juarascio, Shoaib, & Timko, 2010, p. 402)

Scales are evil! But I'm obsessed with them! I'm on the damn thing like 3 times a day!
(adapted from Gavin, Rodham, & Poyer, 2008, pp. 327–328)

As these quotations from "pro-anorexia" social network sites show, **eating disorders** differ from "normal" dieting. Here, eating becomes a person's sole focus in life. Imagine waking up and planning each day around eating (or not eating). You monitor every morsel. You are obsessed with checking and rechecking your weight. Or you have the impulse to gorge every time you approach the refrigerator or buy a box of candy at the store. Let's now explore three classic forms these fixations take: anorexia, bulimia, and binge eating disorder.

Anorexia nervosa, the most serious eating disorder, is defined by self-starvation — specifically to the point of reaching 85 percent of one's ideal body weight or less. (This means that if a girl should weigh 110 pounds, she now weighs less than 95 pounds.)

Interestingly, due to an epigenetic process, this fraternal twin girl may be more insulated from developing an eating disorder as a teen by simply being exposed to the circulating testosterone her brother's body is giving off.

eating disorder A pathological obsession with getting and staying thin. The best-known eating disorders are *anorexia nervosa* and *bulimia nervosa*.

anorexia nervosa A potentially life-threatening eating disorder characterized by pathological dieting (resulting in severe weight loss and, in females, loss of menstruation) and by a distorted body image.

Another common feature of this primarily female disorder is that leptin levels have become too low to support adult fertility and the girl stops menstruating. A hallmark of eating disorders—among both girls and boys—is a distorted body image (Espeset and others, 2011). Even when people look skeletal, they feel fat. They often compulsively exercise, running for hours and abandoning their other commitments to spend every day at the gym (Holland, Brown, & Keel, 2014).

People with eating disorders may be disconnected from reality, denying that their symptoms apply to them ("Oh no, I don't binge and purge") (Gratwick-Sarll and others, 2016). Sometimes they literally don't see their true body size: As a girl named Sarah commented: "I remember . . . passing an open door and saw myself in the mirror . . . and thought 'Oh gosh, she is thin!' But then when I understood that it was actually me, I didn't see me as thin anymore" (quoted in Espeset and others, 2011, p. 183).

Anorexia is a life-threatening disease. People who drop to two-thirds of their ideal weight or less need to be hospitalized and fed—intravenously, if necessary—to stave off death (Diamanti and others, 2008). A student of mine who now runs a self-help group for people with eating disorders provided a vivid reminder of the enduring physical toll anorexia can cause. Alicia informed the class that she had permanently damaged her heart muscle during her bout with this devastating disease.

Bulimia nervosa is typically not life threatening because the person's weight often stays within a normal range. However, because this disorder involves frequent binging (at least once weekly eating sprees in which thousands of calories may be consumed in a matter of hours) and either purging (getting rid of the food by vomiting or misusing laxatives and diuretics) or fasting, bulimia can seriously compromise health. In addition to producing deficiencies of basic nutrients, the purging episodes can cause mouth sores, ulcers in the esophagus, and the loss of tooth enamel due to being exposed to stomach acid.

Binge eating disorder, which first appeared in the *Diagnostic and Statistical Manual (DSM-5)* in 2013, involves recurrent out-of-control eating. The person wolfs down huge quantities of food and then may be wracked by feelings of disgust, guilt, and shame. This mental disorder was added to the *DSM-5* because (no surprise) it is intimately tied to obesity and so presents a serious threat to health (Myers & Wiman, 2014). Binge eating disorder, like anorexia and bulimia, can also wreak havoc on a person's life (Goldschmidt and others, 2014).

How common are these mainly female teenage and young-adult disorders? In one 8-year-long community survey, binge eating was most prevalent, affecting roughly 3 in 100 young women over that time; bulimia ranked second (at 2.6 in 100). Thankfully, the most serious condition, anorexia, struck only 8 out of 1,000 girls. The bad news is that subclinical (less severe) forms of eating disorders may affect an astonishing 18 million people in the United States at some point in their lives (Forbush & Hunt, 2014).

What causes these conditions? Twin studies strongly suggest anorexia and bulimia have a hereditary component (Striegel-Moore & Bulik, 2007). Whether due to shared genetic propensities to develop these disorders or parents with their own eating issues continually reinforcing the message ("There is *nothing* worse than being fat!"), these debilitating preoccupations tend to be passed down from parents to children (Lydecker & Grilo, 2016). One strong, nonspecific risk factor that provokes eating disorders involves internalizing issues—worrying excessively (Sala & Levinson, 2016), being depressed, and experiencing intense mood fluctuations (Lavender and others, 2016; Munch, Hunger, & Schweitzer, 2016). When these temperamentally vulnerable children are teased about their weight and internalize the thin ideal, eating disorders

bulimia nervosa An eating disorder characterized by at least biweekly cycles of binging and purging in an obsessive attempt to lose weight.

binge eating disorder A newly labeled eating disorder defined by recurrent, out-of-control binging.

What causes teenage girls to develop eating disorders? This condition is apt to be provoked by varying forces.

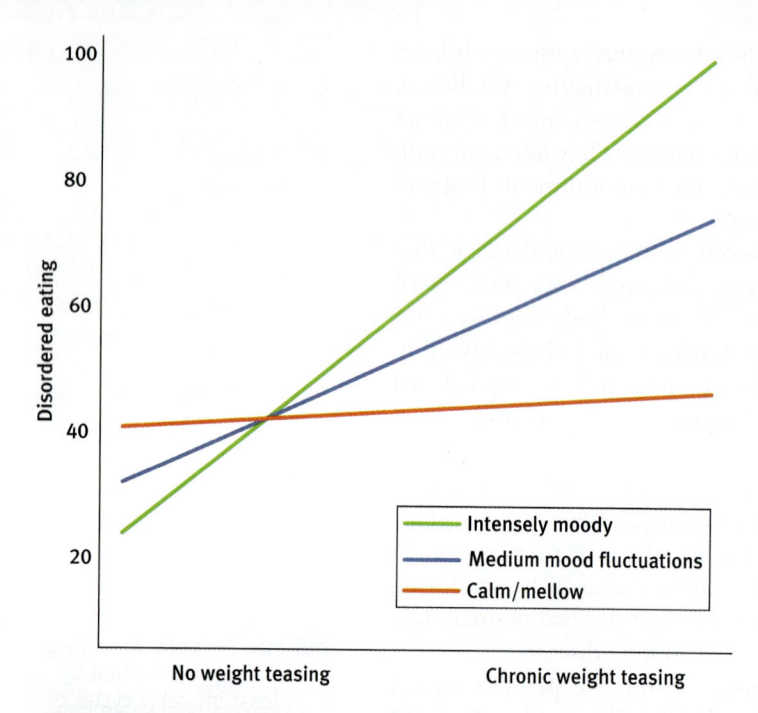

FIGURE 8.6: The interaction between "mood fluctuations," weight teasing, and pathological eating among a sample of girls This chart shows that when girls are intensely moody, being teased about weight is likely to escalate into eating disorder symptoms; but for mellow girls, weight-teasing has no impact on problematic eating.

Data from Douglas and Varnado-Sullivan, 2016, p. 171.

can flare up (Douglas & Varnado-Sullivan, 2016; see Figure 8.6).

Researchers find that teens with eating disorders have other symptoms: insecure attachments (Munch, Hunger, & Schweitzer, 2016) and an extreme need for approval (Abbate-Daga and others, 2010). These children tend to be perfectionists (Lavender and others, 2016), prone to bouts of intensely low self-worth (Fairchild & Cooper, 2010). At bottom, teenagers with eating disorders have low *self-efficacy*—they feel out of control of their lives.

Table 8.2 offers a summary checklist for determining whether a teenager you love is at risk for developing an eating disorder. Still, if you know a young person who is struggling with this issue, there is brighter news. Most adolescents grow out of eating problems as they get older and construct a satisfying adult life (Keel and others, 2007). And, contrary to popular opinion, therapy for eating disorders works!

Table 8.2: Is a Teenager at Risk for an Eating disorder? A Checklist

(Background influences: Has this child reached puberty? Is this child female?)
1. Does this teen have parents with eating issues?
2. Is she prone to worry, and does she have intense mood swings?
3. Does this girl have insecure attachments, set excessively high standards for her behavior, and have an overpowering need to be liked?
4. Does this child have very low self-efficacy?
5. Has this child been continually teased about her weight, and responded by vigorously internalizing the idea, "I *must* be thin"?

INTERVENTIONS: Improving Teenagers' Body Image

Perhaps the best place to begin to treat young people with eating disorders is to examine how girls who embrace their bodies reason and think. These adolescents do not deny their "imperfections," but focus on their physical pluses. They care about their health—eating nutritious foods, appreciating what their bodies can do (Frisén & Holmqvist, 2010). They feel accepted for their bodies and avoid abusing cigarettes or alcohol (Andrew, Tiggemann, & Clark, 2016). They tend to be spiritually oriented (Boisvert & Harrell, 2013) and understand what *really* makes people beautiful in life. As one woman named Heather put it: "You have to remind yourself that even though [the thin ideal] is what [the media are all about] . . . promoting, self-esteem really looks the best" (Wood-Barcalow, Tylka, & Augustus-Horvath, 2010, p. 115).

Heather's remarks explain why a popular eating-disorder treatment (called *dialectic behavior therapy*) teaches meditation and strategies to promote self-efficacy (feeling in control of one's life) (Tanofsky-Kraff and others, 2015). Therapists have devised other creative approaches, such as repeatedly exposing women to video images of themselves, to train them to see their real body size (Trentowska, Svaldi, & Tuschen-Caffier, 2014).

One innovative treatment ignores *any* underlying psychological causes. Some therapists have had success by keeping the girl's body temperature warm and training her in the appropriate amount to eat via a scale under a plate that measures her intake (Bergh and others, 2013).

Although eating disorders have the reputation of being hard to cure, the reverse seems true. This may explain why therapists who treat these young people have lower burnout rates than do their colleagues (Thompson-Brenner, 2013; Warren and others, 2013) and find such personal meaning in this work (Zerbe, 2013).

The same upbeat message is typical of much (but not all) of the research relating to our final topic: teenage sex.

Tying It All Together

1. Kimberly, an eleventh grader, tells you, "I am ugly," but knows she is terrific in sports and academics. According to Harter's studies, is Kimberly likely to have high or low self-esteem?

2. Amy is regularly on a diet, trying for that Barbie-doll figure. Jasmine, who is far below her ideal body weight, is always exercising and has cut her food intake down to virtually nothing. Sophia, whose weight is normal, goes on eating sprees followed by purges every few days. Clara also has regular, out-of-control eating sprees, after which she says she feels like a bloated "blimp." Identify which girls have an eating disorder, and name each person's specific problem.

3. Pick which three female teens seem protected from developing an eating disorder: *Cotonya, whose role model is Beyoncé; Caroline, who has high self-efficacy; Cora, who has a twin brother; Connie, who exercises for an hour every day.*

4. Eating disorders are very hard to treat—*true* or *false*?

Answers to the Tying It All Together questions can be found at the end of this chapter.

Sexuality

548: Immculate ros: Sex sex sex that all you think about?

559: Snowbunny: people who have sex at 16 r sick:

560: Twonky: I agree

564: 00o0CaFfEinNe; no sex until ur happily married—Thtz muh rule

566: Twonky: I agree with that too.

567: Snowbunny: me too caffine!

(quoted in Subrahmanyam, Greenfield, & Tynes, 2004, p. 658)

LEARNING OUTCOMES

- Outline recent trends in teenage sexuality.
- Explore forces influencing the transition to intercourse.
- Critique the sexual double standard and school-based sex education.

Sex is the elephant in the room of teenage life. Everyone knows it's a top-ranking issue, but the adult world often shies away from mentioning it. Celebrated in the media, minimized or ignored by parents ("If I talk about it, I'll encourage my child to do it") (see Elliot, 2012; Hyde and others, 2013), the issue of when and whether to have sex is left for teenagers to decide on their own as they filter through conflicting messages and—as you can see above—vigorously stake out their positions in online chats.

It is a minefield issue that contemporary young people negotiate in different ways. Poll your classmates. Some people, as with the teenagers quoted above, may advocate abstinence, believing that everyone should remain a virgin until marriage. Others probably believe that having sex within a loving relationship is fine. Some students, if they are being honest, will admit, "I want to try out the sexual possibilities, but I promise to use contraception!"

This increasing acceptability (within limits) of carving out our own sexual path was highlighted in sexual surveys polling U.S. high school seniors in 1950, 1972, and 2000 (Caron & Moskey, 2002). Over the years, the number of seniors who decided that it's OK for teenagers to have sex shot up from a minority to more than 70 percent. But in the final, turn-of-the-century poll, more teens agreed that a person could decide to not have sex and still be popular. Most felt confident they would use birth control when they were sexually active and could wait to have intercourse until they got married. How are these efficacious attitudes translated into action? Let's begin our exploration at the sexual starting gate—with desire.

Exploring Sexual Desire

David, age 14: Since a year or so ago, I just think about sex and masturbation ALL THE TIME! I mean I just think about having sex no matter where I am and I'm aroused all the time. Is that normal?

Expert's reply: Welcome to the raging hormones of adolescence!
(adapted from a teenage sexuality online advice forum)

At what age does sexual desire begin? Although scientists had long assumed that the answer was during puberty, when testosterone is pumping through the body, research with homosexual adults caused them to rethink this idea. When gay women and men were asked to recall a watershed event in their lives—the age when they first realized that they were physically attracted to a person of the same sex—their responses centered around age 10. At that age, the output of the adrenal androgens is rising but testosterone production has not yet fully geared up (McClintock & Herdt, 1996). So our first sexual feelings seem programmed by the adrenal androgens and appear before we undergo the visible changes of puberty, by about fourth grade!

How do sex hormone levels relate to teenagers' sexual desires? According to researchers, we need a threshold androgen level to prime our initial feelings of desire (Udry, 1990; Udry & Campbell, 1994). Then, signals from the environment feed back to heighten interest in sex. As children see their bodies changing, they think of themselves in a new, sexual way. Reaching puberty evokes a different set of signals from the outside world. A ninth-grade boy finds love notes in his locker. A seventh-grade girl notices men looking at her differently as she walks down the street. The physical changes of puberty and how outsiders react to those changes usher us into our lives as sexual human beings. Which young people act on those desires by having intercourse as teens?

Who Is Having Intercourse?

Today, the average age of first intercourse in the United States is 17.8 for women and 18 for men (Finer & Philbin, 2014). But about 1 in 8 children make a "sexual debut" by age 15 (Guttmacher Institute, 2014; see also Figure 8.7).

As ecological developmental systems theory suggests, a variety of forces predict what researchers call an earlier *transition to intercourse*. One influence, for both boys and girls, is biological—being on an earlier puberty timetable. Ethnicity and socioeconomic status (SES) also matter. African Americans and lower-income males are more apt to be sexually active at younger ages (Finer & Philbin, 2014; Moilanen and others, 2010; Zimmer-Gembeck & Helfand, 2008).

Personality makes a difference. Teens who are more impulsive—that is, those with externalizing tendencies—are apt to make the transition earlier (Moilanen and others, 2010). For European American girls, one study suggested that having a risk-taking personality and low social self-worth correlated with being advanced sexually—that is, engaging in pre-intercourse activities such as fondling at age 12 (Hipwell and others, 2010). Conversely, also for girls, having religious parents predicts staying a virgin because it makes it more likely that a teen will have close church friends who agree that abstinence is the way to go (Landor and others, 2011).

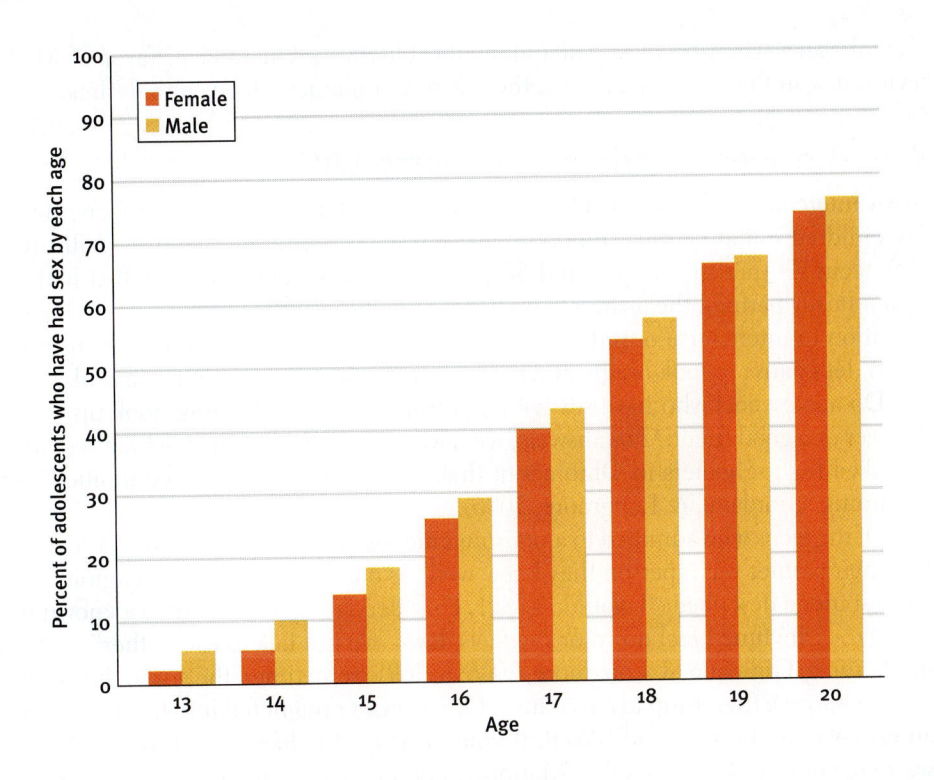

FIGURE 8.7: Percent of U.S. teens who have had intercourse, at different ages This chart pinpoints late adolescence as the tipping point when most American teens have had sex. But it also shows (not unexpectedly) that intercourse rates rise dramatically with age.

Data from Guttmacher Institute, 2014.

This brings up the crucial role of peers. As I described in the discussion of early-maturing girls, we can predict a teenager's chance of having intercourse by looking at the company she (or he) chooses. Having an older boyfriend or girlfriend (no surprise) raises the chance of a child's becoming sexually active (Martin, 1996). In fact, scientists can make precise statistical calculations of a teen's intercourse odds based on the number of people in that child's social circle who have gone "all the way" (Ali & Dwyer, 2011). So, just as with other aspects of human behavior, to understand whether a teen is sexually active, look at the values and behaviors of his (or her) group.

You also might want to look at what a child watches on TV. In one fascinating study, researchers were able to predict which virgin boys and girls became sexually active from looking at their prior TV watching practices. Teens who reported watching a heavy diet of programs with sexually oriented talk, especially in mixed gender groups, were twice as likely to have intercourse in the next year as the children who did not watch such shows (Collins and others, 2004).

Since sexual experiences (affairs, and so on) are a common media theme, we might predict that simply watching a good deal of television would promote an earlier transition to intercourse. We would be wrong. With any media, it's the content that matters—whether a child prefers sex-laced cable channels (Bersamin and others, 2008), gravitates to Internet porn, or avidly consumes magazines like *Cosmo* rather than sticking to *Seventeen* (Walsh, 2008).

Should we blame *Cosmo* reports such as "101 Ways to Drive Him Wild in Bed" for *causing* teenagers to start having sex? A bidirectional influence is probably in operation here. If a teenager is *already* interested in sex, that boy or girl will gravitate toward media that fit this passion. For me, the tip-off was raiding my parents' library to read the steamy scenes in that forbidden book, D. H. Lawrence's *Lady Chatterley's Lover*. Today, parents know that their child has entered a different

Is my teenage daughter having intercourse? Researchers can now offer parents precise odds by determining how many people in this crowd of best buddies have gone "all the way."

mental space when he or she abandons the Discovery Channel in favor of MTV. Swimming in this sea of media sex, then, further inflames a teenager's desires.

Who Are Teens Having Intercourse With?

Many intercourse episodes on TV involve one-night stands (Grube and others, 2008). Are children imitating these models when they start having intercourse? With most U.S. teens (70 percent of girls and 56 percent of boys) reporting they first had sex with a steady partner, the answer is no. But as roughly 1 in 5 teens report making the transition to intercourse outside of a committed relationship (Guttmacher Institute, 2014), let's pause to look briefly at what these nonromantic encounters are like.

Do adolescents who have sex with a person they are not dating hook up with a stranger or a good friend? For answers, we have an interview study in which researchers asked high schoolers in Ohio about their experiences with "noncommitted" sex (Manning, Giordano, & Longmore, 2006).

Of the teens who admitted to a nonromantic sexual encounter, 3 out of 4 reported that their partner was a person they knew well. As one boy, who lost his virginity with his best friend described: "I wouldn't really consider dating her . . . but I've known her so long . . . anytime I feel down or she feels down, we just talk to each other" (quoted in Manning, Giordano, & Longmore, 2006, p. 469). Sometimes, the goal of having sex was to change a friendship to a romance. Or a teenager might fall into having sex with an ex-boyfriend or girlfriend: "Well, it kind of happened like towards the end when we were both friends" (quoted in Manning, Giordano, & Longmore, 2006, p. 470).

So far, I have painted a benign portrait of these more casual, "friends with benefits" experiences. Not so! Having one-night stands or on again/off again relationships is a risk factor for depression (see Chapter 10). This brings up the supposedly clashing sexual agendas of women and men.

Hot in Developmental Science: Is There Still a Sexual Double Standard?

> It's different for boys, it's like . . . if they have sex with somebody and then they are rewarded . . . and all the guys are just like "That's great!" You have sex, and you're a girl and it's like "Slut." That's how it is . . .
>
> (quoted in Martin, 1996, p. 86)

These complaints from a 16-year-old girl named Erin refer to the well-known **sexual double standard.** Boys are supposed to want sex; girls are supposed to resist. Teenage boys get reinforcement for "getting to home base." Intercourse is fraught with ambivalence and danger for girls: "Should I do it? Will he love me if I do it? Will he love me if I don't? Will I get pregnant? What will my friends and my parents think?"

Basic to the stereotype of the double standard is the idea that girls are looking for committed relationships and that boys mainly want sex. The Ohio study, discussed in the previous section, as well as more recent research conducted in South Africa (Bhana, 2016), offer different views. Feeling emotionally intimate, most teens reported, was their main priority. And when a couple did have sex—often in a close relationship—the decision was frequently as difficult for guys as for girls. Read what a boy named Tim had to say:

> That was something that I had been saving. I really wanted to save it for marriage, but I was curious and um she was special enough to me that I could give her this part of my life that I had been saving and um . . . She felt the same way because she wanted to wait till marriage, but we had decided and we was [were] both curious I guess and so it just happened.
>
> (quoted in Giordano, Manning, & Longmore, 2010, p. 1007)

---

sexual double standard A cultural code that gives men greater sexual freedom than women. Specifically, society expects males to want to have intercourse and expects females to remain virgins until they marry and to be more interested in relationships than in having sex.

Moreover, when sex happened too quickly, as this next quotation shows, boys—as much as girls—were turned off:

> She was like . . . moving too fast . . . like she wanted to have sex with me in the car and I'm like "No" and then she starts touching me and I'm like "I'm cool, I'm cool; I got to go". . . . And I did that and I left. . . . I was just, I don't know; she wasn't the girl I wanted to have sex with. . . . She wasn't the right girl.
> (quoted in Giordano, Manning, & Longmore, 2010, p. 1002)

In this study, both male and female teens reported that the decision to have sex was mutual; no one was pressuring anyone else. Or, as another boy named Tim delightfully put it:

> So if a girl says yes and a boy says no; it's a maybe. If a guy doesn't know and a girl says yes, it's yes. . . . If a girl says yes and a guy says yes, it's yes. . . . So I think the women have more control because their opinion matters more in that situation.
> (quoted in Giordano, Manning, & Longmore, 2010, p. 1007)

Is it really true, as Tim implies, that females are the main initiators (aggressors) when it comes to sex? Consider this revealing evidence from the virtual world: When researchers analyzed the profile photo comments on a popular Belgian social network site, they found that girls' sexually oriented responses to boys' posted photos far outnumbered boys' comments to the photos posted by girls.

Here are a few enthusiastic female posts that a boy named Kendeman's photo evoked: "You are **** . . . beautiful!" "I just wanted to say this because I think you are wonderfuuuuuul. Nobody can compete with you!" (Quoted from De Ridder & Van Bauwell, 2013, p. 576.)

What are the teens who avidly scan the photos on a social network site likely to do? The surprise is that girls may decide to post more assertive, sexually oriented comments than boys.

So, even though the double standard seems firmly in operation, when we hear male teens brag about their exploits or listen to people make comments about "sluts and studs," the reality is complex. Boys want sex in a loving relationship—just like girls (Ott and others, 2006). In terms of making the first sexually oriented moves, either online or, sometimes, in the flesh—if anything, an anti-double standard can apply!

Wrapping Up Sexuality: Contemporary Trends

In summary, the news about teenage sexuality is good. Teenagers today feel more confident about charting their sexual path. Most sexual encounters occur in committed love relationships. The decision to have teenage sex is not typically taken

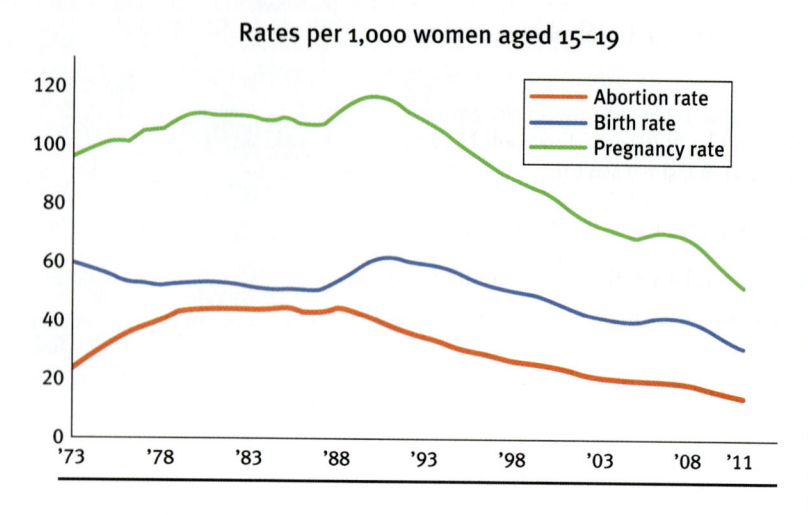

FIGURE 8.8: Encouraging snapshots of twenty-first-century teenage sexuality in the United States The news about adolescent pregnancy is good! For the past 30 years, teen abortion rates and especially adolescent pregnancies and births dramatically declined to reach historic lows in 2011.

Data from American Teens' Sources of Sexual Health Education, 2016.

Because teenagers are passionate for guidelines about how to have loving relationships, this high school couple might love romance education classes!

lightly, but in a climate of caring and mutual decision making for both girls and boys. Girls have far more control in the sexual arena than we think!

These changes are mirrored in the encouraging statistics in Figure 8.8: lower abortion rates and fewer U.S. teenage pregnancies and births. In fact, over the decade spanning the late 1990s to the early twenty-first century, teen pregnancy rates in the United States dipped from more than 5 to 4 per 1,000 girls.

Still, with regard to teenage pregnancy, the United States ranks near the pinnacle of the developed world. While European teens have comparable levels of sexual activity as U.S. adolescents, EU pregnancy rates put the United States to shame (Guttmacher Institute, 2014; McKay & Barrett, 2010). Compared to Western Europe, the prevalence of gonorrhea and chlamydia among U.S. adolescents is very high (Guttmacher Institute, 2011b).

INTERVENTIONS: Toward Teenager-Friendly Sex Education

These less-than-flattering statistics bring us back to the issue I alluded to in my discussion of puberty: sex education. Clearly, in its mission to prevent teenage pregnancy, the United States is falling short. Could *one* reason be that teens are not getting the "correct" information in school sex-education classes?

Actually, around the world, school sex education offers a patchwork of slip-shod strategies. Some school systems and countries teach only abstinence. Others discuss contraception and sexually transmitted infections (STIs). Some teach teens about alternative lifestyles, such as being gay. Other nations have no school sex education at all. The reason comes as no surprise: From Canada to Australia (Goldman & Coleman, 2013) to South Africa (Francis & DePalma, 2014), parents are deeply divided about what to say to teens about sex (Elliot, 2012).

One classic fear is that teaching contraception might encourage teens to have intercourse. This we *know* is not true. Comprehensive sex education, not only helps prevent pregnancy, but it can delay the transition to intercourse (UNFPA, 2015). When Irish researchers compared young people in that nation who had high school sex education versus a group who had received no instruction, girls and boys exposed to the classes became sexually active at an *older age* than their peers (Bourke and others, 2014).

Some of you reading this information might think, "OK, maybe that's true, but having my child's school discuss contraception violates my own moral principles because I believe abstinence is the only way to go." Perhaps everyone might agree with this next approach.

For decades, teens have complained that high school sex education is irrelevant to their lives. Adolescents say they are hungering for different information: "How can I develop a relationship?" "What does it mean to fall in love?" (See Martin, 1996.)

Therefore, controversies about whether to teach contraception may be missing the boat. We now know that most teens, even in permissive EU nations such as Belgium, want to have sex in a committed relationship (Van Damme & Biltereyst, 2013). Young people are passionate to connect with a romantic partner in a fulfilling way. Since teenagers may be reluctant to discuss these embarrassing "adult" yearnings with their parents, to really speak to young people's passions, sex education should center on much more than sex. Schools need romance education classes!

Tying It All Together

1. A mother asks you when her son will have his first sexual feelings. You answer: *around age 10, before the physical signs of puberty occur/around age 13 or 14/in the middle of puberty/toward the end of puberty.*

2. A friend thinks her teenage daughter may be having sex. So she asks for your opinion. All the following questions are relevant for you to ask *except*:
   a. Are your daughter's friends having sex?
   b. Is your daughter watching a lot of TV?
   c. Is your daughter watching sexually explicit cable channels with her male friends and reading *Cosmo*?
   d. Does your daughter have an older boyfriend?

3. Tom is discussing trends in teenage sex and pregnancy. Which *two* statements should he make?
   a. Today, sex often happens in a committed relationship.
   b. Today, the United States has lower teenage pregnancy rates than other Western nations.
   c. In recent decades, rates of teenage births in the United States have declined.
   d. Today, boys are still the sexual initiators.

4. Imagine you are designing a "model" sex-education program. According to this section, you should focus on:
   a. encouraging abstinence.
   b. providing information about birth control and STIs.
   c. discussing how to have loving relationships.

Answers to the Tying It All Together questions can be found at the end of this chapter.

SUMMARY

Puberty

Today, the physical changes of **puberty** occur during early adolescence, and there can be more than a decade between the time children physically mature and when they enter adult life. Because in agrarian societies a person's changing body used to be the signal to get married, many cultures devised **puberty rites** to welcome the physical changes. The **secular trend in puberty** has magnified the separation between puberty and full adulthood, the fact that **menarche** (and **spermarche**) are occurring at much younger ages.

Two hormonal command centers program puberty. The adrenal glands produce **adrenal androgens** starting in middle childhood. The **HPG axis**, the main system that sets the bodily changes in motion, involves the hypothalamus, the pituitary, and the **gonads** (ovaries and testes), which produce estrogens and **testosterone** (found in both males and females). Leptin levels primed by a variety of environmental influences trigger the initial hypothalamic hormone.

The physical changes of puberty are divided into **primary sexual characteristics, secondary sexual characteristics,** and the **growth spurt.** Although in females puberty begins with the growth spurt and menarche occurs late in the process, the rate and sequence of this total body transformation varies from child to child. Because for males the externally visible changes of puberty occur later and the organs of reproduction are the first to start developing, the puberty timetables of the sexes are not as far apart as they appear.

The striking individual differences in pubertal timing are mainly genetically programmed. African American children tend to reach puberty at younger ages. For girls, being overweight and having stressful family relationships are tied to reaching puberty earlier. These "environmental events" push up the hypothalamic timer, but strangely, mainly for females.

How children feel about their changing bodies varies, depending on the social environment. Breast development often evokes positive emotions. Feelings about menstruation may be more positive among upper middle class girls because today's affluent mothers are more apt to celebrate this change. First ejaculation is rarely discussed. Children tend to be embarrassed about their changing bodies around their opposite sex parent.

Girls who mature early are at risk of getting into trouble as teens (for example, taking drugs, getting pregnant, or doing poorly in school)—but mainly if they reach puberty in a stressful environment, live in a permissive culture, and get involved with older friends. Because they often end up heavier and shorter, these girls tend to have a poor body image and are more prone to be anxious and depressed.

Based on early research, developmentalists argued against moving pre-teens to middle school; but in general, the key is to provide nurturing schools at this vulnerable age. Parents should discuss puberty with their children, especially their sons. We need to be alert to potential problems with early-maturing girls. We need to begin puberty education earlier and consider implementing global guidelines for elementary school children that focus on respecting one's body.

Body Image Issues

How children feel about their looks is closely tied to their overall self-esteem. Girls tend to feel worse about their looks than boys do, partly because society expects women to adhere to the **thin ideal.** Boys feel pressured to build up their muscles. The female impulse to be thin may have biological roots, but peer pressures and media images play an important role in this widespread passion.

The three **eating disorders** are **anorexia nervosa** (severe underweight resulting from obsessive dieting), **bulimia nervosa** (chronic binging and often purging), and **binge eating disorder** (binging alone). Family pressures, perfectionistic tendencies, mood swings, and low self-esteem put girls at special risk for these problems. Weight teasing can provoke eating disorders in vulnerable children. Eating-disorder interventions take varied forms, and treatments for these problems often do work.

Sexuality

Teenagers today feel freer to make their own decisions about whether and when to have intercourse. While sexual desire is triggered by the adrenal androgens and first switches on at around age 10, sexual signals from the outside world feed back to cause children to become interested in sex.

Factors that predict making the transition to intercourse include race, SES, family and peer influences, and gravitating to sex-laden media. Most teens have their first intercourse experience in a romantic relationship. Non-committed sex most often takes place with someone an adolescent knows well. Although the **sexual double standard** suggests that boys just want sex and girls are interested in relationships, both males and females are mainly interested in love. Ironically, our image of men as the sexual aggressors may operate in the opposite way in the "real world."

The good news about U.S teenage sexuality is that pregnancy rates are declining, although adolescent births are still markedly higher in the United States than in other Western nations. Rather than arguing about whether to teach contraception, educators should provide sex-education classes relevant to young people's real concerns: relationships and romance.

KEY TERMS

adrenal androgens, p. 226
anorexia nervosa, p. 238
binge eating disorder, p. 239
bulimia nervosa, p. 239
eating disorder, p. 238
gonads, p. 226
growth spurt, p. 227
HPG axis, p. 226
menarche, p. 225
primary sexual characteristics, p. 226
puberty, p. 223
puberty rite, p. 224
secondary sexual characteristics, p. 227
secular trend in puberty, p. 225
sexual double standard, p. 244
spermarche, p. 225
testosterone, p. 226
thin ideal, p. 237

ANSWERS TO Tying It All Together QUIZZES

Puberty

1. Today, puberty occurs a decade or more before we can fully reach adult life.
2. (a) The initial hypothalamic hormone triggers the pituitary to produce its hormones, which cause the ovaries and testes to mature and produce their hormones, which, in turn, produce the body changes. (b) Estrogens, testosterone, and the adrenal androgens.
3. Calista
4. *earlier*
5. An early-maturing girl

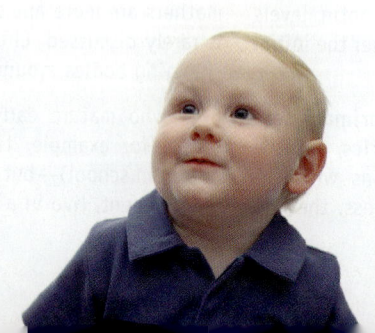

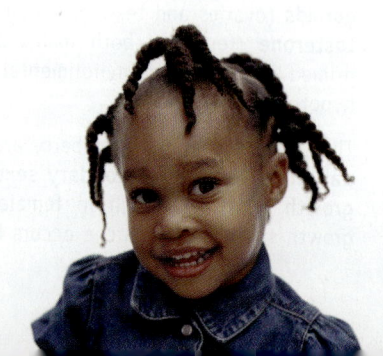

6. *Possible recommendations:* Pay special attention to providing nurturing schools in sixth and seventh grade. Push for more adequate, "honest" puberty education at a younger age, possibly in a format—such as online—where children can talk anonymously about their concerns. Institute a public awareness program encouraging parents to talk about puberty with a same-sex child. Encourage mothers to speak positively about menstruation and have dads discuss events such as spermarche with sons. Make everyone alert to the dangers associated with being an early-maturing girl and develop formal interventions targeted to this at-risk group. Institute sensitive, school-based "respect your body" discussions—based on the UNESCO guidelines—for children beginning in the early elementary school years.

Body Image Issues

1. Unfortunately, low self-esteem
2. Jasmine, Sophia, and Clara have eating disorders. Jasmine has the symptoms of anorexia nervosa; Sophia has the symptoms of bulimia nervosa. Clara has binge eating disorder.
3. Cotonya, Caroline, and Cora (We don't know about Connie—but, if she obsessively exercises just to stay thin, she might be at higher risk.)
4. False, as research suggests eating disorders are treatable.

Sexuality

1. Around age 10, before the physical signs of puberty occur
2. b
3. a and c
4. c, discussing how to have loving relationships

CONNECT ONLINE:

LaunchPad macmillan learning

Check out our videos and additional resources located at: www.macmillanlearning.com

CHAPTER 9

CHAPTER OUTLINE

Setting the Context

Cognitive and Emotional Development: The Mysterious Teenage Mind

Three Classic Theories of Teenage Thinking

Studying Three Aspects of Storm and Stress

HOW DO WE KNOW . . . That Adolescents Make Riskier Decisions When They Are with Their Peers?

HOT IN DEVELOPMENTAL SCIENCE: A Potential Pubertal Problem—Popularity

Different Teenage Pathways

Wrapping Things Up: The Blossoming Teenage Brain

INTERVENTIONS: Making the World Fit the Teenage Mind

EXPERIENCING ADOLESCENCE: Innocently Imprisoned at 16

Another Perspective on the Teenage Mind

Social Development

Separating from Parents

Connecting in Groups

A Note on Adolescence Worldwide

Cognitive, Emotional, and Social Development in Adolescents

Samantha's father began to worry when his daughter was in sixth grade. Suddenly, his sweet little princess was becoming so selfish, so moody, and so rude. She began to question everything, from her 10 o'clock curfew to why poverty exists. She had to buy clothes with the right designer label and immediately download the latest music. She wanted to be an individual, but her clique shaped every decision. She got hysterical if anyone looked at her the wrong way. Worse yet, Samantha was hanging out with the "popular" crowd—smoking, drinking, not doing her homework, cutting class.

Her twin brother, Sam, couldn't have been more different. Sam was obedient, an honor student, captain of the basketball team. He mellowly sailed into his teenage years. Actually, Sam defied the categories. He was smart and a jock. He volunteered to work with disabled children. He effortlessly moved among the brains, the popular kids, and the artsy groups at school. Still, this model child was passionate to vigorously test the limits. The most heart-stopping example happened when the police picked up Sam and a carload of buddies for drag racing. Sam's puzzled explanation: "Something just took over and I stopped thinking, Dad."

If you looked beneath the surface, however, both of his children were great. They were thoughtful, caring, and capable of having deep discussions about life. They just got caught up in the moment and lost their minds when they were with friends. What goes on in the teenage mind?

Think of our contradictory stereotypes about the teenage mind. Teenagers are idealistic, thoughtful, and introspective; concerned with larger issues; pondering life in deep ways; but also impulsive, moody, and out of control. Adolescents are the ultimate radicals, rejecting everything adults say, as well as the consummate conformists, dominated by the crowd and totally influenced by their peers.

These contradictory ideas are mirrored in confusing laws about when society views teens as "adults." In the United States, adolescents can sometimes be tried in adult courts at 14, an age when they are barred from seeing R-rated movies. Mature enough to vote at age 18, U.S. teens are unable to buy liquor until age 21. How is science shedding light on the teenage mind? That is the subject of the chapter you are about to read.

Left: SpeedKingz/Shutterstock.com

LEARNING OUTCOME
- Explain how teenagerhood evolved.

Setting the Context

> Youth are heated by nature as drunken men by wine.
>
> (Aristotle, n.d.)

> I would that there were no age between ten and twenty-three . . . , for there's nothing in between but getting wenches with child, wronging the anciently, stealing, fighting. . . .
>
> (William Shakespeare, *The Winter's Tale*, Act III)

As these quotations illustrate, throughout history, world-class geniuses viewed young people as being hot-headed and out of control. When, in 1904, G. Stanley Hall first identified a life stage characterized by **"storm and stress,"** which he called *adolescence*, he was only echoing these timeless ideas. Moreover, as youths' mission is to view the world in fresh, new ways, it makes sense that most societies would naturally view each new generation in ambivalent terms—praising young people for their passion and energy; fearing them as a threat.

However, until recently, young people never had time to rebel against society because they took on adult responsibilities at an early age. As I described in Chapter 1, adolescence became a distinct stage of life in the United States only during the twentieth century, when—for most children—going to high school became routine (Mintz, 2004; Modell, 1989; Palladino, 1996).

Look into your family history and you may find a great-grandparent who finished high school or college. But a century ago, most U.S. children left school after sixth or seventh grade to find work (Mintz, 2004). Unfortunately, however, in the 1930s, during the Great Depression, there was little work to be found. Idle young people roamed the countryside, angry and depressed. Alarmed by this situation, the Roosevelt administration proposed laws to lure young people to school. The legislation worked. By 1939, 75 percent of all U.S. teenagers were attending high school.

High school boosted the intellectual skills of a whole cohort of Americans. But it produced a generation gap between young people and their less educated, often immigrant parents and encouraged adolescents to spend their days together in isolated, age-segregated groups. Then, during the 1950s, when entrepreneurs began to target products to this new, lucrative "teen" market, we developed our familiar adolescent culture with its distinctive music and dress (Mintz, 2004; Modell, 1989). The sense of young people bonded together (against their elders) peaked during the late 1960s and early 1970s. With "Never trust anyone over 30" as its slogan, the baby-boom cohort rejected the rules relating to marriage and gender roles, and transformed the way we live (see Chapter 1).

This chapter explores adolescence in the contemporary developed world—a time when we expect every teenager to finish high school and so insulate young people from adult responsibilities for almost a decade after they reach puberty. First, I'll examine cognition and teenage emotions, then I'll chart how teenagers separate from their parents and relate to each other in groups.

Before beginning your reading, you might want to take the "Stereotypes About Adolescence: True or False?" quiz in Table 9.1. In the following pages, I'll discuss why each stereotype is right or wrong.

"storm and stress" G. Stanley Hall's phrase for the intense moodiness, emotional sensitivity, and risk-taking tendencies that characterize the life stage he labeled adolescence.

As illustrated in this famous 1930s photograph of a migrant family traveling across the arid Southwest to search for California jobs, during the Great Depression, there was no real adolescence because many children had to work from an early age to help support their families.

Table 9.1: Stereotypes About Adolescence: True or False?

T/F	1. Adolescents think about life in deeper, more thoughtful ways than children do.
T/F	2. Adolescence is when we develop our personal moral code for living.
T/F	3. Adolescents are highly sensitive to what other people think.
T/F	4. Adolescents are unusually susceptible to peer influences.
T/F	5. Adolescents are highly emotional, compared to other age groups.
T/F	6. Adolescents are prone to taking risks.
T/F	7. Most adolescents are emotionally disturbed.
T/F	8. Rates of suicide are at their peak during adolescence.
T/F	9. Adolescents feel more stressed out with their parents than with their peers.
T/F	10. Getting in with a bad crowd makes it more likely for teenagers to "go down the wrong path."

(Answers: 1. T, 2. T, 3. T, 4. T, 5. T, 6. T, 7. F, 8. F, 9. T, 10. T)

Cognitive and Emotional Development: The Mysterious Teenage Mind

LEARNING OUTCOMES
- Outline Piaget's, Kohlberg's, and Elkind's perspectives on adolescence.
- Explore adolescent brain development, teenage risk-taking, and storm and stress.
- Predict which teens are at risk for getting into serious trouble and which teens flourish.
- Evaluate how society and high schools can better fit the teenage mind.

Thoughtful and introspective, but impulsive and out of control; peer-centered conformists and rebellious risk-takers; capable of making mature decisions, but needing to be sheltered from the world: Can teenagers *really* be all these things? In our search to explain these contradictions, let's look at three classic theories of teenage thinking, then explore the research related to teenage storm and stress.

Three Classic Theories of Teenage Thinking

Have a conversation with a 16-year-old and a 10-year-old and you will be struck by the incredible mental growth that occurs during adolescence. It's not so much that teenagers know more than fourth or fifth graders, but that adolescents *think* in a different way. With an elementary school child, you can have a rational conversation about daily life. With a teenager, you can have a rational talk about *ideas*. This ability to reason abstractly about concepts defines Jean Piaget's formal operational stage.

Formal Operational Thinking: Abstract Reasoning at Its Peak

Children in concrete operations look beyond the way objects immediately appear. They realize that when Mommy puts on a mask, she's still Mommy "inside." They understand that when you pour a glass of juice into a different-shaped glass, the amount of liquid remains the same. Piaget believed that during the **formal operational stage**, at around age 12, thinking takes a qualitative leap (see Table 9.2 on page 254). Specifically, according to Piaget, adolescents can think logically in the realm of pure thought.

formal operational stage Jean Piaget's fourth and final stage of cognitive development, reached at around age 12 and characterized by teenagers' ability to reason at an abstract, scientific level.

Table 9.2: Piaget's Stages: Focus on Adolescence

Age	Name of Stage	Description
0–2	Sensorimotor	The baby manipulates objects to pin down the basics of physical reality.
2–7	Preoperations	Children's perceptions are captured by their immediate appearances: "What they see is what is real." They believe, among other things, that inanimate objects are really alive and that if the appearance of a quantity of liquid changes (for example, if it is poured from a short, wide glass into a tall, thin one), the amount of liquid itself changes.
8–12	Concrete operations	Children have a realistic understanding of the world. Their thinking is really on the same wavelength as that of adults. While they can reason conceptually about concrete objects, however, they cannot think abstractly in a scientific way.
12+	Formal operations	Reasoning is at its pinnacle: hypothetical, scientific, flexible, fully adult. Our full cognitive human potential has been reached.

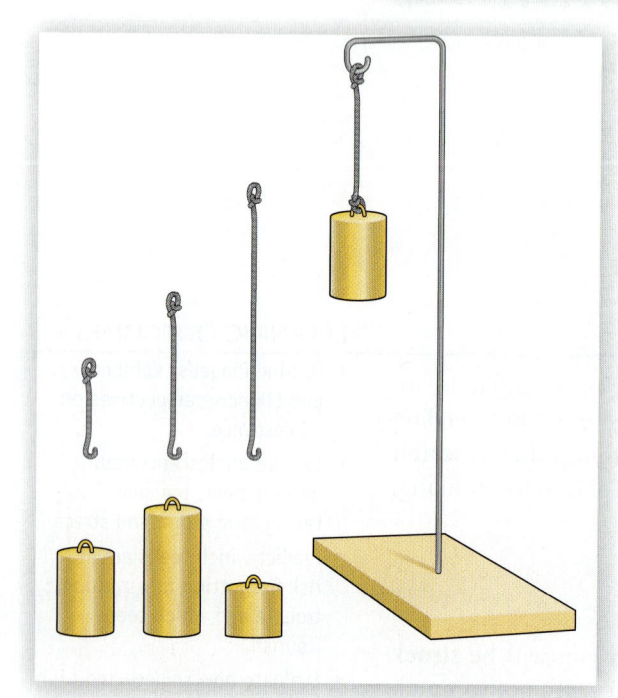

FIGURE 9.1: Piaget's pendulum apparatus: A task to assess whether children can reason scientifically Piaget presents the child with the different weights and string lengths illustrated here and shows the child how to attach them to the pendulum (and to one another). Then he says, "Your task is to discover what makes the pendulum swing more or less rapidly from side to side—is it the length of the string, the heaviness of the weight, or the height (and force) from which you release the pendulum?" and watches to see what happens.

Adolescents Can Think Logically About Concepts and Hypothetical Possibilities

Ask fourth or fifth graders to put objects such as sticks in order from small to large, and they will effortlessly perform this concrete operational task. But present a similar verbal challenge—such as "Bob is taller than Sam, and Sam is taller than Bill. Who is the tallest?"—and children are lost. The reason is that only adolescents can logically manipulate concepts in their minds (Elkind, 1968; Flavell, 1963).

Moreover, if you give a concrete operational child a reasoning task that begins, "Suppose snow is blue," she will refuse to go further, saying, "That's not true!" Adolescents in formal operations have no problem tackling that question because, once our thinking is liberated from concrete objects, we can reason about concepts that may *not* be real.

Adolescents Can Think Like Real Scientists

When our thinking occurs on an abstract plane, we can approach problems in a systematic way, devising a strategy to scientifically prove that something is true.

Piaget designed an exercise to reveal this new scientific thought: He presented children with a pendulum apparatus and unattached strings and weights (see Figure 9.1). Notice that the strings differ in length and that the weights vary in size or heaviness. The children's task was to connect the weights to the strings, then attach them to the pendulum, to decide which influence determined how quickly the pendulum swung from side to side. Was it the length of the string, the heaviness of the weight, or the height from which the string was released?

Think about this problem, and you may realize that being systematic is essential in order to solve this task—keeping everything constant but the factor whose influence you want to assess. (This is the defining characteristic of the experimental method described in Chapter 1.) To test whether it's the heaviness of the weight, keep the string length and the height from which you drop it constant, varying only the weight; then isolate another variable, keeping everything else the same. When you vary just the length of the string, you will realize that string length alone determines how quickly the pendulum swings.

Elementary school children, Piaget discovered, approach these problems haphazardly. Only adolescents adopt a true "experimental" strategy to solve reasoning tasks (Flavell, 1963; Ginsburg & Opper, 1969).

How Does This Change in Thinking Apply to Real Life?

The ability to think hypothetically and scientifically explains why it's not until high school that we can thrill to a poetic metaphor or comprehend chemistry experiments (Kroger, 2000). It's only during high school that we can join the debate team and argue the case for and against capital punishment, no matter what we *personally* believe. In fact, reaching the formal operational stage explains why teenagers are famous for debating *everything* in their lives. A 10-year-old who wants to stay up till 2 A.M. to watch a new movie will just keep saying, "I don't want to go to bed." A teenager will lay out his case point by point: "Mom, I got enough sleep last night. Besides, I only need six hours of sleep. I can go to bed after school tomorrow."

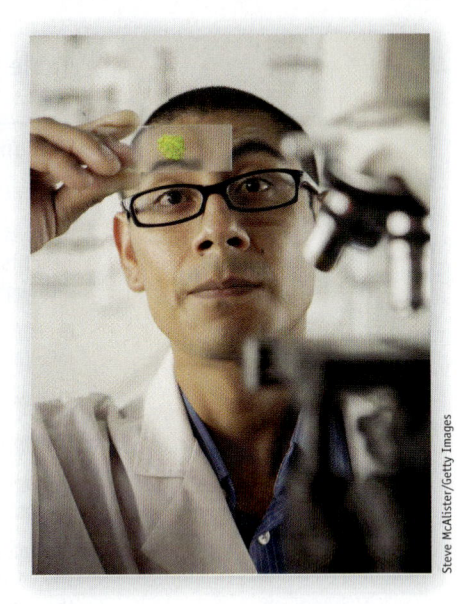

But do *all* adolescents reach formal operations? The answer is no. Rather than being universal, formal operational reasoning mainly occurs in scientifically oriented Western cultures. In fact, most people in *any* society don't make it to Piaget's final stage.

In one late-twentieth-century study, only a fraction of adults approached the pendulum problem scientifically. When asked to debate a controversial issue such as capital punishment, most people did not even realize that they needed to use logic to construct their case (Kuhn, 1989).

Does cognition *ever* change during adolescence in the way Piaget predicts? The answer is yes. Formal operational skills swing into operation when older teens plan their future lives.

Think back to the skills it took to get into college. You may have learned about your options from an adviser, researched possibilities on the Internet, visited campuses, and constructed different applications to showcase your talents. Then, when you got accepted, you needed to reflect on your future self again: "This school works financially, but is it too large? How will I feel about moving far from home?" Would you have been able to mentally weigh these different alternatives at age 10, 12, or 14?

The bottom line is that reaching concrete operations puts us on the same wavelength as adults. Formal operational thinking allows us to *behave* like adults.

Formal operations enables undergraduates like this young man to be a research collaborator in his professor's chemistry lab.

Kohlberg's Stages of Moral Judgment: Developing Internalized Moral Values

This new ability to reflect on our future allows us to reflect on our values. Therefore, drawing on Piaget's theory, developmentalist Lawrence Kohlberg (1981, 1984) argued that, during adolescence, we can develop a moral code that guides our lives. To measure this moral code, Kohlberg constructed ethical dilemmas, had people reason about these scenarios, and asked raters to chart the responses according to the three levels of moral thought outlined in Table 9.3 on page 256. Before looking at the table, take a minute to respond to the "Heinz dilemma," the most famous problem on Kohlberg's moral judgment test:

> A woman was near death from cancer. One drug might save her. The druggist was charging . . . ten times what the drug cost him to make. The . . . husband, Heinz, went to everyone he knew to borrow the money but he could only get together about half of what it cost. [He] asked the . . . druggist to sell it cheaper or let him pay later. But the druggist said NO! Heinz broke into the man's store to steal the drug. . . . Should he have done that? Why?
>
> (adapted from Reimer, Paolitto, & Hersh, 1983)

Discussing your plans with an adviser and realistically assessing your interests and talents involve the future-oriented adult thinking that only becomes possible in late adolescence. So, even if they don't reason at the formal operational level on Piaget's laboratory tasks, these high school seniors are probably firmly formal operational in the way they think about their lives.

Table 9.3: Kohlberg's Three Levels of Moral Reasoning, with Sample Responses to the Heinz Dilemma

Preconventional Thought

Description: Person operates according to a "Will I be punished or rewarded?" mentality.

Reasons given for acting in a certain way: (1) To avoid getting into trouble or to get concrete benefits. (2) Person discusses what will best serve his own needs ("Will it be good for me?"), although he may also recognize that others may have different needs.

Examples: (1) Heinz shouldn't steal the drug because then the police will catch him and he will go to jail. (2) Heinz should steal the drug because his wife will love him more.

Conventional Thought

Description: Person's morality centers on the need to obey society's rules.

Reasons given for acting in a certain way: (1) To be thought of as a "good person." (2) The idea that it's vital to follow the rules to prevent a breakdown in society.

Examples: (1) Heinz should steal the drug because that's what "a good husband" does; or Heinz should not steal the drug because good citizens don't steal. (2) Heinz can't steal the drug—even though it might be best—because, if one person decides to steal, so will another and then another, and then the laws would all break down.

Postconventional Thought

Description: Person has a personal moral code that transcends society's rules.

Reasons given for acting in a certain way: (1) Talks about abstract concepts, such as taking care of all people. (2) Discusses the fact that universally valid moral principles transcend anything society says.

Examples: (1) Although it's wrong for Heinz to steal the drug, there are times when rules must be disobeyed to provide for people's welfare. (2) Heinz must steal the drug because saving a human life is more important than every other consideration.

Information from Reimer, Paolitto, & Hersh, 1983.

---

preconventional thought In Lawrence Kohlberg's theory, the lowest level of moral reasoning, in which people approach ethical issues by only considering the personal punishments or rewards of their actions.

conventional thought In Lawrence Kohlberg's theory, the intermediate level of moral reasoning, in which people respond to ethical issues by discussing the need to uphold social norms.

postconventional thought In Lawrence Kohlberg's theory, the highest level of moral reasoning, in which people respond to ethical issues by applying their own moral guidelines apart from society's rules.

If you thought in terms of whether Heinz would be personally punished or rewarded for his actions, you would be classified at the lowest moral level, **preconventional thought**. Responses such as "Heinz should not take the drug because he will go to jail" or "Heinz should take the drug because then his wife will treat him well" suggest that, because your focus is on external consequences (that is, whether Heinz will get in trouble or be praised), you are not demonstrating *any* moral sense.

If you made comments such as "Heinz shouldn't [or should] steal the drug because it's a person's duty to obey the law [or to stick up for his wife]" or "Yes, human life is sacred, but the rules must be obeyed," your response is classified as **conventional thought**—the moral level right where adults typically rank. This shows your morality centers around the need to uphold society's norms.

People who reason about this dilemma using their own moral guidelines *apart* from society's rules are operating at Kohlberg's highest moral level, **postconventional thought**. A response that shows postconventional reasoning might be "Heinz had to steal the drug because nothing outweighs the universal principle of saving a life."

When Kohlberg conducted studies with different age groups, he discovered that at age 13, preconventional answers were universal. By 15 or 16, most children around the world were reasoning at the conventional stage. Yet many of us stop right there. Although some of Kohlberg's adults did think postconventionally, using his *incredibly* demanding criteria, almost no person consistently made it to the highest moral stage (Reimer, Paolitto, & Hersh, 1983; Snarey, 1985).

How Does Kohlberg's Theory Apply to Real Life?

Kohlberg's categories get us to think deeply about our values. Do you have a moral code that guides your actions? Would you intervene, no matter what the costs, to save a person's life? These categories give us insights into other people's moral priorities, too. While reading about Kohlberg's preconventional level, you might have thought: "I know someone just like this. This person has no ethics. He only cares about whether or not he gets caught!"

However, Kohlberg's idea that children can't go beyond a punishment-and-reward mentality is fundamentally wrong. As I described in Chapter 3, our basic sense of ethics naturally kicks in before we begin to speak!

In a classic late-twentieth-century paper, psychologist Carol Gilligan offered a feminist critique of Kohlberg's ideas. Recall that postconventional thinking requires abstractly weighing ideals of justice. Women's morality, Gilligan believes, revolves around concrete, caring-oriented criteria: "Hurting others is wrong"; "Moral people reach out in a nurturing way" (Gilligan & Attanucci, 1988).

Is Kohlberg's scale valid? Does the way teenagers reason about artificial scenarios mirror their ethical actions in the real world? Not necessarily. When exceptionally prosocial teenagers (for example, community leaders who set up programs for the homeless) took Kohlberg's test, researchers rated their answers at the same conventional stage as nonprosocial teens! (See Reimer, 2003.)

Actually, it makes perfect sense that the way someone *talks* about morality doesn't necessarily reflect actual behavior. We all know adults who spout the highest ethical principles but act despicably—such as the minister who lectures his congregation about the sanctity of marriage while cheating on his wife, or the chairperson of an ethics committee who has been taking bribes for years.

Still, when Kohlberg describes changes in moral reasoning during adolescence, he makes an important point. Teenagers are famous for questioning society's rules, for seeing the world's injustice, and for getting involved in idealistic causes. Unfortunately, this ability to step back and see the world as it should be, but rarely is, may produce the emotional storm and stress of teenage life.

Elkind's Adolescent Egocentrism: Explaining Teenage Storms

This was David Elkind's (1978) conclusion when he drew on Piaget's concept of formal operations to make sense of teenagers' emotional states. Elkind argued that when children make the transition to formal operational thought at about age 12, they see beneath the surface of adult rules. A sixth-grader realizes that his 10 o'clock bedtime, rather than being carved in stone, is an arbitrary number capable of being contested and changed. A socially conscious 14-year-old becomes acutely aware of the difference between what adults say they do and how they act. The same parents and teachers who punish you for missing your curfew or being late to class can't get to the dinner table or arrive at meetings on time.

According to Elkind, the realization that the emperor has no clothes ("Those godlike adults are no better than me") leads to anger, anxiety, and the impulse to rebel. From arguing with a ninth-grade English teacher over a grade to testing the limits by driving fast, teenagers are famous for protesting anything just because it's "a rule."

More tantalizing, Elkind draws on formal operational thinking to make sense of the classic behavior we observe in young teens—their incredible sensitivity to what other people think. According to Elkind, when children first become attuned to other people's flaws, the feeling turns inward to become an obsession with what others think about their *own* personal flaws. This produces **adolescent egocentrism**—the distorted feeling that one's own actions are at the center of everyone else's consciousness.

Therefore, 13-year-old Melody drives her parents crazy. She objects to everything from the way they dress to how they chew their food. When her mother picks her

Taking to the streets to advocate for climate change is apt to be a life-changing experience for these teens. It also is a developmental landmark, as advances in moral reasoning make adolescents exquisitely sensitive to injustice.

adolescent egocentrism David Elkind's term for the tendency of young teenagers to feel that their actions are at the center of everyone else's consciousness.

Look at the worried expressions on the faces of these freshmen cheerleaders and you can almost hear them thinking, "If I make a mistake during the game, everyone will laugh at me for my whole life!" According to David Elkind, the imaginary audience makes daily life intensely humiliating for young teens.

imaginary audience David Elkind's term for the tendency of young teenagers to feel that everyone is watching their every action; a component of adolescent egocentrism.

personal fable David Elkind's term for young teenagers' tendency to believe that their lives are special and heroic; a component of adolescent egocentrism.

up from school, she will not let this humiliating person leave the car: "Mom, I don't know you!" She does not spare herself from equally harsh critiques: A minuscule pimple is a monumental misery; stumbling and spilling her food on the school lunch line is a source of ultimate shame ("Everyone is laughing at me! My life is over!"). According to Elkind, a facet of adolescent egocentrism called the **imaginary audience** evokes this intense self-consciousness. Young teens, such as Melody, literally feel that they are on stage, with everyone watching everything they do.

A second component of adolescent egocentrism is the **personal fable**. Teenagers feel that they are invincible and that their own life experiences are unique. So Melody believes that no one has ever suffered as disgusting a blemish. She has the *most* embarrassing mother in the world.

These mental distortions explain the exaggerated emotional storms we laugh about during the early adolescent years. Unfortunately, the "It can't happen to me" component of the personal fable may lead to tragic acts. Boys put their lives at risk in drag racing contests because they believe they can never die. A girl does not use contraception when she has sex because, she reasons, "Yes, *other* girls can get pregnant, but not me. And, if I do get pregnant, I will be the center of attention, a real heroine."

Studying Three Aspects of Storm and Stress

Are teenagers unusually sensitive to other people's reactions? Is Elkind (like other observers, from Aristotle to Shakespeare to G. Stanley Hall) correct in saying that risk-taking is intrinsic to being a "hot-headed youth"? Are adolescents really highly emotional and/or likely to be emotionally disturbed? For answers, let's turn now to research that explores these three core aspects of teenage storm and stress.

Are Adolescents Exceptionally Socially Sensitive?

In the last chapter, I described that when they reach puberty, children—especially girls—become attuned to their bodies' flaws. In Chapter 6, I discussed how the passion to fit in socially (and target people who don't!) makes relational aggression explode around fifth or sixth grade. In one revealing study, when researchers asked middle schoolers to list their priorities, pre-teens ranked social success as their top concern. Being in the "popular crowd" was more important than being a scholar, being nice, or even having friends (see LaFontana & Cillessen, 2010)!

Moreover, as Elkind would predict, brain-imaging studies suggest that adolescents are unusually hypersensitive to other people's emotions (Monk and others, 2003). Young teens act impulsively, *specifically* in arousing situations involving their friends (Steinberg, 2016). This tendency—illustrated in the study described in the How Do We Know box—is mirrored in neural changes (Blakemore & Mills, 2014; Peake and others, 2013). Reward regions of the cortex spike when teens make risky decisions, but only when friends watch (Smith and others, 2015).

So the answer to the question of whether adolescents are more socially sensitive is absolutely yes, especially around the pubertal years!

Are Adolescents Risk-Takers?

Doing something and getting away with it. . . . You are driving at 80 miles an hour and stop at a stop sign and a cop will turn around the corner and you start giggling. Or you are out drinking or maybe you smoked a joint, and you say "hi" to a police officer and he walks by. . . .

(quoted in Lightfoot, 1997, p. 100)

HOW DO WE KNOW . . .
that adolescents make riskier decisions when they are with their peers?

Teenagers' heightened social sensitivity gives us strong evidence that they do more dangerous things in arousing situations with their friends. A classic, ingenious video study drove this point home scientifically. Researchers (Gardner & Steinberg, 2005) asked younger teenagers (aged 13 to 16), emerging adults (aged 18 to 22), and adults (aged 24 and over) to play a computer game in which they could earn extra points by taking risks, such as continuing to drive a car after a traffic light had turned yellow. They assigned the members of each age group to two conditions: Either play the game alone or in the presence of two friends.

The chart shows the intriguingly different findings for younger teenagers and for people over age 24. Notice that, while being with other people had no impact on risky decision making in the adults, it had an enormous effect on young teens, who were much more likely to risk crashing the car by driving farther after the yellow light appeared when with friends. The bottom line: Watch for risky behavior when groups of teenagers are together—a fact to consider the next time you see a car full of adolescents barreling down the road with music playing full blast!

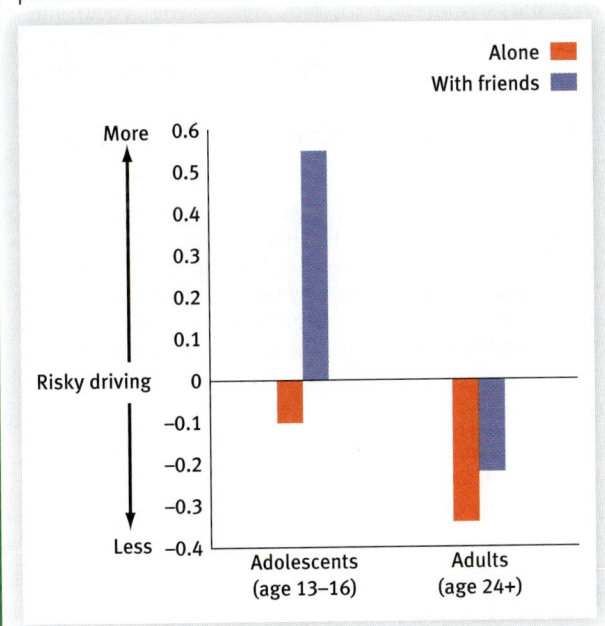

Risky driving tendencies of teens versus adults when in peer situations and when alone.

The quotation from a teen at the bottom of the previous page, and the research in the previous section, suggest (no surprise) that the second storm-and-stress stereotype is *definitely true*. From the thrill of binge drinking to the lure of driving fast, risk-taking is a basic feature of teenage life (Duell and others, 2016; Steinberg, 2016). In laboratory gambling tasks, researchers pinpoint puberty as the age of maximum risky-decision making for both sexes (Icenogle and others, 2016); but, because of their later pubertal timetable (and, as you will see later, slower brain maturation), the male danger zone extends through the teens (Shulman and others, 2015).

Consider, for instance, yearly nationwide University of Michigan–sponsored polls that track U.S. young people's lives. In examining data spanning 1997 to 2008, researchers found that 1 in 6 mainly male teens had been arrested by age 18. By age 23, the arrest rate slid up to an astonishing almost 1 in 3! (See Brame and others, 2012.) In the 2010 survey, roughly 2 in 10 high school seniors admitted to binge drinking (defined as having five or more drinks at a time for males and four or more drinks in a row for females) (Johnston and others, 2011). (Table 9.4 on the next page showcases some interesting research facts related to alcohol and adolescents.)

Who is likely to risk betting all their chips on the off chance they might get a winning hand? All odds are on these teenage boys.

> **Table 9.4:** Stereotypes and Surprising Research Facts About Alcohol and Teens
>
> **Stereotype #1: Teenagers who drink are prone to abuse alcohol later in life.**
>
> *Research answer:* "It depends on *when* you begin." Drinking during puberty is a risk factor for later alcohol problems (Blomeyer and others, 2013). However, during the late teens and early twenties, binge drinking—in Western societies—is often encouraged and then normally tends to decline when people assume adult roles such as marriage and parenthood (Gates, Corbin, & Fromme, 2016). So we can't predict from a person's consumption at these peak-use ages to the rest of adulthood.
>
> **Stereotype #2: Involvement in academics and/or athletics protects a teen from abusing alcohol.**
>
> *Research answer:* "It's complicated." While excelling at academics protects children at high genetic risk from drinking to excess as a teen (Benner and others, 2014), heavy athletic involvement is correlated with binge drinking for boys (Barnes and others, 2007; Peck, Vida, & Eccles, 2008). This research points (again) to the pivotal role of peers. Drinking (no surprise) is a prominent feature of the high school jock culture, and more of a "no-no" in the society of scholars, *specifically* during the high school years.
>
> **Stereotype #3: Middle childhood problems are risk factors for later excessive drinking.**
>
> *Research answer:* "Both true and surprisingly false." As you might expect, impulse control problems predict problem drinking (Lopez-Caneda and others, 2014). However, two longitudinal investigations—conducted in the United States and Great Britain—revealed that, for girls, high academic achievement was a risk factor for heavy drinking in the early twenties (Englund and others, 2008; Maggs, Patrick, & Feinstein, 2008)! To explain this uncomfortable finding, researchers suggest that girls who do well academically tend to go to college, where, again, the peer culture encourages drinking to excess.

The good news is that, in contrast to our images of rampant teenage substance abuse, most high school seniors do not report using *any* drugs, as you can see in Figure 9.2. The most recent 2016 University of Michigan poll found the *lowest* rates of teenage alcohol use since the survey was instituted four decades ago (Johnston and others, 2016)! The bad news is that—for an alarming fraction of young people in the United States—encounters with the criminal justice system are a depressing feature of modern life.

Younger children also rebel, disobey, and test the limits. But, if you have seen a group of teenage boys hanging from a speeding car, you know that the risks adolescents take can be life threatening. At the very age when they are most physically robust, teenagers—especially males—are most likely to die of preventable causes such as accidents (Dahl, 2004; Spear, 2008). So, yes, parents can worry about their children—particularly their sons—when they haven't made it home from a party and it's already 2 A.M.!

Are Adolescents More Emotional, More Emotionally Disturbed, or Both?

Given this information, it's no surprise that the third major storm-and-stress stereotype is also correct: Adolescents are more emotionally intense than adults. Developmentalists could not reach this conclusion by using surveys in which they asked young people to reflect on how they *generally* felt. They needed a method to chart the minute-to-minute ups and downs of teenagers' emotional lives.

Imagine that you could get inside the head of a 16-year-old as that person went about daily life. About 40 years ago, Mihaly Csikszentmihalyi and Reed Larson (1984) accomplished this feat by devising a procedure called the **experience-sampling technique**. The researchers asked students at a suburban Chicago high school to carry pagers programmed to emit a signal at random intervals during each day for a

experience-sampling technique A research procedure designed to capture moment-to-moment experiences by having people carry pagers and take notes describing their activities and emotions whenever the signal sounds.

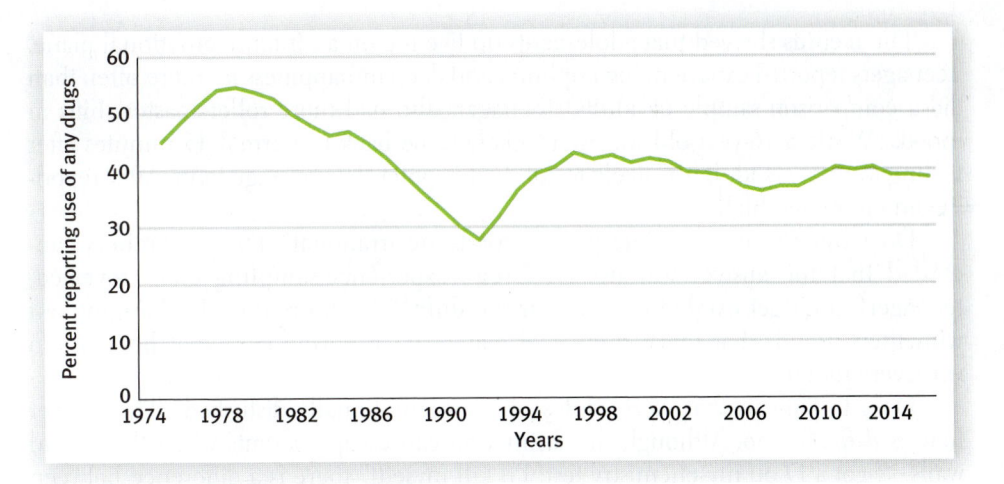

FIGURE 9.2: **Trends in prevalence of illicit drug use, reported by U.S. high school seniors from the mid-1970s to 2016** Contrary to our stereotypes, only 2 in 5 U.S. high school seniors reports using any illicit drugs (including alcohol) over the past year. Notice also that drug use was actually somewhat more common during the late 1970s and early 1980s—among the parents of today's teens, during their own adolescence.

Data from Johnston and others, 2016.

week. When the beeper went off, each teenager filled out a chart like the one shown in Figure 9.3. Notice that when you look at Greg's record, the experience-sampling procedure gives us insights into what experiences make teenagers (and people of other ages) feel joyous or distressed. Let's now look at what the charts revealed about the intensity of adolescents' moods.

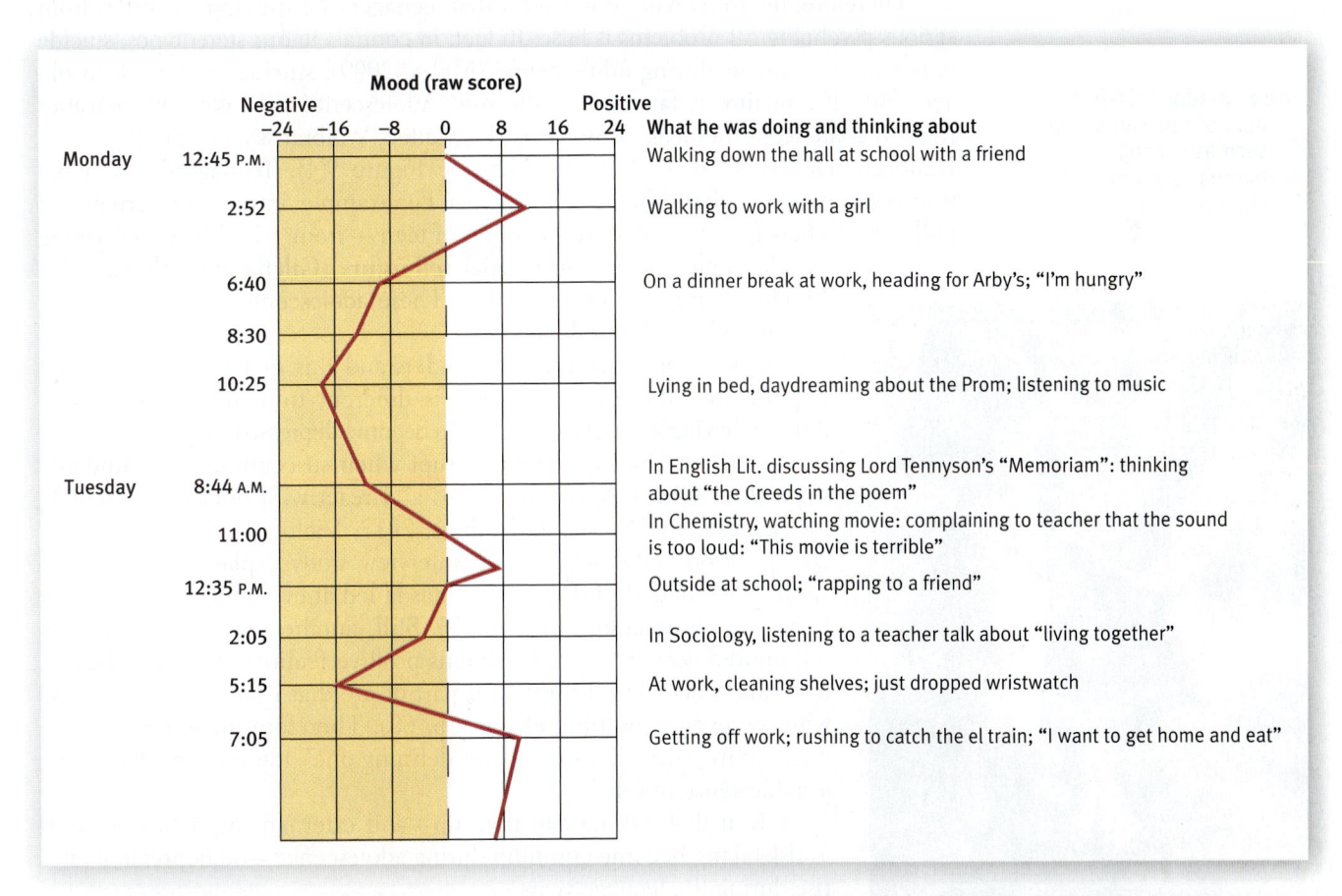

FIGURE 9.3: **Two days in the life of Gregory Stone: An experience-sampling record** This chart is based on two days of self-reports by a teenager named Greg Stone, as he was randomly beeped and asked to rate his moods and what he was doing at that moment. By looking at Greg's mood, can you identify the kinds of activities that he really enjoys or dislikes? Now, as an exercise, you might want to monitor your own moods for a few days and see how they change in response to your own life experiences. What insights does your internal mental checklist reveal about which activities are most enjoyable for you?

Data from Csikszentmihalyi & Larson, 1984, p. 111.

The records showed that adolescents do live life on an intense emotional plane. Teenagers reported experiencing euphoria and deep unhappiness far more often than did a comparison sample of adults. Teenagers also had more roller-coaster shifts in moods. While a 16-year-old was more likely to be back to normal 45 minutes after feeling terrific, an adult was likely to still feel happier than average hours after reporting an emotional high.

Does this mean that adolescents' moods are irrational? The researchers concluded that the answer was no. As Greg's experience-sampling chart revealed, teenagers don't get excited or down in the dumps for no reason. It's hanging out with their friends that make them feel elated. It's a boring class that bores them very, very much.

Does this mean that *most* adolescents are emotionally disturbed? The answer here is *definitely* no. Although the distinction can escape parents when their child wails, "I got a D on my chemistry test; I'll kill myself!" there is a difference between being *emotional* and being emotionally disturbed.

Actually, when developmentalists ask teenagers to evaluate their lives, they get an upbeat picture of how young people generally feel. Most adolescents around the world are confident and hopeful about the future (Gilman and others, 2008; Lewin-Bizan and others, 2010). In one U.S. poll, researchers classified 4 out of 10 adolescents as "flourishing"—efficacious, zestful, connected to family and friends. Only 6 percent were "languishing," totally demoralized about life (Keys, 2007).

Therefore, the stereotypic impression that teenagers are unhappy or suffer from serious psychological problems is false. In fact, in contrast to our stereotypes, suicide is not most common during adolescence (Males, 2009); suicide rates peak in old age! Still, the picture is far from totally rosy. Adolescents' risk-taking propensities make the late teens the peak crime years (DeMatteo, Wolbransky, & LaDuke, 2016; Heilbrun, DeMatteo, & Goldstein, 2016; see Figure 9.4). Teenagers' emotional storms can produce other distressing symptoms. For example, in several international polls, researchers found an alarming fraction of teens—from 1 in 4 to 1 in 6 young people—engaged in **nonsuicidal self-injury** (Giletta and others, 2012; Muehlenkamp and others, 2012). These adolescents cut themselves or perform other self-mutilation acts.

Scientists are passionate to understand this global epidemic. The impulse to self-injure, they find, is different from being addicted to drugs or having a genetic tendency to become depressed (Maciejewski and others, 2017). Cutting episodes erupt when susceptible teens undergo stress (Liu, Cheek & Nestor, 2016) and react with bouts of incredibly low self-esteem (Anestis and others, 2013; Victor, Glenn, & Klonsky, 2012). As one adolescent in an interview study explained, it's due to "pure black hatred of the self that has failed at everything else" (Breen, Lewis, & Sutherland, 2013, p. 59). Still, another child who regularly self-injured admitted to a poisonous positive feeling: "I love looking at my scars. They are an important part of me that I know will always be with me even if nothing else is" (p. 60). Therefore, in some distorted way, cutting may be a strategy for defining one's identity and *preserving* a stable sense of self.

Given that cutting can flare up—and externalizing behaviors such as risk-taking become common during adolescence—do depression rates rise during the teenage years?

Unfortunately, the answer is yes. Moreover, while the prevalence of this mental disorder is about equal for each sex during childhood, by the mid-teens, the adult gender pattern kicks in. Throughout life, women are roughly twice as susceptible to depression as are men. So, while they are worrying about their teenage sons, mothers might be a bit concerned about their daughters, too (see Oldehinkel & Bouma, 2011, for a review).

nonsuicidal self-injury Acts of self-mutilation, such as cutting or burning one's body, to cope with stress.

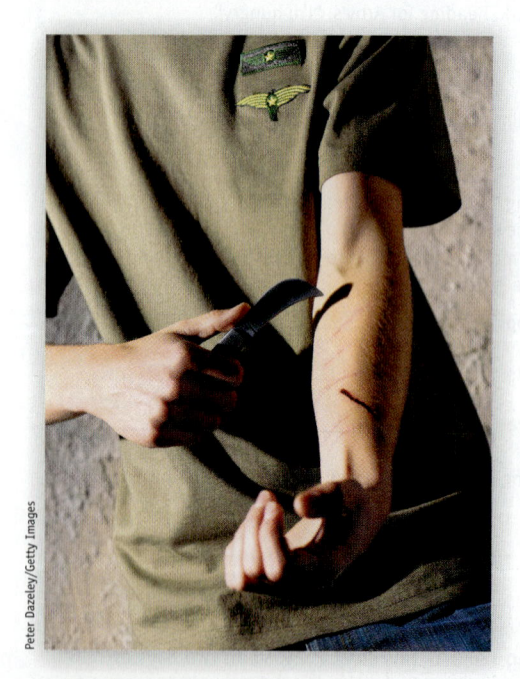

Most teens are upbeat and happy, and suicide is very, very rare during the adolescent years. But cutting, or nonsuicidal self-injury, is upsettingly prevalent at this age.

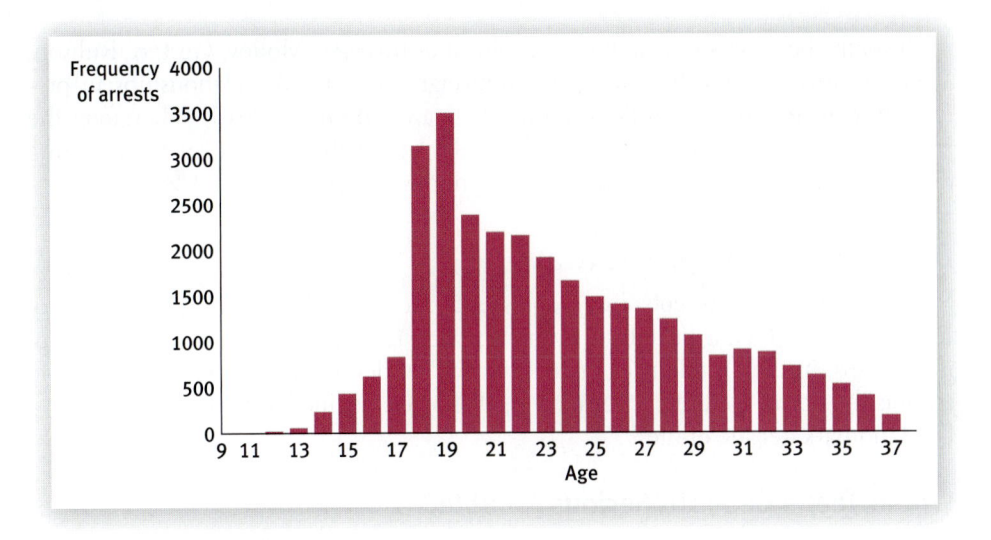

FIGURE 9.4: Frequency of arrests by age in a California study of offenders This chart, although describing California statistics, reflects the standard pattern around the world. The peak years for law breaking are the late teens, after which criminal activity declines.

Data from Natsuaki, Ge, & Wenk, 2008.

Depression rates may escalate during adolescence because the hormonal changes of puberty make the teenage brain more sensitive to stress (Romeo, 2013). But why is depression a mainly female disorder? Are women biologically primed to internalize their problems when under stress? We do not know. What we do know is that if a child's fate is to battle *any* serious mental health disorder, from depression to schizophrenia, that condition often has its onset in late adolescence or the early emerging-adult years.

Moreover, I believe that the push to be socially successful (or popular) may explain *many* classic distressing symptoms during the early teens.

Hot in Developmental Science: A Potential Pubertal Problem—Popularity

Young teens' drive for social status, for instance, accounts for why academic motivation often takes a nosedive in middle school (LaFontana & Cillessen, 2010; Li & Lerner, 2011). Worse yet—because at this age it can be "cool" to rebel—for aggressive children, being in the "popular group" is a risk factor for failing in school (Troop-Gordon, Visconti, & Kuntz, 2011). Therefore, chasing popularity has academic costs. Moreover, young teens may be faced with a difficult choice: "Either be in the 'in crowd' or care about school" (Blakely-McClure & Ostrov, 2016; Wilson, Karimpour, & Rodkin, 2011).

Making it into the in crowd has moral costs. Relational aggression, as I described in Chapter 6, helps propel pre-teens into the high-status group (Kiefer & Wang, 2016). As one Italian study showed, adolescents in the "cool" popular group were more apt than their classmates to view unethical behaviors, such as manipulating and deceiving people, as perfectly acceptable, too (Berger & Caravita, 2016).

Being part of the elite "in crowd" at school is probably a thrilling experience for these girls. But, they may develop some not-so-nice qualities as the price of being at the top of the class status rungs.

Finally, because social standing is critical at this age (Molloy, Gest, & Rulison, 2011), feeling rejected by one's peers outweighs poor family relationships in producing teenage anxiety and depression (Haltigan and others, 2017). Therefore, the intense push to be popular may partly explain both the upsurge in internalizing disorders and the rise in moral disengagement during the early teens!

Different Teenage Pathways

So far, I seem to be stereotyping "adolescents" as a monolithic group. This is absolutely not true! Teenagers differ—in their passion to be popular, in their school connectedness, in their tendencies to take risks or get depressed. As diversity at this life stage is the norm, the critical question is, "Who gets derailed and who thrives during this landmark decade of life?"

Which Teens Get into Serious Trouble?

Without denying that serious adolescent difficulties can unpredictably erupt, here are three thunderclouds that foreshadow stormy weather ahead.

At-Risk Teens Tend to Have Prior Emotion Regulation Problems

It should come as no surprise that one thundercloud relates to elementary school externalizing tendencies (DeMatteo, Wolbransky, & LaDuke, 2016). Not only is the lure of getting into trouble overwhelming when children have problems regulating their behavior, but if preteens are rejected by the mainstream kids, they gravitate to antisocial friends (Ettekal & Ladd, 2015; more about this later).

Therefore, tests of *executive functions*—measures that chart whether girls and boys have difficulty thinking through their behavior—strongly predict adolescent storms. Moreover, getting into trouble at an atypically young age foreshadows delinquent behavior during the teenage years (DeMatteo, Wolbransky, & LaDuke, 2016).

At-Risk Teens Tend to Have Poor Family Relationships

Feeling alienated from one's parents can also be a warning sign of developing storms. When researchers explored the emotions of teens who self-injured, these children often anguished: "My parents are way too critical"; "I can't depend on my mom or dad" (Bureau and others, 2010; You, Lin, & Leung, 2013).

In essence, these young people were describing an insecure attachment. Teenagers want to be listened to and respected. They need to know they are unconditionally loved (Allen and others, 2007). So, to draw on my metaphor about dancing to describe infant attachment in Chapter 4, with adolescents, parents must be exceptionally skillful dancers. They should understand when to back off and when to stay close. In Chapter 7's terms, adolescents require an *authoritative* discipline style.

But since the attachment dance is bidirectional, when we see correlations between teenagers' reporting distant family relationships and having troubles, it's not *simply* parents who are at fault. Imagine that you are a 15-year-old who is having unprotected sex, taking drugs, or withdrawing from the world. Would you tell your parents about your life? And when you withdrew to your room or lied about your activities, wouldn't you feel even more alienated? "My family knows nothing about who I am" (Bradley & Coryn, 2013).

Yes, it's easy to *say* that being authoritative is vital in parenting teens. But take it from me (I've been there!), when your teenager is getting into trouble, confronting him about his activities is apt to backfire. So it can be difficult for frantic parents to understand how to *really* act authoritatively in a much-loved son or daughter's life.

At-Risk Teens Live in a Risk-Taking Environment

Focusing on parent–child relationships neglects the role the social milieu plays in seeding teenage storms. If a child's adored older brother is taking drugs (Solmeyer,

McHale, & Crouter, 2014), and especially if a teen lives in a disorganized, low-efficacy community (Jennings and others, 2016), the chance of getting into trouble accelerates. As ecological developmental systems theory spells out, to *really* help teenagers thrive, we need a nurturing wider world. Now, let's look at who thrives during their teens.

Which Teens Flourish?

> In high school, I connected with my lifelong love of music. I'll never forget that feeling when I got that special prize in band my senior year.

> At about age 15, I decided the best way to keep myself off the streets was to get involved in my church youth group. It was my best time of life.

As the quotations show, these attributes offer a mirror image of the qualities I just described: Teenagers thrive when they have superior executive functions (Gestsdottir and others, 2010; Urban, Lewin-Bizan, & Lerner, 2010). They flourish when parents reinforce their unique strengths ("You are terrific at the drums! I know you can succeed!") (Jach and others, 2017). A mentor or VIP (very important non-parental adult) can be vital: a caring adviser who spends time with a child and is on the same wavelength, in terms of personality (Futch Ehrlich and others, 2016).

Thriving does not mean staying out of trouble. Many adolescents who are flourishing also engage in considerable risk-taking during their early and middle teens (Lerner and others, 2010). Therefore, testing the limits is a *normal* adolescent experience even among the happiest, healthiest teens (Larson & Grisso, 2016).

And let's not give up on children who *do* get seriously derailed. Developmentalists make a distinction between **adolescence-limited turmoil** (antisocial behavior during the teenage years) and **life-course difficulties** (antisocial behaviors that continue into adult life) (Moffitt, 1993). Perhaps you have a friend who used to stay out all night partying and taking drugs, but later became a responsible parent. Or you may know a "troubled teen" who is succeeding incredibly well after finding the right person–environment fit at college or work. (For a compelling example, see the Experiencing Adolescence feature on page 267.) If so, you understand a main message of the next chapter: We do get more mature during the emerging-adult years. (Table 9.5 offers a checklist so you can evaluate whether a child you love might have a stormy or sunny adolescence.)

Suppose this 16-year-old chess whiz had no adults to encourage and nurture his passion. He would probably never have a chance to express his talent and flourish during his teenage years.

adolescence-limited turmoil Antisocial behavior that, for most teens, is specific to adolescence and does not persist into adult life.

life-course difficulties Antisocial behavior that, for a fraction of adolescents, persists into adult life.

Table 9.5: Predicting Whether a Child Is Prone to Teenage Storms or to Flourish: A Section Summary Checklist

Threatening Thunderclouds
1. Does this child have emotion regulation difficulties and is he failing socially?
2. Does this child have distant or conflict-ridden family relationships?*
3. Does this child live in an environment where risk-taking is prized, or is this person being raised in a disorganized, low collective-efficacy neighborhood?

Sunny Signs
1. Does this child have good executive functions and a special talent?
2. Does this child have parents who encourage his or her gifts?
3. Does this boy or girl have an adult mentor?

Information from Masten (2004), p. 315, and the sources in this section.

*As I will describe later in this chapter, conflict (and distancing) from parents predictably occurs during early adolescence.

Wrapping Things Up: The Blossoming Teenage Brain

Now, let's put it all together: the mental growth, the morality, the emotionality, and the sensitivity to what others think. Give teenagers an intellectual problem and they can reason in mature ways. But younger teens tend to be captivated by popularity and get overwhelmed in arousing situations when they are with their friends.

According to Laurence Steinberg (2016), these qualities make sense when we look at the developing brain. Puberty heightens the output of certain neurotransmitters, which provokes the passion to take risks (Guerri & Pascual, 2010). At the same time, the insulating *myelin sheath* continues to grow until our twenties (see Table 9.6). As Steinberg explains, it's like starting the engine of adulthood with an unskilled driver. This heightened activation of the "socioemotional brain," with a cognitive control center still "under construction," makes adolescence a potentially dangerous time.

Studies around the world support Steinberg's dual-brain function explanation for teenage risk-taking (Shulman and others, 2016). From Kenya to China to Colombia, "sensation seeking" peaks during the early teens, while self-control steadily grows into the emerging-adult years (Steinberg, 2016). As I've highlighted in earlier chapters, it takes more than two decades for the frontal lobes to grow up.

Table 9.6: Teenage Brain-Imaging Questions and Findings

Question #1: How does the brain change during adolescence?

Answer: *Dramatically, in different ways.* Frontal lobe gray matter (the neurons and synapses) peaks right before puberty and then gradually declines due to pruning—that is, the cortex "gets thinner" over the teenage years. In contrast, white matter (the myelin sheath) steadily grows into the twenties.

Question #2: Are there gender differences in brain development?

Answer: *Yes.* Because girls reach puberty earlier, they are on a faster brain-development timetable than boys; their gray matter peaks at a younger age (10 for girls and 12 for boys), and white matter increases at an accelerated pace in the female brain. Do these gender differences explain why teenage boys are far more likely to get into trouble with the law? Many researchers believe the answer is yes.

Question #3: Do the brain-imaging findings mirror the behavioral research in this section?

Answer: *Not really.* Although the teen brain generally matures in the ways I've described, studies that explore differences in specific brain-activation patterns of deviant teens versus their more well-adjusted age mates have confusing results.

Conclusion: While we do have good general data on teenage brain development, we still have far to go in neuroscientifically mapping the teenage mind.

Information from Bava and others, 2010; Bjork & Pardini, 2015; Blakemore, Burnett, & Dahl, 2010; Bramen and others, 2011; Burnett and others, 2011; Herting & Sowell, 2017; Koolschijn & Crone, 2013; Lenroot & Giedd, 2010; Luciana, 2010; Moreno & Trainor, 2013; Negriff and others, 2011; Shulman and others, 2015.

But from an evolutionary standpoint, it is logical to start adolescence with an accelerated emotional engine. Teenagers' risk-taking tendencies propel them into the world. Their passion to bond with their peers is vital to leaving their parents and forming new attachments as adults. The teenage brain is beautifully tailored to help young people make the leap from childhood to adult life (Dahl, 2004; Steinberg, 2008).

INTERVENTIONS: Making the World Fit the Teenage Mind

Table 9.7 summarizes these messages in a chart for parents. Now let's explore our discussion's ramifications for society.

Table 9.7: Tips for Parents of Teens

1. Understand that strong emotions may not have the same meaning for your teen as for you. So try not to take comments like "I hate myself" or "I'm the dumbest person in the world" very seriously. Also, during the early teen years, new research—discussed later in this chapter—suggests it's normal for your child to become secretive and rebellious. But just because your teen gets furious at you, don't think she doesn't love you.
2. Understand that, while sampling forbidden activities is normal, if your teen is getting involved in genuinely illegal activities or seems seriously depressed, you do need to be concerned.
3. Understand that your child's peer choices (and peer-group status) offer good hints about his behavior, and that striving to be in the "popular crowd"—while normal—can have unpleasant consequences.
4. Roll with the punches, encourage your child's passions, and enjoy your teenager!

Don't punish adolescents as if they were mentally just like adults. If the adolescent brain is a work in progress, it doesn't make sense to have the same legal sanctions for teenagers who commit crimes that we have for adults. Rather than locking adolescents up, it seems logical that at this young age the focus should be on rehabilitation. As Laurence Steinberg (2016; Shulman & Steinberg, 2016) and virtually every other adolescence expert suggests, with regard to the legal system, "less guilty by reason of adolescence" is the way to go.

Is the U.S. legal system listening to the adolescence specialists? The answer is "a bit." In 2005, the Supreme Court outlawed the death penalty for adolescents and, in 2012, eliminated life sentences without the possibility of parole for teens (Heilbrun, DeMatteo, & Goldstein, 2016). Still, today, as the Experiencing Adolescence box suggests, judges and prosecutors can decide to transfer some children as young as age 13 (!) out of the juvenile justice system and then try them as adults (Larson & Grisso, 2016). Yes, as my amazing interview with Jason suggests, with luck and a resilient temperament, a shockingly punitive approach can help turn a person around. However, there is no evidence that condemning adolescents to the gulag of dysfunctional adult prisons deters later criminal acts (Fabian, 2011). Do you believe that it's *ever* acceptable to try teenagers as adults?

Experiencing Adolescence: Innocently Imprisoned at 16

If you think the U.S. legal system protects 16-year-olds from adult jail and that citizens can't be falsely incarcerated without a trial, think again. Then, after reading Jason's story, you might link his horrific teenage years to the qualities involved in resilience (discussed in Chapter 7).

> I grew up with crazy stuff. My mom was a drug dealer and my dad passed away so I was adopted by my grandparents. I was kicked out of four schools before ninth grade. By age 15, I was involved with a street gang and heavy gun trading in Birmingham, Alabama. I was in a car with some older guys during a drive-by shooting, got pulled over, and that was the last time I saw daylight for over 3 years.
>
> The original charge was carrying a concealed weapon, and I was sent to a juvenile boot camp. Then, two days after being discharged, detectives were knocking on my door with the full charges: three counts of attempted murder. The arresting officers decided to transfer me to county jail, where I ended up for 19 months. If you go to trial and lose, you get the maximum sentence, 20 years to life, so—even though I was innocent—avoiding trial is the thing you want to do. What happens is that your lawyers keep negotiating plea bargains. First, I was offered 20 to life, with the idea I'd be out in 10 years; then 15 years, then 10. Not very appealing for a 16-year-old kid! Finally, by incredible good luck, I got a lawyer who takes kids from prisons and puts them into rehab facilities, and he convinced the judge that was best for me. I quickly had to take what they offered—being sent to the Nashville Rescue Mission and then a halfway house for 2 years—because my trial date was coming up very soon.

Jail was unbelievable. The ninth floor of the Jefferson County Jail is well known because that's where they send criminals from the penitentiary who have committed the most violent crimes to await trial. My first cellmate had cut a guy's head off. Every time you get to know a group, the next week another group arrives in jail and you have to fight them. The guards were no better. If they didn't like a prisoner, they would persuade inmates to beat the living daylights out of that person.

What helped me cope were my dreams, because you are not in jail in your dreams. I wrote constantly, read all the time. What ultimately helped was being sent out of state (so I couldn't get involved with my old friends) and, especially, my counselors at the mission. I never met guys so humble; such amazing people. Also, if I got into trouble again, I knew where I could be heading. Scared the heck out of me. Now, everything I do is dependent on being normal. I'm 22. I have good friends but I haven't told anyone anything about my past. I have a 3.5 average. I'm working two jobs. I'll be the first person in my family to graduate college. I want to go to grad school to get my psychology Ph.D.

Pass laws that are user-friendly to the teenage mind. Putting adolescents in adult prisons is counterproductive, simply because this practice exposes the most socially sensitive age group to adults who are apt to encourage criminal acts (Larson & Grisso, 2016). Therefore, it's best to craft legislation that takes teenagers' mental processes into account. One excellent example is graduated driving laws that limit young people from operating cars at night and while in groups. Since these U.S. rules were instituted in the late 1990s, teenage crash rates have declined dramatically, although adolescents still get into more accidents than adults (McCarty & Teoh, 2015). Another approach is to draw on adolescents' peer sensitivities in a positive way.

Provide group activities that capitalize on adolescents' strengths. How can we help teenagers forge growth-enhancing peer relationships and promote their inner development?

Youth development programs fulfill this mission. They give adolescents a safe place to explore their passions during the unstructured late afternoon hours, when teens are most prone to get into trouble while hanging out with friends (Hoeben and others, 2016). From 4-H clubs to church groups to high school plays, youth development programs ideally foster qualities that developmentalist Richard Lerner has named the five C's: *competence, confidence, character, caring,* and *connections*. They provide an environment that allows young people to thrive (Lerner, Dowling, & Anderson, 2003; Lerner and others, 2016; Tolan, 2016).

I wish I could say that every youth program fostered flourishing. But as anyone who has spent time at a girls' club or the local Y knows, these settings can also encourage group bullying and antisocial acts (Rorie and others, 2011). Therefore, after-school programs must be well structured and supervised. They have to promote the five C's. And, since youth development programs are voluntary and so tend to be utilized by teenagers who are already coping well, they don't help the very at-risk boys and girls most in need (Ciocanel and others, 2017).

Therefore, to really alter the adolescent experience, it seems more effective to embed enriching offerings into the place every child attends: school. In one heartening study, high schools that featured strong arts programs made students feel more engaged in *all* of their classes (Martin and others, 2013). Intense involvement in high school clubs in particular predicts work success years down the road (Gardner, Roth, & Brooks-Gunn, 2008; Linver, Roth, & Brooks-Gunn, 2009)—which brings me to another important issue. For the sake of *both* their present and future, how can we get *every* teenager connected to school?

Change high schools to provide a better adolescent–environment fit. Adolescents who feel embedded in nurturing schools tend to feel good about themselves (Hirschfield

youth development program Any after-school program or structured activity outside of the school day that is devoted to promoting flourishing in teenagers.

& Gasper, 2011; Lewis and others, 2011) and the world (Flanagan & Stout, 2010). Just as with day care, as I described in Chapter 4, excellent high schools can offer at-risk teens a vital haven when they are having problems at home (Loukas, Roalson, & Herrera, 2010).

Unfortunately, however, in one disheartening international poll, although teenagers were generally upbeat about other aspects of their lives, they rated their high school experience as only "so-so" (Gilman and others, 2008). How can we turn this situation around?

In surveys, teenagers say that they are yearning for the experiences that characterize high-quality elementary schools (described in Chapter 7)—autonomy-supporting work that encourages them to think, teachers who respect their abilities (LaRusso, Romer, & Selman, 2008), hands-on courses that are relevant to their lives (Wagner, 2000). Service-learning classes in particular can make an enduring impact on development (McIntosh, Metz, & Youniss, 2005). Here is what one African American young man had to say about volunteering at a soup kitchen: "I was on the brink of becoming one of those hoodlums the world so fears. This class was one of the major factors in my choosing the right path" (quoted in Yates & Youniss, 1998, p. 509).

These teens are taking great pleasure in serving meals to the homeless as part of their community-service project. Was a high school experience like this life-changing for you?

We also might rethink the school day to take into account teenagers' unique sleep requirements. During early adolescence, the sleep cycle is biologically pushed back (Colrain & Baker, 2011; Feinberg & Campbell, 2010). Because they tend to go to bed after 11 P.M. and must wake up for school at 6 or 7 A.M., the typical U.S. teen sleeps fewer than 7 hours each day (Colrain & Baker, 2011). Worse yet, children who strongly show this evening circadian shift are *generally* at risk for a stormy teenage life. They tend to have poorer family relationships (Díaz-Morales and others, 2014), are often lonely, and are less mentally tough (Brand and others, 2014; Doane & Thurston, 2014). Because sleep deprivation throws the cognitive and emotional systems more out of whack, these adolescents are apt to be impulsive (Peach & Gaultney, 2013) and engage in deviant acts (Telzer, Fuligni, and others, 2013), in addition to (no surprise) doing poorly in class. Might experimenting with starting high school at 10 A.M. promote a better body–school fit?

Finally, it's past time to rethink **zero-tolerance policies**, high school rules mandating immediate suspension for any deviant act. This U.S. practice, which exploded during the 1990s, had laudable goals: protecting classmates from violent peers and deterring later criminal acting out. But studies show that being suspended from school *encourages* later delinquency. Schools that take a hard-core zero-tolerance approach make every student feel less connected to their teachers and classes (Daly and others, 2016).

Being expelled, sometimes for infractions as minor as smoking on school grounds, pathologizes normal teenage behavior. It prevents the most vulnerable teens from getting the caring attachment experiences they vitally require (see my discussions in Chapters 4 and 7). What developmentalists evocatively call the **school-to-prison pipeline**—meaning the transition from adolescence-limited turmoil to life-course criminal behavior—can be set in motion when an at-risk, frequently male, teenager is barred from the classroom doors (Daly and others, 2016).

Think back to your high school days. What rules did you find problematic? What allowed you to thrive? How would you change your high school to help teenagers make the most of these special years?

Could this have been you in high school, particularly toward the end of the week? Do you think we are making a mistake by resisting teenagers' biological clocks and insisting that the school day start at 8 A.M.?

zero-tolerance policies The practice in U.S. public high schools of suspending students after one rule infraction.

school-to-prison pipeline Term referring to the way school expulsion may provoke criminal behavior and incarceration for at-risk teens.

Another Perspective on the Teenage Mind

Until now, I've been highlighting the mainstream developmental science message: "Because of their brain immaturity, teens need protection from the world." But might scientists be over-invoking biology to inappropriately label teenagers as out of control?

Consider, for instance, the fact that zero-tolerance school policies can collide with teenagers' natural impulse to sample *all of life*. Furthermore, is teenage risk-taking that dangerous compared to the impulsive activities we engage in *throughout* adulthood—from marrying multiple times, to making unaffordable investments, to starting unprovoked wars (see Willoughby and others, 2013)?

Drawing on these ideas, Robert Epstein has put forth an innovative critique of the immature adolescent brain. Epstein (2010) reminds us that adolescence is an artificial construction. Nature intended us to enter adulthood at puberty. Now young people must languish for a decade under the ill-fitting label "child." How many "predictable" teenage symptoms of storm and stress, Epstein argues, have little to do with faulty frontal lobes and everything to do with a poor contemporary body–environment fit? Do teenagers *really* have immature brains, or are adults to blame for shackling teenagers' minds?

Let's keep these thoughts in mind in the next section, as we turn to explore parent–teenager relationships in depth.

Assuming adult responsibilities right after puberty, like fishing for a living, is what nature intended for our species (see Chapter 8). Therefore, Robert Epstein believes so-called teenage "dysfunction" is produced by a dysfunctional modern society.

Tying It All Together

1. Robin, a teacher, is about to transfer from fourth grade to the local high school, and she is excited by all the things that her older students will be able to do. Based on what you have learned about Piaget's formal operational stage and Kohlberg's theory of moral reasoning, pick which *two* new capacities Robin may find among her students.
    a. The high schoolers will be able to memorize poems.
    b. The high schoolers will be able to summarize the plots of stories.
    c. The high schoolers will be able to debate different ideas even if they don't personally agree with them.
    d. The high schoolers will be able to develop their own moral principles.

2. Eric is a basketball coach. The year-end tournament is tomorrow, and the star forward has the flu and won't be able to play. Terry, last year's number one player, offers to fill in—even though this violates the conference rules. Eric agonizes about the ethical issue. Should he deprive his guys of their shot at the championship, or go against the regulations and put Terry in? How would you reason about this issue? Now, fit your responses into Kohlberg's categories of moral thought.

3. A 14-year-old worries that everyone is watching every mistake she makes; at the same time, she is fearless when her friends dare her to take life-threatening risks like bungee jumping off a cliff. According to Elkind, this feeling that everyone is watching her illustrates _____; the risk-taking is a sign of _____; and both are evidence of the process called _____.

4. Pick which symptom indicates your 15-year-old nephew has a genuine psychological problem: *intense mood swings and social sensitivities/depression/a tendency to engage in risky behavior with friends*.

5. Your child has made it into the popular kids' crowd at school. You should feel (pick one): *proud because that means he is able to get along with the kids/worried because he is at risk for moral disengagement and acting-out behaviors*.

6. There has been a rise in teenage crimes in your town, and you are at the local high school to explore solutions. Given what you know about the teenage mind, which change should you *not* support?
   a. Vigorously implement zero-tolerance policies.
   b. Encourage the school to expand their menu of clubs and service-learning classes.
   c. Think about postponing the beginning of the school day to 10 A.M.

7. Imagine you are a college debater. Use your formal operational skills to argue first for and then against the proposition that society should try teens as adults.

Answers to the Tying It All Together questions can be found at the end of this chapter.

Social Development

What are teenager–parent interactions like? Now it's time to tackle this question, as I focus on those twin adolescent agendas—separating from parents and connecting with peers.

Separating from Parents

> When I'm with my dad fishing, or when my family is just joking around at dinner—it's times like these when I feel completely content, loved, the best about life and myself.

In their original experience-sampling study, Csikszentmihalyi and Larson (1984) discovered that teenagers' most uplifting experiences occurred when with their families—sharing a joke around the dinner table or having a close moment with Mom or Dad. Unfortunately, however, those moments were few and far between. In fact, while peer encounters were more apt to evoke passionate highs, when adolescents were with their families, unhappy emotions outweighed positive ones 10 to 1.

This tendency to lock horns with parents seems built into the universal adolescent experience, as shown in the global poll illustrated in Figure 9.5. Notice that, while the gap differs from nation to nation, teenagers typically rank stress with parents as more upsetting than stress with peers (Persike & Seiffge-Krenke, 2014).

LEARNING OUTCOMES

- Outline how teenagers separate from parents and the special separation issues immigrant teens face.
- Describe cliques, crowds, and teenage peer groups.
- Explain the forces that promote delinquent peer groups, making special reference to gangs.

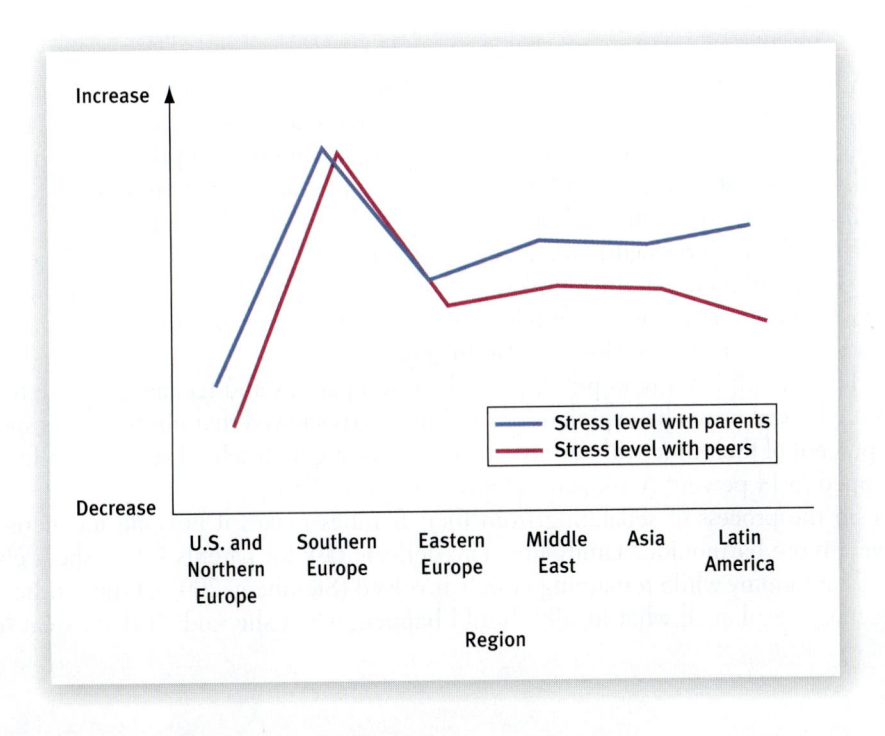

FIGURE 9.5: Mean of parent–child stress versus stress with peers, as reported by teens in various regions of the globe Notice that with the exception of southern Europe, worldwide adolescent stress with parents is more intense than stress with peers.

Data from Persike & Seiffge-Krenke, 2014, p. 499.

The Issue: Pushing for Autonomy

Why does family life produce such teenage pain? As developmentalists point out, if our home life is good, our family is our loving cocoon. However, in addition to being a safe haven, parents are often a source of pain. The reason is that their job is both to love us and to limit us. When this parental limiting function gets into high gear, teenage distress becomes acute.

What do teenagers and their parents argue about? This global poll offers insights into specific cultural parenting priorities in different world regions (Persike & Seiffge-Krenke, 2014). In northern Europe and the United States, arguments around academic issues loom large ("I hate that pressure to get good grades!"). For Japanese and Chinese teens, these kinds of school-related conflicts outweigh everything else.

Perhaps because it's crucial in these societies to marry within "one's own group," in the Middle East, micromanaging peer relationships is a major stress ("My parents won't let me see the friends I want!"). In southern Europe, where children still live with their parents into their early thirties, dependency and general parent–child acrimony is a serious concern ("We fight all the time!" "They won't let me grow up!"). (More about this in Chapter 10.)

But the main issue *every nation* centers around is independence ("Why can't I do what I want? You have too many rules!"). Moreover, most clashes occur just when peer group pressures reach their peak—around the early teens (Daddis, 2011; De Goede, Branje, & Meeus, 2009).

The Process: Exploring the Dance of Autonomy

Actually, parent–adolescent conflict flares up while children are in the midst of puberty (Steinberg, 2005; Steinberg & Hill, 1978). From an evolutionary perspective, the hormonal surges of puberty may propel this struggle for autonomy ("You can't tell me what to do!"), which sets in motion the dance of separation intrinsic to becoming an independent adult.

How does the dance of autonomy unfold? Based on periodically asking teens questions—such as, "Do your parents know what you do in your free time?" or "Do you tell your parents who you hang out with?"—and exploring parental rules, Canadian researchers offered a motion picture of changing parent–child relationships over the teenage years (Keijsers & Poulin, 2013).

As it turns out, children first initiate the push for independence by becoming secretive and distant in their early teens. But parents only respond by steadily granting their children much more freedom beginning after age 15.

Why is mid- to later adolescence a crucial period of granting autonomy? The reason may be that, at this age, parents feel their children are more mature (Wray-Lake, Crouter, & McHale, 2010). As teens get closer to graduation, their priorities shift from rebelling to constructing an adult life. By junior and senior year, it's important to stop rebelling and to think concretely about college and a career (Malin and others, 2014).

Even the major social markers of independence at around age 16 or 17 eliminate sources of family strain. Think about how getting your first job, or your license, removed an important area of family conflict. You no longer had to ask your parents for every dime or rely on Mom or Dad to get around.

These adult landmarks put distance between parents and teenagers in the most basic, physical way. The experience-sampling charts showed that ninth-graders spent 25 percent of their time with family members. Among high school seniors, the figure dropped to 14 percent (Csikszentmihalyi & Larson, 1984).

So the process of separating from their families makes it possible for teens to have a more harmonious family life. The delicate task for parents is to respect children's autonomy while remaining closely involved (Steinberg, 2001). One mother of a teenager explained what ideally should happen, when she said: "I don't treat her like a young child anymore, but we're still very close. Sort of like a friendship, but not really, because I'm still in charge. She's my buddy" (quoted in Shearer, Crouter, & McHale, 2005, p. 674).

This quotation brings up a telling gender difference in the parent–child intimacy dance. The earlier Canadian study showed that boys maintained their new, distant pubertal communication pattern as they traveled into the late teens—not telling mothers much about their activities, avoiding sharing their lives. But girls, after becoming more secretive and distant as young teens, reached out to their mothers during mid- and later adolescence to reconnect.

Figure 9.6 illustrates the striking pubertal decline in family closeness in a national U.S. longitudinal study. Notice, as in the Canadian research I just described, the stark decline in parent–child attachment during the early teens, and how girls—but not boys—grow slightly more attached to their parents after ninth grade (Kim and others, 2015). Does this same dramatic dance of separation apply to immigrant teens from more collectivist regions of the world?

Passing a driving test and finally getting the keys to the car is a joyous late-teenage transition into adult liberation. It's almost the developed-world equivalent of a puberty rite!

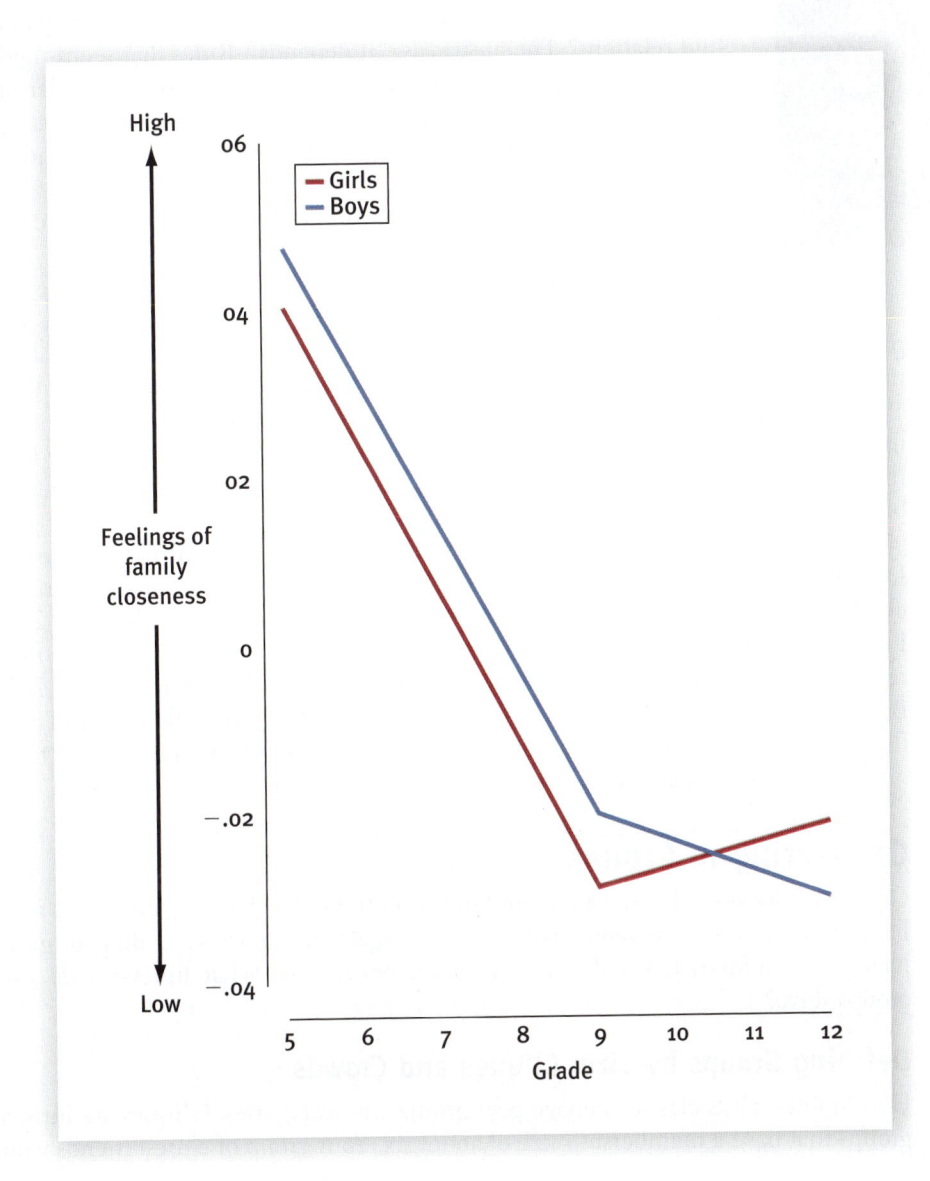

FIGURE 9.6: Changes in feelings of attachment to parents, reported among a sample of 4,407 children, tracked from fifth to twelfth grade In this mammoth multi-site U.S study, notice how the pre-teen dance of separation from parents explodes during middle school. Note also how girls but not boys become slightly more attached to their parents after ninth grade.

Data from Kim and others, 2015.

Cultural Variations on a Theme

My parents won't let me date anyone who isn't Hindi—or go to parties. They never tell me they love me. I have to be at home right after school to do the grocery shopping and other family chores. Why can't they just let me be a normal American kid?

In individualistic societies, we strive for parent–child adult relationships that are less hierarchical, more like friends. But, as the preceding quotation suggests, cultures that stress parental obedience above everything else have different ideas about how teenagers should behave.

Therefore, among immigrant adolescents, the impulse to separate from one's family can provoke intense conflicts relating to *acculturation*. Young people may face the wrenching dilemma of "choosing" between their parents' values and the norms of their new home (Kim & Park, 2011; Kim, Chen, and others, 2013; Park and others, 2010; Wu & Chao, 2011). Straddling two cultures, as described in the quotation above, can also upend the normal parent–child relationship because it catapults some second-generation children into becoming the family adults. As one teacher who worked with Chinese immigrants commented, "The kids may be doing the interpreting and translating . . . , they may be the de facto parents" (quoted in Lim and others, 2009).

Given these strains, are immigrant teens at risk for poor parent–child relations? The answer is, "It depends." Rules that seem rigid to Western eyes have a different meaning when young people understand that their parents have sacrificed everything for their well-being (Wu & Chao, 2011). As one touching, international poll showed, the core quality that makes adolescents feel loved *worldwide* is feeling their parents have gone out of their way to do things that are rare and emotionally hard (McNeely & Barber, 2010).

Therefore, knowing that one's parents made a rare sacrifice ("giving up their happiness and moving for my future") can create unusually close parent–child bonds. Helping a non-English-speaking mother or father negotiate this unfamiliar culture can promote self-efficacy and encourage empathy, too. As one 19-year-old revealingly commented: "My entire childhood, I was translating simple things day to day . . . [It made me feel] . . . empowered, proud, frustrated at times, [but] understanding of my parents' struggle" (Guan, Greenfield, & Orellana, 2014, p. 332).

This quotation may explain a phenomenon called the **immigrant paradox**. Despite coping with an overload of stresses (Cho & Haslam, 2010), many immigrant children living in poverty do better than their peers (van Geel & Vedder, 2011). Identifying with one's cultural roots, as I will describe in the next chapter, fosters resilience and anchors a young person more deeply in life (Telzer and others, 2016). But like all children, immigrant teens take different paths—some flourish and others flounder (Suárez-Orozco and others, 2010). One force is critical in predicting failure or success: not surprisingly, it's a teenager's group of peers.

As she translates an oath of naturalization to her non-English-speaking Iraqi mom, this daughter is engaging in a role reversal that, while distressing, offers a lifelong sense of empathy and self-efficacy.

immigrant paradox The fact that despite living in poverty, going to substandard schools, and not having parents who speak a nation's language, immigrant children do far better than we might expect at school.

Connecting in Groups

Go to your local mall and watch sixth and seventh graders hanging out to get a first-hand glimpse of the pre-teen passion to congregate in groups. How do peer groups change as children travel deeper into adolescence, and what functions do these groups serve?

Defining Groups by Size: Cliques and Crowds

Developmentalists classify teenage peer groups into categories. **Cliques** are intimate groups that have a membership size of about six. Your group of closest friends would

clique A small peer group composed of roughly six teenagers who have similar attitudes and who share activities.

constitute a clique. **Crowds** are larger groupings. Your crowd comprises both your best buddies and a more loose-knit set of people you get together with less regularly.

In a 1960s observational study in Sydney, Australia, one researcher found that these groups serve a crucial purpose: They are the vehicles that convey teenagers to relationships with the other sex (Dunphy, 1963).

As you can see in the photos in Figure 9.7, children enter their pre-teen years belonging to unisex cliques, close associations of same-gender best friends. Relationships start to change when cliques of boys and girls enter a public space and "accidentally" meet. At the mall, notice the bands of sixth- or seventh-grade girls who have supposedly arrived to check out the stores but who really have another agenda: They know that boy best friends will be there. A major mode of interaction when these groups meet is loud teasing. When several cliques get together to walk around the stores, they have melded into that larger, first genuinely mixed-sex group called a *crowd* (Cotterell, 1996).

The crowd is an ideal medium to bridge the gap between the sexes because there is safety in numbers. Children can still be with their own gender while they are crossing into that "foreign" land. Gradually, out of these large-group experiences, small heterosexual cliques form. You may recall this stage during high school, when your dating activities occurred in a small group of girls *and* boys. Finally, at the end of adolescence, the structure collapses. It seems babyish to get together as a group. You want to be with your romantic partner alone.

You might be surprised to know that, although the tempo is slower today (see the next chapter's discussion), the same progression outlined in this 50-year-old research still rings true (Child Trends Data Bank, 2008): First, teenagers get together in large mixed-sex crowds; next, they align into smaller heterosexual groups; then, during their twenties, they get seriously romantically involved.

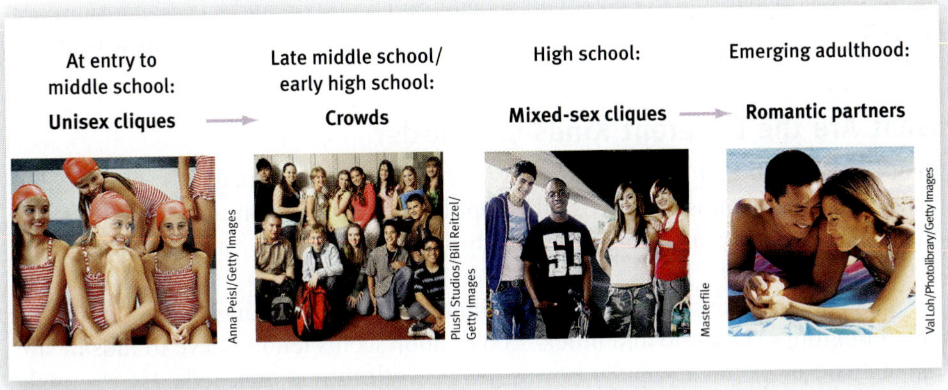

crowd A relatively large teenage peer group.

FIGURE 9.7: The steps from unisex elementary cliques to adult romantic relationships: A visual summary Unisex cliques meld into large heterosexual crowds, then re-form as heterosexual cliques, and then break up into one-to-one dating relationships. Does this sequence match your own experience?

What Is the Purpose of Crowds?

Crowds have other critical functions. They allow teenagers to connect with people who share their values. Just as elementary school children select friends with similar attitudes (see Chapter 6), teenagers gravitate to the crowd that fits their interests. When a particular group's priorities are different from one's own, an adolescent disengages from that group. As one academically focused teenager lamented: "I see some of my friends changing. . . . They are getting into parties and alcohol. . . . We used to be good friends . . . and now, I can't really relate to them. . . . That's kind of sad" (quoted in Phelan, Davidson, & Yu, 1998, p. 60).

Crowds actually serve as a roadmap, allowing teens to connect with "our kind of people" in an overwhelming social world (Smetana, Campione-Barr, & Metzger, 2006). Today, adolescents can immediately find crowds that fit their interests by

As you pass this group of "punks" on the street, you may think, "Why do they dress in this crazy way?" But for this group, their outlandish hair and clothes are a message that "I'm very different, and I don't agree with what society says." Most importantly, they are a signal to attract fellow minds: "I'm like you. I'm safe. I have the same ideas about the world."

going online. In fact, one great benefit of the social media revolution is that technology allows teenagers to instantly forge connections with compatible crowds (Xie, 2014).

In the real world, however, it's mainly in large high schools that young people need special help in sorting themselves into defined crowds. Therefore, one developmentalist suggested that a school's size plays a vital role in promoting defined teenage crowds (Cotterell, 1996). When your classes are filled with unfamiliar faces, it is helpful to develop a mechanism for finding a smaller set of people just like you. Teenagers adopt a specific look—like having weird hair and wearing ornament-studded jeans—to signal: "I'm your type of person. It's okay to be friends with me."

What Are the Different Kinds of Crowds?

In affluent societies, there is consistency in the major crowd categories. The intellectuals (also called brains and nerds), the popular kids, the deviants, and a residual type (such as Goths) appear in high schools throughout the West (Sussman and others, 2007).

How much mixing occurs between different crowds? Although teens do straddle different groups (Lonardo and others, 2009), adolescents tend to have friends in similar status crowds. So a popular boy associates with the popular kids. He shuns the socially more marginal groups, such as the deviants (bad kids) or nerdy brains. Moreover, because being brainy—and, especially, advertising that you work to get high grades—can go against the group norms, intellectuality does not gain teenagers kudos in the peer world in many U.S. public high schools today (Sussman and others, 2007).

A study tracking children's self-esteem as they moved from elementary school into high school documented how being brainy was transformed from a plus to more of a teenage liability during high school (Prinstein & La Greca, 2002). The researchers found that teenagers in the high-status jock crowd reported becoming more self-confident during adolescence. (These are the people who would tell you, "I wasn't very happy in elementary school, but high school was my best time of life.") The brainy group followed the opposite path—happiest during elementary school, less self-confident as teens.

Unfortunately, boys and girls who ended up in the high school deviant peer group were particularly unhappy in elementary school *as well as* during their adolescent years (see also Heaven, Ciarrochi, & Vialle, 2008). Recall that having prior externalizing problems and being rejected by the mainstream kids predict gravitating toward groups of "bad" peers. Now, let's explore why joining that bad crowd makes a teenager more likely to fail.

"Bad" Crowds

The classic defense that parents give for a teenager's delinquent behavior is, "My child got involved with a bad crowd." Without ignoring the principle of selection (birds of a feather flock together), there are powerful reasons why bad crowds *do* cause teenagers to do bad things.

For one thing, as I've been highlighting, teenagers are incredibly swayed by their peers. Moreover, each group has a leader, the person who most embodies the group's goals. So, if a child joins the brains group, his academic performance is apt to improve because everyone is jockeying for status by competing for grades (Cook, Deng, & Morgano, 2007; Molloy, Gest, & Rulison, 2011). However, in delinquent peer groups, members model the most antisocial leader. This most acting-out girl or boy sets the standard for how others want to behave.

Therefore, just as you felt compelled to jump into the icy water at camp when the bravest of your bunkmates took the plunge, if one group member begins selling guns or drugs, the rest must follow the leader or risk being called "chicken." Moreover, when children compete for status by getting into trouble, this creates ever-wilder antisocial modeling and propels the group toward taking increasingly risky acts.

Combine this principle with the impact of just being in a group. When young people get together, a group high occurs. Talk gets louder and more outrageous. People act in ways that would be unthinkable if they were alone. From rioting at rock concerts to being in a car with your buddies during a drive-by shooting (recall the earlier Experiencing Adolescence box), groups *do* cause people to act in dangerous ways (Cotterell, 1996).

By videotaping groups of boys, developmentalists have documented the **deviancy training,** or socialization into delinquency, that occurs as a function of simply talking with friends in a group (Dishion, McCord, & Poulin, 1999; Rorie and others, 2011). The researchers find that at-risk pre-teens forge friendships through specific kinds of conversations: They laugh, egg one another on, and reinforce one another as they discuss committing antisocial acts. So peer interactions in early adolescence are a medium by which problem behavior gets solidified, established, and entrenched.

The lure of entering an antisocial peer group is strong for at-risk kids because they are already feeling "it's me against the world" (Veenstra and others, 2010; see Chapter 6). Put yourself in the place of a child whose impulsive behavior is causing him to get rejected by the "regular" kids (Ettekal & Ladd, 2015). You need to connect with other children like yourself because you have failed at gaining entry anywhere else. Once in the group, your buddies reinforce your *hostile attributional bias*. Your friends tell you that it's fine to go against the system. You are finding acceptance in an unfriendly world.

In middle-class settings, popular kids sometimes get into trouble. "Self-identifying" as a jock is a risk factor for abusing alcohol or having unprotected sex (Cook, Deng, & Morgano, 2007). (At this point, any reader who has lived through adolescence is probably saying, "Duh!") But in affluent communities, children with prior problems tend to gravitate toward the druggy or delinquent groups. In economically

As a group euphoria sets in and people start surging for the stage, these teenagers at an outdoor music festival might trample one another—and then later be horrified that they could ever have acted this way.

deviancy training
Socialization of a young teenager into delinquency through conversations centered on performing antisocial acts.

deprived neighborhoods, there may be *no* positive peer group. Flourishing is impossible because the whole community is a toxic place. The only major crowd may be the antisocial group called a *gang*.

Society's Nightmare Crowd: Teenage Gangs

The **gang**, a close-knit, delinquent peer group, embodies society's worst nightmares. Gang members share a collective identity, which they often express by adopting specific symbols and claiming control over a certain turf (Jennings and others, 2016). This typically male group appears in different cultures and historical eras. However, with gangs, the socioeconomic context looms large: Adverse economic conditions, and especially living in communities low in collective efficacy, promote gangs (again, for a vivid example, turn back to the Experiencing Adolescence box on page 267).

Gangs provide teenagers with status. They offer children physical protection in dangerous neighborhoods. Gangs give teenagers who are disconnected from their families the sense of belonging to a coherent (even far more caring!) group. When young people have few options for making it in the conventional way, gangs provide an avenue for making a living (for example, by selling drugs or stealing). So, a harsh, unfriendly environment can propel time-limited adolescent turmoil into life-course criminal careers.

A Note on Adolescence Worldwide

A kinder, gentler twentieth-century developed world propelled adolescence into a life stage. Adolescence still doesn't exist for the nearly 50 million children who have been displaced from their homes in war-torn, famine-ridden regions of the globe (United Nations Children's Fund, 2016). There is no adolescence for street children or females forced into the sex trade, or for African girls forced into unwanted marriages as early as age 13 (Erulkar, 2013).

There is no life stage called adolescence for the thousands of child soldiers compelled to take up arms in dysfunctional, failed-state civil wars. Many combatants in the poorest regions of the globe are teenage boys. Some are coerced into fighting as young as age 10 or 8 (Child Soldiers International, 2017).

Yes, many teenagers in the world are flourishing. But children in the least-developed countries may not have the chance to be adolescents or construct a decent adult life. Although critics, such as Robert Epstein, bemoan the shackles of Western teens, having an extra decade liberated from grown-up responsibilities can be critical to flourishing during adult life.

How do contemporary, developed-world young people construct an adult life? Stay tuned for answers in the final chapter of this book.

---

gang A close-knit, delinquent peer group. Gangs form mainly in impoverished disorganized communities; they offer their members protection from harm and engage in a variety of criminal activities.

This 14-year-old soldier and devastated child bride in Africa offer a stark testament that, in some regions of the world, young people still are deprived of an adolescence.

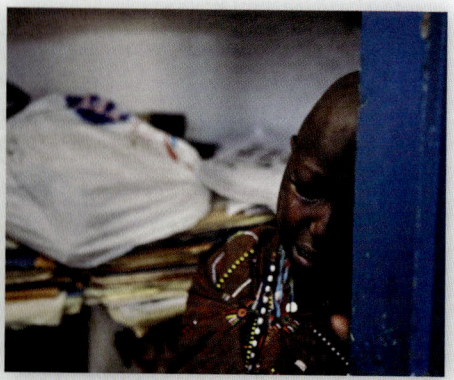

Tying It All Together

1. Chris and her parents are arguing again. Based on this chapter, at what age might arguments between Chris and her parents be most intense? Around what age would Chris's parents have begun to seriously loosen their rules? Choose between ages *12, 16, and 19*.

2. Your niece Heather hangs around with a small group of girlfriends. You see them at the mall giggling at a group of boys. According to the standard pattern, what is the next step?
   a. Heather and her friends will begin going on dates with the boys.
   b. Heather and her clique will meld into a large heterosexual crowd.
   c. Heather and her clique will form another small clique composed of both girls and boys.

3. Mom #1 says, "Getting involved with the 'bad kids' makes teens get into trouble." Mom #2 disagrees: "It's the kid's personality that causes him to get into trouble." Mom #3 says, "You both are correct—but also partly wrong. The kid's personality causes him to gravitate toward the 'bad kids,' and then that peer group encourages antisocial acts." Which mother is right?

4. You want to intervene to help prevent at-risk pre-teens from becoming delinquents. First, devise a checklist to assess who might be appropriate for your program. Then, applying the principles in this chapter, offer suggestions for how you would turn potentially "troublemaking teens" around.

Answers to the Tying It All Together questions can be found at the end of this chapter.

SUMMARY

Cognitive and Emotional Development: The Mysterious Teenage Mind

Wise observers have described the "hot-headed" qualities of youth for millennia. However, adolescence, first identified by G. Stanley Hall in the early 1900s and characterized by **"storm and stress,"** became a life stage in the United States during the twentieth century, when high school became universal and brought teens together as a group.

Jean Piaget believes that when teenagers reach the **formal operational stage,** they can think abstractly about hypothetical possibilities and reason scientifically. Most adults can't reason like scientists, but older teenagers use the skills involved in formal operations to plan their futures.

According to Lawrence Kohlberg, reaching formal operations allows teenagers to develop moral values that guide their lives. By examining how they reason about ethical dilemmas, Kohlberg classified moral development as either **preconventional** (moral judgment in which only punishment and reward are important); **conventional** (moral judgment based on obeying social norms); or **postconventional** (the highest level of moral reasoning, based on having one's own moral ideals, apart from society's rules). Although Kohlberg's theory has serious flaws, children become attuned to society's injustices during adolescence.

According to David Elkind, this ability to evaluate the adult world produces **adolescent egocentrism.** The **imaginary audience** (the feeling that everyone is watching everything one does) and the **personal fable** (feeling invincible and utterly unique) are two components of this intense early-teenage sensitivity to what others think.

Many storm-and-stress stereotypes about teenagerhood are true. Adolescents are highly socially sensitive. In arousing peer situations, they are apt to take dangerous risks. This risk-taking (and sometimes law-breaking) tendency, especially with friends, makes adolescence a dangerous time. Research using the **experience-sampling technique** shows teens are more emotionally intense than adults. Contrary to our stereotypes, however, most adolescents are upbeat and happy. Still, **nonsuicidal self-injury** is not infrequent, and depression rates rise during adolescence—especially among females. The push to be popular may explain many unfortunate behaviors during the pubertal years.

The minority of teenagers who get into *serious* trouble tend to have prior emotional and social problems, feel distant from their families, and live in a risk-taking milieu. Having specific talents, good executive functions, and being connected to caring adults help teens thrive. However, even well-adjusted teenagers experiment with forbidden activities, and serious **adolescence-limited turmoil** may not lead to **life-course difficulties.** Many problem teens construct fulfilling adult lives.

The unique characteristics of the teenage brain make adolescence a relatively dangerous life stage. The frontal lobes are still maturing. Puberty heightens teenagers' social sensitivities and emotional states. The lessons for society are as follows: (1) Don't punish teenagers who break the law in the same ways that adult offenders are punished; (2) pass legislation that takes teenage sensitivities into account; and (3) channel teenage passions in a positive way through high-quality **youth development programs.** Make high schools more appealing, rethink punitive school **zero-tolerance policies** that promote the **school-to-prison pipeline**, and adjust the school day to fit adolescent sleep. While the "immature brain" conception of adolescence is in vogue, critics suggest that it minimizes teenagers' strengths.

Social Development

Teenagers' struggles with parents are most intense during puberty, and issues relating to independence loom large in these conflicts around the world (with cultural variations). After young teens distance themselves from their families, by mid- and later adolescence, parents respond by relaxing their rules. Eventually, young people develop a more friendlike (but still more distant) relationship with their parents. Immigrant adolescents face unique stresses, although the **immigrant paradox** suggests that caring for a non-English-speaking mother or father can make teens self-confident, empathic, and mature.

Cliques and **crowds** convey adolescents, in stages, toward romantic involvement. Crowds, such as the jocks or the brains, also give teenagers an easy way of finding people like themselves in large high schools. The jocks (in contrast to the lower-status brains) feel better about themselves in high school than during elementary school. Children who enter delinquent groups tend to be unhappy before high school and remain distressed during their teenage years.

Entering a "bad" crowd promotes antisocial behavior because group members model the most antisocial leader. **Deviancy training**, in which pre-teens egg one another on by talking about doing dangerous things, leads directly to delinquency as at-risk children travel into high school. **Gangs**, mainly male teenage peer groups that engage in criminal acts, may be the only social group available in disorganized, impoverished communities. In the least developed regions of the world, young people may still not have any adolescence at all.

KEY TERMS

adolescence-limited turmoil, p. 265
adolescent egocentrism, p. 257
clique, p. 274
conventional thought, p. 256
crowd, p. 275
deviancy training, p. 277
experience-sampling technique, p. 260
formal operational stage, p. 253
gang, p. 278
imaginary audience, p. 258
immigrant paradox, p. 274
life-course difficulties, p. 265
nonsuicidal self-injury, p. 262
personal fable, p. 258
postconventional thought, p. 256
preconventional thought, p. 256
school-to-prison pipeline, p. 269
"storm and stress," p. 252
youth development program, p. 268
zero-tolerance policies, p. 269

ANSWERS TO Tying It All Together QUIZZES

Cognitive and Emotional Development: The Mysterious Teenage Mind

1. c and d
2. If your arguments centered on getting punished or rewarded (the coach needs to put Terry in because that's his best shot at winning; or the coach can't put Terry in because if someone finds out, he will be in trouble), you are reasoning at the preconventional level. Comments such as "going against the rules is wrong" might be classified as conventional. If you argued, "Putting Terry in goes against my values, no matter what the team or the rules say," your response might qualify as postconventional.
3. the imaginary audience; the personal fable; adolescent egocentrism
4. depression
5. worried, because he is at risk for moral disengagement and acting-out behaviors
6. a
7. Trying teens as adults. Pro arguments: Kohlberg's theory clearly implies teens know right from wrong, so if teens knowingly do the crime, they should "do the time." Actually, the critical dimension in deciding on adult punishment should be a person's culpability—premeditation, seriousness of the infraction, and so on—not age. Con arguments:

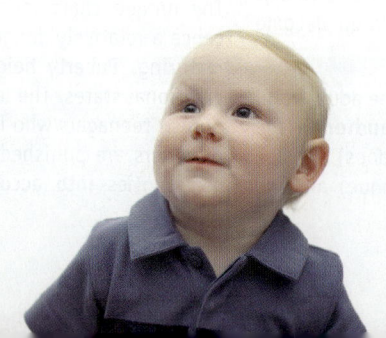

The research in this chapter shows that teens are indeed biologically and behaviorally different, so it is cruel to judge their behavior by adult standards. Moreover, if the U.S. bars young people from voting or serving in the military until age 18, and won't let people buy alcohol until age 21, it's unfair to put teens in adult prisons.

Social Development

1. At age 12, the arguments would be most intense; by age 16, Chris's parents would be giving her much more freedom
2. b
3. Mom #3 is correct.
4. Checklist: (1) Is this child unusually aggressive and does he have poor executive functions? (2) Is he being rejected by the mainstream kids? (3) Does this child have poor relationships with his parents? (4) Does he live in a dangerous, low-efficacy community or a risk-taking environment? Your possible program: Provide positive school activities that nurture the child's interests. Offer service-learning opportunities. Possibly institute group sessions with parents to solve problems around certain issues. Definitely try to get the child connected with caring mentors and a different set of (prosocial) friends.

CONNECT ONLINE:

LaunchPad macmillan learning | Check out our videos and additional resources located at: www.macmillanlearning.com

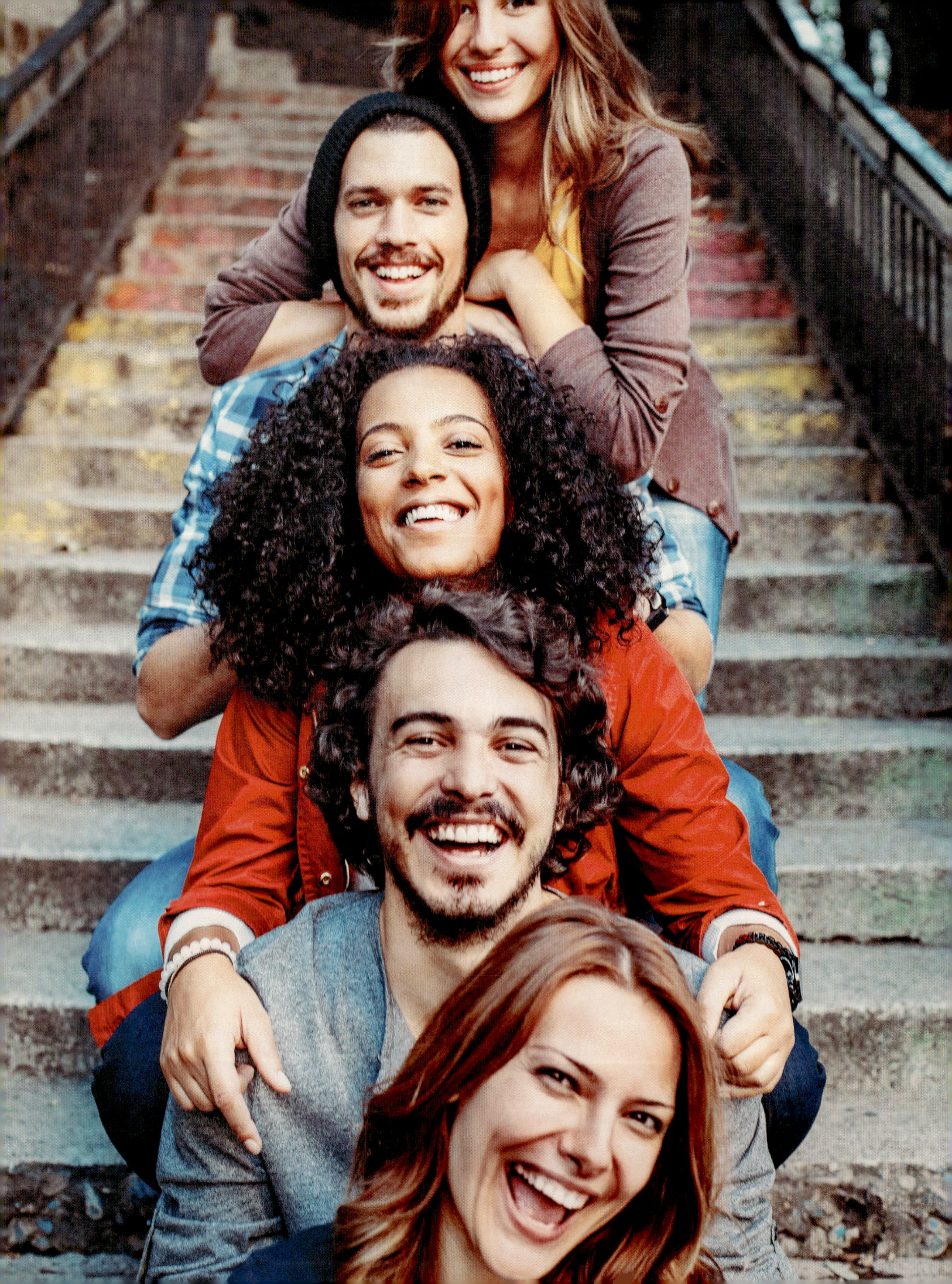

The Next Step: Emerging into Adulthood

PART V

Now it's time to end the journey of childhood by exploring that new life stage called emerging adulthood and reflecting on our field.

Chapter 10—Emerging into Adulthood tackles the challenge of constructing an adult life. Here, among other topics, I'll discuss leaving home, finding an identity, negotiating college, choosing a career, and searching for love. If you are a traditional college student or adult in your twenties, this chapter is for you.

Final Thoughts Here I'll take a step back to reflect on what I've learned in writing this book. After you read my top insights from surveying the research, take a minute to think about what stood out for you during this semester's exploration of children's lives.

CHAPTER 10

CHAPTER OUTLINE

Setting the Context
Culture and History
Beginning and End Points

Constructing an Identity
Marcia's Identity Statuses
The Identity Statuses in Action
Ethnic Identity, a Minority Theme

Finding a Career
Entering with High (But Often Unrealistic) Career Goals
Self-Esteem and Emotional Growth During College and Beyond
EXPERIENCING EMERGING ADULTHOOD: A Surprising Path to Adult Success
Finding Flow
Emerging into Adulthood Without a College Degree (in the United States)
INTERVENTIONS: Smoothing the School Path and School-to-Work Transition
Being in College
INTERVENTIONS: Making College an Inner-Growth Flow Zone

Finding Love
Setting the Context: Seismic Shifts in Searching for Love
HOT IN DEVELOPMENTAL SCIENCE: Same-Sex Romance
Similarity and Structured Relationship Stages: A Classic Model of Love and a Critique
HOT IN DEVELOPMENTAL SCIENCE: Facebook Romance
Love Through the Lens of Attachment Theory
HOW DO WE KNOW . . . That a Person Is Securely or Insecurely Attached?
INTERVENTIONS: Evaluating Your Own Relationship

Emerging into Adulthood

After graduating from high school, Sam looked forward to enjoying college. But his freshman year at State U was a nightmare. His courses felt irrelevant. He zoned out during lectures. Compared to high school, the work seemed impossibly hard. Most important, with his full-time job at the supermarket and five classes a semester, he lost his scholarship after the first year. The only rational solution was to drop out and move back in with his parents, so he could save money and then consider going back.

Six years later, Sam now has enough money to move out of the house. He was promoted to store supervisor (with health insurance!) and drives for a ride-sharing company on weekends. He met a terrific woman on Facebook named Clara. They just moved in together and plan to get married in a few years—if they both can get stable, well-paying jobs.

Clara and Sam share many values, even though, he must admit, she is more mature. He respects Clara's strong work ethic, and the fact that she helps care for her disabled sister while going to nursing school full time. Actually, Clara reminds him of his sister. She even physically resembles Samantha and his mom! Should Sam return to State U and get a business degree? Will having a B.A. allow him to support a family? At 28, it's crunch-time to get serious about life.

Can you identify with Sam's anxieties about finishing college? Perhaps, like Clara, you are trying to balance family demands while getting your degree. No matter what your situation, if you are in your twenties, you probably feel "in between." You are clearly not a child, but you haven't reached those classic adult goals—marriage, parenthood, embarking on your "real" career. You fit into that life-stage Jeffrey Arnett (2004, 2007) labels **emerging adulthood.**

This chapter is devoted to this new life phase. It explores the decade lasting from age 18 to our late twenties, when we are constructing an adult life. First, I'll examine the features of emerging adulthood and describe the challenges we face during this pivotal, transitional life stage. Then I'll focus on three crucial emerging-adult concerns: career, college, and finding love.

emerging adulthood The phase of life that begins after high school and tapers off toward the late twenties, devoted to constructing an adult life.

LEARNING OUTCOMES

- List the core emerging-adult challenges.
- Outline the historical forces that have shaped emerging adulthood, and how this life stage varies in southern Europe, Scandinavia, and the United States.
- Describe nest-leaving changes and social clock issues.

Setting the Context

Emerging adulthood is not a universal life stage. It occurs for the minority of young people living at this point in history in the developed world. Its goal is exploration—trying out options before committing to adult life. Although they often plan to get married (Willoughby and others, 2015; Willoughby & Hall, 2015), most emerging adults are not ready to settle down (Hall & Walls, 2016). They don't feel financially secure. They may move from job to job, enter and then exit college or a parent's home, and test out relationships before they get married and have children (Arnett, 2016).

Exploring different possibilities defines emerging adulthood. Its other core quality is exuberant optimism about what lies ahead (Tanner & Arnett, 2010; Silva, 2016). As Table 10.1 shows, emerging adults are at their physical peak. Their reasoning abilities are in top form. Still, the challenges young people face during this watershed age are more daunting than at any other life stage.

Table 10.1: A Twenty-Something Body at Its Physical Peak: A Brief Summary

The skeleton: Our height peaks at age 20 and then, due to the compression of the joint cartilage and bones, declines as we get older.

The muscles: The contracting skeletal muscle fibers allow us to perform physical tasks. During the late teens these fibers are at top capacity and then slowly atrophy and are replaced by fat.

The heart: During exercise, cardiac output (our heart's pumping capacity) dramatically increases—delivering more oxygen to the muscles. Cardiac function is at a high point during later adolescence, and then also gradually declines.

The lungs: The lungs are the bellows that deliver oxygen to the blood. Our ability to breathe in deeply and exhale forcefully (called *vital capacity*) peaks during youth and falls off year by year.

Information from Spense, 1989; Masoro, 1999.

FIGURE 10.1: Young men (blue bars) and women (pink bars) in the United States completing the classic "benchmarks of adulthood" at age 25, in 1960 and 2010 This chart documents the mammoth shift in the passage to adulthood that I will discuss in this chapter. In 1960, by their mid-twenties, most people had finished school, started a career, gotten married, and had children. Today, getting to these standard adult roles is rare by that age.
Data from Furstenberg, 2015.

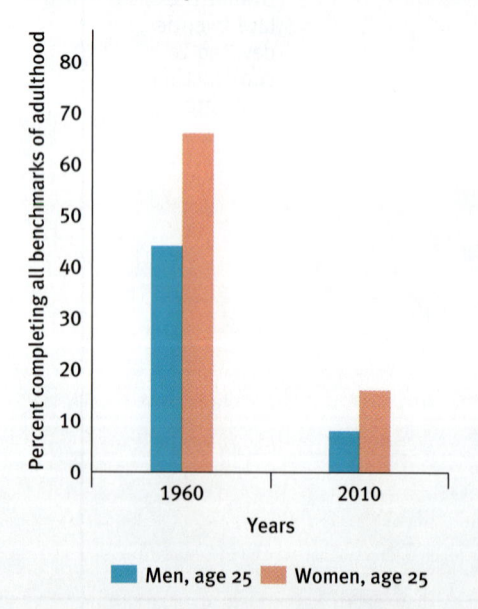

WE NEED TO RE-CENTER OUR LIVES Our parents protect us during adolescence. Now, our task is to take control of ourselves and act like "real adults" (Tanner, 2006; Tanner & Arnett, 2010). We used to count on marriage, parenthood, and supporting a family to make us feel adult. No more! Since only a tiny minority of contemporary U.S. young people have entered these adult roles by age 25 (see Figure 10.1), most people now view the criteria for reaching adulthood in internal terms: Adults accept responsibility for their actions; adults financially support themselves; adults make independent decisions about life (Arnett, 2016; Arnett & Padilla-Walker, 2015).

WE HAVE ENTERED AN UNSTRUCTURED, UNPREDICTABLE PATH During adolescence, high school organizes our days. We wake up, go to class; we are on an identical track. Then, at age 18, our lives diverge. Many of us go to college; others enter the world of work. Emerging adults live alone or with friends, stay with their parents or move far away. For some emerging adults, constructing an adult life takes decades. For people who have children and enter their work lives by age 18, there may be no emerging adulthood at all. So emerging adulthood is defined by variability—as we set sail on our own. Why did this structure-free stage emerge?

Culture and History

Our twentieth-century longevity gains made emerging adulthood possible. Imagine reaching adulthood a century ago. With an average life expectancy in the fifties (Gordon, 2015), you could not have the luxury of spending a decade constructing an adult life. Now, with life expectancy floating up to the late seventies and eighties in developed nations (Central Intelligence Agency, n.d.), putting off adult commitments until an older age makes excellent sense.

Education made emerging adulthood likely. A half-century ago, high school graduates could get high-paying jobs. Today, in the United States, we see college as crucial to career success (Danziger & Ratner, 2010; Silva, 2016). But, although most emerging adults enter college, it typically takes six years to get an undergraduate degree, especially because so many young people need to work to finance school. If we add in graduate school, constructing a career can take until the mid-twenties and beyond (Furstenberg, 2015).

Emerging adulthood was promoted by the fact that staying married and finding well-paying work can be elusive (Furstenberg, 2015; Willoughby & Hall, 2016). It took hold in a late-twentieth-century Western culture that stresses self-expression and "doing your own thing," in which people make dramatic changes *throughout* their adult years.

Longevity, education, and an uncertain modern life propelled emerging adulthood. Still, the forces that drive this life stage vary from place to place. For snapshots of this variability, let's travel to southern Europe, Scandinavia, and then enter the United States.

The Mediterranean Model: Living with Parents and Having Trouble Making the Leap to Adult Life

In southern Europe, the main barrier to reaching adulthood is alarmingly high youth unemployment rates (Crocetti & Tagliabue, 2016). In these Catholic nations, the social norms discourage **cohabitation**, or living together without being married. So young people in Portugal, Italy, Spain, and Greece typically spend their twenties and early thirties in their parents' house (Mendonça & Fontaine, 2013; Seiffge-Krenke, 2013). Unfortunately, as of this writing (2017), family traditions and financial constraints have seriously impeded young people's travels into an independent life.

cohabitation Sharing a household in an unmarried romantic relationship.

The Scandinavian Plan: Living Independently with Government Help

These barriers do not exist in Scandinavia, where jobs are more plentiful (as of this writing in 2017) and getting married is an optional choice (Wängqvist and others, 2016). In Norway, Sweden, and Denmark, the government funds university attendance. A strong social safety net provides free health care and other benefits to citizens of every age. So in these northern European countries, **nest-leaving**—moving out of a parent's home to live independently—often begins at the brink of the emerging-adult years (Furstenberg, 2010; Hendry & Kloep, 2010). In the Nordic nations, the twenties are more of a stress-free interlude—a time for exploring life before having children, and then *perhaps* deciding to marry a life love (Wängqvist & Frisén, 2016).

nest-leaving Moving out of a childhood home and living independently.

Many Greek men in their late twenties and thirties still live with their families because they cannot afford to leave the nest and construct an adult life. How would you react in this situation?

The United States Route(s): Colliding Conceptions and Diverse, SES-Related Paths

Emerging adulthood in the United States has features of both Scandinavia and southern Europe. As in the Nordic nations, a high fraction of U.S. women now give birth without being married (Furstenberg, 2015). However, as the

If you visited this Scandinavian family, these parents might be happily cohabiting without feeling they needed a wedding ring. In the United States, we view a marriage ceremony as a pinnacle life event!

photos above show, like their southern European counterparts, U.S. young people view being married as an important life goal (Willoughby & Hall, 2016; Willoughby and others, 2015). Our individualistic culture strongly encourages people to move out of a parent's home at age 18; but this same focus on self-reliance means that, unlike in Scandinavia, the U.S. government doesn't pay for college and emerging adults have trouble finding decently paying jobs.

The reality is that these colliding conceptions, combined with our dramatic *income inequalities*, produce sharp social-class differences in how U.S. emerging adults construct an adult life. Because people are reluctant to get married until they can support a family, marriage in the United States has become a middle-class achievement. Low-income adults often travel through life without having a spouse (Furstenberg, 2015). And, unless they have fairly well-off parents, U.S. young people may have trouble immediately reaching the first classic benchmark of adult life—moving out of their parents' house (Settersten & Ray, 2010).

Beginning and End Points

This brings up an interesting issue: When *does* emerging adulthood begin and end?

Exploring the Traditional Entry Point: Nest-Leaving

Actually, in the United States and northern Europe, we traditionally see leaving the nest as an important rite of passage. It forces people to take that first important step toward independent adulthood—taking care of their needs on their own. It also causes a change in family relationships, as parents view their children in a different, adult way. Listen to this British mother gushing about her 20-year-old daughter: "To be honest, I'm real proud of her. . . . She keeps her flat tidy which was a total shocker to me; I'd expected to be a laundry and maid service to her, but fair play, she's done all her washing and cleaning" (quoted in Kloep & Hendry, 2010, p. 824).

This quotation hints at two benefits of leaving home: Moving out should produce more harmonious family relationships; it should force young people to "grow up."

Does Leaving Home Produce Better Parent–Child Relationships?

Here, U.S. research suggests that the answer is often yes. In several longitudinal studies, both young people and their parents reported less conflict when children left the nest (Morgan, Thorne, & Zubriggen, 2010; Whiteman, McHale, & Crouter, 2007). However, this is not true in Italy, where young people prize family closeness over friendships (Crocetti & Meeus, 2014) and, as I mentioned

For this mother, being invited to her daughter's first apartment may be a thrilling experience: "My baby did grow up to become a responsible woman!"

earlier, emerging adults typically live in their parents' home. In Portugal, one study showed that parents got more agitated when their children moved out of the house! (See Mendonça & Fontaine, 2013.)

I must emphasize that, even in the United States, physically leaving home does not mean having distant family relationships. Judging by the 24/7 texts that fly back and forth between my students and their parents, the impulse to stay closely connected to mothers and fathers is more intense among this cohort of twenty-somethings than when I was a college student decades ago (see Levine & Dean, 2012). Having close mother–child relationships and calling each other frequently is correlated with adjusting well to college and homing in on a satisfying career (Chih-Yuan, Bryan, & Lauren, 2016). Although they may not be making the meals or doing the laundry, mothers remain a vital support as young people leave the nest and travel into the wider world.

This twenty-first-century college student is more likely to openly share her feelings and rely on her mother's advice than her mother did when she was the girl's age.

Does Leaving Home Make People More Adult?

Here, too, studies imply the answer is yes. When Belgian researchers compared young people in their early twenties who never left home with a same-aged group who moved out, the "nest residers" were less likely to be in a long-term relationship, felt more emotionally dependent on their parents, and were less satisfied with life (Kins & Beyers, 2010; see also Seiffge-Krenke, 2010). One emerging adult named Adam spelled out his feelings: "(It) is comparable to living in a hotel actually. I have no charges . . . my meals are prepared, my laundry is done" (quoted in Kins, de Mol, & Beyers, 2014, p. 104). Another British mother put it more graphically: "He is my little boy, a mummy's boy if you like. . . . And 'cos he lives at home still . . . I do his clothes, his washing, tidy his room . . . and even still do packed lunch for him to take to work" (quoted in Kloep & Hendry, 2010, p. 826).

These quotations reinforce all of our negative images about emerging adults who stay in the nest: They are lazy, babyish, and unwilling to grow up. The problem is that we are confusing consequences with causes. Nest-leaving, as I've been suggesting, has an economic cause (Seiffge-Krenke, 2013). Young people often stay at home, or return to live with their parents, because they cannot afford to live on their own (Berzin & De Marco, 2010; Britton, 2013).

In addition to financial problems, there is another barrier to moving out for some immigrant and ethnic minority youth: values (Furstenberg, 2010; Kiang & Fuligni, 2009). If a young person's collectivist worldview says to put family first, children may stay in the nest for adult-centered reasons—to help with the finances and the chores. As one Latino 20-year-old explained: "I can't leave my mom by herself, she is a single mother. The only person she's got is me. . . ." (quoted in Sánchez and others, 2010, p. 872).

So, is nest-leaving still the beginning of emerging adulthood? Not really, anymore. Do young people *need* to live independently to act mature? The answer is

Table 10.2: **Tips for Getting Along as Co-residing Adults**

1. **For parents:** Don't micromanage or hover (for example, texting or calling) when your child comes home "late." Support your child's goals and encourage your son or daughter to make a financial contribution to the family, as subsidizing everything reinforces the impression that this young person is still a child (Nelson & Luster, 2016).

2. **For children:** Resist being babied (and totally subsidized), but lean on your parents for emotional support. If you have a sense of purpose, you are apt to feel "adult" and also close to your parents, even if you are living "at home" (see Hill, Burrow, & Sumner, 2016).

3. **For parents and children:** Talk openly about your concerns and set up shared rules: How will you divide household tasks? Is living together contingent on staying in school or searching for a job? Then vow to treat each other like loving adults.

social clock The concept that we regulate our passage through adulthood by an inner timetable that tells us which life activities are appropriate at certain ages.

age norms Cultural ideas about the appropriate ages for engaging in particular activities or life tasks.

on time Being on target in a culture's timetable for achieving adult life tasks.

off time Being too late or too early in a culture's timetable for achieving adult life tasks.

definitely no. Parents' task is to construct adult-to-adult relationships with their children no matter where the younger generation lives (see Table 10.2 for suggestions). And young people's challenge is to assemble the building blocks to construct a satisfying adult life. When should this constructing phase end and adulthood arrive? The answer brings up a classic concept in adult development.

Exploring the Fuzzy End Point: The Ticking of the Social Clock

Our feelings about when we should get our adult lives in order reflect our culture's **social clock** (Neugarten, 1972, 1979). This phrase refers to shared **age norms** that act as guideposts to what behaviors are appropriate at particular ages. If our passage matches up with the normal timetable in our society, we are defined as **on time**; if not, we are **off time**—either too early or too late for where we should be at a given age.

So in the twenty-first-century West, exploring different options is considered on time during our twenties, but these activities become off time if they extend well into the next decade of life. A parent whose 35-year-old son is "just dating" and shows no signs of deciding on a career or moves back home for the third or fourth time may become impatient: "Will my child ever grow up?" A woman traveling into her mid-thirties may get uneasy: "I'd better hurry up if I want a family," or "Do I still have time to go to medical school?" Although emerging adults *say* they view adulthood in internal terms, feeling seriously off time in the late direction can cause young people considerable distress (Nelson & Luster, 2016).

Society sets the general social-clock guidelines. Today, with the average age of marriage in most European countries floating up to about the thirties (Shulman & Connolly, 2013), it's fine to date for more than a decade if you live in the West. But in China, where everyone is expected to get married and where the marriage age is lower now than in the past (Yeung & Hu, 2013), it can be embarrassing to be over age 30 without a mate: "The older generation cannot understand why I keep being single . . . ," said one woman. "Many people will think . . . I must have some mental or physical deficiencies" (quoted in Wang & Abbott, 2013, p. 226).

Personal preferences make a difference. In one survey, developmentalists found that they could predict a given undergraduate's social-clock timetable by asking a simple question: "Is having a family your main passion?" People who said that marriage was their top-ranking agenda or that they couldn't wait to be a mom or dad tended

When this not-so-young man in his forties finally proposed to his longtime, 38-year-old girlfriend, both their families were probably thrilled. Feeling "off time" in the late direction in your social-clock timetable can cause everyone considerable distress.

to get married and give birth at younger ages (Carroll and others, 2007). So, the limits of emerging adulthood are set both by our society and our personal goals (see Willoughby & Hall, 2015).

The problem, however, is that our social-clock agendas are not totally under control. People cannot "decide" to find the love of their life at a defined age (Sharon, 2015). This sense of being "out of control" may explain why emerging adulthood is both an exhilarating *and* emotionally challenging time. On the positive side, as I mentioned earlier, emerging adults are remarkably optimistic about their futures (Frye & Liem, 2011; Pryor and others, 2011; Silva, 2016). On the negative side, the twenties are the life stage when anxiety disorders reach their peak (Schwartz, 2016).

For some young people, the issue is failing to take responsibility. As one emerging adult anguished: "My life looks like a . . . gutter and effort to fight that gutter . . . then back in the gutter . . . I just don't have any control over myself" (quoted in Macek, Bejcek, & Vanickova, 2007, p. 466). For others, there may be romantic heartbreaks or understanding that one's career dreams can't be fulfilled (more about both issues soon). Or emerging adults may not have any sense of where they want to go in life: "We do have more possibilities . . . but that's why it's harder" . . . "You study and you wonder what it is good for" (quoted in Macek, Bejcek, & Vanickova, 2007, p. 468). The reason for this inner turmoil is that, during emerging adulthood, we undergo a mental makeover. We decide *who* to be as adults.

The fact that this young woman's passion since childhood was to be a mother could explain why she gave birth at the atypically young age of 24.

Tying It All Together

1. You are giving a toast at your friend Sarah's 20th birthday party, and you want to offer some predictions about what the next years might hold in store for her. Given your understanding of emerging adulthood, which would *not* be a safe prediction?
   a. Sarah may not reach the standard markers of adulthood for many years.
   b. Sarah will have graduated from college in four years.
   c. Sarah might need to move back into the nest or might still be living at home.

2. Which emerging adult is *least* likely to be in the nest?
   a. Manuel, who lives in Madrid
   b. Paula, whose parents live below the poverty line
   c. Silvia, who lives in Stockholm

3. Staying in the nest during the twenties today is a "symptom" of a child's refusing to grow up—*true* or *false*?

4. Which person is most apt to worry about a social-clock issue: Martha, age 50, who wants to apply to nursing school, or Lee, age 28, who has just become a father?

Answers to the Tying It All Together questions can be found at the end of this chapter.

Constructing an Identity

Erik Erikson was the theorist who highlighted the challenge of transforming our childhood self into the person we will be as adults. He named this process the search for **identity** (see Table 10.3 on page 292).

Time spent wandering through Europe to find himself sensitized Erikson to the difficulties young people face in constructing an adult self. Erikson's fascination with identity, however, crystallized when he worked in a psychiatric hospital for troubled

LEARNING OUTCOMES
- Describe the different identity statuses.
- Examine ethnic identity.

identity In Erikson's theory, the life task of deciding who to be as an adult.

Table 10.3: Erikson's Psychosocial Stages of Childhood, Adolescence, and Emerging Adulthood

Life Stage	Primary Task
Infancy (birth to 1 year)	Basic trust versus mistrust
Toddlerhood (1 to 2 years)	Autonomy versus shame and doubt
Early childhood (3 to 6 years)	Initiative versus guilt
Middle childhood (7 to 12 years)	Industry versus inferiority
Adolescence and emerging adulthood (teens into twenties)	**Identity versus role confusion**
Emerging adulthood (twenties)	Intimacy versus isolation

role confusion Erikson's term for a failure in identity formation, marked by the lack of any sense of a future adult path.

teens. Erikson discovered that young patients suffered from a problem he labeled **role confusion.** They had no sense of any adult path:

> [The person feels as] if he were moving in molasses. It is hard for him to go to bed and face the transition into . . . sleep; and it is equally hard for him to get up. . . . Such complaints as . . . "I don't know" . . . "I give up" . . . "I quit" . . . are often expressions of . . . despair.
>
> (Erikson, 1968, p. 169)

Some people felt a frightening sense of falseness: "If I tell a girl I like her, if I make a gesture . . . this third voice is at me all the time—'You're doing this for effect; you're a phony'" (quoted in Erikson, 1968, p. 173). Others could not cope with having any future and planned to end their lives on a symbolic date.

This derailment, which Erikson called *role confusion*—an aimless drifting, or shutting down—differs from the active search process he labeled *moratorium* (1980). Taking time to explore different paths, Erikson argued, is crucial to forming a solid adult identity. Having witnessed Hitler's Holocaust, Erikson believed that young people must discover their own identities. He had seen a destructive process of identity formation firsthand. To cope with that nation's economic problems after World War I, German teenagers leaped into pathological identities by entering totalitarian organizations such as the Hitler Youth.

Can we categorize the ways people tackle the challenge of constructing an adult identity? Decades ago, James Marcia answered yes.

identity statuses Marcia's four categories of identity formation: identity diffusion, identity foreclosure, moratorium, and identity achievement.

identity diffusion According to James Marcia, an identity status in which the person is aimless or feels totally blocked, without any adult life path.

identity foreclosure According to James Marcia, an identity status in which the person decides on an adult life path (often one spelled out by an authority figure) without any thought or active search.

moratorium According to James Marcia, an identity status in which the person actively explores various possibilities to find a truly solid adult life path.

Marcia's Identity Statuses

Marcia (1966, 1987) devised four **identity statuses** to expand on Erikson's powerful ideas:

- **Identity diffusion** best fits Erikson's description of the most troubled teens—young people drifting aimlessly toward adulthood without any goals: "I don't know where I am going," "Nothing has any appeal."

- **Identity foreclosure** describes a person who adopts an identity without any self-exploration or thought. At its violent extreme, foreclosure might apply to a Hitler Youth member or a teenager who becomes a terrorist. In general, however, researchers define young people as being in foreclosure when they adopt an identity handed down by some authority: "My parents want me to take over the family business, so that's what I will do."

- The person in **moratorium** is engaged in the exciting search for an adult self. While this internal process provokes anxiety because it involves wrestling with different philosophies and ideas, Marcia (and Erikson) believed it was critical to arriving at the final stage.

- **Identity achievement** is the end point: "I've weighed the options and I want to be a computer artist, no matter what my family says."

As the photo series shows, Marcia's categories offer a marvelous framework for pinpointing what is going wrong (or right) in a young person's life. Perhaps while reading these descriptions you were thinking, "I have a friend in diffusion. Now I understand exactly what this person's problem is!" How do these statuses play out in life?

identity achievement A fully mature identity status in which the young person chooses a satisfying adult life path.

This young woman may fit Marcia's category of *identity diffusion*. She seems listless and depressed.

This student, forced by his dad to get a degree in computer science in order to get a well-paying job, feels incredibly bored. People who follow their parents' career choices without exploring other possibilities are in *identity foreclosure*. (While Erikson and Marcia linked this status to poor mental health—as you will see on the next page—young people "in foreclosure" can also feel happy about this state.)

This young woman, who has accepted a company internship, is in *identity moratorium* because she wants to figure out if she likes working in this career. We don't know, however, if she is excitedly exploring her options or unproductively obsessing about her choices.

This delighted man is in *identity achievement* because he has discovered that his life passion lies in computer design.

The Identity Statuses in Action

Marcia believed that as teenagers get older, they pass from diffusion to moratorium to achievement. Who thinks much about adulthood in ninth or tenth grade? At that age, your agenda is to cope with puberty. You test the limits. You sometimes act in ways that seem tailor-made to undermine your adult life (see Chapter 9). Then, older adolescents and emerging adults undertake a moratorium search as adulthood looms in full view. At some point during the twenties, people reach achievement, finding a secure adult identity.

However, in real life, people move back and forth across identity statuses *throughout* adulthood (Côté & Bynner, 2008; Schwartz and others, 2015; Waterman, 1999). A woman might enter college exploring different faiths, then become a committed Catholic, start questioning her choice again at 30, and finally settle on her spiritual identity in Bahai at age 45. As many older students are aware, you may have gone through moratorium and believed you were in identity achievement in your career, but then shifted back to moratorium when you realized, "I need a more fulfilling job."

This lifelong shift is appropriate. It's unrealistic to think we reach a final identity as emerging adults. The push to rethink our lives, to have plans and goals, is what makes us human. It is essential at any age. Moreover, revising our identity is vital to living fully since our lives are always being disrupted—as we change careers, become parents, are widowed, or adapt to our children leaving the nest (McAdams, 2013).

The bad news is that young people may get mired in unproductive identity statuses. In some studies, an alarming 1 in 4 undergraduates is locked in diffusion (Côté & Bynner, 2008). They don't have *any* career goals. Or, people may be sampling different paths, but without much Eriksonian moratorium joy. Is your friend who keeps changing his major and putting off graduating excitedly exploring his options, or is he afraid of entering the real world? Are the emerging adults who move from low-wage job to low-wage job really in moratorium or randomly drifting into adult life?

Actually, Erikson's and Marcia's assumptions that people need to sample *many* fields to construct a solid career identity is false. Having a career in mind from childhood, such as knowing you want to be a nurse from age 9 (the status Marcia dismisses as "foreclosure") can be fine. Anxiously obsessing about possibilities—that is, being locked in a state called **ruminative moratorium**—produces poor mental health (Beyers & Luyckx, 2016; Hatano, Sugimura, & Crocetti, 2016): "I don't know if I want to be an anesthesiologist or an actor, and that's driving me crazy."

There can even be problems with being identity achieved. Suppose that after searching various possibilities, you adopt a devalued identity ("Yes, I'll enter medical school, but I'm not convinced being a doctor is me"). It doesn't matter *how* we arrive at achievement. What's crucial is to make a commitment and *feel confident* that this decision expresses our inner self (see Schwartz and others, 2015, for reviews).

Ethnic Identity, a Minority Theme

The emotional advantages of feeling positive about our identity is underscored by **ethnic identity**, a person's sense of belonging to a defined ethnic category, such as Asian American. If you are a member of the dominant culture, you rarely think of your ethnicity. For minority children, categorizing oneself according to a defined label such as Latino or Asian occurs during concrete operations (see Chapter 6), although the salience of this perception waxes and wanes at different ages. For instance, a boy may be acutely aware of his Latino roots if he attends a mainly White high school (Douglass, Wang, & Yip, 2016). While bonding with friends who share her heritage, a girl may feel especially Korean or Vietnamese (Douglass, Mirpuri, & Yip, 2016).

Studies show that being proud of one's ethnic background offers young people a sense of meaning in life (Acevedo-Polakovich and others, 2014; Ajibade and others, 2016). Identifying with being Canadian or Cambodian buffers teenagers from becoming depressed or resorting to risk-taking (Polanco-Roman & Miranda, 2013; Toomey and others, 2013). Ethnic pride is even correlated with doing well in middle school (Santos & Collins, 2016). But it's important to reach out to the wider culture. Actually, firmly connecting with the mainstream culture ("I'm also proud of being American") is one sign that an ethnic minority young person has the skills to reach out fully in love.

---

ruminative moratorium When a young person is unable to decide between different identities, becoming emotionally paralyzed and highly anxious.

ethnic identity How people come to terms with who they are as people in relation to their unique ethnic or racial heritage.

Connecting with his ethnic identity can offer this young man an intense sense of life meaning.

The challenges for **biracial or multiracial** emerging adults—that is, people from mixed racial or ethnic backgrounds (like former President Barack Obama)—are particularly poignant. These young people may feel adrift without any ethnic home (Literte, 2010). But here, too, reaching identity achievement has widespread benefits. Research suggests that having a biracial or bicultural background pushes people to think in more creative ways (Tadmor, Tetlock, & Peng, 2009). It also promotes resilience. As one biracial woman in her early thirties put it: "When I was younger I felt I didn't belong anywhere. But now I've just come to the conclusion that my home is inside myself" (Phinney, 2006, p. 128).

Making sense of one's "place in the world" as an ethnic minority is literally a minority identity theme. But every person grapples with choosing a career and finding love. The rest of this chapter tackles those agendas.

> **biracial or multiracial identity** How people of mixed racial backgrounds come to terms with who they are as people in relation to their heritage.

Tying It All Together

1. You overheard your psychology professor saying that his daughter Emma shows symptoms of Erikson's role confusion. Emma must be _____ (*drifting, actively searching for an identity*), which in Marcia's identity status framework is a sign of _____ (*diffusion, foreclosure, moratorium*).

2. Joe said, "I've wanted to be a lawyer since I was a little boy." Kayla replied, "I don't know what my career will be, and I've been obsessing about the possibilities day and night." Joe's identity status is _____ (*moratorium, foreclosure, diffusion, or achievement*), whereas Kayla's status is _____ (*moratorium, foreclosure, diffusion, or achievement*). According to the latest research, who is apt to have an emotional problem?

3. Your cousin Clara has enrolled in nursing school. To predict her feelings about this decision, pick the right question to ask: *Have you explored different career possibilities?/ Do you feel nursing expresses your inner self?*

4. Having a biracial or multiracial identity makes people think in more rigid ways about the world—*true* or *false*?

Answers to the Tying It All Together questions can be found at the end of this chapter.

Finding a Career

When asked to sum up the definition of ideal mental health, Sigmund Freud famously answered, "The ability to love and work." Let's now look at finding ourselves in the world of work.

When did you begin thinking about your career? What influences are drawing you to psychology, nursing, or business—a compelling class, a caring mentor, or the conviction that this field would fit your talents best? How do young people feel about their careers, their futures, and working itself?

To answer these questions, Mihaly Csikszentmihalyi and Barbara Schneider (2000) conducted a pioneering study of teenagers' career dreams. They selected 33 U.S. schools and interviewed students from sixth to twelfth grade. To chart how young people felt—when at home, with friends, when at school—they used the *experience-sampling method* (discussed in Chapter 9). Now let's touch on their insights and more recent studies as we track young people moving through their emerging adult years.

LEARNING OUTCOMES
- Describe self-esteem changes after young people enter college and emerging adult emotional growth.
- Outline the features and function of flow states.
- Explore higher education, making special reference to issues relating to completing college and the school-to-work transition.
- Summarize strategies for having a fulfilling college experience.

Entering with High (But Often Unrealistic) Career Goals

Almost every teenager dreams of going to college and having a high-paying career. This tendency to aim high appears regardless of gender or social class (Silva, 2016). Whether male or female, rich or poor, adolescents have lofty career goals. Moreover,

FIGURE 10.2: The fading chances of U.S. upward mobility Basic to the "American dream" is having children who are more successful in terms of income (and of course education, too). But, while upward mobility was the birthright of American babies born during World War II (early 1940s) and, to a lesser extent, children born during the early baby boom (late 1940s to 1950), notice from the chart that by the mid-twentieth century, the odds of U.S. newborns earning more than their parents dramatically decreased.

Data from The Equality of Opportunity Project, n.d.

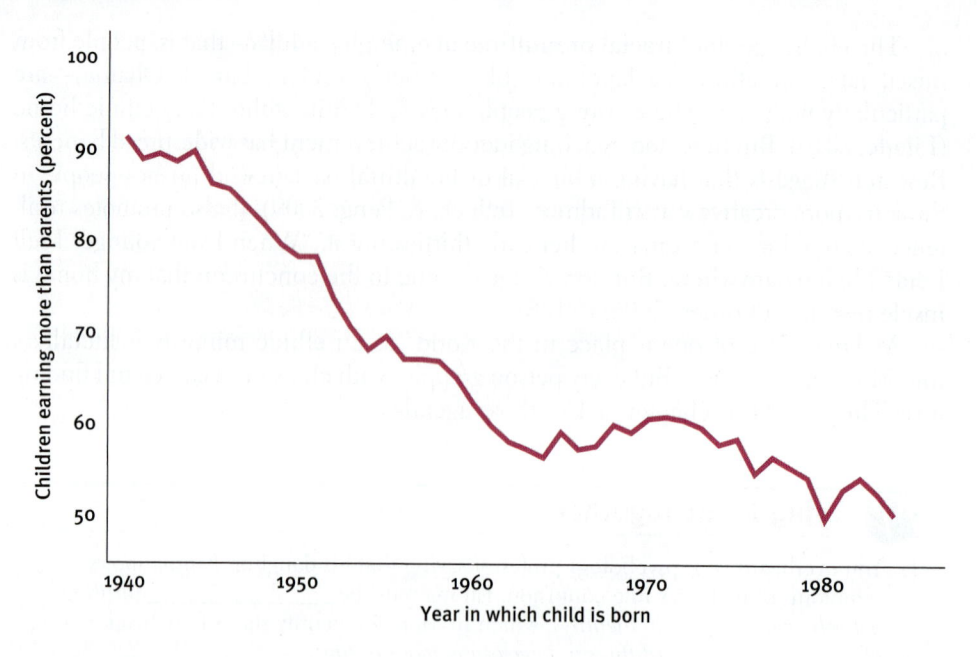

I believe that the experts who view today's young people as overly coddled (Levine & Dean, 2012), narcissistic (Twenge, 2006), and basically unmotivated are wrong. As you can see in Figure 10.2, emerging adults face a more difficult economy than their parents'—and especially their grandparents—confronted at the same age. Therefore, it makes sense that in one survey of U.S. college freshmen, students reported being more driven to work hard than their counterparts in the past (Pryor and others, 2011).

The problem is that teenagers are (naturally) clueless about the objective barriers to reaching their dream careers. Can someone who "hates reading" spend a decade getting a psychology Ph.D.? What happens when my students learn they must earn a GPA close to 3.7 to enter our university's nursing program, or that they can't go to law school because of the astronomical costs? Career disappointment can lurk around the corner for young people as they enter college and confront the real world. How do people react?

Self-Esteem and Emotional Growth During College and Beyond

One U.S. survey showed that self-esteem dips dramatically during the first semester of college (Chung and others, 2014) and then gradually rises over the next few years (Higher Education Research Institute [HERI], 2013; see also Wagner and others, 2013). Because entering students inflate their academic abilities (Chung and others, 2014), it can be a shock when those disappointing first-semester grades arrive. Still, as the research described in Figure 10.3 shows, there is diversity, with some people

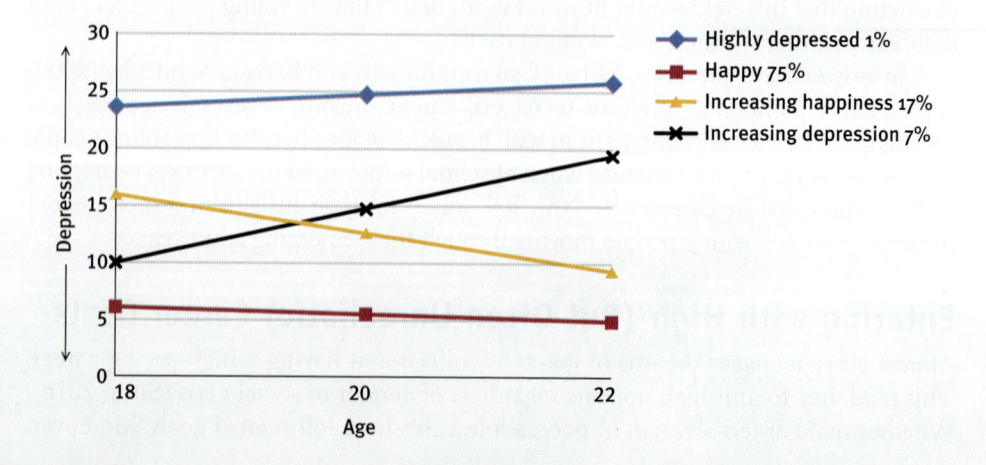

FIGURE 10.3: The ways depression changed in an economically diverse sample of over 1,000 young people traveling from age 18 to age 22 Notice from this chart that the vast majority of young people are happy both during their teens and as they emerge into their early twenties (red line). Teens with major depressive disorders are still battling their condition three years later (blue line). But a reasonable percentage of moderately depressed teens become happier as they make the transition to adult life (yellow line)—although, granted, some do become more depressed (black line).

Data from Frye & Liem, 2011.

getting unhappier and others improving in mental health from age 18 to 22 (Frye & Liem, 2011).

Who thrives? The figure implies that personality matters. Young people who enter emerging adulthood upbeat and competent are set up to flourish when confronting the demands of college life. In their study, Csikszentmihalyi and Schneider (2000) called these efficacious teens "workers." They are the 16-year-olds who amaze you with their ability to balance band, a part-time job, and honors classes.

But even when teenagers don't qualify as workers, emerging adulthood can be a time of tremendous emotional growth (Alessandri and others, 2016; Syed & Seiffge-Krenke, 2015). Growth is most likely to occur in a personality dimension that psychologists call *conscientiousness*—becoming more reliable, developing self-control (see Cramer, 2008; Donnellan, Conger, & Burzette, 2007; Walton and others, 2013). Emerging adults tend to become more resilient (Zimmermann & Iwanski, 2014). They reason in more thoughtful ways (Labouvie-Vief, 2006).

To explain this rise in *executive functions*, neuroscientists might look to the fully developed frontal lobes (Henin & Berman, 2016). But an equally plausible cause lies in the wider world. Finding a job that perfectly fits your talents (see the Experiencing Emerging Adulthood box) can transform even troubled teens into workers (Denissen, Asendorpf, & van Aken, 2008.) Csikszentmihalyi argues that a powerful inner state can lock *anyone* into the right career.

Experiencing Emerging Adulthood: A Surprising Path to Adult Success

Dyslexia caused him serious trouble in elementary school; then, at age 12, he began taking drugs. When, at 15, he took the family car and ran away for a weekend in New Orleans, his frantic father visited the local jail and begged the police to take their son in. Finally, his hysterical parents paid guards to take him to a wilderness program and then a school for troubled teens—where he spent his high school years. After dropping out of college his first semester, during his twenties, he drifted from job to job. He was incredibly talented with people but couldn't get along with his bosses.

At about age 30, he got into real estate—a profession for which you don't need a college degree, where what matters is hard work and world-class people skills. After taking the sales associate test eight times, he finally passed! Today, at age 34, he owns a management company and gets national performance awards. He is on track to out-earn his parents (who both graduated from Ivy League schools). His name is Thomas Belsky, and he is my son.

Am I sharing this story *just to* brag about my son and show that with incredible self-efficacy children can triumph against academic odds? I'll answer no. Suppose that Thomas had grown up with adults who weren't devoted to his well-being. Would he have fulfilled his natural gifts or even be alive today?

Finding Flow

Think back over the past week to the times you felt energized and alive. You might be surprised to discover that events you looked forward to—such as relaxing at home—do not come to mind. Many of life's most uplifting experiences occur when we connect deeply with people. Others take place when we are immersed in some compelling task. Csikszentmihalyi calls this intense task absorption **flow**.

Flow is different from "feeling happy." We enter this state during an activity that stretches our capacities, such as the challenge of decoding a difficult academic problem, or (hopefully) getting absorbed in mastering the material in this class. People also differ in the activities that cause flow. For some of us, it's hiking in the Himalayas that produces this feeling. For me, it has been writing this book. When we are in flow, we enter an altered state of consciousness in which we forget the outside world. Problems disappear. We lose a sense of time. The activity feels infinitely worth doing for its own sake. Flow makes us feel completely alive.

flow Csikszentmihalyi's term for feeling total absorption in a challenging, goal-oriented activity.

Csikszentmihalyi (1990), who has spent his career studying flow, finds that some people rarely experience this feeling. Others feel flow several times a day. If you feel flow only during a rare mountain-climbing experience or, worse yet, when robbing a bank, Csikszentmihalyi argues that it will be difficult to construct a satisfying life. The challenge is to find flow in ways related to a career.

Flow depends on being *intrinsically motivated*. We must be mesmerized by what we are doing right now for its own sake, not for an extrinsic reward. But there also is a future-oriented dimension to feeling flow. Flow, according to Csikszentmihalyi, happens when we are working toward a goal.

For example, the idea that this book will be published a year from now is pushing me to write this page. But what riveted me to my chair this morning is the actual process of writing. Getting into a flow state is often elusive. On the days when I can't construct a paragraph, I get anxious. But if I could not regularly find flow in my writing, I would never be writing this book.

Figure 10.4 shows exactly why finding flow can be difficult. That state depends on a delicate person–environment fit. When a task seems beyond our capacities, we become anxious. When an activity is too simple, we grow bored. Ideally, the activities that make us feel flow can alert us to our ideal careers. Think about some situation in which you recently felt in flow. If you are in ruminative moratorium or worry you may be in career diffusion, can you use this feeling to alert you to a particular field?

Drawing on flow, my discussion of identity, as well as economic concerns, let's now look at two career paths that emerging adults in the United States follow.

For this captivated graduate student, the hours may fly by. Challenging activities that fully draw on our talents and skills produce that marvelous inner state called flow.

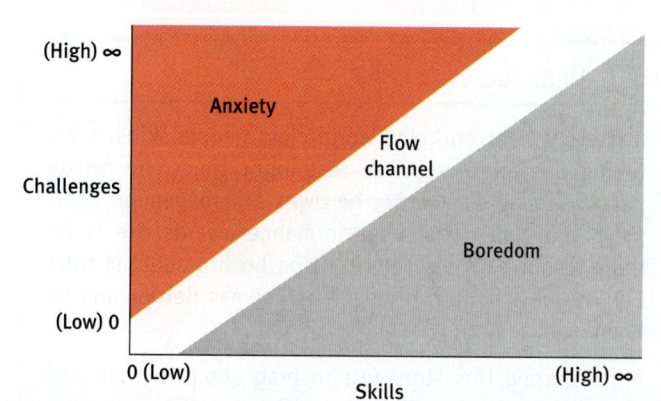

FIGURE 10.4: The zone of flow Notice that the flow zone (white area) depends on a delicate matching of our abilities and the challenge involved in a particular real-world task. If the task is beyond our capacities, we land in the upper red area of the chart and become anxious. If the task is too easy, we land in the lower, gray area of the chart and become bored. Moreover, as our skills increase, the difficulty of the task must also increase to provide us with the sense of being in flow. Which theorist's ideas about teaching and what stimulates mental growth does this model remind you of? (Turn the page upside down for the answer.)
Data from Csikszentmihalyi, 1990.

Answer: Vygotsky

Emerging into Adulthood Without a College Degree (in the United States)

"I never want this kind of job for my kids." This comment, from a 40-year-old high-school graduate construction worker, sums up the general feeling in the United States that college is vital for having a good life (Arnett, 2016). Actually, more than 2 of every 3 U.S. high school graduates enroll in college right after high school. However, as time passes, the ranks thin. For students beginning at four-year institutions, the odds of graduating within the next six years are about 3 in 5 (National Center on Education Statistics, Fast Facts, n.d.). The graduation rates for their community-college counterparts are far lower than this.

People in the United States who don't go to college or who never get their degree can have fulfilling careers. Some, like my son, excel at Robert Sternberg's practical intelligence (described in Chapter 7) but do not do well at academics. When they find their flow in the work world, they blossom.

However, I wouldn't rely on these unusual, anecdotal reports. As Figure 10.5 shows, in 2012, the median income of people aged 25 to 35 with master's degrees, who worked full time, was roughly $70,000 per year. Their counterparts, with only high school diplomas, earned less than one-half of that amount—$30,000 (National Center on Education Statistics, Fast Facts, n.d.). In 2013, in the 25–34 age group, roughly 1 out of 10 non-college graduates were unemployed. The comparable statistic

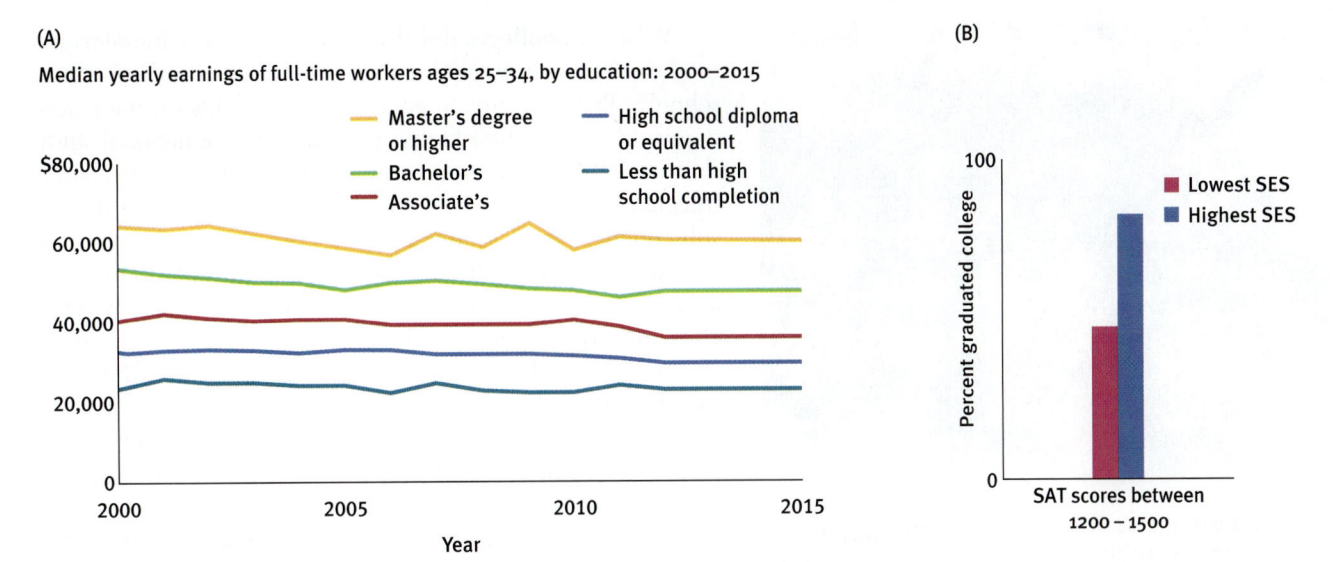

(A)

Median yearly earnings of full-time workers ages 25–34, by education: 2000–2015

— Master's degree or higher
— Bachelor's
— Associate's
— High school diploma or equivalent
— Less than high school completion

(B)

■ Lowest SES
■ Highest SES

Percent graduated college

SAT scores between 1200–1500

FIGURE 10.5: Snapshots of economic inequality, with regard to higher education, earnings, and getting a college degree Chart (A) shows that the high school versus higher-education earnings gap has been pronounced during the twenty-first century, which underscores the fact that people without a college degree are "left behind" economically. Chart (B) shows that for intellectually talented young people, family income makes a huge difference in getting that degree. Bottom line: In the United States, finishing college is vital and low-income, high-ability students are at a severe disadvantage.

(A): Data from National Center on Education Statistics, n.d.; (B): Data from Carnevale & Strohl, 2010.

for young people with a B.A. or higher was 6 percent (National Center on Education Statistics, Fast Facts, n.d.).

Given these facts, why do many emerging adults drop out of school? Our first assumption is that these people are not "college material"—uninterested in academics, poorly prepared in high school, and/or can't do the work.

True, to succeed in college, academic aptitude is important (Ishitani, 2016). A U.S. public school student graduating high school with a C average has less than 1 in 5 odds of finishing a four-year degree (Engle, n.d.). But, as Figure 10.5B shows, economic considerations matter greatly. Academically talented, low-SES young people are far less likely to graduate from college than their affluent peers (Carnevale & Strohl, 2010; Silva, 2016).

When the Gates Foundation surveyed more than 600 twenty-first-century young adults ages 22 to 30 who had dropped out of college, they discovered the same message—money matters. Only 1 in 10 students said they left school because the courses were too difficult or they weren't interested in the work. The main reason was that they had to work full time to finance school, and the strain became too much (Silva, 2016).

The silver lining is that most of these people did plan to return. And, as many nontraditional student readers are aware, there can be emotional advantages to leaving and then coming back. In Sweden, the social clock for college is programmed to start ticking a few years after high school (Arnett, 2007). The reasoning is that time spent in the wider world helps people home in on what to study in school.

This twenty-something college student is at higher risk of dropping out simply because he has to work full time while going to school.

INTERVENTIONS: Smoothing the School Path and School-to-Work Transition

Still, we can't let society off of the hook. The fact that financing college is so difficult for U.S. young people is a national shame (Arnett, 2016). The standard practice of taking out loans means that college graduates face frightening economic futures after earning their degrees (Silva, 2016). In 2012, more than 1 out of every 2 U.S. emerging adults left college owing the government and private lenders $20,000 or more (HERI, 2013).

Triumphing over Hitler's Germany provided a lifelong maturity boost for a whole cohort of 18-year-old boys—and because, during World War II, serving one's nation in the military was mandatory, these young soldiers were apt to develop strong lifelong bonds from sharing this pivotal experience that transcended social class.

school-to-work transition The change from the schooling phase of life to the work world.

What can colleges do? To undercut identity moratorium (and the 6 years until graduation statistic I cited earlier), many schools offer programs to get entering students on track academically. But in their focus on freshmen, one national study showed, U.S. colleges may be neglecting the role of "academic integration" (keeping students connected to college) during subsequent years (Ishitani, 2016).

Another possibility is to require young people to perform a gap year of challenging national service at age 18. As societies intuitively realized when they devised puberty rituals (described in Chapter 8), testing one's talents in the "real world" propels adult maturity. At a minimum, working for a year side by side with peers of every social class might reduce the socioeconomic bubbles that are helping tear the United States apart.

We also should rethink our emphasis on college as the only ticket to a financially secure, successful life. Because some people are skilled at working with their hands, or excel in practical intelligence, why force non-academically oriented emerging adults to endure a poor talent–environment fit? Can't we develop government-sponsored apprentice programs like the ones currently in operation in Germany? In that nation, employers partner with schools that offer on-the-job training. Graduates emerge with a *definite* position in that specific firm (see Buchanan, 2017).

Germany also has a youth unemployment problem. But because its apprenticeship programs offer young people careers outside of college, this nation helps undercut the unproductive ruminative-identity moratorium that produces such angst in the Western world. In one German national survey, having a job or being enrolled in an apprentice program predicted both identity achievement and occupational self-efficacy down the road (Seiffge-Krenke, Persike, & Luyckx, 2013).

How many young people are locked in diffusion or moratorium because the United States lacks a defined **school-to-work transition** (school-to-career path)? Rather than leaving the anxiety-ridden, post-education job-hunt to luck and putting the burden on the "inner" talents of kids, can't we devise strategies to help young people confront this crucial social-clock challenge of adult life?

Table 10.4 summarizes the main messages of this section, by offering suggestions for emerging adults and society. Now it's time to immerse ourselves in the undergraduate experience.

Table 10.4: Succeeding in College/Finding a Career Identity: Tips for Young People and Society

For Young People

1. Understand that when you enter college, you may overestimate your academic abilities. It takes time to get adjusted to the demands of this new life!
2. Focus on finding your flow in selecting a career. Avoid obsessing about different possibilities, but understand that it can take time to formulate a clear career plan.
3. If you need to drop out for some time, understand it's not the end of the world. Having a year or two off may help you home in on a career identity and be a better student.

For Colleges (and Society)

1. Provide support *throughout* college to help students succeed.
2. Reach out to low-income students and offer special services for parents or working adults.
3. Institute a national (ideally, mandatory) year of government service for all young people at age 18 and offer apprenticeship programs linked to jobs—ones that offer a conduit to careers without college.
4. Make negotiating young people's school-to-work transition a national priority!

Being in College

So far, I've been implying that the only purpose of college is to find a career. Thankfully, in surveys, most U.S. college graduates disagree. They report that the main value of being an undergraduate was to help them "grow intellectually and personally" (Hoover, 2011).

If you are a traditional college student, here are tips to make your college experience an inner-growth flow zone.

INTERVENTIONS: Making College an Inner-Growth Flow Zone

GET THE BEST PROFESSORS (AND TALK TO THEM OUTSIDE OF CLASS!) It's a no-brainer that, just as in elementary school (see Chapter 7), an exciting college teacher can make an enduring difference in a young person's life (Komarraju, Musulkin, & Bhattacharya, 2010; Schreiner and others, 2011). Outstanding professors adore their subject and are committed to communicating their passion to students (Bane, 2004). So reach out and talk to your professors. Feeling listened to can be a peak experience in a person's academic life. As one community college student put it:

> You know, what he does more than anything else is that . . . he really listens. I was in his office last semester and I was telling him how I was struggling. . . . He really let me talk myself into doing what I needed to pass. It's like, you know he gives a damn.
>
> (quoted in Schreiner and others, 2011, p. 324)

CONNECT YOUR CLASSES TO POTENTIAL CAREERS Professors' mission is to excite you in their field. But classes can't provide the hands-on experience you need to find your zone of flow. So institute your personal school-to-work transition. Set up independent studies involving volunteer work. If you are interested in science, work in a professor's lab. If your passion is politics, do an internship with a local legislator. In one study, college seniors mentioned that the highlight of their undergraduate experience occurred during a mentored project in the real world (Light, 2001).

IMMERSE YOURSELF IN THE COLLEGE MILIEU Following this advice is easier if you attend a small residential school. At a large university, especially a commuter school, you'll need to make special efforts to get involved in campus life. Join a college organization—or two or three. Working for the college newspaper or becoming active in the drama club will not only provide you with a rich source of friends, but it can help promote your career identity, too.

CAPITALIZE ON THE DIVERSE HUMAN CONNECTIONS COLLEGE OFFERS As I've been highlighting, peer groups are vital in shaping children's development from preschool on. At college, it is tempting to find a single clique and then not reach out to other crowds. Resist this impulse. A major growth experience college provides is the chance to connect with people of different points of view (Hu & Kuh, 2003; see also Leung & Chiu, 2011). Here's what a Harvard undergraduate had to say:

> I have re-evaluated my beliefs. . . . At college, there are people of all different religions around me. . . . Living . . . with these people

College is an ideal time to connect with people from different backgrounds. So go for it!

marks an important difference. . . . [It] has made me reconsider and ultimately reaffirm my faith.

(quoted in Light, 2001, p. 163)

But this community college student summed it up best:

> When I come home and have all these great stories; they think college is the most amazing thing . . . and that's because of all the people I'm surrounded with.

(quoted in Schreiner and others, 2011, p. 337)

Being surrounded by interesting people has another benefit: It promotes Erikson's other emerging adult task—finding love.

Tying It All Together

1. Your 17-year-old cousin is graduating from high school. Given what you learned in this section, you might predict that she has *overly high/overly low* expectations about her academic abilities and that she will become *more mature/remain exactly the same* as she travels through her twenties.

2. Hannah loves her server job—but only during busy times. When the restaurant is hectic, she gets energized. Time flies by. She feels exhilarated, at the top of her form, like a multitasking whiz! Hannah is describing a _____ experience.

3. Josiah says the reason his classmates drop out of college is that they can't do the work. Jocasta says, "Sorry, it's the need to work incredible hours to pay for school." Make each person's case, using the information from this chapter.

4. Your cousin Juan, a new freshman, asks for tips about how to succeed in college. Based on this section, pick the advice you should *not* give:
   a. Get involved in campus activities.
   b. Select friends who have exactly the same ideas as you do.
   c. Get the best professors and reach out to make connections with them.

Answers to the Tying It All Together questions can be found at the end of this chapter.

LEARNING OUTCOMES

- Outline changes in the twenty-first-century search for love.
- Explain Murstein's theory, making reference to critiques of homogamy and the idea that mate selection progresses in defined stages.
- Survey Facebook romance and adult attachment theory.
- Summarize this section's tips for finding fulfilling relationships.

intimacy Erikson's first adult task, which involves connecting with a partner in a mutual loving relationship.

Finding Love

How do emerging adults negotiate Erikson's first task of adult life (see Table 10.5)—**intimacy**, the search for love? Let's first explore some cultural shifts in the ways we choose mates before turning to our main topic: finding fulfilling love.

Table 10.5: Erikson's Life Stages and Their Psychological Tasks

Life Stage	Primary Task
Infancy (birth to 1 year)	Basic trust versus mistrust
Toddlerhood (1 to 2 years)	Autonomy versus shame and doubt
Early childhood (3 to 6 years)	Initiative versus guilt
Middle childhood (7 to 12 years)	Industry versus inferiority
Adolescence and emerging adulthood (teens into twenties)	Identity versus role confusion
Emerging adulthood (twenties)	**Intimacy versus isolation**

Setting the Context: Seismic Shifts in Searching for Love

Daolin Yang lives in Hebie Province, China. . . . At age 15, he married his wife Yufen, then 13. . . . A matchmaker proposed the marriage on behalf of the Yang family. They have been married for 62 years. . . . He says that they married first and dated later. It is "cold at the start and hot in the end." The relationship gets better and better over the years.

(Xia & Zhou, 2003, p. 231)

I got married a month ago to the woman . . . I met on Match a year ago. I met my wife just a week after setting up my profile, and we have been together ever since. . . . Thanks to the profiles, local singles matching, and easy chats, I found the girl of my dreams.

(adapted from Top 10 Best Dating Sites, 2014)

Throughout history, parents chose a child's marital partner (often during puberty), and newlyweds hoped (if they were lucky) to later fall in love. Today, with the explosion of online dating, the Internet has globalized the search for love. By the second decade of the twentieth century, an incredible 1 in 3 married couples in the United States had met online. Moreover, studies suggest that online marriages are more likely to be happy than those in which spouses meet in the traditional way! (See Cacioppo and others, 2013.)

Many More Partner Choices—with Cautions

The twentieth-century lifestyle revolution also produced a remarkable expansion in the *kind* of partners we choose. During the 1950s in the South, interracial marriages were against the law. By the turn of the twenty-first century, 1 in 3 European Americans reported getting romantically involved with someone of a different ethnicity or race (Yancey & Yancey, 2002). In one recent survey, even 3 out of 4 students attending historically Black colleges said they were open to dating someone of a different race (Stackman, Reviere, & Medley, 2016).

However, there are limits to the global assumption that we live in a golden age of diverse partner choices. Yes, during the 1950s, young people risked being shunned by their parents (and society) for marrying outside of their race. But during that era of upward mobility, Americans were far more likely to select partners of a different social class than today. Escalating income inequalities mean that twenty-first-century U.S. children are increasingly likely to be raised in class-based social milieus. Therefore, research suggests that mate choices today are as stratified by income as during the early twentieth century (Mare, 2016)!

Still, one *total* transformation has occurred in the way we select mates: Same sex romance is clearly out of the closet in the Western world.

Hot in Developmental Science: Same-Sex Romance

In the 1990s, when I began teaching at my southern university, I remember being disturbed by the snickering that would erupt when I discussed same-sex relationships. No more! Although the gay rights movement exploded in the late 1960s in New York City, its most amazing strides took place during the early twenty-first century. As one developmentalist put it, within a few years, the announcement "I'm gay" went from evoking shock to producing yawns—"So, what else is new?" (See Savin-Williams, 2001, 2008.) In an era in which emerging adults define themselves as "mostly straight," "sometimes gay," "occasionally bisexual," or "heterosexual but attracted to the other gender," limiting one's sexual identity to a defined category is becoming passé (see Morgan, 2013).

Homophobia, the fear and dislike of gay people, still is not rare. The fact that, as early as elementary school (see Chapter 6), peers reject boys who don't stick

> **homophobia** Intense fear and dislike of gay people.

> **Table 10.6: Stereotypes and Scientific Facts Related to Being Gay**
>
> **Stereotype #1:** Overinvolved mothers and distant fathers—or any parenting issue—"causes" children to be gay.
>
> **Scientific fact:** It's now abundantly clear that childrearing has *nothing* to do with sexual choices. Research suggests that prenatal testosterone may help program a fetus's later sexual orientation (see Chapter 6).
>
> **Stereotype #2:** Same-sex couples have lower-quality relationships—their interactions are "psychologically immature."
>
> **Scientific fact:** This widespread stereotype is also untrue. When same-sex partners have personality issues, they fight a good deal, just like any couple does (Markey and others, 2014). But, in one Swiss study, lesbian couples reported less conflict than a comparable heterosexual group. These women also tended to be more satisfied with their mates (Meuwly and others, 2013).
>
> **Stereotype #3:** Same-sex parents have pathological family interactions and disturbed children.
>
> **Scientific fact:** When British researchers (Golombok and others, 2003) compared lesbian-mother, two-parent-heterosexual, and single-mother families, they found that children raised in lesbian families had no gender identity issues or signs of impaired mental health. In fact, the lesbian mothers showed signs of superior parenting—hitting their children less frequently and engaging in more fantasy play.
>
> **Stereotype #4:** Gay and transgender young people are emotionally disturbed.
>
> **Scientific fact:** Unfortunately, elevated rates of psychological problems (such as suicidal thoughts, depression, and drug abuse) are more common among sexual-minority youth (Harper & Wilson, 2017). However, the massive overt rejection that gay and transgender young people experienced in the past is much rarer today in the West.

to standard gender roles suggests that society still has serious qualms about accepting people who venture outside of the heterosexual norms.

Given this enduring (but covert) social scorn, it makes sense that sexual-minority young people still can undergo considerable emotional turmoil during their teens (see Table 10.6). Because ethnic-minority families are more apt to strongly adhere to traditional gender conceptions, Black and Latino LGBTQ emerging adults frequently have the most difficulty coming out (Budge and others, 2016; Richter, Lindahl, & Malik, 2017). But in one U.S. survey of 165 bisexual and gay young people, the largest group (about 4 in 5 adolescents and emerging adults) was classified as identity achieved. These young people said they felt fully accepted by their families and comfortable with their sexual choices. The concern was the 1 in 5 respondents the researchers labeled as "struggling." While these young people "knew" their identity, they worried about disclosing this fact to disapproving parents and friends (Bregman and others, 2013).

The most at-risk group may be young people who are genuinely "identity confused." When researchers explored the mental health of women who defined themselves as heterosexual but reported having mainly same-sex attractions, this group was as likely to be distressed as their counterparts who openly labeled themselves as bisexual or gay (Johns, Zimmerman, & Bauermeister, 2013).

Again, this research underscores the importance of being identity achieved in a positive way. Once you *embrace* your identity (or self)—whether as a gay person, transgender teen, or ethnic minority—there is a sense of self-efficacy and relief. But problems arise if your attachment figures dislike the person you "really" are (Velkoff and others, 2016), or when you languish untethered in moratorium for an extended time.

A More Erratic, Extended Dating Phase

Unfortunately, however, romantic moratorium is built into Western society because, as I've been highlighting, the untethered phase of mate selection lasts so long. In tracking over 500 economically diverse young people from age 18 to 25, U.S. researchers found that a fraction—about 1 in 4 respondents—did find an enduring, stable relationship soon after leaving their teens. The largest group—almost 1 in 3 people—had only sporadic relationships or no romantic involvements during their college careers (Rauer and others, 2013).

When emerging adults do find a partner, they may have on-again/off-again relationships, a process called **relationship churning**. In one U.S. survey, nearly 1 in 2 couples in their twenties who broke up had gotten back together again at some point. And, after ending the relationship, one-half continued to have sex with their ex (Halpern-Meekin and others, 2013).

In interviews, young people gamely frame their romantic disappointments as learning experiences: "Don't trust someone because they say they love you. Sometimes it's better to let things go" (quoted in Norona, Roberson, & Welsh, 2017, p. 168). But it's no surprise that, after these breakups, people are more likely to binge drink (Bowers, Segrin, & Joyce, 2016). Their health also declines (Barr and others, 2016). One longitudinal study suggested that, after a couple separates, the losses in self-esteem tend to last a full year (Luciano & Orth, 2017). Contrast this with the research suggesting that cohabiting and getting married increases young people's feelings of self-worth (Luciano & Orth, 2017; Mernitz & Dush, 2016)!

I believe that these studies validate Erikson's idea that finding intimacy is important during emerging adulthood. While it may make good sense to be wary about getting married, a high-quality love relationship can buffer young people from the ups and downs of the turbulent twenties (and of any age). How can people achieve this goal?

This once standard campus scene is less typical today, as more undergraduates are putting off romance until they have their careers in place. But, as I mention in the text, traveling through college (and the twenties) without a stable relationship has emotional downsides.

Similarity and Structured Relationship Stages: A Classic Model of Love and a Critique

Bernard Murstein's now-classic **stimulus-value-role theory** (1999) views finding satisfying love as a three-phase process. During the **stimulus phase,** we see a potential partner and make our first decision: "Could this be a good choice for me?" Since we know nothing about the person, our judgment is based on superficial signs, such as looks or the way the individual dresses. In this assessment, we compare our own reinforcement value to the other person's along a number of dimensions (Murstein, 1999): "True, I am not as good-looking, but she may find me desirable because I am better educated." If the person seems of equal value, we decide to go on a date.

When we start seeing each other, we enter the **value-comparison phase.** Here, our goal is to match up in attitudes: "Does this person share my interests and values?" If this partner seems "right," we enter the **role phase,** in which we work out our shared lives.

So, at a party, Aaron scans the room and rejects Sophia with the tattoos. If he is searching on eHarmony he might be put off by Georgette, who looks too gorgeous or has posted photos of her vacation in San Tropez. Aaron gravitates to Ashley because her profile suggests that she is more low maintenance and maybe—like him—a bit shy. When Aaron and Ashley begin seeing each other, they discover that they enjoy the same activities; they both love hiking; they have the same worldview. On their third or tenth date, there may be a revelation that "this person is too different." But, if things go smoothly, Aaron and Ashley plan their future. Should they cohabit or move to California when they graduate? When will they marry and have kids?

The *equal-reinforcement-value partner* aspect of Murstein's theory explains why we expect couples to be similar in "social value" as well as social class (Conroy-Beam & Buss, 2016). When we find serious value mismatches, we search for reasons to explain these discrepancies (Murstein, Reif, & Syracuse-Siewert, 2002): "That handsome

relationship churning Having on-again/off-again romantic relationships in which couples repeatedly get together and then break up.

stimulus-value-role theory Murstein's mate-selection theory that suggests similar people pair up and that our path to commitment progresses through three phases (called the *stimulus, value-comparison,* and *role* phases).

stimulus phase In Murstein's theory, the initial mate-selection stage, in which we make judgments about a potential partner based on external characteristics such as appearance.

value-comparison phase In Murstein's theory, the second mate-selection stage, in which we make judgments about a partner on the basis of similar values and interests.

role phase In Murstein's theory, the final mate-selection stage, in which committed partners work out their future life together.

young lawyer must have low self-esteem to have settled for that unattractive older woman"; "Perhaps he chose that person because she has millions in the bank."

Most important, Murstein's theory suggests that in love relationships, as in childhood friendships, **homogamy** (similarity) is the driving force. We want a soul mate, a person who matches us, not just in external status, but also in interests and attitudes about life.

> **homogamy** The principle that we select a mate who is similar to us.

Actually, because research suggests that identical twins (who have the same DNA) are more likely than fraternal twins to select partners with similar "bonding styles," humans may be biologically primed to gravitate to specific mates (Horwitz and others, 2016). Just like Lorenz's geese (described in Chapter 4), our species might even become attached to the way childhood caregivers *physically* appear. In one fascinating study, young people tended to choose partners who resembled their opposite gender parent—but only if they felt close to that person as a child (Kocsor and others, 2016). So if you have the uncanny sense you chose your lover partly because she looks like your beloved mother, you may be right!

Homogamy is enhanced by the fact that people with identical passions gravitate to similar zones of flow. Political junkies may discover the love of their life when working on election campaigns. Theater majors are apt to find the perfect mate when trying out for plays. Moreover, when couples connect though mutual interests ("I met my love at the theater"), they find an interesting side benefit: Sharing flow activities helps to keep passion alive (Reissman, Aron, & Bergin, 1993).

The Limits to Looking for a Similar Mate

Still, there are important exceptions to the rule that homogamy drives love. In examining happiness among long-married couples, researchers discovered that relationships worked best when one partner was more dominant and the other more submissive (Markey & Markey, 2007).

Logically, matching up two strong personalities might not promote romantic bliss (people would probably fight). Two passive partners might frustrate each other ("Why doesn't my lover take the lead?"). Yes, similarity is important (birds of a feather should flock together). But, as in the other familiar saying that opposites attract, couples get along best when they have a *few* carefully selected opposing personality preferences and styles.

Moreover, suppose a couple is very similar but in unpleasant traits, such as their tendency to fly off the handle or be pathologically shy. What really matters in happiness is not so much objective similarity, but believing that a significant other has terrific personality traits. People who see their partner as outgoing and emotionally stable ("He is a real people person, and open to new things") have better relationships over time (Furler, Gomez, & Grob, 2013; Furler, Gomez, & Grob, 2014).

The bottom-line message is that finding a soul mate does not mean selecting a clone. We don't want a reflection of our current self. We choose people who embody our "ideal self"—the person we would like to be. Moreover, one study showed that when people believe their partner embodies their best self ("I fell in love with him because he's a wonderful actor, and that's always been my goal"), they tend to grow emotionally as people, becoming more like their ideal (Rusbult and others, 2009).

Admiring each other's talents in their shared life passion predicts future happiness for this young couple. It also may make these actors feel as if they are becoming better performers just from being together—and it certainly helps if they inflate each other's talents, too ("My partner is sure to be the next Denzel Washington!").

Actually, rather than objectively matching up, happy couples see their mates through rose-colored glasses (Murray & Holmes, 1997). They inflate their partner's virtues (Murray and others, 2000). They overestimate the extent to which they and that person are alike in values and goals (Murray and others, 2002). So science confirms George Bernard Shaw's classic observation: "Love is a gross exaggeration of the difference between one person and everyone else."

The Limits to Charting Love in Stages

> As soon as I met R, . . . he was just so kind and thoughtful and he was considerate. So we started talking on email and . . . I got back from the trip, and he came over a month after the cruise. . . . I knew like right away. . . . It was just like kind of a confirmation that, I don't know, we were meant to be together.
>
> (quoted in Mackinnon and others, 2011, p. 607)

This quotation suggests that viewing mate selection in static stages minimizes the magical essence of romance. Couples may suddenly fall in love when they meet after months of emails. Or there may be an epiphany, at some point, when people decide, "This is the one."

In a classic study, researchers captured these ups and downs by asking dating couples to graph their chances (from 0 to 100 percent) of marrying their partner. They then had these student volunteers return each month, chart changes in their feelings of commitment, and explain the reasons for any dramatic relationship turning points (Surra & Hughes, 1997; Surra, Hughes, & Jacquet, 1999).

You can see examples of these turning points in Table 10.7. Notice that relationships do often hinge on homogamy issues ("This person is right for me"). Other causes are important, too—from the input of family and friends ("I really dislike that person") to the idea that I'm too young to get involved. Today, an important turning point in commitment is becoming Facebook official with a mate.

Table 10.7: Some Major Positive (+) and Negative (−) Turning Points in a Relationship

Personal Compatibility/Homogamy
We spent a lot of time together. +
We had a big fight. −
We had similar interests. +

Compatibility with Family and Friends
My friends kept saying that Sue was bad for me. −
I fit right in with his family. +
Her dad just hated me. −

Other Random Forces
I just turned 21, so I don't want to be tied down to anyone. −
The guy I used to date started calling me. −

Information from Surra, Hughes, & Jacquet, 1999.

Hot in Developmental Science: Facebook Romance

As ground zero in our contemporary social life, Facebook (and other social media sites) is a research gold mine for exploring the nuances of modern love. Scroll through your daily feed and you will notice that some couples seem invisible on Facebook; others continually broadcast their love. Does Facebook homogamy (shared likes, profile similarities, mutual friends) reflect actual relationship closeness? By comparing couples' attitudes with these virtual love signs, researchers find the answer is yes. More Facebook similarity mirrors the depth of real-world love (Castaneda, Wendel, & Crockett, 2015).

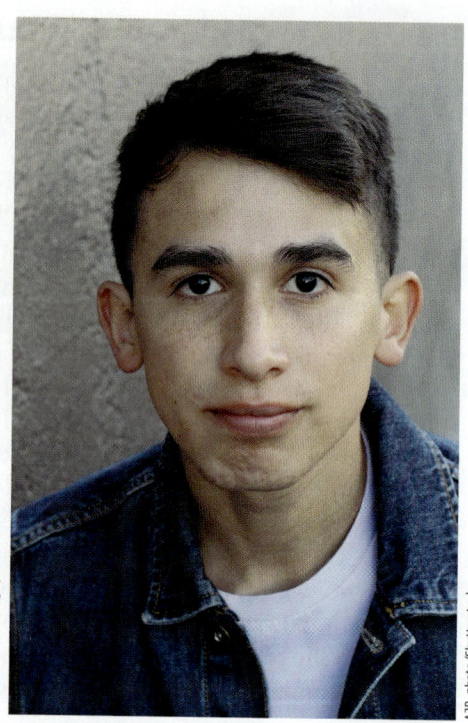

Would you rate the couple on the left as nicer human beings than the person on the right? If you are like most people, your answer would be yes.

Moreover, labeling oneself as "in a relationship" does reflect a major romantic turning point. In surveys, people who take this step report being more committed to their partners and less interested in searching for other mates (Lane, Piercy, & Carr, 2016).

Using simulated profiles, researchers find that posting loving photos of couples makes outsiders judge a given Facebook user as more likeable. On the other hand, putting gushy statements ("I love my sweet baby so much") on a partner's wall is a turnoff. This kind of behavior gets people fewer votes for being personally liked (Emery and others, 2015).

Normally, changing one's status from "single" to "in a relationship" evokes kudos like "Congrats!" But another study using simulated Facebook pages showed that what really matters are the comments others post. If friends make snide comments like, "Too bad," outsiders see the relationship as a negative, rather than as a plus (Ballantine, Lin, & Veer, 2015).

But the greatest danger happens when couples break up, and Facebook users feel compelled to broadcast their failure to the world by changing their online status to "it's complicated" or "single." To cope with their pain, people commonly use cleansing strategies such as deleting mutual photos and, sometimes, defriending a former mate (LeFebvre, Blackburn, & Brody, 2015). But the temptation can be overwhelming to monitor an ex by obsessively checking mutual friends' pages or engage in bouts of relational aggression on one's *own* Facebook page. As one young woman admitted (after breaking up), "I had a lot more status updates and pictures showing how much fun I was having" (quoted in LeFebvre, Blackburn, & Brody, 2015, p. 90).

This is why, in interviews, young people lambast Facebook as "a trap"; "It's a total . . . train wreck" (quoted in Fox, Osborn, & Warber, 2014, p. 531). Although it may not make or break a relationship, the social-media revolution makes love much "more complicated" in Facebook terms. (Check out Table 10.8 for some interesting additional research facts related to online romance.)

What concrete behaviors *really* predict whether a relationship will last? Without denying that couples have ups and downs, relationship churning erodes

Table 10.8: Fascinating Scientific FAQs About Online Love

Question #1: Should I worry if there is a huge assortment of potentially competing romantic possibilities on my partner's Facebook friends list?

Research answer: No, but be concerned if your lover is adding *new* friends. In one study with college students, the sheer number of romantic possibilities on a person's friend list had nothing to do with the odds that a partner would stray; but a person who reported lower feelings of commitment was apt to solicit new Facebook friends (see Drouin, Miller, & Dibble, 2014). Furthermore, women in a relationship should never send winking emoticons to male friends because these implicit tips signal, "I'm interested in having sex" and, therefore, make mates intensely jealous if they are male (Hudson and others, 2015).

Question #2: I must admit that I'm guilty of sexting my partner. Does that mean I'm a loose woman or have personality issues?

Research answer: Contrary to media alarm bells, sexting is not a symptom of mental health problems (Gordon-Messer and others, 2013). People sext for many reasons—such as for fun, as a joke, or to show off their bodies to friends (Burkett, 2015). Actually, the main correlate of sexting is being in a close romantic relationship (Delevi & Weisskirch, 2013; Samimi & Alderson, 2014). Still, among females, unwanted sexting is fairly common—with more than one-half of girls in one study reporting they engaged in this behavior to please their mates (Drouin & Tobin, 2014).

Question #3: My lover texts me millions of times every day. Does that mean he is anxious about my love and generally insecure?

Research answer: Not necessarily, but be alert to whether he prefers texting to contacting you in other ways. In measuring relationship satisfaction among 364 daters, and controlling for physical distance, one psychologist (Luo, 2014) found that the absolute number of texts per day didn't matter. However, overusing this communication mode, compared to calling or meeting face to face, predicted relationship distress. Other research suggests that texting at unusual hours, such as late at night, is symptomatic of being anxious about a relationship (Lepp, Li, & Barkley, 2016). So, when a lover's cyberspace messages pop up at inappropriate times and especially when these virtual communications replace "real life" interactions, your partner may feel uneasy about your love.

Question #4: I get intensely anxious if I haven't checked Facebook every hour. Is that a sign I have emotional problems?

Research answer: As one survey suggested, the average undergraduate spends two hours on social media; so, clearly, virtual reality has taken over young peoples' lives. But in this poll, students who reported getting very agitated when they didn't repeatedly check Facebook did report lower well-being than their peers (Satici & Uysal, 2015). Because face-to-face interactions evoke more happiness than spending time in solitary venues (such as being online) (Coccia & Darling, 2016), feeling *completely* tethered to Facebook can be incompatible with flourishing in life.

---

trust (Ogolsky, Surra, & Monk, 2016). Cycling through breaking up and getting back together signals that things are spiraling out of control (Vennum and others, 2015).

Why are some people prone to repeatedly having stormy, erratic relationships, while others know how to reach out in love? This brings me to the final piece of the puzzle relating to finding fulfilling love: Select someone who is securely attached!

Love Through the Lens of Attachment Theory

Think back to the Chapter 4 discussion of the different infant attachment styles. Mary Ainsworth (1973) found that *securely attached* babies run to their mother with hugs and kisses when she appears in the room. *Avoidant* infants act cold, aloof, and indifferent in the Strange Situation when the caregiver returns. *Anxious-ambivalent* babies are overly clingy, afraid to explore the toys, and angry and inconsolable when their caregiver arrives. Now, think of your own romantic relationships, or the relationships of family members or friends. Wouldn't these same attachment categories apply to adult romantic love? Cindy Hazan and Phillip Shaver (1987) had the same

adult attachment styles The different ways in which adults relate to romantic partners, based on Mary Ainsworth's infant attachment styles. (Adult attachment styles are classified as *secure, preoccupied/ambivalent insecure,* or *avoidant/dismissive insecure.*)

preoccupied/ambivalent adult attachment An excessively clingy, needy style of relating to loved ones.

avoidant/dismissive adult attachment A standoffish, excessively disengaged style of relating to loved ones.

insight: Let's draw on Ainsworth's dimensions to classify people into different **adult attachment styles**.

People with a **preoccupied/ambivalent** type of insecure attachment fall quickly and deeply in love (see the How Do We Know box). But, because they are engulfing and needy, they often end up being rejected or feeling unfulfilled. Adults with an **avoidant/dismissive** insecure attachment are at the opposite end of the spectrum—withholding, aloof, reluctant to engage. You may have dated this kind of person, someone whose mottos are "stay independent," "don't share," "avoid getting close" (Feeney, 1999).

HOW DO WE KNOW...
that a person is securely or insecurely attached?

How do developmentalists classify adults as either securely or insecurely attached? In the current relationship interview, researchers ask participants to describe their romantic relationships. Trained evaluators then code the responses.

People are labeled securely attached if they coherently describe the pluses and minuses of the relationship; if they talk freely about their desire for intimacy; and if they adopt an other-centered perspective, seeing nurturing the other person's development as a primary goal. People who describe their relationship in formal, stilted ways, emphasize "autonomy issues," or talk about the advantages of being together in non-intimate terms ("We are buying a house"; "We go places"), are classified as avoidant/dismissive. Those who express total dependence ("I can't function unless she is nearby"), anger about not being treated correctly, or anxiety about the partner leaving are classified as preoccupied/ambivalent.

This in-depth interview technique is time intensive. But many attachment researchers argue that it reveals a person's attachment style better than questionnaires in which people simply check "yes" or "no" to indicate whether items on a scale apply to them.

Secure adult attachment
- **Definition:** Capable of genuine intimacy in relationships.
- **Signs:** Empathic, sensitive, able to reach out emotionally; balances own needs with those of partner; has affectionate, caring interactions; probably in a loving, long-term relationship.

Avoidant/dismissive adult attachment
- **Definition:** Unable to get close in relationships.
- **Signs:** Uncaring, aloof, emotionally distant; unresponsive to loving feelings; abruptly disengages at signs of involvement; unlikely to be in a long-term relationship.

Preoccupied/ambivalent adult attachment
- **Definition:** Needy and engulfing in relationships.
- **Signs:** Excessively jealous, suffocating; needs continual reassurance of being totally loved; unlikely to be in a loving, long-term relationship.

Securely attached adults are fully open to love. They give their partners space to differentiate, yet are firmly committed. Like Ainsworth's secure infants, their faces light up when they talk about their partner: The joy in their love shines through.

Decades of research show that insecurely attached emerging adults have trouble with relationships (Lapsley & Woodbury, 2016). Securely attached people are more successful in love.

Securely attached adults have happier marriages. They report more satisfying romances (Mikulincer and others, 2002; Morgan & Shaver, 1999). Securely attached adults hang in there during difficult times. They freely support their partner in times of need. Using the metaphor of mother–infant attachment described in Chapter 4, people with secure attachments are wonderful dancers. They excel at being emotionally in tune.

Remember also from Chapter 4 that Bowlby and Ainsworth believe that the dance of attachment between the caregiver and baby is the basis for feeling securely attached in infancy and for dancing well in other relationships. Listen to friends anguishing over their relationship problems, and you will hear similar ideas: "The reason I act clingy is that, during childhood, I felt unloved"; "It's hard for me to warm up because my mom was rejecting and cold." We know that attachment categories are malleable during childhood. Once we enter adulthood, how much can these styles change?

To answer this question, researchers measured the attachment styles of several hundred women at intervals over two years (Cozzarelli and others, 2003). They found that almost one-half of the women had changed categories over that time. So the good news is that we can change our attachment status from insecure to secure. And—as will come as no surprise—we can also move in the opposite direction, temporarily feeling insecurely attached after a terrible experience with love. The best way to understand attachment styles, then, is as somewhat enduring and consistent, arising, in part, from our experiences in love.

One reason attachment styles stay stable is that they operate as a self-fulfilling prophecy. A preoccupied, clingy person does tend to be rejected repeatedly. An avoidant individual remains isolated because piercing that armored shell takes such a heroic effort. A loving person gets more secure over time because his caring behavior evokes warm, loving responses (Davila & Kashy, 2009).

By now, you are probably impressed with the power of the attachment perspective to predict real-world love. But notice that these *correlational* findings have conceptual flaws. Suppose that a person labels his childhood as unhappy, has an insecure attachment style, and experiences relationship distress. It's tempting to say that "poor parenting" caused this insecure worldview, which then produced the current problems; but couldn't this connection operate in the opposite way? "I'm not getting along with my partner, so I believe love can't work out, and it must be my parents' fault." Or couldn't these *self-reports* be caused by a third force—such as being depressed? If you have a gloomy worldview, wouldn't you see both your childhood and current relationship as dissatisfying and also have an avoidant or preoccupied attachment style?

Still, as a framework for understanding people (and ourselves), the attachment-styles framework has great appeal. Who can't relate to having a lover (or friend or parent) with a dismissive or preoccupied attachment? Don't the defining qualities of secure attachment give us a beautiful roadmap for how we should relate to the significant others in our lives?

> **secure adult attachment** The genuine intimacy that is ideal in love relationships.

INTERVENTIONS: Evaluating Your Own Relationship

How can you use *all* of these section insights to ensure smoother sailing in romance? Select someone who is similar in values and interests, but don't necessarily search for a partner with your exact personality traits. Find someone you respect as an individual, a person whose qualities embody the "self" you want to be—but it's best if you each differ on the need to take charge. Focus on the outstanding "special qualities" of your significant other, and to cement your passion, share arousing flow states. Expect bumps along the way, but be cautious if you repeatedly break up and get back together again. Look for someone who is securely attached.

Still, however, notice the other implicit message of Table 10.7 (page 307) describing relationship turning points: If things don't work out, it may have absolutely *nothing* to do with you, your partner, or any problem basic to how well you get along! If you want to evaluate your own relationship, you might take the questionnaire based on these chapter points in Table 10.9.

Table 10.9: Evaluating Your Own Relationship: A Section Summary Checklist

	No	Yes
1. Are you and your partner on the same wavelength in terms of values, and did you connect over similar passions or flow states?	☐	☐
You don't have to be clones, but having mutual passions and *regularly sharing* those interests is a key to keeping passion alive.*		
2. Do you believe that your partner embodies your ideal self?	☐	☐
Looking up to your partner as someone you want to be like predicts staying together happily, as well as growing emotionally toward your ideal.		
3. Do you see your partner as utterly terrific and unique?	☐	☐
Deciding that this person has no human flaws is not necessary—but seeing your partner as "unique and special" also predicts being happy together.		
4. Is your romance moving along steadily (versus being turbulent)?	☐	☐
If you experience minor ups and downs in your feelings of love, that's fine, but it's a bad sign if you repeatedly break up and get together again.		
5. Is your partner able to fully reach out in love, neither intensely jealous nor aloof?	☐	☐
Some jealousy or hesitation about commitment can be normal, but in general, your partner should be securely attached and able to love.		

If you checked "yes" for all six of these questions, your relationship is in excellent shape. If you checked "no" for every question, your "relationship" does not exist! One or two no's mixed in with yes's suggest areas that need additional work.

*Recall that it may be best if one of you has a stronger, or more dominant, personality.

Notice that, in this final chapter, we have come full circle in this book. Just as having a close attachment is the number-one infant agenda, it's crucial to building a successful adult life as well. Attachment and autonomy are the twin agendas of childhood and human life!

Tying It All Together

1. Latoya is discussing how twenty-first-century relationships have changed. Which of the following statements is *incorrect*?
   a. Today, young people are more likely to marry outside of their social class.
   b. Today, same-sex relationships are much more acceptable.
   c. Today, homophobia no longer exists.

2. Today, *more/fewer* people are open to interracial dating, and people who meet on the Internet are *less/more* apt to be happily married than their counterparts who meet in traditional ways.

3. Natasha and Akbar met at a friend's New Year's Eve party and just started dating. They are about to find out whether they share similar interests, backgrounds, and worldviews. This couple is in Murstein's (choose one) *stimulus/value-comparison/role* phase of romantic relationships.

4. Catherine tells Kelly, "To have a happy relationship, find someone as similar to you as possible." Go back and review this section. Then list the ways in which Catherine is somewhat wrong.

5. Kita is clingy and always feels rejected. Rena runs away from intimate relationships. Sam is affectionate and loving. Match the attachment status of each person to one of the following alternatives: *secure*, *avoidant-dismissive*, or *preoccupied*.

Answers to the Tying It All Together questions can be found at the end of this chapter.

SUMMARY

Setting the Context

Psychologists have identified a new life phase called **emerging adulthood**. This in-between, not-quite-fully-adult time of life—which begins after high school and tapers off by the late twenties—involves testing out adult roles. Because young people haven't reached the standard benchmarks of adulthood—finding a career, getting married, becoming parents—for an extended time, we tend to see the essence of adulthood as taking responsibility for one's life. In southern Europe, young people typically live at home until they marry, and they have trouble becoming financially independent. In Scandinavia, **cohabitation** is widely accepted and marriage is optional. In the Nordic nations, better economies, an emphasis on independence, and government assistance make early **nest-leaving** the norm. In the United States, there are striking social-class differences. While most young people plan to marry, low-income adults have trouble making it to that state. Nest-leaving is also difficult when young people don't have the funds to leave home.

We think of the entry point of emerging adulthood as leaving the nest. Although parent–child relationships may improve after emerging adults move out, the idea that people *must* leave home to "act adult" is incorrect. Young people today often live with their parents because they cannot afford to live alone. Ethnic-minority youth, in particular, may stay in the nest as "full adults" to help their families.

Social-clock pressures, or **age norms**, set the boundaries of emerging adulthood. Exploring is **on time**, or appropriate, in the twenties, but **off time** if it extends well into the thirties. Although society sets the overall social-clock guidelines, people also have their own personal timetables for reaching adult markers. Social-clock pressures make emerging adulthood a time of special stress.

Constructing an Identity

Identity, or finding one's true adult self is, according to Erikson, the major challenge facing people on the brink of adulthood. Erikson believed that exploring various possibilities is critical to developing a solid identity. The alternative is **role confusion**—drifting and seeing no adult future.

James Marcia identified four **identity statuses: identity diffusion** (drifting aimlessly), **identity foreclosure** (leaping into an identity without any thought), **moratorium** (exploring different pathways), and **identity achievement** (settling on an identity). In contrast to Marcia's idea that we progress through these stages and reach achievement in the twenties, people shift from status to status throughout life. Emerging adults may not need to sample different fields to develop a secure career identity. Being locked in **ruminative moratorium** produces special pain. In terms of identity—including one's **ethnic (biracial or multiracial) identity**—it's important to feel positive about who you are.

Finding a Career

Teenagers have lofty career goals. The downside is that, because many teens overinflate their abilities, self-esteem often drops when young people enter college. Emerging adults follow diverse emotional paths as they move through their early twenties. While people who enjoy mastering challenges ("workers") are set up to flourish during emerging adulthood, the twenties in general are a time of emotional growth. Troubled teens can be very successful if they find satisfying jobs.

Flow is a feeling of total absorption in a challenging task. The hours pass like minutes, intrinsic motivation is high, and skills are in balance with the demands of a given task. Flow states can alert people to their ideal careers.

Although higher education is important to constructing a middle-class life, and most young people in the United States enroll in college, many drop out before finishing. High-performing youths from low-income backgrounds are less apt to graduate than their affluent counterparts. We need to make it easier for financially strapped young people to get a B.A. and offer non-college alternatives that lead directly to jobs. The absence of a real **school-to-work transition** in the United States is a national crisis.

College should be a time of inner growth. Get the best professors, explore career-relevant work, become involved in campus activities, and reach out to students of different backgrounds.

Finding Love

Erikson's second emerging-adult task, **intimacy**—finding committed love—has changed dramatically in recent decades. People now find romance online and are far more likely to date outside their ethnicity, although partner choices are more stratified by income today. Despite enduring **homophobia**, Western gay and transgender teens feel more comfortable about coming out. The dating phase of life lasts longer, too, with many young people putting off serious romantic involvements until they establish a career. Unfortunately, **relationship churning** has downsides, and romantic breakups take an emotional and physical toll. Having a loving partner is very helpful during the tumultuous emerging adult years.

Stimulus-value-role theory spells out a three-stage process leading to marriage. First, people select a potential partner who looks appropriate (the **stimulus phase**); then, during the **value-comparison phase,** they find out whether they have common interests. Finally, during the **role phase,** couples plan their lives together. **Homogamy,** people's tendency to choose similar partners and people of equivalent status and social value, is the main principle underlying this theory.

A variety of forces (such as genetic predispositions or connecting via similar flow states) make homogamy the underlying force driving romance. However, relationships flourish when people respect their partner's personality, and two very dominant (or submissive) personalities might not mesh. It helps to inflate a lover's virtues and view a partner as embodying one's "ideal self."

While relationships can have dramatic turning points, too much turmoil is a bad sign. Social media sites such as Facebook provide a wealth of insights about modern love.

Researchers have spelled out three **adult attachment styles.** Adults ranked as insecurely attached—either **preoccupied/ambivalent** (overly clingy and engulfing) or **avoidant/dismissive** (overly aloof and detached)—have poorer-quality relationships. **Securely attached** adults tend to be successful in love and marriage. The attachment-styles framework offers additional fascinating insights into the qualities we should search for in finding fulfilling love.

KEY TERMS

adult attachment styles, p. 310
age norms, p. 290
avoidant/dismissive adult attachment, p. 310
biracial or multiracial identity, p. 295
cohabitation, p. 287
emerging adulthood, p. 285
ethnic identity, p. 294

flow, p. 297
homogamy, p. 306
homophobia, p. 303
identity, p. 291
identity achievement, p. 293
identity diffusion, p. 292
identity foreclosure, p. 292
identity statuses, p. 292
intimacy, p. 302

moratorium, p. 292
nest-leaving, p. 287
off time, p. 290
on time, p. 290
preoccupied/ambivalent adult attachment, p. 310
relationship churning, p. 305
role confusion, p. 292
role phase, p. 305

ruminative moratorium, p. 294
school-to-work transition, p. 300
secure adult attachment, p. 311
social clock, p. 290
stimulus phase, p. 305
stimulus-value-role theory, p. 305
value-comparison phase, p. 305

ANSWERS TO Tying It All Together QUIZZES

Setting the Context
1. b. Sarah is likely not to finish college within four years.
2. c. Silvia, who lives in Stockholm
3. false (There are many rational "adult reasons" people stay in the nest.)
4. Martha, who is starting a new career at age 50; she will be most worried about the ticking of the social clock.

Constructing an Identity
1. drifting; diffusion
2. foreclosure; moratorium. Kayla is most apt to have an emotional problem.

3. Do you feel nursing expresses your inner self?
4. False

Finding a Career
1. overly high; get more mature
2. flow
3. Josiah might argue that prior academic performance predicts college completion, with low odds of finishing for high school graduates with a C-average or below. Jocasta should reply that money is crucial because academically talented low-income kids are far less likely to finish college than their affluent peers, and dropouts cite "financial issues" as the main reason for leaving.
4. b

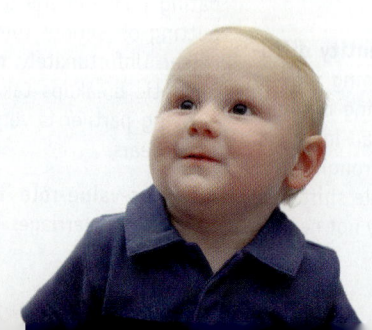

Finding Love

1. a and c.
2. Today *more* people are open to interracial dating, and people who meet on the Internet are *more* apt to be happily married than their counterparts who meet in traditional ways.
3. value-comparison phase
4. Actually, people who have dominant personalities might be better off with more submissive mates (and vice versa). We gravitate to people with good personalities. Rather than searching for a clone, it's best to find a mate who is similar to one's ideal self. Overinflating that person's virtues helps tremendously, too!
5. Kita's status is preoccupied. Rena is avoidant/dismissing. Sam is securely attached.

CONNECT ONLINE:

LaunchPad — macmillan learning | Check out our videos and additional resources located at: www.macmillanlearning.com

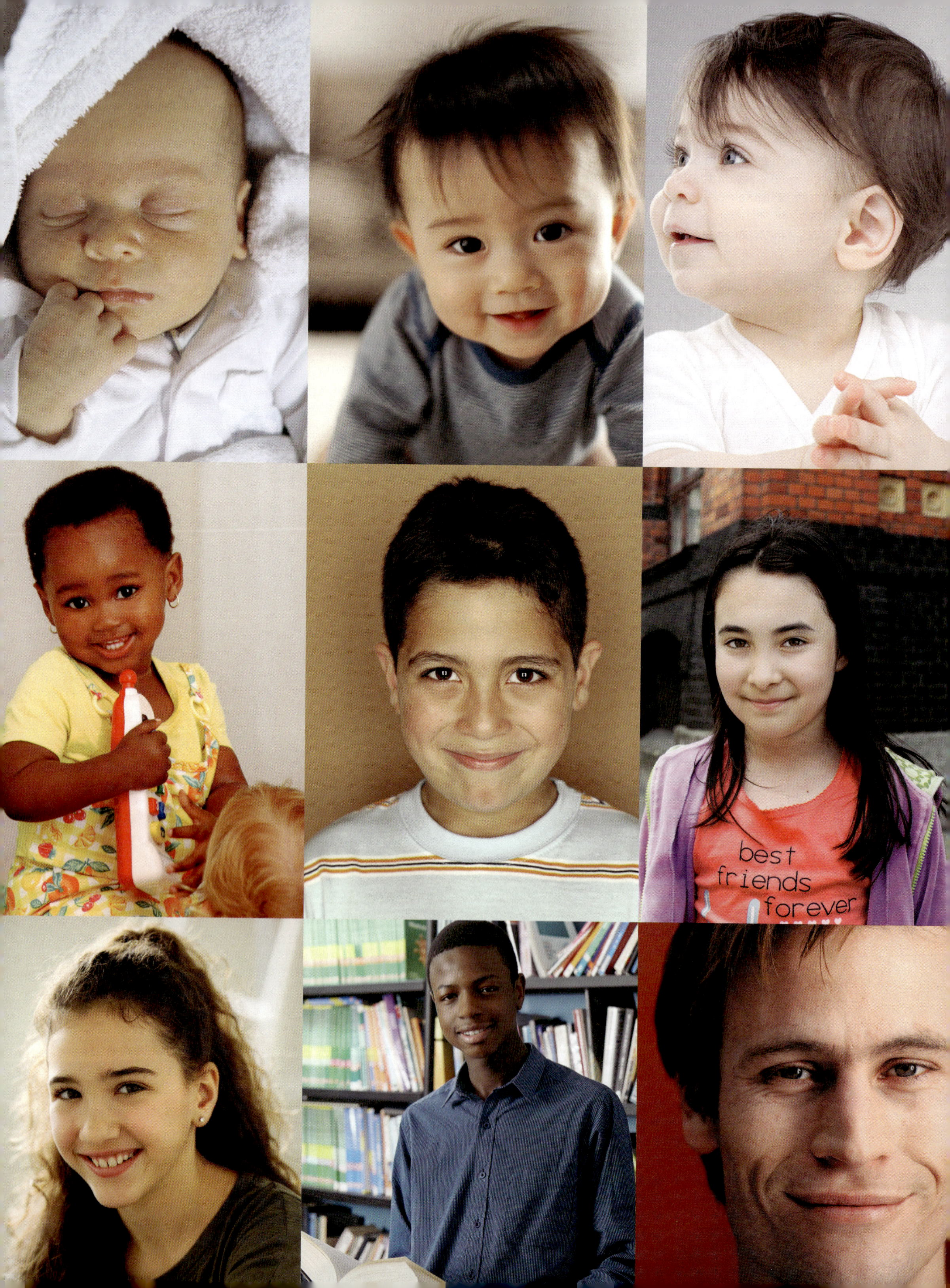
best
friends
forever

Final Thoughts

Writing this book has given me an unparalleled perspective into what motivates human beings. So please indulge me as I share my top insights about people from surveying the science—and make a final comment about our field.

Many qualities that define humanity appear before age 1. As Piaget's pioneering observations demonstrated, our passion to explore the world begins almost from birth. The research in Chapter 3 brings home the fact that newborns are primed to connect with the human world. I am amazed by the findings showing that 8-month-olds have a basic sense of ethics. I am heartened by the fact that toddlers take more pleasure in giving when they *don't* receive rewards. On a negative note, stranger anxiety—that defining quality of toddlerhood—and the studies showing that 9-month-olds become less sensitive to facial expressions of different ethnic groups show that the roots of adult prejudice don't have to be taught. Many human strengths and frailties naturally unfold early in life.

The main quality that makes humanity special takes decades to lock in. On the other hand, as Piaget's research also shows, children don't grasp the basics of adult reality until age 7 or 8 (see Chapter 5). Because the brain's frontal lobes grow into the mid-twenties, teenagers have considerable trouble controlling themselves (see Chapter 9). This book brings home the fact that we can't view children and adolescents as mini-adults. Executive functions—that uniquely human gift—grow *gradually* over years.

Attachment and separation (assertion) are humanity's two agendas. Toddlers, as you read in Chapter 4, are passionate to assert themselves, but they can't let their parents out of sight. The puberty hormones that push young teens to leave their families drive preteens to be incredibly sensitive to their peers (see Chapters 8 and 9). This seesaw between connecting and asserting ourselves plays out during childhood in popularity and friendships (see Chapters 5 and 6). It drives teenagers to bond in groups and reject society's rules (see Chapter 9). Two simple motives underlie human behavior: self-efficacy and the need to connect.

Complex forces shape behavior. At the same time, understanding development requires going beyond simplistic dichotomies such as "it's the parents" or "it's the genes." Peers, schools, and communities influence how children grow. We can't even understand parent–child interactions without considering a caregiver's other relationships, as I pointed out in Chapters 2, 4, and 7. Many different forces shape children's lives.

Developmentalists understand these complexities. We regularly rely on input from researchers around the world to make sense of children's lives. We draw on multiple strategies—from single-person accounts to mammoth thousand-person polls—to discover the scientific truth. As our science moves into its robust second century, we have a rich array of international studies tracing development over decades. Please join us in helping our flourishing, global—finally *genuinely* mature—field grow!

Glossary

A

accommodation In Piaget's theory, enlarging mental capacities to fit input from the wider world.

acculturation Among immigrants, the tendency to become similar to the mainstream culture after time spent living in a new society.

achievement tests Measures that evaluate a child's knowledge in specific school-related areas.

active forces The nature-interacts-with-nurture principle that genetic temperamental tendencies and predispositions cause children to select specific environments.

adolescence Stage of life lasting from puberty through high school graduation (roughly age 12 to 19).

adolescence-limited turmoil Antisocial behavior that is specific to adolescence and does not persist into adult life.

adolescent egocentrism David Elkind's term for the tendency of young teenagers to feel that their actions are at the center of everyone else's consciousness.

adoption study Behavioral genetic research strategy, designed to determine the genetic contribution to a given trait, that involves comparing adopted children with their biological and adoptive parents.

adrenal androgens Hormones produced by the adrenal glands that program puberty.

adult attachment styles The different ways in which adults relate to romantic partners, based on Mary Ainsworth's infant attachment styles. (Adult attachment styles are classified as *secure*, *preoccupied/ambivalent insecure*, or *avoidant/dismissive insecure*.)

age norms Cultural ideas about the appropriate ages for engaging in particular activities or life tasks.

age of viability The earliest point at which a baby can survive outside the womb.

aggression Any hostile or destructive act.

amniocentesis A second-trimester procedure that involves inserting a syringe into a woman's uterus to extract a sample of amniotic fluid, which is tested for genetic and chromosomal conditions.

amniotic sac A bag-shaped, fluid-filled membrane that contains and insulates the fetus.

analytic intelligence In Robert Sternberg's framework on successful intelligence, the facet of intelligence involved in performing well on academic problems.

animism In Piaget's theory, the preoperational child's belief that inanimate objects are alive.

anorexia nervosa A potentially life-threatening eating disorder characterized by pathological dieting (resulting in severe weight loss and, in females, loss of menstruation) and by a distorted body image.

A-not-B error In Piaget's framework, a classic mistake made by infants in the sensorimotor stage, whereby babies approaching age 1 go back to the original hiding place to look for an object even though they have seen it get hidden in a second place.

anxious-ambivalent attachment An insecure attachment style characterized by a child's intense distress when reunited with a primary caregiver after separation.

Apgar scale A quick test used to assess a just-delivered baby's condition by measuring heart rate, muscle tone, respiration, reflex response, and color.

artificialism In Piaget's theory, the preoperational child's belief that human beings make everything in nature.

assimilation In Jean Piaget's theory, the first step promoting mental growth, which involves fitting environmental input to current mental capacities.

assisted reproductive technology (ART) Any infertility treatment in which the egg is fertilized outside the womb.

attachment The powerful bond of love between a caregiver and child (or between any two people).

attachment in the making Second phase of Bowlby's attachment sequence, when, from 4 to 7 months of age, babies slightly prefer the primary caregiver.

attachment theory Theory formulated by John Bowlby centering on the crucial importance to our species' survival of being closely connected with a caregiver during early childhood.

attention-deficit/hyperactivity disorder (ADHD) The most common childhood learning disorder in the United States, disproportionately affecting boys; characterized by inattention and hyperactivity at home and at school.

authoritarian parents In the parenting-styles framework, when parents provide many rules but rank low on love.

authoritative parents In the parenting-styles framework, the best child-rearing style, when parents provide ample love and family rules.

autism spectrum disorders (ASDs) Conditions characterized by persistent, severe, widespread social and conversational deficits; lack of interest in people and their feelings; and repetitive, restricted behavior patterns, such as rocking, ritualized behavior, hypersensitivity to sensory input, and a fixation on inanimate objects. A core characteristic of these disorders is impairments in theory of mind.

autobiographical memories Recollections of events and experiences that make up one's life history.

autonomy Erikson's second psychosocial task, when toddlers confront the challenge of understanding that they are separate individuals.

avoidant attachment An insecure attachment style characterized by a child's indifference to a primary caregiver at being reunited after separation.

avoidant/dismissive adult attachment A standoffish, excessively disengaged style of relating to loved ones.

axon A long nerve fiber that usually conducts impulses away from the cell body of a neuron.

B

babbling The alternating vowel and consonant sounds that babies repeat with variations of intonation and pitch and that precede the first words.

baby boomers Age group born from 1946–1961, after soldiers returned from World War II.

baby-proofing Making the home safe for a newly mobile infant.

behavioral genetics Field devoted to scientifically determining the role that hereditary forces play in determining individual differences.

bidirectionality The crucial principle that people affect one another, or that interpersonal influences flow in both directions.

binge eating disorder An eating disorder defined by recurrent, out-of-control binging.

biracial or multiracial identity How people of mixed racial backgrounds come to terms with who they are as people in relation to their heritage.

birth defect A physical or neurological problem that occurs prenatally or at birth.

blastocyst The hollow sphere of cells formed during the germinal stage in preparation for implantation.

body mass index (BMI) The ratio of a person's weight to height; the main indicator of overweight or underweight.

bulimia nervosa An eating disorder characterized by at least biweekly cycles of binging and purging in an obsessive attempt to lose weight.

bullying A situation in which one or more children (or adults) harass or target a specific child for systematic abuse.

bully-victims Exceptionally aggressive children (with externalizing disorders) who repeatedly bully and get victimized.

C

centering In Piaget's conservation tasks, the preoperational child's tendency to fix on the most visually striking feature of a substance and not take into account other dimensions.

cephalocaudal sequence The developmental principle that growth occurs in a sequence from head to toe.

cerebral cortex The outer, folded mantle of the brain, responsible for thinking, reasoning, perceiving, and all conscious responses.

cervix The neck, or narrow lower portion, of the uterus.

cesarean section (c-section) Delivering a baby surgically by extracting the fetus through incisions in the woman's abdominal wall.

child maltreatment Any act that seriously endangers a child's physical or emotional well-being.

childhood obesity A body mass index at or above the 95th percentile compared to the U.S. norms established for children in the 1970s.

chorionic villus sampling (CVS) A relatively risky first-trimester pregnancy test for fetal genetic disorders.

chromosome A threadlike strand of DNA located in the nucleus of every cell that carries the genes, which transmit hereditary information.

circular reactions In Piaget's framework, repetitive action-oriented schemas (or habits) characteristic of babies during the sensorimotor stage.

class inclusion The understanding that a general category can encompass several subordinate elements.

clear-cut (focused) attachment Critical attachment phase, from 7 months through toddlerhood, defined by the need to have a primary caregiver nearby.

clique A small peer group composed of roughly six teenagers who have similar attitudes and who share activities.

cognitive behaviorism (social learning theory) A behavioral worldview emphasizing that children learn by watching others and that our thoughts about the reinforcers determine behavior. Cognitive behaviorists focus on charting and modifying children's thoughts.

cohabitation Sharing a household in an unmarried romantic relationship.

cohort People born during the same historical time period.

colic A baby's frantic, continual crying during the first three months of life; caused by an immature nervous system.

collaborative pretend play Fantasy play in which children work together to develop and act out scenes.

collective efficacy Communities defined by strong cohesion, a commitment to neighbor-to-neighbor helping, and shared prosocial values among residents.

collectivist cultures Societies that prize social harmony, obedience, and close family connectedness over individual achievement.

concrete operational thinking In Piaget's framework, the type of cognition characteristic of children aged 8 to 11, marked by the ability to reason about the world in logical, adult ways.

conservation tasks Piagetian tasks that involve changing the shape of substances to see whether children can go beyond the way that substance visually appears to understand that the amount remains the same.

contexts of development Basic markers that shape children's (and adults') lives.

conventional thought In Lawrence Kohlberg's theory, the intermediate level of moral reasoning, in which people respond to ethical issues by discussing the need to uphold social norms.

corporal punishment The use of physical force to discipline a child.

correlational study A research strategy that involves relating two or more variables.

cortisol A hormone often measured in saliva by researchers as a biological marker of stress.

co-sleeping The standard custom, in collectivist cultures, of having a child and parent share a bed.

creative intelligence In Robert Sternberg's framework on successful intelligence, the facet of intelligence involved in producing novel ideas or innovative work.

cross-sectional study A developmental research method that involves comparing different age groups at a single time.

crowd A relatively large teenage peer group.

cyberbullying Systematic harassment conducted through electronic media.

D

day care Less academically oriented group programs serving young children, most often infants and toddlers.

day-care center A day-care arrangement in which a large number of children are cared for at a licensed facility by paid providers.

decentering In Piaget's conservation tasks, the concrete operational child's ability to look at several dimensions of an object or substance.

demographic Relating to the statistical study of populations.

dendrite A branching fiber that receives information and conducts impulses toward the cell body of a neuron.

depth perception The ability to see (and fear) heights.

developed world The most affluent countries in the world.

developing world The more impoverished countries of the world.

developmental disorders Learning impairments and behavioral problems during infancy and childhood.

developmentalists (developmental scientists) Researchers and practitioners whose professional interest lies in development.

deviancy training Socialization of a young teenager into delinquency through conversations centered on performing antisocial acts.

disorganized attachment An insecure attachment style characterized by responses such as freezing or fear when a child is reunited with the primary caregiver in the Strange Situation.

DNA (deoxyribonucleic acid) The material that makes up genes, which bear our hereditary characteristics.

dominant disorder An illness that a child gets by inheriting one copy of the abnormal gene that causes the disorder.

dose–response effect Term referring to the fact that the amount (dose) of a substance, in this case the depth and length of deprivation, determines its probable effect or impact on the person. (In the orphanage studies, the "response" is subsequent emotional and/or cognitive problems.)

Down syndrome The most common chromosomal abnormality, causing intellectual disability, susceptibility to heart disease, other health problems, and distinctive physical characteristics including slanted eyes and a stocky build.

dyslexia A learning disorder that is characterized by reading difficulties, lack of fluency, and poor word recognition that is often genetic in origin.

E

early childhood The first phase of childhood, lasting from age 3 through kindergarten, or about age 6.

Early Head Start A federal program that provides counseling and other services to low-income parents and children under age 3.

eating disorder A pathological obsession with getting and staying thin. The best-known eating disorders are *anorexia nervosa* and *bulimia nervosa*.

ecological, developmental systems approach An all-encompassing perspective on children that stresses the need to embrace a variety of approaches, and emphasizes the reality that many influences affect development.

egocentrism In Piaget's theory, the preoperational child's inability to understand that other people have different points of view from one's own.

embryonic stage The second stage of prenatal development, lasting from week 3 through week 8.

emerging adulthood The phase of life that begins after high school, lasts through the late twenties, and is devoted to constructing an adult life.

emotion regulation The capacity to manage one's emotional state.

empathy Feeling the exact emotion that another person is experiencing.

epigenetics Research field exploring how early life events alter the outer cover of our DNA, producing lifelong changes in health and behavior.

Erikson's psychosocial tasks In Erik Erikson's theory, the unique psychological challenges children face at specific ages.

ethnic identity How people come to terms with who they are as people in relation to their unique ethnic or racial heritage.

evocative forces The nature-interacts-with-nurture principle that genetic temperamental tendencies and predispositions evoke, or produce, certain responses from other people.

evolutionary psychology Theory or worldview highlighting the role that inborn, species-specific behaviors play in shaping behavior.

executive functions Abilities that allow us to plan and direct our thinking and control our immediate impulses.

exercise play Running and chasing play that exercises children's physical skills.

experience-sampling technique A research procedure designed to capture moment-to-moment experiences by having people carry pagers and take notes describing their activities and emotions whenever the signal sounds.

externalizing tendencies A personality style that involves acting on one's immediate impulses and behaving disruptively and aggressively.

extrinsic motivation The drive to take an action because that activity offers external reinforcers such as praise, money, or a good grade.

F

face-perception studies Research using preferential looking and habituation to explore what very young babies know about faces.

fallopian tube One of a pair of slim, pipelike structures that connect the ovaries with the uterus.

family day care A day-care arrangement in which a neighbor or relative cares for a small number of children in his or her home for a fee.

family–work conflict A common developed-world situation, in which parents are torn between the demands of family and a career.

fantasy play Pretend play in which a child makes up a scene, often with a toy or other prop.

fear bias The human tendency to be hypersensitive to fearful facial cues that, by alerting us to danger, may prevent us from getting injured or killed.

fertility rate In a specific nation, the average number of children a woman gives birth to during her lifetime.

fertilization The union of sperm and egg.

fetal alcohol syndrome (FAS) A cluster of birth defects caused by the mother's alcohol consumption during pregnancy.

fetal programming research New research discipline exploring the impact of traumatic pregnancy events and stress on producing low birth weight, obesity, and long-term physical problems.

fetal stage The final phase of prenatal development, lasting seven months, characterized by physical refinements, massive growth, and the development of the brain.

fine motor skills Physical abilities that involve small, coordinated movements, such as drawing and writing one's name.

flow Csikszentmihalyi's term for feeling total absorption in a challenging, goal-oriented activity.

Flynn effect Remarkable rise in overall performance on IQ tests that has been occurring around the world over the past century.

food insecurity According to U.S. Department of Agriculture surveys, the number of households that report needing to serve unbalanced meals, worrying about not having enough food at the end of the month, or having to go hungry due to lack of money (latter is *severe food insecurity*).

formal operational stage Jean Piaget's fourth and final stage of cognitive development, reached at around age 12 and characterized by teenagers' ability to reason at an abstract, scientific level.

frontal lobes The area at the front uppermost part of the brain, responsible for reasoning and planning our actions.

G

g Charles Spearman's term for a general intelligence factor that he claimed underlies all cognitive activities.

gang A close-knit, delinquent peer group. Gangs form mainly in impoverished disorganized communities; they offer their members protection from harm and engage in a variety of criminal activities.

gender schema theory Explanation for gender-stereotyped behavior that emphasizes the role of cognitions; specifically, the idea that once children know their own gender label (girl or boy), they selectively watch and model their own sex.

gender-segregated play Play in which boys and girls associate only with members of their own sex—typical of childhood.

gene A segment of DNA that contains a chemical blueprint for manufacturing a particular protein.

genetic counselor A professional who counsels parents-to-be about their children's risk of developing genetic disorders and about available treatments.

genetic testing A blood test to determine whether a person carries the gene for a given genetic disorder.

germinal stage The first 14 days of prenatal development, from fertilization to full implantation.

gestation The period of pregnancy.

gifted The label for superior intellectual functioning characterized by an IQ score of 130 or above, showing that a child ranks in the top 2 percent of his age group.

gonads The sex organs—the ovaries in girls and the testes in boys.

goodness of fit An ideal parenting strategy that involves arranging children's environments to suit their temperaments, by minimizing their vulnerabilities and accentuating their strengths.

grammar The rules and word-arranging systems that every human language employs to communicate meaning.

gross motor skills Physical abilities that involve large muscle movements, such as running and jumping.

growth spurt A dramatic increase in height and weight that occurs during puberty.

guilt Feeling upset about having caused harm to a person or about having violated one's internal standard of behavior.

H

habituation The predictable loss of interest that develops once a stimulus becomes familiar; used to explore infant sensory capacities and thinking.

Head Start A federal program offering high-quality day care at a center and other services to help preschoolers aged 3 to 5 from low-income families prepare for school.

holophrase First clear evidence of language, when babies use a single word to communicate a sentence or complete thought.

homogamy The principle that we select a mate who is similar to us.

homophobia Intense fear and dislike of gay people.

hormones Chemical substances released in the bloodstream that target and change organs and tissues.

hostile attributional bias The tendency of highly aggressive children to see motives and actions as threatening when they are actually benign.

HPG axis The main hormonal system that programs puberty; it involves a triggering hypothalamic hormone that causes the pituitary to secrete its hormones, which in turn cause the ovaries and testes to develop and secrete the hormones that produce the major body changes.

I

identity In Erikson's theory, the life task of deciding who to be as an adult.

identity achievement A fully mature identity status in which the young person chooses a satisfying adult life path.

identity constancy In Piaget's theory, the preoperational child's inability to grasp that a person's core "self" stays the same despite changes in external appearance.

identity diffusion According to James Marcia, an identity status in which the person feels aimless or totally blocked, without any adult life path.

identity foreclosure According to James Marcia, an identity status in which the person decides on an adult life path (often one spelled out by an authority figure) without any thought or active search.

identity statuses Marcia's four categories of identity formation: identity diffusion, identity foreclosure, moratorium, and identity achievement.

imaginary audience David Elkind's term for the tendency of young teenagers to feel that everyone is watching their every action; a component of adolescent egocentrism.

immigrant paradox The fact that despite living in poverty, going to substandard schools, and not having parents who speak a nation's language, immigrant children do far better than we might expect at school.

implantation The process in which a blastocyst becomes embedded in the uterine wall.

income inequality The gap between the very rich (or top 1 percent of the population) and everyone else.

individualistic cultures Societies that promote personal achievement and independence as keys to successful adult lives.

induction The ideal discipline style for socializing prosocial behavior, which involves getting a child who has behaved hurtfully to empathize with the pain he has caused the other person.

industry Erik Erikson's term for the middle childhood psychosocial task involving bending to adult reality and needing to work for what we want.

infant mortality Death during the first year of life.

infant-directed speech (IDS) The simplified, exaggerated, high-pitched tones that adults and children use to speak to infants that function to help teach language.

infertility The inability to conceive after a year of unprotected sex. (Includes the inability to carry a child to term.)

information-processing approach A perspective on understanding cognition that divides thinking into specific steps and component processes, much like a computer.

initiative Erik Erikson's term for the early childhood psychosocial task that involves exuberantly testing skills.

inner speech In Vygotsky's theory, the way in which human beings learn to regulate their behavior and master cognitive challenges, through silently repeating information or talking to themselves.

insecure attachment Deviation from the normally joyful response of being reunited with a primary caregiver, signaling problems in the caregiver–child relationship.

intellectual disability The label for significantly impaired cognitive functioning, measured by deficits in behavior accompanied by having an IQ of 70 or below.

intelligence quotient (IQ) Measure designed to evaluate a child's overall cognitive ability, or general aptitude for mastering academic work.

internalizing tendencies A personality style that involves intense fear, social inhibition, and often depression.

intimacy Erikson's first adult task, which involves connecting with a partner in a mutual loving relationship.

intrinsic motivation The drive to act based on the pleasure of taking that action in itself, not for an external reinforcer or reward.

in vitro fertilization An infertility treatment in which conception occurs outside the womb.

K

kangaroo care Carrying a young baby in a sling close to the caregiver's body. This technique is most useful for soothing an infant.

L

language acquisition device (LAD) Chomsky's term for a hypothetical brain structure that enables our species to learn and produce language.

learned helplessness A state that develops when a person feels incapable of affecting the outcome of events, and so gives up without trying.

life-course difficulties Antisocial behavior that, for a fraction of adolescents, persists into adult life.

little-scientist phase The time around age 1 when babies use tertiary circular reactions to actively explore the properties of objects, experimenting with them like scientists.

longitudinal study A developmental research strategy that involves testing the same group repeatedly over years.

low birth weight (LBW) A weight at birth of less than 5½ pounds.

M

mass-to-specific sequence The developmental principle that large structures (and movements) precede increasingly detailed refinements.

mean length of utterance (MLU) The average number of morphemes per sentence.

means–end behavior In Piaget's framework, performing a different action to get to a goal—an ability that emerges in the sensorimotor stage as babies approach age 1.

menarche A girl's first menstruation.

micronutrient deficiency Chronically inadequate level of a specific nutrient important to development and disease prevention, such as vitamin A, zinc, and/or iron.

middle childhood The second phase of childhood, comprising the ages from roughly 7 to 12 years.

miscarriage The naturally occurring loss of a pregnancy and death of the fetus.

modeling Learning by watching and imitating others.

moral disengagement Rationalizing moral or ethical lapses by invoking justifications, such as "He deserved that."

moratorium According to James Marcia, an identity status in which the person actively explores various possibilities to find a truly solid adult life path.

morpheme The smallest unit of meaning in a particular language—for example, *boys* contains two morphemes: *boy* and the plural suffix *-s*.

multiple intelligences theory In Howard Gardner's perspective on intelligence, the principle that there are eight separate kinds of intelligence—verbal, mathematical, interpersonal, intrapersonal, spatial, musical, kinesthetic, naturalist—plus a possible ninth type, called spiritual intelligence.

myelination Formation of a fatty layer encasing the axons of neurons. This process, which speeds the transmission of neural impulses, continues from birth into early adulthood.

N

natural childbirth Labor and birth without medical interventions.

naturalistic observation A measurement strategy that involves directly watching and coding behaviors.

nature Biological or genetic causes of development.

neonatal intensive care unit (NICU) A special hospital unit that treats at-risk newborns, such as low-birth-weight and very-low-birth-weight babies.

nest-leaving Moving out of a childhood home and living independently.

neural tube A cylindrical structure that forms along the back of the embryo and develops into the brain and spinal cord.

neuron A nerve cell.

nonsuicidal self-injury Acts of self-mutilation, such as cutting or burning one's body, to cope with stress.

nurture Environmental causes of development.

O

object permanence In Piaget's framework, the understanding that objects continue to exist even when we can no longer see them, which gradually emerges during the sensorimotor stage.

off time Being too late or too early in a culture's timetable for achieving adult life tasks.

on time Being on target in a culture's timetable for achieving adult life tasks.

operant conditioning Learning that determines any voluntary response. Specifically, children behave the way they do when they are reinforced for acting in a certain way.

ovary One of a pair of almond-shaped organs that contain a woman's ova, or eggs.

overextension An error in early language development in which young children apply verbal labels too broadly.

overregularization An error in early language development, in which young children apply the rules for plurals and past tenses even to exceptions, so irregular forms sound like regular forms.

ovulation The moment during a woman's monthly cycle when an ovum is expelled from the ovary.

ovum An egg cell containing the genetic material contributed by the mother to the baby.

oxytocin The hormone whose production is centrally involved in bonding, nurturing, and caregiving behaviors in our species and other mammals.

P

parental alienation The practice among divorced parents of bad-mouthing a former spouse, with the goal of turning a child against that person.

parenting style In Diana Baumrind's framework, how parents align on love and discipline.

permissive parents In the parenting-styles framework, when parents provide few rules but lots of love.

personal fable David Elkind's term for young teenagers' tendency to believe that their lives are special and heroic; a component of adolescent egocentrism.

person–environment fit The extent to which the environment is tailored to our biological tendencies and talents.

phoneme The sound units that convey meaning in a given language—for example, in English, the *c* sound of *cat* and the *b* sound of *bat*.

Piaget's cognitive developmental theory Jean Piaget's principle that from infancy to adolescence, children progress through four qualitatively different stages of intellectual growth.

placenta The structure projecting from the wall of the uterus during pregnancy through which the developing baby absorbs nutrients.

plastic Malleable, or capable of being changed (refers to neural or cognitive development).

postconventional thought In Lawrence Kohlberg's theory, the highest level of moral reasoning, in which people respond to ethical issues by applying their own moral guidelines apart from society's rules.

power assertion An ineffective socialization strategy that involves yelling, screaming, or hitting a child.

practical intelligence In Robert Sternberg's framework on successful intelligence, the facet of intelligence involved in knowing how to act competently in real-world situations.

preattachment phase The first phase of John Bowlby's developmental attachment sequence, during the first three months of life, when infants show no visible signs of attachment.

preconventional thought In Lawrence Kohlberg's theory, the lowest level of moral reasoning, in which people approach ethical issues by only considering the personal punishments or rewards of their actions.

preferential-looking paradigm A research technique to explore early infant sensory capacities and cognition, drawing on the principle that we are attracted to novelty and prefer to look at new things.

preoccupied/ambivalent adult attachment An excessively clingy, needy style of relating to loved ones.

preoperational thinking In Piaget's theory, the type of cognition characteristic of children aged 2 to 7, marked by an inability to step back from one's immediate perceptions and think conceptually.

preschool A teaching-oriented group setting for children aged 3 to 5.

primary attachment figure The closest person in a child's or adult's life.

primary circular reactions In Piaget's framework, the first infant habits during the sensorimotor stage, centered on the body.

primary sexual characteristics Physical changes of puberty that directly involve the reproductive organs, such as growth of the penis and onset of menstruation.

proactive aggression A hostile or destructive act initiated to achieve a goal.

prosocial behavior Sharing, helping, and caring actions.

proximity-seeking behavior Acting to maintain physical contact or to be close to an attachment figure.

proximodistal sequence The developmental principle that growth occurs from the most interior parts of the body outward.

puberty The hormonal and physical changes by which children become sexually mature human beings and reach their adult height.

puberty rite A "coming of age" ritual held in traditional cultures to celebrate children's transition to adulthood.

Q

qualitative research Occasional developmental science data-collection strategy that involves personal interviews.

quantitative research Standard developmental science data-collection strategy that involves testing groups and using numerical scales and statistics.

quickening A pregnant woman's first feeling of the fetus moving inside her body.

R

reactive aggression A hostile or destructive act carried out in response to being frustrated or hurt.

recessive disorder An illness that a child gets by inheriting two copies of the abnormal gene that causes the disorder.

reflex A response or action that is automatic and programmed by noncortical brain centers.

rehearsal A learning strategy in which people repeat information to embed it in memory.

reinforcement Behavioral term for reward.

rejecting-neglecting parents In the parenting-styles framework, the worst child-rearing approach, when parents provide little discipline or love.

relational aggression A hostile or destructive act designed to cause harm to a person's relationships.

relationship churning Having on-again/off-again romantic relationships in which couples repeatedly get together and then break up.

reliability In measurement terminology, a basic criterion for a test's accuracy that scores must be fairly similar when a person takes the same test more than once.

REM sleep The phase of sleep involving rapid eye movements, when the EEG looks almost like it does during waking. REM sleep decreases as infants mature.

representative sample A group that reflects the characteristics of the overall population.

resilient children Children who rebound from serious early life traumas to construct successful adult lives.

reversibility In Piaget's conservation tasks, the concrete operational child's knowledge that a specific change in the way a given substance looks can be reversed.

role confusion Erikson's term for a failure in identity formation, marked by the lack of any sense of a future adult path.

role phase In Murstein's theory, the final mate-selection stage, in which committed partners work out their future life together.

rooting reflex Newborns' automatic response to a touch on the cheek, involving turning toward that location and beginning to suck.

rough-and-tumble play Play that involves shoving, wrestling, and hitting, but in which no actual harm is intended; especially characteristic of boys.

ruminative moratorium When a young person is unable to decide between different identities, becoming emotionally paralyzed and highly anxious.

S

scaffolding The process of teaching new skills by entering a child's zone of proximal development and tailoring one's efforts to that person's competence level.

school-to-prison pipeline Term referring to the way school expulsion may provoke criminal behavior and incarceration for at-risk teens.

school-to-work transition The change from the schooling phase of life to the work world.

secondary circular reactions In Piaget's framework, habits of the sensorimotor stage lasting from about 4 months of age to the baby's first birthday, centered on exploring the external world.

secondary sexual characteristics Physical changes of puberty not directly involved in reproduction, such as female breast development and male facial hair.

secular trend in puberty A decline in the average age at which children reach puberty.

secure adult attachment The genuine intimacy that is ideal in love relationships.

secure attachment Ideal attachment response when a child responds with joy at being reunited with a primary caregiver.

selective attention A learning strategy in which people manage their awareness so as to attend only to what is relevant and to filter out unneeded information.

self-awareness The capacity to observe our abilities and actions from an outside frame of reference and to reflect on our inner state.

self-conscious emotions Feelings of pride, shame, or guilt, which first emerge around age 2 and show the capacity to reflect on the self.

self-efficacy According to cognitive behaviorism, an internal belief in one's competence that predicts whether children initiate activities or persist in the face of failures.

self-esteem Evaluating oneself as either "good" or "bad" as a result of comparing the self to other people.

self-report strategy A measurement technique in which people report on their feelings and activities through questionnaires.

self-soothing Children's ability, usually beginning at about 6 months of age, to put themselves back to sleep when they wake up during the night.

semantics The meaning system of a language—that is, what the words stand for.

sensitive period The time when a body structure is most vulnerable to damage by a teratogen, typically when that organ or process is rapidly developing or coming "on line."

sensorimotor stage Piaget's first stage of cognitive development, lasting from birth to age 2, when babies' agenda is to pin down the basics of physical reality.

separation anxiety When a baby gets upset as a primary caregiver departs.

sex-linked single-gene disorder An illness, carried on the mother's X chromosome, that typically leaves the female offspring unaffected but has a fifty-fifty chance of striking each male child.

sexual double standard A cultural code that gives men greater sexual freedom than women. Specifically, society expects males to want to have intercourse and expects females to remain virgins until they marry and to be more interested in relationships than in having sex.

shame A feeling of being personally humiliated.

single-gene disorder An illness caused by a single gene.

skin-to-skin contact An effective calming strategy that involves holding a young infant next to a caregiver's body.

social clock The concept that we regulate our passage through adulthood by an inner timetable that tells us which life activities are appropriate at certain ages.

social cognition Any skill related to understanding feelings and negotiating interpersonal interactions.

social networking sites Internet sites whose goal is to forge personal connections among users.

social referencing A baby's monitoring a caregiver for cues as to how to behave.

social smile The first real smile, occurring at about 2 months of age.

social-interactionist perspective An approach to language development that emphasizes its social function, specifically that babies and adults have a mutual passion to communicate.

socialization How children are taught to behave in socially appropriate ways.

socioeconomic status (SES) A basic marker referring to status on educational and, especially, income rungs.

specific learning disorder The label for any impairment in language or any deficit related to listening, thinking, speaking, reading, writing, spelling, or understanding mathematics.

spermarche A boy's first ejaculation of live sperm.

stimulus phase In Murstein's theory, the initial mate-selection stage, in which we make judgments about a potential partner based on external characteristics such as appearance.

stimulus-value-role theory Murstein's mate-selection theory that suggests similar people pair up and that our path to commitment progresses through three phases (called the *stimulus*, *value-comparison*, and *role* phases).

"storm and stress" G. Stanley Hall's phrase for the intense moodiness, emotional sensitivity, and risk-taking tendencies that characterize the life stage he labeled adolescence.

stranger anxiety Beginning at about age 7 months, when a baby grows wary of people other than a caregiver.

Strange Situation Procedure to measure attachment at age 1, involving separations and reunions with a caregiver.

stunting Excessively short stature in a child, caused by chronic lack of adequate nutrition.

subject attrition The fact that people drop out at each testing point in longitudinal research.

successful intelligence In Robert Sternberg's framework, the optimal form of cognition, which involves striking the right balance of analytic, creative, and practical intelligence.

sucking reflex The automatic, spontaneous sucking movements newborns produce, especially when anything touches their lips.

sudden infant death syndrome (SIDS) The unexplained death of an apparently healthy infant, often while sleeping, during the first year of life.

sympathy A state necessary for acting prosocially, involving feeling upset for a person who needs help.

synapse The gap between the dendrites of one neuron and the axon of another, over which impulses flow.

synaptogenesis Forming of connections between neurons at the synapses. This process, responsible for all perceptions, actions, and thoughts, is most intense during infancy and childhood but continues throughout life.

synchrony The reciprocal aspect of the attachment relationship, with a caregiver and infant responding emotionally to each other in a sensitive, exquisitely attuned way.

syntax The system of grammatical rules in a particular language.

T

telegraphic speech First stage of combining words in which a toddler pares down a sentence to its essential words.

temperament A person's characteristic, inborn style of dealing with the world.

teratogen A substance that crosses the placenta and harms the fetus.

tertiary circular reactions In Piaget's framework, "little-scientist" activities of the sensorimotor stage, beginning around age 1, involving flexibly exploring the properties of objects.

testes Male organs that manufacture sperm.

testosterone The hormone responsible for maturation of the male reproductive organs and other signs of puberty in men, and for hair and skin changes and sexual desire in both sexes.

theory Any perspective explaining why people act the way they do. Theories allow us to predict behavior and also suggest how to intervene to improve behavior.

theory of mind Children's first cognitive understanding, which appears at about age 4, that other people have different beliefs and perspectives from their own.

thin ideal Media-driven cultural idea that females need to be abnormally thin.

toddlerhood The important transitional stage after babyhood, from roughly age 1 year to 2½.

traditional behaviorism The original behavioral worldview that focused on charting and modifying only "objective," visible behaviors.

trimester One of the 3-month-long segments into which pregnancy is divided.

true experiment The only research strategy that can determine that something causes something else; involves randomly assigning children to different treatments and then looking at the outcome.

twin study Behavioral genetic research strategy, designed to determine the genetic contribution of a given trait, that involves comparing identical twins with fraternal twins (or with other people).

twin/adoption study Behavioral genetic research strategy that involves comparing the similarities of identical twin pairs adopted into different families, to determine the genetic contribution to a given trait.

U

ultrasound In pregnancy, an image of the fetus in the womb that helps to date the pregnancy, assess the fetus's growth, and identify abnormalities.

umbilical cord The structure that attaches the placenta to the fetus, through which nutrients are passed and fetal wastes are removed.

underextension An error in early language development in which young children apply verbal labels too narrowly.

undernutrition A chronic lack of adequate food.

upward mobility Rising in social class and/or economic status from one's childhood.

uterus The pear-shaped muscular organ in a woman's abdomen that houses the developing baby.

V

validity In measurement terminology, a basic criterion for a test's accuracy involving whether that measure reflects the real-world quality it is supposed to measure.

value-comparison phase In Murstein's theory, the second mate-selection stage, in which we make judgments about a partner on the basis of similar values and interests.

very low birth weight (VLBW) A weight at birth of less than 3¼ pounds.

visual cliff A table that appears to "end" in a drop-off at its midpoint; used to test infant depth perception.

W

WISC (Wechsler Intelligence Scale for Children) The standard intelligence test used in childhood, consisting of different subtests.

working memory In information-processing theory, the limited-capacity gateway system, containing all the material that we can keep in awareness at a single time. The material in this system is either processed for more permanent storage or lost.

working model In Bowlby's theory, the mental representation of a caregiver that enables children over age 3 to be physically apart from their caregiver.

Y

youth development program Any after-school program or structured activity outside of the school day that is devoted to promoting flourishing in teenagers.

Z

zero-tolerance policies The practice in U.S. public high schools of suspending students after one rule infraction.

zone of proximal development (ZPD) In Vygotsky's theory, the gap between a child's ability to solve a problem totally on his own and his potential knowledge if taught by a more accomplished person.

zygote A fertilized ovum.

References

Abbate-Daga, G., Gramaglia, C., Amianto, F., Marzola, E., & Fassino, S. (2010). Attachment insecurity, personality, and body dissatisfaction in eating disorders. *The Journal of Nervous and Mental Disease, 198*(7), 520–524.

Abramson, L. Y., Seligman, M. E., & Teasdale, J. D. (1978). Learned helplessness in humans: Critique and reformulation. *Journal of Abnormal Psychology, 87,* 49–74.

Abu-Akel, A., & Shamay-Tsoory, S. (2011). Neuroanatomical and neurochemical bases of theory of mind. *Neuropsychologia, 49,* 2971–2984.

Abubakar, A., Holding, P., Vijver, F. J. R., Newton, C., & Baar, A. V. (2010). Children at risk for developmental delay can be recognised by stunting, being underweight, ill health, little maternal schooling or high gravity. *Journal of Child Psychology and Psychiatry, 51*(6), 652–659.

Abubakar, A. A., Vijver, F., Suryani, A., Handayani, P., & Pandia, W. (2015). Perceptions of parenting styles and their associations with mental health and life satisfaction among urban Indonesian adolescents. *Journal of Child & Family Studies, 24*(9), 2680–2692. doi:10.1007/s10826-014-0070-x

Acevedo-Polakovich, I. D., Cousineau, J. R., Quirk, K. M., Gerhart, J. I., Bell, K. M., & Adomako, M. S. (2014). Toward an asset orientation in the study of U.S. Latina youth: Biculturalism, ethnic identity, and positive youth development. *Counseling Psychologist, 42*(2), 201–222.

Adair, L. S. (2008). Child and adolescent obesity: Epidemiology and developmental perspectives. *Physiology & Behavior, 94,* 8–16.

Adi-Japha, E., Berberich-Artzi, J., & Libnawi, A. (2010). Cognitive flexibility in drawings of bilingual children. *Child Development, 81*(5), 1356–1366.

Adolph, K. E. (2008). Learning to move. *Current Directions in Psychological Science, 17*(3), 213–218.

Adolph, K., & Berger, S. E. (2006). Motor development. In D. Kuhn, R. S. Siegler, W. Damon, & R. M. Lerner (Eds.), *Handbook of child psychology: Vol. 2, Cognition, perception, and language* (6th ed., pp. 161–213). Hoboken, NJ: Wiley.

Agency for Healthcare Research and Quality. (2014). Evidence report/technology assessment Number 214: Smoking cessation interventions in pregnancy and postpartum care executive summary. Effective Health Care Program, Rockville, MD: Author.

Ahn, S. J., Kyeong, S., Suh, S. H., Kim, J., Chung, T., & Seok, J. (2016). What is the impact of child abuse on gray matter abnormalities in individuals with major depressive disorder: A case control study. *BMC Psychiatry, 16,* 161–167. doi:10.1186/s12888-016-1116-y

Ahnert, L., Pinquart, M., & Lamb, M. (2006). Security of children's relationships with nonparental care providers: A meta-analysis. *Child Development, 74*(3), 664–679.

Ainsworth, M. D. S. (1967). *Infancy in Uganda: Infant care and the growth of love.* Baltimore, MD: Johns Hopkins Press.

Ainsworth, M. D. S. (1973). The development of infant–mother attachment. In B. M. Caldwell & H. N. Ricciuti (Eds.), *Review of child development research* (Vol. 3, pp. 1–94). Chicago, IL: University of Chicago Press.

Ainsworth, M. D. S., Blehar, M. C., Waters, E., & Wall, S. (1978). *Patterns of attachment: A psychological study of the strange situation.* Hillsdale, NJ: Erlbaum.

Ajibade, A., Hook, J. N., Utsey, S. O., Davis, D. E., & Tongeren, D. V. (2016). Racial/ethnic identity, religious commitment, and well-being in African Americans. *Journal of Black Psychology, 42*(3), 244–258.

Aknin, L. B., Hamlin, J. K., & Dunn, E. W. (2012). Giving leads to happiness in young children. *Plos ONE, 7*(6).

Aksan, N., & Kochanska, G. (2004). Links between systems of inhibition from infancy to preschool years. *Child Development, 75*(5), 1477–1490.

Al Gharaibeh, F. (2015). The effects of divorce on children: Mothers' perspectives in UAE. *Journal of Divorce and Remarriage, 56*(5), 347–368. doi:10.1080/10502556.2015.1046800

Alderson, R. M., Hudec, K. L., Patros, C. G., & Kasper, L. J. (2013). Working memory deficits in adults with attention-deficit/hyperactivity disorder (ADHD): An examination of central executive and storage/rehearsal processes. *Journal of Abnormal Psychology, 122*(2), 532–541.

Aldred, H. E. (1997). *Pregnancy and birth sourcebook: Basic information about planning for pregnancy, maternal health, fetal growth and development.* Detroit, MI: Omnigraphics.

Alea, N., & Wang, Q. (2015). Going global: The functions of autobiographical memory in cultural context. *Memory, 23*(1), 1–10. doi:10.1080/09658211.2014.972416

Aleni Sestito, L., & Sica, L. S. (2014). Identity formation of Italian emerging adults living with parents: A narrative study. *Journal of Adolescence, 371,* 435–447.

Alessandri, G., Eisenberg, N., Vecchione, M., Caprara, G. V., & Milioni, M. (2016). Ego-resiliency development from late adolescence to emerging adulthood: A ten-year longitudinal study. *Journal of Adolescence, 50,* 91–102.

Ali, M. M., & Dwyer, D. S. (2011). Estimating peer effects in sexual behavior among adolescents. *Journal of Adolescence, 34,* 183–190.

Allen, J. P., Porter, M., McFarland, C., McElhaney, K. B., & Marsh, P. (2007). The relation of attachment security to adolescents' paternal and peer relationships, depression, and externalizing behavior. *Child Development, 78*(4), 1222–1239.

Allison, C. M., & Hyde, J. S. (2013). Early menarche: Confluence of biological and contextual factors. *Sex Roles, 68*(1–2), 55–64.

Alloway, T. P., McCallum, F., Alloway, R. G., & Hoicka, E. (2015). Liar, liar, working memory on fire: Investigating the role of working memory in childhood verbal deception. *Journal of Experimental Child Psychology, 137,* 30–38. doi:10.1016/j.jecp.2015.03.013

Almas, A. N., Degnan, K. A., Nelson, C. A., Zeanah, C. H., & Fox, N. A. (2016). IQ at age 12 following a history of institutional care: Findings from the Bucharest Early Intervention Project. *Developmental Psychology, 52*(11), 1858–1866.

Almqvist, A., & Duvander, A. (2014). Changes in gender equality? Swedish fathers' parental leave, division of childcare and housework. *Journal of Family Studies, 20*(1), 19–27.

Alt, D. (2016). Using structural equation modeling and multidimensional scaling to assess female college students' academic adjustment as a function of perceived parenting styles. *Current Psychology: A Journal for Diverse Perspectives on Diverse Psychological Issues, 35*(4), 549–561. doi:10.1007/s12144-015-9320-3

American Academy of Pediatrics. (2005). Breastfeeding and the use of human milk. *Pediatrics, 115,* 496–506.

American Academy of Pediatrics, Committee on Drugs. (2000). Use of psychoactive medication during pregnancy and possible effects on the fetus and newborn. *Pediatrics, 105,* 880–887.

American Psychiatric Association. (2013). *Diagnostic and statistical manual of mental disorders* (5th ed.). Arlington, VA: American Psychiatric Publishing.

American Teens' Sources of Sexual Health Education. (2016, October 27). Retrieved April 4, 2017, from https://www.guttmacher.org/fact-sheet/facts-american-teens-sources-information-about-sex

Anakwenze, U., & Zuberi, D. (2013). Mental health and poverty in the inner city. *Health & Social Work, 38*(3), 147–157.

Andero, A. A., & Stewart, A. (2002). Issue of corporal punishment: Re-examined. *Journal of Instructional Psychology, 29,* 90–96.

Anders, T., Goodlin-Jones, B. L., & Zelenko, M. (1998). Infant regulation and sleep–wake state development. *Zero to Three, 19*(2), 9–14.

Anderson, J. W. (1972). Attachment behavior out of doors. In N. Blurton Jones (Ed.), *Ethological studies of child behaviour* (pp. 199–215). London, England: Cambridge University Press.

Anderson, R., & Mitchell, E. M. (1984). Children's health and play in rural Nepal. *Social Science & Medicine, 19,* 735–740.

Andrew, R., Tiggemann, M., & Clark, L. (2016). Predictors and health-related outcomes of positive body image in adolescent girls: A prospective study. *Developmental Psychology, 52*(3), 463–474. doi:10.1037/dev0000095

Andrews, T., & Knaak, S. (2013). Medicalized mothering: Experiences with breastfeeding in Canada and Norway. *The Sociological Review, 61*(1), 88–110.

Anestis, M. D., Pennings, S. M., Lavender, J. M., Tull, M. T., & Gratz, K. L. (2013). Low distress tolerance as an indirect risk factor for suicidal behavior: Considering the explanatory role of non-suicidal self-injury. *Comprehensive Psychiatry, 54*(7), 996–1002.

Annerbäck, E.-M., Svedin, C.-G., & Gustafsson, P. A. (2010). Characteristic features of severe child physical abuse—A multi-informant approach. *Journal of Family Violence, 25,* 165–172.

Archibald, A. B., Graber, J. A., & Brooks-Gunn, J. (2003). Pubertal processes and physiological growth in adolescence. In G. R. Adams & M. D. Berzonsky (Eds.), *Blackwell handbook of adolescence* (pp. 24–47). Malden, MA: Blackwell.

Ariès, P. (1962). *Centuries of childhood: A social history of family life.* New York, NY: Knopf.

Arnett, J. J. (2004). *Emerging adulthood: The winding road from the late teens through the twenties.* New York, NY: Oxford University Press.

Arnett, J. J. (2007). The long and leisurely route: Coming of age in Europe today. *Current History: A Journal of Contemporary Affairs, 106,* 130–136.

Arnett, J. J. (2016). Does emerging adulthood theory apply across social classes? National data on a persistent question. *Emerging Adulthood, 4*(4), 227–235.

Arnett, J. J., & Padilla-Walker, L. M. (2015). Brief report: Danish emerging adults' conceptions of adulthood. *Journal of Adolescence, 38,* 39–44.

AVERT. (2005). *AIDS and HIV statistics for sub-Saharan Africa.* Retrieved from http://www.avert.org/subadults.htm., November 2005.

Axelsson, A., Andersson, R., & Gulz, A. (2016). Scaffolding executive function capabilities via play-&-learn software for preschoolers. *Journal of Educational Psychology, 108*(7), 969–981. doi:10.1037/edu0000099

Baddeley, A. D. (1992). Working memory: The interface between memory and cognition. *Journal of Cognitive Neuroscience, 4,* 281–288.

Bahrick, L. B., Todd, J. T., Castellanos, I., & Sorondo, B. M. (2016). Enhanced attention to speaking faces versus other event types emerges gradually across infancy. *Developmental Psychology, 52*(11), 1705–1720. doi:10.1037/dev0000157

Baibazarova, E., van de Beek, C., Cohen-Kettenis, P. T., Buitelaar, J., Shelton, K. H., & van Goozen, S. M. (2013). Influence of prenatal maternal stress, maternal plasma cortisol and cortisol in the amniotic fluid on birth outcomes and child temperament at 3 months. *Psychoneuroendocrinology, 38*(6), 907–915.

Baijot, S., Slama, H., Soderlund, G., Ban, B., Colin, C., Deitnre, P., & Deconnick, N. (2016). Neuropsychological and neurophysiological benefits in children without and with ADHD. *Behavioral Brain Function, 12*(11).

Baillargeon, R. (1993). The object concept revisited: New direction in the investigation of infants' physical knowledge. In C. Granrud (Ed.), *Visual perception and cognition in infancy* (pp. 265–315). Hillsdale, NJ: Erlbaum.

Baillargeon, R., & DeVos, J. (1991). Object permanence in young infants: Further evidence. *Child Development, 62,* 1227–1246.

Baillargeon, R., & Graber, M. (1987). Where's the rabbit? 5.5-month-old infants' representation of the height of a hidden object. *Cognitive Development, 2,* 375–392.

Baillargeon, R., Scott, R. M., & Bian, L. (2016). Psychological reasoning in infancy. *Annual Review of Psychology, 67*(1), 159–186. doi:10.1146/annurev-psych-010213-115033

Ball, H. L., & Volpe, L. E. (2013). Sudden Infant Death Syndrome (SIDS) risk reduction and infant sleep location—Moving the discussion forward. *Social Science & Medicine, 79,* 84–91.

Ballantine, P. W., Lin, Y., & Veer, E. (2015). The influence of user comments on perceptions of Facebook relationship status updates. *Computers in Human Behavior, 49,* 50–55.

Ballard, R. H., Holtzworth-Munroe, A., Applegate, A. G., D'Onofrio, B. M., & Bates, J. E. (2013). A randomized controlled trial of child-informed mediation. *Psychology, Public Policy, and Law, 19*(3), 271–281.

Banducci, A. N., Gomes, M., MacPherson, L., Lejuez, C. W., Potenza, M. N., Gelernter, J., & Amstadter, A. B. (2014). A preliminary examination of the relationship between the 5-HTTLPR and childhood emotional abuse on depressive symptoms in 10–12-year-old youth. *Psychological Trauma: Theory, Research, Practice, and Policy, 6*(1), 1–7.

Bandura, A. (1977). *Social learning theory.* Englewood Cliffs, NJ: Prentice Hall.

Bandura, A. (1986). *Social foundations of thought and action: A social cognitive theory.* Englewood Cliffs, NJ: Prentice-Hall.

Bandura, A. (1989). Human agency in social cognitive theory. *American Psychologist, 44,* 1175–1184.

Bandura, A. (1992). Exercise of personal agency through the self-efficacy mechanism. In R. Schwarzer (Ed.), *Self-efficacy: Thought control of action* (pp. 3–38). Washington, DC: Hemisphere.

Bandura, A. (1997). *Self-efficacy: The exercise of control.* New York, NY: Freeman.

Bane, K. (2004). *What the best college teachers do.* Cambridge, MA: President and Fellows of Harvard College.

Barkin, S., Scheindlin, B., Ip, E. H., Richardson, I., & Finch, S. (2007). Determinants of parental discipline practices: A national sample from primary care practices. *Clinical Pediatrics, 46*(1), 64–69.

Barkley, R. A. (1998). *Attention-deficit hyperactivity disorder: A handbook for diagnosis and treatment* (2nd ed.). New York, NY: Guilford Press.

Barkley, R. A., & Murphy, K. R. (2006). *Attention-deficit hyperactivity disorder: A clinical workbook* (3rd ed.). New York, NY: Guilford Press.

Barnes, G. M., Hoffman, J. H., Welte, J. W., Farrell, M. P., & Dintcheff, B. A. (2007). Adolescents' time use: Effects on substance use, delinquency and sexual activity. *Journal of Youth and Adolescence, 36,* 697–710.

Barnett, L. M., van Beurden, E., Morgan, P. J., Brooks, L. O., & Beard, J. R. (2009). Childhood motor skill proficiency as a predictor of adolescent physical activity. *Journal of Adolescent Health, 44,* 252–259.

Barnett, S. M., Ceci, S. J., & Williams, W. M. (2006). Is the ability to make a bacon sandwich a mark of intelligence? And other issues: Some reflections on Gardner's theory of multiple intelligences. In J. A. Schaler (Ed.), *Howard Gardner under fire: The rebel psychologist faces his critics* (pp. 95–114). Chicago, IL: Open Court.

Barnett, W. S., & Friedman-Krauss, A. H. (2016). *State(s) of Head Start.* New Brunswick, NJ: National Institute for Early Education Research.

Barnhart, S., & Maguire-Jack, K. (2016). Single mothers in their communities: The mediating role of parenting stress and depression between social cohesion, social control and child maltreatment. *Children & Youth Services Review, 70,* 37–45. doi:10.1016/j.childyouth.2016.09.003

Baron, I. S., & Rey-Casserly, C. (2010). Extremely preterm birth outcome: A review of four decades of cognitive research. *Neuropsychology Review, 20*(4), 430–425.

Barr, A. B., Lorenz, F. O., Sutton, T. E., Gordon Simons, L., Wickrama, K. S., & Simons, L. G. (2016). Romantic relationship transitions and changes in health among rural, White young adults. *Journal of Family Psychology, 30*(7), 832–842.

Barrera, C. M., Perrine, C. G., Li, R., & Scanlon, K. S. (2016). Age at introduction to solid foods and child obesity at 6 years. *Childhood Obesity, 12*(3), 188–192.

Barry, R. A., & Kochanska, G. (2010). A longitudinal investigation of the affective environment in families with young children: From infancy to early school age. *Emotion, 10*(2), 237–249.

Bashe, P., & Greydanus, D. E. (2003). *Caring for your teenager: The complete and authoritative guide.* New York, NY: Bantam Books.

Batool, S. S., & de Visser, R. O. (2016). Experiences of infertility in British and Pakistani women: A cross-cultural qualitative analysis. *Health Care for Women International, 37*(2), 180–196.

Baumeister, R. F., Campbell, J. D., Krueger, J. I., & Vohs, K. D. (2003). Does high self-esteem cause better performance, interpersonal success, happiness, or healthier lifestyles? *Psychological Science in the Public Interest, 4*(1), 1–44.

Baumrind, D. (1971). Current patterns of parental authority. *Developmental Psychology, 4*(1, Pt. 2), 1–103.

Baumrind, D., Larzelere, R. E., & Cowan, P. A. (2002). Ordinary physical punishment: Is it harmful? Comment on Gershoff. *Psychological Bulletin, 128,* 580–589.

Bava, S., Thayer, R., Jacobus, J., Ward, M., Jernigan, T. L., & Tapert, S. F. (2010). Longitudinal characterization of white matter maturation during adolescence. *Brain Research, 1327,* 38–46.

Becker, S. P., Fite, P. J., Luebbe, A. M., Stoppelbein, L., & Greening, L. (2013). Friendship intimacy exchange buffers the relation between ADHD symptoms and later social problems among children attending an after-school care program. *Journal of Psychopathology and Behavioral Assessment, 35*(2), 142–152.

Becker-Blease, K. A., Turner, H. A., & Finkelhor, D. (2010). Disasters, victimization, and children's mental health. *Child Development, 81*(4), 1040–1052.

Beckmann, C. R. B., Ling, F. W., Laube, D. W., Smith, R. P., Barzansky, B. M., & Herbert, W. N. P. (2002). *Obstetrics and gynecology* (4th ed.). Baltimore, MD: Lippincott Williams & Wilkins.

Beernick, A. C. E., Swinkels, S. H. N., & Buitelaar, J. K. (2007). Problem behavior in a community sample of 14- and 19-month-old children. *European Child and Adolescent Psychiatry, 16,* 271–280.

Behboodi-Moghadam, Z., Salsali, M., Eftekhar-Ardabily, H., Vaismoradi, M., & Ramezanzadeh, F. (2013). Experiences of infertility through the lens of Iranian infertile women: A qualitative study. *Japan Journal of Nursing Science, 10*(1), 41–46.

Behrens, K. Y., Haltigan, J. D., & Bahm, N. I. (2016). Infant attachment, adult attachment, and maternal sensitivity: Revisiting the intergenerational transmission gap. *Attachment & Human Development, 18*(4), 337–353. doi:10.1080/14616734.2016.1167095

Behrens, K. Y., Parker, A. C., & Haltigan, J. D. (2011). Maternal sensitivity assessed during the Strange Situation Procedure predicts child's attachment quality and reunion behaviors. *Infant Behavior and Development, 34*(2), 378–381.

Beijers, R., Cillessen, L., & Zijlmans, M. A. (2016). An experimental study on mother–infant skin-to-skin contact in full-terms. *Infant Behavior and Development, 43,* 58–65. doi:10.1016/j.infbeh.2016.01.001

Beijers, R., Riksen-Walraven, J. M., & deWeerth, C. (2013). Cortisol regulation in 12-month-old human infants: Associations with the infants' early history of breastfeeding and co-sleeping. *Stress: The International Journal on the Biology of Stress, 16*(3), 267–277.

Bell, A. S. (2011). A critical review of ADHD diagnostic criteria: What to address in the *DSM-V. Journal of Attention Disorders, 15*(1), 3–10.

Bellinger, D., Leviton, A., Waternaux, C., Needleman, H., & Rabinowitz, M. (1987). Longitudinal analyses of prenatal and postnatal lead exposure and early cognitive development. *New England Journal of Medicine, 316,* 1037–1043.

Belsky, D. W., Moffitt, T. E., Corcoran, D. L., Domingue, B., Harrington, H. L., Houts, R., Ramrakha, S., Sugden, K., Williams, B. S., Poulton, R., Caspi, A. (2016). The genetics of success: How single nucleotide polymorphisms associated with educational attainment relate to life-course development. *Psychological Science, 27*(7), 957–972.

Belsky, J. (2016). *Experiencing the lifespan* (4th ed.). New York, NY: Worth.

Belsky, J., Houts, R. M., & Pasco Fearon, R. M. (2010). Infant attachment security and the timing of puberty: Testing an evolutionary hypothesis. *Psychological Science, 21,* 1195–1201.

Belsky, J., & Pluess, M. (2009). Beyond diathesis stress: Differential susceptibility to environmental influences. *Psychological Bulletin, 135*(6), 885–908.

Belsky, J., & Pluess, M. (2011). Beyond adversity, vulnerability, and resilience: Individual differences in developmental plasticity. In D. Cicchetti & G. I. Roisman (Eds.), *The Origins and Organization of Adaptation and Maladaptation* (pp. 379–422). Hoboken, NJ: Wiley.

Belsky, J., & Pluess, M. (2013). Genetic moderation of early child-care effects on social functioning across childhood: A developmental analysis. *Child Development, 84*(4), 1209–1225.

Belsky, J., & Pluess, M. (2016). Differential susceptibility to environmental influences. In D. Cicchetti (Ed.), *Developmental Psychopathology* (3rd ed.). New York, NY: Wiley.

Belsky, J., Ruttle, P. L., Boyce, W. T., Armstrong, J. M., & Essex, M. J. (2015). Early adversity, elevated stress physiology, accelerated sexual maturation, and poor health in females. *Developmental Psychology, 51*(6), 816–822. doi:10.1037/dev0000017

Belsky, J., Steinberg, L. D., Houts, R. M., Friedman, S. L., DeHart, G., Cauffman, E., . . . Susman, E. (2007a). Family rearing antecedents of pubertal timing. *Child Development, 78*(4), 1302–1321.

Belsky, J., Vandell, D. L., Burchinal, M., Clarke-Stewart, K. A., McCartney, K., Owen, M. T., & The NICHD Early Child Care Research Network. (2007b). Are there long-term effects of early child care? *Child Development, 78*(2), 681–701.

Bem, S. L. (1981). Gender schema theory: A cognitive account of sex typing. *Psychological Review, 88*, 354–364.

Beneventi, H., Tønnessen, F. E., Ersland, L., & Hugdahl, K. (2010). Working memory deficit in dyslexia: Behavioral and fMRI evidence. *International Journal of Neuroscience, 120*, 51–59.

Ben-Itzchak, E., Zukerman, G., & Zachor, D. A. (2016). Having older siblings is associated with less severe social communication symptoms in young children with autism spectrum disorder. *Journal of Abnormal Child Psychology, 44*(8), 1613–1620. doi:10.1007/s10802-016-0133-0

Benjet, C., & Kazdin, A. E. (2003). Spanking children: The controversies, findings and new directions. *Clinical Psychology Review, 23*, 197–224.

Benner, A. D., Kretsch, N., Harden, P., & Crosnoe, R. (2014). Academic achievement as a moderator of genetic influences on alcohol use in adolescence. *Developmental Psychology, 50*(4), 1170–1178.

Benoit, A., Lacourse, E., & Claes, M. (2013). Pubertal timing and depressive symptoms in late adolescence: The moderating role of individual, peer, and parental factors. *Development and Psychopathology, 25*(2), 455–471.

Berger, A., Alyagon, U., Hadaya, H., Atzaba-Poria, N., & Auerbach, J. G. (2013). Response inhibition in preschoolers at familial risk for attention deficit hyperactivity disorder: A behavioral and electrophysiological stop signal study. *Child Development, 84*(5), 1616–1632.

Berger, C., & Caravita, S. C. (2016). Why do early adolescents bully? Exploring the influence of prestige norms on social and psychological motives to bully. *Journal of Adolescence, 46*, 45–56.

Bergh, C., Callmar, M., Danemar, S., Hölcke, M., Isberg, S., Leon, M., . . . Södersten, P. (2013). Effective treatment of eating disorders: Results at multiple sites. *Behavioral Neuroscience, 127*(6), 878–889.

Berk, L. E., & Winsler, A. (1999). *NAEYC research into practice series: Vol. 7. Scaffolding children's learning: Vygotsky and early childhood education.* Washington, DC: National Association for the Education of Young Children.

Berko, J. (1958). The child's learning of English morphology. *Word, 14*, 150–177.

Berlin, L. J., Appleyard, K., & Dodge, K. (2011). Intergenerational continuity in child maltreatment: Mediating mechanisms and implications for prevention. *Child Development, 82*(1), 162–176.

Berry, D., Blair, C., & Granger, D. A. (2016). Child care and cortisol across infancy and toddlerhood: Poverty, peers, and developmental timing. *Family Relations, 65*(1), 51–72. doi:10.1111/fare.12184

Berry, D., Blair, C., Ursache, A., Willoughby, M. T., & Granger, D. A. (2014). Early childcare, executive functioning, and the moderating role of early stress physiology. *Developmental Psychology, 50*(4), 1250–1261.

Bersamin, M., Bourdeau, B., Fisher, D. A., Hill, D. L., Walker, S., Grube, J. W., & Grube, E. L. (2008). Casual partnerships: Media exposure and relationship status at last oral sex and vaginal intercourse. Paper presented at the Biennial Meeting of the Society for Research in Adolescence, Chicago, 2008.

Berthelsen, D., & Brownlee, J. (2007). Working with toddlers in child care: Practitioners' beliefs about their role. *Early Childhood Research Quarterly, 22*, 347–362.

Berzin, S. C., & De Marco, A. C. (2010). Understanding the impact of poverty on critical events in emerging adulthood. *Youth & Society, 43*(2), 278–300.

Best, J. R., & Miller, P. H. (2010). A developmental perspective on executive function. *Child Development, 81*(6), 1641–1660.

Beyers, W., & Luyckx, K. (2016). Ruminative exploration and reconsideration of commitment as risk factors for suboptimal identity development in adolescence and emerging adulthood. *Journal of Adolescence, 47*, 169–178.

Bhana, D. (2016). "Sex isn't better than love": Exploring South African Indian teenage male and female desires beyond danger. *Childhood, 23*(3), 362–377. doi:10.1177/0907568216642828

Bjork, J. M., & Pardini, D. A. (2015). Who are those "risk-taking adolescents"? Individual differences in developmental neuroimaging research. *Developmental Cognitive Neuroscience, 11* (Proceedings from the inaugural Flux Congress; towards an integrative developmental cognitive neuroscience), 56–64.

Bjorklund, D. F. (2005). *Children's thinking: Cognitive development and individual differences* (4th ed.). Belmont, CA: Wadsworth.

Bjorklund, D. F., & Bjorklund, B. R. (1992). *Looking at children: An introduction to child development.* Monterey, CA: Brooks-Cole.

Bjorklund, D. F., & Pellegrini, A. D. (2002). *The origins of human nature: Evolutionary developmental psychology.* Washington, DC: American Psychological Association.

Bjorklund, D. F., & Rosenblum, K. E. (2001). Children's use of multiple and variable addition strategies in a game context. *Developmental Science, 4*, 184–194.

Blair, C. (2017). Educating executive function. Wiley Interdisciplinary Reviews. *Cognitive Science, 8*(1–2). doi:10.1002/wcs.1403

Blakely-McClure, S., & Ostrov, J. (2016). Relational aggression, victimization and self-concept: Testing pathways from middle childhood to adolescence. *Journal of Youth & Adolescence, 45*(2), 376–390.

Blakemore, S., & Mills, K. L. (2014). Is adolescence a sensitive period for sociocultural processing? *Annual Review of Psychology, 65*, 187–207.

Blakemore, S.-J., Burnett, S., & Dahl, R. E. (2010). The role of puberty in the developing adolescent brain. *Human Brain Mapping, 31*, 926–933.

Blatney, M., Jelinek, M., & Osecka, T. (2007). Assertive toddler, self-efficacious adult: Child temperament predicts personality over forty years. *Personality and Individual Differences, 43*, 2127–2136.

Blomeyer, D., Friemel, C. M., Buchmann, A. F., Banaschewski, T., Laucht, M., & Schneider, M. (2013). Impact of pubertal stage at first drink on adult drinking behavior. *Alcoholism: Clinical and Experimental Research, 37*(10), 1804–1811.

Blum, D. (2002). *Love at Goon Park: Harry Harlow and the science of affection.* Cambridge, MA: Perseus.

Bohlin, G., Eninger, L., Brocki, K. C., & Thorell, L. B. (2012). Disorganized attachment and inhibitory capacity: Predicting externalizing problem behaviors. *Journal of Abnormal Child Psychology, 40*(3), 449–458.

Boisvert, J. A., & Harrell, W. A. (2013). The impact of spirituality on eating disorder symptomatology in ethnically diverse Canadian women. *International Journal of Social Psychiatry, 59*(8), 729–738.

Bonanno, R. A., & Hymel, S. (2013). Cyberbullying and internalizing difficulties: Above and beyond the impact of traditional forms of bullying. *Journal of Youth and Adolescence, 42*(5), 685–697.

Boonpleng, W., Park, C. G., Gallo, A. M., Corte, C., McCreary, L., & Bergren, M. D. (2013). Ecological influences of early childhood obesity: A multilevel analysis. *Western Journal of Nursing Research, 35*(6), 742–759.

Booth-LaForce, C., & Oxford, M. L. (2008). Trajectories of social withdrawal from grades 1 to 6: Prediction from early parenting, attachment, and temperament. *Developmental Psychology, 44*, 1298–1313.

Borko, H., Wolf, S. A., Simone, G., & Uchiyama, K. P. (2003). Schools in transition: Reform efforts and school capacity in Washington state. *Educational Evaluation and Policy Analysis, 25*, 171–201.

Bornstein, M. (2017). The specificity principle in Acculturation Science. *Perspectives on Psychological Science, 12*(1), 3–45.

Bourke, A., Boduszek, D., Kelleher, C., McBride, O., & Morgan, K. (2014). Sex education, first sex and sexual health outcomes in adulthood: Findings from a nationally representative sexual health survey. *Sex Education, 14*(3), 299–309.

Bowers, J. R., Segrin, C., & Joyce, N. (2016). The role of transitional instability, psychological distress, and dysfunctional drinking in emerging adults' involvement in risky sex. *Journal of Social & Personal Relationships, 33*(8), 1097–1119.

Bowlby, J. (1969). *Attachment and loss: Vol. 1. Attachment.* New York, NY: Basic Books.

Bowlby, J. (1973). *Attachment and loss: Vol. 2. Separation: Anxiety and anger.* New York, NY: Basic Books.

Bowlby, J. (1980). *Attachment and loss: Vol. 3. Loss: Sadness and depression.* New York, NY: Basic Books.

Boyle, D. E., Marshall, N. L., & Robeson, W. W. (2003). Gender at play: Fourth grade girls and boys on the playground. *American Behavioral Scientist, 46*, 1326–1345.

Bradley, R. H., & Coryn, R. (2013). From parent to child to parent . . . : Paths in and out of problem behavior. *Journal of Abnormal Child Psychology, 41*(4), 515–529.

Bradley, R. H., McRitchie, S., Houts, R. M., Nader, P., & O'Brien, M. (2011). Parenting and the decline of physical activity from age 9 to 15. *The International Journal of Behavioral Nutrition and Physical Activity, 8*, ArtID: 33.

Brame, R., Turner, M. C., Paternoster, R., & Bushway, S. (2012). Cumulative prevalence of arrest from ages 8 to 23 in a national sample. *Pediatrics, 129*(1), 21–27.

Bramen, J. E., Hranilovich, J. A., Dahl, R. E., Forbes, E. E., Chen, J., Toga, A. W., . . . Sowell, E. R. (2011). Puberty influences medial temporal lobe and cortical gray matter maturation differently in boys than girls matched for sexual maturity. *Cerebral Cortex, 21*(3), 636–646.

Brand, S., Gerber, M., Kalak, N., Kirov, R., Lemola, S., Clough, P. J., . . . Holsboer-Trachsler, E. (2014). Adolescents with greater mental toughness show higher sleep efficiency, more deep sleep and fewer awakenings after sleep onset. *Journal of Adolescent Health, 54*(1), 109–113.

Braun, S. S., & Davidson, A. J. (2016). Gender nonconformity in middle childhood: A mixed methods approach to understanding gender-typed behavior, friendship and peer preference. *Sex Roles, 44*, 1–14.

Breaux, R. P., Brown, H. R., & Harvey, E. A. (2016). Mediators and moderators of the relation between parental ADHD symptomatology and the early development of child ADHD and ODD symptoms. *Journal of Abnormal Child Psychology.* doi:10.1007/s10802-016-0213-1

Breen, A. V., Lewis, S. P., & Sutherland, O. (2013). Brief report: Non-suicidal self-injury in the context of self and identity development. *Journal of Adult Development, 20*(1), 57–62.

Bregman, H. R., Malik, N. M., Page, M. L., Makynen, E., & Lindahl, K. M. (2013). Identity profiles in lesbian, gay, and bisexual youth: The role of family influences. *Journal of Youth and Adolescence, 42*(3), 417–430.

Brenning, K., Soenens, B., & Vansteenkiste, M. (2015). What's your motivation to be pregnant? Relations between motives for parenthood and women's prenatal functioning. *Journal of Family Psychology, 29*(5), 755–765.

Bretherton, I. (2005). In pursuit of the internal working model construct and its relevance to attachment relationships. In K. E. Grossmann, K. Grossmann, & E. Waters (Eds.), *Attachment from infancy to adulthood: The major longitudinal studies* (pp. 13–47). New York, NY: Guilford Press.

Britton, M. L. (2013). Race/ethnicity, attitudes, and living with parents during young adulthood. *Journal of Marriage and Family, 75*(4), 995–1013.

Brody, N. (2006). Geocentric theory: A valid alternative to Gardner's theory of intelligence. In J. A. Schaler (Ed.), *Howard Gardner under fire: The rebel psychologist faces his critics* (pp. 73–94). Chicago, IL: Open Court Publishing Co.

Bronfenbrenner, U. (1977). Toward an experimental ecology of human development. *American Psychologist, 32*, 513–531.

Brooks-Gunn, J., Newman, D. L., Holderness, C. C., & Warren, M. P. (1994). The experience of breast development and girls' stories about the purchase of a bra. *Journal of Youth and Adolescence, 23*, 539–565.

Brooks-Gunn, J., & Ruble, D. N. (1982). The development of menstrual-related beliefs and behaviors during early adolescence. *Child Development, 53*, 1567–1577.

Brooks-Gunn, J., & Warren, M. P. (1985). The effects of delayed menarche in different contexts: Dance and nondance students. *Journal of Youth and Adolescence, 14*, 285–300.

Brooks-Gunn, J., & Warren, M. P. (1988). The psychological significance of secondary sexual characteristics in nine- to eleven-year-old girls. *Child Development, 59*, 1061–1069.

Brotman, L. M., O'Neal, C. R., Huang, K., Gouley, K. K., Rosenfelt, A., & Shrout, P. E. (2009). An experimental test of parenting practices as a mediator of early childhood physical aggression. *Journal of Child Psychology and Psychiatry, 50*(3), 235–245.

Brown, A., Rance, J., & Bennett, P. (2016). Understanding the relationship between breastfeeding and postnatal depression: The role of pain and physical difficulties. *Journal of Advanced Nursing, 72*(2), 273–282. doi:10.1111/jan.12832

Buchanan, C. (2017). What U.S. companies can learn from Germany's apprenticeship program, INC. Retrieved from www.inc.com, May 2017.

Budge, S. L., Thai, J. L., Tebbe, E. A., & Howard, K. S. (2016). The intersection of race, sexual orientation, socioeconomic status, trans identity, and mental health outcomes. *Counseling Psychologist, 47*(3), 404–433.

Bukowski, W. M. (2001). Friendship and the worlds of childhood. In D. W. Nangle & C. A. Erdley (Eds.), *New directions for child and adolescent development: No. 91. The role of friendship in psychological adjustment* (pp. 93–105). San Francisco: Jossey-Bass.

Burchinal, M., Skinner, D., & Reznick, J. S. (2010). European American and African American mothers' beliefs about parenting and disciplining infants: A mixed-method analysis. *Parenting: Science and Practice, 10*, 79–96.

Bureau, J.-F., Martin, J., Freynet, N., Poirier, A. A., Lafontaine, M.-F., & Cloutier, P. (2010). Perceived dimensions of parenting and non-suicidal self-injury in young adults. *Journal of Youth and Adolescence, 39*, 484–494.

Burkett, M. (2015). Sex(t) talk: A qualitative analysis of young adults' negotiations of the pleasures and perils of sexting. *Sexuality & Culture, 19*(4), 835–863.

Burnett, S., Thompson, S., Bird, G., & Blakemore, S. (2011). Pubertal development of the understanding of social emotions: Implications for education. *Learning and Individual Differences, 21*(6), 681–689.

Burns, R., Brusseau, T., Fu, Y., & Hannon, J. (2015). Predictors and trends of gross motor skill performance in at-risk elementary school-aged children. *Perceptual and Motor Skills, 121*(1), 284–299.

Bushnell, I. W. R. (1998). The origins of face perception. In F. Simion & G. Butterworth (Eds.), *The development of sensory, motor and cognitive capacities in early infancy: From perception to cognition* (pp. 69–86). Hove, England: Psychology Press.

Buttelmann, D., Call, J., & Tomasello, M. (2009). Do great apes use emotional expressions to infer desires? *Developmental Science, 12*(5), 688–698.

Cacioppo, J. T., Cacioppo, S., Gonzaga, G. C., Ogburn, E. L., & Vander Weele, T. J. (2013). Marital satisfaction and break-ups differ across on-line and offline meeting venues. *PNAS Proceedings of the National Academy of Sciences of the United States of America, 110*(25), 10135–10140.

Campos, J. J., Anderson, D. I., Barbu-Roth, M. A., Hubbard, E. M., Hertenstein, M. J., & Witherington, D. (2000). Travel broadens the mind. *Infancy, 1*, 149–219.

Canário, C., & Figueiredo, B. (2016). Partner relationship from early pregnancy to 30 months postpartum: Gender and parity effects. *Couple and Family Psychology: Research and Practice, 5*(4), 226–239.

Canter, A. S. (1997). The future of intelligence testing in the schools. *School Psychology Review, 26*, 255–261.

Caplan, A. L., Blank, R. H., & Merrick, J. C. (Eds.). (1992). *Compelled compassion: Government intervention in the treatment of critically ill newborns.* Totowa, NJ: Humana Press.

Caravita, S. C., & Cillessen, A. H. (2012). Agentic or communal? Associations between interpersonal goals, popularity, and bullying in middle childhood and early adolescence. *Social Development, 21*(2), 376–395. doi:10.1111/j.1467-9507.2011.00632.x

Carlson, A. G., Rowe, E., & Curby, T. W. (2013). Disentangling fine motor skills' relations to academic achievement: The relative contributions of visual-spatial integration and visual-motor coordination. *The Journal of Genetic Psychology: Research and Theory on Human Development, 174*(5), 514–533.

Carlson, S. M, Claxton, L. J., & Moses, L. J. (2016). The relation between executive function and theory of mind is more than skin deep. *Journal of Cognition and Development, 16*(1), 186–197.

Carnevale, A., & Strohl, J. (2010). How increasing college access is increasing inequality and what to do about it. In R. D. Kahlenberg (Ed.), *Rewarding strivers: Helping low-income students succeed in college.* New York, NY: The Century Foundation Press.

Caron, S. L., & Moskey, E. G. (2002). Changes over time in teenage sexual relationships: Comparing the high school class of 1950, 1975, and 2000. *Adolescence, 37*, 515–526.

Carroll, J. S., Willoughby, B., Badger, S., Nelson, L. J., Barry, C. M., & Madsen, S. D. (2007). So close, yet so far away: The impact of varying marital horizons on emerging adulthood. *Journal of Adolescent Research, 22*(3), 219–247.

Case, R. (1999). Conceptual development. In M. Bennett (Ed.), *Developmental psychology: Achievements and prospects* (pp. 36–54). New York, NY: Psychology Press.

Cashmore, J., & Parkinson, P. (2008). Children's and parents' perceptions on children's participation in decision making after parental separation and divorce. *Family Court Review, 46*(1), 91–104.

Castaneda, A. M., Wendel, M. L., & Crockett, E. E. (2015). Overlap in Facebook profiles reflects relationship closeness. *Journal of Social Psychology, 155*(4), 395–401.

Castel, A. D., Lee, S. S., Humphreys, K. L., & Moore, A. N. (2010). Memory capacity, selective control, and value-directed remembering in children with and without attention-deficit/hyperactivity disorder (ADHD). *Neuropsychology, 25*(1), 15–24.

Castellanos-Ryan, N., Parent, S., Vitaro, F., Tremblay, R. E., & Séguin, J. R. (2013). Pubertal development, personality, and substance use: A 10-year longitudinal study from childhood to adolescence. *Journal of Abnormal Psychology, 122*(3), 782–796.

Caulfield, L., Richard, S. A., Rivera, J. A., Musgrove, P., & Black, R. E. (2006). *Disease control priorities in developing countries* (2nd ed.). New York, NY: Oxford University Press.

Ceci, S. J., Rosenblum, T., de Bruyn, E., & Lee, D. Y. (1997). A bio-ecological model of intellectual development: Moving beyond h-sup-2. In R. J. Sternberg & E. L. Grigorenko (Eds.), *Intelligence, heredity, and environment* (pp. 303–322). New York, NY: Cambridge University Press.

Cenk, D. S., & Demir, A. (2016). The relationship between parenting style, gender and academic achievement with optimism among Turkish adolescents. *Current Psychology: A Journal for Diverse Perspectives on Diverse Psychological Issues, 35*(4), 720–728. doi:10.1007/s12144-015-9375-1

Centers for Disease Control and Prevention. (2010a). *What is assisted reproductive technology?* Retrieved from http://www.cdc.gov/art/

Centers for Disease Control and Prevention. (2010b). Increasing prevalence of parent-reported attention-deficit/hyperactivity disorder among children: United States, 2003–2007. *Morbidity and Mortality Weekly Report (MMWR)*, 59(44). Retrieved from http://www.ncbi.nlm.nih.gov/pubmed/21063274

Centers for Disease Control and Prevention. (2016). Fast Stats: Births—method of delivery. Retrieved from http//www.cdc.gov, November 2016.

Centers for Disease Control and Prevention. (2017). Vaccines do not cause autism. Retrieved from https://www.cdc.gov/vaccinesafety/concerns/autism.html, May 2017.

Centers for Disease Control and Prevention. (n.d.). *Attention deficit hyperactivity disorder*. In CDC Fast Stats. Retrieved from http://www.cdc.gov/nchs/fastats/adhd.htm

Centers for Disease Control and Prevention (CDC), U.S. Department of Health and Human Services. (2015). *Results from the school health policies and practices study 2014*. Retrieved from https://www.cdc.gov/healthyyouth/data/shpps/pdf/shpps-508-final_101315.pdf

Central Intelligence Agency. (2015). CIA World Factbook. Retrieved from https://www.cia.gov/library/publications/the-world-factbook/rankorder/2127rank.html, November 2016.

Central Intelligence Agency. (2017). The World Factbook, Infant mortality rate. Retrieved from https://www.cia.gov//library/publications/, April 2017.

Central Intelligence Agency. (n.d.). World Factbook, Life Expectancy at Birth, https://www.cia.gov/library/publications/the-world-factbook/rankorder/2102rank.html

Chang, H. H., Larson, J., Blencowe, H., Spong, C. Y., Howson, C. P., Cairns-Smith, S., . . . Lawn, J. E. (2013). Preventing preterm births: Analysis of trends and potential reductions with interventions in 39 countries with very high human development index. *The Lancet*, 381(9862), 223–234.

Chang, Y., & Locke, J. (2016). A systematic review of peer-mediated interventions for children with autism spectrum disorder. *Research in Autism Spectrum Disorders*, 27, 1–10. doi:10.1016/j.rasd.2016.03.010

Chen, B., & Santo, J. B. (2016). The relationships between shyness and unsociability and peer difficulties. *International Journal of Behavioral Development*, 40(4), 346–358. doi:10.1177/0165025415587726

Chen, Y., McAnally, H. M., & Reese, E. (2013). Development in the organization of episodic memories in middle childhood and adolescence. *Frontiers in Behavioral Neuroscience*, 7, 84.

Chertkow, H., Whitehead, V., Phillips, N., Wolfson, C., Atherton, J., & Bergman, H. (2010). Multilingualism (but not always bilingualism) delays the onset of Alzheimer disease: Evidence from a bilingual community. *Alzheimer Disease and Associated Disorders*, 24(2), 118–125.

Chetty, R., Friedman, J. N., & Rockoff, J. E. (2014). Measuring the impacts of teachers ii: Teacher value-added and student outcomes in adulthood. *American Economic Review*, 104(9), 2633–2679. doi:10.1257/aer.104.9.2633

Chetty, R., & Hendren, N. (2016). The impacts of neighborhoods on intergenerational mobility I: Childhood exposure effects. Working paper.

Chetty, R., & Hendren, N. (2017). The impacts of neighborhoods on intergenerational mobility ii: county-level estimates. NBER Working Papers, 1.

Chetty, R., Hendren, N., & Katz, L. (2016). The effects of exposure to better neighborhoods on children: New evidence from the moving to opportunity experiment. *American Economic Review*, 106(4), 855–902.

Cheung, C. (2016). Preventing physical child abuse by legal punishment and neighbor help. *Children and Youth Services Review*, 71, 545–557.

Cheung, P. C., Cunningham, S. A., Narayan, K. V., & Kramer, M. R. (2016). Childhood obesity incidence in the United States: A systematic review. *Childhood Obesity*, 12(1), 1–11. doi:10.1089/chi.2015.0055

Chih-Yuan, S. L., Bryan, J. D., & Lauren, A. B. (2016). Intergenerational solidarity and individual adjustment during emerging adulthood. *Journal of Family Issues*, 37(10), 1412–1432.

Child Soldiers International. (2017, April 01). Central African Republic. Retrieved from https://www.child-soldiers.org/central-african-republic

Child Trends Data Bank. (2008). Retrieved from http://www.childtrends.org/databank/

Child Trends Data Bank. (2016a). Data bank indicator, Racial and ethnic composition of the child population. Retrieved from www.Childtrends.org, March 2017.

Child Trends Data Bank. (2016b). Retrieved from www.childtrends.org, November 2016.

Cho, Y., & Haslam, N. (2010). Suicidal ideation and distress among immigrant adolescents: The role of acculturation, life stress, and social support. *Journal of Youth and Adolescence*, 39(4), 370–379.

Choi, J., Johnson, D. W., & Johnson, R. (2011). The roots of social dominance: Aggression, prosocial behavior, and social interdependence. *Journal of Educational Research*, 104(6), 442–454.

Choi, Y., Kim, Y. S., Kim, S. Y., & Park, I. K. (2013). Is Asian American parenting controlling and harsh? Empirical testing of relationships between Korean American and Western parenting measures. *Asian American Journal of Psychology*, 4(1), 19–29.

Chong, A., Biehle, S. N., Kooiman, L. Y., & Mickelson, K. D. (2016). Postnatal depression: The role of breastfeeding efficacy, breastfeeding duration, and family–work conflict. *Psychology of Women Quarterly*, 40(4), 518–531. doi:10.1177/0361684316658263

Christensen, J., Grønborg, T. K., Sørensen, M. J., Schendel, D., Parner, E. T., Pedersen, L. H., & Vestergaard, M. (2013). Prenatal valproate exposure and risk of autism spectrum disorders and childhood autism. *Journal of the American Medical Association*, 309(16), 1696–1703.

Chua, A. (2011). *Battle hymn of the tiger mother.* New York, NY: Penguin Press.

Chung, J. M., Robins, R. W., Trzesniewski, K. H., Noftle, E. E., Roberts, B. W., & Widaman, K. F. (2014). Continuity and change in self-esteem during emerging adulthood. *Journal of Personality and Social Psychology*, 106(3), 469–483.

Cicchetti, D. (2016). Socioemotional, personality, and biological development: Illustrations from a multilevel developmental psychopathology perspective on child maltreatment. *Annual Review of Psychology*, 67(1), 187–211. doi:10.1146/annurev-psych-122414-033259

Ciocanel, O., Power, K., Eriksen, A., & Gillings, K. (2017). Effectiveness of positive youth development interventions: A meta-analysis of randomized controlled trials. *Journal of Youth & Adolescence*, 46(3), 483–504. doi:10.1007/s10964-016-0555-6

Class, Q. A., Khashan, A. S., Lichtenstein, P., Långström, N., & D'Onofrio, B. M. (2013). Maternal stress and infant mortality: The importance of the preconception period. *Psychological Science*, 24(7), 1309–1316.

Clearfield, M. W., & Jedd, K. E. (2013). The effects of socio-economic status on infant attention. *Infant and Child Development, 22*(1), 53–67.

Coccia, C., & Darling, C. A. (2016). Having the time of their life: College student stress, dating and satisfaction with life. *Stress & Health: Journal of the International Society for the Investigation of Stress, 32*(1), 28–35.

Cohen, O., Leichtentritt, R. D., & Volpin, N. (2014). Divorced mothers' self-perception of their divorce-related communication with their children. *Child & Family Social Work, 19*(1), 34–43.

Coie, J. D., & Dodge, K. A. (1998). Aggression and antisocial behavior. In W. Damon (Series Ed.) & N. Eisenberg (Vol. Ed.), *Handbook of child psychology: Vol. 3. Social, emotional, and personality development* (5th ed., pp. 779–862). Hoboken, NJ: Wiley.

Colasante, T., Zuffianó, A., & Malti, T. (2016). Daily deviations in anger, guilt, and sympathy: A developmental diary study of aggression. *Journal of Abnormal Child Psychology, 44*(8), 1515–1526. doi:10.1007/s10802-016-0143-y

Coley, R. L., Votruba-Drzal, E., Miller, P. L., & Koury, A. (2013). Timing, extent, and type of child care and children's behavioral functioning in kindergarten. *Developmental Psychology, 49*(10), 1859–1873.

Collignon, O., Vandewalle, G., Voss, P., Albouy, G., Charbonneau, G., Lassonde, M., & Lepore, F. (2011). Functional specialization for auditory-spatial processing in the occipital cortex of congenitally blind humans. *Proceedings of the National Academy of Sciences of the United States of America, 108*(11), 4435–4440.

Collins, R. L. (2011). Content analysis of gender roles in media: Where are we now and where should we go? *Sex Roles, 64,* 290–298.

Collins, R. L., Elliott, M. N., Berry, S. H., Kanouse, D. E., Kunkel, D., Hunter, S. B., & Miu, A. (2004). Watching sex on television predicts adolescent initiation of sexual behavior. *Pediatrics, 114,* e280–e289.

Colrain, I. M., & Baker, F. C. (2011). Changes in sleep as a function of adolescent development. *Neuropsychology Review, 21,* 5–21.

Compian, L., Gowen, L. K., & Hayward, C. (2004). Peripubertal girls' romantic and platonic involvement with boys: Associations with body image and depression symptoms. *Journal of Research on Adolescence, 14,* 23–47.

Conroy-Beam, D., & Buss, D. M. (2016). How are mate preferences linked with actual mate selection? Tests of mate preference integration algorithms using computer simulations and actual mating couples. *Plos ONE, 6.*

Cook, C. R., Williams, K. R., Guerra, N. G., Kim, T. E., & Sadek, S. (2010). Predictors of bullying and victimization in childhood and adolescence: A meta-analytic investigation. *School Psychology Quarterly, 25*(2), 65–83.

Cook, T. D., Deng, Y., & Morgano, E. (2007). Friendship influences during early adolescence: The special role of friends' grade point average. *Journal of Research on Adolescence, 17*(2), 325–356.

Cooley, J. L., & Fite, P. J. (2016). Peer victimization and forms of aggression during middle childhood: The role of emotion regulation. *Journal of Abnormal Child Psychology, 44*(3), 535–546. doi:10.1007/s10802-015-0051-6

Cormier, D. C., Kennedy, K. E., & Aquilina, A. M. (2016). Test review: "Wechsler Intelligence Scale for Children, Fifth Edition: Canadian 322 (WISC-V^{CDN}) by D. Wechsler." *Canadian Journal of School Psychology, 31*(4), 322–334.

Corsaro, W. A. (1985). *Friendship and peer culture in the early years.* Norwood, NJ: Ablex.

Corsaro, W. A. (1997). *The sociology of childhood.* Thousand Oaks, CA: Pine Forge Press/Sage.

Costos, D., Ackerman, R., & Paradis, L. (2002). Recollections of menarche: Communication between mothers and daughters regarding menstruation. *Sex Roles, 46,* 49–59.

Côté, J., & Bynner, J. M. (2008). Changes in the transition to adulthood in the UK and Canada: The role of structure and agency in emerging adulthood. *Journal of Youth Studies, 11,* 251–268.

Cotterell, J. (1996). *Social networks and social influences in adolescence.* New York, NY: Routledge.

Cowan, N. (2016). Exploring the possible and necessary in working memory development. *Monographs of the Society for Research in Child Development, 81*(3), 149–158. doi:10.1111/mono.12257

Cowan, P. A., Cowan, C. P., & Mehta, N. (2009). Adult attachment, couple attachment, and children's adaptation to school: An integrated attachment template and family risk model. *Attachment & Human Development, 11*(1), 29–46.

Cozzarelli, C., Karafa, J. A., Collins, N. L., & Tagler, M. J. (2003). Stability and change in adult attachment styles: Associations with personal vulnerabilities, life events, and global construals of self and others. *Journal of Social & Clinical Psychology, 22,* 315–346.

Crade, M., & Lovett, S. (1988). Fetal response to sound stimulation: Preliminary report exploring use of sound stimulation in routine obstetrical ultrasound examinations. *Journal of Ultrasound in Medicine, 7,* 499–503.

Cramer, P. (2008). Identification and the development of competence: A 44-year longitudinal study from late adolescence to late middle age. *Psychology and Aging, 23,* 410–421.

Crawford, A. M., & Manassis, K. (2011). Anxiety, social skills, friendship quality, and peer victimization: An integrated model. *Journal of Anxiety Disorders, 25*(7), 924–937.

Crick, N. R., & Dodge, K. A. (1996). Social information-processing mechanisms on reactive and proactive aggression. *Child Development, 67,* 993–1002.

Crocetti, E., & Meeus, W. (2014). "Family comes first!" Relationships with family and friends in Italian emerging adults. *Journal of Adolescence, 371,* 463–1473.

Crocetti, E., & Tagliabue, S. (2016). Are being responsible, having a stable job, and caring for the family important for adulthood? Examining the importance of different criteria for adulthood in Italian emerging adults. In R. Žukauskienė (Ed.), *Emerging adulthood in a European context* (pp. 33–53). New York, NY: Routledge/Taylor & Francis Group.

Csikszentmihalyi, M. (1990). *Flow: The psychology of optimal experience.* New York, NY: Harper & Row.

Csikszentmihalyi, M., & Larson, R. (1984). *Being adolescent: Conflict and growth in the teenage years.* New York, NY: Basic Books.

Csikszentmihalyi, M., & Schneider, B. L. (2000). *Becoming adult: How teenagers prepare for the world of work.* New York, NY: Basic Books.

Culbert, K. M., Breedlove, S. M., Sisk, C. L., Burt, S. A., & Klump, K. L. (2013). The emergence of sex differences in risk for disordered eating attitudes during puberty: A role for prenatal testosterone exposure. *Journal of Abnormal Psychology, 122*(2), 420–432.

CysticFibrosis.com. (n.d.). Retrieved from http://www.cysticfibrosis.com/home/

Daddis, C. (2011). Desire for increased autonomy and adolescents' perceptions of peer autonomy: "Everyone else can; why can't I?" *Child Development, 82*(4), 1310–1326.

Dahl, R. E. (2004). Adolescent brain development: A period of vulnerabilities and opportunities. In R. E. Dahl & L. P. Spear (Eds.), *Adolescent brain development: Vulnerabilities and opportunities, Volume 1021* (pp. 1–22). New York, NY: Academy of Sciences.

Daly, B. P., Hildenbrand, A. K., Haney-Caron, E., Goldstein, N. S., Galloway, M., & DeMatteo, D. (2016). Disrupting the school-to-prison pipeline: Strategies to reduce the risk of school-based zero tolerance policies resulting in juvenile justice involvement. In K. Heilbrun, D. DeMatteo, & N. S. Goldstein (Eds.), *APA handbook of psychology and juvenile justice* (pp. 257–275). Washington, DC: American Psychological Association. doi:10.1037/14643-012

Damaraju, E., Caprihan, A., Lowe, J. R., Allen, E. A., Calhoun, V. D., & Phillips, J. P. (2014). Functional connectivity in the developing brain: A longitudinal study from 4 to 9 months of age. *Neuro-Image, 84*, 169–180.

Danese, A., & Baldwin, J. R. (2017). Hidden wounds? Inflammatory links between childhood trauma and psychopathology. *Annual Review of Psychology, 68*(1), 517–544. doi:10.1146/annurev-psych-010416-044208

Danziger, S., & Ratner, D. (2010). Labor market outcomes and the transition to adulthood. *The Future of Children, 20*, 1–24. Retrieved from http://www.futureofchildren.org/publications/journals/article/index.xml?journalid=72&articleid=524

Darwiche, J., Favez, N., Maillard, F., Germond, M., Guex, P., Despland, J., & deRoten, Y. (2013). Couples' resolution of an infertility diagnosis before undergoing in vitro fertilization. *Swiss Journal of Psychology, 72*(2), 91–102.

Dasen, P. R. (1977). *Piagetian psychology: Cross-cultural contributions.* New York, NY: Gardner Press.

Dasen, P. R. (1984). The cross-cultural study of intelligence: Piaget and the Baoule. *International Journal of Psychology, 19*, 407–434.

Davila, J., & Kashy, D. A. (2009). Secure base processes in couples: Daily associations between support experiences and attachment security. *Journal of Family Psychology, 23*, 76–88.

De Goede, I. H. D., Branje, S. J. T., & Meeus, W. H. J. (2009). Developmental changes in adolescents' perceptions of relationships with their parents. *Journal of Youth and Adolescence, 38*, 75–88.

de Onis, M., Blössner, M., & Borghi, E. (2012). Prevalence and trends of stunting among preschool children, 1990–2020. *Public Health Nutrition, 15*, 142–148.

De Ridder, S., & Van Bauwel, S. (2013). Commenting on pictures: Teens negotiating gender and sexualities on social networking sites. *Sexualities, 16*(5–6), 565–586.

De Schipper, E. J., Riksen-Walraven, J. M., & Geurts, S. A. E. (2006). Effects of child–caregiver ratio on the interactions between caregivers and children in child-care centers: An experimental study. *Child Development, 77*(4), 861–874.

De Schipper, J. C., Tavecchio, L. W. C., & van IJzendoorn, M. H. (2008). Children's attachment relationships with day care caregivers: Associations with positive caregiving and the child's temperament. *Social Development, 17*(3), 454–470.

Dean, D. C., O'Muircheartaigh, J., Dirks, H., Waskiewicz, N., Walker, L., Doernberg, E., ... Deoni, S. L. (2014). Characterizing longitudinal white matter development during early childhood. *Brain Structure & Function, 220*(4), 1921–1933.

Dean, R. S., & Davis, A. S. (2007). Relative risk of perinatal complications in common childhood disorders. *School Psychology Quarterly, 22*(1), 13–23.

Deardorff, J., Cham, H., Gonzales, N. A., White, R. B., Tein, J., Wong, J. J., & Roosa, M. W. (2013). Pubertal timing and Mexican-origin girls' internalizing and externalizing symptoms: The influence of harsh parenting. *Developmental Psychology, 49*(9), 1790–1804.

Deary, I. J., Whalley, L. J., Lemmon, H., Crawford, J. R., & Starr, J. M. (2000). The stability of individual differences in mental ability from childhood to old age: Follow-up of the 1932 Scottish Mental Survey. *Intelligence, 28*, 49–55.

Deater-Deckard, K., Beekman, C., Wang, Z., Kim, J., Petrill, S., Thompson, L., & DeThorne, L. (2010). Approach/positive anticipation, frustration/anger, and overt aggression in childhood. *Journal of Personality, 78*(3), 991–1010.

DeCasper, A. J., & Fifer, W. P. (1980, June 6). Of human bonding: Newborns prefer their mothers' voices. *Science, 208*, 1174–1176.

Deci, E. L., & Ryan, R. M. (1985). The general causality orientations scale: Self-determination in personality. *Journal of Research in Personality, 19*, 109–134.

Deci, E. L., & Ryan, R. M. (2000). The "what" and "why" of goal pursuits: Human needs and the self-determination of behavior. *Psychological Inquiry, 11*, 227–268.

DeGarmo, D. S. (2010). Coercive and prosocial fathering, antisocial personality, and growth in children's post-divorce noncompliance. *Child Development, 81*(2), 503–516.

Degnan, K. A., Almas, A. N., & Fox, N. A. (2010). Temperament and the environment in the etiology of childhood anxiety. *Journal of Child Psychology and Psychiatry, 51*(4), 497–517.

Del Giudice, M. (2011). Alone in the dark? Modeling the conditions for visual experience in human fetuses. *Developmental Psychobiology, 53*(2), 214–219.

Delevi, R., & Weisskirch, R. S. (2013). Personality factors as predictors of sexting. *Computers in Human Behavior, 29*(6), 2589–2594.

Deligiannidis, K. M., Byatt, N., & Freeman, M. P. (2014). Pharmacotherapy for mood disorders in pregnancy: A review of pharmacokinetic changes and clinical recommendations for therapeutic drug monitoring. *Journal of Clinical Psychopharmacology, 34*(2), 244–255. doi:10.1097/JCP.0000000000000087

DeMatteo, D., Wolbransky, M., & LaDuke, C. (2016). Risk assessment with juveniles. In K. Heilbrun, D. DeMatteo, & N. S. Goldstein (Eds.), *APA handbook of psychology and juvenile justice* (pp. 365–384). Washington, DC: American Psychological Association.

Denham, S. A. (1998). *Emotional development in young children.* New York, NY: Guilford Press.

Denham, S. A., Blair, K. A., DeMulder, E., Levitas, J., Sawyer, K., Auerbach-Major, S., & Queenan, P. (2003). Preschool emotional competence: Pathway to social competence. *Child Development, 74*, 238–256.

Deniz Can, D., Richards, T., & Kuhl, P. K. (2013). Early gray-matter and white-matter concentration in infancy predict later language skills: A whole brain vowel-based morphometry study. *Brain and Language, 124*(1), 34–44.

Dennis, C., Gagnon, A., Van Hulst, A., Dougherty, G., & Wahoush, O. (2013). Prediction of duration of breastfeeding among migrant and Canadian-born women: Results from a multi-center study. *Journal of Pediatrics, 162*(1), 72–79.

Dennison, M. J., Sheridan, M. A., Busso, D. S., Jenness, J. L., Peverill, M., Rosen, M. L., & McLaughlin, K. A. (2016). Neurobehavioral markers of resilience to depression amongst adolescents exposed to child abuse. *Journal of Abnormal Psychology, 125*(8), 1201–1212. doi:10.1037/abn0000215

Dennissen, J. J. A., Asendorpf, J. B., & van Aken, M. A. G. (2008). Childhood personality predicts long-term trajectories of shyness and aggressiveness in the context of demographic transitions in emerging adulthood. *Journal of Personality, 76*(1), 67–99.

Deoni, S. L., Dean, D. I., Piryatinsky, I., O'Muircheartaigh, J., Waskiewicz, N., Lehman, K., . . . Dirks, H. (2013). Breastfeeding and early white matter development: A cross-sectional study. *Neuro Image, 82*, 77–86.

Dequinzio, J. A., Poulson, C. L., Townsend, D. B., & Taylor, B. A. (2016). Social referencing and children with autism. *The Behavior Analyst, 39*(2), 319–331. doi:10.1007/s40614-015-0046-1

Diamanti, A., Basso, M. S., Castro, M., Bianco, G., Ciacco, E., Calce, A., . . . Gambarara, M. (2008). Clinical efficacy and safety of parental nutrition in adolescent girls with anorexia nervosa. *Journal of Adolescent Health, 42*, 111–118.

Diamond, A. (2009). The interplay of biology and the environment broadly defined. *Developmental Psychology, 45*, 1–8.

Díaz-Morales, J. F., Escribano, C., Jankowski, K. S., Vollmer, C., & Randler, C. (2014). Evening adolescents: The role of family relationships and pubertal development. *Journal of Adolescence, 37*(4), 425–432.

Dietz, P. M., Homa, D., England, L. J., Burley, K., Tong, V. T., Dube, S. R., & Bernert, J. T. (2011). Estimates of nondisclosure of cigarette smoking among pregnant and nonpregnant women of reproductive age in the United States. *American Journal of Epidemiology, 173*(3), 355–359.

Dimidjian, S., Goodman, S. H., Felder, J. N., Gallop, R., Brown, A. P., & Beck, A. (2016). Staying well during pregnancy and the postpartum: A pilot randomized trial of mindfulness-based cognitive therapy for the prevention of depressive relapse/recurrence. *Journal of Consulting and Clinical Psychology, 84*(2), 134–145. doi:10-1037/ccp0000068

Dishion, T. J., McCord, J., & Poulin, F. (1999). When interventions harm: Peer groups and problem behavior. *American Psychologist, 54*, 755–764.

Dishion, T. J., & Tipsord, J. M. (2011). Peer contagion in child and adolescent social and emotional development. *Annual Review of Psychology, 62*, 189–214.

Doane, L. D., & Thurston, E. C. (2014). Associations among sleep, daily experiences, and loneliness in adolescence: Evidence of moderating and bidirectional pathways. *Journal of Adolescence, 37*(2), 145–154.

Dodge, K. A., Coie, J. D., & Lynam, D. (2006). Aggression and antisocial behavior in youth. In N. Eisenberg, W. Damon, & R. M. Lerner (Eds.), *Handbook of child psychology: Vol. 3. Social, emotional, and personality development* (6th ed., pp. 719–788). Hoboken, NJ: Wiley.

Donnellan, M. B., Conger, R. D., & Burzette, R. G. (2007). Personality development from late adolescence to young adulthood: Differential stability, normative maturity, and evidence for the maturity-stability hypothesis. *Journal of Personality, 75*(2), 237–263.

Doucet, S., Soussignan, R., Sagot, P., & Schaal, B. (2007). The "smellscape" of mother's breast: Effects of odor masking and selective unmasking on neonatal arousal, oral and visual responses. *Developmental Psychobiology, 49*, 129–138.

Douglas, P. S., & Hill, P. S. (2013). Behavioral sleep interventions in the first six months of life do not improve outcomes for mothers or infants: A systematic review. *Journal of Developmental and Behavioral Pediatrics, 34*(7), 497–507.

Douglas, V., & Varnado-Sullivan, P. (2016). Weight stigmatization, internalization, and eating disorder symptoms: The role of emotion dysregulation. *Stigma and Health, 1*(3), 166–175. doi:10.1037/sah0000029

Douglass, S., Mirpuri, S., & Yip, T. (2017). Considering friends within the context of peers in school for the development of ethnic/racial identity. *Journal of Youth and Adolescence, 46*(2), 300–316.

Douglass, S., Wang, Y., & Yip, T. (2016). The everyday implications of ethnic-racial identity processes: Exploring variability in ethnic-racial identity salience across situations. *Journal of Youth & Adolescence, 45*(7), 1396–1414.

Drouin, M., & Tobin, E. (2014). Unwanted but consensual sexting among young adults: Relations with attachment and sexual motivations. *Computers in Human Behavior, 31*, 412–418.

Drouin, M., Miller, D. A., & Dibble, J. L. (2014). Ignore your partners' current Facebook friends; beware the ones they add! *Computers in Human Behavior, 35*, 483–488.

Duell, N., Chein, J., Bacchini, D., Chaudhary, N., Dodge, K. A., Lansford, J. E., . . . Peña Alampay, L. (2016). Interaction of reward seeking and self-regulation in the prediction of risk taking: A cross-national test of the dual systems model. *Developmental Psychology, 52*(10), 1593–1605.

Duffy, A. L., Penn, S., Nesdale, D., & Zimmer-Gembeck, M. J. (2016). Popularity: Does it magnify associations between popularity prioritization and the bullying and defending behavior of early adolescent boys and girls? *Social Development, 26*(2), 263–277. doi:10.1111/sode.12206

Duffy, D., & Reynolds, P. (2011). Babies born at the threshold of viability: Attitudes of paediatric consultants and trainees in South East England. *Acta Paediatrica, 100*, 42–46.

Duh, S., Paik, J. H., Miller, P. H., Glick, S. C., Li, H., & Himmelfarb, I. (2016). Theory of mind and executive function in Chinese children. *Developmental Psychology, 52*(4), 582–591.

Duncan, G. J., Magnuson, K., & Votruba-Drzal, E. (2017). Moving beyond correlations in assessing the consequences of poverty. *Annual Review of Psychology, 68*(1), 413–434. doi:10.1146/annurev-psych-010416-044224

Dunfield, K. A., & Kuhlmeier, V. A. (2013). Evidence for partner choice in toddlers: Considering the breadth of other oriented behaviors. *Behavioral and Brain Sciences, 36*(1), 88–89.

Dunn, J., & Hughes, C. (2001). "I got some swords and you're dead!" Violent fantasy, antisocial behavior, friendship, and moral sensibility in young children. *Child Development, 72*, 491–505.

Dunn, J., Wooding, C., & Hermann, J. (1977). Mothers' speech to young children: Variation in context. *Developmental Medicine & Child Neurology, 19*, 629–638.

Dunphy, D. C. (1963). The social structure of urban adolescent peer groups. *Sociometry, 26*, 230–246.

Duvander, A. (2014). How long should parental leave be? Attitudes to gender equality, family, and work as determinants of women's and men's parental leave in Sweden. *Journal of Family Issues, 35*(7), 909–926.

Dwairy, M. (2010). Parental inconsistency: A third cross-cultural research on parenting and psychological adjustment of children. *Journal of Child and Family Studies, 19*, 23–29.

Dweck, C. S. (1986). Motivational processes affecting learning. *American Psychologist, 41*, 1040–1048.

Eccles, J. S., & Roeser, R. W. (2003). Schools as developmental contexts. In G. R. Adams & M. D. Berzonsky (Eds.), *Blackwell handbook of adolescence* (pp. 129–148). Malden, MA: Blackwell.

Economic Policy Institute. (2011). State of Working America, Washington, D.C.: Author.

Edwards, R. C., & Hans, S. L. (2016). Prenatal depressive symptoms and toddler behavior problems: The role of maternal sensitivity and child sex. *Child Psychiatry and Human Development, 47*(5), 696–707.

Egeli, N., & Rinaldi, C. (2016). Facets of adult social competence as predictors of parenting style. *Journal of Child & Family Studies, 25*(11), 3430–3439. doi:10.1007/s10826-016-0484-8

Eisenberg, N. (1992). *The caring child*. Cambridge, MA: Harvard University Press.

Eisenberg, N. (2003). Prosocial behavior, empathy, and sympathy. In M. H. Bornstein, L. Davidson, C. L. M. Keyes, & K. A. Moore (Eds.), *Well-being: Positive development across the life course* (pp. 253–265). Mahwah, NJ: Erlbaum.

Eisenberg, N., & Fabes, R. A. (1998). Prosocial development. In W. Damon (Series Ed.) & N. Eisenberg (Vol. Ed.), *Handbook of child psychology: Vol 3. Social, emotional, and personality development* (5th ed., pp. 701–778). Hoboken, NJ: Wiley.

Eisenberg, N., Hofer, C., Sulik, M. J., & Liew, J. (2014). The development of prosocial moral reasoning and a prosocial orientation in young adulthood: Concurrent and longitudinal correlates. *Developmental Psychology, 50*(1), 58–70.

Eisner, E. W. (2004). Multiple intelligences: Its tensions and possibilities. *Teachers College Record, 106*, 31–39.

Elkind, D. (1968). Cognitive development in adolescence. In J. F. Adams (Ed.), *Understanding adolescence* (pp. 128–158). Boston: Allyn and Bacon.

Elkind, D. (1978). Understanding the young adolescent. *Adolescence, 13*, 127–134.

Elliot, S. (2012). *Not my kid: What parents believe about the sex lives of their teenagers*. New York, NY: University Press.

Ellis, B. J. (2004). Timing of pubertal maturation in girls: An integrated life history approach. *Psychological Bulletin, 130*, 920–958.

Ellis, B. J., Boyce, W. T., Belsky, J., Bakermans-Kranenburg, M. J., & van IJzendoorn, M. H. (2011a). Differential susceptibility to the environment: An evolutionary-neurodevelopmental theory. *Development and Psychopathology, 23*(1), 7–28.

Ellis, B. J., Shirtcliff, E. A., Boyce, W., Deardorff, J., & Essex, M. J. (2011b). Quality of early family relationships and the timing and tempo of puberty: Effects depend on biological sensitivity to context. *Development and Psychopathology, 23*(1), 85–99.

Emery, L. F., Muise, A., Alpert, E., & Le, B. (2015). Do we look happy? Perceptions of romantic relationship quality on Facebook. *Personal Relationships, 22*(1), 1–7.

Engle, S. (n.d.). Degree attainment rates at colleges and universities: College completion declining, taking longer, UCLA study shows. *Higher Education Research Institute*. Retrieved from http://www.gseis.ucla.edu/heri/darcu_pr.html

Englund, M. M., Egeland, B., Olivia, E. M., & Collins, W. A. (2008). Childhood and adolescent predictors of heavy drinking and alcohol use disorders in early adulthood: A longitudinal development analysis. *Addiction, 103* (Suppl. 1), 23–35.

Epstein, R. (2010). *Teen 2.0: Saving our children and families from the torment of adolescence*. New York, NY: Linton.

Erikson, E. H. (1963). *Childhood and society* (2nd ed.). New York, NY: Norton.

Erikson, E. H. (1968). *Identity: Youth and crisis*. New York, NY: Norton.

Erikson, E. H. (1980). *Identity and the life cycle*. New York, NY: Norton.

Erulkar, A. (2013). Adolescence lost: The realities of child marriage. *Journal of Adolescent Health, 52*(5), 513–514.

Espelage, D. L., & De La Rue, L. (2013). School bullying: Its nature and ecology. In J. C. Srabstein & J. Merrick (Eds.), *Bullying: A public health concern* (pp. 23–37). Hauppauge, NY: Nova Science.

Espeset, E. M. S., Nordbø, R. H. S., Gulliksen, K. S., Skårderud, F., Geller, J., & Holte, A. (2011). The concept of body image disturbance in anorexia nervosa: An empirical inquiry utilizing patients' subjective experiences. *Eating Disorders, 19*(2), 175–193.

Ettekal, I., & Ladd, G. W. (2015). Developmental pathways from childhood aggression-disruptiveness, chronic peer rejection, and deviant friendships to early-adolescent rule breaking. *Child Development, 86*(2), 614–631. doi:10.1111/cdev.12321

Evans, A. D., Xu, F., & Lee, K. (2011). When all signs point to you: Lies told in the face of evidence. *Developmental Psychology, 47*(1), 39–49.

Evans, G. W., & Kim, P. (2013). Childhood poverty, chronic stress, self-regulation, and coping. *Child Development Perspectives, 7*(1), 43–48.

Fabes, R. A., Martin, C. L., & Hanish, L. D. (2003). Young children's play qualities in same-, other-, and mixed-sex peer groups. *Child Development, 74*, 921–932.

Fabian, J. (2011). Applying Roper v. Simmons in juvenile transfer and waiver proceedings: A legal and neuroscientific inquiry. *International Journal of Offender Therapy and Comparative Criminology, 55*(5), 732–755.

Faguy, K. (2016). Obesity in children and adolescents: Health effects and imaging implications. *Radiologic Technology, 87*(3), 279–302.

Fairchild, H., & Cooper, M. (2010). A multidimensional measure of core beliefs relevant to eating disorders: Preliminary development and validation. *Eating Behaviors, 11*, 239–246.

Farmer, T. W., Hamm, J. V., Leung, M., Lambert, K., & Gravelle, M. (2011). Early adolescent peer ecologies in rural communities: Bullying in schools that do and do not have a transition during the middle grades. *Journal of Youth and Adolescence, 40*(9), 1106–1117.

Farroni, T., Massaccesi, S., & Simion, F. (2002). La direzione dello sguardo di un'altra persona puo dirigere l'attenzione del neonato? [Can the direction of the gaze of another person shift the attention of a neonate?] *Giornale Italiano di Psicologia, 29*, 857–864.

Feeney, J. A. (1999). Adult romantic attachment and couple relationships. In J. Cassidy & P. R. Shaver (Eds.), *Handbook of attachment: Theory, research, and clinical applications* (pp. 355–377). New York, NY: Guilford Press.

Feinberg, I., & Campbell, I. G. (2010). Sleep EEG changes during adolescence: An index of a fundamental brain reorganization. *Brain and Cognition, 72*, 56–65.

Feixa, C. (2011). Past and present of adolescence in society: The "teen brain" debate in perspective. *Neuroscience and Biobehavioral Reviews, 35*(8), 1634–1643.

Feldman, R., & Eidelman, A. I. (2003). Skin-to-skin contact (kangaroo care) accelerates autonomic and neurobehavioural maturation in preterm infants. *Developmental Medicine & Child Neurology, 45*, 274–281.

Ferber, R. (1985). Sleep, sleeplessness, and sleep disruptions in infants and young children. *Annals of Clinical Research, 17*(5). Special issue: Sleep research and its clinical implications, 227–234.

Ferland, P., & Caron, S. L. (2013). Exploring the long-term impact of female infertility: A qualitative analysis of interviews with postmenopausal women who remained childless. *The Family Journal, 21*(2), 180–188.

Fernandez, M., Blass, E. M., Hernandez-Reif, M., Field, T., Diego, M., & Sanders, C. (2003). Sucrose attenuates a negative electroencephalographic response to an aversive stimulus for newborns. *Journal of Developmental & Behavioral Pediatrics, 24*, 261–266.

Field, T., Diego, M., & Hernandez-Reif, M. (2007). Massage therapy research. *Developmental Review, 27*, 75–89.

Field, T., Diego, M., & Hernandez-Reif, M. (2011). Potential underlying mechanisms for greater weight gain in massaged preterm infants. *Infant Behavior and Development, 34*(3), 383–389.

Figueiredo, B., Dias, C. C., Pinto, T. M., & Field, T. (2016). Infant sleep–wake behaviors at two weeks, three and six months. *Infant Behavior and Development, 44*, 169–178. doi:10.1016/j.infbeh.2016.06.011

Finegood, E. D., Wyman, C., O'Connor, T. G., & Blair, C. B. (2017). Salivary cortisol and cognitive development in infants from low-income communities. *Stress: The International Journal on the Biology of Stress, 20*(1), 112–121. doi: 10.1080/10253890.2017.1286325

Finer, L. B., & Philbin, J. M. (2014). Trends in ages at key reproductive transitions in the United States, 1951–2010. *Women's Health Issues 24*(3), 1–9.

Fink, E., Begeer, S., Peterson, C. C., Slaughter, V., & Rosnay, M. D. (2015). Friendlessness and theory of mind: A prospective longitudinal study. *British Journal of Developmental Psychology, 33*(1), 1–17. doi:10.1111/bjdp.12060

Finkel, D., & Pedersen, N. L. (2004). Processing speed and longitudinal trajectories of change for cognitive abilities: The Swedish Adoption/Twin Study of Aging. *Aging, Neuropsychology, and Cognition, 11*, 325–345.

Fischbach, R. L., Harris, M. J., Ballan, M. S., Fischbach, G. D., & Link, B. G. (2016). Is there concordance in attitudes and beliefs between parents and scientists about autism spectrum disorder? *Autism, 20*(3), 353–363. doi:10.1177/1362361315585310

Fitzpatrick, M. J., & McPherson, B. J. (2010). Coloring within the lines: Gender stereotypes in contemporary coloring books. *Sex Roles, 62*, 127–137.

Fivush, R. (2011). The development of autobiographical memory. *Annual Review of Psychology, 62*, 559–582.

Flanagan, C. A., & Stout, M. (2010). Developmental patterns of social trust between early and late adolescence: Age and school climate effects. *Journal of Research on Adolescence, 20*(3), 748–773.

Flanders, J., Herman, L., Kahalisa, N., & Paquette, D. (2013). Rough-and-tumble play and the cooperation–competition dilemma. In D. Navaez, J. Panksepp, A. Schore, & T. Gleason (Eds.), *Evolution, early experience and human development: From research to practice* (pp. 371–387). New York: Oxford University Press.

Flavell, J. H. (1963). *The developmental psychology of Jean Piaget*. New York, NY: Van Nostrand.

Flavell, J. H., Beach, D. R., & Chinsky, J. M. (1966). Spontaneous verbal rehearsal in a memory task as a function of age. *Child Development, 37*, 283–299.

Flower, K. B., Willoughby, M., Cadigan, R. J., Perrin, E. M., & Randolph, G. (2008). Understanding breastfeeding initiation and continuation in rural communities: A combined qualitative/quantitative approach. *Maternal and Child Health Journal, 12*(3), 402–414.

Flynn, J. R. (2007). *What is intelligence? Beyond the Flynn effect*. New York, NY: Cambridge University Press.

Fonseca, A., Nazaré, B., & Canavarro, M. C. (2014). Parenting an infant with a congenital anomaly: An exploratory study on patterns of adjustment from diagnosis to six months post birth. *Journal of Child Health Care, 18*(2), 111–122.

Forbush, K. T., & Hunt, T. K. (2014). Characterization of eating patterns among individuals with eating disorders: What is the state of the plate? *Physiology & Behavior, 134*, 92–109.

Ford, D. H., & Lerner, R. M. (1992). *Developmental systems theory: An integrative approach*. Newbury Park, CA: Sage.

Forster, S., Robertson, D. J., Jennings, A., Asherson, P., & Lavie, N. (2014). Plugging the attention deficit: Perceptual load counters increased distraction in ADHD. *Neuropsychology, 28*(1), 91–97.

Foster, R. E., Stone, F. P., Linkh, D. J., Besetsny, L. K., Collins, P. S., Saha, T., . . . Milner, J. S. (2010). Substantiation of spouse and child maltreatment reports as a function of referral source and maltreatment type. *Military Medicine, 175*(8), 560–566.

Fothergill, A. (2013). Managing childcare: The experiences of mothers and childcare workers. *Sociological Inquiry, 83*(3), 421–447.

Fox, J., Osborn, J. L., & Warber, K. M. (2014). Relational dialectics and social networking sites: The role of Facebook in romantic relationship escalation, maintenance, conflict, and dissolution. *Computers in Human Behavior, 35*, 527–534.

Fox, S. E., Levitt, P., & Nelson, C. A. (2010). How the timing and quality of early experiences influence the development of brain architecture. *Child Development, 81*(1), 28–40.

Francis, D. A., & DePalma, R. (2014). Teacher perspectives on abstinence and safe sex education in South Africa. *Sex Education, 14*(1), 81–94.

Frans, E. M., Sandin, S., Reichenberg, A., Långström, N., Lichtenstein, P., McGrath, J. J., & Hultman, C. M. (2013). Autism risk across generations: A population-based study of advancing grandpaternal and paternal age. *JAMA Psychiatry, 70*(5), 516–521.

Frey, K. S., & Ruble, D. N. (1985). What children say when the teacher is not around: Conflicting goals in social comparison and performance assessment in the classroom. *Journal of Personality and Social Psychology, 48*, 550–562.

Frey, K. S., & Ruble, D. N. (1990). Strategies for comparative evaluation: Maintaining a sense of competence across the life span. In R. J. Sternberg & J. Kolligian, Jr. (Eds.), *Competence considered* (pp. 167–189). New Haven, CT: Yale University Press.

Frisén, A., & Holmqvist, K. (2010). What characterizes early adolescents with a positive body image? A qualitative investigation of Swedish girls and boys. *Body Image, 7*, 205–212.

Frye, A. A., & Liem, J. H. (2011). Diverse patterns in the development of depressive symptoms among emerging adults. *Journal of Adolescent Research, 26*(5), 570–590.

Fu, R., Chen, X., Wang, L., & Yang, F. (2016). Developmental trajectories of academic achievement in Chinese children: Contributions of early social-behavioral functioning. *Journal of Educational Psychology, 108*(7), 1001–1012. doi:10.1037/edu0000100

Furler, K., Gomez, V., & Grob, A. (2013). Personality similarity and life satisfaction in couples. *Journal of Research in Personality, 47*(4), 369–375.

Furler, K., Gomez, V., & Grob, A. (2014). Personality perceptions and relationship satisfaction in couples. *Journal of Research in Personality, 50,* 33–41.

Furstenberg, F. F. Jr. (2010). On a new schedule: Transitions to adulthood and family change. *The Future of Children, 20,* 67–87. Retrieved from http://www.futureofchildren/futureofchildren/publications/docs/20_01_04.pdf

Furstenberg, F. F. Jr. (2015). Becoming adults: Challenges in the transition to adult roles. *American Journal of Orthopsychiatry, Special Issue: Generations in Conflict: Responding to Sociocultural and Socioeconomic Trends, 85*(5), S14–S21.

Futch Ehrlich, V. A., Deutsch, N. L., Fox, C. V., Johnson, H. E., & Varga, S. M. (2016). Leveraging relational assets for adolescent development: A qualitative investigation of youth–adult "connection" in positive youth development. *Qualitative Psychology, 3*(1), 59–78. doi:10.1037/qup0000046

Gagne, M. H., Tourigny, M., Joly, J., & Pouliot-Lapointe, J. (2007). Predictors of adult attitudes toward corporal punishment of children. *Journal of Interpersonal Violence, 22*(10), 1285–1304.

Gardner, H. (1998). A multiplicity of intelligences. *Scientific American Presents, 9*(4), 18–23.

Gardner, H. (2004). *Frames of mind: The theory of multiple intelligences.* New York, NY: Basic Books.

Gardner, H., & Moran, S. (2006). The science of multiple intelligences theory: A response to Lynn Waterhouse. *Educational Psychologist, 41*(4), 227–232.

Gardner, M., Roth, J., & Brooks-Gunn, J. (2008). Adolescents' participation in organized activities and developmental success 2 and 8 years after high school: Do sponsorship, duration, and intensity matter? *Developmental Psychology, 44,* 814–830.

Gardner, M., & Steinberg, L. (2005). Peer influence on risk taking, risk preference and risky decision-making in adolescence and adulthood: An experimental study. *Developmental Psychology, 41,* 625–635.

Gartstein, M. A., Bridgett, D. J., Young, B. N., Panksepp, J., & Power, T. (2013). Origins of effortful control: Infant and parent contributions. *Infancy, 18*(2), 149–183.

Gates, J. R., Corbin, W. R., & Fromme, K. (2016). Emerging adult identity development, alcohol use, and alcohol-related problems during the transition out of college. *Psychology of Addictive Behaviors, 30*(3), 345–355. doi:10.1037/adb0000179

Gath, A. (1993). Changes that occur in families as children with intellectual disability grow up. *International Journal of Disability, Development and Education, 40,* 167–174.

Gaul, D., & Issartel, J. (2016). Fine motor skill proficiency in typically developing children: On or off the maturation track? *Human Movement Science, 46,* 78–85.

Gavin, J., Rodham, K., & Poyer, H. (2008). The presentation of "pro-anorexia" in online group interactions. *Qualitative Health Research, 18*(3), 325–333.

Gazelle, H., & Ladd, G. W. (2003). Anxious solitude and peer exclusion: A diathesis-stress model of internalizing trajectories in childhood. *Child Development, 74,* 257–278.

Geary, D. C. (1998). *Male, female: The evolution of human sex differences.* Washington, DC: American Psychological Association.

Gentile, K. (2014). Exploring the troubling temporalities produced by fetal personhood. *Psychoanalysis, Culture & Society, 19*(3), 279–296.

Gerber, E. B., Whitebook, M., & Weinstein, R. S. (2007). At the heart of child care: Predictors of teacher sensitivity in center-based child care. *Early Childhood Research Quarterly, 22,* 327–346.

Gershoff, E. T., & Grogan-Kaylor, A. (2016). Race as a moderator of associations between spanking and child outcomes. *Family Relations, 3,* 490. doi:10.1111/fare.12205

Gervain, J., & Mehler, J. (2010). Speech perception and language acquisition in the first year of life. *Annual Review of Psychology, 61,* 191–218.

Gestsdottir, S., Bowers, E., von Eye, A., Napolitano, C. M., & Lerner, R. M. (2010). Intentional self-regulation in middle adolescence: The emerging role of loss-based selection in positive youth development. *Journal of Youth and Adolescence, 39,* 764–782.

Gibbins, S., & Stevens, B. (2001). Mechanisms of sucrose and nonnutritive sucking in procedural pain management in infants. *Pain Research & Management, 6,* 21–28.

Gibson, E. J., & Walk, R. D. (1960). The "visual cliff." *Scientific American, 202*(4), 64–71.

Giedd, J. N., Stockman, M., Weddle, C., Liverpool, M., Alexander-Bloch, A., Wallace, G. L., & Lenroot, R. K. (2010). Anatomic magnetic resonance imaging of the developing child and adolescent brain and effects of genetic variation. *Neuropsychology Review, 20*(4), 349–361.

Gilbert-Barness, E. (2000). Maternal caffeine and its effect on the fetus. *American Journal of Medical Genetics, 93,* 253.

Giletta, M., Scholte, R. J., Engels, R. E., Ciairano, S., & Prinstein, M. J. (2012). Adolescent non-suicidal self-injury: A cross-national study of community samples from Italy, the Netherlands and the United States. *Psychiatry Research, 197*(1–2), 66–72.

Gilligan, C., & Attanucci, J. (1988). Two moral orientations: Gender differences and similarities. *Merrill-Palmer Quarterly: Journal of Developmental Psychology, 34*(3), 223–237.

Gilman, R., Huebner, E. S., Tian, L., Park, N., O'Byrne, J., Schiff, M., . . . Langknecht, H. (2008). Cross-national adolescent multidimensional life satisfaction reports: Analysis of mean scores and response style differences. *Journal of Youth and Adolescence, 37,* 142–154.

Ginsburg, H., & Opper, S. (1969). *Piaget's theory of intellectual development: An introduction.* Englewood Cliffs, NJ: Prentice-Hall.

Giordano, P. C., Manning, W. D., & Longmore, M. A. (2010). Affairs of the heart: Qualities of adolescent romantic relationships and sexual behavior. *Journal of Research on Adolescence, 20*(4), 983–1013.

Goldberg, W. A., Lucas-Thompson, R. G., Germo, G. R., Keller, M. A., Davis, E. P., & Sandman, C. A. (2013). Eye of the beholder? Maternal mental health and the quality of infant sleep. *Social Science & Medicine, 79,* 101–108.

Goldman, J. G., & Coleman, S. J. (2013). Primary school puberty/sexuality education: Student-teachers' past learning, present professional education, and intention to teach these subjects. *Sex Education, 13*(3), 276–290.

Goldschmidt, A. B., Wall, M. M., Loth, K. A., Bucchianeri, M. M., & Neumark-Sztainer, D. (2014). The course of binge eating from adolescence to young adulthood. *Health Psychology, 33*(5), 457–460.

Golombok, S., Perry, B., Burston, A., Murray, C., Mooney-Somers, J., Stevens, M., & Golding, J. (2003). Children with lesbian parents: A community study. *Developmental Psychology, 39*, 20–33.

Gooch, D., Snowling, M., & Hulme, C. (2011). Time perception, phonological skills and executive function in children with dyslexia and/or ADHD symptoms. *Journal of Child Psychology and Psychiatry, 52*(2), 195–203.

Goodlin-Jones, B. L., Burnham, M. M., Gaylor, E. E., & Anders, T. F. (2001). Night waking, sleep–wake organization, and self-soothing in the first year of life. *Journal of Developmental and Behavioral Pediatrics, 22*(4), 226–233.

Gopnik, A. (2010). How babies think: Even the youngest children know, experience and learn far more than scientists ever thought possible. *Scientific American, 303*, 76–81.

Gordon, R. J. (2015). *The rise and fall of American growth.* Princeton, NJ: Princeton University Press.

Gordon-Messer, D., Bauermeister, J. A., Grodzinski, A., & Zimmerman, M. (2013). Sexting among young adults. *Journal of Adolescent Health, 52*(3), 301–306.

Gore, T., & Dubois, R. (1998). The "Back to Sleep" campaign. *Zero to Three, 19*(2), 22–23.

Gould, L. A., & Pate, M. (2010). Discipline, docility, and disparity: A study of inequality and corporal punishment. *British Journal of Criminology, 50*, 185–205.

Gould, S. J. (1981). *The mismeasure of man.* New York, NY: Norton.

Graber, J. A., Nichols, T. R., & Brooks-Gunn, J. (2010). Putting pubertal timing in developmental context: Implications for prevention. *Developmental Psychobiology, 52*(3), 254–262.

Graham, J., Banaschewski, T., Buitelaar, J., Coghill, D., Danckaerts, M., Dittmann, R. W., . . . Taylor, E. (2011). European guidelines on managing adverse effects of medication for ADHD. *European Child & Adolescent Psychiatry, 20*, 17–37.

Gratwick-Sarll, K., Bentley, C., Harrison, C., & Mond, J. (2016). Poor self-recognition of disordered eating among girls with bulimic-type eating disorders: Cause for concern? *Early Intervention in Psychiatry, 10*(4), 316–333.

Greenfield, E. A. (2010). Child abuse as a life-course social determinant of adult health. *Maturitas, 66*, 51–55.

Groen, Y., Wijers, A. A., Tucha, O., & Althaus, M. (2013). Are there sex differences in ERPs related to processing empathy-evoking pictures? *Neuropsychologia, 51*(1), 142–155.

Groeneveld, M. G., Vermeer, H. J., van IJzendoorn, M. H., & Linting, M. (2010). Children's well-being and cortisol levels in home-based and center-based childcare. *Early Childhood Research Quarterly, 25*(4), 502–514.

Grossman, T., & Jessen, S. (2017). When in infancy does the "fear bias" develop? *Journal of Experimental Child Psychology, 153*, 149–154.

Grube, J. W., Bourdeau, B., Fisher, D. A., & Bersamin, M. (2008). *Television exposure and sexuality among adolescents: A longitudinal survey study.* Paper presented at the Biennial Meeting of the Society for Research in Adolescence: Chicago, IL.

Grych, J., Hamby, S., & Banyard, V. (2015). The resilience portfolio model: Understanding healthy adaptation in victims of violence. *Psychology of Violence, 5*(4), 343–354. doi:10.1037/a0039671

Guan, S. A., Greenfield, P. M., & Orellana, M. F. (2014). Translating into understanding: Language brokering and prosocial development in emerging adults from immigrant families. *Journal of Adolescent Research, 29*(3), 331–355.

Guardino, C. M., & Schetter, C. D. (2014). Coping during pregnancy: A systematic review and recommendations. *Health Psychology Review, 8*(1), 70–94.

Guendelman, S., Kosa, J. L., Pearl, M., Graham, S., Goodman, J., & Kharrazi, M. (2009). Juggling work and breastfeeding: Effects of maternity leave and occupational characteristics. *Pediatrics, 123*, e38–e46.

Guerra, N. G., Williams, K. R., & Sadek, S. (2011). Understanding bullying and victimization during childhood and adolescence: A mixed methods study. *Child Development, 82*(1), 295–310.

Guerri, C., & Pascual, M. (2010). Mechanisms involved in the neurotoxic, cognitive, and neurobehavioral effects of alcohol consumption during adolescence. *Alcohol, 44*(1), 15–26.

Guttmacher Institute. (2011b). *In brief: Facts on American teens' sexual and reproductive health.* New York, NY: Guttmacher Institute.

Guttmacher Institute. (2014). *Contraceptive use in the United States.* Retrieved from http://www.guttmacher.org/pubs/fb_contr_use.html

Haapala, E. A., Poikkeus, A.-M., Kukkonen-Harjula, K., Tompuri, T., Lintu, N., Väistö, J., Leppänen, P. H. T., Laaksonen, D. E., Lindi, V., & Lakka, T. A. (2014). Associations of physical activity and sedentary behavior with academic skills—A follow-up study among primary school children. *PLoS One, 9*(9), ArtID: e107031.

Habermas, T., Negele, A., & Mayer, F. B. (2010). "Honey, you're jumping about"—Mothers' scaffolding of their children's and adolescents' life narration. *Cognitive Development, 25*, 339–351.

Haga, M., Gísladóttír, T., & Sigmundsson, H. (2015). The relationship between motor competence and physical fitness is weaker in the 15–16 yr. adolescent age group than in younger age groups (4–5 yr. and 11–12 yr.). *Perceptual and Motor Skills, 121*(3), 900–912.

Hall, G. S. (1969). *Adolescence.* New York, NY: Arno Press. (Original work published 1904)

Hall, S. (2011). "It's going to stop in this generation": Women with a history of child abuse resolving to raise their children without abuse. *Harvard Educational Review, 81*(1), 24–49.

Hall, S., & Walls, J. (2015). Exploring family-oriented markers of adulthood: Political and personal variations among emerging adults. *Emerging Adulthood, 4*(3), 192–199.

Halperin, J. M., & Healey, D. M. (2011). The influences of environmental enrichment, cognitive enhancement, and physical exercise on brain development: Can we alter the developmental trajectory of ADHD? *Neuroscience and Biobehavioral Reviews, 35*, 621–634.

Halpern, H. P., & Perry-Jenkins, M. (2016). Parents' gender ideology and gendered behavior as predictors of children's gender-role attitudes: A longitudinal exploration. *Sex Roles, 74*(11–12), 527–542. doi:10.1007/s11199-015-0539-0

Halpern-Meekin, S., Manning, W. D., Giordano, P. C., & Longmore, M. A. (2013). Relationship churning in emerging adulthood: On/off relationships and sex with an ex. *Journal of Adolescent Research, 28*(2), 166–188.

Haltigan, J., Roisman, G., Cauffman, E., & Booth-LaForce, C. (2017). Correlates of childhood vs. adolescence internalizing symptomatology from infancy to young adulthood. *Journal of Youth & Adolescence, 46*(1), 197–212.

Hamlin, J. K. (2013a). Failed attempts to help and harm: Intention versus

Hamlin, J. K. (2013b). Moral judgment and action in preverbal infants and toddlers: Evidence for an innate moral core. *Current Directions in Psychological Science, 22*(3), 186–193.

Hamlin, J. K., & Wynn, K. (2011). Young infants prefer prosocial to antisocial others. *Cognitive Development, 26,* 30–39.

Hamlin, J. K., Mahajan, N., Liberman, Z., & Wynn, K. (2013). Not like me = bad: Infants prefer those who harm dissimilar others. *Psychological Science, 24*(4), 589–594.

Harbourne, R. T., Lobo, M. A., Karst, G. M., & Galloway, J. C. (2013). Sit happens: Does sitting development perturb reaching development, or vice versa? *Infant Behavior and Development, 36*(3), 438–450.

Harley, K., & Reese, E. (1999). Origins of autobiographical memory. *Developmental Psychology, 35,* 1338–1348.

Harlow, C. M. (Ed.). (1986). *From learning to love: The selected papers of H. F. Harlow.* New York, NY: Praeger.

Harlow, H. F. (1958). The nature of love. *American Psychologist, 13,* 673–685.

Harlow, H. F., Harlow, M. K., Dodsworth, R. O., & Arling, G. L. (1966). Maternal behavior of rhesus monkeys deprived of mothering and peer associations in infancy. *Proceedings of the American Philosophical Society, 110,* 58–66.

Harper, G. W., & Wilson, B. M. (2017). Situating sexual orientation and gender identity diversity in context and communities. In M. A. Bond, I. Serrano-García, C. B. Keys, M. Shinn (Eds.), *APA handbook of community psychology: Theoretical foundations, core concepts, and emerging challenges* (pp. 387–402). Washington, DC, US: American Psychological Association.

Harriger, J. A., Calogero, R. M., Witherington, D. C., & Smith, J. E. (2010). Body size stereotyping and internalization of the thin ideal in preschool girls. *Sex Roles, 63,* 609–620.

Harris, J. R. (1995). Where is the child's environment? A group socialization theory of development. *Psychological Review, 102,* 458–489.

Harris, J. R. (1998). *The nurture assumption: Why children turn out the way they do.* New York, NY: Free Press.

Harris, J. R. (2002). Beyond the nurture assumption: Testing hypotheses about the child's environment. In J. G. Borkowski, S. L. Ramey, & M. Bristol-Power (Eds.), *Parenting and the child's world: Influences on academic, intellectual, and social-emotional development* (pp. 3–20). Mahwah, NJ: Erlbaum.

Harris, J. R. (2006). *No two alike: Human nature and human individuality.* New York, NY: Norton.

Harrist, A. W., Thompson, S. D., & Norris, D. J. (2007). Defining quality childcare: Multiple stakeholder perspectives. *Early Education and Development, 18*(2), 305–336.

Harter, S. (1981). A new self-report scale of intrinsic versus extrinsic orientation in the classroom: Motivational and informational components. *Developmental Psychology, 17,* 300–312.

Harter, S. (1999). *The construction of the self: A developmental perspective.* New York, NY: Guilford Press.

Hartup, W. W., & Stevens, N. (1997). Friendships and adaptation in the life course. *Psychological Bulletin, 121,* 355–370.

Hashimoto-Torii, K., Kawasawa, Y. I., Kuhn, A., & Rakic, P. (2011). Combined transcriptome analysis of fetal human and mouse cerebral cortex exposed to alcohol. *Proceedings of the National Academy of Sciences of the United States of America, 108*(10), 4212–4217.

Haskett, M. E., Neupert, S. D., & Okado, Y. (2014). Factors associated with 3-year stability and change in parenting behavior of abusive parents. *Journal of Child and Family Studies, 23*(2), 263–274.

Hatano, K., Sugimura, K., & Crocetti, E. (2016). Looking at the dark and bright sides of identity formation: New insights from adolescents and emerging adults in Japan. *Journal of Adolescence, 141,* 156–168.

Hazan, C., & Shaver, P. (1987). Romantic love conceptualized as an attachment process. *Journal of Personality and Social Psychology, 52,* 511–524.

Healthychildren.org. (n.d.). Retrieved from http/www/Healthychildren.org

Healy, E., Reichenberg, A., Nam, K. W., Allin, M. G., Walshe, M., Rifkin, L., ... Nosarti, C. (2013). Preterm birth and adolescent social functioning—Alterations in emotion-processing brain areas. *Journal of Pediatrics, 163*(6), 1596–1604.

Heatherton, T. F. (2011). Neuroscience of self and self-regulation. *Annual Review of Psychology, 62,* 363–390.

Heaven, P. C. L., Ciarrochi, J., & Vialle, W. (2008). Self-nominated peer crowds, school achievement, and psychological adjustment in adolescents: Longitudinal analysis. *Personality and Individual Differences, 44,* 977–988.

Hedley, D., Brewer, N., Nevill, R., Uljarević, M., Butter, E., & Mulick, J. A. (2016). The relationship between clinicians' confidence and accuracy, and the influence of child characteristics, in the screening of autism spectrum disorder. *Journal of Autism and Developmental Disorders, 46*(7), 2340–2348. doi:10.1007/s10803-016-2766-9

Heilbrun, K., DeMatteo, D., & Goldstein, N. S. (2016). *APA handbook of psychology and juvenile justice.* Washington, DC: American Psychological Association.

Hellerstein, S., Feldman, S., & Duan, T. (2016). Survey of obstetric care and cesarean delivery rates in Shanghai, China. *Birth: Issues in Perinatal Care, 43*(3), 193–199.

Hendry, A., Jones, E. J., & Charman, T. (2016). Executive function in the first three years of life: Precursors, predictors and patterns. *Developmental Review, 42,* 1–33. doi:10.1016/j.dr.2016.06.005

Hendry, L. B., & Kloep, M. (2010). How universal is emerging adulthood? An empirical example. *Journal of Youth Studies, 13*(2), 169–179.

Hengartner, M. P., Müller, M., Rodgers, S., Rössler, W., & Ajdacic-Gross, V. (2013). Can protective factors moderate the detrimental effects of child maltreatment on personality functioning? *Journal of Psychiatric Research, 47*(9), 1180–1186.

Henin, A., & Berman, N. (2016). The promise and peril of emerging adulthood: Introduction to the special issue. *Cognitive and Behavioral Practice, 23*(3), 263–269. doi:10.1016/j.cbpra.2016.05.005

Hennekam, S. (2016). Identity transition during pregnancy: The importance of role models. *Human Relations, 69*(9), 1765. doi:10.1177/0018726716631402

Henrique, R. S., Alessandro, H. N., Stodden, D. F., Fransen, J., Campos, C. M. C., Queiroz, D. R., & Cattuzzo, M. T. (2016). Association between sports participation, motor competence and weight status: A longitudinal study. *Journal of Science and Medicine in Sport, 19*(10), 825–829.

Henry, L. A., Messer, D. J., & Nash, G. (2012). Executive functioning in children with specific language impairment. *Journal of Child Psychology and Psychiatry, 53,* 37–45.

Hensler, B. S., Schatschneider, C., Taylor, J., & Wagner, R. K. (2010). Behavioral genetic approach to the study of dyslexia. *Journal of Developmental and Behavioral Pediatrics, 31*(7), 525–532.

Hepach, R., Vaish, A., & Tomasello, M. (2013). A new look at children's prosocial motivation. *Infancy, 18*(1), 67–90.

Herbert, A. C., Ramirez, A. M., Lee, G., North, S. J., Askari, M. S., West, R. L., Sommer, M. (2016). Puberty experiences of low-income girls in the United States: A systematic review of qualitative literature from 2000 to 2014. *Journal of Adolescent Health, 60*(4), 363–379.

Herrnstein, R. J., & Murray, C. A. (1994). *The bell curve: Intelligence and class structure in American life.* New York, NY: Free Press.

Herting, M. M., & Sowell, E. R. (2017). Puberty and structural brain development in humans. *Frontiers in Neuroendocrinology, 44*, 122–137.

Hertzog, C. (1996). Research design in studies of aging and cognition. In J. E. Birren, K. W. Schaie, R. P. Abeles, M. Gatz, & T. A. Salthouse (Eds.), *Handbook of the psychology of aging* (4th ed., pp. 24–37). San Diego, CA: Academic Press.

Hesse-Biber, S., Livingstone, S., Ramirez, D., Barko, E. B., & Johnson, A. L. (2010). Racial identity and body image among black female college students attending predominately white colleges. *Sex Roles, 63*, 697–711.

Higher Education Research Institute. (2013). Class of 2012: Findings from the college senior survey. *HERI Research Brief.* Retrieved from http://www.heri.ucla.edu/

Hill, P., Burrow, A., & Sumner, R. (2016). Sense of purpose and parent–child relationships in emerging adulthood. *Emerging Adulthood, 4*(6), 436–439.

Hilmert, C. J., Kvasnicka-Gates, L., Teoh, A. N., Bresin, K., & Fiebiger, S. (2016). Major flood related strains and pregnancy outcomes. *Health Psychology, 35*(11), 1189–1196. doi:10.1037/hea0000386

Hinde, R. A. (2005). Ethology and attachment theory. In K. E. Grossmann, K. Grossmann, & E. Waters (Eds.), *Attachment from infancy to adulthood: The major longitudinal studies* (pp. 1–12). New York, NY: Guilford Press.

Hipwell, A. E., Keenan, K., Loeber, R., & Battista, D. (2010). Early predictors of sexually intimate behaviors in an urban sample of young girls. *Developmental Psychology, 46*(2), 366–378.

Hirschfield, P. J., & Gasper, J. (2011). The relationship between school engagement and delinquency in late childhood and early adolescence. *Journal of Youth and Adolescence, 40*(1), 3–22.

Hoeben, E. M., Meldrum, R. C., Walker, D., & Young, J. T. (2016). The role of peer delinquency and unstructured socializing in explaining delinquency and substance use: A state-of-the-art review. *Journal of Criminal Justice, 47*, 108–122.

Hoff-Ginsberg, E. (1997). *Language development.* Belmont, CA: Brooks/Cole.

Hoffman, M. L. (1994). Discipline and internalization. *Developmental Psychology, 30*, 26–28.

Hoffman, M. L. (2001). Toward a comprehensive empathy-based theory of prosocial moral development. In A. C. Bohart & D. J. Stipek (Eds.), *Constructive and destructive behavior: Implications for family, school, and society* (pp. 61–86). Washington, DC: American Psychological Association.

Hofstede, G. (1981). Cultures and organizations. *International Studies of Management and Organization, 10*(4), 15–41.

Hofstede, G. (2001). *Culture's consequences: Comparing values, behaviors, institutions, and organizations across nations* (2nd ed.). Thousand Oaks, CA: Sage.

Holland, L. A., Brown, T. A., & Keel, P. K. (2014). Defining features of unhealthy exercise associated with disordered eating and eating disorder diagnoses. *Psychology of Sport and Exercise, 15*(1), 116–123.

Hoogman, M., Onnink, M., Cools, R., Aarts, E., Kan, C., Arias Vasquez, A., . . . Franke, B. (2013). The dopamine transporter haplotype and reward-related striatal responses in adult ADHD. *European Neuropsychopharmacology, 23*(6), 469–478.

Hoover, E. (2011). *The Chronicle of Higher Education: Surveys of the public and presidents.* In *College's value goes deeper than the degree, graduates say.* Retrieved from http://www.chronicle.com/article/Its-More-Than_the/127534

Horwitz, B. N., Reynolds, C. A., Walum, H., Ganiban, J., Spotts, E. L., Reiss, D., . . . Neiderhiser, J. M. (2016). Understanding the role of mate selection processes in couples' pair-bonding behavior. *Behavior Genetics, 46*(1), 143–149.

House, B. R., Silk, J. B., Henrich, J., Barrett, H. C., Scelza, B. A., Boyette, A. H., . . . Laurence, S. (2013). Ontogeny of prosocial behavior across diverse societies. *Proceedings of the National Academy of Sciences of the United States of America, 110*(36), 14586–14591.

Hrdy, S. B. (1999). *Mother nature: A history of mothers, infants, and natural selection.* New York, NY: Pantheon Books.

Hu, S., & Kuh, G. D. (2003). Diversity experiences and college student learning and personal development. *Journal of College Student Development, 44*, 320–334.

Huang, H., Coleman, S., Bridge, J. A., Yonkers, K., & Katon, W. (2014). A meta-analysis of the relationship between antidepressant use in pregnancy and the risk of preterm birth and low birth weight. *General Hospital Psychiatry, 36*(1), 13–18.

Huddleston, J., & Ge, X. (2003). Boys at puberty: Psychosocial implications. In C. Hayward (Ed.), *Gender differences at puberty* (pp. 113–134). New York, NY: Cambridge University Press.

Hudson, M. B., Nicolas, S. C., Howser, M. E., Lipsett, K. E., Robinson, I. W., Pope, L. J., . . . Friedman, D. R. (2015). Examining how gender and emoticons influence Facebook jealousy. *Cyberpsychology, Behavior & Social Networking, 18*(2), 87–92.

Hughes, C., & Devine, R. T. (2015). Individual differences in theory of mind from preschool to adolescence: Achievements and directions. *Child Development Perspectives, 9*(3), 149–153. doi:10.1111/cdep12124

Huizink, A. J. (2015). Prenatal maternal substance use and offspring outcomes: Overview of recent findings and possible interventions. *European Psychologist,* Special Issue: Prenatal Adversity: Impact and Potential Interventions, 20(2), 90–101.

Hunger and Poverty Facts and Statistics. (n.d.). Retrieved from http://www.feedingamerica.org/hunger-in-america/impact-of-hunger/hunger-and-poverty/hunger-and-poverty-fact-sheet.html?referrer=https://www.google.com/, December 2016.

Huttenlocher, P. R. (2002). *Neural plasticity: The effects of environment on the development of the cerebral cortex.* Cambridge, MA: Harvard University Press.

Hyde, A., Drennan, J., Butler, M., Howlett, E., Carney, M., & Lohan, M. (2013). Parents' constructions of communication with their children about safer sex. *Journal of Clinical Nursing, 22*(23–24), 3438–3446.

Icenogle, G., Steinberg, L., Olino, T. M., Shulman, E. P., Chein, J., Alampay, L. P., . . . Uribe Tirado, L. M. (2016). Puberty predicts approach but not avoidance on the Iowa gambling task in a multinational sample. *Child Development.* doi:10.1111/cdev.12655

Imuta, K., Henry, J. D., Slaughter, V., Selcuk, B., & Ruffman, T. (2016). Theory of mind and prosocial behavior in childhood: A meta-analytic view. *Developmental Psychology, 54*(8), 1192–1205.

Ishitani, T. T. (2016). Time-varying effects of academic and social integration on student persistence for first and second year of college. National data approach. *Journal of College Student Retention, 18*(3), 263–286.

Ito, M., & Sharts-Hopko, N. C. (2002). Japanese women's experience of childbirth in the United States. *Health Care for Women International, 23*, 666–677.

Jach, H. K., Sun, J., Loton, D., Chin, T., & Waters, L. E. (2017). Strengths and subjective well-being in adolescence: Strength-based parenting and the moderating effect of mindset. *Journal of Happiness Studies.*

Jackson, D. B. (2016). Breastfeeding duration and offspring conduct problems: The moderating role of genetic risk. *Social Science & Medicine, 166*, 128–136. doi:10.1016/j.socscimed.2016.08.014

Jackson, T., & Chen, H. (2008). Predicting changes in eating disorder symptoms among Chinese adolescents: A 9-month prospective study. *Journal of Psychosomatic Research, 64*, 87–95.

Jaffe, J., & Diamond, M. O. (2011). *Reproductive trauma: Psychotherapy with infertility and pregnancy loss clients.* Washington, DC: American Psychological Association.

Jaffee, S. R., Bowes, L., Ouellet-Morin, I., Fisher, H. L., Moffitt, T. E., Merrick, M. T., & Arseneault, L. (2013). Safe, stable, nurturing relationships break the intergenerational cycle of abuse: A prospective nationally representative cohort of children in the United Kingdom. *Journal of Adolescent Health, 53*(4, Suppl.), S4–S10.

Jang, H., Reeve, J., & Deci, E. L. (2010). Engaging students in learning activities: It is not autonomy support or structure but autonomy support and structure. *Journal of Educational Psychology, 102*(3), 588–600.

Janssen, I. (2015). Hyper-parenting is negatively associated with physical activity among 7- to 12-year-olds. *Preventative Medicine, 73*, 55–59.

Janssen, T. W., Bink, M., Geladé, K., Mourik, R. V., Maras, A., & Oosterlaan, J. (2016). A randomized controlled trial into the effects of neurofeedback, methylphenidate, and physical activity on EEG power spectra in children with ADHD. *Journal of Child Psychology and Psychiatry, 57*(5), 633–644. doi:10.1111/jcpp.12517

Jennings, W. G., Gonzalez, J. R., Piquero, A. R., Bird, H., Canino, G., & Maldonado-Molina, M. (2016). The nature and relevance of risk and protective factors for violence among Hispanic children and adolescents: Results from the Boricua Youth Study. *Journal of Criminal Justice, 45*, 41–47.

Jensen, C., Steinhausen, H., & Lauritson, M. B. (2014). Time trends over 16 years in incidence rates of autism spectrum disorders across the lifespan based on nationwide Danish register data. In *Journal of Autism Development Disorders, 44*(8), 1808–1818.

Jensen, H., Grøn, R., Lidegaard, Ø., Pedersen, L., Andersen, P., & Kessing, L. (2013). The effects of maternal depression and use of antidepressants during pregnancy on risk of a child small for gestational age. *Psychopharmacology, 228*(2), 199–205.

Jenson, W. R., Olympia, D., Farley, M., & Clark, E. (2004). Positive psychology and externalizing students in a sea of negativity. *Psychology in the Schools, 41*, 67–79.

Jiang, Y., Ekono, M., & Skinner, C. (2016). Basic facts about low-income children: Children under 18 years, 2014. National Center for Children in Poverty, 1–8.

Jiang, Y., Granja, M., Koball, H., & National Center for Children in Poverty. (2017). Basic facts about low-income children: Children under 18 years, 2015. Fact Sheet.

Johns, M. M., Zimmerman, M., & Bauermeister, J. A. (2013). Sexual attraction, sexual identity, and psychosocial well-being in a national sample of young women during emerging adulthood. *Journal of Youth and Adolescence, 42*(1), 82–95.

Johnson, A. M., Kirk, R., Rooks, A. J., & Muzik, M. (2016). Enhancing breastfeeding through healthcare support: Results from a focus group study of African American mothers. *Maternal and Child Health Journal, 20*(S1), 92–102. doi:10.1007/s10995-016-2085-y

Johnson, K. M. (2013). Making families: Organizational boundary work in US egg and sperm donation. *Social Science & Medicine, 99*, 64–71.

Johnston, L. D., Miech, R. A., O'Malley, P. M., Bachman, J. G., & Schulenberg, J. E. (2016). Monitoring the Future, 2016 overview: Key findings on adolescent drug use, p. 10.

Johnston, L. D., O'Malley, P. M., Bachman, J. G., & Schulenberg, J. E. (2011). *Marijuana use continues to rise among U.S. teens, while alcohol use hits historic lows.* In *University of Michigan New Service: Ann Arbor, MI.* Retrieved from http://www.monitoringthefuture.org

Jokhi, R. P., & Whitby, E. H. (2011). Magnetic resonance imaging of the fetus. *Developmental Medicine & Child Neurology, 53*, 18–28.

Juarascio, A. S., Shoaib, A., & Timko, C. A. (2010). Pro-eating disorder communities on social networking sites: A content analysis. *Eating Disorders, 18*, 393–407.

Julian, M. M. (2013). Age at adoption from institutional care as a window into the lasting effects of early experiences. *Clinical Child and Family Psychology Review, 16*(2), 101–145.

Kagan, J. (1984). *The nature of the child.* New York, NY: Basic Books.

Kagan, J. (1994). *Galen's prophecy: Temperament in human nature.* New York, NY: Basic Books.

Kagan, J. (1998). *Galen's prophecy: Temperament in human nature.* Boulder, CO: Westview Press.

Kalmijn, M. (2013). Adult children's relationships with married parents, divorced parents, and stepparents: Biology, marriage, or residence? *Journal of Marriage and Family, 75*(5), 1181–1193.

Karen, R. (1998). *Becoming attached: First relationships and how they shape our capacity to love.* London, England: Oxford University Press.

Karni, E., Leshno, M., & Rapaport, S. (2014). Helping patients and physicians reach individualized medical decisions: Theory and application to prenatal diagnostic testing. *Theory and Decision, 76*(4), 451–467.

Karns, J. T. (2001). Health, nutrition, and safety. In G. Bremner & A. Fogel (Eds.), *Blackwell handbook of infant development* (pp. 693–725). Malden, MA: Blackwell.

Kato, K., & Pedersen, N. L. (2005). Personality and coping: A study of twins reared apart and twins reared together. *Behavior Genetics, 35*, 147–158.

Katz, I., Kaplan, A., & Gueta, G. (2010). Students' needs, teachers' support, and motivation for doing homework: A cross-sectional study. *Journal of Experimental Education, 78*(2), 246–267.

Keefe, M. R., Karlsen, K. A., Lobo, M. L., Kotzer, A. M., & Dudley, W. N. (2006). Reducing parenting stress in families with irritable infants. *Nursing Research, 55*(3), 198–205.

Keel, P. K., Baxter, M. G., Heatherton, T. F., & Joiner, T. E. (2007). A 20-year longitudinal study of body weight, dieting, and eating disorder symptoms. *Journal of Abnormal Psychology, 116*(2), 422–432.

Keijsers, L., & Poulin, F. (2013). Developmental changes in parent–child communication throughout adolescence. *Developmental Psychology, 49*(12), 2301–2308.

Kellman, P. J., & Banks, M. S. (1998). Infant visual perception. In W. Damon (Series Ed.) & D. Kuhn & R. S. Siegler (Vol. Eds.), *Handbook of child psychology: Vol. 2, Cognition, perception, and language* (pp. 103–146). Hoboken, NJ: Wiley.

Keys, C. L. (2007). Promoting and protecting mental health as flourishing: A complementary strategy for improving national mental health. *American Psychologist, 61*, 95–108.

Kiang, L., & Fuligni, A. J. (2009). Ethnic identity and family processes among adolescents from Latin American, Asian, and European backgrounds. *Journal of Youth and Adolescence, 38*, 228–241.

Kiefer, S. M., & Wang, J. H. (2016). Associations of coolness and social goals with aggression and engagement during adolescence. *Journal of Applied Developmental Psychology, 44*, 52–62.

Killewald, A. (2013). A reconsideration of the fatherhood premium: Marriage, coresidence, biology, and fathers' wages. *American Sociological Review, 78*(1), 96–116.

Kim, B. K. E., Oesterle, S., Catalano, R. F., & Hawkins, J. D. (2015). Change in protective factors across adolescent development. *Journal of Applied Developmental Psychology, 40*, 31.

Kim, M., & Park, I. J. K. (2011). Testing the moderating effect of parent–adolescent communication on the acculturation gap-distress relation in Korean American families. *Journal of Youth and Adolescence, 40*, 1661–1673.

Kim, S. Y., Chen, Q., Wang, Y., Shen, Y., & Orozco-Lapray, D. (2013). Longitudinal linkages among parent–child acculturation discrepancy, parenting, parent–child sense of alienation, and adolescent adjustment in Chinese immigrant families. *Developmental Psychology, 49*(5), 900–912.

Kim, S. Y., Wang, Y., Orozco-Lapray, D., Shen, Y., & Murtuza, M. (2013). Does "tiger parenting" exist? Parenting profiles of Chinese Americans and adolescent developmental outcomes. *Asian American Journal of Psychology, 4*(1), 7–18.

Kim, S., Yun, I., & Kim, J. (2016). Associations between body weight and bullying among South Korean adolescents. *The Journal of Early Adolescence, 36*(4), 551–574. doi:10.1177/0272431615577204

King, E. K., Pierro, R. C., Li, J., Porterfield, M. L., & Rucker, L. (2016). Classroom quality in infant and toddler classrooms: Impact of age and programme type. *Early Child Development & Care, 186*(11), 1821–1835. doi:10.1080/03004430.2015.1134521

Kinniburgh-White, R., Cartwright, C., & Seymour, F. (2010). Young adults' narratives of relational development with stepfathers. *Journal of Social and Personal Relationships, 27*(7), 890–907.

Kins, E., & Beyers, W. (2010). Failure to launch, failure to achieve criteria for adulthood. *Journal of Adolescence Research, 25*(5), 743–777.

Kins, E., de Mol, J., & Beyers, W. (2014). "Why should I leave?" Belgian emerging adults' departure from home. *Journal of Adolescent Research, 29*(1), 89–119.

Kitahara, M. (1989). Childhood in Japanese culture. *Journal of Psychohistory, 17*, 43–72.

Kitzinger, S. (2000). *Rediscovering birth*. New York, NY: Pocket Books.

Kloep, M., & Hendry, L. B. (2010). Letting go or holding on? Parents' perceptions of their relationships with their children during emerging adulthood. *British Journal of Developmental Psychology, 28*(4), 817–834.

Knopik, V. S., Marceau, K., Palmer, R. H., Smith, T. F., & Heath, A. C. (2016). Maternal smoking during pregnancy and offspring birth weight: A genetically-informed approach comparing multiple raters. *Behavior Genetics, 46*(3), 353–364.

Knox, M. (2010). On hitting children: A review of corporal punishment in the United States. *Journal of Pediatric Health Care, 24*(2), 103–107.

Kobayashi, M., Cassia, V. M., Kanazawa, S., Yamaguchi, M. K., & Kakigi, R. (2016). Perceptual narrowing towards adult faces is a cross-cultural phenomenon in infancy: A behavioral and near-infrared spectroscopy study with Japanese infants. *Developmental Science*. doi:10.1111/desc.12498

Kobel, S., Kettner, D. K., Erkelenz, N., Drenowatz, C., & Steinacker, J. M. (2015). Correlates of habitual physical activity and organized sports in German primary school children. *Public Health, 129*, 237–243.

Kochanska, G., Aksan, N., Penney, S. J., & Boldt, L. J. (2007). Parental personality as an inner resource that moderates the impact of ecological adversity on parenting. *Journal of Personality and Social Psychology, 92*(1), 136–150.

Kochanska, G., Coy, K. C., & Murray, K. T. (2001). The development of self-regulation in the first four years of life. *Child Development, 72*, 1091–1111.

Kochanska, G., & Kim, S. (2013). Early attachment organization with both parents and future behavior problems: From infancy to middle childhood. *Child Development, 84*(1), 283–296.

Kochanska, G., & Knaack, A. (2003). Effortful control as a personality characteristic of young children: Antecedents, correlates, and consequences. *Journal of Personality, 71*, 1087–1112.

Kochanska, G., Woodard, J., Kim, S., Koenig, J. L., Yoon, J. E., & Barry, R. A. (2010). Positive socialization mechanisms in secure and insecure parent–child dyads: Two longitudinal studies. *Journal of Child Psychology and Psychiatry, 51*(9), 998–1009.

Kocsor, F., Saxton, T. K., Lang, A., & Bereczkei, T. (2016). Preference for faces resembling opposite-sex parents is moderated by emotional closeness in childhood. *Personality and Individual Differences, 93*, 23–29.

Kohlberg, L. (1966). Moral education in the schools: A developmental view. *School Review, 74*, 1–30.

Kohlberg, L. (1981). *The meaning and measurement of moral development*. Worcester, MA: Clark University Press.

Kohlberg, L. (1984). *The psychology of moral development: The nature and validity of moral stages*. San Francisco: Harper & Row.

Komarraju, M., Musulkin, S., & Bhattacharya, G. (2010). Role of student-faculty interactions in developing college students' academic self-concept, motivation, and achievement. *Journal of College Student Development, 51*(1), 332–342.

Konner, M. (2010). *The evolution of childhood*. Cambridge, MA: Harvard University Press.

Koolschijn, P. C., & Crone, E. A. (2013). Sex differences and structural brain maturation from childhood to early adulthood. *Developmental Cognitive Neuroscience, 5*, 106–118.

Kover, S. T., Edmunds, S. R., & Weismer, S. E. (2016). Brief report: Ages of language milestones as predictors of developmental trajectories in young children with autism spectrum disorder. *Journal of Autism and Developmental Disorders*, 46(7), 2501–2507. doi:10.1007/s10803-016-2756-y

Kraft, I., Schreiber, J., Cafiero, R., Metere, R., Schaadt, G., Brauer, J., . . . Skeide, M. A. (2016). Predicting early signs of dyslexia at a preliterate age by combining behavioral assessment with structural MRI. *Neuroimage*, 143, 378–386.

Kreppner, J., Rutter, M., Marvin, R., O'Conner, T., & Sonuga-Barke, E. (2011). Assessing the concept of the "insecure-other" category in the Cassidy-Marvin scheme: Changes between 4 and 6 years in the English and Romanian adoptee study. *Social Development*, 20(1), 1–16.

Kretsch, N., & Harden, K. P. (2014). Pubertal development and peer influence on risky decision making. *The Journal of Early Adolescence*, 34(3), 339–359.

Kroger, J. (2000). *Identity development: Adolescence through adulthood*. Thousand Oaks, CA: Sage.

Kronenberg, M. E., Hansel, T. C., Brennan, A. M., Osofsky, H. J., Osofsky, J. D., & Lawrason, B. (2010). Children of Katrina: Lessons learned about post disaster symptoms and recovery patterns. *Child Development*, 81(4), 1241–1259.

Krstev, S., Marinković, J., Simić, S., Kocev, N., & Bondy, S. J. (2013). The influence of maternal smoking and exposure to residential ETS on pregnancy outcomes: A retrospective national study. *Maternal and Child Health Journal*, 17(9), 1591–1598.

Kuhn, D. (1989). Children and adults as intuitive scientists. *Psychological Review*, 96, 674–689.

Kuhnert, R., Begeer, S., Fink, E., & Rosnay, M. D. (2017). Gender-differentiated effects of theory of mind, emotion understanding, and social preference on prosocial behavior development: A longitudinal study. *Journal of Experimental Child Psychology*, 154, 13–27. doi:10.1016/j.jecp.2016.10.001

Kwon, M., Setoodehnia, M., Baek, J., Luck, S. J., & Oakes, L. M. (2016). The development of visual search in infancy: Attention to faces versus salience. *Developmental Psychology*, 52(4), 537–555.

La Paro, K. M., & Gloeckler, L. (2016). The context of child care for toddlers: The "experience expectable environment." *Early Childhood Education Journal*, 44(2), 147–153. doi:10.1007/s10643-015-0699-0

Labouvie-Vief, G. (2006). Emerging structures of adult thought. In J. J. Arnett & J. L. Tanner (Eds.), *Emerging adults in America: Coming of age in the 21st century* (pp. 59–84). Washington, DC: American Psychological Association.

LaFontana, K. M., & Cillessen, A. H. N. (2010). Developmental changes in the priority of perceived status in childhood and adolescence. *Social Development*, 19(1), 130–147.

Lahey, J. (2014). Birthing a nation: The effect of fertility control access on the nineteenth-century demographic transition. *Journal of Economic History*, 74, 482–508.

Laible, D. J. (2004). Mother–child discourse surrounding a child's past behavior at 30 months: Links to emotional understanding and early conscience development at 36 months. *Merrill-Palmer Quarterly*, 50, 159–180.

Lamela, D., Figueiredo, B., Bastos, A., & Feinberg, M. (2016). Typologies of post-divorce coparenting and parental well-being, parenting quality and children's psychological adjustment. *Child Psychiatry & Human Development*, 47(5), 716–728. doi:10.1007/s10578-015-0604-5

Landerl, K., & Moll, K. (2010). Comorbidity of learning disorders: Prevalence and familial transmission. *Journal of Child Psychology and Psychiatry*, 51(3), 287–294.

Landor, A., Simons, L. G., Simons, R. L., Brody, G. H., & Gibbons, F. X. (2011). The role of religiosity in the relationship between parents, peers, and adolescents in risky sexual behavior. *Journal of Youth and Adolescence*, 40, 296–309.

Lane, B. L., Piercy, C. W., & Carr, C. T. (2016). Making it Facebook official: The warranting value of online relationship status disclosures on relational characteristics. *Computers in Human Behavior*, 56, 561–568.

Lapsley, D., & Woodbury, R. D. (2016). Social cognitive development in emerging adulthood. In J. J. Arnett (Ed.), *The Oxford handbook of emerging adulthood* (pp. 142–159). New York, NY: Oxford University Press.

Larson, K., & Grisso, T. (2016). Transfer and commitment of youth in the United States: Law, policy, and forensic practice. In K. Heilbrun, D. DeMatteo, & N. S. Goldstein (Eds.), *APA handbook of psychology and juvenile justice* (pp. 445–466). Washington, DC: American Psychological Association.

Larsson, H., Andkarsater, H., Rastam, M., Chang, Z., & Lichtenstein, O. (2012). Childhood attention-deficit hyperactivity disorder as an extreme of a continuous trait: A quantitative genetic study of 8,500 twin pairs. *Journal of Child Psychology and Psychiatry*, 53(1), 73–80.

LaRusso, M. D., Romer, D., & Selman, R. L. (2008). Teachers as builders of respectful school climates: Implications for adolescent drug use norms and depressive symptoms in high school. *Journal of Youth and Adolescence*, 37, 386–398.

Larzelere, R. E., & Knowles, S. J. (2015, August). Toddlers need both positive parenting and consistent consequences from mothers. Paper presented at the American Psychological Association, Toronto, ON.

Larzelere, R. E., & Kuhn, B. R. (2005). Comparing child outcomes of physical punishment and alternative disciplinary tactics: A meta-analysis. *Clinical Child and Family Psychology Review*, 8, 1–37.

Latz, S., Wolf, A. W., & Lozoff, B. (1999). Cosleeping in context: Sleep practices and problems in young children in Japan and the United States. *Archives of Pediatrics & Adolescent Medicine*, 153, 339–346.

Lavadera, A. L., Caravelli, L., & Togliatti, M. M. (2013). Child custody in Italian management of divorce. *Journal of Family Issues*, 34(11), 1536–1562.

Lavender, J. M., Utzinger, L. M., Li, C., Wonderlich, S. A., Engel, S. G., Mitchell, J. E., & Cao, L. (2016). Reciprocal associations between negative affect, binge eating, and purging in the natural environment in women with bulimia nervosa. *Journal of Abnormal Psychology*, 125(3), 381–386. doi:10.1037/abn0000135

Lavezzi, A. M., Corna, M., Mingrone, R., & Matturri, L. (2010). Study of the human hypoglossal nucleus: Normal development and morpho-functional alterations in sudden unexplained late fetal and infant death. *Brain & Development*, 32, 275–284.

Lavezzi, A. M., Matturri, L., Del Corno, G., & Johanson, C. E. (2013). Vulnerability of fourth ventricle choroid plexus in sudden unexplained fetal and infant death syndromes related to smoking mothers. *International Journal of Developmental Neuroscience*, 31(5), 319–327.

Lawler, M., & Nixon, E. (2011). Body dissatisfaction among adolescent boys and girls: The effects of body mass, peer appearance culture and internalization of appearance ideals. *Journal of Youth and Adolescence, 40*, 59–71.

Lawn, J. E., Blencowe, H., Pattinson, R., Cousens, S., Kumar, R., Ibiebele, I., . . . Stanton, C. (2011). Stillbirths: Where? When? Why? How to make the data count? *The Lancet, 377*(9775), 1448–1463.

Leavitt, J. W. (1986). *Brought to bed: Childbearing in America, 1750 to 1950.* New York, NY: Oxford University Press.

Lecanuet, J. P., Graniere-Deferre, C., Jacquet, A. Y., & DeCasper, A. J. (2000). Fetal discrimination of low-pitched musical notes. *Developmental Psychobiology, 36*, 29–39.

Lee, A. (2016). Implementing character education program through music and integrated activities in early childhood settings in Taiwan. *International Journal of Music Education, 34*(3), 340–351.

Lee, E. A. E., & Troop-Gordon, W. (2011). Peer processes and gender role development: Changes in gender atypicality related to negative peer treatment and children's friendships. *Sex Roles, 64*, 90–102.

Lee, J. (2008). "A Kotex and a smile": Mothers and daughters at menarche. *Journal of Family Issues, 29*, 1325–1347.

Lee, S. J., & Altschul, I. (2015). Children: Do immigrant and U.S.-born Hispanic parents differ? *Journal of Interpersonal Violence, 30*(3), 475–498. doi: 10.1177/0886260514535098

Lee, V. E., & Burkam, D. T. (2002). *Inequality at the starting gate: Social background differences in achievement as children begin school.* Washington, D.C. Economic Policy Institute.

Lee, Y., & Styne, D. (2013). Influences on the onset and tempo of puberty in human beings and implications for adolescent psychological development. *Hormones and Behavior, 64*(2), 250–261.

LeFebvre, L., Blackburn, K., & Brody, N. (2015). Navigating romantic relationships on Facebook: Extending the relationship dissolution model to social networking environments. *Journal of Social and Personal Relationships, 32*(1), 78–98.

Lenroot, R. K., & Giedd, J. N. (2010). Sex differences in the adolescent brain. *Brain and Cognition, 72*, 46–55.

Lepp, A., Li, J., & Barkley, J. E. (2016). College students' cell phone use and attachment to parents and peers. *Computers in Human Behavior, 64*, 401–408.

Leppänen, P. H. T., Hämäläinen, J. A., Salminen, H. K., Eklund, K. M., Guttorm, T. K., Lohvansuu, K., . . . Lyytinen, H. (2010). Newborn brain event-related potentials revealing atypical processing of sound frequency and the subsequent association with later literacy skills in children with familial dyslexia. *Cortex, 46*, 1362–1376.

Lepper, M. R., Greene, D., & Nisbett, R. E. (1973). Undermining children's intrinsic interest with extrinsic reward: A test of the "overjustification" hypothesis. *Journal of Personality and Social Psychology, 28*, 129–137.

Lerner, R. M. (1998). Theories of human development: Contemporary perspectives. In W. Damon (Series Ed.) & R. M. Lerner (Vol. Ed.). *Handbook of child psychology: Vol. 1. Theoretical models of human development* (5th ed., pp. 1–24). Hoboken, NJ: Wiley.

Lerner, R. M., Dowling, E. M., & Anderson, P. M. (2003). Positive youth development: Thriving as the basis of personhood and civil society. *Applied Developmental Science, 7*, 172–180.

Lerner, R. M., Dowling, E., & Roth, S. L. (2003). Contributions of life span psychology to the future elaboration of developmental systems theory. In U. M. Staudinger & U. Lindenberger (Eds.), *Understanding human development: Dialogues with lifespan psychology* (pp. 413–422). Dordrecht, Netherlands: Kluwer Academic.

Lerner, R. M., Lerner, J. V., Urban, J. B., & Zaff, J. (2016). Evaluating programs aimed at promoting positive youth development: A relational development systems-based view. *Applied Developmental Science, 20*(3), 175–187.

Lerner, R. M., von Eye, A., Lerner, J. V., Lewin-Bizan, S., & Bowers, E. P. (2010). Special issue introduction: The meaning and measurement of thriving: A view of the issues. *Journal of Youth and Adolescence, 39*, 707–719.

Lessard, G., Flynn, C., Turcotte, P., Damant, D., Vézina, J., Godin, M., & Rondeau-Cantin, S. (2010). Child custody issues and co-occurrence of intimate partner violence and child maltreatment: Controversies and points of agreement amongst practitioners. *Child & Family Social Work, 15*(4), 492–500.

Lester, F., Benfield, N., & Fathalla, M. M. F. (2010). Global women's health in 2010: Facing the challenges. *Journal of Women's Health, 19*(11), 2081–2089.

Leung, A. K., & Chiu, C. (2011). Multicultural experience fosters creative conceptual expansion. In A. K. Leung, C. Chiu, & Y. Y. Hong (Eds.), *Cultural processes: A social psychological perspective* (pp. 263–285). New York, NY: Cambridge University Press.

Leve, L. D., Kerr, D. C. R., Shaw, D., Ge, X., Neiderhiser, J. M., Scaramella, L. V., . . . Reiss, D. (2010). Infant pathways to externalizing behavior: Evidence of genotype X environmental interaction. *Child Development, 81*(1), 240–356.

Leventhal, T., & Newman, S. (2010). Housing and child development. *Children and Youth Services Review, 32*(9), 1165–1174.

Levine, A., & Dean, D. (2012). Generation on a tightrope: A portrait of today's college students. San Francisco: Jossey-Bass.

Lewin-Bizan, S., Lynch, A. D., Fay, K., Schmid, K., McPherran, C., Lerner, J. V., & Lerner, R. M. (2010). Trajectories of positive and negative behaviors from early- to middle-adolescence. *Journal of Youth and Adolescence, 39*, 751–763.

Lewis, A. D., Huebner, E. S., Malone, P. S., & Valois, R. F. (2011). Life satisfaction and student engagement in adolescents. *Journal of Youth and Adolescence, 40*, 249–262.

Li, X., Ling, H., Zhang, J., Si, X., & Ma, X. (2013). Influence of timing of puberty on boys' self-concept and peer relationship. *Chinese Journal of Clinical Psychology, 21*(3), 512–514.

Li, Y., & Lerner, R. M. (2011). Trajectories of school engagement during adolescence: Implications for grades, depression, delinquency, and substance use. *Developmental Psychology, 4*(1), 233–247.

Lickenbrock, D. M., Braungart-Rieker, J. M., Ekas, N. V., Zentall, S. R., Oshio, T., & Planalp, E. M. (2013). Early temperament and attachment security with mothers and fathers as predictors of toddler compliance and noncompliance. *Infant and Child Development, 22*(6), 580–602.

Lieberman, A. F. (1993). *The emotional life of the toddler.* New York: Free Press.

Liebschutz, J. M., Crooks, D., Rose-Jacobs, R., Cabral, H. J., Heeren, T. C., Gerteis, J., . . . Frank, D. A. (2015). Prenatal substance exposure: What predicts behavioral resilience by early adolescence? *Psychology of Addictive Behaviors, 29*(2), 329–337. doi:10.1037/adb0000082

Light, R. J. (2001). *Making the most of college: Students speak their minds.* Cambridge, MA: Harvard University Press.

Lightfoot, C. (1997). *The culture of adolescent risk-taking.* New York, NY: Guilford Press.

Lim, S. L., Yeh, M., Liang, J., Lau, A. S., & McCabe, K. (2009) Acculturation gap, intergenerational conflict, parenting style, and youth distress in immigrant Chinese American families. *Marriage & Family Review, 45*, 84–106.

Lin, Y., Tsai, Y., & Lai, P. (2013). The experience of Taiwanese women achieving post-infertility pregnancy through assisted reproductive treatment. *The Family Journal, 21*, 189–197.

Lin, Y., Xu, J., Huang, J., Jia, Y., Zhang, J., Yan, C., & Zhang, J. (2017). Effects of prenatal and postnatal maternal emotional stress on toddlers' cognitive and temperamental development. *Journal of Affective Disorders, 207*, 9–17. doi:10.1016/j.jad.2016.09.010

Linares, R., Bajo, M. T., & Pelegrina, S. (2016). Age-related differences in working memory updating components. *Journal of Experimental Child Psychology, 147*, 39–52. doi:10.1016/j.jecp.2016.02.009

Lindberg, L. D., Maddow-Zimet, I., & Boonstra, H. (2016). Changes in adolescents' receipt of sex education, 2006–2013. *The Journal of Adolescent Health: Official Publication of the Society for Adolescent Medicine, 58*(6), 621–627. doi:10.1016/j.jadohealth.2016.02.004

Lindsey, E. W. (2014). Physical activity play and preschool children's peer acceptance: Distinctions between rough-and-tumble and exercise play. *Early Education and Development, 25*(3), 277–294. doi:10.1080/10409289.2014.890854

Linver, M. R., Roth, J. L., & Brooks-Gunn, J. (2009). Patterns of adolescents' participation in organized activities: Are sports best when combined with other activities? *Developmental Psychology, 45*, 354–367.

Literte, P. E. (2010). Revising race: How biracial students are changing and challenging student services. *Journal of College Student Development, 51*(2), 115–135.

Liu, R. T., Cheek, S. M., & Nestor, B. A. (2016). Non-suicidal self-injury and life stress: A systematic meta-analysis and theoretical elaboration. *Clinical Psychology Review, 47*, 1–14.

Lonardo, R. A., Giordano, P. C., Longmore, M. A., & Manning, W. D. (2009). Parents, friends, and romantic partners: Enmeshment in deviant networks and adolescent delinquency involvement. *Journal of Youth and Adolescence, 38*, 367–383.

Lopes, L., Santos, R., Pereira, B., & Lopes, V. P. (2013). Associations between gross motor coordination and academic achievement in elementary school children. *Human Movement Science, 32*(1), 9–20.

Lopez-Caneda, E., Holguin, S., Rodrigues, C., Cadaveira, F., Corral, M., & Doallo, S. (2014). The impact of alcohol use on inhibitory control (and vice versa) during adolescence and young adulthood: A review. *Alcohol and Alcoholism, 49*(2), 173–184.

López-Guimerà, G., Levine, M. P., Sánchez-Carracedo, D., & Fauquet, J. (2010). Influence of mass media on body image and eating disordered attitudes and behaviors in females: A review of effects and processes. *Media Psychology, 13*(4), 387–416.

Lorber, M. F., Mitnick, D. M., & Slep, A. M. (2016). Parents' experience of flooding in discipline encounters: Associations with discipline and interplay with related factors. *Journal of Family Psychology, 30*(4), 470–479. doi:10.1037/fam0000176

Lorber, M. F., O'Leary, S. G., & Smith Slep, A. M. (2011). An initial evaluation of the role of emotion and impulsivity in explaining racial/ethnic differences in the use of corporal punishment. *Developmental Psychology, 47*(6), 1744–1749.

Lorenz, K. (1935). Der Kumpan in der Umwelt des Vogels. Der Artgenosse als auslosendes Moment sozialer Verhaltungsweisen. [The companion in the bird's world. The fellow-member of the species as releasing factor of social behavior.]. *Journal für Ornithologie. Beiblatt. (Leipzig), 83*, 137–213.

Loukas, A., Roalson, L. A., & Herrera, D. E. (2010). School connectedness buffers the effects of negative family relations and poor effortful control on early adolescent conduct problems. *Journal of Research on Adolescence, 20*(1), 13–22.

Lu, S. (2015). Fetal alcohol spectrum disorders are more common than thought, say researchers at congressional briefing. Retrieved from http://www.apa.org/monitor/2015/06/upfront-fasd.aspx, June 2015.

Lubans, D. R., Morgan, P. J., Cliff, D. P., Barnett, L. M., & Okeley, A. D. (2010). Fundamental movement skills in children and adolescents: Review of associated health benefits. *Sports Medicine, 40*(12), 1019–1035.

Lubold, A. M. (2016). Breastfeeding and employment: A propensity score matching approach. *Sociological Spectrum, 36*(6), 391–405. doi:10.1080/02732173.2016.1227286

Luciana, M. (2010). Adolescent brain development: Current themes and future directions. Introduction to the special issue [Editorial]. *Brain and Cognition, 72*, 1–5.

Luciano, E. C., & Orth, U. (2017). Transitions in romantic relationships and development of self-esteem. *Journal of Personality and Social Psychology, 122*(2), 307–328.

Lui, P. R., & Rollock, D. (2013). Tiger mother: Popular and psychological scientific perspectives on Asian culture and parenting. *American Journal of Orthopsychiatry, 83*(4), 450–456.

Luo, S. (2014). Effects of texting on satisfaction in romantic relationships: The role of attachment. *Computers in Human Behavior, 33*, 145–152.

Lydecker, J. A., & Grilo, C. M. (2016). Fathers and mothers with eating-disorder psychopathology: Associations with child eating-disorder behaviors. *Journal of Psychosomatic Research, 86*, 63–69. doi:10.1016/j.jpsychores.2016.05.006

Lynch, R. J., Kistner, J. A., Stephens, H. F., & David-Ferdon, C. (2016). Positively biased self-perceptions of peer acceptance and subtypes of aggression in children. *Aggressive Behavior, 42*(1), 82–96. doi:10.1002/ab.21611

Lynne-Landsman, S. D., Graber, J. A., & Andrews, J. A. (2010). Do trajectories of household risk in childhood moderate pubertal timing effects on substance initiation in middle school? *Developmental Psychology, 46*(4), 853–868.

Ma, F., Evans, A. D., Liu, Y., Luo, X., & Xu, F. (2015). To lie or not to lie? The influence of parenting and theory-of-mind understanding on three-year-old children's honesty. *Journal of Moral Education, 44*(2), 198–212. doi:10.1080/03057240.2015.1023182

Ma, J. (2016). Neighborhood and parenting both matter: The role of neighborhood collective efficacy and maternal spanking in early behavioral problems. *Children and Youth Services Review, 61*, 250–260.

Maccoby, E. E. (1990). Gender and relationships: A developmental account. *American Psychologist, 45*, 513–520.

Maccoby, E. E. (1998). *The two sexes: Growing up apart, coming together.* Cambridge, MA: Belknap Press of Harvard University Press.

Maccoby, E. E. (2002). Gender and group process: A developmental perspective. *Current Directions in Psychological Science, 11*, 54–58.

Macek, P., Bejcek, J., & Vanickova, J. (2007). Contemporary Czech emerging adults: Generation growing up in the period of social changes. *Journal of Adolescent Research, 22*(5), 444–474.

Maciejewski, D. F., Renteria, M. E., Abdellaoui, A., Medland, S. E., Few, L. R., Gordon, S. D., . . . Verweij, K. J. (2017). The association of genetic predisposition to depressive symptoms with non-suicidal and suicidal self-injuries. *Behavior Genetics, 47*(1), 3–10.

Mackinnon, S. P., Nosko, A., Pratt, M. W., & Norris, J. E. (2011). Intimacy in young adults' narratives of romance and friendship predicts Eriksonian generativity: A mixed method analysis. *Journal of Personality, 79*(3), 587–617.

MacMillan, H. L., Tanaka, M., Duku, E., Vaillancourt, T., & Boyle, M. H. (2013). Child physical and sexual abuse in a community sample of young adults: Results from the Ontario Child Health Study. *Child Abuse & Neglect: The International Journal, 37*(1), 14–21.

Maggs, J. L., Patrick, M. E., & Feinstein, L. (2008). Childhood and adolescent predictors of alcohol use and problems in adolescence and adulthood in the National Child Development Study. *Addiction, 103* (Suppl. 1), 7–22.

Malacrida, C., & Boulton, T. (2014). The best laid plans? Women's choices, expectations and experiences in childbirth. *Health: An Interdisciplinary Journal for the Social Study of Health, Illness and Medicine, 18*(1), 41–59.

Males, M. (2009). Does the adolescent brain make risk taking inevitable? *Journal of Adolescent Research, 24*, 3–20.

Malin, H., Reilly, T. S., Quinn, B., & Moran, S. (2014). Adolescent purpose development: Exploring empathy, discovering roles, shifting priorities, and creating pathways. *Journal of Research on Adolescence, 24*(1), 186–199.

Mandler, J. M. (2007). On the origins of the conceptual system. *American Psychologist, 62*(8), 741–751.

Manfra, L., & Winsler, A. (2006). Preschool children's awareness of private speech. *International Journal of Behavioral Development, 30*(6), 537–549.

Manning, W. D., Giordano, P. C., & Longmore, M. A. (2006). Hooking up: The relationship contexts of "nonrelationship" sex. *Journal of Adolescent Research, 21*(5), 459–483.

Marcia, J. E. (1966). Development and validation of ego-identity status. *Journal of Personality and Social Psychology, 3*, 551–558.

Marcia, J. E. (1987). The identity status approach to the study of ego identity development. In T. Honess & K. Yardley (Eds.), *Self and identity: Perspectives across the lifespan* (pp. 161–171). New York, NY: Routledge.

Mare, R. D. (2016). Educational homogamy in two gilded ages: Evidence from intergenerational social mobility data. *Annals of the American Academy of Political and Social Science, 663*(1), 117–139.

Marieb, E. N. (2004). *Human anatomy & physiology* (6th ed.). New York, NY: Pearson Education.

Markey, P. M., & Markey, C. N. (2007). Romantic ideals, romantic obtainment, and relationship experiences: The complementarity of interpersonal traits among romantic partners. *Journal of Social and Personal Relationships, 24*(4), 517–533.

Markey, P., Markey, C., Nave, C., & August, K. (2014). Interpersonal problems and relationship quality: An examination of gay and lesbian romantic couples. *Journal of Research in Personality, 51*, 1–8.

Markin, R. D. (2016). What clinicians miss about miscarriages: Clinical errors in the treatment of early term perinatal loss. *Psychotherapy, 53*(3), Special Issue: Clinical Errors, 347–353.

Marlier, L., Schaal, B., & Soussignan, R. (1998). Neonatal responsiveness to the odor of amniotic and lacteal fluids: A test of perinatal chemosensory continuity. *Child Development, 69*, 611–623.

Martin, A. J., Mansour, M., Anderson, M., Gibson, R., Liem, G. D., & Sudmalis, D. (2013). The role of arts participation in students' academic and nonacademic outcomes: A longitudinal study of school, home, and community factors. *Journal of Educational Psychology, 105*(3), 709–727.

Martin, C. L., & Ruble, D. N. (2010). Patterns of gender development. *Annual Review of Psychology, 61*, 353–381.

Martin, C. L., & Dinella, L. M. (2002). Children's gender cognitions, the social environment, and sex differences in cognitive domains. In A. McGillicuddy-De Lisi & R. De Lisi (Eds.), *Biology, society, and behavior: The development of sex differences in cognition* (pp. 207–239). Westport, CT: Ablex.

Martin, C. L., & Fabes, R. A. (2001). The stability and consequences of young children's same-sex peer interactions. *Developmental Psychology, 37*, 431–446.

Martin, J. A., Hamilton, B. E., & Osterman, M. K. (2016). Births in the United States, 2015. *NCHS Data Brief, (258)*, 1–8.

Martin, K. A. (1996). *Puberty, sexuality, and the self: Boys and girls at adolescence.* New York, NY: Routledge.

Martin, M. A., Garcia, G., Kaplan, H. S., & Gurven, M. D. (2016). Conflict or congruence? Maternal and infant-centric factors associated with shorter exclusive breastfeeding durations among the Tsimane. *Social Science & Medicine, 170*, 9–17. doi:10.1016/j.socscimed.2016.10.003

Marysko, M., Finke, P., Wiebel, A., Resch, F., & Moehler, E. (2010). Can mothers predict childhood behavioral inhibition in early infancy? *Child and Adolescent Mental Health, 15*(2), 91–96.

Masoro, E. (1999). *Challenges of biological aging.* New York, NY: Springer.

Masten, A. S. (2004). Regulatory processes, risk, and resilience in adolescent development. In R. E. Dahl & L. P. Spear (Eds.), *Adolescent brain development: Vulnerabilities and opportunities* (Vol. 1021, pp. 310–319). New York, NY: New York Academy of Sciences.

May, P. A., Hamrick, K. J., Corbin, K. D., Hasken, J. M., Marais, A., Blankenship, J., . . . Gossage, J. P. (2016). Maternal nutritional status as a contributing factor for the risk of fetal alcohol spectrum disorders. *Reproductive Toxicology, 59*, 101–108. doi:10.1016/j.reprotox.2015.11.006

Mayberry, M. L., & Espelage, D. L. (2007). Associations among empathy, social competence, & reactive/proactive aggression subtypes. *Journal of Youth and Adolescence, 36*, 787–798.

Mayeux, L., & Cillessen, A. H. N. (2008). It's not just being popular, it's knowing it, too: The role of self-perceptions of status in the associations between peer status and aggression. *Social Development, 17*, 871–888.

Maynard, A. E., & Greenfield, P. M. (2003). Implicit cognitive development in cultural tools and children: Lessons from Maya Mexico. *Cognitive Development, 18*, 489–510.

McAdams, D. P. (2013). The psychological self as actor, agent, and author. *Perspectives on Psychological Science, 8*(3), 272–295.

McAlister, A. R., & Peterson, C. C. (2013). Siblings, theory of mind, and executive functioning in children aged 3–6 years:

New longitudinal evidence. *Child Development, 84*(4), 1442–1458.

McCall, R. B., Muhamedrahimov, R. J., Groark, C. J., Palmov, O. I, Nikiforova, N. V., Salaway, J. L., & Julian, M. M. (2016). The development of children placed into different types of Russian families following an institutional intervention. *International Perspectives in Psychology: Research, Practice, Consultation, 5*(4), 255–270. doi:10.1037/ipp0000060

McCarthy, M. C., & Lumley, M. N. (2012). Sources of emotional maltreatment and the differential development of unconditional and conditional schemas. *Cognitive Behavior Therapy, 41*(4), 288–297.

McCarty, A. T., & Teoh, E. R. (2015). Tracking progress in teenage driver crash risk in the United States since the advent of graduated driver licensing programs. *Journal of Safety Research, 53*, 1–9.

McClintock, M. K., & Herdt, G. (1996). Rethinking puberty: The development of sexual attraction. *Current Directions in Psychological Science, 5*, 178–183.

McCloskey, L. A. (2013). The intergenerational transfer of mother–daughter risk for gender-based abuse. *Psychodynamic Psychiatry, 41*(2), 303–328.

McCreight, B. S. (2004). A grief ignored: Narratives of pregnancy loss from a male perspective. *Sociology of Health and Illness, 26*, 326–350.

McDonald, K. L., Malti, T., Killen, M., & Rubin, K. H. (2014). Best friends' discussions of social dilemmas. *Journal of Youth and Adolescence, 43*(2), 233–244.

McDonnell, C. G., Valentino, K., Comas, M., & Nuttall, A. K. (2016). Mother–child reminiscing at risk: Maternal attachment, elaboration, and child autobiographical memory specificity. *Journal of Experimental Child Psychology, 143*, 64–84. doi:10.1016/j.jecp.2015.10.012

McElwain, N. L., Booth-LaForce, C., & Wu, X. (2011). Infant–mother attachment and children's friendship quality: Maternal mental-state talk as an intervening mechanism. *Developmental Psychology, 47*(5), 1295–1311.

McGeown, K. (2005). *Life in Ceausescu's institutions.* Retrieved from http://news.bbc.co.uk/2/hi/europe/4630855.stm

McIntosh, H., Metz, E., & Youniss, J. (2005). Community service and identity formation in adolescents. In J. L. Mahoney, R. W. Larson, & J. S. Eccles (Eds.), *Organized activities as contexts of development: Extracurricular activities, after-school and community programs* (pp. 331–351). Mahwah, NJ: Erlbaum.

McKay, A., & Barrett, M. (2010). Trends in teen pregnancy rates from 1996–2006: A comparison of Canada, Sweden, U.S.A., and England/Wales. *Canadian Journal of Human Sexuality, 19*(1–2), 43–52.

McLaughlin, K. A., Fox, N. A., Zeanah, C. H., Sheridan, M. A., Marshall, P., & Nelson, C. A. (2010). Delayed maturation in brain electrical activity partially explains the association between early environmental deprivation and symptoms of attention-deficit/hyperactivity disorder. *Biological Psychiatry, 68*(4), 329–336.

McLaughlin, K. A., Zeanah, C. H., Fox, N. A., & Nelson, C. A. (2012). Attachment security as a mechanism linking foster care placement to improved mental health outcomes in previously institutionalized children. *Journal of Child Psychology and Psychiatry, 53*(1), 46–55.

McLeskey, J., Waldron, N. L., & Redd, L. (2014). A case study of a highly effective, inclusive elementary school. *Journal of Special Education, 48*(1), 59–70.

McNeely, C. A., & Barber, B. K. (2010). How do parents make adolescents feel loved? Perspectives on supportive parenting from adolescents in 12 cultures. *Journal of Adolescent Research, 25*(4), 601–631.

McNiel, M. E., Labbok, M. H., & Abrahams, S. W. (2010). What are the risks associated with formula feeding? A re-analysis and review. *Birth: Issues in Prenatal Care, 37*(1), 50–58.

Meier, M. H., Hall, W., Caspi, A., Belsky, D. W., Cerda, M., Harrington, H. L., Houts, R., Poulton, R., & Moffitt, T. E. (2016). Which adolescents develop persistent substance dependence in adulthood? Using population-representative longitudinal data to inform universal risk assessment. *Psychological Medicine, 46*(4), 877–889.

Melinder, A., Baugerud, G. A., Ovenstad, K. S., & Goodman, G. S. (2013). Children's memories of removal: A test of attachment theory. *Journal of Traumatic Stress, 26*(1), 125–133.

Mellor, D., Fuller-Tyszkiewicz, M., McCabe, M. P., & Ricciardelli, L. A. (2010). Body image and self-esteem across age and gender: A short-term longitudinal study. *Sex Roles, 63*(9–10), 672–681.

Menard, J. L., & Hakvoort, R. M. (2007). Variations of maternal care alter offspring levels of behavioral defensiveness in adulthood: Evidence for a threshold model. *Behavioral Brain Research, 176*, 302–313.

Mendle, J., Harden, K. P., Brooks-Gunn, J., & Graber, J. A. (2010). Development's tortoise and hare: Pubertal timing, pubertal tempo, and depressive symptoms in boys and girls. *Developmental Psychology, 46*(5), 1341–1353.

Mendle, J., Moore, S. R., Briley, D. A., & Harden, K. P. (2016). Puberty, socioeconomic status, and depression in girls: Evidence for gene × environment interactions. *Clinical Psychological Science, 4*(1), 3–16.

Mendonça, M., & Fontaine, A. M. (2013). Late nest leaving in Portugal: Its effects on individuation and parent–child relationships. *Emerging Adulthood, 1*(3), 233–244.

Mernitz, S. E., & Dush, C. K. (2016). Emotional health across the transition to first and second unions among emerging adults. *Journal of Family Psychology, 30*(2), 233–244.

Messler, C. F., Holmberg, H., & Sperlich, B. (2016). Multimodal therapy involving high-intensity interval training improves the physical fitness, motor skills, social behavior, and quality of life of boys with ADHD: A randomized controlled study. *Journal of Attention Disorders.* doi:10.1177/1087054716636936

Meuwly, N., Feinstein, B. A., Davila, J., Nuñez, D. G., & Bodenmann, G. (2013). Relationship quality among Swiss women in opposite-sex versus same-sex romantic relationships. *Swiss Journal of Psychology, 72*(4), 229–233.

Mikkelsen, A. T., Madsen, S. A., & Humaidan, P. (2013). Psychological aspects of male fertility treatment. *Journal of Advanced Nursing, 69*(9), 1977–1986.

Mikulincer, M., Florian, V., Cowan, P. A., & Cowan, C. P. (2002). Attachment security in couple relationships: A systemic model and its implications for family dynamics. *Family Process, 41*, 405–434.

Miller, D., & Daniel, B. (2007). Competent to cope, worthy of happiness? How the duality of self-esteem can inform a resilience-based classroom environment. *School Psychology International, 28*(5), 605–622.

Miller, W. D., Sadegh-Nobari, T., & Lillie-Blanton, M. (2011). Healthy starts for all: Policy prescriptions. *American Journal of Preventive Medicine, 40*(1), S19–S37.

Miniño, A. M., Arias, E., Kochanek, K. D., Murphy, S. L., & Smith, B. L. (2002, September 16). Deaths: Final data for 2000. *National Vital Statistics Reports, 50*(16).

Mintz, S. (2004). *Huck's raft: A history of American childhood*. Cambridge, MA: Belknap Press of Harvard University Press.

Mirkovic, K. R., Perrine, C. G., & Scanlon, K. S. (2016). Paid maternity leave and breastfeeding outcomes. *Birth*, *43*(3), 233–239. doi:10.1111/birt.12230

Modell, J. (1989). *Into one's own: From youth to adulthood in the United States, 1920–1975*. Berkeley, CA: University of California Press.

Moehler, E., Kagan, J., Oelkers-Ax, R., Brunner, R., Poustka, L., Haffner, J., & Resch, F. (2008). Infant predictors of behavioural inhibition. *British Journal of Developmental Psychology*, *26*(1), 145–150.

Moffitt, T. E. (1993). Adolescence-limited and life-course-persistent antisocial behavior: A developmental taxonomy. *Psychological Review*, *100*, 674–701.

Moilanen, K. L., Crockett, L. J., Raffaelli, M., & Jones, B. L. (2010). Trajectories of sexual risk from middle adolescence to early adulthood. *Journal of Research on Adolescence*, *20*(1), 114–139.

Molden, D. C., & Dweck, C. S. (2006). Finding "meaning" in psychology: A lay theories approach to self-regulation, social perception, and social development. *American Psychologist*, *61*, 192–203.

Molina, M. F., & Musich, F. M. (2015). Perception of parenting style by children with ADHD and its relation with inattention, hyperactivity/impulsivity and externalizing symptoms. *Journal of Child and Family Studies*, *25*(5), 1656–1671. doi:10.1007/s10826-015-0316-2

Molloy, L. E., Gest, S. D., & Rulison, K. L. (2011). Peer influences on academic motivation: Exploring multiple methods of assessing youths' most "influential" peer relationships. *The Journal of Early Adolescence*, *31*(1), 13–40.

Monk, C. S., McClure, E. B., Nelson, E. E., Zarahn, E., Bilder, R. M., Leibenluft, E., . . . Pine, D. S. (2003). Adolescent immaturity in attention-related brain engagement to emotional facial expressions. *Neuroimage*, *20*(1), 420–428.

Moore, D. S. (2015). *The developing genome: An introduction to behavioral epigenetics*. Oxford, UK: Oxford University Press.

Moore, S. R., & Thoemmes, F. (2016). What is the biological reality of gene–environment interaction estimates? An assessment of bias in developmental models. *Journal of Child Psychology and Psychiatry*, *11*, 1258. doi:10.1111/jcpp.12579

Moreno, M., & Trainor, M. E. (2013). Adolescence extended: Implications of new brain research on medicine and policy. *Acta Paediatrica*, *102*(3), 226–232.

Morgan, E. M. (2013). Contemporary issues in sexual orientation and identity development in emerging adulthood. *Emerging Adulthood*, *1*(1), 52–66.

Morgan, E. M., Thorne, A., & Zubriggen, E. L. (2010). A longitudinal study of conversations with parents about sex and dating during college. *Developmental Psychology*, *46*(1), 139–150.

Morgan, H. J., & Shaver, P. R. (1999). Attachment processes and commitment to romantic relationships. In J. M. Adams & W. H. Jones (Eds.), *Handbook of interpersonal commitment and relationship stability* (pp. 109–124). Dordrecht, Netherlands: Kluwer Academic.

Mori, A., & Cigala, A. (2016). Perspective taking: Training procedures in developmentally typical preschoolers. Different intervention methods and their effectiveness. *Educational Psychological Review*, *28*(2), 267–294. doi:10.1007/s10648-015-9306-6

Moss, E., Cyr, C., Bureau, J.-F., Tarabulsy, G. M., & Dubois-Comtois, K. (2005). Stability of attachment during the preschool period. *Developmental Psychology*, *41*, 773–783.

Motsa, L. F., Ibisomi, L., & Odimegwu, C. (2016). The influence of infant feeding practices on infant mortality in southern Africa. *Maternal and Child Health Journal*, *20*(10), 2130–2141. doi:10.1007/s10995-016-2033-x

Mountain, G., Cahill, J., & Thorpe, H. (2017). Sensitivity and attachment interventions in early childhood: A systematic review and meta-analysis. *Infant Behavior and Development*, *46*, 14–32. doi:10.1016/j.infbeh.2016.10.006

Muehlenkamp, J. J., Claes, L., Havertape, L., & Plener, P. L. (2012). International prevalence of adolescent non-suicidal self-injury and deliberate self-harm. *Child and Adolescent Psychiatry and Mental Health*, *6*, 1–9.

Mueller, C. M., & Dweck, C. S. (1998). Praise for intelligence can undermine children's motivation and performance. *Journal of Personality and Social Psychology*, *75*(1), 33–52.

Mulvey, K. L., & Killen, M. (2016). Keeping quiet just wouldn't be right: Children's and adolescents' evaluations of challenges to peer relational and physical aggression. *Journal of Youth and Adolescence*, *45*(9), 1824–1835. doi:10.1007/s10964-016-0437-y

Mumford, K. H., & Kita, S. (2016). At 10–12 months, pointing gesture handedness predicts the size of receptive vocabularies. *Infancy*, *21*(6), 751–765. doi:10.1111/infa.12138

Munch, A. L., Hunger, C., & Schweitzer, J. (2016). An investigation of the mediating role of personality and family functioning in the association between attachment styles and eating disorder status. *BMC Psychology*, *4*(ARTD), 36.

Munroe, R. L. (2010). Following the Whitings: The study of male pregnancy symptoms. *Journal of Cross-Cultural Psychology*, *41*(4), 592–604.

Murray, A. L., Scratch, S. E., Thompson, D. K., Inder, T. E., Doyle, L. W., Anderson, J. I., & Anderson, P. J. (2014). Neonatal brain pathology predicts adverse attention and processing speed outcomes in very preterm and/or very low birth weight children. *Neuropsychology*, *28*(4), 552–562.

Murray, S. L., & Holmes, J. G. (1997). A leap of faith? Positive illusions in romantic relationships. *Personality and Social Psychology Bulletin*, *23*, 586–604.

Murray, S. L., Holmes, J. G., Dolderman, D., & Griffin, D. W. (2000). What the motivated mind sees: Comparing friends' perspectives to married partners' views of each other. *Journal of Experimental Social Psychology*, *36*, 600–620.

Murstein, B. I. (1999). The relationship of exchange and commitment. In J. M. Adams & W. H. Jones (Eds.), *Handbook of interpersonal commitment and relationship stability* (pp. 205–219). Dordrecht, Netherlands: Kluwer Academic.

Murstein, B. I., Reif, J. A., & Syracuse-Siewert, G. (2002). Comparison of the function of exchange in couples of similar and differing physical attractiveness. *Psychological Reports*, *91*, 299–314.

Must, A., Naumova, E. N., Phillips, S. M., Blum, M., Dawson-Hughes, B., & Rand, W. M. (2005). Childhood overweight and maturational timing in the development of adult overweight and fatness: The Newton Girls Study and its follow-up. *Pediatrics*, *116*, 620–627.

Must, O., Must, A., & Mikk, J. (2016). Predicting the Flynn effect through word abstractness: Results from the national intelligence tests support Flynn's explanation. *Intelligence*, *57*, 7–14. doi:10.1016/j.intell.2016.03.003

Myers, L. L., & Wiman, A. M. (2014). Binge eating disorder: A review of a new DSM diagnosis. *Research on Social Work Practice*, *24*(1), 86–95.

National Center on Education Statistics, Fast Facts. (n.d.). *Employment rates of college graduates*. Retrieved from http://www.nces.ed.gov/fastfacts

National Down Syndrome Society. (2017). Down syndrome facts. Retrieved from http//www.ndss.org, April 2017.

Natsuaki, M. N., Leve, L. D., Harold, G. T., Neiderhiser, J. M., Shaw, D. S., Ganiban, J., . . . Reiss, D. (2013). Transactions between child social wariness and observed structured parenting: Evidence from a prospective adoption study. *Child Development, 84*(5), 1750–1765.

Natsuaki, M., Ge, X., & Wenk, E. (2008). Continuity and changes in the developmental trajectories of criminal career: Examining the roles of timing of first arrest and high school graduation. *Journal of Youth and Adolescence, 37*, 431–444.

Naughton, F., Eborall, H., & Sutton, S. (2013). Dissonance and disengagement in pregnant smokers: A qualitative study. *Journal of Smoking Cessation, 8*(1), 24–32. doi:10.1017/jsc.2013.4

Neberich, W., Penke, L., Lehnart, J., & Asendorpf, J. B. (2010). Family of origin, age at menarche, and reproductive strategies: A test of four evolutionary developmental models. *European Journal of Developmental Psychology, 7*(2), 153–177.

Negriff, S., Dorn, L. D., Pabst, S. R., & Susman, E. J. (2011). Morningness/eveningness, pubertal timing, and substance use in adolescent girls. *Psychiatry Research, 185*, 408–413.

Nelson, K. (1974). Concept, word, and sentence: Interrelations in acquisition and development. *Psychological Review, 81*, 267–285.

Nelson, K., & Fivush, R. (2004). The emergence of autobiographical memory: A social cultural developmental theory. *Psychological Review, 111*, 486–511.

Nelson, L. J., & Luster, S. S. (2016). "Adulthood" by whose definition? The complexity of emerging adults' conceptions of adulthood. In J. J. Arnett (Ed.), *The Oxford handbook of emerging adulthood* (pp. 421–437). New York, NY: Oxford University Press.

Nerini, A. (2015). Media influence and body dissatisfaction in preadolescent ballet dancers and non-physically active girls. *Psychology of Sport and Exercise, 20*, 76–83. doi:10.1016/j.psychsport.2015.04.011

Neugarten, B. (1972). Personality and the aging process. *The Gerontologist, 12*(1, Pt. 1), 9–15.

Neugarten, B. L. (1979). Time, age, and the life cycle. *American Journal of Psychiatry, 136*, 887–894.

Newcomb, A. F., & Bagwell, C. L. (1995). Children's friendship relations: A meta-analytic review. *Psychological Bulletin, 117*, 306–347.

Newland, R. P., Parade, S., Dickstein, S., & Seifer, R. (2016). Goodness of fit between maternal and infant sleep: Associations with maternal depressive symptoms and attachment security. *Infant Behavior and Development, 44*, 179–188.

Nicolopoulou, A., Barbosa de Sá, A., Ilgaz, H., & Brockmeyer, C. (2010). Using the transformative power of play to educate hearts and minds: From Vygotsky to Vivian Paley and beyond. *Mind, Culture, and Activity, 17*, 42–58.

Nmyanzi, L. A. (2016). Combating childhood obesity: Reactions of children aged 10–11 years toward the National Child Measurement Programme. *Journal of Child Health Care, 20*(4), 464–472. doi:10.1177/1367493515604493

Nolvi, S., Karlsson, L., Bridgett, D. J., Korja, R., Huizink, A. C., Kataja, E., & Karlsson, H. (2016). Maternal prenatal stress and infant emotional reactivity six months postpartum. *Journal of Affective Disorders, 199*, 163–170. doi:10.1016/j.jad.2016.04.020

Nomaguchi, K. M., & DeMaris, A. (2013). Nonmaternal care's association with mother's parenting sensitivity: A case of self-selection bias? *Journal of Marriage and Family, 75*(3), 760–777.

Nomaguchi, K., & House, A. N. (2013). Racial-ethnic disparities in maternal parenting stress: The role of structural disadvantages and parenting values. *Journal of Health and Social Behavior, 54*(3), 386–404.

Normand, S., Schneider, B., Lee, M., Maisonneuve, M., Chupetlovska-Anastasova, A., Kuehn, S., & Robaey, P. (2013). Continuities and changes in the friendships of children with and without ADHD: A longitudinal, observational study. *Journal of Abnormal Child Psychology, 41*(7), 1161–1175.

Norona, J. C., Roberson, P. E., & Welsh, D. P. (2017). I learned things that make me happy, things that bring me down: Lessons from romantic relationships in adolescence and emerging adulthood. *Journal of Adolescent Research, 32*(2), 155–182.

Obradović, J., Burt, K. B., & Masten, A. S. (2010). Testing a dual cascade model linking competence and symptoms over 20 years from childhood to adulthood. *Journal of Clinical Child and Adolescent Psychology, 39*(1), 90–102.

Oddo, S., Lux, S., Weiss, P. H., Schwab, A., Welzer, H., Markowitsch, H. J., & Fink, G. R. (2010). Specific role of medial prefrontal cortex in retrieving recent autobiographical memories: An fMRI study of young female subjects. *Cortex, 46*, 29–39.

Ogolsky, B. G., Surra, C. A., & Monk, J. K. (2016). Pathways of commitment to wed: The development and dissolution of romantic relationships. *Journal of Marriage and Family, 78*(2), 293–310.

Oldehinkel, A. J., & Bouma, E. C. (2011). Sensitivity to the depressogenic effect of stress and HPA-axis reactivity in adolescence: A review of gender differences. *Neuroscience and Biobehavioral Reviews, 35*(8), 1757–1770.

Olweus, D., Limber, S., & Mihalic, S. F. (1999). *Blueprints for violence prevention, Book 9: Bullying prevention program*. Boulder, CO: Center for the Study and Prevention of Violence, Institute of Behavioral Science, University of Colorado at Boulder.

Omar, H., McElderry, D., & Zakharia, R. (2003). Educating adolescents about puberty: What are we missing? *International Journal of Adolescent Medicine and Health, 15*, 79–83.

Ostrov, J. M., & Godleski, S. A. (2010). Toward an integrated gender-linked model of aggression subtypes in early and middle childhood. *Psychological Review, 117*(1), 233–242.

Ostrov, J. M., Murray-Close, D., Godleski, S. A., & Hart, E. J. (2013). Prospective associations between forms and functions of aggression and social and affective processes during early childhood. *Journal of Experimental Child Psychology, 116*(1), 19–36.

Ott, M. A., Millstein, S. G., Ofner, S., & Halpern-Felsher, B. L. (2006). Greater expectations: Adolescents' positive motivations for sex. *Perspectives on Sexual and Reproductive Health, 38*, 84–89.

Otterman, G., Lainpelto, K., & Lindblad, F. (2013). Factors influencing the prosecution of child physical abuse cases in a Swedish metropolitan area. *Acta Paediatrica, 102*(12), 1199–1203.

Owens, E. B., & Hinshaw, S. P. (2013). Perinatal problems and psychiatric comorbidity among children with ADHD. *Journal of Clinical Child and Adolescent Psychology, 42*(6), 762–768.

Paek, H.-J., Nelson, M. R., & Vilela, A. M. (2011). Examination of gender-role portrayals in television advertising across seven countries. *Sex Roles, 64*, 192–207.

Paikoff, R. L., & Brooks-Gunn, J. (1991). Do parent–child relationships change during puberty? *Psychological Bulletin, 110*, 47–66.

Palladino, G. (1996). *Teenagers: An American history.* New York, NY: Basic Books.

Panicker, A. S., & Chelliah, A. (2016). Resilience and stress in children and adolescents with specific learning disability. *Journal of the Canadian Academy of Child & Adolescent Psychiatry, 25*(1), 17–23.

Panter-Brick, C., Grimon, M., Kalin, M., & Eggerman, M. (2015). Trauma memories, mental health, and resilience: A prospective study of Afghan youth. *Journal of Child Psychology & Psychiatry, 56*(7), 814–825. doi:10.1111/jcpp.12350

Parackal, S. M., Parackal, M. K., & Harraway, J. A. (2013). Prevalence and correlates of drinking in early pregnancy among women who stopped drinking on pregnancy recognition. *Maternal and Child Health Journal, 17*(3), 520–529.

Paredes, M. F., James, D., Gil-Perotin, S., Kim, H., Cotter, J. A., Ng, C., . . . Alvarez-Buylia, A. (2016). Extensive migration of young neurons into the infant human frontal lobe. *Science, 354*(6308), aaf 7073 1–7.

Parent, A.-S., Teilmann, G., Juul, A., Skakkebaek, N. E., Toppari, J., & Bourguignon, J.-P. (2003). The timing of normal puberty and the age limits of sexual precocity: Variations around the world, secular trends, and changes after migration. *Endocrine Reviews, 24*, 668–693.

Parent, M. C., & Moradi, B. (2011). His biceps become him: A test of objectification theory's application to drive for muscularity and propensity for steroid use in college men. *Journal of Counseling Psychology, 58*, 246–256.

Park, Y. S., Kim, B. S. K., Chiang, J., & Ju, C. M. (2010). Acculturation, enculturation, parental adherence to Asian cultural values, parenting styles, and family conflict among Asian American college students. *Asian American Journal of Psychology, 1*(1), 67–79.

Parrish, D. E., von Sternberg, K., Castro, Y., & Velasquez, M. M. (2016). Processes of change in preventing alcohol exposed pregnancy: A mediation analysis. *Journal of Consulting and Clinical Psychology, 84*(9), 803–812.

Pasco Fearon, R., Bakermans-Kranenburg, M. J., van IJzendoorn, M. H., Lapsley, A., & Roisman, G. I. (2010). The significance of insecure attachment and disorganization in the development of children's externalizing behavior: A meta-analytic study. *Child Development, 81*(2), 435–456.

Pasco Fearon, R. M., & Belsky, J. (2011). Infant–mother attachment and the growth of externalizing problems across the primary-school years. *Journal of Child Psychology and Psychiatry, 52*(7), 782–791.

Passini, C. M., Pihet, S., & Favez, N. (2014). Assessing specific discipline techniques: A mixed-methods approach. *Journal of Child and Family Studies, 23*(8), 1389–1402. doi:10.1007/s10826-013-9796-0

Pastorelli, C., Lansford, J. E., Luengo Kanacri, B. P., Malone, P. S., DiGiunta, L., Bacchini, D., . . . Sorbring, E. (2016). Positive parenting and children's prosocial behavior in eight countries. *Journal of Child Psychology and Psychiatry, 57*(7), 824–834. doi:10.1111/jcpp.12477

Patall, E. A., Cooper, H., & Robinson, J. C. (2008). The effects of choice on intrinsic motivation and related outcomes: A meta-analysis of research findings. *Psychological Bulletin, 134*(2), 270–300.

Paul, A. M. (2010). *Origins: How the nine months before birth shape our lives.* New York, NY: Free Press.

Paulus, M., & Moore, C. (2014). The development of recipient-dependent sharing behavior and sharing expectations in preschool children. *Developmental Psychology, 50*(3), 914–921.

Paulussen-Hoogeboom, M. C., Stams, G. J. J. M., Hermanns, J. M. A., & Peetsma, T. T. D. (2007). Child negative emotionality and parenting from infancy to preschool: A meta-analytic review. *Developmental Psychology, 43*(2), 438–453.

Peach, H. D., & Gaultney, J. F. (2013). Sleep, impulse control, and sensation-seeking predict delinquent behavior in adolescents, emerging adults, and adults. *Journal of Adolescent Health, 53*(2), 293–299.

Peake, S. J., Dishion, T. J., Stormshak, E. A., Moore, W. E., & Pfeifer, J. H. (2013). Risk-taking and social exclusion in adolescence: Neural mechanisms underlying peer influences on decision-making. *Neuroimage, 82*, 23–34.

Peasgood, T., Bhardwaj, A., Biggs, K., Brazier, J. E., Coghill, D., Cooper, C. L., . . . Sonuga-Barke, E. S. (2016). The impact of ADHD on the health and well-being of ADHD children and their siblings. *European Child & Adolescent Psychiatry, 11*, 1217–1231. doi:10.1007/s00787-016-0841-6

Peck, S. C., Vida, M., & Eccles, J. S. (2008). Adolescent pathways to adulthood drinking: Sport activity involvement is not necessarily risky or protective. *Addiction, 103* (Suppl. 1), 69–83.

Pedersen, N. L. (1996). Gerontological behavior genetics. In J. E. Birren, K. W. Schaie, R. P. Abeles, M. Gatz, & T. A. Salthouse (Eds.), *Handbook of the psychology of aging* (4th ed., pp. 59–77). San Diego, CA: Academic Press.

Pellegrini, A. D. (2006). The development and function of rough-and-tumble play in childhood and adolescence: A sexual selection theory perspective. In A. Göncü & S. Gaskins (Eds.), *Play and development: Evolutionary, sociocultural, and functional perspectives. The Jean Piaget Symposium Series* (pp. 77–98). Mahwah, NJ: Erlbaum.

Pellegrini, A. D., Long, J. D., Roseth, C. J., Bohn, C. M., & Van Ryzin, M. (2007). A short-term longitudinal study of preschoolers' (*Homo sapiens*) sex segregation: The role of physical activity, sex, and time. *Journal of Comparative Psychology, 121*(3), 282–289.

Pellegrini, A. D., & Smith, P. K. (Eds.). (2005). *The nature of play: Great apes and humans.* New York, NY: Guilford Press.

Peper, J. S., & Dahl, R. E. (2013). The teenage brain: Surging hormones—Brain–behavior interactions during puberty. *Current Directions in Psychological Science, 22*(2), 134–139.

Pérez-Edgar, K., Bar-Haim, Y., McDermott, J. M., Chronis-Tuscano, A., Pine, D. S., & Fox, N. A. (2010a). Attention biases to threat and behavioral inhibition in early childhood shape adolescent social withdrawal. *Emotion, 10*, 349–357.

Pérez-Edgar, K., McDermott, J. N., Korelitz, K., Degnan, K. A., Curby, T. W., Pine, D. S., & Fox, N. A. (2010b). Patterns of sustained attention in infancy shape the developmental trajectory of social behavior from toddlerhood through adolescence. *Developmental Psychology, 46*(6), 1723–1730.

Persike, M., & Seiffge-Krenke, I. (2014). Is stress perceived differently in relationships with parents and peers? Inter- and intra-regional comparisons on adolescents from 21 nations. *Journal of Adolescence, 37*(4), 493–504.

Peskin, J. (1992). Ruse and representations: On children's ability to conceal information. *Developmental Psychology, 28*, 84–89.

Peters, E., Riksen-Walraven, J. M., Cillessen, A. H., & Weerth, C. D. (2011). Peer rejection and HPA activity in middle childhood:

Friendship makes a difference. *Child Development, 82*(6), 1906–1920. doi:10.1111/j.1467-8624.2011.01647.x

Petraglia, F., Serour, G. I., & Chapron, C. (2013). The changing prevalence of infertility. *International Journal of Gynecology Obstetrics, 123* (Suppl. 2), S4-8.

Pettigrew, S., Jongenelis, M., Chikritzhs, T., Pratt, I. S., Slevin, T., & Glance, D. (2016). A comparison of alcohol consumption intentions among pregnant drinkers and their nonpregnant peers of child-bearing age. *Substance Use & Misuse, 51*(11), 1421–1427.

Pfinder, M., Kunst, A. E., Feldmann, R., van Eijsden, M., & Vrijkotte, T. M. (2014). Educational differences in continuing or restarting drinking in early and late pregnancy: Role of psychological and physical problems. *Journal of Studies on Alcohol and Drugs, 75*(1), 47–55.

Phelan, P., Davidson, A. L., & Yu, H. C. (1998). *Adolescents' worlds: Negotiating family, peers, and school.* New York, NY: Teachers College Press.

Philbrook, L. E., & Teti, D. M. (2016). Associations between bedtime and nighttime parenting and infant cortisol in the first year. *Developmental Psychobiology, 58*(8), 1087–1100. doi:10.1002/dev.21442

Phillips, D. A., & Lowenstein, A. E. (2011). Early care, education and child development. *American Review of Psychology, 62*, 483–500.

Phinney, J. S. (2006). Acculturation is not an independent variable: Approaches to studying acculturation as a complex process. In M. H. Bornstein & L. R. Cote (Eds.), *Acculturation and parent–child relationships: Measurement and development* (pp. 79–95). Mahwah, NJ: Erlbaum.

Piaget, J. (1950). *The psychology of intelligence.* Oxford, England: Harcourt.

Piaget, J. (1962). *Play, dreams and imitation in childhood.* New York, NY: Norton. (Original work published 1951).

Piaget, J. (1965). *The moral judgment of the child* (Paperback ed.). New York, NY: Free Press.

Piaget, J. (1971). *The psychology of intelligence.* London, England: Routledge & Kegan Paul. (Original work published 1950)

Pieloch, K. A., McCullough, M. B., & Marks, A. K. (2016). Resilience of children with refugee statuses: A research review. *Canadian Psychology, 57*(4), 330–339. doi:10.1037/cap0000073

Pinker, S. (2011). *The better angels of our nature: Why violence has declined.* New York, NY: Viking.

Pinquart, M. (2013). Do the parent–child relationship and parenting behaviors differ between families with a child with and without chronic illness? A meta-analysis. *Journal of Pediatric Psychology, 38*(7), 708–721.

Pinquart, M., Feubner, C., & Ahnert, L. (2013). Meta-analytic evidence for stability in attachments from infancy to early adulthood. *Attachment & Human Development, 15*(2), 189–218.

Plant, C. P., Donohue, B., & Holland, J. M. (2016). Examination of life satisfaction, child maltreatment potential and substance use in mothers referred for treatment by child protective services for child neglect and substance abuse: Implications for intervention planning. *Applied Research in Quality of Life, 3*, 805. doi:10.1007/s11482-015-9398-7

Plant, T. M. (2015). The hypothalamo-pituitary-gonadal axis. *Journal of Endocrinology, 226*(2), T41. doi:10.1530/JOE-15-0113

Plomin, R., & Bergeman, C. S. (1991). The nature of nurture: Genetic influence on "environmental" measures. *Behavioral and Brain Sciences, 14*, 373–427.

Plomin, R., & Spinath, F. M. (2004). Intelligence: Genetics, genes, and genomics. *Journal of Personality and Social Psychology, 86*, 112–129.

Pnevmatikos, D., & Trikkaliotis, I. (2013). Intra-individual differences in executive functions during childhood: The role of emotions. *Journal of Experimental Child Psychology, 115*(2), 245–261.

Poirier, F. E., & Smith, E. O. (1974). Socializing functions of primate play. *American Zoologist, 14*, 275–287.

Polanco-Roman, L., & Miranda, R. (2013). Culturally related stress, hopelessness, and vulnerability to depressive symptoms and suicidal ideation in emerging adulthood. *Behavior Therapy, 44*(1), 75–87.

Pölkki, P. L., & Vornanen, R. H. (2016). Role and success of Finnish early childhood education and care in supporting child welfare clients: Perspectives from parents and professionals. *Early Childhood Education Journal, 44*(6), 581–594. doi:10.1007/s10643-015-0746-x

Posada, G., Trumbell, J., Noblega, M., Plata, S., Peña, P., Carbonell, O. A., & Lu, T. (2016). Maternal sensitivity and child secure base use in early childhood: Studies in different cultural contexts. *Child Development, 87*(1), 297–311. doi:10.1111/cdev.12454

Potts, M., Prata, N., & Sahin-Hodoglugil, N. N. (2010). Maternal mortality: One death every 7 min. *The Lancet, 375*(9728), 1762–1763.

Poulin, F., & Chan, A. (2010). Friendship stability and change in childhood and adolescence. *Developmental Review, 30*(3), 257–272.

Poulton, R., Moffitt, T. E., & Silva, P. A. (2015). The Dunedin Multidisciplinary Health and Development Study: Overview of the first 40 years, with an eye to the future. *Social Psychiatry and Psychiatric Epidemiology, 50*(5), 679–693.

Prazen, A., Wolfinger, N. H., Cahill, C., & Kowaleski-Jones, L. (2011). Joint physical custody and neighborhood friendships in middle childhood. *Sociological Inquiry, 2*, 247.

Preston, S. H. (1991). *Fatal years: Child mortality in late nineteenth-century America.* Princeton, NJ: Princeton University Press.

Prinstein, M. J., & La Greca, A. M. (2002). Peer crowd affiliation and internalizing distress in childhood and adolescence: A longitudinal follow-back study. *Journal of Research on Adolescence, 12*, 325–351.

Pryor, J. H., Hurtado, S., DeAngelo, L., Blake, L. P., & Tran, S. (2011). *The American freshman: National norms, Fall 2010.* Los Angeles, Higher Education Research Institute, UCLA.

Puhl, R. M., & Latner, J. D. (2007). Stigma, obesity, and the health of the nation's children. *Psychological Bulletin, 133*(4), 557–580.

Rabin, J. S., Gilboa, A., Stuss, D. T., Mar, R. A., & Rosenbaum, R. S. (2010). Common and unique neural correlates of autobiographical memory and theory of mind. *Journal of Cognitive Neuroscience, 22*(6), 1095–1111.

Ramsay, S. M., & Santella, R. M. (2011). The definition of life: A survey of obstetricians and neonatologists in New York City hospitals regarding extremely premature births. *Maternal and Child Health Journal, 15*, 446–452.

Ramsey, E., Kelly-Vance, L., Allen, J. A., Rosol, O., & Yoerger, M. (2016). Autism spectrum disorder prevalence rates in the United States: Methodologies, challenges, and implications for individual states. *Journal of Developmental and Physical Disabilities, 28*(6), 803–820. doi:10.1007/s10882-016-9510-4

Ratner, N. B. (2013). Why talk with children matters: Clinical implications of infant- and child-directed speech research. *Seminars in Speech and Language, 34*(4), 203–214.

Rauer, A. J., Pettit, G. S., Lansford, J. E., Bates, J. E., & Dodge, K. A. (2013). Romantic relationship patterns in young adulthood and their developmental antecedents. *Developmental Psychology, 49*(11), 2159–2171.

Reijneveld, S. A., van der Wal, M. F., Brugman, E., Sing, R. A. H., & Verloove-Vanhorick, S. P. (2004). Infant crying and abuse. *Lancet, 364*, 1340–1342.

Reijntjes, A., Vermande, M., Olthof, T., Goossens, F. A., Aleva, L., & Meulen, M. V. (2016). Defending victimized peers: Opposing the bully, supporting the victim, or both? *Aggressive Behavior, 42*(6), 585–597. doi:10.1002/ab.21653

Reimer, J., Paolitto, D. P., & Hersh, R. H. (1983). *Promoting moral growth: From Piaget to Kohlberg* (2nd ed.). New York, NY: Longman.

Reimer, K. (2003). Committed to caring: Transformation in adolescent moral identity. *Applied Developmental Science, 7*, 129–137.

Reindl, M., Gniewosz, B., & Reinders, H. (2016). Socialization of emotion regulation strategies through friends. *Journal of Adolescence, 49*, 146–157. doi:10.1016/j.adolescence.2016.03.008

Reissman, C., Aron, A., & Bergen, M. R. (1993). Shared activities and marital satisfaction: Causal direction and self-expansion versus boredom. *Journal of Social and Personal Relationships, 10*, 243–254.

Ren, R., Guo, F., & Chen, Z. (2015). Early puberty and delinquent behaviors among adolescent girls: Moderating of parenting. *Chinese Journal of Clinical Psychology, 23*(1), 178–181.

Richter, B., Lindahl, K., & Malik, N. (2017). Examining ethnic differences in parental rejection of LGB youth sexual identity. *Journal of Family Psychology, 31*(2), 244–249.

Rigoli, D., Piek, J., Kane, R., Whillier, A., Baxter, C., & Wilson, P. (2013). An 18-month follow-up investigation of motor coordination and working memory in primary school children. *Human Movement Science, 32*(5), 1116–1126.

Rilling, J. K. (2013). The neural and hormonal bases of human parental care. *Neuropsychologia, 51*(4), 731–747.

Rinehart, M. S., & Kiselica, M. S. (2010). Helping men with the trauma of miscarriage. *Psychotherapy: Theory, Research, Practice, Training, 47*(3), 288–295.

Rispoli, K. M., McGoey, K. E., Koziol, N. A., & Schreiber, J. B. (2013). The relation of parenting, child temperament, and attachment security in early childhood to social competence at school entry. *Journal of School Psychology, 51*(5), 643–658.

Rizzo, M. T., Elenbaas, L., Cooley, S., & Killen, M. (2016). Children's recognition of fairness and others' welfare in a resource allocation task: Age-related changes. *Developmental Psychology, 52*(8), 1307–1317. doi:10.1037/dev0000134

Roache, R. (2016). Infertility and non-traditional families. *Journal of Medical Ethics: Journal of the Institute of Medical Ethics, 42*(9), 557–558.

Roberts, A. L., Lyall, K., Rich-Edwards, J. W., Ascherio, A., & Weisskopf, M. G. (2013). Association of maternal exposure to childhood abuse with elevated risk for autism in offspring. *JAMA Psychiatry, 70*(5), 508–515.

Roberts, C. (2016). Tanner's puberty scale: Exploring the historical entanglements of children, scientific photography and sex. *Sexualities, 19*(3), 328–346. doi:10.1177/1363460715593477

Rodkin, P. C., & Roisman, G. I. (2010). Antecedents and correlates of the popular-aggressive phenomenon in elementary school. *Child Development, 81*(3), 837–850.

Rodkin, P. C., Ryan, A. M., Jamison, R., & Wilson, T. (2013). Social goals, social behavior, and social status in middle childhood. *Developmental Psychology, 49*(6), 1139–1150.

Rodriguez, C. M., & Henderson, R. C. (2010). Who spares the rod? Religious orientation, social conformity, and child abuse potential. *Child Abuse & Neglect, 34*, 84–94.

Roffwarg, H. P., Muzio, J. N., & Dement, W. C. (1966, April 29). Ontogenetic development of the human sleep–dream cycle. *Science, 152*, 604–619.

Rogoff, B., Paradise, R., Arauz, R. M., Correa-Chavez, M., & Angelillo, C. (2003). Firsthand learning through intent participation. *Annual Review of Psychology, 54*, 175–203.

Rohlf, H., Busching, R., & Krahé, B. (2016). The socializing effect of classroom aggression on the development of aggression and social rejection: A two-wave multilevel analysis. *Journal of School Psychology, 58*, 57–72. doi:10.1016/j.jsp.2016.05.002

Rojas-Flores, L., Herrera, S., Currier, J. M., Lin, E. Y., Kulzer, R., & Foy, D. W. (2013). "We are raising our children in fear": War, community violence, and parenting practices in El Salvador. *International Perspectives in Psychology: Research, Practice, Consultation, 2*(4), 269–285.

Romano, E., Babchishin, L., Pagani, L. S., & Kohen, D. (2010). School readiness and later achievement: Replication and extension using a nationwide Canadian survey. *Developmental Psychology, 46*(5), 995–1007.

Romeo, R. D. (2013). The teenage brain: The stress response and the adolescent brain. *Current Directions in Psychological Science, 22*(2), 140–145.

Rorie, M., Gottfredson, D. C., Cross, A., Wilson, D., & Connell, N. M. (2011). Structure and deviancy training in after-school programs. *Journal of Adolescence, 34*, 105–117.

Rose, A. J., & Asher, S. R. (2000). Children's friendships. In C. Hendrick & S. S. Hendrick (Eds.), *Close relationships: A sourcebook* (pp. 47–57). Thousand Oaks, CA: Sage.

Rose, J., Vassar, R., Cahill-Rowley, K., Guzman, X., Stevenson, D. K., & Barnea-Goraly, N. (2014). Brain microstructural development at near-term age in very-low-birth-weight preterm infants: An atlas-based diffusion imaging study. *Neuroimage, 86*, 244–256.

Rosenfield, R. L., Lipton, R. B., & Drum, M. L. (2009). Thelarche, pubarche, and menarche attainment in children with normal and elevated body mass index. *Pediatrics, 123*, 84–88.

Rosenthal, M., Wallace, G. L., Lawson, R., Wills, M. C., Dixon, E., Yerys, B. E., & Kenworthy, L. (2013). Impairments in real-world executive function increase from childhood to adolescence in autism spectrum disorders. *Neuropsychology, 27*(1), 13–18.

Roussotte, F., Soderberg, L., & Sowell, E. (2010). Structural, metabolic and functional brain abnormalities as a result of prenatal exposure to drugs of abuse: Evidence from neuroimaging. *Neuropsychology Review, 20*(4), 376–397.

Rowe, D. C. (2003). Assessing genotype–environment interactions and correlations in the postgenomic era. In R. Plomin, J. C. DeFries, I. W. Craig, & P. McGuffin (Eds.), *Behavioral genetics in the postgenomic era* (pp. 71–86). Washington, DC: American Psychological Association.

Rowe, M. L., Levine, S. C., Fisher, J. A., & Goldin-Meadow, S. (2009). Does linguistic input play the same role in language learning for children with and without early brain injury? *Developmental Psychology, 45*, 90–102.

Royal College of Obstetricians and Gynaecologists. (1999). *Alcohol consumption in pregnancy*. Retrieved from http://www.rcog.org/uk/index.asp?PageID=509

Royer, N., & Moreau, C. (2016). A survey of Canadian early childhood educators' psychological well-being at work. *Early Childhood Education Journal, 44*(2), 135–146. doi:10.1007/s10643-015-1696-3

Ruble, D. N., Martin, C., & Berenbaum, S. A. (2006). Gender development. In N. Eisenberg, W. Damon, & R. M. Lerner (Eds.), *Handbook of child psychology: Vol. 3. Social, emotional, and personality development* (6th ed., pp. 858–932). Hoboken, NJ: Wiley.

Runions, K. C. (2013). Toward a conceptual model of motive and self-control in cyber-aggression: Rage, revenge, reward, and recreation. *Journal of Youth and Adolescence, 42*(5), 751–771.

Rusbult, C. E., Kumashiro, M., Kubacka, K. E., & Finkel, E. J. (2009). "The part of me that you bring out": Ideal similarity and the Michelangelo phenomenon. *Journal of Personality and Social Psychology, 96*, 61–82.

Rushton, J. P., & Jensen, A. R. (2005). Thirty years of research on race differences in cognitive ability. *Psychology, Public Policy, and Law, 11*, 235–294.

Ryan, J. J., Glass, L. A., & Bartels, J. M. (2010). Stability of the WISC-IV in a sample of elementary and middle school children. *Applied Neuropsychology, 17*(1), 68–72.

Ryan, R. M., Deci, E. L., Grolnick, W. S., & La Guardia, J. G. (2006). The significance of autonomy and autonomy support in psychological development and psychopathology. In D. Cicchetti & D. J. Cohen (Eds.), *Developmental psychopathology: Vol. 1. Theory and method* (2nd ed., pp. 795–849). Hoboken, NJ: John Wiley & Sons Inc.

Ryan-Krause, P. (2011). Attention deficit hyperactivity disorder: Part III. *Journal of Pediatric Health Care, 25*(1), 50–53.

Sabik, N. J., Cole, E. R., & Ward, L. M. (2010). Are all minority women equally buffered from negative body image? Intra-ethnic moderators of the buffering hypothesis. *Psychology of Women Quarterly, 34*(2), 139–151.

Saenz, J., & Alexander, G. M. (2013). Postnatal testosterone levels and disorder relevant behavior in the second year of life. *Biological Psychology, 94*(1), 152–159.

Saigal, S., Day, K. L., Lieshout, R. J., Schmidt, L. A., Morrison, K. M., & Boyle, M. H. (2016). Health, wealth, social integration, and sexuality of extremely low-birth-weight prematurely born adults in the fourth decade of life. *JAMA Pediatrics, 170*(7), 678. doi:10.1001/jamapediatrics.2016.0289

Sakyi, K., Surkan, P. J., Fombonne, E., Cholett, A., & Melchior, M. (2016). Childhood friendships and psychological difficulties in young adulthood: An 18-year follow up study. *European Child and Adolescent Psychiatry, 24*(7), 815–826.

Sala, M., & Levinson, C. A. (2016). The longitudinal relationship between worry and disordered eating: Is worry a precursor or consequence of disordered eating? *Eating Behaviors, 23*, 28–32.

Salmon, K., & Reese, E. (2015). Talking (or not talking) about the past: The influence of parent–child conversation about negative experiences on children's memories. *Applied Cognitive Psychology, 29*(6), 791–801. doi:10.1002/acp.3186

Samimi, P., & Alderson, K. G. (2014). Sexting among undergraduate students. *Computers in Human Behavior, 31*, 230–241.

Sánchez, B., Esparza, P., Cölon, Y., & Davis, K. E. (2010). Tryin' to make it during the transition from high school: The role of family obligation attitudes and economic context for Latino emerging adults. *Journal of Adolescent Research, 25*(6), 858–884.

Sandler, I. N., Wheeler, L. A., & Braver, S. L. (2013). Relations of parenting quality, interparental conflict, and overnights with mental health problems of children in divorcing families with high legal conflict. *Journal of Family Psychology, 27*(6), 915–924.

Santesso, D. L., Schmidt, L. A., & Trainor, L. J. (2007). Frontal brain electrical activity (EEG) and heart rate in response to affective infant-directed (ID) speech in 9-month-old infants. *Brain and Cognition, 65*, 14–21.

Santos, C. E., & Collins, M. A. (2016). Ethnic identity, school connectedness, and achievement in standardized tests among Mexican-origin youth. *Cultural Diversity & Ethnic Minority Psychology, 22*(3), 447–452.

Satici, S. A., & Uysal, R. (2015). Well-being and problematic Facebook use. *Computers in Human Behavior, 49*, 185–190.

Sato, K., Oikawa, M., Hiwatashi, M., Sato, M., & Oyamada, N. (2016). Factors relating to the mental health of women who were pregnant at the time of the Great East Japan earthquake: Analysis from month 10 to month 48 after the earthquake. *BioPsychoSocial Medicine, 10*(1). doi:10.1186/s13030-016-0072-6

Sattler, J. M. (2001). *Assessment of children: Cognitive applications* (4th ed.). La Mesa, CA: Sattler.

Savin-Williams, R. C. (2001). *Mom, Dad, I'm gay. How families negotiate coming out*. Washington, DC: American Psychological Association.

Savin-Williams, R. C. (2008). Then and now: Recruitment, definition, diversity, and positive attributes of same-sex populations. *Developmental Psychology, 44*(1), 135–138.

Scahill, L., Bearss, K., Lecavalier, L., Smith, T., Swiezy, N., Aman, M. G., . . . Johnson, C. (2016). Effect of parent training on adaptive behavior in children with autism spectrum disorder and disruptive behavior: Results of a randomized trial. *Journal of the American Academy of Child & Adolescent Psychiatry, 55*(7), 602–609. doi:10.1016/j.jaac.2016.05.001

Scarr, S. (1997). Behavior-genetic and socialization theories of intelligence: Truce and reconciliation. In R. J. Sternberg & E. L. Grigorenko (Eds.), *Intelligence, heredity, and environment* (pp. 3–41). New York, NY: Cambridge University Press.

Scarr, S., & Deater-Deckard, K. (1997). Family effects on individual differences in development. In S. S. Luthar, J. A. Burack, D. Cicchetti, & J. R. Weisz (Eds.), *Developmental psychopathology: Perspectives on adjustment, risk, and disorder* (pp. 115–136). New York, NY: Cambridge University Press.

Schellinger, K., & Talmi, A. (2013). Off the charts? Considerations for interpreting parent reports of toddler hyperactivity. *Infant Mental Health Journal, 34*(5), 417–419.

Scheres, A., Tontsch, C., & Lee Thoeny, A. (2013). Steep temporal reward discounting in ADHD-Combined type: Acting upon feelings. *Psychiatry Research, 209*(2), 207–213.

Schirduan, V., & Case, K. (2004). Mindful curriculum leadership for students with attention deficit hyperactivity disorder: Leading in elementary schools by using multiple intelligences theory (SUMIT). *Teachers College Record, 106*, 87–95.

Schlegel, A. (1995). The cultural management of adolescent sexuality. In P. R. Abramson & S. D. Pinkerton (Eds.), *Sexual nature, sexual culture* (pp. 177–194). Chicago, IL: University of Chicago Press.

Schlegel, A., & Barry, H., III. (1991). *Adolescence: An anthropological inquiry.* New York, NY: Free Press.

Schlinger, H. D. (2003). The myth of intelligence. *Psychological Record, 53,* 15–32.

Schmid, G., Schreier, A., Meyer, R., & Wolke, D. (2010). A prospective study in the persistence of infant crying, sleeping and feeding problems and preschool behavior. *Acta Pædiatrica, 99,* 286–290.

Scholte, R., Sentse, M., & Granic, I. (2010). Do actions speak louder than words? Classroom attitudes and behavior in relation to bullying in early adolescence. *Journal of Clinical Child & Adolescent Psychology, 39*(6), 789–799.

Schramm, D. G., Harris, S. M., Whiting, J. B., Hawkins, A. J., Brown, M., & Porter, R. (2013). Economic costs and policy implications associated with divorce: Texas as a case study. *Journal of Divorce & Remarriage, 54*(1), 1–24.

Schreiner, L. A., Noel, P., Anderson, E., & Cantwell, L. (2011). The impact of faculty and staff on high-risk college student persistence. *Journal of College Student Development, 52*(3), 321–338.

Schueler, C. M., & Prinz, R. J. (2013). The role of caregiver contingent responsiveness in promoting compliance in young children. *Child Psychiatry and Human Development, 44*(3), 370–381.

Schwartz, C. E., Wright, C. I., Shin, L. M., Kagan, J., & Rauch, S. L. (2003, June 20). Inhibited and uninhibited infants "grown up": Adult amygdalar response to novelty. *Science, 300,* 1952–1953.

Schwartz, S. J, Meca, A., Hardy, S., Zamboanga, B., Waterman, A., Picariello, S., . . . Forthun, L. (2015). Identity in young adulthood: Links with mental health and risky behavior. *Journal of Applied Developmental Psychology, 36,* 39–52.

Schwartz, S. J. (2016). Turning point for a turning point: Advancing emerging adulthood theory and research. *Emerging Adulthood, 4*(5), 307–317.

Schwartz, S. J., Zambotanga, B. L., Luyckx, Meca A., & Riche, R. (2016). Identity in emerging adulthood: Reviewing the field and looking forward. In J. J. Arnett (Ed.), *The Oxford handbook of emerging adulthood* (pp. 401–420). New York, NY: Oxford University Press.

Scrimgeour, M. B., Davis, E. L., & Buss, K. A. (2016). You get what you get and you don't throw a fit!: Emotion socialization and child physiology jointly predict early prosocial development. *Developmental Psychology, 52*(1), 102–116.

Scrimsher, S., & Tudge, J. (2003). The teaching/learning relationship in the first years of school: Some revolutionary implications of Vygotsky's theory. *Early Education and Development, 14,* 293–312.

Sebastián-Enesco, C., Hernández-Lloreda, M. V., & Colmenares, F. (2013). Two and a half-year-old children are prosocial even when their partners are not. *Journal of Experimental Child Psychology, 116*(2), 186–198.

Seiffge-Krenke, I. (2010). Predicting the timing of leaving home and related developmental tasks: Parents' and children's perspectives. *Journal of Social and Personal Relationships, 27*(4), 495–518.

Seiffge-Krenke, I. (2013). "She's leaving home . . ." Antecedents, consequences, and cultural patterns in the leaving home process. *Emerging Adulthood, 1*(2), 114–124.

Seiffge-Krenke, I., Persike, M., & Luyckx, K. (2013). Factors contributing to different agency in work and study: A view on the "forgotten half." *Emerging Adulthood, 1*(4), 283–292.

Self-Brown, S. R., & Mathews, S. (2003). Effects of classroom structure on student achievement goal orientation. *Journal of Educational Research, 97,* 106–111.

Settersten, R. A., & Ray, B. (2010). *What's going on with young people today? The long and twisting path to adulthood.* In *The Future of Children, 20*(1), 1–21. Retrieved from www.princeton.edu/futureofchildren/publications/docs/20_01_02.pdf

Shahaeian, A., Peterson, C. C., Slaughter, V., & Wellman, H. M. (2011). Culture and the sequence of steps in theory of mind development. *Developmental Psychology, 47*(5), 1239–1247. doi:10.1037/a0023899

Shalev, I., Moffitt, T. E., Braithwaite, A. W., Danese, A., Fleming, N. I., Goldman-Mellor, S., . . . Caspi, A. (2014). Internalizing disorders and leukocyte telomere erosion: A prospective study of depression, generalized anxiety disorder and post-traumatic stress disorder. *Molecular Psychiatry, 19*(11), 163–1170.

Shao, S., Kong, R., Zou, L., Zhong, R., Lou, J., Zhou, J., . . . Song, R. (2016). The roles of genes in the neuronal migration and neurite outgrowth network in developmental dyslexia: Single- and multiple-risk genetic variants. *Molecular Neurobiology, 53*(6), 3967–3975. doi:10.1007/s12035-015-9334-8

Sharon, T. (2015). Constructing adulthood: Markers of adulthood and well-being among emerging adults. *Emerging Adulthood, 4*(3), 161–167.

Shaywitz, S. E., Morris, R., & Shaywitz, B. A. (2008). The education of dyslexic children from childhood to young adulthood. *Annual Review of Psychology, 59,* 451–475.

Shearer, C. L., Crouter, A. C., & McHale, S. M. (2005). Parents' perceptions of changes in mother–child and father–child relationships during adolescence. *Journal of Adolescent Research, 20,* 662–684.

Sheehan, A., Schmied, V., & Barclay, L. (2013). Exploring the process of women's infant feeding decisions in the early post-birth period. *Qualitative Health Research, 23*(7), 989–998.

Sheridan, A., Murray, L., Cooper, P. J., Evangeli, M., Byram, V., & Halligan, S. L. (2013). A longitudinal study of child sleep in high- and low-risk families: Relationship to early maternal settling strategies and child psychological functioning. *Sleep Medicine, 14*(3), 266–273.

Shonkoff, J. P., & Phillips, D. A. (2000). Growing up in child care. In J. P. Shonkoff & D. A. Phillips (Eds.), *From neurons to neighborhoods: The science of early childhood development* (pp. 297–327). Washington, DC: National Academy Press.

Shulman, E. P., & Steinberg, L. (2016). Human development and juvenile justice. In K. Heilbrun, D. DeMatteo, & N. S. Goldstein (Eds.), *APA handbook of psychology and juvenile justice* (pp. 69–90). Washington, DC: American Psychological Association.

Shulman, E. P., Harden, K. P., Chein, J. M., & Steinberg, L. (2015). Sex differences in the developmental trajectories of impulse control and sensation-seeking from early adolescence to early adulthood. *Journal of Youth and Adolescence, 44*(1), 1–17.

Shulman, S., & Connolly, J. (2013). The challenge of romantic relationships in emerging adulthood: Reconceptualization of the field. *Emerging Adulthood, 1*(1), 27–39.

Sieswerda-Hoogendoorn, T., Bilo, R. A., van Duurling, L. L., Karst, W. A., Maaskant, J. M., van Aalderen, W. M., & van Rijn, R. R. (2013). Abusive head trauma in young children in the Netherlands:

Evidence for multiple incidents of abuse. *Acta Paediatrica, 102*(11), e497–501.

Silk, T. J., Genc, S., Anderson, V., Efron, D., Hazell, P., Nicholson, J. M., . . . Sciberras, E. (2016). Developmental brain trajectories in children with ADHD and controls: A longitudinal neuroimaging study. *BMC Psychiatry, 16*(1). doi:10.1186/s12888-016-0770-4

Silva, J. M. (2016). High hopes and hidden inequalities: How social class shapes pathways to adulthood. *Emerging Adulthood, 4*(4), 239–241.

Silventoinen, K., Haukka, J., Dunkel, L., Tynelius, P., & Rasmussen, F. (2008). Genetics of pubertal timing and its associations with relative weight in childhood and adult height: The Swedish young male twins study. *Pediatrics, 121*(4), 885–891.

Silvetti, M., Castellar, E. N., Roger, C., & Verguts, T. (2014). Reward expectation and prediction error in human medial frontal cortex: An EEG study. *Neuroimage, 84*, 376–382.

Simmons, R. G., & Blyth, D. A. (1987). *Moving into adolescence: The impact of pubertal change and school context.* Hawthorne, NY: Aldine.

Simons, D. A., & Wurtele, S. K. (2010). Relationships between parents' use of corporal punishment and their children's endorsement of spanking and hitting other children. *Child Abuse & Neglect, 34*, 639–646.

Sjörs, G. (2010). Treatment decisions for extremely preterm newborns: Beyond gestational age. *Acta Paediatrica, 99*(12), 1761–1762.

Skinner, B. F. (1960). *The behavior of organisms: An experimental analysis.* New York, NY: Appleton-Century-Crofts.

Skinner, B. F. (1974). *About behaviorism.* New York, NY: Knopf.

Skoog, T., Stattin, H., Ruiselova, Z., & Özdemir, M. (2013). Female pubertal timing and problem behaviour: The role of culture. *International Journal of Behavioral Development, 37*(4), 357–365.

Slater, A. (2001). Visual perception. In G. Bremner & A. Fogel (Eds.), *Blackwell handbook of infant development* (pp. 5–34). Malden, MA: Blackwell.

Slater, A., Quinn, P. C., Kelly, D. J., Lee, K., Longmore, C. A., McDonald, P. R., & Pascalis, O. (2010). The shaping of the face space in early infancy: Becoming a native face processor. *Child Development Perspectives, 4*(5), 201–211.

Slaughter, V., Peterson, C. C., & Moore, C. (2013). I can talk you into it: Theory of mind and persuasion behavior in young children. *Developmental Psychology, 49*(2), 227–231.

Slavin, R. E., Cheung, A., Holmes, G., Madden, N. A., & Chamberlain, A. (2013). Effects of a data-driven district reform model on state assessment outcomes. *American Educational Research Journal, 50*(2), 371–396.

Slobin, D. I. (1972). Children and language: They learn the same way all around the world. *Psychology Today, 6*(2), 71–74, 82.

Smetana, J. G., Campione-Barr, N., & Metzger, A. (2006). Adolescent development in interpersonal and societal contexts. *Annual Review of Psychology, 57*, 255–284.

Smetana, J. G., Kochanska, G., & Chuang, S. (2000). Mothers' conceptions of everyday rules for young toddlers: A longitudinal investigation. *Merrill-Palmer Quarterly, 46*, 391–416.

Smith, A. K., Rhee, S. H., Corley, R. P., Friedman, N. P., Hewitt, J. K., & Robinson, J. L. (2012). The magnitude of genetic and environmental influences on parental and observational measures of behavioral inhibition and shyness in toddlerhood. *Behavior Genetics, 42*(5), 764–777.

Smith, A. R., Steinberg, L., Strang, N., & Chein, J. (2015). Age differences in the impact of peers on adolescents' and adults' neural response to reward. *Developmental Cognitive Neuroscience, 11*, 75–82.

Smith, J. P., & Ellwood, M. (2011). Feeding patterns and emotional care in breastfed infants. *Social Indicators Research, 101*, 227–231.

Smith, K., Colquhoun, D., Ernst, E., Sampson, W., & Jonas, M. (2016). Child health advice and parental obligation: The case of safe sleep recommendations and sudden unexpected death in infancy. *Bioethics, 2*, 129. doi:10.1111/bioe.12174

Smith, L., Gardner, B., Aggio, D., & Hamer, M. (2015). Association between participation in outdoor play and sport at 10 years old with physical activity in adulthood. *Preventive Medicine: An International Journal Devoted to Practice and Theory, 74*, 31–35.

Smith, M. E. (1926). An investigation of the development of the sentence and the extent of vocabulary in young children. *University of Iowa Studies: Child Welfare, 3*, 92.

Smith, R. L., Rose, A. J., & Schwartz-Mette, R. A. (2010). Relational and overt aggression in childhood and adolescence: Clarifying mean-level gender differences and associations with peer acceptance. *Social Development, 19*(2), 243–269.

Smolak, L., & Stein, J. A. (2010). A longitudinal investigation of gender role and muscle building in adolescent boys. *Sex Roles, 63*, 738–746.

Smolucha, L., & Smolucha, F. (1998). The social origins of mind: Post-Piagetian perspectives on pretend play. In O. N. Saracho & B. Spodek (Eds.), *Multiple perspectives on play in early childhood education* (pp. 34–58). Albany, NY: State University of New York Press.

Snarey, J. R. (1985). Cross-cultural universality of social-moral development: A critical review of Kohlbergian research. *Psychological Bulletin, 97*, 202–232.

Soenens, B., & Vansteenkiste, M. (2010). A theoretical upgrade of the concept of parental psychological control: Proposing new insights on the basis of self-determination theory. *Developmental Review, 30*(1), 74–99.

Solmeyer, A. R., McHale, S. M., & Crouter, A. C. (2014). Longitudinal associations between sibling relationship qualities and risky behavior across adolescence. *Developmental Psychology, 50*(2), 600–610.

Sonuga-Barke, E. J. S., & Halperin, J. M. (2010). Developmental phenotypes and causal pathways in attention deficit/hyperactivity disorder: Potential targets for early intervention? *Journal of Child Psychology & Psychiatry, 51*(4), 368–389.

Spear, L. P. (2008). The psychology of adolescence. In K. K. Kline (Ed.), *Authoritative communities: The scientific cases for nurturing the whole child* (pp. 263–280). New York, NY: Springer-Verlag.

Spencer, S. V., Bowker, J. C., Rubin, K. H., Booth-LaForce, C., & Laursen, B. (2013). Similarity between friends in social information processing and associations with positive friendship quality and conflict. *Merrill-Palmer Quarterly, 59*(1), 106–131.

Spense, A. (1989). *The biology of human aging.* Englewood Cliffs, NJ: Prentice Hall.

Spinath, B., & Steinmayr, R. (2008). Longitudinal analysis of intrinsic motivation and competence beliefs: Is there a relation over time? *Child Development, 49*, 1555–1569.

Sroufe, L. A. (2000). Early relationships and the development of children. *Infant Mental Health Journal, 21*, 67–74.

Sroufe, L. A., Egeland, B., Carlson, E., & Collins, W. A. (2005). Placing early attachment experiences in developmental context: The Minnesota Longitudinal Study. In K. E. Grossman, K. Grossman, & E. Waters (Eds.), *Attachment from infancy to adulthood: The major longitudinal studies* (pp. 48–70). New York: Guilford Press.

St. James-Roberts, I. (2007). Helping parents to manage infant crying and sleeping: A review of the evidence and its implications for services. *Child Abuse Review, 16*, 47–69.

Stackman, V. R., Reviere, R., & Medley, B. C. (2016). Attitudes toward marriage, partner availability, and interracial dating among black college students from historically black and predominantly white institutions. *Journal of Black Studies, 47*(2), 169–192.

Staikova, E., Gomes, H., Tartter, V., McCabe, A., & Halperin, J. M. (2013). Pragmatic deficits and social impairment in children with ADHD. *Journal of Child Psychology and Psychiatry, 54*(12), 1275–1283.

Stallman, H. M., & Ohan, J. L. (2016). Parenting style, parental adjustment, and co-parental conflict: Differential predictors of child psychosocial adjustment following divorce. *Behaviour Change, 33*(2), 112–126. doi:10.1017/bec.2016.7

Stark, R., Bauer, E., Merz, C. J., Zimmermann, M., Reuter, M., Plichta, M. M., . . . Herrmann, M. J. (2011). ADHD related behaviors are associated with brain activation in the reward system. *Neuropsychologia, 49*, 426–434.

Stattin, H., & Magnusson, D. (1990). *Pubertal maturation in female development*. Hillsdale, NJ: Erlbaum.

Steigler, H., & Thaler, L. (2106). Eating disorders, gene–environment interactions and the genome: Roles of stress exposures and nutritional status. *Physiology and Behavior, 162*, 181–185.

Stein, A., Malmberg, L., Leach, P., Barnes, J., & Sylva, K. (2013). The influence of different forms of early childcare on children's emotional and behavioural development at school entry. *Child: Care, Health and Development, 39*(5), 676–687.

Stein, J. H., & Reiser, L. W. (1994). A study of White middle-class adolescent boys' responses to "semenarche" (the first ejaculation). *Journal of Youth and Adolescence, 23*, 373–384.

Steinberg, L. (2001). We know somethings: Parent–adolescent relationships in retrospect and prospect. *Journal of Research on Adolescence, 11*, 1–19.

Steinberg, L. (2005). Cognitive and affective development in adolescence. *Trends in Cognitive Sciences, 9*, 69–74.

Steinberg, L. (2008). A social neuroscience perspective on adolescent risk-taking. *Developmental Review, 28*, 78–106.

Steinberg, L. (2016). Commentary: Commentary on special issue on the adolescent brain: Redefining adolescence. *Neuroscience and Biobehavioral Reviews, 70*, 343–346.

Steinberg, L., & Hill, J. P. (1978). Patterns of family interaction as a function of age, the onset of puberty, and formal thinking. *Developmental Psychology, 14*, 683–684.

Sternberg, R. J. (1984). Toward a triarchic theory of human intelligence. *Behavioral and Brain Sciences, 7*, 269–315.

Sternberg, R. J. (1996). *Successful intelligence: How practical and creative intelligence determine success in life*. New York, NY: Simon & Schuster.

Sternberg, R. J. (1997). The triarchic theory of intelligence. In D. P. Flanagan, J. L. Genshaft, & P. L. Harrison (Eds.), *Contemporary intellectual assessment: Theories, tests, and issues* (pp. 92–104). New York, NY: Guilford Press.

Sternberg, R. J. (2007). Who are the bright children? The cultural context of being and acting intelligent. *Educational Researcher, 36*(3), 148–155.

Sternberg, R. J. (2010). WICS: A new model for school psychology. *School Psychology International, 31*(6), 599–616.

Sternberg, R. J., Grigorenko, E. L., & Kidd, K. K. (2005). Intelligence, race, and genetics. *American Psychologist, 60*, 46–59.

Sternberg, R. J., Grigorenko, E. L., & Bundy, D. A. (2001). The predictive value of IQ. *Merrill-Palmer Quarterly, 47*, 1–41.

Sternberg, R. J., Jarvin, L., Birney, D. P., Naples, A., Stemler, S. E., Newman, T., . . . Grigorenko, E. L. (2014). Testing the theory of successful intelligence in teaching grade 4 language arts, mathematics, and science. *Journal of Educational Psychology, 106*(3), 881–899.

Sticca, F., & Perren, S. (2013). Is cyberbullying worse than traditional bullying? Examining the differential roles of medium, publicity, and anonymity for the perceived severity of bullying. *Journal of Youth and Adolescence, 42*(5), 739–750.

Stiles, J., & Jernigan, T. L. (2010). The basics of brain development. *Neuropsychology Review, 20*(4), 327–348.

Stipek, D. J. (1996). Motivation and instruction. In D. C. Berliner & R. C. Calfee (Eds.), *Handbook of educational psychology* (pp. 85–113). New York, NY: Macmillan.

Stipek, D. J. (1997). Success in school— For a head start in life. In S. S. Luthar, J. A. Burack, D. Cicchetti, & J. R. Weisz (Eds.), *Developmental psychopathology: Perspectives on adjustment, risk, and disorder* (pp. 75–92). New York, NY: University Press.

Stöckel, T., & Hughes, C. M. L. (2016). The relation between measures of cognitive and motor functioning in 5- to 6-year-old children. *Psychological Research, 80*(4), 543–554.

Stoltenborgh, M., Bakermans-Kranenburg, M. J., van IJzendoorn, M. H., & Alink, L. A. (2013). Cultural–geographical differences in the occurrence of child physical abuse. A meta-analysis of global prevalence. *International Journal of Psychology, 48*(2), 81–94.

Stremler, R., Hodnett, E., Kenton, L., Lee, K., Weiss, S., Weston, J., & Willan, A. (2013). Effect of behavioural–educational intervention on sleep for primiparous women and their infants in early postpartum: Multisite randomised controlled trial. *BMJ (British Medical Journal), 346*.

Striegel-Moore, R. H., & Bulik, C. M. (2007). Risk factors for eating disorders. *American Psychologist, 62*(3), 181–198.

Strohmeier, D., Kärnä, A., & Salmivalli, C. (2010). Intrapersonal and interpersonal risk factors for peer victimization in immigrant youth in Finland. *Developmental Psychology, 47*, 248–258.

Suárez-Orozco, C., Gaytán, F. X., Bang, H. J., Pakes, J., O'Connor, E., & Rhodes, J. (2010). Academic trajectories of newcomer immigrant youth. *Developmental Psychology, 46*(3), 602–618.

Subrahmanyam, K., Greenfield, P. M., & Tynes, B. (2004). Constructing sexuality and identity in an online teen chatroom. *Journal of Applied Developmental Psychology. Special Issue: Developing Children, Developing Media: Research from Television to the Internet from the Children's Digital Media Center, 25*, 651–666.

Sugiyama, T., Horino, M., Inoue, K., Kobayashi, Y., Shapiro, M. F., & McCarthy, W. J. (2016). Trends of child's weight perception by children, parents, and healthcare professionals during the time of terminology change in childhood obesity in the United States, 2005–2014.

Childhood Obesity, 12(6), 463–473. doi:10.1089/chi.2016.0128

Sulaiman, Z., Liamputtong, P., & Amir, L. H. (2016). The enablers and barriers to continue breast milk feeding in women returning to work. *Journal of Advanced Nursing, 72*(4), 825–835. doi:10.1111/jan.12884

Sullivan, H. S. (1953). *The interpersonal theory of psychiatry.* New York, NY: Norton.

Sun, S. S., Schubert, C. M., Chumlea, W. C., Roche, A. F., Kulin, H. E., Lee, P. A., . . . Ryan, A. S. (2002). National estimates of the timing of sexual maturation and racial differences among U.S. children. *Pediatrics, 110,* 911–919.

Suomi, S. J. (2004). How gene–environment interactions shape biobehavioral development: Lessons from studies with rhesus monkeys. *Research in Human Development, 1,* 205–222.

Super, C. M., & Harkness, S. (2003). The metaphors of development. *Human Development, 46,* 3–23.

Surra, C. A., & Hughes, D. K. (1997). Commitment processes in accounts of the development of premarital relationships. *Journal of Marriage and Family, 59,* 5–21.

Surra, C. A., Hughes, D. K., & Jacquet, S. E. (1999). The development of commitment to marriage: A phenomenological approach. In J. M. Adams & W. H. Jones (Eds.), *Handbook of interpersonal commitment and relationship stability* (pp. 125–148). Dordrecht, Netherlands: Kluwer Academic.

Sussman, S., Pokhrel, P., Ashmore, R. D., & Brown, B. B. (2007). Adolescent peer group identification and characteristics: A review of the literature. *Addictive Behaviors, 32,* 1602–1627.

Svensson, B., Bornehag, C.-G., & Janson, S. (2011). Chronic conditions in children increase the risk for physical abuse—but vary with socio-economic circumstances. *Acta Paediatrica, 100,* 407–412.

Swann, W. B., Chang-Schneider, C., & McClarty, K. L. (2007). Do people's self-views matter? *American Psychologist, 62*(2), 84–94.

Syed, M., & Seiffge-Krenke, I. (2015). Change in ego development, coping, and symptomatology from adolescence to emerging adulthood. *Journal of Applied Developmental Psychology, 41,* 110–119.

Tadmor, C. T., Tetlock, P. E., & Peng, K. (2009). Acculturation strategies and integrative complexity: The cognitive implications of biculturalism. *Journal of Cross-Cultural Psychology, 40,* 105–139.

Takeo, F., Yui, Y., & Ichiro, K. (2016). Neighborhood social capital and infant physical abuse: A population-based study in Japan. *International Journal of Mental Health Systems.* doi:10.1186/s13033-016-0047-9

Tanner, J. L. (2006). Recentering during emerging adulthood: A critical turning point in life span human development. In J. J. Arnett & J. L. Tanner (Eds.), *Emerging adults in America: Coming of age in the 21st century* (pp. 21–55). Washington, DC: American Psychological Association.

Tanner, J. L., & Arnett, J. J. (2010). Presenting "emerging adulthood": What makes it developmentally distinctive. In J. J. Arnett, M. Kloep, L. B. Hendry, & J. L. Tanner (Eds.), *Debating emerging adulthood: Stage or process?* (pp. 13–30). New York, NY: Oxford University Press.

Tanner, J. M. (1955). *Growth at adolescence.* Oxford, England: Blackwell.

Tanner, J. M. (1978). *Foetus into man: Physical growth from conception to maturity.* Cambridge, MA: Harvard University Press.

Tanofsky-Kraff, M., Shomaker, L. B., Young, J. F., & Wilfley, D. E. (2015). Interpersonal psychotherapy for eating disorders and the prevention of excess weight gain. In H. Thompson-Brenner (Ed.), *Casebook of evidence-based therapy for eating disorders* (pp. 195–219). New York, NY: Guilford Press.

Tasimi, A., & Young, L. (2016). Memories of good deeds past: The reinforcing power of prosocial behavior in children. *Journal of Experimental Child Psychology, 147,* 159–166. doi:10.1016/j.jecp.2016.03.001

Taveras, E. M. (2016). Childhood obesity risk and prevention: Shining a lens on the first 1000 days. *Childhood Obesity, 12*(3), 159–161. doi:10.1089/chi.2016.0088

Taylor, C. A., Hamvas, L., & Paris, R. (2011). Perceived instrumentality and normativeness of corporal punishment use among black mothers. *Family Relations, 60,* 60–72.

Tebeka, S., Le Strat, Y., & Dubertret, C. (2016). Developmental trajectories of pregnant and postpartum depression in an epidemiologic survey. *Journal of Affective Disorders, 203,* 62–68.

Telzer, E. H., Flannery, J., Shapiro, M., Humphreys, K. L., Goff, B., Gabard-Durman, L., . . . Tottenham, N. (2013). Early experience shapes amygdala sensitivity to race: An international adoption design. *Journal of Neuroscience, 33*(33), 13484–13488.

Telzer, E. H., Fuligni, A. J., Lieberman, M. D., & Galván, A. (2013). The effects of poor quality sleep on brain function and risk taking in adolescence. *Neuroimage, 71,* 275–283.

Telzer, E., Yuen, C., Gonzales, N., & Fuligni, A. (2016). Filling gaps in the acculturation gap-distress model: Heritage cultural maintenance and adjustment in Mexican-American families. *Journal of Youth & Adolescence, 45*(7), 1412–1425. doi:10.1007/s10964-015-0408-8

Terry-McElrath, Y. M., Maslowsky, J., O'Malley, P. M., Schulenberg, J. E., & Johnston, L. D. (2016). Sleep and substance use among U.S. adolescents, 1991–2014. *American Journal of Health Behavior, 40*(1), 77–91.

Teskereci, G., & Oncel, S. (2013). Effect of lifestyle on quality of life of couples receiving infertility treatment. *Journal of Sex & Marital Therapy, 39*(6), 476–492.

Teti, D. M., Kim, B., Mayer, G., & Countermine, M. (2010). Maternal emotional availability at bedtime predicts infant sleep quality. *Journal of Family Psychology, 24,* 307–315.

Teti, D. M., Shimizu, M., Crosby, B., & Kim, B. (2016). Sleep arrangements, parent–infant sleep during the first year, and family functioning. *Developmental Psychology, 52*(8), 1169–1181. doi:10.1037/dev0000148

Thapar, A., & Cooper, M. (2016). Attention deficit hyperactivity disorder. *Lancet, 387*(10024, North American Edition), 1240–1250. doi:10.1016/s0140-6736(15)00238-x

The Equality of Opportunity Project. (n.d.). http://www.equality-of-opportunity.org/, Chart #2.

Thiessen, E. D., Hill, E. A., & Saffran, J. R. (2005). Infant-directed speech facilitates word segmentation. *Infancy, 7,* 53–71.

Thomaes, S., Stegge, H., & Olthof, T. (2007). Externalizing shame responses in children: The role of fragile-positive self-esteem. *British Journal of Developmental Psychology, 25*(4), 559–577.

Thomas, A., & Chess, S. (1977). *Temperament and development.* Oxford, England: Brunner/Mazel.

Thomas, A., Chess, S., & Birch, H. G. (1968). *Temperament and behavior disorders in children.* New York, NY: New York University Press.

Thomas, J. R., & French, K. E. (1985). Gender differences across age in motor performance: A meta-analysis. *Psychological Bulletin, 98*, 260–282.

Thompson, R. A., & Newton, E. K. (2013). Baby altruists? Examining the complexity of prosocial motivation in young children. *Infancy, 18*(1), 120–133.

Thompson-Brenner, H. (2013). The good news about psychotherapy for eating disorders: Comment on Warren, Schafer, Crowley, and Olivardia. *Psychotherapy, 50*(4), 565–567.

Tolan, P. (2016). Positive youth development interventions: Advancing evaluation theory and practice. *Applied Developmental Science, 20*(3), 147–149. doi:10.1080/10888691.2015.1014485

Tomlinson, M., Cooper, P., & Murray, L. (2005). The mother–infant relationship and infant attachment in a South African peri-urban settlement. *Child Development, 76*, 1044–1054.

Tompkins, V. (2015). Improving low-income preschoolers' theory of mind: A training study. *Cognitive Development, 36*, 1–19. doi:10.1016/j.cogdev.2015.07.001

Toomey, R. B., Umaña-Taylor, A. J., Updegraff, K. A., & Jahromi, L. B. (2013). Ethnic identity development and ethnic discrimination: Examining longitudinal associations with adjustment for Mexican-origin adolescent mothers. *Journal of Adolescence, 36*(5), 825–833.

Top 10 Best Dating Sites. (2014). *10 best dating sites, dating site reviews of Match.com*. Retrieved from http://www.top10bestdtingsites.com/index

Trentowska, M., Svaldi, J., & Tuschen-Caffier, B. (2014). Efficacy of body exposure as treatment component for patients with eating disorders. *Journal of Behavior Therapy and Experimental Psychiatry, 45*(1), 178–185.

Triandis, H. C. (1995). *Individualism & collectivism*. Boulder, CO: Westview Press.

Troop-Gordon, W., Visconti, K. J., & Kuntz, K. J. (2011). Perceived popularity during early adolescence: Links to declining school adjustment among aggressive youth. *The Journal of Early Adolescence, 31*(1), 125–151.

Turkheimer, E. (2004). Spinach and ice cream: Why social science is so difficult. In L. F. DiLalla (Ed.) *Behavior genetic principles: Perspectives in development, personality, and psychopathology*. Washington, DC: American Psychological Association Press.

Turkheimer, E., Haley, A., Waldron, M., D'Onofrio, B., & Gottesman, I. I. (2003). Socioeconomic status modifies heritability of IQ in young children. *Psychological Science, 14*, 623–628.

Turkington, C., & Alper, M. M. (2001). *The encyclopedia of fertility and infertility*. New York, NY: Facts on File.

Twenge, J. M. (2006). *Generation me: Why today's young Americans are more confident, assertive, entitled—and more miserable than ever before*. New York, NY: Free Press.

U.S. Department of Agriculture, Food and Nutrition Service. (2014). Retrieved from http://www.fns.usda.gov/snap/supplemental-nutrition-assistance-program

U.S. Department of Labor Statistics, Fertility. (2017). Women's bureau. Retrieved from https://www.dol.gov/wb/stats/Fertility.htm, February 2017.

Udry, J. R. (1990). Biosocial models of adolescent problem behaviors. *Social Biology, 37*, 1–10.

Udry, J. R. (2000). Biological limits of gender construction. *American Sociological Review, 65*, 443–457.

Udry, J. R., & Campbell, B. C. (1994). Getting started on sexual behavior. In A. S. Rossi (Ed.), *Sexuality across the life course* (pp. 187–207). Chicago, IL: University of Chicago Press.

Uji, M., Sakamoto, A., Adachi, K., & Kitamura, T. (2014). The impact of authoritative, authoritarian, and permissive parenting styles on children's later mental health in Japan: Focusing on parent and child gender. *Journal of Child and Family Studies, 23*(2), 293–302.

Umemura, T., Jacobvitz, D., Messina, S., & Hazen, N. (2013). Do toddlers prefer the primary caregiver or the parent with whom they feel more secure? The role of toddler emotion. *Infant Behavior and Development, 36*(1), 102–114.

UNFPA. (2015). *Emerging evidence, lessons and practice in comprehensive sexuality education, a global review*. Paris, France: UNESCO.

UNICEF (United Nations Children's Fund). (2009). *The state of the world's children: Maternal and newborn health, 2009*. Retrieved from http://www.unicef.org/publications/index_47127.html

United Nations Children's Fund (UNICEF). (2016). *Uprooted: The growing crisis for refugee and migrant children*. Retrieved from https://data.unicef.org/topic/child-migration-and-displacement/migration/. doi:10.18356/f5cc00a0-en

Urban, J. B., Lewin-Bizan, S., & Lerner, R. M. (2010). The role of intentional self-regulation, lower neighborhood ecological assets, and activity involvement in youth developmental outcomes. *Journal of Youth and Adolescence, 39*, 783–800.

Valentino, K., Nuttall, A. K., Comas, M., McDonnell, C. G., Piper, B., Thomas, T. E., & Fanuele, S. (2014). Mother–child reminiscing and autobiographical memory specificity among preschool-age children. *Developmental Psychology, 50*(4), 1197–1207.

van Aken, C., Junger, M., Verhoeven, M., van Aken, M. A. G., & Deković, M. (2008). The longitudinal relations between parenting and toddlers' attention problems and aggressive behaviors. *Infant Behavior and Development, 31*, 432–446.

Van Damme, E., & Biltereyst, D. (2013). Let's talk about sex: Audience research of Flemish teenage television viewers and their view on sexuality. *Journal of Youth Studies, 16*(3), 287–303. doi:10.1080/13676261.2012.710744

van der Fels, I. M. J., te Wierike, S. C. M., Hartman, E., Elferink-Gemser, M. T., Smith, J., & Visscher, C. (2015). The relationship between motor skills and cognitive skills in 4–16 year old typically developing children: A systematic review. *Journal of Science and Medicine in Sport, 18*(6), 697–703.

van IJzendoorn, M. H., & Sagi, A. (1999). Cross-cultural patterns of attachment: Universal and contextual dimensions. In J. Cassidy & P. R. Shaver (Eds.), *Handbook of attachment: Theory, research, and clinical applications* (pp. 713–734). New York, NY: Guilford Press.

van Lawick, J., & Visser, M. (2015). No kids in the middle: Dialogical and creative work with parents and children in the context of high conflict divorces. *Australian and New Zealand Journal of Family Therapy, 36*(1), 33–50. doi:10.1002/anzf.1091

Vandell, D. L., Burchinal, M., Vandergrift, N., Belsky, J., & Steinberg, L. (2010). Do effects of early child care extend to age 15 years? Results from the NICHD Study of Early Child Care and Youth Development. *Child Development, 81*(3), 737–756.

Vanderloo, L. M., & Mandich, G. (2013). Battling bullying: Do obese children face the same fight? *Canadian Journal of Mental Health, 32*(4), 85–88.

Vandorpe, B., Vandendriessche, J., Lefevre, J., Pion, J., Vaeyens, R., Matthys, S., Philippaerts, R., & Lenoir, M. (2011). The Körperkoordinations Test für Kinder: Reference values and suitability for 6- to 12-year-old children in Flanders. *Scandinavian Journal of Medicine and Science in Sports, 21*(3), 378–388.

van Geel, M., & Vedder, P. (2011). The role of family obligations and school adjustment in explaining the immigrant paradox. *Journal of Youth and Adolescence, 40,* 187–196.

Vaughn, L. M., Ireton, C., Geraghty, S. R., Diers, T., Niño, V., Falciglia, G. A., . . . Mosbaugh, C. (2010). Sociocultural influences on the determinants of breast-feeding by Latina mothers in the Cincinnati area. *Family & Community Health, 33*(4), 318–328.

Veenstra, R., Huitsing, G., Dijkstra, J., & Lindenberg, S. (2010). Friday on my mind: The relation of partying with antisocial behavior of early adolescents. The TRAILS Study. *Journal of Research on Adolescence, 20*(2), 420–431.

Velkoff, E. A., Forrest, L. N., Dodd, D. R., & Smith, A. R. (2016). Predicting suicide risk among sexual minority women. *Psychology of Women Quarterly, 40*(2), 261–274.

Vennum, A., Hardy, N., Sibley, D. S., & Fincham, F. D. (2015). Dedication and sliding in emerging adult cyclical and non-cyclical romantic relationships. *Family Relations, 64*(3), 407–419.

Verhaeghe, L., Dereu, M., Warreyn, P., Groote, I. D., Vanhaesebrouck, P., & Roeyers, H. (2016). Extremely preterm born children at very high risk for developing autism spectrum disorder. *Child Psychiatry & Human Development, 47*(5), 729–739. doi:10.1007/s10578-015-0606-3

Verhage, M. L., Schuengel, C., Madigan, S., Fearon, R. M. P., Oosterman, M., Cassibba, R., . . . van IJzendoorn, M. H. (2016). Narrowing the transmission gap: A synthesis of three decades of research on intergenerational transmission of attachment. *Psychological Bulletin, 142,* 337–366.

Verweij, E., Oepkes, D., de Vries, M., van den Akker, M., van den Akker, E. S., & de Boer, M. A. (2013). Non-invasive prenatal screening for trisomy 21: What women want and are willing to pay. *Patient Education and Counseling, 93*(3), 641–645.

Vianna, E., & Stetsenko, A. (2006). Embracing history through transforming it: Contrasting Piagetian versus Vygotskian (activity) theories of learning and development to expand constructivism within a dialectical view of history. *Theory & Psychology, 16*(1), 81–108.

Victor, S. E., Glenn, C. R., & Klonsky, E. D. (2012). Is non-suicidal self-injury an "addiction"? A comparison of craving in substance use and non-suicidal self-injury. *Psychiatry Research, 197*(1–2), 73–77.

Virmani, E. A., & Ontai, L. L. (2010). Supervision and training in childcare: Does reflective supervision foster caregiver insightfulness? *Infant Mental Health Journal, 31*(1), 16–32.

Visconti, K. J., Ladd, G. W., & Kochenderfer-Ladd, B. (2015). The role of moral disengagement in the associations between children's social goals and aggression. *Merrill-Palmer Quarterly, 1,* 101. doi:10.13110/merrpalmquar1982.61.1.0101

Volk, H. E., Lurmann, F., Penfold, B., Hertz-Picciotto, I., & McConnell, R. (2013). Traffic-related air pollution, particulate matter, and autism. *JAMA Psychiatry, 70*(1), 71–77.

Volkmar, F., Siegel, M., Woodbury-Smith, M., King, B., McCracken, J., & State, M. (2014). Practice parameter for the assessment and treatment of children and adolescents with autism spectrum disorder. *Journal of the American Academy of Child & Adolescent Psychiatry, 53*(2), 237–257.

von der Lippe, A., Eilertsen, D. E., Hartmann, E., & Killèn, K. (2010). The role of maternal attachment in children's attachment and cognitive executive functioning: A preliminary study. *Attachment & Human Development, 12*(5), 429–444.

Von Raffler-Engel, W. (1994). *The perception of the unborn across the cultures of the world.* Seattle, WA: Hogrefe & Huber.

Votruba-Drzal, E., Coley, R. L., Koury, A. S., & Miller, P. (2013). Center-based child care and cognitive skills development: Importance of timing and household resources. *Journal of Educational Psychology, 105*(3), 821–838.

Vouloumanos, A., Werker, J. F., Hauser, M. D., & Martin, A. (2010). The tuning of human neonates' preference for speech. *Child Development, 81*(2), 517–527.

Vreeswijk, C. M., Maas, A. M., Rijk, C. M., & van Bakel, H. A. (2014). Fathers' experiences during pregnancy: Paternal prenatal attachment and representations of the fetus. *Psychology of Men & Masculinity, 15*(2), 129–137.

Vygotsky, L. S. (1962). *Thought and language* (E. Hanfmann & G. Vakar, Eds. & Trans.). New York, NY: MIT Press and Wiley. (Original work published 1934)

Vygotsky, L. S. (1978). *Mind in society: The development of higher psychological processes* (M. Cole, V. John-Steiner, S. Scribner, & E. Souberman, Eds.). Cambridge, MA: Harvard University Press. (Original work published 1935)

Waasdorp, T. E., Baker, C. N., Paskewich, B. S., & Leff, S. S. (2013). The association between forms of aggression, leadership, and social status among urban youth. *Journal of Youth and Adolescence, 42*(2), 263–274.

Waasdorp, T. E., Bradshaw, C. P., & Duong, J. (2011). The link between parents' perceptions of the school and their responses to school bullying: Variation by child characteristics and the forms of victimization. *Journal of Educational Psychology, 103*(2), 324–335.

Wadsworth, B. J. (1996). *Piaget's theory of cognitive and affective development: Foundations of constructivism* (5th ed.). White Plains, NY: Longman.

Wagner, J., Lüdtke, O., Jonkmann, K., & Trautwein, U. (2013). Cherish yourself: Longitudinal patterns and conditions of self-esteem change in the transition to young adulthood. *Journal of Personality and Social Psychology, 104*(1), 148–163.

Wagner, M., Darko, J., Worth, A., & Woll, A. (2016). Elaboration of the environmental stress hypothesis—Results from a population-based 6-year follow-up. *Frontiers in Psychology,* http://journal.frontiersin.org/journal.

Wagner, T. (2000). *How schools change: Lessons from three communities revisited* (2nd ed.). New York, NY: Routledge Falmer.

Walsh, J. L. (2008, March). *Magazine reading as a longitudinal predictor of women's sexual norms and behaviors.* Paper presented at 12th Biennial Meeting of Society for Research on Adolescence, Chicago, IL.

Walton, K. E., Huyen, B. T., Thorpe, K., Doherty, E. R., Juarez, B., D'Accordo, C., & Reina, M. T. (2013). Cross-sectional personality differences from age 16–90 in a Vietnamese sample. *Journal of Research in Personality, 47*(1), 36–40.

Walvoord, E. C. (2010). The timing of puberty: Is it changing? Does it matter? *Journal of Adolescent Health, 47,* 433–439.

Wang, H., & Abbott, D. A. (2013). Waiting for Mr. Right: The meaning of being a single educated Chinese female over 30 in Beijing and Guangzhou. *Women's Studies International Forum, 40*, 222–229.

Wang, J. J., Ali, M., Frisson, S., & Apperly, I. A. (2016). Language complexity modulates 8- and 10-years-olds' success at using their theory of mind abilities in a communication task. *Journal of Experimental Child Psychology, 149*, 62–71. doi:10.1016/j.jecp.2015.09.006

Wang, M., & Saudino, K. J. (2013). Genetic and environmental influences on individual differences in emotion regulation and its relation to working memory in toddlerhood. *Emotion, 13*(6), 1055–1067.

Wang, S., Yang, Y., Xing, W., Chen, J., Liu, C., & Luo, X. (2013). Altered neural circuits related to sustained attention and executive control in children with ADHD: An event-related fMRI study. *Clinical Neurophysiology, 124*(11), 2181–2190.

Wang, Z., Devine, R. T., Wong, K. K., & Hughes, C. (2016). Theory of mind and executive function during middle childhood across cultures. *Journal of Experimental Child Psychology, 149*, 6–22. doi:10.1016/j.jecp.2015.09.028

Wängqvist, M., & Frisén, A. (2016). Swedish emerging adults' sense of identity and perceptions of adulthood. In R. Žukauskienė (Ed.), *Emerging adulthood in a European context* (pp. 154–174). New York, NY: Routledge/Taylor & Francis Group.

Wängqvist, M., Carlsson, J., van der Lee, M., & Frisén, A. (2016). Identity development and romantic relationships in the late twenties. *Identity: An International Journal of Theory and Research, 16*(1), 124–144.

Warren, C. S., Schafer, K. J., Crowley, M. J., & Olivardia, R. (2013). Demographic and work-related correlates of job burnout in professional eating disorder treatment providers. *Psychotherapy, 50*(4), 553–564.

Waterman, A. S. (1999). Identity, the identity statuses, and identity status development: A contemporary statement. *Developmental Review, 19*, 591–621.

Watson, J. B. (1930). *Behaviorism* (Revised ed.). New York, NY: Norton.

Watson, J. B. (with the assistance of Watson, R. R.). (1972). *Psychological care of infant and child*. New York, NY: Arno Press. (Original work published 1928)

Weaver, J. M., & Schofield, T. J. (2015). Mediation and moderation of divorce effects on children's behavior problems. *Journal of Family Psychology, 29*(1), 39–48. doi:10.1037/fam0000043

Wedding, D., Kohout, J., Mengel, M. B., Ohlemiller, M., Ulione, M., Cook, K., . . . Braddock, S. (2007). Psychologists' knowledge and attitudes about fetal alcohol syndrome, fetal alcohol spectrum disorders, and alcohol use during pregnancy. *Professional Psychology: Research and Practice, 38*(2), 208–213.

Weisfeld, G. (1997). Puberty rites as clues to the nature of human adolescence. *Cross-Cultural Research: The Journal of Comparative Social Science, 31*, 27–54.

Weisgram, E. S., Fulcher, M., & Dinella, L. M. (2014). Pink gives girls permission: Exploring the roles of explicit gender labels and gender-typed colors on preschool children's toy preferences. *Journal of Applied Developmental Psychology, 35*(5), 401–409. doi:10.1016/j.appdev.2014.06.004

Wender, P. H., Reimherr, F. W., Marchant, B. K., Sanford, M. E., Czajkowski, L. A., & Tomb, D. A. (2011). A one-year trial of methylphenidate in the treatment of ADHD. *Journal of Attention Disorders, 15*(1), 36–45.

Werner, N. E., & Hill, L. G. (2010). Individual and peer group normative beliefs about relational aggression. *Child Development, 81*(3), 826–836.

Werner-Lin, A., McCoyd, J. L. M., & Bernhardt, B. A. (2016). Balancing genetics (science) and counseling (art) in prenatal chromosomal microarray testing. *Journal of Genetic Counseling, 25*(5), 855–867.

Werth, B., & Tsiaras, A. (2002). *From conception to birth: A life unfolds*. New York, NY: Doubleday.

Wertz, R. W., & Wertz, D. C. (1989). *Lying-in: A history of childbirth in America* (expanded ed.). New Haven, CT: Yale University Press.

White, B. A., Jarrett, M. A., & Ollendick, T. H. (2013). Self-regulation deficits explain the link between reactive aggression and internalizing and externalizing behavior problems in children. *Journal of Psychopathology and Behavioral Assessment, 35*(1), 1–9.

White, J. (2006). Multiple invalidities. In J. A. Schaler (Ed.), *Howard Gardner under fire: The rebel psychologist faces his critics* (pp. 45–71). Chicago, IL: Open Court.

Whiteman, S. D., McHale, S. M., & Crouter, A. C. (2007). Longitudinal changes in marital relationships: The role of offspring's pubertal development. *Journal of Marriage and Family, 69*(4), 1005–1020.

Wiebe, S. A., Clark, C. A., Jong, D. M., Chevalier, N., Espy, K. A., & Wakschlag, L. (2015). Prenatal tobacco exposure and self-regulation in early childhood: Implications for developmental psychopathology. *Development and Psychopathology, 27*(2), 397–409. doi:10.1017/s095457941500005x

Wiik, K. L., Loman, M. M., Van Ryzin, M. J., Armstrong, J. M., Essex, M. J., Pollak, S. D., & Gunnar, M. R. (2011). Behavioral and emotional symptoms of post-institutionalized children in middle childhood. *Journal of Child Psychology and Psychiatry, 52*(1), 56–63.

Williams, K. E., Nicholson, J. M., Walker, S., & Berthelsen, D. (2016). Early childhood profiles of sleep problems and self-regulation predict later school adjustment. *British Journal of Educational Psychology, 86*(2), 331–350. doi:10.1111/bjep.12109

Willoughby, B., & Hall, S. (2015). Enthusiasts, delayers, and the ambiguous middle: Marital paradigms among emerging adults. *Emerging Adulthood, 3*(2), 123–135.

Willoughby, B., Medaris, M., James, S., & Bartholomew, K. (2015). Changes in marital beliefs among emerging adults: Examining marital paradigms over time. *Emerging Adulthood, 3*(4), 219–228.

Willoughby, T., Good, M., Adachi, P. C., Hamza, C., & Tavernier, R. (2013). Examining the link between adolescent brain development and risk taking from a social–developmental perspective. *Brain and Cognition, 83*(3), 315–323.

Wilson, S. M., Ngige, L. W., & Trollinger, L. J. (2003). Connecting generations: Paths to Maasai and Kamba marriage in Kenya. In R. R. Hamon & B. B. Ingoldsby (Eds.), *Mate selection across cultures* (pp. 95–118). Thousand Oaks, CA: Sage.

Wilson, T., Karimpour, R., & Rodkin, P. C. (2011). African American and European American students' peer groups during early adolescence: Structure, status, and academic achievement. *The Journal of Early Adolescence, 31*(1), 74–98.

Wimmer, H., & Perner, J. (1983). Beliefs about beliefs: Representation and constraining function of wrong beliefs in young children's understanding of deception. *Cognition, 13*, 103–128.

Wolfe, D. A. (2011). Risk factors for child abuse perpetration. In J. W. White,

M. P. Koss, & A. E. Kazdin (Eds.), *Violence against women and children: Vol. 1. Mapping the terrain* (pp. 31–53). Washington, D.C.: American Psychological Association.

Woltering, S., & Shi, Q. (2016). On the neuroscience of self-regulation in children with disruptive behavior problems: Implications for education. *Review of Educational Research, 86*(4), 1085–1110. doi:10.3102/0034654316673722

Wood, D., Bruner, J. S., & Ross, G. (1976). The role of tutoring in problem solving. *Journal of Child Psychology and Psychiatry, 17*, 89–100.

Wood-Barcalow, N. L., Tylka, T. L., & Augustus-Horvath, C. L. (2010). "But I like my body": Positive body image characteristics and a holistic model for young-adult women. *Body Image, 7*, 106–116.

Woody, M. L., Burkhouse, K. L., & Gibb, B. E. (2015). Overgeneral autobiographical memory in children of depressed mothers. *Cognition and Emotion, 29*(1), 130–137. doi:10.1080/02699931.2014.891972

World Health Organization. (2003). *Kangaroo mother care: A practical guide.* Geneva, Switzerland: Department of Reproductive Health and Research, World Health Organization.

World Health Organization. (2006). Retrieved from http://www.who.int/childgrowth/standards/mm_windows_graph.pdf?ua=1

World Health Organization. (2016). Media Centre, Maternal Mortality Fact Sheet. Retrieved from http://www.who.int/mediacentre/factsheets/fs348/en/, November 2016.

Wray-Lake, L., Crouter, A. C., & McHale, S. M. (2010). Developmental patterns in decision-making autonomy across middle childhood and adolescence: European American parents' perspectives. *Child Development, 81*(2), 636–651.

Wright, M. O., & Masten, A. S. (2005). Resilience processes in development: Fostering positive adaptation in the context of adversity. In S. Goldstein & R. B. Brooks (Eds.), *Handbook of resilience in children* (pp. 17–37). New York, NY: Kluwer Academic/Plenum.

Wu, C., & Chao, R. K. (2011). Intergenerational cultural dissonance in parent–adolescent relationships among Chinese and European Americans. *Developmental Psychology, 47*(2), 493–508.

Wymbs, B. T., & Pelham, Jr., W. E. (2010). Child effects on communication between parents of youth with and without attention-deficit/hyperactivity disorder. *Journal of Abnormal Psychology, 119*(2), 366–375.

Xia, Y. R., & Zhou, Z. G. (2003). The transition of courtship, mate selection, and marriage in China. In R. R. Hamon & B. B. Ingoldsby (Eds.), *Mate selection across cultures* (pp. 231–246). Thousand Oaks, CA: Sage.

Xie, W. (2014). Social network site use, mobile personal talk and social capital among teenagers. *Computers in Human Behavior, 41*, 228–235.

Xu, H., Wen, L. M., Hardy, L. L., & Rissel, C. (2016). A 5-year longitudinal analysis of modifiable predictors for outdoor play and screen-time of 2- to 5-year-olds. *International Journal of Behavioral Nutrition and Physical Activity, 13*(1). doi:10.1186/s12966-016-0

Yancey, G. A., & Yancey, S. W. (2002). *Just don't marry one: Interracial dating, marriage, and parenting.* Valley Forge, PA: Judson Press.

Yang, C. K., & Hahn, H. M. (2002). Cosleeping in young Korean children. *Journal of Developmental & Behavioral Pediatrics, 23*, 151–157.

Yang, F., Chen, X., & Wang, L. (2014). Relations between aggression and adjustment in Chinese children: Moderating effects of academic achievement. *Journal of Clinical Child and Adolescent Psychology, 43*(4), 656–669. doi:10.1080/15374416.2013.782816

Yang, J., Granja, M. R., & Koball, H. (2017). Basic facts about low-income children. *Children under 18 Years, 2015.* National Center for Children in Poverty. http://nccp.org/publications/pub_1170.html

Yang, P., Chen, Y., Yen, C., & Chen, H. (2014). Psychiatric diagnoses, emotional–behavioral symptoms and functional outcomes in adolescents born preterm with very low birth weights. *Child Psychiatry and Human Development, 46*, 358–366.

Yaros, A., Lochman, J. E., & Wells, K. (2015). Parental aggression as a predictor of boys' hostile attribution across the transition to middle school. *International Journal of Behavioral Development, 40*(5), 452–458. doi:10.1177/0165025415607085

Yates, M., & Youniss, J. (1998). Community service and political identity development in adolescence. *Journal of Social Issues, 54*, 495–512.

Yeung, W. J., & Hu, S. (2013). Coming of age in times of change: The transition to adulthood in China. *Annals of the American Academy of Political and Social Science, 646*(1), 149–171.

Ying, L., & Loke, A. Y. (2016). An analysis of the concept of partnership in the couples undergoing infertility treatment. *Journal of Sex & Marital Therapy, 42*(3), 243–256.

You, J., Lin, M., & Leung, F. (2013). Functions of non-suicidal self-injury among Chinese community adolescents. *Journal of Adolescence, 36*(4), 737–745.

Young, S., & Amarasinghe, J. M. (2010). Practitioner review: Non-pharmacological treatments for ADHD: A lifespan approach. *Journal of Child Psychology and Psychiatry, 51*(2), 116–133.

Zaichkowsky, L. D., & Larson, G. A. (1995). Physical, motor, and fitness development in children and adolescents. *Journal of Education, 177*, 55–79.

Zayas, V., Mischel, W., Shoda, Y., & Aber, J. L. (2011). Roots of adult attachment: Maternal caregiving at 18 months predicts adult peer and partner attachment. *Social Psychological and Personality Science, 2*(3), 289–297.

Zeanah, C. H., Berlin, L. J., & Boris, N. W. (2011). Practitioner review: Clinical applications of attachment theory and research for infants and young children. *Journal of Child Psychology and Psychiatry, 52*(8), 819–833.

Zerbe, K. (2013). Personal meaning and eating disorder treatment: Comment on Warren et al. *Psychotherapy, 50*(4), 573–575.

Zeskind, P. S., & Lester, B. M. (2001). Analysis of infant crying. In L. T. Singer & P. S. Zeskind (Eds.), *Biobehavioral assessment of the infant* (pp. 149–166). New York, NY: Guilford Press.

Zettergren, P. (2007). Cluster analysis in sociometric research: A pattern-oriented approach to identifying temporally stable peer status groups of girls. *The Journal of Early Adolescence, 27*, 90–114.

Zimmer-Gembeck, M. J., & Helfand, M. (2008). Ten years of longitudinal research on U.S. adolescent sexual behavior: Developmental correlates of sexual intercourse, and the importance of age, gender and ethnic background. *Developmental Review, 28*, 153–224.

Zimmermann, P., & Iwanski, A. (2014). Emotion regulation from early adolescence to emerging adulthood and middle adulthood: Age differences, gender differences, and emotion-specific developmental variations. *International Journal of Behavioral Development, 38*(2), 182–194.

Name Index

A

Aarts, E., 170
Abbate-Daga, G., 240
Abdellaoui, A., 262
Aber, J. L., 113
Abrahams, S. W., 76
Abramson, L. Y., 174
Abu-Akel, A., 151
Abubakar, A., 78
Abubakar, A. A., 195
Acevedo-Polakovitch, I. D., 294
Ackerman, R., 233
Adachi, K., 195
Adachi, P. C., 270
Adair, L. S., 234
Adi-Japha, E., 150
Adolph, K. E., 89
Adomako, M. S., 294
Agency for Healthcare Research and Quality (AHRQ), 47
Ahn, S. J., 201
Ahnert, L., 113, 119, 120
Ainsworth, M. D. S., 108, 110, 309
Ajdacic-Gross, V., 201
Ajibade, A., 294
Aknin, L. B., 127
Aksan, N., 117, 123
Alampay, L. P., 259
Albouy, G., 73
Alderson, K. G., 309
Alderson, R. M., 170
Aldred, H. E., 34
Alea, N., 148
Alessandri, G., 297
Alessandro, H. N., 166
Aleva, L., 176
Alexander, G. M., 156
Alexander-Bloch, A., 74
Al Gharaibeh, F., 202
Ali, M., 149
Ali, M. M., 243
Alink, L. A., 200
Allen, E. A., 72
Allen, J. A., 158
Allen, J. P., 264
Allin, M. G., 62
Allison, C. M., 231, 234
Alloway, R. G., 168
Alloway, T. P., 168
Almas, A. N., 114, 124, 184, 185
Alper, M. M., 55
Alpert, E., 308
Alt, D., 195
Althaus, M., 176
Altschul, I., 194
Alvarez-Buylia, A., 72, 82
Alyagon, U., 170
Aman, M. G., 158
Amarasinghe, J. M., 171
American Academy of Pediatrics (AAP), 76
American Academy of Pediatrics (AAP), Committee on Drugs, 45
American Psychiatric Association, 158
American Teens' Sources of Sexual Health Education, 236
Amianto, F., 240
Amir, L. H., 76
Amstadter, A. B., 201
Anakwenze, U., 116
Andero, A. A., 199
Anders, T. F., 81
Andersen, P., 47
Anderson, D. I., 90
Anderson, E., 301
Anderson, J. I., 62
Anderson, J. W., 108
Anderson, M., 268
Anderson, P. J., 62
Anderson, P. M., 268
Anderson, R., 137
Anderson, V., 171
Andersson, R., 137
Andkarsater, H., 171
Andrew, R., 240
Andrews, J. A., 234
Andrews, T., 77
Anestis, M. D., 262
Angelillo, C., 144
Annerbäck, E.-M., 200
Apperly, I. A., 149
Applegate, A. G., 203
Appleyard, K., 201
Aquilina, A. M., 205
Arauz, R. M., 144
Archibald, A. B., 224, 229
Arias, E., 59
Arias Vasquez, A., 170
Ariés, P., 5, 6
Arling, G. L., 107
Armstrong, J. M., 114, 231, 232
Arnett, J. J., 6, 278, 286, 298, 299
Aron, A., 306
Arseneault, L., 201
Ascherio, A., 158
Asendorpf, J. B., 231, 297
Asherson, P., 171
Ashmore, R. D., 276
Askari, M. S., 233
Ataba-Poria, N., 170
Atherton, J., 150
Attanucci, J., 257
Auerbach, J. G., 170
Auerbach-Major, S., 182
Augustus-Horvath, C. L., 240
Axelsson, A., 137

B

Baar, A. V., 78
Babchishin, L., 180
Bacchini, D., 177, 194, 259
Bachman, J. G., 259, 260, 261
Back, J., 86
Baddeley, A. D., 168
Badger, S., 291
Bagwell, C. L., 182
Bahm, N. I., 110
Bahrick, L. B., 86
Baibazarova, E., 48
Baijot, S., 171
Baillargeon, R., 94, 95
Bajo, M. T., 168
Baker, F. C., 269
Bakermans-Kranenburg, M. J., 113, 126, 200
Baldwin, J. R., 201
Ball, H. L., 84
Ballan, M. S., 158
Ballantine, P. W., 308
Ballard, R. H., 203
Ban, B., 171
Banaschewski, T., 171, 260
Banducci, A. N., 201
Bandura, A., 12
Bane, K., 301
Bang, H. J., 274
Banks, M. S., 86
Banyard, V., 196
Barber, B. K., 274
Barbosa de Sá, A., 153
Barbu-Roth, M. A., 90
Barclay, L., 77
Bar-Haim, Y., 124
Barkin, S., 199
Barkley, J. E., 309
Barkley, R. A., 170, 171
Barko, E. B., 238
Barnea-Goraly, N., 62
Barnes, G. M., 260
Barnes, J., 118
Barnett, L. M., 165, 166
Barnett, S. M., 211
Barnett, W. S., 117
Barnhart, S., 200
Baron, I. S., 63
Barr, A. B., 305
Barrera, C. M., 167
Barrett, M., 246
Barry, C. M., 291
Barry, H., III, 224
Barry, R. A., 113, 121
Bartels, J. M., 207
Bartholomew, K., 286, 288
Barzansky, B. M., 41
Bastos, A., 202, 203
Bates, J. E., 203, 305
Batool, S. S., 55, 56

Battista, D., 242
Bauer, E., 171
Bauermeister, J. A., 304
Baugerud, G. A., 148
Baumeister, J. A., 309
Baumeister, R. F., 175
Baumrind, D., 193, 199
Bava, S., 266
Baxter, C., 166
Baxter, M. G., 240
Beach, D. R., 168
Beard, J. R., 166
Bearss, K., 158
Beck, A., 49
Becker, S. P., 182
Becker-Blease, K. A., 196
Beckman, C. R. B, 41
Beekman, C., 179, 185
Begeer, S., 151
Behboodi-Moghadam, Z., 55
Behrens, K. Y., 110
Beijers, R., 76, 80
Bejcek, J., 291
Bell, A. S., 171
Bell, K. M., 294
Belsky, D. W., 27
Belsky, J., 17, 49, 83, 113, 118, 120, 126, 231, 232
Belsky, J. K., 43
Bem, S. L., 157
Beneventi, H., 207
Benfield, N., 61
Ben-Itzchak, E., 158
Benjet, C., 199
Benner, A. D., 260
Bennett, P., 77
Benoit, A., 233
Bentley, C., 239
Berberich-Artzi, J., 150
Bereczkei, T., 306
Berenbaum, S. A., 155
Bergeman, C. S., 16
Bergen, M. R., 306
Berger, A., 170
Berger, C., 263
Berger, S. E., 89
Bergh, C., 241
Bergman, H., 150
Bergren, M. D., 231
Berk, L. E., 145
Berko, J., 146

Berlin, L. J., 109, 110, 201
Berman, N., 297
Bernert, J. T., 47
Bernhardt, B. A., 53
Berry, D., 117, 118
Berry, S. H., 243
Bersamin, M., 243, 244
Berthelsen, D., 82, 119
Berzin, S. C., 289
Besetsny, L. K., 200
Best, J. R., 168
Beyers, W., 289, 294
Bhana, D., 244
Bhattacharya, G., 301
Bian, L., 94, 95
Biehle, S. N., 76, 77
Biggs, K., 171
Bilder, R. M., 258
Bilo, R. A., 200
Biltereyst, D., 246
Bink, M., 171
Birch, H. G., 111, 125
Bird, G., 266
Bird, H., 265, 278
Bjardwaj, A., 171
Bjork, J. M., 266
Bjorklund, D. F., 42, 76, 144, 152, 156, 169
Black, R. E., 77
Blackburn, K., 308
Blair, C., 116, 117, 118
Blair, K. A., 182
Blake, L. P., 291, 296
Blakely-McClure, S., 263
Blakemore, S., 258, 266
Blakemore, S.-J., 266
Blank, R. H., 62
Blankenship, J., 47
Blass, E. M., 86
Blatney, M., 181
Blehar, M. C., 108, 110
Blencowe, H., 39, 62
Blomeyer, D., 260
Blum, D., 106
Blum, M., 234
Blyth, D. A., 234, 235
Boduszek, D., 246
Bohlin, G., 113
Bohn, C. M., 155
Boisvert, J. A., 240
Boldt, L. J., 117

Bonanno, R. A., 185
Bondy, S. J., 47
Boonpleng, W., 231
Boonstra, H., 236
Booth-LaForce, C., 113, 182, 184, 264
Boris, N. W., 109, 110
Borko, H., 212
Bornehag, C.-G., 200
Bornstein, M., 196
Boulton, T., 61
Bouma, E. C., 262
Bourdeau, B., 243, 244
Bourguignon, J.-P., 225, 231
Bourke, A., 246
Bowers, E., 265
Bowes, L., 201
Bowker, J. C., 182
Bowlby, J., 14, 82, 107, 108, 110, 113, 114
Boyce, W. T., 126, 231, 232
Boyle, D. E., 155
Boyle, M. H., 62, 63, 200
Braddock, S., 48
Bradley, R. H., 166, 264
Bradshaw, C. P., 185
Braithwaite, A., 27
Brame, R., 259
Bramen, J. E., 266
Brand, S., 269
Branje, S. J. T., 272
Brauer, J., 207
Braun, S. S., 184
Braungart-Ricker, J. M., 123
Braver, S. L., 203
Brazier, J. E., 171
Breaux, R. P., 171
Breedlove, S. M., 238
Breen, A. V., 262
Brennan, A. M., 196
Brenning, K., 43
Bresin, K., 49
Bretherton, I., 108, 113
Bridge, J. A., 47
Bridgett, D. J., 111, 122
Briley, D. A., 234
Britton, M. L., 289
Brocki, K. C., 113
Brockmeyer, C., 153
Brody, G. H., 242
Brody, N., 209, 308

Brooks, L. O., 166
Brooks-Gunn, J., 224, 227, 229, 231, 232, 233, 234, 236, 268
Brotman, L. M., 125
Brown, A., 77
Brown, A. P., 49
Brown, B. B., 276
Brown, H. R., 171
Brown, T. A., 239
Brownlee, J., 119
Brugman, E., 200
Bruner, J. S., 144, 148
Brunner, R., 124
Brusseau, T., 165
Bryan, J. D., 289
Bucchianeri, M. M., 239
Buchanan, C., 300
Buchmann, A. F., 260
Budge, S. L., 304
Buitelaar, J., 48, 171
Bukowski, W. M., 182
Bulik, C. M., 239
Bundy, D. A., 209
Burchinal, M., 118, 199
Bureau, J.-F., 111, 264
Burkam, D. T., 205
Burkett, M., 309
Burley, K., 47
Burnett, S., 266
Burnham, M. M., 81
Burns, R., 165
Burt, K. B., 126
Burt, S. A., 238
Burzette, R. G., 297
Buschining, R., 186
Bushnell, I. W. R., 86
Bushway, S., 259
Buss, D. M., 305
Buss, K. A., 123
Butler, M., 235, 241
Buttelmann, D., 134
Byatt, N., 47
Bynner, J. M., 294
Byram, V., 83, 114

C

Cabral, H. J., 47
Cacioppo, J. T., 303
Cacioppo, S., 303
Cadaveira, F., 260

Name Index

Cadigan, R. J., 76
Cafiero, R., 207
Cahill, J., 113
Cahill-Rowley, K., 62
Cairns-Smith, S., 62
Calhoun, V. D., 72
Call, J., 134
Callmar, M., 241
Calogero, R. M., 238
Campbell, B. C., 242
Campbell, I. G., 269
Campbell, J. D., 175
Campione-Barr, N., 275
Campos, J. J., 90
Canário, C., 43
Canavarro, M. C., 54
Canino, G., 265, 278
Canter, A. S., 207
Cantwell, L., 301
Cao, L., 239, 240
Caplan, A. L., 62
Caprara, G. V., 297
Caprihan, A., 72
Caravelli, L., 202
Caravita, S. C., 183, 263
Carbonell, O. A., 110
Carlson, A. G., 136
Carlson, E., 113
Carlson, S. M., 151
Carlsson, J., 287
Carnevale, A., 299
Carney, M., 235, 241
Caron, S. L., 55, 56, 242
Carr, C. T., 308
Carroll, J. S., 291
Cartwright, C., 204
Case, K., 211
Case, R., 168
Cashmore, J., 203
Caspi, A., 27
Cassia, V. M., 87
Cassibba, R., 110
Castaneda, A. M., 307
Castel, A. D., 170
Castellanos, I., 86
Castellanos-Ryan, N., 233
Castro, Y., 49
Catalano, R. F., 273
Cattuzzo, M. T., 166
Cauffman, E., 231, 264
Caulfield, L., 77

Ceci, S. J., 198, 211
Cenk, D. S., 195
Centers for Disease Control and Prevention, 57, 60, 158, 170, 172, 236
Central Intelligence Agency (CIA), 7, 63, 287
Cham, H., 234
Chamberlain, A., 215
Chan, A., 181
Chang, H. H., 62
Chang, Y., 158
Chang, Z., 171
Chang-Schneider, C., 175
Chao, R. K., 274
Chapron, C., 55
Charbonneau, G., 73
Charman, T., 116
Cheek, S. M., 262
Chein, J. M., 258, 259
Chelliah, A., 207
Chen, B., 172, 174
Chen, H., 62, 238
Chen, J., 170, 266
Chen, Q., 274
Chen, X., 172
Chen, Y., 62, 148
Chen, Z., 234
Chertkow, H., 150
Chess, A., 111
Chess, S., 125
Chetty, R., 22, 117, 215, 216
Cheung, A., 215
Cheung, P., 202
Cheung, P. C., 167
Chevalier, N., 47
Chiang, J., 274
Chih-Yuan, S. L., 289
Chikritzhs, T., 48
Child Soldiers International, 278
Child Trends Databank, 7, 9, 275
Chin, T., 265
Chinsky, J. M., 168
Chiu, C., 301
Cho, Y., 274
Choi, J., 215
Choi, Y., 195
Cholett, A., 185
Chong, A., 76

Christensen, J., 158
Chronis-Tuscano, A., 124
Chua, A., 194
Chuang, S., 122
Chumlea, W. C., 231
Chung, J. M., 296
Chung, T., 201
Chupetlovska-Anastasova, A., 171
Ciairano, S., 262
Ciarrochi, J., 277
Cicchetti, D., 200, 201
Cigala, A., 151
Cillessen, A. H. N., 179, 182, 183, 258, 263
Cillessen, L., 80
Ciocanel, O., 268
Claes, L., 262
Claes, M., 233
Clark, C. A., 47
Clark, L., 240
Clarke-Stewart, K. A., 118
Class, Q. A., 48
Claxton, L. J., 151
Clearfield, M. W., 116
Cliff, D. P., 165, 166
Clough, P. J., 269
Cloutier, P., 264
Coccia, C., 309
Coghill, D., 171
Cohen, O., 202
Cohen-Kettenis, P. T., 48
Coie, J. D., 178
Colasante, T., 178
Cole, E. R., 238
Coleman, S., 47
Coleman, S. J., 236, 246
Coley, R. L., 117, 118
Colin, C., 171
Collignon, O., 73
Collins, M. A., 294
Collins, N. L., 311
Collins, P. S., 200
Collins, R. L., 156, 243
Collins, W. A., 113, 260
Colmenares, F., 127
Cölon, Y., 289
Colquhoun, D., 83
Colrain, I. M., 269
Comas, M., 148
Compian, L., 238

Compos, C. M. C., 166
Conger, R. D., 297
Connell, N. M., 268, 277
Connolly, J., 290
Conroy-Beam, D., 305
Cook, C. R., 185
Cook, K., 48
Cook, T. D., 277
Cooley, J. L., 180
Cooley, S., 177
Cools, R., 170
Cooper, C. L., 171
Cooper, H., 213, 214
Cooper, M., 170, 240
Cooper, P. J., 83, 112, 114
Corbin, K. D., 47
Corbin, W. R., 260
Corcoran, D. L., 27
Corley, R. P., 124
Cormier, D. C., 205
Corna, M., 84
Corral, M., 260
Correa-Chavez, M., 144
Corsaro, W. A., 153, 154
Corte, C., 231
Coryn, R., 264
Costos, D., 233
Côté, J., 294
Cotter, J. A., 72, 82
Cotterell, J., 276, 277
Countermine, M., 83
Cousens, S., 39
Cousineau, J. R., 294
Cowan, C. P., 111, 311
Cowan, N., 168
Cowan, P. A., 111, 199, 311
Coy, K. C., 122
Cozzarelli, C., 311
Crade, M., 39
Cramer, P., 297
Crawford, A. M., 185
Crawford, J. R., 207
Crick, N. R., 180
Crocetti, E., 287, 288, 294
Crockett, E. E., 307
Crockett, L. J., 242
Crone, E. A., 266
Crooks, D., 47
Crosby, B., 83
Crosnoe, R., 260

Cross, A., 268, 277
Crouter, A. C., 265, 272, 273, 288
Crowley, M. J., 241
Csikszentmihalyi, M., 260, 261, 271, 272, 295, 297, 298
Culbert, K. M., 238
Cunningham, S. A., 167
Curby, T. W., 124, 136
Currier, J. M., 195
Cyr, C., 111
CysticFibrosis.com, 51
Czajkowski, L. A., 171

D
D'Accordo, C., 297
Daddis, C., 272
Dahl, R. E., 227, 260, 266
Daly, B. P., 269
Damant, D., 203
Damaraju, E., 72
Danckaerts, M., 171
Danemar, S., 241
Danese, A., 27, 201
Daniel, B., 175
Danziger, S., 287
Darling, C. A., 309
Darwich, J., 56
Dasen, P. R., 143
David-Ferdon, C., 173
Davidson, A. J., 184
Davidson, A. L., 275
Davila, J., 311
Davis, A. S., 47
Davis, D. E., 294
Davis, E. L., 122
Davis, E. P., 82
Davis, K. E., 289
Dawson-Hughes, B., 234
Day, K. L., 62, 63
Dean, D., 289, 296
Dean, D. C., 72, 99
Dean, D. I., 76
Dean, R. S., 47
DeAngelo, L., 291, 296
Deardorff, J., 231, 234
Deary, I. J., 207
Deater-Deckard, K., 179, 185, 197
de Boer, M. A., 54
de Bruyn, E., 198

DeCasper, A. J., 86
Deci, E. L., 214
Deconnick, N., 171
DeGarmo, D. S., 203
Degnan, K. A., 114, 124, 184, 185
De Goede, I. H. D., 272
DeHart, G., 231
Deitnre, P., 171
Deković, M., 178
De La Rue, L., 186
Del Corno, G., 84
Delevi, R., 309
Del Giudice, M., 39
Deligiannidis, K. M., 47
De Marco, A. C., 289
DeMaris, A., 118
DeMatteo, D., 262, 264, 267, 269
Demir, A., 195
de Mol, J., 289
DeMulder, E., 182
Deng, Y., 277
Denham, S. A., 176, 182
Deniz Can, D., 99
Dennis, C., 76
Deoni, S. L., 72, 76, 99
DePalma, R., 246
Dequinzio, J. A., 158
Dereu, M., 158
De Ridder, S., 245
de Roten, Y., 56
De Shipper, J. C., 119
Despland, J., 56
DeThorne, L., 179, 185
Deutsch, N. L., 265
Devine, R. T., 149, 151
de Visser, R. O., 55, 56
de Vries, M., 54
de Weerth, C., 76
Diamond, A., 21
Diamond, M. O., 43, 57
Dian, T., 61
Dias, C. C., 80
Díaz-Morales, J. F., 269
Dibble, J. L., 309
Dickstein, S., 82
Diego, M., 80, 86
Diers, T., 76
Dietz, P. M., 47
DiGiunta, L., 177, 194

Dimidjian, S., 49
Dinella, L. M., 157
Dintcheff, B., 260
Dirks, H., 72, 76, 99
Dishion, T. J., 178, 181, 258, 277
Dittmann, R. W., 171
Dixon, E., 158
Doallo, S., 260
Doane, L. D., 269
Dodd, D. R., 304
Dodge, K. A., 178, 180, 201, 259, 305
Dodsworth, R. O., 107
Doernberg, E., 72, 99
Doherty, E. R., 297
Dolderman, D., 306
Domingue, B., 27
Donnellan, M. B., 297
D'Onofrio, B. M., 48, 203, 209
Donohue, B., 200
Dorn, L. D., 266
Doucet, S., 86
Dougherty, G., 76
Douglas, P. S., 82
Douglas, V., 238, 240
Douglass, S., 294
Dowling, E. M., 21, 268
Doyle, L. W., 62
Drennan, J., 235, 241
Drenowatz, C., 166
Druin, M., 309
Drum, M. L., 231
Dube, S. R., 47
Dubertret, C., 47
Dubois-Comtois, K., 111
Dudley, W. N., 79
Duell, N., 259
Duffy, A. L., 176
Duffy, D., 62
Duh, S., 151
Duku, E., 200
Duncan, G. J., 116, 205
Dunfield, K. A., 126
Dunkel, L., 231
Dunn, E. W., 127
Dunn, J., 152, 154
Dunphy, D. C., 275
Duong, J., 185

Dush, C. K., 305
Duvander, A., 43
Dwairy, M., 194
Dweck, C. S., 175, 213
Dwyer, D. S., 243

E
Eborall, H., 47
Eccles, J. S., 235, 260
Economic Policy Institute, 7, 116
Edmunds, S. R., 158
Edwards, R. C., 43
Efron, D., 171
Eftekhar-Ardabily, H., 55
Egeland, B., 113, 260
Egeli, N., 195
Eggerman, M., 196
Eidelman, A. I., 80
Eilertsen, D. E., 113
Eisenberg, N., 176, 177, 297
Eisner, E. W., 209, 211
Ekas, N. V., 123
Eklund, K. M., 207
Ekono, M., 115
Elenbaas, L., 177
Elferink-Gemser, M. T., 166
Elkind, D., 254, 257
Elliot, S., 235, 241, 246
Elliott, M. N., 243
Ellis, B. J., 126, 231
Elwood, M., 76
Emery, L. F., 308
Engel, S. G., 239, 240
Engels, R. E., 262
England, J. L., 47
Engle, S., 299
Englund, M. M., 260
Eninger, L., 113
Epstein, R., 270
The Equality of Opportunity Project, 296
Eriksen, A., 268
Erikson, E., 18, 20, 82, 121, 134, 164, 173, 291–292, 302
Erkelenz, N., 166
Ernst, E., 83
Ersland, L., 207
Erulkar, A., 278
Escribano, C., 269

Esparza, P., 289
Espelage, D. L., 183, 186
Espeset, E. M. S., 239
Espy, K. A., 47
Essex, M. J., 114, 231, 232
Ettekal, I., 180, 264, 277
Evangeli, M., 83, 114
Evans, A. D., 149
Evans, G. W., 116

F

Fabes, R. A., 155, 156, 176
Fabian, J., 267
Faguy, K., 167
Fairchild, H., 240
Falciglia, G. A., 76
Fanuele, S., 148
Farmer, T. W., 235
Farrell, M. P., 260
Farroni, T., 86
Fassino, S., 240
Fathalla, M. M. F., 61
Fauquet, J., 238
Favez, N., 56, 125
Fay, K., 262
Fearon, R. M. P., 110
Feeney, J. A., 310
Feinberg, I., 269
Feinberg, M., 202, 203
Feinstein, L., 260
Felder, J. N., 49
Feldman, R., 48, 80
Feldman, S., 61
Ferber, R., 83
Ferland, P., 55, 56
Fernandez, M., 86
Feubner, C., 113
Few, L. R., 262
Fexia, C., 224
Fiebiger, S., 49
Field, T., 80, 86
Fifer, W. P., 86
Figueiredo, B., 43, 80, 202, 203
Finch, S., 199
Fincham, F. D., 309
Finegood, E. D., 116
Finer, L. B., 242
Fink, E., 151
Fink, G. R., 151
Finke, P., 124

Finkel, D., 15
Finkel, E. J., 306
Finkelhor, D., 196
Fischbach, G. D., 158
Fischbach, R. L., 158
Fisher, D. A., 243, 244
Fisher, H. L., 201
Fisher, J. A., 73
Fite, P. J., 180, 182
Fitzpatrick, M. J., 156
Fivush, R., 148
Flanagan, C. A., 269
Flanders, J., 152
Flannery, J., 87
Flavell, J. H., 19, 91, 142, 168, 254
Fleming, N. I., 27
Florian, V., 311
Flower, K. B., 76
Flynn, C., 203
Flynn, J. R., 17, 209
Fombonne, E., 185
Fonseca, A., 54
Fontaine, A. M., 287, 289
Forbes, E. E., 266
Forbush, K. T., 239
Ford, D. H., 21
Forrest, L. N., 304
Forster, S., 171
Forthun, L., 294
Foster, R. E., 200
Fothergill, A., 118
Fox, C. V., 265
Fox, J., 308
Fox, N. A., 114, 124, 184, 185
Fox, S. E., 73
Foy, D. W., 195
Francis, D. A., 246
Frank, D. A., 47
Franke, B., 170
Frans, E. M., 158
Fransen, J., 166
Freeman, M. P., 47
French, K. E., 136
Freud, S., 13
Frey, K. S., 173
Freynet, N., 264
Friedman, D. R., 309
Friedman, J. N., 215
Friedman, N. P., 124

Friedman, S. I., 231
Friedman-Krauss, A. H., 117
Friemel, C. M., 260
Frisén, A., 240, 287
Frisson, S., 149
Fromme, K., 260
Frye, A. A., 291, 296, 297
Fu, R., 172
Fu, Y., 165
Fulcher, M., 157
Fuligni, A. J., 196, 269, 274, 289
Fuller-Tyszkiewicz, M., 237
Furler, K., 306
Fürstenberg, F. F., 288
Fürstenberg, F. F., Jr., 287, 288, 289
Futch Ehrlich, V. A., 265

G

Gabard-Durman, L., 87
Gagne, M. H., 199
Gallo, A. M., 231
Gallop, R., 49
Galloway, J. C., 90
Galloway, M., 269
Galván, A., 269
Ganiban, J., 124, 306
Garcia, G., 76, 77
Gardner, H., 211
Gardner, M., 259, 268
Gartstein, M. A., 122
Gasper, J., 269
Gates, J. R., 260
Gath, A., 50
Gaul, D., 165
Gaultney, J. F., 269
Gavin, J., 238
Gaylor, E. E., 81
Gaytán, F. X., 274
Gazelle, H., 187
Ge, X., 125, 230
Geary, D. C., 136
Geladé, K, 171
Gelernter, J., 201
Geller, J., 239
Genc, S., 171
Gentile, K., 57
Geraghty, S. R., 76
Gerber, E. B., 120
Gerber, M., 269

Gerhart, J. L., 294
Germo, G. R., 82
Germond, M., 56
Gershoff, E. T., 199
Gershoff, J., 199
Gerteis, J., 47
Gervain, G., 98
Gest, S. D., 264, 277
Gestsdottir, S., 265
Geurts, S. A. E., 119
Gibbins, S., 86
Gibbons, F. X., 242
Gibson, E. J., 87
Gibson, R., 268
Giedd, J. N., 74, 266
Gilbert-Barness, E., 45
Giletta, M., 262
Gilligan, C., 257
Gillings, K., 268
Gilman, R., 262, 269
Gil-Perotin, S., 72
Ginsburg, H., 254
Giordano, P. C., 244, 245, 276, 305
Gísladóttír, T., 166
Glance, D., 48
Glass, L. A., 207
Glenn, C. R., 262
Glick, S. C., 151
Gloeckler, L., 119
Gniewosz, B., 182
Godin, M., 203
Godleski, S. A., 179, 183
Goff, B., 87
Goldberg, W. A., 82
Goldin-Meadow, S., 73
Goldman, J. G., 236, 246
Goldman-Mellor, S., 27
Goldschmidt, A. B., 239
Goldstein, N. S., 262, 267, 269
Gomes, H., 171
Gomes, M., 201
Gomez, V., 306
Gonzaga, G. C., 303
Gonzales, J. R., 278
Gonzales, N. A., 196, 234, 274
Gonzales, N. A., 234
Gonzalez, J. R., 265
Gooch, D., 170, 207
Good, M., 270

Goodlin-Jones, B. L., 81
Goodman, G. S., 148
Goodman, J., 77
Goodman, S. H., 49
Goossens, F. A., 176
Gopnik, A., 94
Gordon, R. J., 5, 6, 76, 286
Gordon, S. D., 262
Gordon-Messer, D., 309
Gordon Simons, L., 305
Gore, T., 84
Gossage, J. P., 47
Gottesman, I. I., 209
Gottfredson, D. C., 268, 277
Gould, L. A., 198
Gould, S. J., 209
Gouley, K. K., 125
Gowen, L. K., 238
Graber, J. A., 224, 227, 229, 231, 234, 236
Graham, J., 171
Graham, S., 77
Gramaglia, C., 240
Granger, D. A., 117, 118
Granic, I., 185, 186
Graniere-Deferre, C., 86
Gratwick-Sarll, K., 239
Gratz, K. L., 262
Gravelle, M., 235
Greene, D., 213
Greenfield, E. A., 200
Greenfield, P. M., 143, 241, 274
Greening, L., 182
Griffin, D. W., 306
Grigorenko, E. L., 205, 209
Grilo, C. M., 239
Grimon, M., 196
Grisso, T., 267, 268
Groark, C. J., 114
Grob, A., 306
Grodzinski, A., 309
Groen, Y., 176
Groenveld, M. G., 118, 120
Grogan-Kaylor, A., 199
Grolnick, W. S., 214
Grøn, R., 47
Grønborg, T. K., 158
Groote, I. D., 158
Grossman, T., 87
Grube, E. L., 243

Grube, J. W., 243, 244
Grych, J., 196
Guan, S. A., 274
Guardino, C. M., 48
Guendelman, S., 77
Guerra, N. G., 185
Guerri, C., 266
Gueta, G., 214
Guex, P., 56
Gulliksen, K. S., 239
Gulz, A., 137
Gunnar, M. R., 114
Guo, F., 234
Gurven, M. D., 76, 77
Gustafsson, P. A., 200
Guttmacher Institute, 242, 244, 246
Guttorm, T. K., 207
Guzman, X., 62

H
Habermas, T., 148
Hadaya, H., 170
Haffner, J., 124
Haga, M., 166
Hahn, H. M., 83
Hakvoort, R. M., 80
Haley, A., 209
Hall, S., 201, 286, 287, 288, 291
Halligan, S. L., 83, 114
Halperin, J. M., 170, 171
Halpern, H. P., 156
Halpern-Felsher, B. L., 245
Halpern-Meekin, S., 305
Haltigan, J. D., 110, 264
Hämäläinen, J. A., 207
Hamby, S., 196
Hamlin, J. K., 96, 127
Hamm, J. V., 235
Hamrick, K. J., 47
Hamvas, L., 199
Hamza, C., 270
Handayani, P., 195
Haney-Caron, E., 269
Hanish, L. D., 155, 156
Hannon, J., 165
Hans, S. L., 43
Hansel, T. C., 196
Harbourne, R. T., 90
Harden, K. P., 227, 234, 259

Harden, P., 260
Hardy, L. L., 137
Hardy, N., 309
Hardy, S., 294
Harkness, S., 173
Harley, K., 148
Harlow, C. M., 107
Harlow, H. F., 106, 107
Harlow, M. K., 107
Harold, G. T., 124
Harraway, J. A., 48
Harrell, W. A., 240
Harriger, J. A., 238
Harrington, H. L., 27
Harris, J. R., 197
Harris, M. J., 158
Harrison, C., 239
Harrist, A. W., 119
Hart, E. J., 183
Harter, S., 214, 237
Hartman, E., 166
Hartmann, E., 113
Hartup, W. W., 182
Harvey, E. A., 171
Hashimoto-Torii, K., 48
Hasken, J. M., 47
Haskett, M. E., 202
Haslam, N., 274
Hatano, K., 294
Haukka, J., 231
Hauser, M. D., 98
Havertape, L., 262
Hawkins, J. D., 273
Hayward, C., 238
Hazan, C., 309
Hazell, P., 171
Hazen, N., 112
Healey, D. M., 170
Healy, E., 62
Heath, A. C., 47
Heatherton, T. F., 151, 240
Heaven, P. C. L., 277
Heeren, T. C., 47
Heilbrun, K., 262, 267
Helfand, M., 242
Hellerstein, S., 61
Henderson, R. C., 199
Hendren, N., 22, 117, 216
Hendry, A., 116
Hendry, L. B., 287, 288, 289
Hengartner, M. P., 201

Henin, A., 297
Hennekam, S., 42
Henrique, R. S., 166
Henry, J. D., 151
Henry, L. A., 207
Hensler, B. S., 207
Hepach, R., 126, 127
Herbert, A. C., 233
Herbert, W. N. P., 41
Herdt, G., 242
Herman, L., 152
Hermann, J., 152
Hermans, J. M. A., 116
Hernández-Lloreda, M. V., 127
Hernandez-Reif, M., 80, 86
Herrera, D. E., 269
Herrera, S., 195
Herrmann, M. J., 171
Herrstein, R. J., 209
Hersh, R. H., 255, 256
Hertenstein, M. J., 90
Herting, M. M., 224, 226, 227, 266
Hertzog, C., 25
Hertz-Picciotto, I., 158
Hesse-Biber, S., 238
Hewitt, J. K., 124
Higher Education Research Institute (HERI), 296, 299
Hildenbrand, A. K., 269
Hill, D. L., 243
Hill, E. A., 99
Hill, J. P., 272
Hill, L. G., 186
Hill, P. S., 82
Hilmert, C. J., 49
Himmelfarb, I., 151
Hinde, R. A., 107
Hinshaw, S. P., 170
Hipwell, A. E., 242
Hirschfield, P. J., 268
Hiwatashi, M., 49
Hodnett, E., 82
Hoeben, E. M., 268
Hofer, C., 176
Hoff-Ginsberg, E., 97, 98
Hoffman, J. H., 260
Hoffman, M. L., 177
Hofstede, G., 8

Hoicka, E., 168
Hölcke, M., 241
Holderness, C. C., 232
Holding, P., 78
Holland, J. M., 200
Holland, L. A., 239
Hollguin, S., 260
Holmberg, H., 171
Holmes, G., 215
Holmes, J. G., 306
Holmqvist, K., 240
Holsboer-Trachsler, E., 269
Holte, A., 239
Holtzworth-Munroe, A., 203
Homa, D., 47
Hoogman, M., 170
Hook, J. N., 294
Horowitz, B. N., 306
House, A. N., 195
Houts, R. M., 27, 166, 231, 232
Howard, K. S., 304
Howlett, E., 235, 241
Howser, M. E., 309
Howson, C. P., 62
Hranilovich, J. A., 266
Hrdy, S. B., 5
Hu, S., 290, 301
Huang, H., 47
Huang, J., 48
Huang, K., 125
Hubbard, E. M., 90
Huddleston, J., 230
Hudec, K. L., 170
Hudson, M. B., 309
Huebner, E. S., 262, 269
Hugdahl, K., 207
Hughes, C., 149, 151, 154
Hughes, C. M. L., 166
Hughes, D. K., 307
Huizink, A. C., 111
Huizink, A. J., 47, 48
Hulme, C., 170, 207
Hultman, C. M., 158
Humaidan, P., 55
Humphreys, K. L., 87, 170
Hunger, C., 239, 240
Hunger and Poverty Facts and Statistics, 79
Hunt, T. K., 239
Hunter, S. B., 243

Hurtado, S., 291, 296
Huttenlocher, P. R., 46
Huyen, B. T., 297
Hyde, A., 235, 241
Hyde, J. S., 231, 234
Hymel, S., 185

I
Ibiebele, I., 39
Ibisomi, L., 76
Icenogle, G., 259
Ilgaz, H., 153
Imuta, K., 151
Inder, T. E., 62
Ip, E. H., 199
Ireton, C., 76
Isberg, S., 241
Ishitani, T. T., 299, 300
Issartel, J., 165
Ito, M., 34
Iwanski, A., 297

J
Jach, H. K., 265
Jackson, D. B., 76
Jackson, T., 238
Jacobus, J., 266
Jacobvitz, D., 112
Jacquet, A. Y., 86
Jacquet, S. E., 307
Jaffe, J., 43, 57
Jaffee, S. R., 201
Jahromi, L. B., 294
James, D., 72
James, S., 286, 288
Jamison, R., 184
Jang, Y., 214
Jankowski, K. S., 269
Janson, S., 200
Janssen, I., 166
Janssen, T. W., 171
Jarrett, M. A., 180
Jedd, K. E., 116
Jelinek, M., 181
Jennings, A., 171
Jennings, W. G., 265, 278
Jensen, A. R., 209
Jensen, H., 47
Jernigan, T. L., 39, 72, 73, 266
Jessen, S., 84, 87
Jia, Y., 48

Jiang, Y., 115
Johanson, C. E., 84
Johns, M. M., 304
Johnson, A. L., 238
Johnson, A. M., 76
Johnson, C., 158
Johnson, D. W., 215
Johnson, H. E., 265
Johnson, K. M., 57
Johnson, R., 215
Johnston, L. D., 259, 260, 261
Joiner, T. E., 240
Jokhi, R. P., 53
Joly, J., 199
Jonas, M., 83
Jones, B. L., 242
Jones, E. J., 116
Jong, D. M., 47
Jongenelis, M., 48
Jonkmann, K., 296
Ju, C. M., 274
Juarascio, A. S., 238
Juarez, B., 297
Julian, M. M., 114
Junger, M., 178
Juul, A., 225, 231

K
Kagan, J., 111, 124, 198
Kahalisa, N., 152
Kakigi, R., 87
Kalak, N., 269
Kalin, M., 196
Kalmign, M., 204
Kan, C., 170
Kanazawa, S., 87
Kane, R., 166
Kanouse, D. E., 243
Kaplan, A., 214
Kaplan, H. S., 76, 77
Karafa, J. A., 311
Karen, R., 14, 106
Karimpour, R., 263
Karlsen, K. A., 79
Karlsson, H., 111
Karlsson, L., 111
Kärnä, A., 185
Karni, E., 54
Karst, G. M., 90
Karst, W. A., 200

Kashan, A. S., 48
Kashy, D. A., 311
Kasper, L. J., 170
Kataja, E., 111
Kato, K., 15
Katon, W., 47
Katz, I., 214
Katz, L., 22
Kawasawa, Y. I., 48
Kazdin, A. E., 199
Keefe, M. R., 79
Keel, P. K., 239, 240
Keenan, K., 242
Keijsers, L., 272
Kelleher, C., 246
Keller, M. A., 82
Kellman, P. J., 86
Kelly, D. J., 86, 87
Kelly-Vance, L., 158
Kennedy, K. E., 205
Kenton, L., 82
Kenworthy, L., 158
Kerr, D. C. R., 125
Kessing, L., 47
Kettner, D. K., 166
Keys, C. L., 262
Kharrazi, M., 77
Kiang, L., 289
Kidd, K. K., 205, 209
Kiefer, S. M., 263
Killèn, K., 113
Killen, M., 176, 177, 182, 186
Killewald, A., 43
Kilzer, R., 195
Kim, B., 83
Kim, B. K. E., 273
Kim, B. S. K., 274
Kim, H., 72, 82
Kim, J., 167, 179, 185, 201
Kim, M., 274
Kim, P., 116
Kim, S., 113, 125, 167
Kim, S. Y., 195, 274
Kim, T. E., 185
Kim, Y. S., 195
King, B., 158
King, E. K., 119
Kinniburgh-White, R., 204
Kins, E., 289
Kirk, R., 76

Kirov, R., 269
Kiselica, M. S., 43
Kistner, J. A., 173
Kita, S., 99
Kitamura, T., 195
Kitzinger, S., 34, 59
Kloep, M., 287, 288, 289
Klonsky, E. D., 262
Klump, K. L., 238
Knaack, A., 123, 125
Knaak, S., 77
Knopik, V. S., 47
Knowles, S. J., 125
Knox, M., 198, 199
Kobayashi, M., 87
Kobel, S., 166
Kocev, N., 47
Kochanek, K. D., 59
Kochanska, G., 113, 117, 121, 122, 123, 125
Kochenderfer-Ladd, B., 177
Kocsor, F., 306
Koenig, J. L., 113
Kohen, D., 180
Kohlberg, L., 157, 255
Kohout, J., 48
Komarraju, M., 301
Kong, R., 207
Konner, M., 5
Kooiman, L. Y., 76, 77
Koolschijn, P. C., 266
Korja, R., 111
Kosa, J. L., 77
Kotzer, A. M., 79
Koury, A. S., 117, 118
Kover, S. T., 158
Kraft, I., 207
Krahé, B., 186
Kramer, M. R., 167
Kreppner, J., 114
Kretsch, N., 234, 260
Kriziol, N. A., 113
Kroger, J., 255
Kronenberg, M. E., 196
Krstev, S., 47
Krueger, J. I., 175
Kubacka, K. E., 306
Kuehn, S., 171
Kuh, G. D., 301
Kuhl, P. K., 99
Kuhlmeier, V. A., 126

Kuhn, A., 48
Kuhn, B. R., 199
Kuhn, D., 255
Kuhnert, R., 151
Kulin, H. E., 231
Kumar, S., 39
Kumashiro, M., 306
Kunkel, D., 243
Kunst, A. E., 48
Kuntz, K. J., 263
Kvasnicka-Gates, L., 49
Kwon, M., 86
Kyeong, S., 201

L
Labbock, M. H., 76
Labouvie-Vief, G., 297
Lacourse, E., 233
Ladd, G. W., 177, 180, 187, 264, 277
LaDuke, C., 262, 264
Lafontaine, M.-F., 264
LaFontana, K. M., 258, 263
La Greca, A. M., 276
La Guardia, J. G., 214
Lahey, J., 6
Lai, P., 57
Laible, D. J., 145
Lainpelto, K., 202
Lamb, M., 119, 120
Lambert, K., 235
Lamela, D., 202, 203
Landerl, K., 207
Landor, A., 242
Lane, B. L., 308
Lang, A., 306
Langknecht, H., 262, 269
Långström, N., 48, 158
Lansford, J. E., 177, 194, 259, 305
La Paro, K. M., 119
Lapsley, A., 113
Lapsley, D., 311
Larson, G. A., 136
Larson, J., 62
Larson, K., 267, 268
Larson, R., 260, 261, 271, 272
Larsson, H., 171
LaRusso, M. D., 269
Larzelere, R. E., 125
Lassonde, M., 73
Latner, J. D., 167

Latz, S., 83
Lau, A. S., 274
Laube, D. W., 41
Laucht, M., 260
Lauren, A. B., 289
Laursen, B., 182
Lavadera, A. L., 202
Lavender, J. M., 239, 240, 262
Lavezzi, A. M., 84
Lavie, N., 171
Lawler, M., 237, 238
Lawn, J. E., 39, 62
Lawrason, B., 196
Lawson, R., 158
Lazelere, R. E., 199
Le, B., 308
Leach, P., 118
Leavitt, J. W., 59
Lecanuet, J. P., 86
Lecavalier, L., 158
Lee, A., 117
Lee, D. Y., 198
Lee, E. A. E., 156
Lee, G., 233
Lee, J., 233
Lee, K., 82, 86, 87, 149
Lee, M., 171
Lee, P. A., 231
Lee, S. S., 170
Lee, V. E., 194, 205
Lee, Y., 225, 227, 230, 231
Lee Thoeny, A., 171
LeFebvre, L., 308
Lefevre, J., 166
Lehman, K., 76
Lehnart, J., 231
Leibenluft, E., 258
Leichtentritt, R. D., 202
Lejuez, C. W., 201
Lemmon, H., 207
Lemola, S., 269
Lenoir, M., 166
Lenroot, R. K., 74, 266
Leon, M., 241
Lepore, F., 73
Lepp, A., 309
Leppänen, P. H. T., 207
Lepper, M. R., 213
Lerner, J. V., 262, 268

Lerner, R. M., 4, 21, 262, 263, 265, 268
Leshno, M., 54
Lessard, G., 203
Lester, B. M., 79
Lester, F., 61
Le Strat, Y., 47
Leung, A. K., 301
Leung, F., 264
Leung, M., 235
Leve, L. D., 124, 125
Leventhal, T., 116
Levine, A., 289, 296
Levine, M. P., 238
Levine, S. C., 73
Levinson, C. A., 239
Levitas, J., 182
Levitt, P., 73
Lewin-Bizan, S., 262, 265
Lewis, A. D., 269
Lewis, S. P., 262
Li, C., 239, 240
Li, H., 151
Li, J., 119, 309
Li, X., 234
Li, Y., 263
Liam, J. H., 296, 297
Liamputtong, P., 76
Liang, J., 274
Liberman, Z., 96
Libnawi, A., 150
Lichtenstein, O., 171
Lichtenstein, P., 48, 158
Lickenbrock, D. M., 123
Lidegaard, Ø., 47
Lieberman, A. F., 123
Lieberman, M. D., 269
Liebschutz, J. M., 47
Liem, G. D., 268
Liem, J. H., 291
Lieshout, R. J., 62, 63
Liew, J., 176
Lightfoot, C., 258
Lillie-Blanton, M., 116, 117
Lim, S. L., 274
Limber, S., 186
Lin, E. Y., 195
Lin, M., 264
Lin, Y., 48, 57, 308
Linares, R., 168
Lindahl, K., 304

Name Index

Lindberg, L. D., 236
Lindblad, F., 202
Lindsey, E. W., 137, 152, 157
Ling, F. W., 41
Ling, H., 234
Link, B. G., 158
Linkh, D. J., 200
Linting, M., 119
Linver, M. R., 268
Lipsett, K. E., 309
Lipton, R. B., 231
Literte, P. E., 295
Liu, C., 170
Liu, R. T., 262
Liu, Y., 149
Liverpool, M., 74
Livingstone, S., 238
Lobo, M. A., 90
Lobo, M. L., 79
Lochman, J. E., 180
Locke, J., 158
Loeber, R., 242
Lohan, M., 235, 241
Lohvansuu, K., 207
Loke, A. Y., 56
Loman, M. M., 114
Lonardo, R. A., 276
Long, J. D., 155
Longmore, C. A., 86, 87
Longmore, M. A., 244, 245, 276, 305
Lopes, L., 166
Lopes, V. P., 166
Lopez-Caneda, E., 260
López-Guimerà, G., 238
Lorber, M. F., 199
Lorenz, F. O., 305
Lorenz, K., 106, 306
Loth, K. A., 239
Loton, D., 265
Lou, J., 207
Loucas, A., 269
Lovett, S., 39
Lowe, J. R., 72
Lowenstein, A. E., 117, 118
Lozoff, B., 83
Lu, T., 110
Lubans, D. R., 165, 166
Lubold, A. M., 77
Lucas-Thompson, R. G., 82

Luciana, M., 266
Luciano, E. C., 305
Luck, S. J., 86
Lüdtke, O., 296
Luebbe, A. M., 182
Luengo Kanacri, B. P., 177, 194
Lui, P. R., 194
Lumley, M. N., 200
Luo, S., 309
Luo, X., 149, 170
Lurmann, F., 158
Luster, S. S., 290
Lux, S., 151
Luyckx, K., 294
Lyall, K., 158
Lydecker, J. A., 239
Lynam, D., 178
Lynch, A. D., 262
Lynch, R. J., 173
Lynne-Landsman, S. D., 234
Lyytinen, H., 207

M

Ma, F., 149
Ma, X., 234
Maas, A. M., 43
Maaskant, J. M., 200
Macek, P., 291
Maciejewski, D. F., 262
MacIntosh, H., 269
Mackinnon, S. P., 307
MacMillan, H. L., 200
Macoby, E. E., 155, 156, 198
MacPherson, L., 201
Madden, N. A., 215
Maddow-Zimet, I., 236
Madigan, S., 110
Madsen, S. A., 55
Madsen, S. D., 291
Maggs, J. L., 260
Magnuson, K., 116, 205
Magnusson, D., 234
Mahajan, N., 96
Mahalic, S. F., 186
Maillard, F., 56
Maisonneuve, M., 171
Malacrida, C., 61
Maldonado-Molina, M., 265, 278

Males, M., 262
Malik, N., 304
Malin, H., 272
Malmberg, L., 118
Malone, P. S., 177, 194, 269
Malti, T., 178, 182
Manassis, K., 185
Mandich, G., 167
Mandler, J. M., 96
Manfra, L., 146
Manning, W. D., 244, 245, 276, 305
Mansour, M., 268
Marais, A., 47
Maras, A., 171
Marceau, K., 47
Marchant, B. K., 171
Marcia, J. E., 292
Mare, R. D., 303
Marinković, J., 47
Markey, C. N., 306
Markey, P. M., 306
Markin, R. D., 42
Markowitsch, H. J., 151
Marks, A. K., 196
Marlier, L., 86
Marrieb, E. N., 36
Marsh, P., 264
Marshall, N. L., 155
Marshall, P., 114
Martin, A., 98
Martin, A. J., 268
Martin, C. L., 155, 156, 157
Martin, J., 264
Martin, K. A., 237, 243, 246
Martin, M. A., 76, 77
Marvin, R., 114
Marysko, M., 124
Marzola, E., 240
Massaccesi, S., 86
Masten, A. S., 126, 196, 265
Mathews, S., 214
Matthys, S., 166
Matturi, L., 84
May, P. A., 47
Mayberry, M. L., 183
Mayer, F. B., 148
Mayer, G., 83
Mayeux, L., 179

Maynard, A. E., 143
McAdams, D. P., 294
McAlister, A. R., 150
McAnally, H. M., 148
McBride, O., 246
McCabe, A., 171
McCabe, K., 274
McCabe, M. P., 237
McCall, R. B., 114
McCallum, F., 168
McCarthy, M. C., 200
McCartney, K., 118
McCarty, A. T., 268
McClarty, K. L., 175
McClintock, M. K., 242
McCloskey, L. A., 201
McClure, E. B., 258
McConnell, R., 158
McCord, J., 277
McCoyd, J. L. M., 53
McCracken, J., 158
McCreary, L., 231
McCreight, B. S., 43
McCullough, M. B., 196
McDermott, J. M., 124
McDermott, J. N., 124
McDonald, K. L., 182
McDonald, P. R., 86, 87
McDonnell, C. G., 148
McElderry, D., 235
McElhaney, K. B., 264
McElwain, N. L., 113
McFarland, C., 264
McGeown, K., 114
McGoey, K. E., 113
McGrath, J. J., 158
McGuire-Jack, K., 200
McHale, S. M., 265, 272, 273, 288
McKay, A., 246
McLaughlin, K. A., 114
McLeskey, J., 213
McNeely, C. A., 274
McNiel, M. E., 76
McPherran, C., 262
McPherson, B. J., 156
McRitchie, S., 166
Meca, A., 294
Medaris, M., 286, 288
Medland, S. E., 262

Medley, B. C., 303
Meeus, W. H. J., 272, 288
Mehler, J., 98
Mehta, N., 111
Melchior, M., 185
Meldrum, R. C., 268
Melinder, A., 148
Mellor, D., 237
Menard, J. L., 80
Mendle, J., 227, 234
Mendonça, M., 287, 289
Mengel, M. B., 48
Mernitz, S. E., 305
Merrick, J. C., 62
Merrick, M. T., 201
Merz, C. J., 171
Messer, D. J., 207
Messina, S., 112
Messler, C. F., 171
Metere, R., 207
Metz, E., 269
Metzger, A., 275
Meulen, M. V., 176
Meyer, R., 79
Mickelson, K. D., 76, 77
Miech, R. A., 260, 261
Mikk, J., 209
Mikkelsen, A. T., 55
Mikulincer, M., 311
Milioni, M., 297
Miller, D., 175
Miller, D. A., 309
Miller, P., 117
Miller, P. H., 151, 168
Miller, P. L., 118
Miller, W. D., 116, 117
Mills, K. L., 258
Millstein, S. G., 245
Milner, J. S., 200
Mingrone, R., 84
Miniño, A. M., 59
Mintz, S., 5, 6, 252
Miranda, R., 294
Mirkovic, K. R., 76
Mirpuri, S., 294
Mischel, W., 113
Mitchell, E. M., 137
Mitchell, J. E., 239, 240
Miu, A., 243
Modell, J., 252
Moehler, E., 124

Moffitt, T. E., 26, 27, 201, 265
Moilanen, K. L., 242
Molden, D. C., 175
Molina, M. F., 171
Moll, K., 207
Molloy, L. E., 264, 277
Mond, J., 239
Monk, C. S., 258
Monk, J. K., 309
Moore, A. N., 170
Moore, C., 149, 151, 176
Moore, D. S., 18, 50, 64
Moore, S. R., 234
Moore, W. E., 258
Moradi, B., 237
Moran, S., 211, 272
Moreau, C., 119
Moreno, M., 266
Morgan, E. M., 288, 303
Morgan, H. J., 311
Morgan, K., 246
Morgan, P. J., 165, 166
Morgano, E., 277
Mori, A., 151
Morris, R., 206, 207
Morrison, K. M., 62, 63
Moses, L. J., 151
Moskey, E. G., 242
Moss, E., 111
Motsa, L. F., 76
Mountain, G., 113
Mourik, R. V., 171
Muchlenkamp, J. J., 262
Mueller, C. M., 175
Muhamedrahimov, R. J., 114
Muise, A., 308
Müller, M., 201
Mulvey, K. L., 176, 186
Mumford, K. H., 99
Munch, A. L., 239, 240
Munroe, R. L., 41
Murphy, K. R., 171
Murphy, S. L., 59
Murray, A. L., 62
Murray, C. A., 209
Murray, K. T., 122
Murray, L., 83, 112, 114
Murray, S. L., 306
Murray-Close, D., 183
Murstein, B. I., 305

Musgrove, P., 77
Musich, F. M., 171
Must, A., 209, 234
Must, O., 209
Musulkin, S., 301
Muzik, M., 76
Myers, L. L., 239

N
Nader, P., 166
Nam, K. W., 62
Napolitano, C. M., 265
Narayan, K. V., 167
Nash, G., 207
National Center on Education Statistics, Fast Facts, 298, 299
National Down Syndrome Society (NDSS), 50
Natsuaki, M. N., 124
Naughton, F., 47
Naumova, E. N., 234
Nazaré, B., 54
Neberich, W., 231
Negele, A., 148
Negriff, S., 266
Neiderhiser, J. M., 124, 125, 306
Nelson, C. A., 73, 114
Nelson, E. E., 258
Nelson, K., 98, 148
Nelson, L. J., 290, 291
Nelson, M. R., 156
Nerini, A., 238
Nesdale, D., 176
Nestor, B. A., 262
Neumark-Sztainer, D., 239
Neupert, S. D., 202
Newcomb, A. F., 182
Newland, R. P., 82
Newman, D. L., 232
Newman, S., 116
Newton, C., 78
Newton, E. K., 126
Ng, C., 72, 82
Ngige, L. W., 224
NICHD Early Child Care Research Network, 118
Nichols, T. R., 231, 234, 236
Nicholson, J. M., 82, 171
Nicolas, S. C., 309
Nicolopoulou, A., 153

Nikiforova, N. V., 114
Niño, V., 76
Nisbett, R. E., 213
Nixon, E., 237, 238
Nmyanzi, L. A., 167
Noblega, M., 110
Noel, P., 301
Noftle, E. E., 296
Nolvi, S., 111
Nomaguchi, K. M., 118, 195
Nordbø, R. H. S., 239
Normand, S., 171
Norris, D. J., 119
Norris, J. E., 307
North, S. J., 233
Nosarti, C., 62
Noska, M. W., 307
Nuttall, A. K., 148

O
Oakes, L. M., 86
Obradović, J., 126
O'Brien, M., 166
O'Byrne, J., 262, 269
O'Connor, E., 274
O'Connor, T. G., 114, 116
Oddo, S., 151
Odimegwe, C., 76
Oelkers-Ax, R., 124
Oepkes, D., 54
Oesterle, S., 273
Ofner, S., 245
Ogburn, E. L., 303
Ogolsky, B. G., 309
Ohan, J. L., 203
Ohlemiller, M., 48
Oikawa, M., 49
Okado, Y., 202
Okeley, A. D., 165, 166
Oldenhinkel, A. J., 262
O'Leary, S. G., 199
Olino, T. M., 259
Olivardia, R., 241
Olivia, E. M., 260
Ollendick, T. H., 180
Olthof, T., 175, 176, 178
Olweus, D., 186
O'Malley, P. M., 259, 260, 261
Omar, H., 235
O'Muircheartaigh, J., 72, 76, 99

Oncel, S., 55
O'Neal, C. R., 125
Onnink, M., 170
Ontai, L. L., 119
Oosterlaan, J., 171
Oosterman, M., 110
Opper, S., 254
Orellana, M. F., 274
Orozco-Lapray, D., 274
Orth, U., 305
Osborn, J. L., 308
Osecka, T., 181
Oshio, T., 123
Osofsky, H. J., 196
Osofsky, J. D., 196
Ostrov, J. M., 179, 183, 263
Ott, M. A., 245
Otterman, G., 202
Ouellet-Morin, I., 201
Ovenstad, K. S., 148
Owen, M. T., 118
Owens, E. B., 170
Oxford, M. L., 184
Oyamada, N., 49
Özdemir, M., 235

P
Pabst, S. R., 266
Pack, H.-J., 156
Padilla-Walker, L. M., 286
Pagani, L. S., 180
Paik, J. H., 151
Pakes, J., 274
Palladino, G., 252
Palmer, R. H., 47
Palmov, O. I., 114
Pandia, W., 195
Panicker, A. S., 207
Panksepp, J., 122
Panter-Brick, C., 196
Paolitto, D. P., 255, 256
Paquette, D., 152
Parackal, M. K., 48
Parackal, S. M., 48
Parade, S., 82
Paradis, L., 233
Paradise, R., 144
Pardini, D. A., 266
Paredes, M. F., 72
Parent, A.-S., 225, 231

Parent, M. C., 237
Parent, S., 233
Paris, R., 199
Park, C. G., 231
Park, I. J. K., 195, 274
Park, N., 262, 269
Park, Y. S., 274
Parker, A. C., 110
Parkinson, P., 203
Parner, E. T., 158
Parrish, D. E., 49
Pascalis, O., 86, 87
Pasco Fearon, R. M., 113, 232
Pascual, M., 266
Passini, C. M., 125
Pastorelli, C., 177, 194
Patall, E. A., 213, 214
Pate, M., 198
Paternoster, R., 259
Patrick, M. E., 260
Patros, C. G., 170
Pattinson, R., 39
Paukoff, R. L., 236
Paul, A. M., 48, 49, 54
Paulssen-Hoogeboom, M. C., 116
Paulus, M., 176
Peach, H. D., 269
Peake, S. J., 258
Pearl, M., 77
Peasgood, T., 171
Peck, S. C., 260
Pedersen, L., 47
Pedersen, L. H., 158
Pedersen, N. L., 15
Peetsma, T. T. D., 116
Pelegrina, S., 168
Pelham, W. E., Jr., 171
Pellegrini, A. D., 42, 76, 152, 153, 155, 156
Peña, P., 110
Peña Alampay, L., 259
Penfold, B., 158
Peng, K., 295
Penke, L., 231
Penn, S., 176
Penney, S. J., 117
Pennings, S. M., 262
Peper, J. S., 227
Pereira, B., 166

Pérez-Edgar, K., 124
Perner, J., 149
Perren, S., 185
Perrin, E. M., 76
Perrine, C. G., 76, 167
Perry-Jenkins, M., 156
Persike, M., 271, 272
Peskin, J., 149
Peters, E., 182
Peterson, C. C., 149, 150, 151
Petraglia, F., 55
Petrill, S., 179, 185
Pettigrew, S., 48
Pettit, G. S., 305
Pfeifer, J. H., 258
Pfinder, M., 48
Phelan, P., 275
Philbin, J. M., 242
Philippaerts, R., 166
Phillips, D. A., 117, 118
Phillips, J. P., 72
Phillips, N., 150
Phillips, S. M., 234
Phinney, J. S., 295
Piaget, J., 19, 20, 91–95, 107, 138–145, 164, 213, 253–255
Picariello, S., 294
Piek, J., 166
Pielock, K. A., 196
Piercy, C. W., 308
Pierro, R. C., 119
Pihet, S., 125
Pine, D. S., 124, 258
Pinker, S., 5, 6, 17, 198, 202
Pinquart, M., 113, 119, 120, 194
Pinto, T. M., 80
Piper, B., 148
Piquero, A. R., 265, 278
Piryatinsky, I., 76
Planalp, E., 123
Plant, C. P., 200
Plant, T. M., 226
Plener, P. L., 262
Plichta, M. M., 171
Plomin, R., 16, 17
Pluess, M., 17, 49, 120, 126
Pnevmatikos, D., 169

Poirier, A. A., 264
Poirier, F. E., 134
Pokhrel, P., 276
Polanco-Roman, L., 294
Pölkki, P. L., 117, 119
Pollak, S. D., 114
Pope, L. J., 309
Porter, M., 264
Porterfield, M. L., 119
Posada, G., 110
Potenza, N. M., 201
Potts, M., 61
Poulin, F., 181, 272, 277
Pouliot-Lapointe, J., 199
Poulson, C. L., 158
Poulton, R., 26, 27
Poustka, L., 124
Power, K., 268
Power, T., 122
Poyer, H., 238
Prata, N., 61
Pratt, I. S., 48
Pratt, M. W., 307
Preston, S. H., 76
Prinstein, M. J., 262, 276
Prinz, R. J., 123
Pryor, J. H., 291, 296
Puhl, R. M., 167

Q
Queenan, P., 182
Queiroz, D. R., 166
Quinn, B., 272
Quinn, P. C., 86, 87
Quirk, K. M., 294

R
Raffaelli, M., 242
Rakic, P., 48
Ramezanzadeh, F., 55
Ramirez, A. M., 233
Ramirez, D., 238
Ramrakha, S., 27
Ramsay, S. M., 62
Ramsey, E., 158
Rance, J., 77
Rand, W. M., 234
Randler, C., 269
Randolph, G., 76
Rapaport, S., 54

Rasmussen, F., 231
Rastam, M., 171
Ratner, D., 287
Ratner, N. B., 99
Rauch, S. L., 124
Rauer, A. J., 305
Ray, B., 288
Redd, L., 213
Reese, E., 148
Reeve, J., 214
Reichenberg, A., 62, 158
Reif, J. A., 305
Reijneveld, S. A., 200
Reijntjes, A., 176
Reilly, T. S., 272
Reimer, J., 255, 256
Reimer, K., 257
Reimherr, F. W., 171
Reina, M. T., 297
Reinders, H., 182
Reindl, M., 182
Reiser, L. W., 230, 233
Reiss, D., 124, 125, 306
Reissman, C., 306
Ren, R., 234
Renteria, M. E., 262
Resch, F., 124
Reuter, M., 171
Reviere, R., 303
Rey-Casserly, C., 63
Reynolds, C. A., 306
Reynolds, P., 62
Reznick, J. S., 199
Rhee, S. H., 124
Rhodes, J., 274
Ricciardelli, L. A., 237
Richard, S. A., 77
Richards, T., 99
Richardson, L., 199
Rich-Edwards, J. W., 158
Richter, B., 304
Rifkin, L., 62
Rigoli, D., 166
Rijk, C. M., 43
Riksen-Walraven, J. M., 76, 119, 182
Rilling, J. K., 113
Rinaldi, C., 195
Rinehart, M. S., 43
Rispoli, K. M., 113

Rissel, C., 137
Risso, M. T., 177
Rivera, J. A., 77
Roache, R., 57
Roalson, L. A., 269
Robaey, P., 171
Roberts, A. L., 158
Roberts, B. W., 296
Roberts, C., 228
Robertson, D. J., 171
Robeson, W. W., 155
Robins, R. W., 296
Robinson, I. W., 309
Robinson, J. C., 213, 214
Robinson, J. L., 124
Roche, A. F., 231
Rockoff, J. E., 215
Rodgers, S., 201
Rodham, K., 238
Rodkin, P. C., 183, 184, 263
Rodrigues, C., 260
Rodriguez, C. M., 199
Roeser, R. W., 235
Roeyers, H., 158
Rogoff, B., 144
Rohlf, H., 186
Roisman, G., 264
Roisman, G. I., 113, 183
Rojas-Flores, L., 195
Rollock, D., 194
Romano, E., 180
Romeo, R. D., 263
Romer, D., 269
Rondeau-Cantin, S., 203
Rooks, A. J., 76
Roosa, M. W., 234
Rorie, M., 268, 277
Rose, A. J., 156, 179
Rose, J., 62
Rose-Jacobs, R., 47
Rosenblum, K. E., 144
Rosenblum, T., 198
Rosenfelt, A., 125
Rosenfield, R. L., 231
Rosenthal, M., 158
Roseth, C. J., 155
Rosnay, M. D., 151
Rosol, O., 158
Ross, G., 144, 148

Rössler, W., 201
Roth, J. L., 268
Roth, S. L., 21
Roussotte, F., 47
Rowe, D. C., 16
Rowe, E., 136
Rowe, M. L., 73
Royal College of Obstetricians and Gynaecologists (RCOG), 48
Royer, N., 119
Rubin, K. H., 182
Ruble, D. N., 155, 157, 173, 233
Rucker, L., 119
Ruffman, T., 151
Ruiselova, Z., 235
Rulison, K. L., 264, 277
Runions, K. C., 185
Rusbult, C. E., 306
Rushton, J. P., 209
Rutter, M., 114
Ruttle, P. L., 231, 232
Ryan, A. M., 184
Ryan, A. S., 231
Ryan, J. J., 207
Ryan, R. M., 214
Ryan-Krause, P., 171

S
Sabik, N. J., 238
Sadegh-Nobari, T., 116, 117
Sadek, S., 185
Saenz, J., 156
Saffran, J. R., 99
Sagi, A., 112
Sagot, P., 86
Saha, T., 200
Sahin-Hodoglugil, N. N., 61
Saigal, S., 62, 63
Sakamoto, A., 195
Sakyi, K., 185
Sala, M., 239
Salminen, H. K., 207
Salmivalli, C., 185
Salmon, K., 148
Salsali, M., 55
Salway, J. L., 114
Samimi, P., 309

Sampson, W., 83
Sánchez, B., 289
Sánchez-Carracedo, D., 238
Sanders, C., 86
Sandin, S., 158
Sandler, I. N., 203
Sandman, C. A., 82
Sanford, M. E., 171
Santella, R. M., 62
Santesso, D. L., 98
Santo, J. B., 172, 174
Santos, C. E., 294
Santos, R., 166
Satici, S. A., 309
Sato, K., 49
Sato, M., 49
Sattler, J. M., 206, 207
Saudino, K. J., 122
Savin-Williams, R. C., 303
Sawyer, K., 182
Saxton, T. K., 306
Scahill, L., 158
Scanlon, K. S., 76, 167
Scaramella, L. V., 125
Scarr, S., 17, 197
Schaadt, G., 207
Schaal, B., 86
Schafer, K. J., 241
Schatschneider, C., 207
Scheindlin, B., 199
Schellinger, K., 121
Schendel, D., 158
Scheres, A., 171
Schetter, C. D., 48
Schiff, M., 262, 269
Schirduan, V., 211
Schlegel, A., 224
Schlinger, H. D., 209
Schmid, G., 79
Schmid, K., 262
Schmidt, L. A., 62, 63, 98
Schmied, V., 77
Schneider, B., 171
Schneider, B. L., 295, 297
Schneider, M., 260
Schofield, T. J., 202, 203
Scholte, R. J., 185, 186, 262
Schreiber, J. B., 113, 207

Name Index

Schreier, A., 79
Schreiner, L. A., 301
Schubert, C. M., 231
Schueler, C. M., 123
Schuengel, C., 110
Schulenberg, J. E., 259, 260, 261
Schwab, A., 151
Schwartz, C. E., 124
Schwartz, S. J., 291, 294
Schwartz-Mette, R. A., 156, 179
Schweitzer, J., 239, 240
Sciberras, E., 171
Scott, R. M., 94, 95
Scratch, S. E., 62
Scrimgeour, M. B., 122
Scrimsher, S., 144
Sebastián-Enesco, C., 127
Séguin, J. R., 233
Seiffge-Krenke, I., 271, 272, 287, 289, 297
Selcuk, B., 151
Self-Brown, S. R., 214
Seligman, M. E., 174
Selman, R. L., 269
Sentse, M., 185, 186
Seok, J., 201
Serour, G. I., 55
Setoodehnia, M., 86
Settersten, R. A., 288
Seymour, F., 204
Shahaeian, A., 149
Shalev, I., 27
Shamay-Tsoory, S., 151
Shao, S., 207
Shapiro, M., 87
Sharon, T., 291
Sharts-Hopko, N. C., 34
Shaver, P. R., 309, 311
Shaw, D. S., 124, 125
Shaywitz, B. A., 206, 207
Shaywitz, S. E., 206, 207
Shearer, C. L., 273
Sheehan, A., 77
Shelton, K. H., 48
Shen, Y., 274
Sheridan, A., 83, 114
Sheridan, M. A., 114
Shi, Q., 173

Shimizu, M., 83
Shin, L. M., 124
Shirtcliff, E. A., 231
Shoaib, A., 238
Shoda, Y., 113
Shomaker, L. B., 240
Shrout, P. E., 125
Shulman, E. P., 259, 266, 267
Shulman, S., 290
Si, X., 234
Sibley, D. S., 309
Siegel, M., 158
Sieswerda-Hoogendoorn, T., 200
Sigmundsson, H., 166
Silk, T. J., 171
Silva, J. M., 287, 291, 295, 299
Silva, P. A., 26
Silventoinen, K, 231
Simić, S., 47
Simion, F., 86
Simmons, R. G., 234, 235
Simone, G., 212
Simons, D. A., 199, 200
Simons, L. G., 242, 305
Simons, R. L., 242
Sing, R. A. H., 200
Sisk, C. L., 238
Sjörs, G., 62
Skakkeback, N. E., 225, 231
Skårderud, F., 239
Skeide, M. A., 207
Skinner, B. F., 11
Skinner, C., 115
Skinner, D., 199
Skoog, T., 235
Slama, H., 171
Slater, A., 86, 87, 88
Slaughter, V., 149, 151
Slavin, R. E., 215
Slevin, T., 48
Slobin, D. I., 146
Smetana, J. G., 122, 275
Smith, A. K., 124
Smith, A. R., 258, 304
Smith, B. L., 59
Smith, E. O., 134
Smith, J., 166

Smith, J. E., 238
Smith, J. P., 76
Smith, K., 83
Smith, M. E., 146
Smith, P. K., 153
Smith, R. L., 156, 179
Smith, R. P., 41
Smith, T., 158
Smith, T. F., 47
Smith Slep, A. M., 199
Smolak, L., 237
Smolucha, F., 153
Smolucha, L., 153
Snarey, J. R., 256
Snowling, M., 170, 207
Soderberg, L., 47
Soderlund, G., 171
Södersten, P., 241
Soenens, B., 43, 214
Solmeyer, A. R., 264
Sommer, M., 233
Sonuga-Barke, E. J. S., 114, 170, 171
Sorbring, E., 177, 194
Sorondo, B. M., 86
Soussignan, R., 86
Sowell, E., 47
Sowell, E. R., 224, 226, 227, 266
Spath, F. M., 17
Spear, L. P., 260
Spencer, S. V., 182
Sperlich, B., 171
Spinath, B., 214
Spong, C. Y., 62
Spotts, E. L., 306
Sroufe, L. A., 112, 113
St. James-Roberts, I., 79, 83
Stackman, V. R., 303
Staikova, E., 171
Stallman, H. M., 203
Stams, G. J. J. M., 116
Stanton, C., 39
Stark, R., 171
Starr, J. M., 207
State, M., 158
Stattin, H., 234, 235
Stegge, H., 175, 178
Steigler, H., 238

Stein, A., 118
Stein, J. A., 237
Stein, J. H., 230, 233
Steinacker, J. M., 166
Steinberg, L. D., 118, 231, 258, 259, 266, 267, 272
Steinmayr, R., 214
Stephens, H. F., 173
Steppelbein, L., 182
Sternberg, R. J., 205, 209, 210
Stetsenko, A., 145
Stevens, B., 86
Stevens, N., 182
Stevenson, D. K., 62
Stewart, A., 199
Sticca, F., 185
Stiles, J., 39, 72, 73
Stipek, D. J., 213
Stöckel, T., 166
Stockman, M., 74
Stodden, D. F., 166
Stoltenborgh, M., 200
Stone, F. P., 200
Stormshak, E. A., 258
Stout, M., 269
Strang, N., 258
Stremler, R., 82
Striegel-Moore, R. H., 239
Strohl, J., 299
Strohmeier, D., 185
Styne, D., 225, 227, 230, 231
Suárez-Orozco, C., 274
Subrahmanyam, K., 241
Sudmalis, D., 268
Sugden, K., 27
Sugimura, K., 294
Suh, S. H., 201
Sulaiman, Z., 76
Sulik, M. J., 176
Sun, J., 265
Sun, S. S., 231
Suomi, S. J., 156
Super, C. M., 173
Surkan, P. J., 185
Surra, C. A., 307, 309
Suryani, A., 195
Susman, E. J., 231, 266
Sussman, S., 276

Sutherland, O., 262
Sutton, S., 47
Sutton, T. E., 305
Svaldi, J., 240
Svedin, C.-G., 200
Svensson, B., 200
Swann, W. B., 175
Swiezy, N., 158
Syed, M., 297
Sylva, K., 118
Syracuse-Siewert, G., 305

T
Tadmor, C. T., 295
Tagler, M. J., 311
Tagliabue, S., 287
Talmi, A., 121
Tanaka, M., 200
Tanner, J. L., 6, 286
Tanner, J. M., 225, 227, 229, 230
Tanofsky-Kraff, M., 240
Tapert, S. F., 266
Tarabulsy, G. M., 111
Tartter, V., 171
Tavecchio, L. W. C., 119
Taveras, E. M., 167
Tavernier, R., 270
Taylor, B. A., 158
Taylor, C. A., 199
Taylor, E., 171
Taylor, J., 207
Teasdale, J. D., 174
Tebbe, E. A., 304
Tebeka, S., 47
Teilmann, G., 225, 231
Tein, J., 234
Telzer, E. H., 87, 196, 269, 274
Teoh, A. N., 49
Teoh, E. R., 268
Teskereci, G., 55
Teti, D. M., 83
Tetlock, P. E., 295
te Wierike, S. C. M., 166
Thai, J. L., 304
Thaler, L., 238
Thapar, A., 170
Thayer, R., 266
Thiessen, E. D., 99

Thomaes, S., 175, 178
Thomas, A., 111, 125
Thomas, J. R., 136
Thomas, T. E., 148
Thomasello, M., 127
Thompson, D. K., 62
Thompson, L., 179, 185
Thompson, R. A., 126
Thompson, S., 266
Thompson, S. D., 119
Thompson-Brenner, H., 241
Thorell, L. B., 113
Thorne, A., 288
Thorpe, H., 113
Thorpe, K., 297
Thurston, E. C., 269
Tian, L., 262, 269
Tiggemann, M., 240
Timko, C. A., 238
Tipsord, J. M., 178, 181
Todd, J. T., 86
Toga, A. W., 266
Togliatti, M. M., 202
Tolan, P., 268
Tomasello, M., 126, 134
Tomb, D. A., 171
Tomlinson, M., 112
Tompkins, V., 151
Tong, V. T., 47
Tongeren, D. V., 294
Tønnessen, F. E., 207
Tontsch, C., 171
Toomey, R. B., 294
Top 10 Best Dating Sites, 303
Toppari, J., 225, 231
Tottenham, N., 87
Tourigny, M., 199
Townsend, D. B., 158
Trainor, L. J., 98
Trainor, M. E., 266
Tran, S., 291, 296
Trautwein, U., 296
Tremblay, R. E., 233
Trentowska, M., 240
Triandis, H. C., 8
Trikkaliotis, I., 169
Trollinger, L. J., 224
Troop-Gordon, W., 156, 263

Trumbell, J., 110
Trzesniewski, K. H., 296
Tsai, Y., 57
Tsiaras, A., 36
Tucha, O., 176
Tudge, J., 144
Tull, M. T., 262
Turcotte, P., 203
Turkheimer, E., 16, 209
Turkington, C., 55
Turner, H. A., 196
Turner, M. C., 259
Tuschen-Caffier, B., 240
Twenge, J. M., 296
Tylka, T. L., 240
Tynelius, P., 231
Tynes, B., 241

U
Uchiyama, K. P., 212
Udry, J. R., 156, 242
Uji, M., 195
Ulione, M., 48
Umaña-Taylor, A. J., 294
Umemura, T., 112
UNFPA, 246
UNICEF, 76, 78
United Nations Children's Fund, 278
Updegraff, K. A., 294
Urban, J. B., 265, 268
Uribe Tirado, L. M., 259
Ursache, A., 117
U.S. Department of Labor Statistics, 117
Utsey, S. O., 294
Utzinger, L. M., 239, 240
Uysal, R., 309

V
Vaeyens, R., 166
Vaillancourt, T., 200
Vaish, A., 126, 127
Vaismoradi, M., 55
Valentino, K., 148
Valois, R. F., 269
van Aalderen, W. M., 200
van Aken, C., 178
van Aken, M. A. G., 178, 297

van Bakel, H. A., 43
Van Bauwel, S., 245
van Beurden, E., 166
Van Damme, E., 246
van de Beek, C., 48
Vandell, D. L., 118
van den Akker, E. S., 54
van den Akker, M., 54
Vandendriessche, J., 166
van Der Fels, I. M. J., 166
Vandergrift, N., 118
van der Lee, M., 287
Vanderloo, L. M., 167
van der Wal, M. F., 200
VanderWeele, T. J., 303
Vandewalle, G., 73
Vandorpe, B., 166
van Duurling, L. L., 200
van Eijsden, M., 48
van Geel, M., 274
van Goozen, S. M., 48
Vanhaesebrouck, P., 158
Van Hulst, A., 76
Vanickova, J., 291
van IJzendoorn, M. H., 110, 112, 113, 118, 119, 120, 126, 200
van Lawick, J., 202
van Rijn, R. R., 200
Van Ryzin, M. J., 114, 155
Vansteenkiste, M., 43, 214
Varga, S. M., 265
Varnado-Sullivan, P., 238, 240
Vassar, R., 62
Vaughn, L. M., 76
Vecchione, M., 297
Vedder, P., 274
Veer, E., 308
Velasquez, M. M., 49
Velkoff, E. A., 304
Vennum, A., 309
Verhaeghe, L., 158
Verhage, M. L., 110
Verhoeven, M., 178
Verloove-Vanhorick, S. P., 200
Vermande, M., 176
Vermeer, H. J., 118, 120
Verweij, E., 54

Name Index

Verweij, K. J., 262
Vestergaard, M., 158
Vézina, J., 203
Vialle, W., 277
Vianna, E., 145
Victor, S. E., 262
Vida, M., 260
Vijver, F., 195
Vijver, F. J. R., 78
Vilela, A. M., 156
Virmani, E. A., 119
Visconti, K. J., 177, 263
Visscher, C., 166
Visser, M., 202
Vitaro, F., 233
Vohs, K. D., 175
Volk, H. E., 158
Volkmar, F., 158
Vollmer, C., 269
Volpe, L. E., 84
Volpin, N., 202
von der Lippe, A., 113
von Eye, A., 265
Von Raffler-Engel, W., 34
von Sternberg, K., 49
Vornanen, R. H., 117, 119
Voss, P., 73
Votruba-Drzal, E., 116, 117, 118, 205
Vouloumanos, A., 98
Vreeswijk, C. M., 43
Vrijkotte, T. M., 48
Vygotsky, L., 144–146, 153, 154

W

Waasdorp, T. E., 185
Wadsworth, B. J., 19
Wagner, J., 296
Wagner, R. K., 207
Wagner, T., 269
Wahoush, O., 76
Wakschlag, L., 47
Waldron, M., 209
Waldron, N. L., 213
Walk, R. D., 87
Walker, D., 268
Walker, L., 72, 99
Walker, S., 82, 243
Wall, M. M., 239
Wall, S., 108, 110
Wallace, G. L., 74, 158
Walls, J., 286
Walsh, J. L., 243
Walshe, M., 62
Walton, K. E., 297
Walum, H., 306
Walvoord, E. C., 231
Wang, J. H., 263
Wang, J. J., 149
Wang, L., 172
Wang, M., 122
Wang, Q., 148
Wang, S., 170
Wang, Y., 274, 294
Wang, Z., 151, 179, 185
Wängqvist, M., 287
Warber, K. M., 308
Ward, L. M., 238
Ward, M., 266
Warren, C. S., 241
Warren, M. P., 232, 233
Warreyn, P., 158
Waskiewicz, N., 72, 76, 99
Waterman, A. S., 294
Waters, E., 108, 110
Waters, L. E., 265
Watson, J. B., 10, 106
Weaver, J. M., 202, 203
Wedding, D., 48
Weddle, C., 74
Weerth, C. D., 182
Weinstein, R. S., 120
Weisfeld, G., 224
Weisgram, E. S., 157
Weismer, S. E., 158
Weiss, P. H., 151
Weiss, S., 82
Weisskirch, R. S., 309
Weisskopf, M. G., 158
Wellman, H. M., 149
Wells, K., 180
Welte, J. W., 260
Welzer, H., 151
Wen, L. M., 137
Wendel, M. L., 307
Wender, P. H., 171
Werker, J. F., 98
Werner, N. E., 186
Werner-Lin, A., 53
Werth, B., 36
Wertz, D. C., 59
Wertz, R. W., 59
West, R. L., 233
Weston, J., 82
Whalley, L. J., 207
Wheeler, L. A., 203
Whillier, A., 166
Whitby, E. H., 53
White, B. A., 180
White, J., 211
White, R. B., 234
Whitebrook, M., 120
Whitehead, V., 150
Whiteman, S. D., 288
Wickrama, K. S., 305
Widaman, K. F., 296
Wiebe, S. A., 47
Wiebel, A., 124
Wiik, K. L., 114
Wijers, A. A., 176
Wilfley, D. E., 240
Willan, A., 82
Williams, B. S., 27
Williams, K. E., 82
Williams, K. R., 185
Williams, W. M., 211
Willoughby, B., 286, 287, 288, 291
Willoughby, M., 76
Willoughby, M. T., 117
Willoughby, T., 270
Wills, M. C., 158
Wilson, D., 268, 277
Wilson, P., 166
Wilson, S. M., 224
Wilson, T., 184, 263
Wiman, A. M., 239
Wimmer, H., 149
Winsler, A., 145, 146
Witherington, D., 90
Witherington, D. C., 238
Wolbransky, M., 262, 264
Wolf, A. W., 83
Wolf, S. A., 212
Wolfe, D. A., 200
Wolfson, C., 150
Wolke, D., 79
Woltering, S., 173
Wonderlich, S. A., 239, 240
Wong, J. J., 234
Wong, K. K., 151
Wood, D., 144
Woodard, J., 113
Wood-Barcalow, N. L., 240
Woodbury, R. D., 311
Woodbury-Smith, M., 158
Wooding, C., 152
Woody, D., 148
World Health Organization (WHO), 61, 80
Wray-Lake, L., 272
Wright, C. I., 124
Wright, M. O., 196
Wu, C., 274
Wu, X., 113
Wurtele, S. K., 199, 200
Wyman, C., 116
Wymbs, B. T., 171
Wynn, K., 96

X

Xia, Y. R., 303
Xie, W., 276
Xing, W., 170
Xu, F., 149
Xu, H., 137
Xu, J., 48

Y

Yamaguchi, M. K., 87
Yan, C., 48
Yancey, G. A., 303
Yancey, S. W., 303
Yang, C. K., 83
Yang, F., 172
Yang, P., 62
Yang, Y., 170
Yaros, A., 180
Yates, M., 269
Yeh, M., 274
Yen, C., 62
Yerys, B. E., 158
Ying, L., 56
Yip, T., 294
Yoerger, M., 158
Yonkers, K., 47
Yoon, J. E., 113

You, J., 264
Young, B. N., 122
Young, J. F., 240
Young, J. T., 268
Young, S., 171
Young, W. J., 290
Youniss, J., 269
Yu, H. C., 275
Yuen, C., 196, 274
Yun, I., 167

Z

Zachor, D. A., 158
Zaff, J., 268
Zaichkowsky, L. D., 136
Zakharia, R., 235
Zamboanga, B., 294
Zarahn, E., 258
Zayas, V., 113
Zeanah, C. H., 109, 110, 114
Zelenko, M., 81
Zentall, S. R., 123
Zerbe, K., 241
Zeskind, P. S., 79
Zettergren, P., 184
Zhang, J., 48, 234
Zhong, R., 207
Zhou, J., 207
Zhou, Z. G., 303
Zijlmans, M. A., 80
Zimmer-Gembeck, M. J., 176, 242
Zimmerman, M., 304, 309
Zimmerman, P., 297
Zimmermann, M., 171
Zou, L., 207
Zuberi, D., 116
Zubriggen, E. L., 288
Zuffianó, A., 178
Zukerman, G., 158

Subject Index

A

abstract conceptualization, 143
academics
  achievement and authoritative parents, 195
  reproducing images to enhance abilities, 136
accommodation, 138
acculturation, 196, 274
achievement tests, 205, 207–210
  analytic intelligence, 210
  decoding meaning of, 207–209
  g, 209
  measuring genetic gifts, 208–209
  reliability, 207
  valid, 207–208
  WISC (Wechsler Intelligence Scale for Children), 205–207
acting out issues, 113
actions, predicting, 10
active forces, 17
ADHD. *See* Activity Attention-deficit/ hyperactivity disorder
adolescence, 6, 7t, 164, 252
  See also teens
  adult gender pattern, 262
  adult prisons, 267–268
  authoritative discipline, 264
  autonomy, 272–274
  body image issues, 237–241
  career goals, 295–296
  cognitive and emotional development, 253–258
  concepts and hypothetical possibilities, 254
  depression, 262–263
  emotional plane, 260–264
  groups, 268, 274–278
  high schools, 268–269
  laws user-friendly to, 268
  making world fit teen mind, 266–269
  nonsuicidal self-injury, 262

parent–child conflict, 272–274
parents and stress, 271
physical developments, 223–246
punishing as adults, 267
rehabilitation, 267
risk takers, 258–260
sampling all of life, 270
school-to-prison pipeline, 269
self-esteem, 237
separating from parents, 271–274
sexuality, 241–247
sleep requirements, 269
social development, 271–278
socially sensitive, 258
stereotypes, 253t
storm and stress, 258–265
thinking like scientists, 254
upbeat, 262
zero-tolerance policies, 269
adolescence-limited turmoil, 265
adolescence stage, 18t, 121t, 164t, 292t
adolescent egocentrism, 257–258
adoption studies, 15
adrenal androgens, 226
adulthood, 6
adults
  attachment styles, 310
  brain, 74
  securely attached, 311
  shaping children's lives, 197
affluent nations
  declining births, 6–7
  developed-world, 8
Afghanistan, 44
  prohibitions during pregnancy, 44
Africa, 8
  attachment security, 112f
African Americans
  age of menarche among, 225

body image concerns among, 238
and puberty timetables, 231
spanking among, 199
age
  of beginning sexual desire, 242
  of first intercourse, 242–244, 243f
  of puberty, decline in, 225, 225f
age groups, comparing, 25–26
age norms, 290
age of viability, 39–40
age-linked theories, 18–20
age-related disease, low birthweight and, 62
aggression, 178
  direct aggression, 179t
  excessive, 180–181
  frustration-aggression hypothesis, 179
  highly aggressive children, 180
  hostile attribution bias, 180
  middle childhood, 178
  proactive aggression, 178–179, 179t
  reactive aggression, 178–179, 179t
  relational aggression, 179, 179t
AIDS, 46
Ainsworth, Mary, 107, 309
alcohol, 47–48
  stereotypes, facts and teens, 260t
Alzheimer's disease, 50
American Academy of Pediatrics, 84, 199
American College of Nurse Midwives, 60
amniocentesis, 54
amniotic sac, 40
amygdala, 87
anal stage, 13
analytic intelligence, 210
androgens, 242
anencephaly, 46

animism, 141, 143
anorexia nervosa, 238–239
A-not-B error, 93–94
anthropologists, 4
antibiotics, 46
antidepressants, 46–47
anti-psychotic drugs, 46
anti-seizure drugs, 46
anxiety
  in early-maturing girls, 234
  separation, 108
  social, 184, 187
  stranger, 108
anxious-ambivalent attachment, 109
anxious-ambivalent babies, 309
Apgar scale, 62
Arnett, Jeffrey, 285
artificialism, 141
Asia, 8
assimilation, 19, 138, 141
assisted reproductive technology (ART), 56–57
athletic skills, 173–174
at-risk teens, 264–265
  antisocial peer group, 277
attachment, 105–115, 107
  anxious-ambivalent attachment, 109
  avoidant infants, 109
  babies mirroring mother's, 109
  basic life bond, 106–115
  caregiver, 109, 111, 112, 119
  children, 111
  clear-cut (focused) attachment, 107
  critical period for, 107
  dance, 110–111

383

Subject Index

attachment (continued)
  developmentalists and, 106–107
  disorganized attachment, 109
  dose–response effect, 114
  geese, 106
  genetics, 107
  infants, 106
  insecurely attached, 109, 109t
  later relationships and mental health, 113
  milestones, 107–108
  monkeys, 106–107
  preattachment phase, 107
  primary attachment figure, 107
  proximity-seeking behavior, 107
  reactive attachment disorder, 114
  relations and poverty, 21–22
  securely attached, 109, 109t
  separation anxiety, 107
  social referencing, 107
  social smile, 107
  stability and change genetics, 113–114
  stranger anxiety, 107
  Strange Situation, 107–108
  styles, 107–108
  toddlers, 112
  transforming status of, 113
  universality of, 112–113
  working model, 107
attachment in the making, 107
attachment response, 14
attachment theory, 14, 20–21, 20t
  love, 309–311
attention-deficit/hyperactivity disorder (ADHD), 170–172, 182
Australia
  affluence, 8
  alcohol during pregnancy, 48
authoritarian parents, 193
authoritative discipline, 264
authoritative parents, 193–194

autism spectrum disorders (ASDs), 158–159
autobiographical memories, 148–149
autonomy, 18, 121–122
  adolescents, 272–274
average children, 183
average intelligence, 17
avoidant/dismissive insecure attachment, 310f
avoidant infants, 109, 309
axons, 72

B
babbling, 98
babies, 8
  See also infants, newborns
  anxious-ambivalent, 109
  attachment, 109
  avoidant, 109
  body size, 88
  caregivers, 98
  child care, 117–118
  cognition, 90–96
  crying, 79–80
  cuddling, 80
  difficult babies, 111
  easy babies, 111
  emerging language, 98–99
  face perception, 86–87
  hitting, 199
  human speech, 98
  insecure attachment, 109, 113
  intentions, 95–96
  kangaroo care, 80
  massaging, 80
  mother, 106–107
  motor milestones, 89–90
  naturally developing gifts, 6
  orphanages, 106
  pointing, 99
  preattachment phase, 107
  quieting, 80
  REM sleep, 81
  secondary circular reactions, 91–92
  securely attached, 309
  self-soothing, 81, 82–83
  separation anxiety, 107
  sleeping, 80–83

  slow to warm up, 111
  social smile, 107
  stranger anxiety, 107
  sudden infant death syndrome (SIDS), 83–84
  temperament, 111
baby boom, 7, 7t
baby-proofing environment, 90
babysitters, 118
baby sleeping-basket, 84
Back to Sleep campaign, 84
bad crowds, 277–278
Baillargeon, Renée, 94
Bambi (movie), 154
Bandura, Albert, 12, 238
  moral disengagement, 177
  self-efficacy, 12
  social learning theory/framework, 12, 238
barren, 55
basic newborn states
  crying, 79–80, 84–85
  eating, 75–79, 84
  newborn reflexes, 75–76
  sleeping, 80–83, 85
  two-year-old food cautions, 75–76
basic trust, 18, 82
The Battle Hymn of The Tiger Mother (Chua), 194
Baumrind, Diana, 193, 194, 199
Beacon Elementary School, 212
behavior
  conscience, 122
  different causes for, 20–22
  inborn biological forces, 14
  nature explaining, 14
  nature *versus* nurture theory, 10–12
  problems with toddlers, 121
  reinforcing, 11
  variable reinforcement schedules, 11
behavioral conduct, 173–174
behavioral genetics, 14–16, 20
behavioral genetics theory, 20t
behaviorism, 10–12, 21
behaviorists, 106

bidirectional, 17
bidirectional education, 144
bidirectional relationships, 111
bigger means more, 140
bilingual preschoolers, 150–151
Binet, Alfred, 19
binge eating disorder, 239
biracial or multiracial emerging adults, 295
birth
  birth defects, 44–54
  Bradley method, 59, 60t
  certified midwives, 59, 60t
  cesarean section (C-section), 60–61
  crowning, 58
  doula, 59, 60
  electronic fetal monitor, 60t
  epidural, 60t
  episiotomy, 60t
  family leave, 43
  id, 13
  labor, 58
  Lamaze technique, 59, 60t
  limiting, 6–7
  medical interventions, 60t
  natural childbirth, 59–60
  natural childbirth providers, 60t
  placenta, 58
  social event, 59
  threats at, 59
  waiting for, 42
birth defects, 44–54
blastocyst, 37, 41
blended families, 192
blood tests, 53
body, expanding size of, 88
body image
  adolescence, 237–241
  boys, 237–238
  eating disorders, 238–241
  girls, 237–238
  improving, 240–241
  thin ideal, 237
body mass index (BMI), 166
  obesity, 231
Botswana
  holding newborns to reduce stress, 80

Subject Index

Bowlby, John, 14, 82, 107, 114
boys
    attachment problems, 114
    autism spectrum disorders (ASDs), 158
    body hair, 229
    body image issues, 237–238
    brains, 74
    dominance, 155
    early-maturing, 233–234
    estrogen, 226
    excitedly running around, 155
    gender barriers, 155
    gender-segregated play, 154–158
    gender-stereotyped play, 156
    gross motor skills, 136
    groups, 155
    growth spurt, 229–230
    hormone levels, 156
    packs, 155
    prosocial behavior, 176–177
    puberty, 229–230
    roped-off gender world, 155
    rough-and-tumble play, 152
    strength, 229
    testes, 229
    testosterone, 226
    voice deepening, 229
    warrior, superhero, 155
Bradley, Robert, 60
brain
    adults, 74
    amygdala, 87
    axons, 72
    boys, 74
    cerebral cortex, 72, 166
    cortex, 72
    dendrites, 72
    development, 39–40, 45
    environmental stimulation and, 73
    facts about, 74t
    frontal lobes, 72, 166
    gender differences, 266
    girls, 74
    growth outside womb, 72
    language development, 74
    left hemisphere, 73
    maturing, 72
    medial frontal cortex, 151
    middle childhood, 166
    myelination, 72
    myelin sheath, 166, 266
    neural pruning, 72–74
    neurotransmitters, 266
    plastic, 73–74
    synapses, 72
    synaptogenesis, 72
    teens, 266–270
    teratogens, 45
    variability in, 74
    visual cortex, 72–73, 73
brain scans, 53, 73
breast-feeding, 76–77
breasts, 232–233
breech birth, 59
Bronfenbrenner, Urie, 20–22
    ecological, developmental systems theory, 21, 197–198
Bronfenbrenner's ecological model, 21f
bulimia nervosa, 239
bullying, 185
    aggressive boys and girls, 185
    appreciative audience, 186
    attacking, 186–187
    attention-deficit/hyperactivity disorder (ADHD), 171
    best friends, 182
    bully-victims, 185
    cyberbullying, 185–186
    early-maturing girls, 234
    eliminating, 11
    middle-aged reflections on, 186f
    recreation, 185
    revenge, 185
    social rewards, 185
    status, 187
    stress, 182
bully-victims, 185

C

Canada
    affluence, 8
    child abuse in, 200
    preschool caregivers, 119
careers
    emerging adulthood, 295–302
    goals, 295–296
    without college degree, 298–299
    women, 7
caregivers
    attachment, 105, 109
    outdoor activities, 166
    power-assertion, 180
    power of, 14
    reminiscing with young children, 148, 149
    separation anxiety, 98, 108
caregiver-to-baby bonding, 111t
centering, 140
cephalocaudal sequence, 38, 39, 88–89, 135
cerebral cortex, 72, 166
cerebral palsy (CP), 63
certified midwives, 59, 60
cervix, 34
cesarean section (C-section), 60–61
Chetty, Raz, 215
child abuse, 200–202
Child and Adult Care Food Program (CACFP), 79t
child care, 117–120
child development, 4
    changes, 25–26
    child care, 118
    contexts, 4
    environmental influences, 20–22
    individual children, 26
    poverty, 115–117
    society shaping, 21
    socioeconomic status (SES), 105
    tracking into adulthood, 26
child maltreatment, 200–202
childbed fever, 59
childhood
    See also early childhood, middle childhood
    brain development during, 151
    cognitive development during, 138–147
    concrete operational stage during, 19t, 91t, 138–140, 138t
    context for, 134–135
    evolution of, 5–6
    growth, 88–89
    health, 6
    home, 193–204
    information-processing perspective on, 168–172, 170t
    mortality rates, 5
    motor abilities during, 136–137, 136t
    obesity during. *See* childhood obesity
    older children's classic problems during, 11
    physical development during, 135–137, 136t
    preoperational stage during, 19t, 91t, 138–140, 138t
    school, 205–217
    social cognition during, 134
    zone of proximal development during, 144–145, 144f
childhood obesity, 166–167, 167t
child-rearing
    permissive, 6
    practices, 4
    toddlers, 125
children
    abandoning, 5
    acculturation, 196
    actively selecting environment, 17
    attachment, 14, 105, 111
    authoritative parents, 194
    causes for actions, 21
    center of the universe, 141–142
    child abuse, 200–201
    communities and, 216
    contexts, 5–9

Subject Index

children (*continued*)
  co-residing adults and, 290t
  erogenous zones, 13
  friendless, 185
  genetic tendencies, 16–17
  inborn talents and temperament, 16–17
  incorrect responses, 19
  intellectual skills, 95
  low-income, 8
  modeling, 12
  moral children, 177
  nature, 14
  object permanence, 94
  play societies, 156
  poverty, 22
  resilient, 196
  shaping lives of, 6
  shunting, 78
  sleep problems, 81–82
  socially anxious, 184
  sports-oriented, 166
  testing, 26–27
  theory of mind, 149
  undernutrition, 78
  working, 5–6
child-shapes-parenting relationship, 16
China
  adopting from orphanages in, 114
  attachment security, 112f
  cesarean sections (C-sections), 60–61
  child-centered parenting and, 194
  prohibitions during pregnancy, 44
  socializing obedience, 149
Chomsky, Noam, 97
chorionic villus sampling (CVS), 54
chromosomes, 36
  abnormal number of, 49–50
  genes, 36
Churchill, Winston, 196, 210
Chutes and Ladders (game), 144, 145, 146
circular reactions, 91–93, 92t
class inclusion, 140
classroom learning, 212–216

clear-cut (focused) attachment, 107
cliques, 274–275
cocaine, 46
cognition
  babies, 90–96
  gender-stereotyped play, 157–158
  sensorimotor stage, 91–92
  tracking early thinking, 93
cognitive behaviorism, 12, 20
cognitive behaviorism theory, 20t
cognitive development
  accommodation, 138
  adolescence, 253–258
  animism, 141
  artificialism, 141
  assimilation, 138, 141
  bigger means more, 140
  centering, 140
  classic theories, 253–255
  concrete operational stage, 138, 142
  conservation tasks, 138–139
  decenter, 140
  early childhood, 138–142
  egocentrism, 142, 257–258
  formal operational stage, 253–255
  identity constancy, 140
  immediate appearances, 140
  information-processing perspective, 168–169
  middle childhood, 167–172
  moral judgment, 255–257
  peculiar perceptions about people, 140–142
  preoperational stage, 138–142
  reversibility, 139
  strange ideas about substances, 138–140
cognitive developmental theory, 19–20
cohabitation, 287
cohort, 5
colic, 79
collaborative pretend play, 153
collective efficacy, 197

collectivist cultures, 8
collectivist worldview, 151
college, 7t, 301–302
  academic aptitude, 299
  career without degree, 298–299
  connecting classes to potential careers, 301
  human connections, 301–302
communities
  collective efficacy, 197
  mattering in children's success, 216
  promoting upward mobility, 216
competition and popularity, 182
concrete operational thinking, 138
concrete operations stage, 19, 19t, 91t, 142, 164t, 253
conscience, 122
conscientiousness, 297
conservation tasks, 138–139
contagious diseases, 59
contexts
  demographic shifts, 6–8
  evolution of childhood, 5–6
  shaping lives of children, 5–9
contexts of development, 4
  for adolescence, 252–253, 253t
  for attachment, 106–107
  cohort and, 5–8
  culture and ethnicity and, 8–9
  gender and, 9, 9t
  for home, 192, 192f, 193, 193t
  for puberty, 224–226, 225f
  for school, 205–206, 205f
  socioeconomic status and, 8
contractions, 58
control intervention, 24
conventional thought, 256, 256t
cooing, 98
corporal punishment, 198–200
correlation study, 23–24
Corsaro, William, 154

cortex, 72–73
  pruning, 87
  voluntary processes replacing newborn reflexes, 75
cortisol, 4, 48, 116
co-sleeping, 83–84
Cosmo, 243
cotinine, 47
couvade, 41
crawling, 90
creative intelligence, 210
cross-sectional study, 25–26
crowds, 275
  bad crowds, 277–278
  deviants, 276–277
  fitting interest of teens, 275–276
  intellectuals, 276
  popular kids, 276
  purpose of, 275–276
  residual types, 276
  straddling different groups, 276
  teenage gangs, 278
crowning, 58
crying, 79–80, 84–85
  basic trust, 82
  self-soothing, 81–83
cultural norms and alcohol, 48
culture
  adolescent–parent relationships and, 272–274
  attitudes toward obesity and, 165–167, 167t
  child maltreatment and, 198–202
  collectivist cultures, 8
  co-sleeping in infancy and, 83–85, 84t
  emerging adulthood, 286–288
  impact of, 8–9
  individualistic cultures, 8
  menstruation and, 233
  parent–child conflict, 274
  parenting styles varying depending on, 194–195
  puberty and, 224–225
  resilient children and, 196
  theory of mind variations, 151

cultures
  prohibitions during pregnancy, 44
cyberbullying, 185–186
cystic fibrosis (CF), 51, 52t
cytomegalovirus, 46

D
Darwin, Charles, 4
day care, 117, 118–120
day-care centers, 118, 120t
decenter, 140
Deci, Edward, 214
delinquency, socialization into, 277
demographic, 6
  shifts, 6–8
dendrites, 72
depression
  adolescents, 262–263
  best friends and, 182
  early-maturing girls, 234–235
depth perception, 87
developed-world nations
  socioeconomic status, 8
developing-world nations
  socioeconomic status (SES), 8, 77–79
developmental disorders, 45
developmentalists, 3
  aggression, 178
  attachment, 106–107
  classifying toddlers, 125–126
  deviancy training, 277
  extrinsic motivation, 213
  false-belief task, 149
  family stress and early puberty, 231
  history and, 4
  insecure attachments, 109
  intrinsic motivation, 213
  nature and nurture, 16–17
  parents, 197–198
  shame versus guilt, 177
  social-interactionist perspective, 97
  socialization, 122
  spontaneous sharing, 176
  sympathy, 176
  tracing language to its roots, 98

developmental science, 4
developmental scientists, 3
deviancy training, 277
deviants, 276–277
Diagnostic and Statistical Manual (DSM-5), 158, 239
  and autism spectrum disorders, 158
  and eating disorders, 239
dialectic behavior therapy, 240
diethylstilbestrol (DES), 45, 47
difficult babies, 111, 125
diphtheria, 6
disorganized attachment, 109
divorce, 202–204
  parents advice relating to, 204t
DNA (deoxyribonucleic acid), 36
dominant disorders, 50–51, 52t
dose–response effect, 114
double-insecure children, 112
doubt and toddlers, 121
Douglass, Richard, 77
doula, 59, 60
down syndrome, 50
dramatic play, 152
drugs, impact of, 47–48
Druids, 141
DSM-5. See *Diagnostic and Statistical Manual*
Dumbo (movie), 154
Dunedin study, 26–27
Dweek, Carol, 175
dysentery, 6
dyslexia, 206–207
  adult success, 297
  facts about, 207t
  overcoming, 208

E
eager students, 213–216
earlier transition to intercourse, 242–243
early childhood, 13–14, 133, 164
  cognitive development, 138–142
  constructing personal past, 148–149
  ego, 13

emotional development, 148–152
  exploration age, 134
  fine motor skills, 136
  gender-segregated play, 155
  gross motor skills, 136
  initiative, 134
  language, 145–147
  lying, 149
  mind reading talents, 134
  motor talents, 136
  outdoor play, 137
  past-talk conversations, 148
  physical development, 135–137
  physical skills threats, 136
  play, 152–154
  social development, 152–158
  stress, 154
  undernutrition, 137
early-childhood poverty, 116–118
  day care, 117–118
  high school success, 205
  intellectual and social boost, 117
early childhood stage, 18t, 121t, 164t, 292t
Early Head Start, 117
early-maturing boys and girls, 233–235
early puberty, 231–232
East Asian birth rates, 7
easy babies, 111
eating, 75–79, 84t
  breast-feeding, 76–77
  food insecurity, 78–79
  malnutrition, 77–79
  newborn reflexes, 75–76
  two-year-old food cautions, 75–76
eating disorders
  anorexia nervosa, 238–239
  binge eating disorder, 239
  bulimia nervosa, 239
  dialectic behavior therapy, 240
  distorted body image, 239
  emotions, 239–240
  hereditary component, 239
ecological, developmental systems approach, 21

economists, 4, 22
education
  bidirectional, 144
  college, 7t
  demographic shifts, 6
  importance of, 6
  poverty, 116
  socioeconomic status (SES), 8
Efé and attachment, 112
efface, 58
ego, 13
egocentrism, 142, 143
elasticity, 97
elementary school children
  physical proficiency, 165–166
  popularity, 182–183
  self-esteem, 173, 276
  theory-of-mind capacities and, 168
  WISC (Wechsler Intelligence Scale for Children), 205–206
  working memory, 168
Elkind, David, 257–258
embryo, 38–39
embryonic stage, 37–38, 45, 54t
emerging adulthood, 6, 7t, 164, 285
  career, 295–302
  cohabitation, 287
  college, 296–297, 301–302
  constructing identity, 291–295
  culture, 286–288
  exploration, 286
  extended dating phase, 304–305
  flow, 297–298
  heart, 286t
  history, 286–288
  income inequalities, 288
  life expectancy, 286–287
  love, 302–312
  lungs, 286t
  marriage, 288
  Mediterranean model, 287
  negative images of, 289
  nest-leaving, 287, 288–290
  partner choices, 302–303

emerging adulthood (continued)
- re-centering lives, 286
- Scandinavian plan, 287
- school-to-work transition, 300
- self-esteem, 296–297
- skeleton, 286t
- smoothing school path, 299–300
- social clock, 290–291
- United States, 287–288
- unstructured, unpredictable path, 286
- without college degree, 298–299

emerging adulthood stage, 18t, 121t, 164t, 292t
emotional abuse, 200
emotional development
- adolescence, 253–258
- aggression, 178–181
- autobiographical memories, 148–149
- constructing personal past, 148–149
- early childhood, 148–152
- emotional regulation, 172
- externalizing tendencies, 172
- identity, 148
- internalizing tendencies, 172
- making sense of other people's minds, 149–152
- middle childhood, 172–181
- morality, 175–178
- prosocial behavior, 175–178
- self-awareness, 172–173
- self-esteem, 173–175
- theory of mind, 149–152

emotional regulation, 172
emotions
- eating disorders, 239–240
- managing and decoding, 95–96

empathy, 176
endometrium, 34
England
- good luck charms during pregnancy, 34

environment
- assimilation and, 19
- Bronfenbrenner's ecological model and, 20–22, 21f
- effect on development, 197
- epigenetics and, 17–18
- high-quality, 17
- intelligence quotient (IQ), 208–209
- lifetime effects, 17–18
- nurture, 10, 12
- parenting styles related to, 197–198
- person–environment fit, 16–18
- societal pressures, 9
- upbringing and, 16

environmental toxins, 46
epidural, 60
epigenetics, 18
- attention-deficit/ hyperactivity disorder and, 170
- child maltreatment and, 201
- childhood obesity and, 167t
- play and, 156

episiotomy, 60
Epstein, Robert, 270
equal-reinforcement-value partner, 305
Erikson, Erik, 18–19, 82, 121
- identity, 291–292
- preschoolers, 154
- psychosocial stages of childhood, adolescence, and emerging adulthood, 18t, 82t, 121t, 164t, 292t
- shame versus guilt, 177

Erikson's psychosocial stages, 18, 18t, 82t, 121t, 164t, 292t
- in adolescence, 18, 18t, 292t
- in early childhood, 18t, 82t
- in infancy, 18, 18t
- in middle childhood, 164t
- in toddlerhood, 121t

Erikson's theory, 20, 20t
erogenous zones, 13
estrogen, 226

ethnic identity, 294–295
ethnicity
- impact of, 8–9
- intercourse and, 242

ethnologists, 106
European nations
- childcare, 117
- fertility rates, 7

evocative forces, 16–17
evolutionary psychologists, 14
evolutionary psychology, 21, 231
evolutionary theory, 20, 20t
executive functions, 168, 297
- attention-deficit/ hyperactivity disorder (ADHD), 170
- highly aggressive children, 180
- predicting adolescent problems, 264

exercise play, 152
existential (spiritual) intelligence, 211
experience-sampling technique, 260–263, 295
exploration age, 134
extended dating phase, 304–305
externalizing tendencies, 172
extinction, 11
extrinsic learning, 214–216
extrinsic motivation, 213
exuberant toddlers, 123–125, 123t

F

Facebook, 8
- cyberbullying, 185
- romance, 307–309

face perception, 86–87
fainting, 41
fallopian tubes, 34–35
false-belief task, 149, 151–152
families
- alternate forms of, 7
- blended families, 192
- child abuse, 200–202
- co-sleeping, 83–84
- decline of traditional, 7t
- divorce, 202–204

- home, 193–204
- inconsistent rules, 194
- size of, 6–7
- traditional nuclear family, 192

family day care, 118
family leave, 43
family stress and early puberty, 231–232
family–work conflict, 43
fantasy play, 152–154, 155
fathers
- custody, 203, 203f
- and divorce, 202
- parenting styles, 193
- and pregnancy, 43–44
- and puberty, 232–233, 236

fear bias, 87, 107
feelings and goals, 95
females
- conception and birth of, 36
- early-maturing, 233–234
- infertility in, 55
- menstruation and, 225, 233
- physical changes of puberty in, 227–228, 230f
- reproductive system of, 34–35, 35f

fertility, decline in, 7t
fertility drugs, 56
fertility rates, 7
fertilization, 35–37
fetal alcohol syndrome (FAS), 47–48
fetal programming research, 49
fetal stage, 39–40, 54t
fetus
- age of viability, 39–40
- hearing, 86
- impaired growth, 49
- tobacco-exposed, 47

Finding Nemo (movie), 154
fine motor skills, 136
Finland
- caregivers, 119
- childcare, 117

first trimester, 41–42, 55t
- chorionic villus sampling (CVS), 54

flow, 297–298

Flynn, James, 208
Flynn effect, 208–209
focused attachment. *See* clear-cut (focused) attachment
food
　maternal reinforcement stimulus, 106
　two-year-old food cautions, 75–76
food insecurity, 78–79, 116
Food Stamp program, 79
formal operational stage, 19, 19t, 91t, 164t, 253–255
foster autonomy, 215t
foster relatedness, 215t
foster relevance, 215t
Franklin, Benjamin, 5
fraternal (dizygotic) twins, 15
Freud, Sigmund, 13, 49, 75, 148, 295
friendless during childhood, 185
friendships
　conflicts, 182
　developing self, 182
　emotions, 182
　loyalty, 182
　middle childhood, 181–182
　preschoolers, 181–182
　relational aggression, 182
　shared morals, 182
　theory of mind, 151
frontal lobes, 72
　middle childhood, 166
　self-control, 168
　theory of mind and, 151
frustration-aggression hypothesis, 179

G
g, 209
games
　attention-deficit/ hyperactivity disorder (ADHD), 171
　false-belief task, 151–152
gametes, 36
gangs, 278
Gardner, Howard, 211
Gates Foundation, 299

gays, 303–304
　See also lesbian
　gay parenting, 192
　sexuality in adolescence, 242
　stereotypes and scientific facts, 304t
gender
　boys, 9t
　color in toy preferences, 157
　girls, 9t
　impact of, 9
　roles, 7, 9
　understanding label, 157
gender differences
　in adolescent–parent relationships, 272–273
　in aggression, 178–180, 179t, 183, 183t
　in ASDs, 158
　in body image concerns, 237–238
　in depression, 262–263
　in eating disorders, 238–239
　in play, 154–158
　in prosocial behavior, 176–177
　in puberty timetable, 230–232, 230t
　sexual double standard and, 244–245
　in sports-related activities, 136
gender-schema theory, 157–158
gender-segregated play, 154–158
gender-stereotyped play, 156–158
genes, 27, 36
genetic counselor, 53
genetic disorders, 50–52
genetic tendencies, 16–17
genetic testing, 51–52
genetics
　attachment, 107, 113–114
　attention-deficit/ hyperactivity disorder (ADHD), 170
　autism spectrum disorders (ASDs), 158

fertilization, 36–37
　puberty, 231
　social skills, 24
Germany and refugees, 193t
germinal stage, 37, 54f
gestation, 41
Ghana, eliminating Kwashiorkor, 77
Gibson, Elinor, 87
gifted, 206–207
Gilligan, Carol, 257
girls
　attachment problems, 114
　autism spectrum disorders (ASDs), 158
　body image issues, 237–238
　brains, 74
　breasts, 227
　collaboration, 155
　estrogen, 226
　fine motor skills, 136
　gender-segregated play, 154–158
　groups, 155
　growth spurt, 227
　internal changes, 227, 229
　maturing early, 233–235
　menarche, 227
　mothers, 238
　nurturing themes, 155–156
　obesity and early puberty, 231–232
　opposite sex and, 155
　permission to act like boys, 157
　playing collaboratively, 155
　predicting early puberty, 232t
　prosocial behavior, 176–177
　puberty, 227, 229
　pubic hair, 227
　rate of change variability, 227
　relational aggression, 183
　strength, 229
　testosterone, 226
　thin ideal, 237–238
　girl-to-girl fantasy play, 155
gonads, 226

goodness of fit, 126
grammar, 97
Great Depression, 6
gross motor skills, 136
groups
　adolescents, 274–278
　cliques, 274–275
　crowds, 275–278
　differences, 26
growth, 88–89
growth spurt, 227
Guatemala
　good luck charms during pregnancy, 34
guilt, 177–178

H
habituation, 86
Hall, G. Stanley, 4, 6, 252
Hansel and Gretel (movie), 154
happiness, 237, 296, 306
Harlow, Harry, 106
Harris, Julie, 197
Harter, Susan, 25–26, 172–173, 214, 237
Harter's five domains, 174t
Hazan, Cindy, 309
Head Start, 117
health
　childhood, 6
　middle childhood, 165–166
hearing, 86
hemophilia, 51, 52, 52t
Hepburn, Audrey, 237
Hereditary Disease Foundation, 53
heredity, impact of, 15
heritability, 15. *See also* genetics
herpes, 46
Hidden Figures (movie), 175
highly aggressive children, 180
high school, 6
　adolescent–environment fit, 268–269
　formal operational stage, 255
　mandating attendance, 6
　self-esteem, 276

Hispanic/Latino Americans
  body image concerns among, 238
  puberty timetable of, 231
HIV/AIDS, teratogenic effects of, 46t
Holland
  difficult behaviors rates, 122f
  miscarriages during World War II, 49
  preschool caregivers, 119
holophrase, 98
Holt, Aimee, 208
home, 193–204
Home Alone (movie), 143
homogamy, 306, 307
homophobia, 303–304
hormones, 41
  adrenal androgens, 226
  cortisol, 48
  estrogen, 226
  hormonal sequence triggering puberty, 227f
  puberty, 226–230
  testosterone, 226
hostile attribution bias, 180, 277
HPG axis, 226
human chorionic gonadotropin (HCG), 41
humans
  genetic contribution to differences, 14–16
  growth, 4
  managing and decoding people's emotions, 95–96
  mind reading talents, 134
  tabula rasa, 6
Hunger Winter, 49
Huntington's disease (HD), 51, 52t, 53f
hypothalamus, 226

I

id, 13
identical (monozygotic) twins, 15
identity, 18, 291–292
  carrying through life, 148
  emerging adulthood, 291–295
  role confusion, 292
identity achievement, 293, 294f
identity constancy, 140
identity diffusion, 292, 293f
identity foreclosure, 292, 293f
identity moratorium, 293f
identity statuses, 292
  adulthood, 294
  biracial or multiracial emerging adults, 295
  ethnic identity, 294–295
  identity achievement, 293
  identity diffusion, 292
  identity foreclosure, 292
  moratorium, 292–293
  ruminative moratorium, 294
imaginary audience, 258
immediate appearances, 140
immigrant(s)
  See also specific immigrant groups
  acculturation and, 196
  adolescent–parent relationships among, 274
  collective efficacy issues and, 196–197
  parenting styles of, 194–195
immigration, 193t
implantation, 37
impotent, 55
inadequate nutrition, 78
income and socioeconomic status (SES), 8
income inequalities, 7, 288
independent variable, 24
India, pregnancy ritual, 34f
individualist cultures, 8–9
individualistic worldview, 151
Indonesia
  prohibitions during pregnancy, 44
induction, 177
Industrial Revolution, 6
industry, 18, 134, 173
infancy, 69–100
  See also newborns
  attachment during, 105, 106–115. *See also* attachment
  attachment styles, 108–110. *See also* attachment
  basic trust in, 18, 18t
  birth and. *See* birth
  brain development during, 72–74, 74t
  categorization during, 96t
  child care and, 117–118, 118f
  cognitive development during, 90–97, 96t
  context for, 72–74
  and co-sleeping, 83
  crying during, 79–80, 84t
  Early Head Start during, 117
  eating during, 75–76, 84t
  growth during, 88
  infant mortality, 63–64
  language development during, 73, 97–100, 98t, 99f
  malnutrition during, 77–79, 78f, 79t
  memory during, 96t
  motor development during, 88f, 89–90
  sensorimotor stage during, 91t, 91–93, 92t
  sleeping during, 80f, 80–82, 81f
  social development during, 113, 117, 122–123, 124
  and sudden infant death syndrome (SIDS), 84
  synchrony in attachment, 110
  temperament during, 111, 123, 124–125, 125t
  understanding of numbers during, 96t
  vision during, 85–87
infancy stage, 18t, 121t, 164t, 292t
infant-directed speech (IDS), 98–99, 144
infant–mother relationship, 109
infant–parent bond, 79–80
infants, 8
  See also newborns
  acting out issues, 113
  anxious-ambivalent, 309
  attachment, 109
  avoidant, 309
  body size, 88
  caregivers, 98
  child care, 117–118
  cognition, 90–96
  crying, 79–80, 84t–85t
  cuddling, 80
  difficult babies, 111
  Early Head Start, 117
  easy babies, 111
  eating, 84t
  emerging language, 98–99
  face perception, 86–87
  forming categories, 96t
  hitting, 199
  human speech, 98
  insecure attachment, 109, 113
  intentions, 95–96
  kangaroo care, 80
  language, 98t
  malnutrition, 77–79
  massaging, 80
  memory, 96t
  mobility, 89
  mother, 106–107
  motor milestones, 89–90
  naturally developing gifts, 6
  nineteenth century, 6
  orphanages, 106
  physical reality, 94–95
  pointing, 99
  preattachment phase, 107
  quieting, 80
  REM sleep, 81
  secondary circular reactions, 91–92
  securely attached, 309
  self-soothing, 81, 82–83
  separation anxiety, 107
  sleeping, 80–83, 85t
  slow to warm up, 111
  social cognition, 95–96
  social smile, 107

stranger anxiety, 107
sudden infant death syndrome (SIDS), 83–84
temperament, 111
understanding numbers, 96t
infectious diseases, 46
inferiority, 173
infertility, 55–56
information-processing perspective, 167
  executive functions, 168
  inhibition, 169
  intellectual growth, 168–169
  memory, 168
  rehearsal, 168
  selective attention, 168–169
  teachers' and parents' guidelines, 170t
inhibition, 169–170
initiative, 18, 134
inner speech, 146
insecurely attached, 109, 113, 114
Instagram, 8
  cyberbullying, 185
institutionalized syndrome, 114
intellectual growth, 168–169
intellectually disabled, 206
intellectual potential, 209
intellectuals, 276
intelligence, 17, 210–211
  analytic, 210
  creative, 210
  g, 209
  heritability of, 208–209
  and IQ tests, 205
  multiple intelligences theory (Gardner), 211
  practical, 210
  successful intelligence (Sternberg), 210
intelligence quotient (IQ), 205
  defining, 205–206
  dyslexia, 206–207
  environment, 208–209
  Flynn effect, 208–209
  gifted, 206–207

intellectually disabled, 206
  predicting real-world performance, 209
  specific learning disorder, 206
intercourse
  changing friendship to romance, 244
  earlier transition to, 242
  one-night stands, 244
  sexual double standard, 244–245
  teens, 244–245
internalizing tendencies, 172
interpersonal intelligence, 211
intimacy, 302
intrapersonal intelligence, 211
intrinsic motivation, 213–214, 298
in vitro fertilization (IVF), 56–57
Iran
  socializing obedience, 149
Israel
  foreign-born residents, 193
Italy
  cohabitation, 287
  relationships, 288

J
James, William, 86, 87
Japan
  affluence, 8
  attachment security, 112f
  collectivist culture of, 9
  good luck charms during pregnancy, 34
  preschoolers with mental health problems, 49
Johnson, Lyndon, 117

K
Kagan, Jerome, 124
kangaroo care, 80
Kaplan, Janet, 186
kindergartners and disruptive behavior, 76
kinesthetic intelligence, 211
King, Stephen, 141
Kohlberg, Lawrence, 255–257
Kwashiorkor, 77

L
labor, 58
Lady Chatterley's Lover (Lawrence), 243
Lamaze, Ferdinand, 60
Lamaze technique, 59, 60
language, 97–99
  babbling, 98
  developing speech, 146–147
  development, 73–74
  early childhood, 145–147
  elasticity, 97
  grammar, 97
  holophrase, 98
  important words, 98
  infant directed speech (IDS), 98–99
  infants, 98t
  inner speech, 146
  language acquisition device (LAD), 97
  mean length of utterance (MLU), 146
  morphemes, 146
  neurological roots of, 99
  overextensions, 147
  overregularization, 146–147
  passion to learn, 97
  phonemes, 146
  pointing, 99
  semantics, 146
  social-interactionist perspective, 97
  syntax, 146
  telegraphic speech, 98
  tracking emerging, 98–99
  underextensions, 147
language acquisition device (LAD), 97
latency, 13
Lawrence, D.H., 243
lead, 46
learned helplessness, 174
learned responses, 11
learning
  context-specific, 197
  extrinsic, 214
  pacing interventions to child's capacity, 144
  scaffolding, 144–145

  zone of proximal development (ZPD), 144–147
left hemisphere, 73
Lerner, Richard, 268
lesbian, gay, transgender, bisexual, queer (LGBTQ)
  See also gays
  emerging adults, 304
  gay parenting, 192
  same-sex romance, 303–304
  stereotypes, 303t
libido, 13
life conditions, 4
life-course difficulties, 265
life expectancy, 6
  lengthening, 7t
life experiences, 16–17
life stress accompanied by social isolation, 200
The Lion King (movie), 154
little-scientist phase, 92
Locke, John, 6
longitudinal studies, 26–27
Lorenz, Konrad, 106
love
  attachment theory, 309–311
  charting in stages, 307
  emerging adulthood, 302–312
  extended dating phase, 304–305
  Facebook romance, 307–309
  focus on, 14
  partner choices, 302–303
  role phase, 305
  scientific answers about online love, 309t
  similarity, 305–307
  stimulus phase, 305
  structured relationship stages, 305–307
  value-comparison stage, 305
low birth weight (LBW), 62
low-income children
  commonality of, 115–116
  problems, 8
  upward mobility, 22
loyalty and friendships, 182

Subject Index

Luxembourg's foreign-born residents, 193t
lying in early childhood, 149

M

magic and toddlers, 95
males
  conception and birth of, 36
  first ejaculation, 233
  infertility in, 55
  intellectual growth, 168–169
  memory, 168
  physical changes of puberty in, 229–230, 230f
  reproductive system of, 35, 35f
malnutrition, 77–79
  global, 77–79
  during infancy, 77–78
  during pregnancy, 46t, 49
  U.S. government-sponsored programs to combat, 79
maltreated children, 201
marriage
  emerging adulthood, 288
  gender roles, 7
  partner choices, 302–303
  puberty, 6
  traditional, 7–8
Masai of Africa, 225
massaging babies, 80
mass-to-specific sequence, 38, 39, 89, 136
maternal reinforcement stimulus, 106
Mather, Cotton, 59
mean length of utterance (MLU), 146
Mean Monkey, 149
means-end behavior, 93
medial frontal cortex, 151
medical interventions, 60
medications, 46–48
memory
  infants, 96t
  making sense of, 168
  rehearsal, 168
  sensory store, 168
  toddlers, 96
  working memory, 168

men
  infertility, 55
  salary raise, 43
  sex-linked disorders, 51
menarche, 225, 227
menstruation, 233
mental health
  attachment, 113
  corporal punishment, 199
mercury, 46
methamphetamine, 46
Methodist Church, 199
Mexico
  new immigrants and spanking, 194
micronutrient deficiencies, 78
middle childhood, 134, 163, 164
  academic motivation, 263
  aggression, 178
  attention-deficit/hyperactivity disorder (ADHD), 170–172
  brain, 166
  cognitive development, 167–172
  emotional development, 172–181
  friendships, 181–182
  health, 165–166
  industry, 134
  information-processing perspective, 168–169, 170t
  motor skills, 165–166
  obesity, 166, 167
  physical development, 165–166
  physical proficiency, 165–166
  play, 166
  popularity, 263
  prosocial behavior, 176
  social development, 181–187
middle childhood stage, 18t, 121t, 164t, 292t
middle-class toddlers, 118
mind
  making sense of other people's, 149–152
  teens, 266–270

mind reading talents, 134
miscarriage, 42–43
modeling, 12
moral code, 255–257
moral disengagement, 177
moral reasoning
  Kohlberg's three levels of, 256t
morality, 175–178
moratorium, 292–293
morning sickness, 41–42
morphemes, 146
mother–child bond, 64
mothers
  attachment to babies, 106, 111
  autobiographical memories, 148
  breast-feeding, 76–77
  dysfunctional early lives, 109
  paid maternity leave, 76–77
  stress during pregnancy, 238
  work demands, 76–77
motivation
  extrinsic, 213–214
  infant social cognition and, 96
  intrinsic, 213–214
motor milestones, 89–90
motor skills
  early childhood, 136
  middle childhood, 165–166
  preschool physical skills, 137
  undernutrition, 137
multiple intelligences theory, 211
Murphy, Susie, 212
Murstein, Bernard, 305–306
musical intelligence, 211
myelination, 72
myelin sheath, 166, 266

N

nannies, 118
National Institute of Child Health and Development (NICHD) Study of Early Child Care, 118
natural childbirth, 59–60

naturalistic intelligence, 211
naturalistic observation, 23, 24t
nature, 10
  affecting upbringing, 16
  explaining behavior, 14
  focus on, 14
  learning language, 97
  combines with nurture, 16–18
nature versus nurture theory, 10–12, 20t
Navajo Kinaalda ceremony, 225
neglect, 200
neonatal intensive care unit, 62
Nepal, 137
nest-leaving, 287
  making people more adult, 289–290
  parent–child relationships, 288–289
Netherlands
  alcohol during pregnancy, 48
neural pruning, 72–74
neural tube, 38
neurons, 38
neuroscience. See brain
neurotransmitters, 266
New Zealand
  affluence, 8
  alcohol during pregnancy, 48
  minimizing SIDS risk, 84
newborns
  See also infancy, infants
  born too small and too soon, 62–63
  breast-feeding, 76–77
  cooing, 98
  disabilities, 63
  habituation, 86
  hearing, 86t
  low birth weight (LBW), 62
  malnutrition, 77–79
  primary circular reactions, 91
  rooting reflex, 75

smell, 86t
stepping, 75
sucking reflex, 75
taste, 86t
testing, 61–62
very low birth weight (VLBW), 62
vision, 85–88
nicotine, 47
nondisjunction, 50
nonsuicidal self-injury, 262
nurture, 10
See also environment, nature versus nurture theory
focus on, 14
learning language, 97
nature and, 16–18
nutrition, 78

O

Obama, Barack, 295
obesity, 49
body mass index (BMI), 231
early-maturing girls, 234
early puberty, 231–232
middle childhood, 166, 167
teens, 24
object permanence, 93–94
observer reports, 24t
obstetrics, 59
Oedipus complex, 13
off time, 290
Olweus Bully Prevention Program, 186
online love
facts about, 309t
on time, 290
operant conditioning, 11, 75
oral stage, 13, 75
orphanages
babies, 106
caregivers, 114
outdoor play, 137
ova, 34, 35–36
ovaries, 34, 226
overextensions, 147
overregularization, 146–147
ovulation, 35
oxytocin, 113–114

P

paid maternity leave, 76–77
parental alienation, 202
parent–child conflict, 272–274
parent–child relationships, 23–24
crawling, 90
nest-leaving, 288–289
parenting styles
authoritarian parents, 193
authoritative parents, 193
divorce, 203
identifying priorities, 195
permissive parents, 193
rejecting-neglecting parents, 193
varying depending on culture, 194–195
parents
See also fathers, mothers, and parenting
abandoning children, 5
adolescents and stress, 271
adolescents separating from, 271–274
advice relating to divorce, 204t
authoritarian, 193
authoritative, 193
best possible environment, 198
co-residing adults and, 290t
goodness of fit, 126
importance of, 196–198
lessons for, 197–198
misreading baby's signals, 109
not mattering, 197–198
permissive, 193
personality problems and child abuse, 200
physically punishing children, 5
power assertion, 198
priorities, 195
rejecting-neglecting, 193
spanking, 198–200
superior, 198
teens alienated from, 264
temperamentally friendly childrearing, 125–126
thinking about, 195
tips about teens, 267t
traditional roles, 7
partner choices, 302–304
past-talk conversations, 148
PCBs, 46
peculiar perceptions about people, 140–142
peer likeability, 173–174
peers
adolescent risk-taking, 259
earlier transition to intercourse, 243
effect of socialization, 156–157
preferences and social goals, 184t
socializing children to become adults, 197
swaying teens, 277
perceptions, 175
permissive childrearing, 6
permissive parents, 193
person–environment fit, 17, 82
personal fable, 258
personal past, 148–149
personality, 172–174
See also temperament
aggression and, 178–181, 179t
resilient, 196
self-awareness and, 172
self-esteem and, 173–175
phallic stage, 13
phonemes, 146
physical abuse, 200
physical appearance, 173–174
physical development
adolescents, 223–246
early childhood, 135–137
frontal lobes, 166
health, 165–166
middle childhood, 165–166
motor skills, 165–166
obesity, 165–166
puberty, 224–236
physical reality, 94–95

Piaget, Jean, 19, 21
adolescents, 253
animism, 143
babies' actions, 94
centering, 140
children are center of the universe, 141–142
conservation tasks, 138–139
critiquing, 94–95
early thinking, 93
egocentrism, 142
evaluating, 143
how children think, 167
object permanence, 93–94
overstating egocentrism, 143
perspectives on life and learning, 145
preoperational stage, 138–142
sensorimotor stage, 91–92
stages, 91, 164, 253
transition from preoperations, 142
young children and immediate perceptions, 164
Piaget's theory, 20, 20t
pituitary gland, 226
placenta, 37, 40
expulsion of, 58
human chorionic gonadotropin (HCG), 41
plastic, 73–74
play
boundaries and rules in, 154
collaborative pretend play, 153
early childhood, 152–154
exercise play, 152
fantasy play, 152–154
gender-segregated play, 154–158
gender-stereotyped play, 156–157
middle childhood, 166
pretending, 152–154
rough-and-tumble play, 152
social norms, 154
popular children, 183

popularity
  average children, 183
  competition, 182
  decoding, 183–184
  popular children, 183
  rejected children, 183–185
  relational aggression, 183
popular kids, 276
population birth rates, 6–7
postconventional thought, 256, 256t, 257
poverty
  achievement tests, 208–209
  artificially depressing test scores, 209
  attachment relations, 21–22
  brain-stimulating activities, 116
  child care, 117–120
  child development, 115–117
  divorce, 202
  education, 116
  before entering kindergarten, 116
  food insecure, 116
  high school graduation and, 116
  insulation from negative effects of, 22
  intellectual and social boost, 117
  physiology and, 116
  single mothers, 116
  young children, 7
power assertion, 124–125, 180, 198, 231
practical intelligence, 210, 211
preattachment phase, 107
preconventional thought, 256, 256t
preferential-looking paradigm, 85–86
pregnancy
  alcohol, 48
  celebrating milestones, 34
  cultural prohibitions, 44
  emotional connections, 42
  fainting, 41
  fathers, 43–44
  gestation, 41
  hormones, 41
  intercourse, 36
  medicines and drugs, 47–48
  miscarriage, 42
  morning sickness, 41–42
  quickening, 42
  relationship issues, 43
  smoking, 47–48
  stress, 48–49
  sub-Saharan Africa, 8
  terminating, 54
  trimesters, 41, 54t
  waiting for birth, 42
  work worries, 43
prejudice, 87
premature babies, 61–64
prenatal development
  age of viability, 39–40
  amniotic sac, 40
  blastocyst, 37
  brain, 39–40
  cephalocaudal sequence, 38, 39
  embryonic stage, 37–38, 54t
  fetal stage, 39–40, 54t
  germinal stage, 37, 54t
  mass-to-specific sequence, 38, **39**
  neural tube, 38
  neurons, 38
  placenta, 37, 40
  principles, 38–39
  proximodistal sequence, 38
  umbilical cord, 40
  zygote, 37
prenatal tests, 53–55
preoccupied/ambivalent insecure attachment, 310t
preoperational stage, 19, 91t, 164t, 253
  cognitive development, 138–142
preoperational thinking, 138
preoperations stage, 19t
preschoolers
  bilingual and theory of mind, 150–151
  fantasy play, 154
  friendships, 181–182
  frontal lobe, 74
  gender-segregated play, 155
  perspective-taking, 151
  physical abilities, 136
  sleeping, 81
  spanking, 199
  sports-related abilities, 136
  synapses, 74
preschools, 117
pretending, 152–154
primary attachment figure, 107
primary circular reactions, 91, 92t
primary school, 6
primary sexual characteristics, 226
proactive aggression, 178–179
progesterone, 41
prosocial behavior, 176–178, 178t
proximity-seeking behavior, 107
proximodistal sequence, 38, 89
psychoanalysis, 13
psychoanalytic theory, 13, 20, 20t
psychologists, 4
psychosocial stages of childhood, adolescence, and emerging adulthood, 82
psychosocial tasks, 18–19
puberty, 223
  boys, 229–230
  breasts, 232–233
  declining age of, 225–226
  differences in timetables for, 230–231
  education about, 236
  first ejaculation, 233
  genetics, 231
  girls, 227, 229
  gonads, 226
  growth spurt, 227
  hormones, 226–230
  HPG axis, 226
  intercourse, 242
  marriage, 6
  menarche, 225
  menstruation, 233
  minimizing distress, 235–236
  neurotransmitters, 266
  obesity and early puberty, 231
  parent–child conflict, 272–274
  parent's lessons, 235–236
  physical changes, 226–230
  primary sexual characteristics, 226
  progression, 228t
  puberty rites, 224–225
  school, 236
  secondary sexual characteristics, 227
  sequence of major events in, 230f
  society's lessons, 236
  spermarche, 225
puberty rites, 224–225

Q

qualitative research, 27
quantitative research, 27
quickening, 42

R

race. See culture(s), ethnicity, *and specific groups*
radiation, 46
rambunctious toddlers, 124–125
reaching, 90
reactive aggression, 178–179, 184
reactive attachment disorder, 114
reading, dyslexia and, 206–208, 207t
realistic perceptions about self, 175
recessive disorders, 50–51, 52t
recreational drugs, 46–47
reflexes, 75
rehearsal, 168
reinforcement, 11
rejected children
  exploring fate of, 185
  externalizing and internalizing problems, 183
  helping, 186–187

Subject Index

not fitting in with dominant group, 184–185
popularity, 183–185
reactive aggression, 184
rejecting-neglecting parents, 193
relational aggression, 179, 202
relationship churning, 305
relationships
  attachment predicting, 113
  bidirectional, 17, 111
  child-shapes-parenting relationship, 16
  evaluating one's own, 311–312, 311t
  friendships and, 151, 155, 181–182
  issues during pregnancy, 43
  popularity and, 182–184, 183f, 184t
  positive and negative turning points, 307t
  same-sex, 303–304
  teens and family, 265, 272–273, 273f
  theory of mind and, 151–152
reliability, 207
REM sleep, 81
repeating interesting acts, 91–93
representative sample, 23
repression, 148
reproductive systems, 34
research, 27
  critiquing, 27
  information-processing, 95
research methods
  control intervention, 24
  correlation study, 23, 24
  cross-sectional study, 25–26
  independent variable, 24
  longitudinal studies, 26–27
  measuring variables, 23
  naturalistic observation, 23
  qualitative research, 27
  quantitative research, 27
  randomly assigning people to different groups, 24
  representative sample, 23
  self-report strategy, 23

testing children periodically, 26–27
true experiment, 24
resilient children, 196
reversibility, 139, 142
Roe v. Wade, 54
role confusion, 292
role phase, 305
Roosevelt, Eleanor, 185
Roosevelt, Franklin, 6
rooting reflex, 75
rough-and-tumble play, 152
Rousseau, Jean Jacques, 6
Rubella (German measles), 45, 46
ruminative moratorium, 294
Russia, 114
Ryan, Richard, 214

S

same-sex romance, 303–304
scaffolding, 144–145
  actively instructing, 144
  effective scaffolders, 145
  pretending, 152
  societal ideas, 148
Scandinavia
  adolescent sex, 235
schemas, 19–20
scholastic competence, 173–174
school
  achievement tests, 205–212
  children starting several years behind others, 205
  classroom learning, 212–216
  eager students, 213–216
  early-maturing girls, 235
  extrinsic learning, 214–216
  extrinsic reinforcers, 214
  intelligence quotient (IQ), 205
  intrinsic motivation, 213–214
  puberty, 236
  successful, 212–213
school-to-prison pipeline, 269
school-to-work transition, 300
second trimester, 42, 54, 55t

secondary circular reactions, 91–92, 93
secondary sexual characteristics, 227
secular trend in puberty, 225–226
secure attachment, 113
securely attached, 109
securely attached adults, 310f, 311
securely attached babies, 309
selective attention, 168–169
self-awareness, 158–159, 172–173
self-conscious emotions, 121–122
self-efficacy, 12, 175
self-esteem, 173
  accurate perceptions, 175
  adolescence, 237
  athletic skills, 173–174
  behavioral conduct, 173–174
  distortions, 173–174, 174t
  elementary school, 276
  emerging adulthood, 296–297
  externalizing tendencies, 173
  high school, 276
  internalizing tendencies, 174, 174t
  peer likeability, 173–174
  physical appearance, 173–174
  realistic perceptions about self, 175
  scholastic competence, 173–174
  self-efficacy, 175
self-report strategy, 23
self-reports, 24t
self-soothing, 81, 82–83
self-understanding, 13–14
semantics, 146
sensitive period, 45
sensorimotor stage, 19, 19t, 91–93, 91t, 164t, 253
sensory and motor development

expanding body size, 88
motor milestones, 89–90
sight in newborns, 85–88
separation anxiety, 107
separation/reunion scenarios, 154
Seventeen (magazine), 243
sex-linked disorders, 50–51, 52t
sexual abuse, 200
sexual desire, 242–243
sexual double standard, 244–245
sexuality
  adolescence, 241–247
  contemporary trends, 245–246
  sexual desire, 242
  teenager-friendly sex education, 246
sexually-transmitted diseases, 55
shame, 121, 177
Shaver, Phillip, 309
Shaw, George Bernard, 306
shyness
  social rejection and, 184, 185
  in toddlerhood, 123–124
sickle cell anemia, 51, 52t
sight in newborns. *See* vision
single-gene disorders, 50–51
single mothers and poverty, 116
single parents' attachment to babies, 111
Skinner, B. F., 11, 97
skin-to-skin contact, 80
sleeping
  bedtime routines, 83
  co-sleeping, 83–84
  difficulties at age 5, 83
  noise and, 80
  patterns shifting, 81
  person–environment fit, 82
  preschoolers, 81
  problems with, 81–82
  REM sleep, 81
  through the night, 82
Sleeping Beauty (movie), 154

Slovakia
  adolescent sex, 235
  culture and pubertal timing predicting problem behavior, 235f
slow-to-warm-up babies, 111
smell and newborns, 86
smoking, 47
social class and breast-feeding, 76
social clock, 290–291
social cognition, 95–96
  attachment and, 107–108
  autism spectrum disorders and, 158–159, 159f
  autobiographical memories and, 148–149, 151t
  brain development and, 134, 138
  in childhood, 148–149
  in infancy, 95–96, 107–108
  play and, 152–156
  theory of mind and, 151–152
social cognitive skills, 134
social development
  adolescents, 271–278
  bullying, 185–187
  early childhood, 152–158
  friendships, 181–182
  middle childhood, 181–187
  popularity, 182–185
social goals and peer preferences, 184t
social impairments and repetitive behavior, 158
social-interactionist perspective, 97
social isolation, 200
social learning theory, 12, 20, 20t
social networking sites, 8
social norms, 154
social problems and corporal punishment, 198
social referencing, 107
social skills, 23–24
social smile, 107

socialization, 122–123
  into delinquency, 277
  gender-stereotyped play, 156–157
  inhibition, 169
  moral children, 177
  secure attachment and, 125
socially anxious children, 184
society
  shaping child development, 21
  social-clock guidelines, 290
socioeconomic status (SES), 8
  children's development, 105
  education, 8
  income, 8
  intercourse, 242
South African puberty ritual, 225f
South America
  collectivist cultures, 8
spanking, 198–200
spatial intelligence, 211
Spearman, Charles, 209
Special Supplemental Nutrition Program for Women, Infants, and Children (WIC), 79t
specific learning disorder, 206
speech
  babbling, 98
  infant-directed (IDS), 98
  inner, 146
  grammar, 97
  language acquisition device (LAD), 97
  telegraphic, 98
sperm, 36
spermarche, 225
spina bifida, 46
sports-oriented children, 166
stages of moral judgment, 255–257
state of disequilibrium, 20
Steinberg, Laurence, 266, 267
stepparents, advice relating to divorce, 204t
stepping reflex, 75
Sternberg, Robert, 210, 212
stimulus phase, 305

stimulus-value-role theory, 305–306
storm and stress, 252
  adolescents, 258–265
  experience-sampling technique, 260–263
  social environment, 264–265
  social sensitivity, 258–260
strange ideas about substances, 138–140
stranger anxiety, 107
Strange Situation, 107–108, 111, 124
stress
  bullying, 182
  early childhood, 154
  pregnancy, 48–49
  during pregnancy, 238
students
  concrete operations, 214
  eager students, 213–216
  intrinsic motivation, 213–214
stunting, 78
subject attrition, 26
sub-Saharan Africa
  fertility, 8
  pregnancy, 8
substance abuse
  in adolescence, 260t, 260, 261f
  fetal alcohol syndrome due to, 47–48
  teratogenic effects of, 46t, 47–48
successful intelligence, 210
sucking reflex, 75
sudden infant death syndrome (SIDS), 83–84
superego, 13
Supplemental Nutrition Assistance Program (SNAP), 79t
Supreme Court, 267
Swaziland
  nursing newborns, 76
Sweden, 43
  culture and pubertal timing predicting problem behavior, 235f
Swedish Twin/Adoption Study, 15, 16, 17

Switzerland
  foreign-born residents, 193t
sympathy, 176
synapses, 72, 74
synaptogenesis, 72, 73
synchrony, 109
syntax, 146

T

tabula rasa, 6
Tanner, Robert, 228
Tanner's five pubertal stages, 228f
taste and newborns, 86
Tay-Sachs disease, 51, 52t
teaching tips, 215t
teenage delinquency
  reducing, 11
teenager-friendly sex education, 246
teens
  See also adolescents
  adolescence-limited turmoil, 265
  alcohol stereotypes and facts, 260t
  brain, 266–270
  brain-imaging questions and findings, 266t
  delinquent behavior, 277
  eating disorders, 240t
  emotional regulation problems, 264
  externalizing tendencies, 242
  flourishing, 265
  high school, 252
  inconsistent family rules, 194
  intercourse, 244–245
  life-course difficulties, 265
  low social self-worth, 242
  minds, 266–270
  obesity, 24
  peers, 243, 277
  poor family relationships, 264
  religious parents, 242
  risk-taking environment, 264–265
  risk-taking personality, 242
  sensation seeking, 266
  serious trouble, 264–265

social status, 263
storms or flourish, 265t
workers, 297
telegraphic speech, 98
temperament, 111, 123–126
   child rearing to suit, 125
   evoking harsh discipline, 180–181
   exuberant versus shy toddler, 123–124, 125t
   in infancy, 111
   and socialization, 124
   styles, 111
temperamentally friendly childrearing, 125–126
teratogens, 45
   alcohol, 47–48
   developing brain and, 45
   developmental disorders, 45
   embryonic stage, 45
   environmental toxins, 46, 48t
   infectious diseases, 46t
   measurement issues, 48–49
   medicines and drugs, 46t, 47–48
   principles, 45–46
   recreational drugs, 46t
   rubella (German measles), 45
   sensitive period, 45
   smoking, 47
   threshold level, 45
   vitamin deficiencies, 46t
tertiary circular reactions, 92, 92t
testes, 35, 226, 229
testing newborns, 61–62
testosterone, 226
   female fetuses, 156
   gender-stereotyped play, 156
   girls becoming weight obsessed, 238
Thalidomide, 46
theories, 10
   age-linked, 18–20
   attachment theory, 14, 20
   behavioral genetics, 14–16, 20
   behaviorism, 10–12
   cognitive behaviorism, 12, 20
   cognitive developmental theory, 19–20
   early childhood, 13–14
   Erikson's theory, 20
   evolutionary psychologists, 14
   evolutionary theory, 20
   nature *versus* nurture, 10–12
   Piaget's theory, 20
   psychoanalytic theory, 13, 20
   psychosocial tasks, 18–19
   reinforcement, 11
   social learning theory, 12, 20
   traditional behaviorism, 20
   unconscious motivations, 13–14
theory of mind
   bilingual preschoolers, 150–151
   children, 149, 151
   cultural variations, 151
   deficits, 158–159
   early or late development, 151
   false-belief tasks, 151
   friendships, 151
   frontal-lobe activity, 151
   individual differences in, 149–151
   lying, 149
   making sense of other people's minds, 149–152
   Mean Monkey, 149
   opposing sibling perspectives, 150
   people may not have your best interests at heart, 149
   sharing and helping, 151
   stimulating, 151–152
   variations, 151
thin ideal, 237
thinking
   A-not-B error, 93–94
   adolescent, 253–255, 254t
   concepts and hypothetical possibilities, 254
   concrete operational, 19t, 138, 138t
   deferred imitation, 93
   different steps to retrieve items, 93
   formal operational, 91t, 253–254, 254t
   high school, 255
   in infancy, 93
   means-end behavior, 93
   object permanence, 93–94
   preoperational, 138–140, 138t
   real scientists, 254
   scientific reasoning and, 254–255
   sensorimotor, 91t, 91–93
   tracking early, 93
third trimester, 42, 54t
threats
   at birth, 59
   preschool physical skills, 137
   survival, 107
threats to developing baby
   chromosomal problems, 49–50
   genetic disorders, 50–52
   interventions, 53–55
   prenatal tests, 53–55
   teratogens, 45–49
toddlerhood, 105, 164
toddlerhood stage, 18t, 121t, 164t, 292t
toddlers
   attachment, 112
   autonomy, 121–122
   behavior problems, 121
   child-rearing strategies, 125
   confrontation, 126
   day care, 117
   doubt, 121
   Early Head Start, 117
   exuberant, 123–125, 123t
   familiar foods, 76
   help, comfort, and share, 126–127
   inhibited, 124
   magic and, 95
   managing disappointment, 122–123
   memory, 96
   raising rambunctious, 124–125
   self-conscious emotions, 121–122
   self-control differences, 122–123
   shame, 121
   shy, 123–125, 123t
   socialization, 122–123
   Strange Situation, 124
   tantrums, 94
   temperament-socialization fit, 124–125
   tertiary circular reactions, 92
toxoplasmosis, 46
traditional
   marriages, 7–8
   nuclear family, 192
traditional behaviorism, 20
traditional behaviorism theory, 20t
traditional behaviorists, 11
trimesters, 41–42
true experiment, 24
twin/adoption studies, 15
twin studies, 15
Twitter, 8
two-year-olds
   conscience, 122
   food cautions, 75–76
   socialization, 122–123
   tantrums, 122

U

ultrasound, 53–54
umbilical cord, 40
uncaring actions, 177
unconscious motivations, 13–14
underextensions, 147
undernutrition, 78
   early childhood, 137
UNESCO, 236
United States
   affluence, 8
   attachment security, 112f
   attention-deficit/hyperactivity disorder (ADHD), 170
   autism spectrum disorders (ASDs), 158

United States (continued)
  babies sleeping in same room as parents, 83
  career without college degree, 298–299
  child care, 117–118
  chronically hungry children, 78–79
  collectivism, 9
  collectivist cultures, 9
  day care, 119–120
  Down syndrome children, 50
  early-childhood poverty, 115–117
  eating disorders, 239
  emerging adulthood, 287–288
  Head Start, 117
  individualism, 8–9
  infant mortality, 63–64
  intercourse, 242
  legal system and adolescents, 267–268
  nutrition programs, 79
  pregnancy-related maternal deaths, 59
  primary school, 6
  spanking, 199
  stunting, 78
  sudden infant death syndrome (SIDS), 84
  teachers following rigid set of learning requirements, 214
  unmarried women with children, 7
  unmarried women with children, 7
  upward mobility, 22
    communities promoting, 216
    genes promoting, 27
uterus, 34, 37

V
vaccines and autism spectrum disorders (ASDs), 158
valid, 207–208
value-comparison stage, 305
variable reinforcement schedules, 11
Venezuela
  Huntington's disease and, 53
very low birth weight (VLBW), 62
Vietnam, puberty and adult responsibilities, 226f
vision, 85–88
Vista School, 212
visual cliff, 87–88
visual cortex, 72–73
vitamin deficiencies, 46
Vygotsky, Lev
  clear boundaries and rules in play, 154
  how children think, 167
  inner speech, 146
  perspectives on life and learning, 145
  zone of proximal development (XPD), 144–147

W
walking schema, 90
Walmart, 11
Washington, George, 5
Watson, John, 10–11, 106
Wechsler, David, 205
Western Europe, 6, 8
  attachment security, 112f
Western nations, 6, 8
Wexler, Milton, 53
Wexler, Nancy, 51–52, 53
WISC (Wechsler Intelligence Scale for Children), 205–207
  subtest sampler, 206t
wisdom, 210
women
  careers, 7
  infertility, 55
Women's March (2017), 157
women's movement, 7
work demands and breast-feeding, 76–77
work worries during pregnancy, 43
workers, 297
working at young age, 5–6
working memory, 168, 170, 171
working model, 107

X
X chromosomes, 36

Y
Y chromosomes, 36
young children and poverty, 7
youth development programs, 268

Z
Zambia
  breast feeding, 76
zero-tolerance policies, 269
Zeus, 141
Zika virus, 46
Zimbabwe
  breast feeding, 76
zone of proximal development (XPD), 144–147
zygote, 37